The Second Vermont Volunteer Infantry Regiment, 1861–1865

Also by Paul G. Zeller

The Ninth Vermont Infantry: A History and Roster (McFarland, 2008)

The Second Vermont Volunteer Infantry Regiment, 1861–1865

by Paul G. Zeller

McFarland & Company, Inc., Publishers
Jefferson, North Carolina, and London

The present work is a reprint of the illustrated case bound edition of The Second Vermont Volunteer Infantry Regiment, 1861–1865, *first published in 2002 by McFarland.*

All maps by George F. Skoch.

Library of Congress Cataloguing-in-Publication Data

Zeller, Paul G., 1946–
The Second Vermont Volunteer Infantry Regiment, 1861–1865 / by Paul G. Zeller.
p. cm.
Includes bibliographical references and index.

ISBN **978-0-7864-4345-1**
softcover : 50# alkaline paper ♾

1. United States. Army. Vermont Infantry Regiment, 2nd (1861–18
2. Vermont—History—Civil War, 1861–1865—Regimental histories.
3. United States—History—Civil War, 1861–1865—Regimental histories.
4. Vermont—History—Civil War, 1861–1865—Personal narratives.
5. United States—History—Civil War, 1861–1865—Personal narratives.
6. Soldiers—Vermont—Registers. I. Title.
E533.5 2nd .Z45 2009 973.7'443—dc21 2002006187

British Library cataloguing data are available

Cover photographs: Captain Volney S. Fullam, commander of Company I (USAMHI); the Grapevine Bridge spanning the Chickahominy River (Library of Congress)

Manufactured in the United States of America

McFarland & Company, Inc., Publishers
Box 611, Jefferson, North Carolina 28640
www.mcfarlandpub.com

This book is dedicated to the memory of
First Lieutenant Henry Leach Franklin
March 4, 1839–May 2, 1913
Co. C, Second Vermont Volunteer Infantry Regiment

Acknowledgments

When I started this book I had no idea of the amount of help that I would need to complete it. Nor did I believe so many individuals would willingly share their letters, diaries and photographs without asking anything in return, or that so many institutions would open their collections to me and their staffs give me so much of their time. To all, I am eternally indebted. I sincerely hope I have not left anyone out of this acknowledgment. If I have, I apologize now.

Breaking with the tradition of thanking one's spouse at the end of the acknowledgments, I must thank my wife, Sally, first. Not only did she give me her moral support during the eight long years that it took me to write this book, but she was my travel agent, editor, critic and most importantly my research assistant. I am sorry that after all the hours we spent poring through old dusty records in the National Archives she felt like a giant silverfish. Without her love and support this book would never have happened.

I am deeply indebted to the following organizations and institutions: Jeffrey D. Marshall and staff, Special Collections, Bailey-Howe Library, University of Vermont; Paul Carnahan and Marjorie Strong, Vermont Historical Society; Vermont State Library, Montpelier, Vt.; Arthur and Elizabeth Schlesinger Library, Radcliffe College; Jerri Knihnicki and Dianne Forbes, U. S. Army Transportation School Library, Fort Eustis, Va.; Mary Dalton, Lincoln Memorial Shrine, Redlands, Calif.; Mary Bort, Manchester Historical Society, Manchester, Vt.; Elaine Dixon, Putney Historical Society, Putney, Vt.; Jean S. Davies, Pittsford Historical Society, Pittsford, Vt.; Pat Carmichael, Dorset Historical Society, Dorset, Vt.; Peter S. Mallett, Georgia Historical Society, Georgia, Vt.; Tunbridge Historical Society, Tunbridge, Vt.; Joann Nichols, Brattleboro Historical Society; Brattleboro, Vt.; William Lizotte, Morristown Historical Society, Morristown, Vt.; Sheldon Museum, Sheldon, Vt.; Sarah Goldberger and J. Michael Moore, Lee Hall Mansion Museum, Newport News, Va.; Jerry Bocheck, Newport News Park, Newport News, Va.; Clay Marshia, Vermont Public Records; Brooks Memorial Library, Brattleboro, Vt.; Kathie Gilman, Vermont Veteran's Home, Bennington, Vt.; Bennington Museum, Bennington, Vt.; Casemate Museum, Fort Monroe, Va.; Swem Library, College of William and Mary; York County Public Library, Yorktown, Va.; Dr. Darrell Beauchamp, Navarro College, Corsicana, Texas; David A. Keough and staff, Manuscript Archives, U.S Army Military History Institute, U.S. Army War College, Carlisle Barracks, Pa.; Denis Delja and the boys in Co. E, Second Vermont Volunteer Infantry Regiment reenactment group; Krista W. Ainsworth, Special Collections, Krietzberg Library, Norwich University, Northfield, Vt.; Duke University; Armed Forces Institute of Pathology, Washington, D.C.; U.S. Naval Historical Center, Washington, D.C.

I thank the following historians who took time out of their busy schedules to review my chapters and maps to insure they were accurate: Donald C. Pfanz, Fredericksburg and Spotsylvania National Military Park; Robert E. L. Krick, Richmond National Battlefield Park; Ted Alexander, Antietam National Battlefield Park; Chris Calkins, Petersburg National Battlefield; James Burgess, Manassas National Battlefield Park; Lt. Col. Joseph W. A. Whitehorne (Ret.), Lord Fairfax Community College, Middletown, Va.;

John Quarstein, administrator of Museums and Historical Services for the City of Newport News, Va.; Howard Coffin, Montpelier, Vt.; Timothy J. Reese, Burkittsville, Md.

I also owe thanks to my friends and co-workers who listened to my ramblings about the Second Vermont and graciously, or maybe to make me go away, read over various parts of my manuscript and loaned me books. CWO 3 Brian Bajsert; CWO 4 Charles D. Brooks; Sharon Browning; Mary Gartman; Lewis Hamner; Maj. William Kroeger; John Raimonde; Joe Shepard; John C. Shulson; Lt. Col. Larry Smith; Maj. Kari H. St. John; Kim Villarreal; and my relic hunting buddy, Stephen Hawkins.

I am grateful for the time my former boss, mentor and friend, Richard W. Van Deren, spent giving my manuscript a final scrub before submission to my publisher. His talent, finely honed during years of having his pen bleed red ink over my correspondence, was put to good use and is much appreciated.

Thanks also go to Barbara F. Earle; Ed Italo; Tony O'Connor; Kenneth E. Proehl; Peter B. Talbot; Tom Ledoux, Webmaster of Vermont in the Civil War; Dr. Thomas P. and Beverly Lowry; Russell and Sue Slora; and John Thomas.

I especially want to thank my good friends Brad Limoge of Morrisville, Vt., and Euclid and Priscilla Farnham of Tunbridge, Vt., for helping me locate photographs, letters, and diaries, helping me with research, reading and commenting on my manuscript, cheering me on, and opening their homes to my wife and me. We love them very much.

I owe a special thanks to the descendants of the men of the Second Vermont who shared with me copies of their ancestors' letters, diaries, military papers and photographs: Thomas R. Baine; Gerry Chittick; Dorothy Goldman; Susan Hunziker; Lucille J. Klynstra; Jeffery S. Jones; the late Dorothy S. Melville and her son Joseph A. Melville; Bob Norris; Alan Poore; Bert Ramage; Leroy Smithson; Steve Taylor; Douglas L. Williams; Mary Jane Williams; Dennis Devereux; Nancy D. Wilson; Roland O. Anderson; Kermit Glines; Douglas W. Ronaldson; Kelly Dolan; Jeffery Bean; William Phipps; Sharon Hammond; Marilyn B. Zimmer; T. J. Lathe; Carl Culham; Karl "Woody" Woodcock; LeRoy P. Graham; Frank Pulaski; Don Streeter; Jo Ann Tellez; Larry Peck; Gary Walker; and Linda Sery.

George F. Skoch drew all the maps, which greatly improved the quality of the book. To George I am eternally grateful.

TABLE OF CONTENTS

Preface

I was introduced to the Second Vermont Volunteer Infantry Regiment on the morning of Christmas Eve, 1977. Stealing a few hours of Civil War relic hunting with my metal detector before doing some last minute Christmas shopping, I was hunting near the Warwick River in Newport News, Virginia, and in the general area occupied by the Vermont Brigade from April 5 to May 4, 1862. The small patch of woods in which I was hunting had previously yielded a number of Civil War buttons and minié balls. The site of my search that morning was a small spot where I was finding Civil War–era coins. I had dug up about a half a dozen pieces of change when out popped a coin with bits of gold shining through the encrusted dirt. I just knew I had finally found a gold coin. After finding several more coins, I decided the spot was played out, and I headed for home, walking on air.

After I got home, the first piece I cleaned, of course, was my gold coin. As the 115 years of dirt melted away I noticed the coin had a hole drilled through it near the rim, and I saw the words *WAR OF 1861* and the raised impression of an eagle.

At first I was crestfallen. I didn't have a gold coin after all. As I cleaned the reverse side, however, there appeared the words H. L. FRANKLIN, BRATTLEBORO, Co. C, 2nd REG., VT., VOL. Although I had been hunting Civil War relics for only a little over a year, I knew I had found a soldier's identification disk, and it was much more valuable than a gold coin.

Sometime later I learned that Union soldiers' records were stored at the National Archives and I might be able to get a copy of Franklin's. I filled out the necessary forms, and one month and $20 later, I had a copy of Franklin's service and pension records. When I tried to find out more about the Second Vermont I discovered it had no regimental history.

Nearly twenty years passed, but I never stopped thinking about it. Finally, I decided that I would attempt to write the history of the unit.

While involved in this endeavor I obtained copies of Henry Franklin's photograph, 11 of his Civil War–era letters, copies of personal papers such as his marriage and death certificates, and a transcript of his court martial.

Henry Leach Franklin, the son of Charles A. and Emily Fletcher Franklin, was born March 4, 1839, in Westmoreland, New Hampshire. Sometime before 1861 the Franklin family moved to Brattleboro, Vermont. Like a lot of young men, he had bounced around from job to job in his teenage years. He had initially worked as a farm hand, but in the winter of 1857, he went on the road with a ventriloquist for three months. From March until October 1858, he worked in a factory. Then in March 1859, he went on the road with a vaudeville company for six months. After returning to Brattleboro, he went to work in a sewing machine shop, where he was working at the outbreak of the Civil War. Caught up in the war fever, he and eight other mechanics were the first men to sign up for the company being formed in Brattleboro.

At the time of his enlistment, May 16, 1861, Henry was 22 years old and stood five feet ten inches tall. He had blue eyes, light brown hair and a light complexion. Soon after enlisting he was chosen as one of the company's corporals.

In February of 1862, Franklin bought two identifica-

Henry L. Franklin's identification disk. Excavated by the author December 24, 1977, near the Warwick River in Newport News, Va. Photograph by author.

tion disks from the sutler (Civil War version of the present day PX). The disks came with an eagle on the front; the back was blank. The sutler would stamp the man's name, unit and hometown on the back. Franklin sent one of the disks home to his mother on February 20, 1862, writing, "Enclosed you will find a medal that are made for soldiers to wear around their neck in time of battle and if they get killed they will know who and where they belong. I have 2 and I send you one of them." Franklin lost his disk—the one I found—on the Virginia Peninsula three months later. I have no idea what happened to the one he sent his mother.

Henry Franklin was typical of the men and boys who joined the Second Vermont. The vast majority of them were farmers and factory workers, and like Franklin most were in their early 20s. Many had never been very far from the village in which they had grown up, much less out of the state. Most of them had joined the army to save the Union, not to free the slaves. Although there was an abolition movement in Vermont at the time, most of the men had never seen a Negro, much less developed any concern about their plight in the South. This attitude would change, however, as the Vermonters spent more and more time in Virginia and Maryland and saw the way slaves were treated.

I have in no way tried to gloss over the men's offensive and sometimes insulting remarks about Negroes as written in their letters and diaries, but neither do I condone it. For the purpose of understanding from where we have come, and to be historically accurate, the passages from the men's letters and diaries remain as written. They are in no way meant to insult African Americans today.

In writing this book, I have tried to let the men of the Second Vermont tell their own stories as much as possible. I have also left the spelling and punctuation in the passages from the men's letters and diaries as they appeared, except where they had very long run-on sentences, in which cases I added periods for ease of reading. I omitted "[*sic*]" where words were misspelled because in many cases there were so many misspelled words it would have become distracting. In the case of William H. Bond's letters I used a version that was "translated" by Thomas R. Baine, Bond's descendant. Bond only had a fourth grade education and wrote phonetically, making his letters extremely difficult to read. Bond himself was self conscious of his writing and more than once in his letters asked that only his family members be allowed to read them.

I have made every effort to ensure this book's historical accuracy, and I accept full responsibility for any inaccuracies that may be found. I sincerely hope this work does justice to the record and memory of the members of the regiment and will make their descendants, as well as the citizens of Vermont, proud of them.

Paul G. Zeller
Yorktown, Virginia
April 2002

List of Maps

CHAPTER 1

OFF TO SAVE THE UNION

To tell the history of the 2nd Vermont Volunteer Infantry Regiment, one begins with the Vermont militia where regiment roots are deeply embedded.

Before the Civil War, Vermont's military reputation was based in the American Revolution. Vermont had pledged to the Continental Congress the service of "more than five thousand hardy soldiers, capable of bearing arms in defense of American Liberty." This was the entire fighting population of the infant state. The Green Mountain Boys under Ethan Allen and Benedict Arnold captured Fort Ticonderoga, May 10, 1775, demanding the British surrender "in the name of the Great Jehovah and the Continental Congress." Vermonters also fought with John Stark at the battle of Bennington August 16, 1777, helping seal British General John Burgoyne's fate in the war's decisive campaign.[1]

The Vermont militia rose to the occasion again during the War of 1812; with the end of that war, interest in and relevance of the militia declined until 1856 when it was virtually nonexistent. The time had passed when every Vermonter was as handy with a rifle as with an axe. The state stopped appropriating funds to support the militia and annual "June trainings" became social occasions rather than a time of military drills.[2]

By 1856, the mood of the nation was changing. Southern states were becoming more vocal and militant concerning the issues of slavery and states' rights, and influential Vermonters took the Southerners' threats seriously enough to make possible the passage of a law reviving the militia. The law provided $3 for each armed and uniformed man who would drill at least three days a year. Because individuals would have to provide their own uniforms, provisions and lodging, few companies were raised, and those that were numbered fewer than 50 men apiece.[3]

In the summer of 1858 Governor Ryland Fletcher, who had been an officer in the Vermont militia during its heyday, invited the companies to muster at Brandon for inspection and drill. Nine companies responded, bringing 450 men. The men had no tents and had to be quartered in village halls and houses. Lacking an officer experienced in drilling a large body of troops, the governor invited Ebenezer Stone, the adjutant general of Massachusetts, to assist. Stone took charge and gave the men their first instruction in battalion drill. Several thousand spectators surrounded the green where the troops were drilling, and in the evening there was a torchlight parade in honor of the troops and speeches by prominent citizens. On the second day, an inspection and review was followed by a simulated charge led by the governor, delighting the spectators. The muster had its desired effect, and during the following year, enough companies were raised to form a brigade of four regiments under the command of General Alonzo Jackman, a professor at Norwich Military Academy.[4]

Another muster was held at Montpelier in August, 1860. Fourteen of 17 companies attended, bringing nearly 900 men. This time the units camped in tents supplied by the state. The militia grew to 22 companies by the close of the year.[5]

While Vermont was getting its militia in shape, the federal government was having serious trouble with its military. On January 9, 1861, the relief ship *Star of the West* had been forced, under fire, to abandon its attempt to resupply Fort Sumter located in the harbor at Charleston, S.C. By the time Abraham Lincoln was inaugurated on March 4, 1861, seven southern states had seceded from the Union. Facing the distinct possibility of armed conflict, Lincoln had a standing army of only 16,000 men who were spread all over the United States. His general in chief of the army, Lt. Gen. Winfield Scott, was so aged and infirm that he was unable to mount a horse.[6]

On April 12, as the *Star of the West* again tried to resupply Sumter, the Confederate batteries ringing Charleston Harbor opened fire on the ship and the fort. On April 15 Lincoln called for 75,000 three month volunteers to save the nation. As a result Virginia seceded on April 17 and Arkansas, Tennessee and North Carolina followed. The formation of the Confederate States of America was complete.[7]

In Vermont, the call for troops was acted upon immediately. Governor Erastus Fairbanks issued a proclamation announcing the outbreak of armed rebellion and the president's call for troops, and issued the orders necessary to raise troops. A special session of the legislature, in a firm commitment to support the president, passed a bill appropriating the staggering sum of $1 million to organize, arm, and equip the militia. Realizing that an army private's pay of $13 a month would not support an established family, the legislature authorized an additional $7 a month supplement to be paid out of state funds to each Vermont soldier.[8]

A circular from the Secretary of War Simon Cameron, accompanying the president's requisition, called for one 780-man infantry regiment from Vermont to serve for three months. By order of the Vermont adjutant general, H. Henry Baxter, several senior militia officers met in Burlington on April 19 to select companies for the 1st Regiment of Vermont Volunteers.[9]

While the militia was mobilizing, so were Vermont's citizens. Town halls filled to capacity for patriotic meetings in support of the war effort. Hundreds of thousands of dollars were raised to equip the militia and, more importantly, to support the families of the men who were giving up their jobs and professions to defend their country.[10]

The 10 companies of the 1st Vermont rendezvoused at Rutland on May 2, 1861, where they trained and were mustered into active service on May 8. John W. Phelps, a native Vermonter and West Point graduate, was chosen as its colonel. A prominent lawyer and active militia officer from Woodstock, Peter T. Washburn, was selected as the lieutenant colonel. On May 9, the regiment left Vermont on its journey south to Virginia, where it had been assigned. The 1st Vermont's entire three months of active duty would be spent in Hampton and Newport News, Va., performing picket and scouting duty.[11]

The only real combat the 1st Vermont participated in was the ill-fated battle at Big Bethel, June 10, 1861, the first major land engagement of the Civil War. The Union force was soundly whipped and retreated to Fort Monroe. The affair cost the Federals two men killed and 21 wounded. The 1st Vermont lost three men wounded and one captured in the fiasco. In a speech at the 1882 reunion of Vermont officers, George G. Benedict, the author of *Vermont in the Civil War*, said of the battle, "It was an inglorious affair, but noteworthy because it exhibited at the outset the mettle of our Vermont soldiers...."[12]

The 1st Vermont returned home to a heroes' welcome on August 7 and mustered out of service on the August 25. Although they had honorably served their country, many of the veterans of the regiment were not finished with military service. One hundred and fifty became field or company grade officers in other Vermont regiments and batteries. A number of the men received commissions in other than Vermont units, making a total of over 250 veterans to be commissioned. Of the 753 rank and file of the 1st Vermont, over 600 reentered the army in some capacity during the war.[13]

While the 1st Vermont was being formed, President Lincoln called for 42,034 volunteers to serve for three years. Toward that call, the 2nd and 3rd Vermont regiments were recruited. The 2nd Vermont was to be formed as soon as possible, the 3rd at a later date. In early May, 60 companies offered themselves for the 2nd regiment. From that pool, Adjutant General Baxter chose 10 companies from the towns of Bennington, Brattleboro, Burlington, Castleton, Fletcher, Ludlow, Montpelier, Tunbridge, Winooski and Waterbury.[14]

On June 3, Baxter ordered all companies of the 2nd Vermont to report to Burlington on or before June 6 for mustering into Federal service:[15]

State of Vermont
Adjutant & Inspector General's Office
Rutland, June 3, 1861

General Order No. 14

A requisition having been made by the President of the United States upon the Governor of this State for a Volunteer Force of Infantry, "to aid in the enforcement of the laws and the suppression of insurrection," and twenty companies having been formed, two Regiments are hereby organized, each regiment consisting of ten companies of 83 officers and enlisted men each.

The following named persons are commissioned as the officers of the several Companies, composing the Second Regiment of Vermont Volunteers:

Company A, James H. Walbridge, Captain; Newton Stone, 1st Lieut.; William H. Cady, 2d Lieut., Bennington.

Company B, James Hope, Captain; John Howe, 1st Lieut.; Enoch Johnson, 2d Lieut., Castleton.

Company C, Edward A. Todd, Captain; John S. Tyler, 1st Lieut.; Forester A. Prouty, 2d Lieut., Brattleboro.

Company D, Charles Dillingham, Captain; Wm. W. Henry, 1st Lieut.; Charles C. Gregg, 2d Lieut.; Waterbury.

Company E, Richard Smith, Captain; Lucius O. Whitney, 1st Lieut.; Orville Bixby, 2d Lieut., Tunbridge.

Company F, Francis V. Randall, Captain; Walter A. Philips, 1st Lieut.; Horace C. Crossman, 2d Lieut., Montpelier.

Company G, John T Drew, Captain; David L. Sharpley, 1st Lieut.; Anson H. Weed, 2d Lieut., Burlington.

Company H, Zerah W. Strait, Captain; Jerome B. Case, 1st Lieut.; Chester K. Leach, 2d Lieut., Fletcher.

Company I, Volney S. Fullam, Captain; Sherman W. Parkhurst, 1st Lieut.; Isaac N. Wadleigh, 2d Lieut., Ludlow.

Company K, John Lonergan, Captain; Christopher M. Dolon, 1st Lieut.; John Bascom, 2d Lieut., Winooski.

The commanding officers of Companies comprising the 2d Regiment, as stated above, will report themselves with the men under their command, to Lieutenant Colonel George J. Stannard, Commanding at Camp "Underwood," Burlington, on or before Thursday, the 6th inst.

Strict subordination will be inforced through the camp, and the troops diligently exercised and instructed in military duty and discipline, until mustered into the service of the United States and sent forward into active service.

Arms, uniforms, equipments, and clothing will be carved out to the Regiment, and as soon as possible.

The utmost diligence in the performance of all duties involved in preparing this regiment for immediate service, is hereby enjoined on all officers and soldiers connected therewith.

H. Henry Baxter
Adj. & Insp. Gen'l.[16]

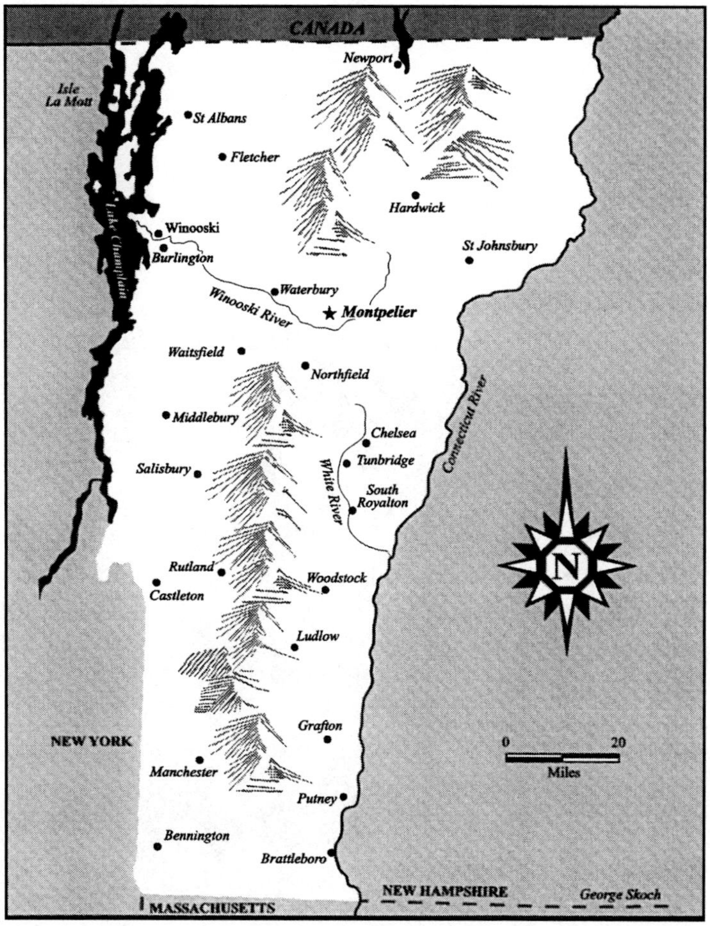

The State of Vermont

In the Civil War, an infantry regiment consisted of 10 companies lettered A through K, minus J. In hand written orders and reports it was too easy to confuse I and J, so J was not used. A captain commanded each company. The company was divided, for command and control purposes, into two platoons: one platoon commanded by a first lieutenant and the other by a second lieutenant. Each platoon was divided into two squads, each under the supervision of a sergeant. The company was also authorized one first sergeant, four sergeants, eight corporals, two musicians, one wagoner, and from 64 to 82 privates.[17]

The regimental staff was made up of a colonel, lieutenant colonel, major, adjutant (first lieutenant), quartermaster (first lieutenant), surgeon, assistant surgeon, chaplain, sergeant major, quartermaster sergeant, commissary sergeant, hospital steward, two principal musicians, and a 24-piece band.[18]

The demographics of the 10 companies were similar. Company I, for example, recruited in Ludlow, consisted of 86 officers and men with an average age of 24. They represented all walks of life. There were 36 farmers, 25 mechanics, three shoemakers, three railroad workers, two lawyers, two teachers, two painters, two teachers, two printers, two salesmen, one carpenter, one merchant, one sawyer, one store clerk, and one student. The occupations of two of the men were not recorded.[19]

To command the 2nd Vermont, the governor wanted a man with a formal military education and regular army experience. The command was first offered to Israel B. Richardson, a Vermont native who was a U.S. Military Academy graduate and had served in the regular army in the war with Mexico. Richardson, living in Michigan at the time, had already been given command of the 1st Michigan Infantry Regiment, but recommended a West Point classmate, Henry Whiting.[20]

Whiting, a 43-year-old native of Bath, N.Y., graduated from West Point in 1841. He was commissioned a second lieutenant in the 5th U.S. Infantry and served five years on the northwestern frontier. In the fall of 1845, war with Mexico was imminent, and Whiting reported to Corpus Christi, Tex. In February 1846, just before the U.S. Army

Left: **Colonel Henry Whiting, first commander of the 2nd Vermont. USAMHI.** ***Right:*** **Lieutenant Colonel George J. Stannard, the first man to offer his services to the State of Vermont in defense of the Union; he is pictured here as a brigadier general. Roger D. Hunt Collection, USAMHI.**

crossed the Rio Grande, Whiting resigned his commission and returned to St. Clair, Mich., where he had been stationed earlier in his career and had married a local girl. On returning to Michigan, he went into the lumber business. Accepting Governor Fairbanks's offer of command, Whiting reported to St. Johnsbury, Vt., where, on June 6 he was commissioned a colonel and given command of the 2nd Vermont.[21]

While Col. Whiting was being commissioned in St. Johnsbury, the regiment's lieutenant colonel, major, and quartermaster were commissioned at Camp Underwood.

Forty-one-year-old businessman George J. Stannard of St. Albans, Vt., was appointed lieutenant colonel. He had been active in the reorganization of the Vermont militia and had commanded one of the best militia companies in the state. Immediately after the assault on Ft. Sumter, he offered his services to the governor of Vermont, becoming the first man in Vermont to volunteer for the war.[22]

Charles H. Joyce, a 31-year-old lawyer from Northfield, was appointed major. Born in Andover, England on January 30, 1830, Joyce and his parents immigrated to the United States when he was six years old and settled in Waitsfield, Vt. After completing his education in Northfield, he read law under three different attorneys, one of them being Francis V. Randall, the commander of the 2nd Vermont's Co. F. Joyce was admitted to the Vermont State Bar in 1852 and practiced law from 1853 until 1861 when he volunteered for military service. In the early 1850s, he married Randall's sister, Rowena M. Randall. Joyce had been active in the Vermont militia and had been elected colonel of the militia's 1st regiment six months prior to joining the 2nd Vermont.[23]

Capt. Perley P. Pitkin, of Montpelier, was selected as the regiment's quartermaster. Unfortunately his superior abilities were recognized early and, by the fall of 1861, Pitkin was assigned to a higher-level staff position. By the summer of 1864, he was promoted to colonel and put in charge of the main base of supply of the Army of the Potomac, at City Point, Va.[24]

Camp Underwood, named for Vermont's Lieutenant Governor Levi Underwood, who lived in Burlington, was located on the northern edge of town on the county fairground. Life there for the men of the 2nd Vermont was structured and busy, but good. They lived in new white six-

Left: **Major Charles H. Joyce, a lawyer from Northfield, Vermont. USAMHI.** ***Right:*** **Quartermaster Perley P. Pitkin; his expertise in logistics soon propelled him to higher level staff jobs. USAMHI.**

man "A" tents located on the west side of the fair-grounds. The enlisted men were supplied with a wool blanket and rubber blanket, but had to sleep on the hard ground for several days until Captain Pitkin was able to procure cornhusk mattresses. By the second week, the men were improving their living conditions by making awnings for their tents with evergreen boughs.[25]

Lt. Col. Stannard had designed a rigorous training schedule for the regiment that was rigidly enforced throughout its two-week stay at Camp Underwood. A copy of the schedule was published in the June 6 edition of the Burlington *Daily Free Press*:

Calls

Reveille	5 A.M.
Police	5:30 A.M.
Surgeon	6:30 A.M.
Breakfast	7 A.M.
Company Drill	7:30 to 8:30 A.M.
Guard Mounting	9 A.M.
Battalion Drill	10 to 12 A.M.
Dinner-(Peas on Trencher)	1 P.M.
Company Drill	2:30 to 3:30 P.M.
Dress Parade-(Retreat)	6:30 P.M.
Tattoo	9 P.M.[26]

Drum rolls signaled calls for daily activities. Probably the most despised was the reveille roll, which sounded at 5 A.M. Hearing it, men pulled on their uniforms and hurried into company formation. While they stood shivering in the cool Vermont morning air, rubbing the sleep from their eyes, first sergeants called roll. After the first formation, save for those detailed for police call, the men were allowed to go back to their tents to wash, use the sink (Civil War term for latrine), spruce up their uniforms, write letters home, or get a few more winks of sleep. At 6:30 A.M., men feeling sick reported in front of the company area to be marched to the hospital for treatment. Breakfast call was at 7 A.M. after which the training day began.[27]

Morning company drill was usually broken down into squad drill, where the men learned individual skills, such as how to stand at attention, how to march, and to perform facing movements. Afternoon company drill included maneuvering the company as a whole, with the captain or one of the lieutenants in charge.[28]

Daily at 6:30 P.M. the drums sounded the call for dress parade, with the men required to be in full dress uniform. This formal formation was the occasion for reading orders, court-martial sentences, or any other types of official communications. In a typical dress parade, the regiment was formed in line of battle, and then each company was given the command "parade rest" by its commander. The band would play and briskly march down and back the entire length of the regiment. The officers then stepped four paces forward, led by the lieutenant colonel and major. Then the company first sergeants marched to the center of the formation and made their reports to the regimental adjutant, who then reported to the colonel and took a position behind him. The men were then put through the manual of arms in unison and again placed at "parade rest." The officers then sheathed their swords, marched to the colonel, saluted, and encircled him to receive his remarks and orders. Afterwards, the officers returned to their companies, dismissed them, and had them marched back to the company areas. The dress parade was a spectacular event and was enthusiastically attended by the local citizens.[29]

Supper immediately followed dress parade. All of the meals for the regiment were served in Mechanic's Hall, one of the permanent buildings on the fairground. The men marched into the building in two ranks, and took each side of the waist high tables. There were no benches, as 2nd Lt. Chester Leach of Co. H, a 32-year-old farmer from Fletcher, put it in a letter home: "When we eat, we sit standing." Although a few of the men complained, the food generally was passable and they could have all they wanted. A typical supper consisted of meat, beans, potatoes, bread, butter, and coffee. The coffee, served at breakfast and supper in large tin coffeepots, was presweetened and piping hot.[30]

Second Lieutenant Chester K. Leach, Company H. USAMHI.

Tattoo sounded at 9 P.M. signaling the time to go to bed. Lights were required to be out 10 minutes later except in the commissioned officers' tents. This time was for officers to study their manuals for the next day's drill. Since most of the junior officers had no prior military training, they stayed one step ahead of their men only by burning the midnight oil. Col. Whiting apparently went through several drill manuals before deciding on Maj. William J. Hardee's *Rifle and Light Infantry Tactics*, one of the most popular drill manuals of the day. One 2nd Vermont officer wrote, "We are drilled thoroughly every day in the manual of arms, according to Hardee's Tactics, having settled down to this mode of drill, and changed, I hope, for the last time."[31]

Not all the enlisted men followed the policy of going to bed after lights out. Many of the 800 plus men, mostly in their late teens and early 20s, were away from home and out of mother's sight for the first time and were in the largest city in Vermont. Many had only two things on their minds—drinking and women. The problem was exacerbated by the lack of a fence around the camp. Guards were at strategic locations, but after lights out, some men ran the guards and headed for town. On June 8, Lt. Leach wrote to his wife, "...have put as many as 25 men in the guard house," and on June 11 after having been officer of the guard the night before, he complained, "I did not go to bed last night until 12 o'clock. The boys kept running the guards, so the Col. ordered a roll call between 11 and 12. Larabee and Walter Chase in our company were absent. They got into the guard house before morning." Pvt. Jerome Cutler, a 24-year-old member of Co. H and a Waterville native, wrote to his fiancée, Emily Bailey, of his displeasure at the men's behavior. "When I lay me down to sleep and rise in the morning I bend my knee to my Heavenly Father and I shall do so though irreligious comrades are around me."[32]

The problem was partly solved toward the end of their two-week stint at Camp Underwood when the guards arrested two local men with a wagonload of liquor they had been selling to the soldiers. The two were put in the guardhouse, though one escaped out a window. The remaining man was taken away by a local policeman the next day and jailed. Finally, Col. Whiting held a courts-marital, and in

Private Jerome Cutler, Company H. Herbert Klynstra Collection, USAMHI.

addition to time spent confined in the guardhouse, men who had been caught AWOL were fined $5.[33]

On Sundays, the one day the army traditionally set aside for inspection, the training schedule was altered. It was generally held several hours after breakfast, and in the intervening time, the men were busy. Uniforms were brushed, leather items blackened, and brass buttons and belt plates shined. Just before to the hour of inspection, the companies marched, with full knapsacks, to the drill field and were put into regimental formation to await the arrival of the inspecting officer. On arrival, the lieutenant colonel or major would get an overall impression of the regiment by slowly walking up and down its entire length. He then conducted a detailed inspection checking the arms, equipment, and uniform of each soldier, starting with Co. A and, one by one, inspected every company. As the inspecting officer approached a company, its commander would order his men to stack arms, unsling and open their knapsacks, and lay out the contents. The inspecting officer then checked the contents of each knapsack, using the tip of his sword, looking for dirty clothing or contraband. Any soldier found deficient in any area was reprimanded on the spot. This was but a preview of what he would receive upon return to the company area. After each company had been inspected, the men were ordered to repack and sling their knapsacks, recover their arms, and then were marched back to their company areas. They were generally free of duty the rest of the day, except for religious services which they were required to attend on Sunday evening.[34]

In the afternoon, some in the ranks were given passes and were able to leave camp for a few hours. Some went swimming in Lake Champlain or walked downtown, perhaps having their "likenesses" taken at a photographer's studio.[35]

Col. Whiting arrived from St. Johnsbury on June 7 and formally took command of the regiment at the morning formation the next day. Before the resulting change of command ceremony, Capt. John T. Drew, commander of Co. G and a 25-year-old Burlington resident, learned that two of his men had decided to go home. Drew was incensed, since the men had already been given several chances to back out of military service. The two men were berated in front of the rest of the company and they, along with another member of the company who had been arrested the day before for being drunk, were dropped from the rolls. The three were drummed out of camp amid the hisses and boos of the rest of the company. Eager volunteers quickly replaced all three men the next day.[36]

After the morning formation, on June 8 physical examinations were begun, as required by army regulations before the regiment could be mustered into federal service. Performed by Lt. Col. Gabriel J. Rains, they consisted of questions about the men's general health, and an inspection of the body, including watching them sit, walk, and run. Meager compared to today's armed forces physical examinations, the exams were rigid by Civil War standards. Examinations were completed on June 11 with some men being rejected, including two officers. Second Lt. Forester A. Prouty of Co. C was replaced by Henry C. Campbell from Putney, who was promoted from the ranks. Capt. Zerah W. Strait, commander of Co. H, was determined, at age 49, to be too old for active service. Elected to replace Strait was William T. Burnham, the popular proprietor of Burnham's Hotel in Montpelier and commander of the newly formed Montpelier company that was scheduled to be mustered into the 3rd Vermont. Burnham received the overwhelming majority of the company, with 67 votes to 4. Voting for captains and lieutenants was a common practice in volunteer units, with the governors issuing commissions to those so selected. In the Union Army, however, this practice was pretty much abandoned by the second year of the war.[37]

Left: **Captain John T. Drew, commander of Company G, who spent most of his time in the army as a POW. USAMHI.** ***Right:*** **Captain William T. Burnham, commander of Company H, pictured here in civilian clothes. USAMHI.**

Lt. Col. Rains, ordered to Vermont by the War Department to muster the Vermont regiments into federal service, had mustered in the 1st Vermont regiment on May 8. Army regulations required the ceremony be conducted by a regular army commissioned officer. Lieutenant Col. Rains, a North Carolinian, had served in the army since graduating from West Point in 1827. It turned out that, during his stay in Vermont, he was a troubled and melancholy man. Being a Southerner, he was torn between remaining faithful to the U.S. Army or casting his lot with the Confederacy. Rains resigned from the army in July and was soon after commissioned a colonel in the Confederate Army. He had earned a reputation in the army for experimenting with explosives, and before war's end, he would be named the head of the Confederate Torpedo Bureau. The 2nd Vermont would run into Rains's handiwork the next spring on the Virginia Peninsula.[38]

The men had asked for religious services, and since the regiment did not yet have a chaplain, Col. Whiting arranged for a service to be performed by the Third Congregational Society. On Sunday afternoon, June 9, the regiment was marched to a 2,000 seat open-air theater on the fairground. The *Daily Free Press* reported that local citizens took the seats not filled by the regiment. The reporter went on to describe the scene. "The broad expanse of sward dotted with the white tents, the throng of citizens, composed largely of ladies and brilliant gay colors, the mass of hearty and sunburned troops in somber gray, relieved in spots by the white havelocks, and all respectful and attentive, made a striking scene."[39]

Fifty members of the regiment were selected for a choir. The preacher held forth for an hour on the righteousness and duty of Christians to participate in war against the evils of the Southern cause. The finale was an admonishment to the men to study their bibles, prepare for death in battle, obey orders, and resist the temptations of a soldier's life.[40]

Left: **Surgeon Newton Ballou, who performed amputations in a cooper's shop during the First Battle of Bull Run, July 21, 1861. Vermont Historical Society.** ***Right:*** **Assistant Surgeon Benjamin W. Carpenter left the 2nd Vermont in August, 1862, to become the surgeon of the 9th Vermont Infantry Regiment. USAMHI.**

Although they had been officially installed several days before, Col. Whiting formally announced his selections of the remaining staff positions at dress parade on June 12. They were:

ADJUTANT: Guilford S. Ladd of Bennington.

SURGEON: Newton H. Ballou of Burlington.

ASSISTANT SURGEON: Benjamin W. Carpenter of Burlington.

CHAPLAIN: Claudius B. Smith of Brandon, a Baptist clergyman and principal of the Literary and Scientific Institute of Brandon.

SERGEANT MAJOR: William Guinan of Montpelier, who was a veteran of the Mexican War where he had served in the 9th U.S. Volunteer Infantry.

COMMISSARY SERGEANT: Lauriston L. Stone of Stowe.

HOSPITAL STEWARD: Eli Z. Stearns of Burlington, a recent medical school graduate who had studied the last two years with Dr. Carpenter.[41]

At the end of dress parade, all of the companies save for Co. K were sworn into federal service by taking the oath of allegiance. During the ceremony, apparently with his war fever cooling, Pvt. Wesley Spaulding of Co. H refused to take the oath. That evening Spaulding and Pvt. Alexis Mead, a recruit in Co. H who had proven disobedient and mutinous, were drummed out of camp.[42]

Capt. John Lonergan's Co. K could not be sworn in because half of his company was AWOL. Lonergan was given until 10 A.M. the next day to round them up to take the oath. The captain managed to get them all in by 10 A.M. the next day and they were sworn in. By the second week, Col. Whiting had dealt with the Winooski boys long enough and recommended to the governor they disband, which was so ordered. Though Capt. Lonergan was furious and protested vigorously, the order stood. On June 18, Lonergan and his company left for home and were immediately replaced with Capt. Solon Eaton's Vergennes company. Although Lonergan would follow the 2nd Vermont to war as a civilian, and once even come under fire, he never received an official military position in the regiment. Yet he badgered the War Department so long that it finally ordered the Vermont adjutant general to allow Lonergan to raise another company. As commander of Co. A of the 13th

Vermont Infantry Regiment, Lonergan would become a hero of the battle of Gettysburg and would be awarded the Medal of Honor.[43]

Top: **Captain John Lonergan, commander of Company K. His company was disbanded for being too rebellious before the 2nd Vermont left for war. USAMHI. *Bottom:* Vermont coat and cuff buttons excavated by the author in Newport News, Virginia. Photograph by author.**

Delivery of uniforms and equipment for the 2nd Vermont began piecemeal starting on June 7 and was completed on June 17. The uniforms consisted of a gray frock coat, gray trousers, two gray flannel shirts, and a cap of gray doe skin with a blue cord. Also issued was a gray overcoat with an attached cape. On the frock coat were gilt buttons bearing the seal of Vermont. Smaller gilt buttons with the buck's head, from the state seal, were on the coat's cuffs. Although normally associated with the Confederate Army, gray was popular with early Union volunteer units. Not until fall would the men of the 2nd Vermont don the more traditional blue uniform.[44]

The soldiers' equipment included a black leather accouterment belt and a black leather shoulder belt worn over the left shoulder to help support the weight of the accouterment belt. That belt was fastened by a lead-filled, stamped brass oval belt plate with the letters "US" on the front. On the shoulder belt was affixed a circular lead-filled brass plate stamped with the impression of an eagle. On the waist belt was carried a bayonet in a leather sheath, a leather cartridge box for 40 rounds of ammunition, and a small leather box for percussion caps. Once assembled, the entire contraption was referred to as one's "equipments."[45]

The women of the towns provided the men with havelocks, white linen coverings for the cap, with a small cape in the back to protect the neck from sunburn. They were very popular with volunteer units, both North and South, in the early months of the war.[46]

Rations were carried in a haversack. The ones issued to the 2nd Vermont were made of jappaned cloth, similar to oil cloth, used to make them waterproof, and were usually black. Haversacks had an inner cloth lining that could be removed and washed. Usually the linings did not last long, and the inside of the haversack became greasy, grimy, and smelly from carrying cooked meats, butter, and other foods.[47]

In addition to seeing that their men were being properly drilled and outfitted, the officers interviewed and selected personal servants. Army regulations allowed two servants for each colonel, lieutenant colonel, and major, and one servant for captains and lieutenants. Field grade officers received an additional $49 a month in pay to employ them and company grade officers an additional $24.50. The servants became an integral part of the unit and were authorized a tent and free medical care. They were not allowed to wear uniforms and were required to carry on their person at all times a certificate, signed by the officer for whom they worked, verifying their employment. Most of the servants appear to have been teenage boys and young men from Vermont. A number of the officers took advantage of this perk, but after the first year of the war most of the servants had tired of army life and quit. By the beginning of the Peninsula Campaign in the spring of 1862, the novelty of having civilian servants seems to have died away.[48]

On Saturday, June 15, the Bennington town band arrived at the Burlington train depot, having volunteered *en masse* to be the regiment's band. A 24-piece brass band under the direction of Capt. Franklin M. Crossett was met by Co. A, the Bennington company, and escorted to Camp Underwood. *The Rutland Daily Herald*, in reporting the occasion stated, "Its members are well trained, and show evidences of thorough practice. Its selection is a very judicious one, although made to the disappointment of our own [Rutland town band] most excellent corps of musicians."[49]

Also on Saturday, the ladies of Burlington delivered more than 400 homemade pies, several hundred cakes, and numerous rounds of Vermont cheese to the camp. The pies were eaten for desert at Sunday dinner on tables the ladies had decorated with bouquets of flowers.[50]

Religious services were held on Sunday, June 16, at 5 P.M.. The sermon was titled "The Christian Soldier." As on the previous Sunday, the men were told of the need for the military to support the civil government, and reminded that a man could be a soldier for his country and at the same time be a soldier for the Lord.[51]

The 2nd Vermont's arms arrived on June 19 and to the disappointment of the men, most proved to be Model 1842 smoothbore muskets rather than the rifled weapons they had expected. Enough of the newer rifled muskets were rounded up so that Co. A could be equipped.[52]

The Model 1842 musket was a .69 caliber smoothbore muzzle loading weapon, weighing a little over nine pounds. It fired a round called a "buck and ball" that consisted of a solid round lead ball packaged with three small lead pellets. Because smoothbore muskets were so inaccurate, buck and ball gave the weapon a good spread and a better likelihood of hitting the intended target. The musket had an effective range of only 200 yards.[53]

Co. A was issued Model 1855 rifled muskets that fired minié balls. The American minié ball was in fact not a ball at all, but a soft lead conical bullet with a cone-shaped cavity in the base and three external rings cut into its lower body. When the rifle was fired, gasses forced the sides of the bullet into the barrel's rifling, causing the bullet to spin, giving it considerable accuracy. The model 1855 rifle could be deadly up to 800 yards, and very accurate up to 250. When its bullet hit a man, the result was not a small hole like a modern jacketed bullet. The minié ball struck at a high velocity and expanded like a dum-dum bullet, splintering bone, and leaving a large exit wound.[54]

Although the rifled musket was introduced into the U.S. Army in 1855, the doctrine for tactical formations did not change. During the Civil War, and even up to and through World War I, tactical offensive formations remained shoulder to shoulder close order formations in two ranks. The two ranks allowed the attacking force to throw its fire power along a broad front, have the sustaining power of the second rank, and allow commanders greater command and control. Unfortunately, once the rifled musket was introduced, the two rank offense could not overcome the firepower of the defender. The defenders could engage the attacking force at a greater distance, pour in a more accurate fire, and keep the attackers under fire for a longer time. The wholesale bloodletting caused by this mismatch between technology and doctrine would be repeated battle after battle during the four years of the Civil War.[55]

The rifled musket also made the bayonet ineffective; however, the bayonet was still attached to the musket on every charge during the war, though it seldom drew blood. Until the Civil War, the foot soldier was actually a spear-carrier in disguise. An advancing regiment was a compact mass of men projecting steel points ahead of them, striving to get to close quarters where they could either impale their opponents or force them to run away. Although the rifled musket made that tactic obsolete, it was continued throughout the war, causing charging units to be shot to shreds before they ever got close enough to the defenders to skewer them.[56]

Co. A was issued the better weapons not because it happened to be designated by the first letter of the alphabet, but because of its place in battle formation. In line of battle, the companies were arranged from left to right as follows: B, G, K, E, H, C, I, D, F, and A. As one of the two flank companies, Co. A was protecting one of the regiment's two most vulnerable spots: its flanks. Co. B protected the other flank and would have been issued the newer weapons had there been enough.[57]

The governor of Vermont had been trying to get good weapons for his regiment. In late May, he wrote to the U.S. registrar of the treasury almost begging for rifled muskets, but the pleading by the governor for decent weapons went unanswered by a government which, at the moment, was totally incapable of raising and equipping the number of troops called for by the president. Many Vermonters thought the arms that had been issued were sufficient for training, but would surely be replaced before the regiment faced the rebels. This would prove not to be the case.[58]

Lt. Col. Rains mustered the regiment into federal service on Thursday evening, June 20, at dress parade. After the mustering ceremony, Governor Fairbanks presented the regiment's U.S. colors to Col. Whiting. The governor made a speech emphasizing the high expectations he and the citizens of Vermont had for the regiment. Col. Whiting then spoke promising that neither he or the men under his command would dishonor the flag. Then Whiting handed the colors to the man selected as the color bearer,

Sgt. Ephriam W. Harrington. Harrington, a 28-year-old carpenter from Waterford, was an impressive looking man. He stood six feet five inches in his stocking feet and would carry the regiment's flag through every battle for the next two years.[59]

The regiment was the object of much attention during its two-week stay at Camp Underwood. Excursion trains brought visitors by the thousands who were captivated by the sight of their husbands, sons, and boyfriends in full uniform, particularly during the evening dress parade. The stirring airs of the regiment's band only heightened the excitement. This all came to an end, however, on Sunday, June 23. With orders in hand to move to Washington the next morning, Col. Whiting closed the camp. With the men having just been paid, Whiting wanted to make sure no one had second thoughts about deserting. Nevertheless, not being totally insensitive to everyone's feelings, he let some men out, or families in, to visit on an individual basis as families approached the guards and asked about a particular soldier by name.[60]

The regiment arose before daylight on Monday, June 24, and the camp was a beehive of activity. An early formation was called and duties were assigned. At 6 A.M., the tents, still damp with dew, were struck. At precisely 7 A.M., with the regimental band leading the way and the U.S. flag flying, the 2nd Vermont moved out of Camp Underwood for the last time.[61]

The departing regiment totaled 866 officers and men. Five sick enlisted men were left in a temporary hospital established in a house just outside the camp on Champlain Street. Twenty-year-old 1st Lt. Walter A. Philips of Co. F and Montpelier was ordered to remain behind and bring the sick men south as soon as they were well enough to rejoin the regiment, which he did on July 6.[62]

Although loaded down with heavy knapsacks with a tightly rolled blanket on top, full canteen, haversack with a full day's rations, and rifle, the men still stepped lively. With the band blaring military marching tunes, the regiment proudly marched down Burlington's St. Paul Street, with gray ranks stretching from gutter to gutter, and swept around the town square on its way to the Rutland & Burlington Railroad depot. The long column with its brightly polished gun barrels and bayonets flashing in the sunlight must have been a splendid sight. Every man wore a sprig of evergreen in his cap: the Green Mountain Boys badge.[63]

An immense throng of people on foot and in carriages lined the streets and accompanied the troops to the depot where the tearful good-byes started.[64]

The train that had been obtained for the regiment's move south consisted of four freight cars for tents and baggage and 20 passenger cars. Drawn by two powerful steam locomotives, the forward engine had a poster affixed to the side bearing a likeness of Lt. Gen. Winfield Scott. Some men had to stand in line for nearly an hour as the companies filed into the cars The extra time gave them a chance for a few more last minute embraces. As the cars were being loaded, one excited soldier leaned out of an open window and displayed a rope with a noose on the end and exclaimed to the delight of the crowd that it was destined for the neck of Jefferson Davis. At 9 A.M., the whistle blew and the train rumbled out of the depot. The crowd cheered, hats and handkerchiefs were waved; and tears flowed. With that, the 2nd Vermont was off to do its part in saving the Union.[65]

Sergeant Ephriam W. Harrington, Company G. Color bearer for the 2nd Vermont for nearly three years. He was awarded the Medal of Honor for bravery May 3, 1863. Pictured here as a captain and commander of Company G. USAMHI.

Pvt. Moses C. Glines, a 27-year-old Tunbridge native in Co. E, confessed to his wife two months later, "I did not think when I left you that I haid so many tears to shede in verginia fore I cood note help sheding a few when we left Vermont. My native land, my home and Everything that I hold dear to me."[66]

The regiment passed through Rutland at noon and arrived in Troy, N.Y., at 5:30 P.M. completing the first leg of its journey. At Troy's train depot, it was met by a delegation of the Sons of Vermont and thousands of local citizens who gave them a very enthusiastic welcome. Each

Private Moses C. Glines, Company E, pictured here in his Grand Army of the Republic uniform near the turn of the century. Kermit Glines.

company was placed in a separate room in the depot. Sandwiches, cold meats, pies, and hot coffee were served and haversacks were filled with cake and sandwiches. The officers were entertained in private homes. The regiment left Troy at 8 P.M. bound for New York City, the men in coaches and the officers in sleeping cars.[67]

The 2nd Vermont arrived in New York City at 6 A.M. on June 25 and was met at the foot of Canal Street by a committee of Vermonters and thousands of New Yorkers. It marched to the Park Barracks where breakfast and lunch were provided. At 2 P.M., the regiment formed in front of city hall and was presented a magnificent regimental standard. Senator Solomon Foote of Vermont replied to the presentation with a patriotic speech on behalf of Colonel Whiting.[68]

The banner was made of blue silk, trimmed with yellow fringe. On both sides was an American shield. On the right side of the shield was the American flag and on the other side was the coat of arms of Vermont. On a scroll above the shield, in gold letters, was inscribed, "Second Regiment Vermont Volunteers." Below was the motto of the state, "Freedom and Unity." A buck's head topped the shield. The staff was made of hickory, tipped with a spearhead, from which red, white, and blue cords and tassels were suspended.[69]

After the ceremony the regiment took a ferry to New Jersey where it transferred to a train. Chugging south through New Jersey, it reached Camden where it again transferred to a ferryboat to cross the Delaware River. It reached the wharf at Philadelphia around midnight and was met by cheering crowds that accompanied the regiment to the railroad station where refreshments, again, were served. At about 1:30 A.M. the men boarded a train on the Philadelphia, Wilmington, and Baltimore Railroad.[70]

On June 26 at 6:30 A.M., the Vermonters reached Perryville, Md., where the train was loaded aboard the 238-foot iron ferry, *Maryland*, and ferried across the Susquehanna River to Havre de Grace. This feat of transportation fascinated the Vermont farm boys. The transfer took an hour and a half, and then they were again on their way. But now there were no cheering crowds at the depots as they passed by. The state of Maryland, being a border state, was divided in its loyalties, and in this part of the state, Harford County, the populace tended to side with the South. The men must have felt they were in enemy territory. The feeling was reinforced when they saw Union soldiers guarding strategic points along the railroad at Perrymanville, Bush River, Gunpowder River, and Back River. The local citizens of Harford County had recently burned the bridges over the Bush and Gunpowder rivers and they had just been rebuilt.[71]

Just before reaching Baltimore, Col. Whiting had the train stopped and ordered the men to load and cap their muskets. The train pulled into Baltimore around 9:30 A.M. Due to an ordinance forbidding locomotives from running through the city, the men had to detrain so horses could pull the cars. The regiment was thus forced to march down Pratt Street from President Street Station to the Baltimore and Ohio Railroad's Camden Street Station. Pvt. Lucius Savage, a 23-year-old Waitsfield farmer in Co. F, noted in his diary:

> On arriving at Baltimore we left the cars and marched in two ranks through the city to the Baltimore and Washington Depot. Orders very strict while in B. Would not allow us to have anything to eat or drink for fear (they said) of our being poisoned. Saw the first Confederate flag before we got to Baltimore and saw a good many in marching through B. No resistance was offered to our passing through although many expressions from the crowd were anything but loyal—it seemed evident to them that we were well fixed for them and seemed

> to us they thought discretion the better part of valor and they concluded not to play the role they did when the 6th Massachusetts passed through on the 19th of April past.[72]

The 6th Massachusetts Infantry Regiment had been attacked by armed citizens while marching between the two stations and lost four men killed and 31 wounded. Other than angry scowls from some of the citizens, the transfer for the 2nd Vermont took place without incident.[73]

The Vermonters arrived, exhausted and hungry, in Washington at 3 P.M. June 26. To the likely bewilderment of the weary soldiers, there were no cheering crowds greeting them in the city they had come to save. Troops had been arriving there since the middle of April, and the locals now saw soldiers more as nuisances than as saviors.[74]

The Green Mountain Boys detrained and were fed a dinner of bread and cold boiled pork. Then they marched a mile from the railroad station to a field off Maryland Avenue between Tenth and Eleventh Streets (present day site of the Forrestal building), where they pitched camp. After seeing New York and Philadelphia, the sight around their camp must have been a disappointment. In 1861, the nation's capital was a ramshackle, dirty town with hogs running loose on its unpaved streets. The smell was worse than the sight, for the city's sanitary conditions were appalling. A defective sewage system that drained directly onto tidal river flats, and the city's numerous privies had always been odorous in warm weather, and newly arrived regiments, whose camps lacked adequate latrine facilities, only added to the filth.[75]

Aside from the smell, the Vermonters' campsite was in a fairly good location. Within a couple of days, the men had it in good shape. Using Yankee ingenuity, the country boys built cooking stoves in the ground by digging a hole over which to set kettles in the clay soil. Although the arrangements for cooking were in place, the food was not. The War Department was totally unprepared to supply the large number of troops who quickly filled Washington. The ration shortage grew so bad that many units, including the 2nd Vermont, were near insurrection. On Sunday, June 30, Co. A refused to attend drill until given sufficient rations. Fortunately, rations were received the next day and everything quickly returned to normal.[76]

It was during their stay in Washington that the men of the 2nd Vermont started to develop a dislike for their commander. This was not an uncommon problem in the newly formed Union volunteer regiments that were made up mainly of independent minded farmers, who did not like taking orders. Yet with Whiting it intensified, probably because he was not a Vermonter and because he believed in firm discipline.

"Our old Col. is very strict," Lt. Leach complained to his wife. "He has forbidden all selling of eatables around the camp & our Capt. was officer of the day yesterday & and he permitted a woman to sell her stuff so the Col. Has ordered him under arrest today." Later Leach would find this was not the only reason Burnham was placed under arrest.

"There is quite a disaffection among the men towards the Col.," Leach wrote several days later. "They think he is rather cross & severe. The most fault I find with him is that anyone can get no instructions from him, but when his orders come out he wants them done right."[77]

One private in the 2nd Vermont penned, "Our camp discipline is pretty rigid, and our Vermont boys chafe under it some. Our Colonel don't seem to exactly understand how to get along with us and some dissatisfaction exists, but I hope all will come out well."[78]

The routine at this camp, named Camp Fairbanks, was less structured than in Burlington. The regiment had but two drills a day, two hours in the morning and two hours in the afternoon. Some days the regiment had target practice down by the Potomac River.

Capt. Drew wrote:

> We also practice some at target shooting. Several of the boys make rather bungling work at this; for instance, one boy in loading a day or two since, put in his first cartridge wrong side up, and afterwards put the loads top of that. The target wasn't hit by nary-a-one of these shots. We have hardly become reconciled to our guns yet; that is, if we are to retain them, which seems to be the general opinion. One thing is certain, we shall never do but little execution with these "popguns."

Lt. Leach expressed the same sentiment writing, "The company all went out to target shoot this forenoon, marched about a mile. Our old muskets shoot all over the safeworks."[79]

The more relaxed routine at Camp Fairbanks gave the men more time to enjoy themselves. Many went swimming in the Potomac or sightseeing around the city. Because of the camp's proximity to the center of the city, the men could easily visit its famous buildings on foot. The Capitol was quite an attraction not only because of its historical significance, but because it was nearing completion of a 10-year long upgrade, and they could watch the new cast iron dome being constructed. The men also visited the Smithsonian Institution and the U. S. Patent Office.[80]

The extra free time also had its down side. Drinking became a problem again. Edson Emery, a 27-year-old Tunbridge farmer turned corporal in Co. E, stated in his diary on July 7 that, "A good many drunk and some fighting."

Lt. Leach, describing what he had observed on a trip downtown, wrote "The street was filled with soldiers all sorts and sizes, drunk and sober. It is no job to get drunk here for there are liquor holes in every direction." Hard drinking was not limited to the enlisted men as Leach detailed in the same letter:

> You say Zina [Leach's cousin] wants to know how well we like our Capt. [Burnham] Well, he is just as good as no Captain at all. He has not done more than two days drill since we have been here, except he was Officer-of-the-Day one day. The next day after he was Officer-of-the-Day he was put under arrest. It was said, "for permitting a woman to sell groceries across the line." But that was not the cause. It was for being intoxicated while on duty. The Col. wrote him a letter which I copied before he got it giving him a choice of two things: either to resign his commission, or leave off drinking. I believe the Col. has his commission which is to be handed over to President Lincoln whenever he does not live up to his agreement.[81]

Pvt. Sanford R. Barnes, a 28-year-old carpenter from Bakersfield in Co. H, also noted Burnham's behavior, "Our Capt. Is about as good as a ___ stick. He smokes & drinks then drinks & smokes. Then changes the programme, smokes & drinks together." Drinking would not be Burnham's only problem.[82]

Another vice prevalent in Washington was prostitution. With the influx of troops into the city, there came a proportional influx of prostitutes. Although nothing remains to document that any members of the 2nd Vermont indulged in the pleasures of the flesh, they probably were little different from lads in other regiments. The houses of ill repute were in the near vicinity of the camp, as noted in one of Lt. Leach's letters "Yesterday [July 7] there was a building burned about 50 rods from our camp. It was set on fire by some soldiers from another camp. They say it was a woman house [Civil War euphemism for a house of prostitution]—of course I don't know. There was two or three of them burned in the city a few days ago."[83]

Apparently during their term of service, most of the men in the 2nd Vermont, at one time or another, visited houses of prostitution, as mentioned in a letter by the 2nd Vermont's surgeon toward the end of the war:

> Well I have one thing to console me—I shall leave this army with a system as pure as when God created it so far as regards prostitutes, for I have neither sought them in city or town hence my skin is as smooth, and free from lothesome venerial sores as ever. Thank Heaven my system has never been contaminated with that most foul of all diseases—.... There is scarcely an Officer or man in this army can say as much—hence *I say it with more pride.* Most of the privates and Officers are *now* or *have been* rotten with it.... Speaking about venerial disease reminds me of a certain Officer of Isle La Mott who smelt so strong of this disease last summer that he became offensive to every one he approached.[84]

Pvt. Chauncey Dickinson of Co. B and Georgia, Vt., also took advantage of this less structured period, on July 3, and deserted. He was never seen in the ranks again.[85]

Despite all the temptations of the big city, Col. Whiting, a devout Christian, tried to provide for the men's religious needs. Pvt. Cutler lamented, "Oh Emily, I miss very much the religious privileges that I was blessed with at home, but still with God's assisting grace I shall hold fast my integrity. Our church here is the open field, its dome the broad canopy of heaven. Every morning we are paraded on the ground to attend prayers, and on Sunday we have preaching."[86]

The sicknesses that had started at Camp Underwood reappeared at Camp Fairbanks with a vengeance. Lt. Leach wrote on July 2, "There is three or four of our company sick with the measles." On July 8 he added:

> Our regt. has been pretty sickly for about a week past. They most all have had diarrhea. I think it is the water as much as anything that does it, and then quite a few have had the measles. Five or six from our company have them but are getting better. Taking out sick, guard, and mess there is not more than half of the company left for parade, but I think within a week their health will be better.[87]

Capt. Drew, commander of Co. G, wrote on July 2, "We have about 20 down with measles, many of which are in the hospital in the city." Measles were so bad in Co. E that when calling for a company formation the first sergeant would yell, "Fall in you measley cusses!"[88]

On July 9, the regiment experienced the first of its many deaths from disease. Pvt. Frederick A. Stoddard of Co. C, a 19-year-old boy of Townshend, died at 11 A.M. of putrid sore throat [diphtheria]. His father, Judge Abishai Stoddard, notified by telegram the day before of young Stoddard's illness, arrived in Washington the next day only to find his son dead. Judge Stoddard had his son's body embalmed and took it home for burial.[89]

While the 2nd Vermont was being formed and trained, important things were happening in Washington. The primary task for the federal government was to defend the nation's capital. Since the majority of the regular army was strung out in various posts across the western frontier, the recently mobilized volunteer units would have to be used in the East. Lt. Gen. Winfield Scott wanted troops across the Potomac as soon as possible to push the Confederates out of Alexandria, Va. This would relieve the tension of having the enemy just across the river, give Scott a base in

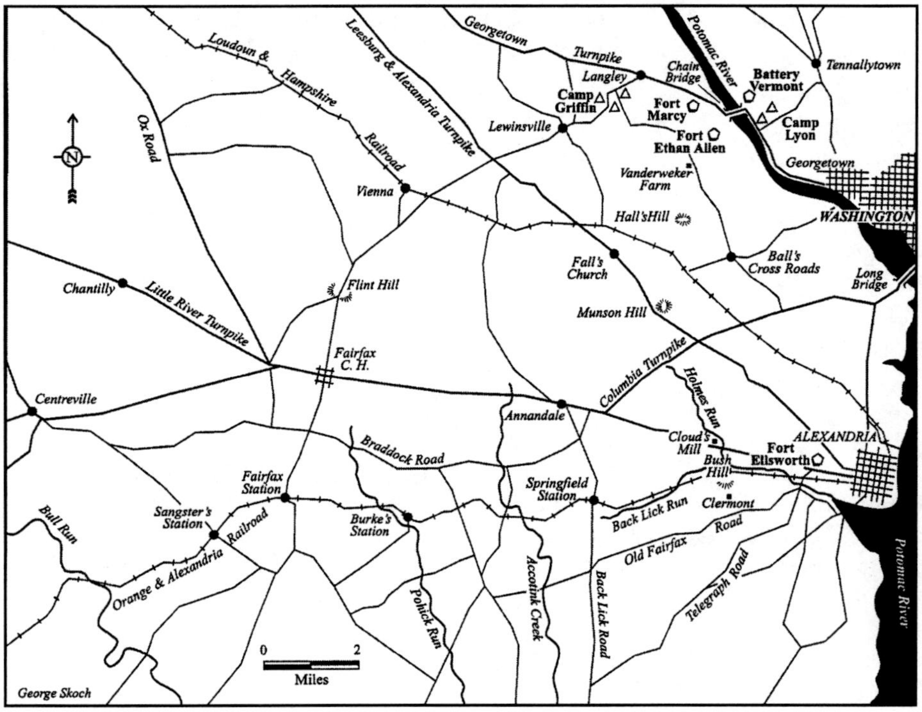

Northern Virginia

Virginia from which to launch other military operations, and would remove from the eyes of the capital the insulting sight of Confederate flags flying from Alexandria's rooftops. On the morning of May 24, federal forces took Alexandria and Arlington with virtually no resistance.[90]

The only unfortunate casualty during the occupation was the murder of Col. Elmer E. Ellsworth, commander of the 11th New York Fire Zouaves. While marching his regiment from the docks to occupy the city's telegraph office, he passed a hotel named the Marshall House at the corner of Duke and Pitt Streets. Atop the hotel there flew a Confederate flag, and the sight incensed the young colonel. Ellsworth took a detail and left the column bent on removing the flag. As he descended the stairs from the roof with the flag in his arms, the proprietor, James Jackson, shot him dead. Instantly one of Ellsworth's men shot Jackson dead. The news of the incident was telegraphed nationwide and Ellsworth became the war's first martyr.[91]

With Alexandria secured and thousands of troops pouring across the Potomac, the federal government had to select a commander to lead them. Irvin McDowell was the man selected.[92]

Irvin McDowell, 42 years old and a West Pointer, had always been a staff officer and had never had command experience. He had served on Brig. Gen. John E. Wool's staff during the war with Mexico. In the spring of 1861, he was serving on Scott's staff in Washington.[93]

McDowell was promoted to brigadier general on May 27. That afternoon he crossed the Potomac to review his new command, and what he found was disquieting. No defensive fortifications around Alexandria had been started or even planned. The men complained of inadequate supplies, a lack of wagons and bad communications with Washington.[94]

McDowell immediately started organizing his units and requisitioning necessary transportation. He formed his regiments into brigades for better command and control. As more and more regiments arrived, he formed the brigades into divisions.[95]

On July 7, Col. Oliver O. Howard, commander of the 3rd Maine Infantry Regiment, was chosen as commander of the Third Brigade of Col. Samuel P. Heintzelman's division. As soon as he received the War Department note appointing him a brigade commander, Howard visited and selected three other units for his brigade—the 4th and 5th Maine regiments and the 2nd Vermont. Finally by July 8, McDowell had his army which he formed into five divisions.[96]

Colonel Oliver O. Howard, pictured here as a major general. Library of Congress.

Colonel Samuel P. Heintzelman, pictured here as a major general. Library of Congress.

The 2nd Vermont received orders on July 8 to be ready to move to Alexandria the next day. Early next morning tents were struck and equipment was packed to move, but the order was countermanded due to an insufficient number of wagons. Later the same day, orders were received to move July 10. By daylight the next morning the wagons had arrived. The tents were struck at 8 A.M., and the regiment moved at nine o'clock for the Potomac River docks to embark for transport to Alexandria. The distance from the camp to the docks was only about two-and-a-half miles, but Col. Whiting moved his men at nearly a double-quick pace. With the morning extremely sultry and the men under full load, many were overcome with the heat and fell out by the roadside. The docks were reached a little after 10 A.M. and the regiment boarded steamers to cross the river.[97]

The Vermonters reached Alexandria by mid-afternoon, unloaded their baggage and equipment, then waited a couple of hours for the train that was to take them to their next destination. During the layover, hundreds of the men rushed to the Marshall House where Col. Ellsworth had been killed, trying to grab something for a souvenir. Because of the national notoriety of Ellsworth's killing, the Marshall House had already been plundered by Union soldiers seeking curios, but not to be denied a souvenir, the Vermont boys whipped out their pocket knives and whittled away. Pvt. Elijah S. Brown, a young man from Woodbury in Co. F, sent his souvenir home in a letter, bragging, "I went to where Col. Ellsworth was shot & this is a piece of the pole that he took the flag from...." Finally by 6 P.M. everyone was rounded up and loaded aboard the train.[98]

The regiment arrived just after sundown at Bush Hill, four miles west of Alexandria. The men were marched a half mile to their new campsite on Confederate Commodore French Forrest's plantation, Clermont. During the march, a terrific thunderstorm erupted and the men pitched tents in a driving rain. Most were bedded down by 10 P.M., tired, wet, and hungry.[99]

The regiment awoke the next morning to a bright day that soon dried the camp. Soon after dawn's first light, everyone was able to see the beauty surrounding the camp. The 360-acre Clermont, located between the Orange and Alexandria Railroad and the Old Fairfax Road, was quite a showplace. The house was a typical two-story wood frame structure, but unlike many houses in northern Virginia, it had been well maintained. The grounds were manicured and boasted exotic plants and numerous shade trees. There was plenty of cool water, the orchard was large, and patches of blackberries were everywhere. The Vermonters took full advantage. Col. Whiting immediately put guards around the house. In fact, he forbade the men to touch the split rail fences, causing them to have to carry firewood from up to a mile away.[100]

The owner of Clermont, French Forrest, had been a captain in the U.S. Navy before the war, but resigned his commission in June to become a captain in the Confederate Navy. He was soon promoted to commodore and put in charge of the Norfolk shipyard. On the morning of May 24, Mrs. Forrest, leaving her breakfast on the table, fled from her farm to Richmond as soon as she heard that Union troops were crossing the Potomac.[101]

The 3rd, 4th, and 5th Maine infantry regiments joined the 2nd Vermont over the next several days, rounding out Howard's brigade.[102]

On July 11, the Vermonters also commenced their first combat operation. Early in the morning, Col. Whiting was ordered to move a force several miles toward Manassas to inspect the Orange and Alexandria Railroad for damage. He sent companies A and B under the command of Maj. Joyce. The reconnaissance force moved down the line to where it crossed Back Lick Creek, near a plantation called Springfield. There the retreating rebels had burned the bridge, leaving only the masonry and iron portions of the structure. Maj. Joyce had been instructed to hold the bridge, if it had been damaged, until work crews could be sent to make repairs. He sent a detachment, under 2nd Lt. Enoch E. Johnson of Co. B, from Castleton, farther down the tracks to determine if there was more damage. Joyce then moved his

Confederate Commodore French Forrest's farm Clermont. University of Vermont.

to the west. McDowell finally submitted a plan of operations that was quickly approved by Gen. Scott. However, one major provision of the plan was that Maj. Gen. Robert Patterson would keep Maj. Gen. Joseph E. Johnston's army of 9,000 rebels locked in place in the Shenandoah Valley so he could not reinforce Beauregard. Scott assured him this would be done. After several false starts and some foot dragging, McDowell issued orders to prepare three days' rations and be ready to move on Manassas on July 16.

With the warning order issued, the 2nd Vermont's camp was suddenly a beehive of activity. Rations were cooked, knap-

main body into the cover of surrounding woods to await Johnson's return. Noticing several well-used paths leading through the woods to the railroad, Joyce sent a messenger back to camp for reinforcements. Co. F was dispatched and arrived at Joyce's location just before dark.[103]

In the meantime, Johnson's detachment returned reporting more damage down the line. Joyce had the companies occupy the surrounding hilltops and prepared to hold the position for the night. It was an anxious night for the men in enemy territory for the first time. Sunrise, however, found them undisturbed by rebels. The detachment returned to camp the next day after being relieved by several companies of the 3rd Maine. During the next week-and-a-half, the regiment was kept busy with daily reconnaissance missions, but the enemy was unseen.[104]

During McDowell's occupation of Virginia, many in the government and the army thought him too lenient toward secessionist property. Officers were verbally abused in soldier gossip and newspapers for using soldiers to guard private property. This securing of private property did not come from Southern sympathy. McDowell knew that a lack of discipline would turn his army into a horde of marauders. As will be seen later, the best efforts of the command to control the plundering of private property were never wholly successful.[105]

In the camps that ringed Alexandria, McDowell's men were learning to become soldiers. McDowell himself was being pressured by the federal government, and the Northern press, to stop the training and attack Gen. P. G. T. Beauregard's Confederate Army, located at Manassas 25 miles

First Lieutenant Enoch E. Johnson, Company B, pictured here as major of the 2nd Vermont. USAMHI.

sacks packed and repacked, and weapons were cleaned and inspected. Pvt. Cutler wrote, "I sat up all last night cooking provisions to carry on the march."[106]

Sure of their success in the upcoming battle, Pvt. James W. Bromley, a 24-year-old farmer from Danby, wrote that evening:

> we are going to start for Manatia [Manassas] Gap tomorrow morning at 1 o'clock. I think that we shall have a little brush. then if the southerers have got any spunk they will have left the Court house and I think that they will leave richmond or Else they will get whiped we have 35 thousand men within five miles of us. we are all going to start and march right along. There is 2 thousand in the same meadow with us here now ... they must run or die or surender. One of the three pretty soon.... I will tell you the particulars when I get back.[107]

Caught up in the excitement, Pvt. Victor Goodrich, a 23-year-old Roxbury native in Co. F, jumped on a wooden box, started dancing, and exclaimed, "Boys, I am going to have one more good dance and it may be my last."[108]

CHAPTER 2

THE DISGRACEFUL AFFAIR AT BULL RUN

Early Tuesday morning, July 16, 1861, McDowell issued orders to move his army. All units were to move that afternoon to reach their first destination by dark. Brig. Gen. Daniel Tyler's First Division was to move to Vienna by the Georgetown Turnpike and the Leesburg Stone Road. Col. David Hunter's Second Division would go by the Columbia Turnpike to where it intersected the Little River Turnpike. Brig Gen. Samuel P. Heintzelman's Third Division was to proceed on the Old Fairfax Court House Road south of the Orange and Alexandria Railroad to either Accotink or Pohick Creek; the final destination being left to his discretion. Col. Dixon Miles's Fifth Division was to move by the Little River Turnpike as far as Annandale. Brig. Gen. Theodore Runyon's Fourth Division was to remain in the defenses of Washington, to protect, and assist in the repair of the railroads leading to Manassas.

On July 17, the First, Second and Fifth Divisions' objective was Fairfax Court House. Heintzelman was to bivouac at Sangster's Station on the Orange and Alexandria Railroad.

The intelligence portion of the order warned of enemy forces at Centreville, Germantown, Fairfax Court House, and Fairfax Station and went on to say that rebels had been obstructing roads and throwing up breastworks. McDowell also noted his concern for not being able to distinguish friendly forces from the enemy, and he cautioned commanders to take great care to avoid firing at each other. Because a number of units like the 2nd Vermont wore gray uniforms similar to those of the Confederates, confusion as to who was who would occur several times during the upcoming battle. McDowell directed each unit to display the national colors at all times, and if possible, to have small U.S. flags placed on the cannons.[1]

At 2 P.M. on Tuesday, July 16, Howard's brigade, with the 2nd Vermont bringing up the rear, started toward Manassas. Col. Whiting and his field and staff officers were as yet without horses and therefore marched on foot with the men. Maj. Joyce, somewhere along the way, bought a horse and was the only mounted officer in the regiment.[2]

Col. Heintzelman's command moved south of the railroad as planned without incident. Rebels were occasionally seen, but were seldom within musket range. Due to the indirect route planned by McDowell, the Confederates seemed not to have expected a Federal column on this road. Local civilians soon spread the word, however, and the rebels felled trees across the roads forcing the troops to take to the fields. The most significant obstacle to the march came at Accotink Creek. Col. Howard recalled the incident in his autobiography:

> When I came to the Accotink I found many men of the preceding brigade sitting down and taking off their shoes—not to wade the shallow stream, but for fear they might slip off the narrow bridge which was made of two logs placed side by side, and so wet their shoes and socks. Regiment after regiment had

> been crossing in this way by file, so that each brigade before mine had taken a full two hours to pass a stream not more than twenty yards wide and the water nowhere above their knees. This delayed my crossing till night. My men were somewhat incensed because I made them close up and march straight through the ford. They surely would not have been so fresh and happy the next morning if they had been three hours later than they were in getting into camp. In such small things as this West Point officers appeared to be too severe with new troops.[3]

It was after midnight before the regiment stopped for a three-hour rest. Pvt. Lucius Savage noted, "After crossing this stream as soon as we reached our proper places and got well closed up we were halted and remained on a piece of very stony ground until morning. The small cobble stone was so thick here that we had to remove them before we could lay down."[4]

The next day, Wednesday, July 17, Howard's brigade marched at daylight and by 5 P.M. had reached Sangster's Station. Wearing wool uniforms and carrying loaded knapsacks and muskets made for a grueling march in the sweltering July heat. Troubles with the division baggage train caused constant delays, and the men, tired from the 15-mile march the day before, were in no hurry. Fatigue, coupled with inadequate training, caused several accidents along the march. In one of the Maine regiments, one man accidentally shot a companion. In another, a soldier attempting to knock apples off a tree with his inverted musket, somehow discharged the weapon, mortally wounding himself. In spite of the heat and the fatiguing march, the pious Howard was appalled by the men's language as he expressed in a letter, "In consequence of hearing much profanity, I wished our men had more regard for the Lord; we might then expect his blessing."[5]

As is typical of green troops, Howard's men had eaten their three days' rations in a day-and-a-half. The shortage was somewhat alleviated that night when they camped at Sangster's Station. About a mile before reaching the station they passed the deserted camp of an Alabama regiment. In their hasty retreat, the rebels had attempted to destroy their store of rations but had not done a thorough job. Howard's men noticed this as they passed and as soon as they stopped for the night, a number of them returned to the camp and gathered up flour, cornmeal, and salt pork. One Vermont soldier wrote, "And taking our tin plates for frying pans we fried the pork with the gravy stirred in some flour and made us some pancakes." Along with the chickens and pigs they had stolen along the route of march, Whiting's boys ate well that night.[6]

The Vermonters, like most soldiers during the Civil War, continued to supplement their "marching rations" with whatever they could buy or steal. After all, marching rations consisted of only a three-day supply of hardtack, salt pork, coffee, sugar, and salt per man. Hardtack, a cracker made of flour and water about three inches square and nearly half an inch thick, was solid and very hard though nourishing. Some 10 slabs usually constituted a day's ration. When on the march or when time was short, hardtack was often crumbled in a cup of coffee and eaten with a spoon. When time permitted, the cracker would be toasted over a fire, soaked in water and fried in pork fat, or beaten into a powder and mixed with boiled rice and served as a griddlecake.[7]

Salt pork was usually fried in a skillet made by the soldier from half a canteen with a wire handle. On the march, pork was often eaten raw or broiled on a stick over a fire and eaten with hardtack. Occasionally, salt pork was issued rancid and sometimes was crawling with worms, which would bring loud complaints from the ranks.[8]

Coffee was the mainstay of the army. Once they became veterans, the soldiers learned to carry a small canvas bag in which they mixed ground coffee and sugar. The ration was ample for three or four pints of coffee a day. On the march, a halt of more than five minutes was sure to see men making little fires and boiling coffee. If rest halts were too far apart, men would often fall out, build a fire, boil coffee, drink it, and then plod along to catch up to their regiment at nightfall.[9]

On Thursday, July 18, Heintzelman's division remained at rest at Sangster's Station most of the day. During the morning, division commanders received an intelligence report and new instructions from McDowell. The general indicated each column had run into obstructions such as felled trees and breastworks and that many of the rebel pickets had been captured with a loss of only four men wounded in Miles's division. McDowell again complained about the men's destruction of secessionist property, stating, "I am distressed to have to report excesses by our troops. The excitement of the men found vent in burning and pillaging, which distressed us all greatly." McDowell's new instructions to the army were few: Miles's division was to camp at Centreville, four miles east of Bull Run; Hunter's division was to get as near Centreville as it could, yet have access to a supply of water; and Heintzelman's division was to move up to Little Rocky Run on the road to Centreville. A postscript gave zest to his message to Tyler, who was in front of Miles: "Observe well the roads to Bull Run and to Warrenton.... Do not bring on an engagement, but keep up the impression that we are moving on Manassas."

With this additional note, McDowell had just changed his battle plan. Until that time, it had been his plan to move on Manassas by a rapid push from his left, but his engineers had found the roads of approach "too narrow and crooked for a large body to move over and the distance around (southward) too great to admit of it with any safety."[10]

During the afternoon, everyone's attention was drawn to cannons booming as Tyler and Richardson attacked Confederate forces guarding Blackburn's Ford of Bull Run in a premature and inconclusive fight. It was the first time the men of the 2nd Vermont had heard combat.[11]

At 5 P.M., Howard's brigade moved down Braddock Road five or six miles to Little Rocky Run about a mile south of Centreville. During the march, a rumor ran down the column that Tyler had been defeated. It proved true. Tyler's orders were to occupy Centreville, which he did without firing a shot. But instead of stopping there, he ordered Col. Richardson's brigade down a road leading to Manassas to determine Confederate strength at Blackburn's Ford. At the ford, Richardson got into sharp fight with Brig. Gen. James Longstreet's and Col. Jubal A. Early's brigades, losing 83 men. Pvt. Elijah S. Brown went down to Blackburn's Ford after the battle and reported, "the 8 that was killed was mangled awful. legs torn of[f] and to tel the fact they were all mangled to peices & we had to let them lay there two nights and one day for the flies to blow. it was the most horrible thing that I ever saw. I went over to see them yesterday to see them buried it made me heart sick."[12]

As the 2nd Vermont prepared to leave Sangster's Station, companies B and G, with Maj. Joyce in charge, were ordered to bring up the rear and guard the baggage and ammunition wagons. Near dark, lagging two miles behind the main column, the horses and mules pulling the wagons balked at climbing a steep hill. No amount of threats or swearing could move them. Finally, in desperation, the troops were ordered to unload the wagons and carry the contents up the one-mile grade. At the top of the hill the wagons were reloaded, and the column proceeded on. Several hours later it caught up with the main body.[13]

The 2nd Vermont bivouacked just after dark. Again the men were out of rations, as related by Pvt. Savage: "Halted about one mile east of Centreville and laid down for the night nothing in our stomachs nothing in our haversacks and nothing we can steal it being in the night. And we being strangers in a strange place we had to content ourselves as best we could and wait for day light."

Next morning, in complete defiance of McDowell's order against foraging, the Vermonters were at it again. Savage continued:

> Our first business this morning was to look about us and see if we could find anything to eat as our trains are not up with us. Early blackberries are quite plenty here now and many of us wandered around and picked berries. Others stole the honey from the neighboring plantations. Others shot some cattle and got some meat while others obtained some ducks, chickens & c. The beef, ducks & c. we roasted on some sticks over the fires. Eat it without salt, bread or anything by way of seasoning.[14]

Pvt. Elijah S. Brown added, "if we had not been lucky enough to found a few beef cattle & a few hogs & poultry that the boys shot on the road we should have all starved to death."[15]

McDowell spent the next two days at Centreville completing the organization of his army, bringing supplies forward, and reconnoitering Confederate positions across Bull Run, where he found the rebels in strength at six of the seven crossing points. The only crossing left unguarded was on the Confederates' extreme left flank at Sudley Springs Ford. With his newly gathered intelligence, McDowell devised another plan of operations which he revealed to a council of war on the evening of Saturday, July 20. Tyler's division, minus Richardson's brigade, was to move along the Warrenton Turnpike early on the morning of July 21 and make a serious demonstration against the Confederates in the vicinity of the Stone Bridge. Meanwhile, Hunter's division would march northwest by a circuitous route and cross Bull Run at Sudley Ford. Heintzelman would follow, but cross Bull Run at Poplar (Red House) Ford south of Sudley Ford. Once across Bull Run, Hunter and Heintzelman would roll up the Confederate line, driving it to the southeast and away from the Manassas Gap Railroad, which was Johnston's probable route of approach from the Shenandoah Valley, if he were able to join Beauregard. When the Stone Bridge was uncovered by the progress of the Federal flanking column, Tyler was to send his brigades across Bull Run. Miles's division was to provide rear area security by holding Centreville and guarding the road to Mitchell's and Blackburn's Fords. Runyon's division would protect the army's line of communication to Washington. Much depended upon Patterson's keeping Johnston in the Shenandoah Valley.[16]

The two days that McDowell's army sat at Centreville gave the Confederates an opportunity to increase their forces along Bull Run. At 1 A.M., July 18, Johnston received orders to transfer his army from the Shenandoah Valley to Manassas. Masking his intentions with a cavalry screen, he moved his units to a station on the Manassas Gap Railroad 34 miles from Manassas Junction. His forces would start arriving at Manassas late the next day.[17]

On Saturday evening, July 20, Howard assembled his brigade for the usual dress parade. The chaplain of one of the Maine regiments gave them a prayer. Howard said, "Every soldier of my command seemed thoughtful and reverent that night." Then Howard addressed the troops telling them that, in all probability, this was the last time they would all meet on dress parade and expressed the hope that they would all behave like men and not turn their backs to the enemy in tomorrow's battle. He was answered with a cheer and a loud "never!"[18]

Sunday morning, July 21, the 2nd Vermont was awakened between 1 and 2 A.M. and told to prepare to move. Canteens and haversacks were filled, a breakfast of coffee and hardtack quickly devoured, and the troops were formed for the march. The men had been instructed to leave their knapsacks in their tents and wear only a rolled blanket over their shoulder. In addition to the rolled blanket, each man carried his canteen, haversack with two day's rations, 40 rounds of ammunition, and his musket.[19]

According to McDowell's movement order, Tyler's division was to be on the road at 2:30 A.M., but he lost an hour getting his inexperienced troops out of their tents. At dawn his skirmishers had reached the Stone Bridge, but the rest of his, as well as other Federal troops, were backed up blocking the Warrenton Turnpike. With lost minutes ticking away, McDowell finally ordered the troops off the pike to allow Hunter's and Heintzelman's divisions to move through. Tyler began his prescribed demonstration in the area of the Stone Bridge around 6 A.M. and for several hours he poured artillery and small arms fire into the woods across Bull Run. Col. Nathan G. Evans, whose brigade faced Tyler, was for a while concerned, but after several hours of hostile fire and no troop movement on Tyler's part, he became suspicious. With no attack by 8:30 A.M., Evans was convinced that all he faced was a feint. Within a short time he received two messages that confirmed that fact. Both messages indicated that a large Federal column was moving around his left flank toward Sudley Ford.[20]

Hunter's division, followed by Heintzelman's, moved several miles down the Warrenton Turnpike before turning onto a small country lane leading to Sudley Ford. As Howard's brigade, bringing up the rear of Heintzelman's column, made the turn it was halted by McDowell, who told the colonel his men were to be held in reserve. The brigade moved off the road to the left where the men found what cover they could for shade. Hunter and Heintzelman continued on toward Sudley Ford. (This was the column that had been reported to Evans.)[21]

Evans left four companies to confront Tyler and marched his other troops north to engage Hunter and Heintzelman. The Federal plan called for reaching Sudley Ford at 7 A.M., but Hunter was more than two hours late crossing the stream. The men had started that morning excited and full of fight, singing "John Brown's Body," but by midmorning, heat, fatigue, tension, and lack of sleep caused a great number of them to fall out. McDowell hurried Hunter's and Heintzelman's men as best he could across Bull Run and then south down the Manassas-Sudley Road. Evans, however, had beaten the Federals to the punch and had his 1,000 men and two guns deployed in the woods on Matthew's Hill, less than a mile south of Sudley Springs Ford. On top of the hill, the rebel troops were protected by a grove of trees, while to their front they had a clear field of fire down the slope toward the open road the Yankees would have to use, and from this position they hit them as soon as they came into range. Rather than bringing all their force to bear and overwhelm Evans, the two Federal commanders threw regiments in piecemeal, allowing Evans to hold out for over an hour. Eventually the Federals flanked Evans's men and threatened to destroy them. Although he was outnumbered six to one, Evans tenaciously held on to his position.[22]

While Evans was being hammered on Matthews Hill, General Beauregard, on the Confederate right, was organizing an attack in that sector to counter the Federal advance. To ensure his left flank did not collapse, he directed Gen. Barnard E. Bee and Col. Francis Bartow to take their brigades to the Confederate left to reinforce Evans and Col. P. St. George Cocke. Brig. Gen. Thomas J. Jackson's brigade also was sent to the left, but not as far as Bee and Bartow.[23]

As Bee and Bartow neared Matthews Hill, Evans was about to be overrun. Quickly sizing up the gravity of the situation, Bee wasted no time getting his men into the fray. Although the reinforcements brought up the total rebel force on Matthews Hill to about 4,500 men, they were still outnumbered. At about 11 A.M., Col. William T. Sherman started crossing his brigade across Bull Run at a farm ford north of the Stone Bridge (going in single file it took nearly an hour) and came in on the Confederate left flank. Sherman's presence, along with the arrival of some of Heintzelman's men, finally overwhelmed the Confederates. They were forced to withdraw across the Warrenton Turnpike and Young's Branch and reform on Henry Hill. From this position they commanded the Warrenton Turnpike and the Manassas-Sudley Road and made ready to take on the Federals again.[24]

McDowell sent an officer to bring up Howard's brigade, and between noon and 1 P.M. it moved forward. The guide had been instructed to bring Howard's brigade straight to the fight, but not knowing about the crossing at Poplar Ford, he brought them the long seven-mile roundabout way, crossing at Sudley Ford, and headed on down Manassas-Sudley Road. It was an exhausting march in the heat of the day. The brigade had made about two miles when word came from Heintzelman to come at the double-quick. In an attempt to keep pace, the men started throwing away their rolled-up blankets, haversacks, and even their canteens.

Howard kept up this pace only for a short while since so many men were dropping out. Captain Burnham was one of the first members of the 2nd Vermont to fall out, leaving the command of Co. H to First Lt. Jerome B. Case. "Our double quick through the hot sun," explained Private Cutler, "about winded many of us up so that we were hardly fit for action when we got their many actually falling so exhausted and nearly melted...." Some of the companies in the 2nd Vermont lost as many as one-quarter of their men from fainting and sunstroke.[25]

McDowell now seemed to have the battle going his way. All along the Confederate line commanders had fought their units gallantly, but they were now at the point of collapse. A final blow by McDowell could result in a Union victory and possibly bring a quick end to the rebellion.[26]

As McDowell's units started to apply pressure to the Confederates on Henry Hill, Bee discovered that Jackson's brigade and several artillery batteries, yet uncommitted, were also on the hill. Jackson had marched his brigade to the sound of the firing and had kept his men under cover while awaiting the coming Federal assault. Bee rode over to Jackson and asked for support to which Jackson agreed. Bee then rode back to his own unit and ordered them to fall in with the Virginians, making the now famous statement, "There is Jackson standing like a stone wall," changing Jackson's name in history forever.[27]

By 1:30 P.M. Beauregard had been reinforced by units forwarded to him by Johnston until his troop strength had been increased by about 7,000 men, but still he was outnumbered. McDowell was now ready to strike his decisive blow. To weaken Confederate resistance he sent Capt. J. B. Ricketts's and Capt. Charles Griffin's batteries to the crest of Henry Hill to pound the enemy line. Ricketts and Griffin both felt they would be too exposed on the bare plateau on the top of the hill, but were assured they would be supported by two regiments of infantry. They reached the top of the hill and unlimbered around 2 P.M.[28]

For a while, Ricketts and Griffin held their own. Then a cavalry charge by Col. James E. B. "Jeb" Stuart's 1st Virginia Cavalry Regiment and a volley from Jackson's men caused the Federal gunners' infantry support to fall back. The 33rd Virginia Infantry took advantage of the Union batteries' vulnerability by moving to within fifty yards of the guns and opening fire. Captain Griffin had wanted to fire on them as soon as they were sighted, but McDowell's chief of artillery, Maj. William Barry, held him in check. Because the 33rd Virginia was wearing blue uniforms he feared they might be their own infantry support. (There continues to be controversy over the uniforms the rebels wore. Colonel Arthur C. Cummings, the 33rd Virginia's commander, and perhaps one or two of his companies may have been in blue, but a number of sources, to include Heintzelman, indicate that the other companies were in "citizen's" clothes. Regardless, Major Barry thought they were Federals.) The rebels' volley instantly revealed their true identity, and the two Federal batteries were destroyed. Most of the Federal gunners were downed in a matter of minutes. Only two of the guns were successfully brought off the hill.[29]

As the battle raged, Howard's brigade continued moving rapidly down Manassas-Sudley Road. The brigade was near the area of Matthews and Henry hills when Colonel Whiting noticed Willcox's brigade had disbanded. Later Whiting recalled, "As we approached the field we met many ambulances and litters with the dying and wounded. We were greeted by the crowds of returning stragglers, telling us to hurry on; that they had driven them a mile." One of the Vermont soldiers had a slightly different memory of this incident. After the battle he wrote, "Many of whom we met told us we must hasten if we wished to bear a part, for the enemy were running." But he remembered the enemy "running toward us."[30]

As his brigade neared the Warrenton Turnpike Howard noted:

> ambulances in long columns leaving the field with the wounded ... there were men with broken arms, faces with bandages stained with blood; bodies pierced; many walking or limping to the rear—meanwhile shells were shrieking and breaking in the heated air. I was sorry, indeed, that those left of my men had to pass that ordeal.[31]

Maj. Joyce was also shocked as he neared the battlefield. He wrote:

> Now we have arrived at a road which leads up along the skirt of a piece of woods, we enter it and go on upon the run. Now. Oh God! What sights meet our eyes! Here are the hospitals for friends and foes. All thrown together; here are the surgeons in the woods sawing off legs and arms from the poor fellows who have been wounded—some they have on the ground and some on a board, they shriek, they groan, they swear, in their delirium of agony. Here comes the carts bringing in the wounded, the blood running from the cart like water from your street sprinkler. It is awful; it is terrible, but yet our brave boys press on.[32]

At about 3 P.M. as the brigade was nearing the Warrenton Turnpike it was met by one of McDowell's aides who led it to Chinn Ridge to support Capt. Ricketts's battery on Henry Hill. The aide led Howard and his men off to the right through the fields between the Manassas-Sudley Road and the John Dogan House and then across the Warrenton Turnpike where the brigade came to a halt behind Chinn Ridge. To the left, near the Henry House, the men could still hear the rattle of muskets and the boom of cannons.[33]

While traversing this area between the Dogan House and Chinn Ridge, the brigade came under a heavy artillery fire. A piece of one of the first Confederate shells to burst in the midst of the 2nd Vermont hit Corp. Russel H. Benjamin of Co. C, shredding one of his legs and throwing him several feet into the air. He landed behind the rear rank of the regiment, dead.[34]

Corp. Benjamin was a 30-year-old resident of Brattleboro who, prior to enlisting, had been employed by the Vermont and Massachusetts Railroad Company. He was a member of Co. C's color guard and gave promise of being a good soldier. His comrades laid his body under a tree where it was found later by the rebels and buried. He left a widow and two small children.[35]

The same shell fragment that killed Benjamin also took down Urban A. Woodbury, 1st Sgt. of Co. H, tearing off the lower part of his right arm. Woodbury, age 23, of Elmore, had just graduated with a medical degree from the University of Vermont before enlisting in the spring of 1861. After being wounded, he was taken to the regimental hospital that had been set up in a cooper's shop near Sudley Church. There the remaining part of his right arm was amputated three inches below the shoulder by Surgeon Ballou, giving Woodbury the distinction of being Vermont's first "empty sleeve" of the war. He was captured with the rest of the severely wounded left in the hospital during the retreat. Woodbury remained in the cooper's shop for a week under the care of the Confederate surgeons before being taken to Richmond as a prisoner of war. He was paroled on October 18, 1861, and honorably discharged from the service. He returned the next year as a captain in the 11th Vermont Infantry. After the war Woodbury became a successful businessman and politician, and in 1894, he was elected for one term as the governor of Vermont.[36]

Several more men of the 2nd Vermont were hit before the brigade reached the shelter of a ravine behind Chinn Ridge. Here 1st Lt. Case fell out from the heat, leaving Chester Leach to lead Co. H. Co. G was also having its problems. Their commander, Capt. John T. Drew, had been left in the camp at Centreville too sick to make the march. Fifty-seven-year-old 1st Lt. David L. Sharpley was leading the company until he went down. Maj. Joyce saw him drop and thought he had been hit. He rushed over to Sharpley and found him stunned; one of the incoming cannon balls had hit so close to him that it knocked the breath out of him, but he was otherwise unhurt. Several of Sharpley's men carried him to safety. 2nd Lt. Anson H. Weed replaced Sharpley.[37]

First Sergeant Urban A. Woodbury, Company H. The note on the photograph to his daughter reads, "Gertrude with much love, Father. This picture is a reproduction of one taken of Urban A. Woodbury in June 1861 when he was First Sergeant of Company H, 2nd Regiment Vermont Volunteers. The chevrons had not been placed on the coat. U.A.W." Morristown Historical Society.

In the ravine behind Chinn Ridge, Col. Howard formed his regiments into two lines of battle: the first composed of the 2nd Vermont and 4th Maine and the second formed by the 3rd and 5th Maine. As the regiments formed in line, Howard sat on his horse in a position where he could see the men as they passed by. "Most people were pale and thoughtful," he recalled later. He also noticed some of the men tried to hide their fear behind a weak smile. When formed, he ordered the first line forward.[38]

Before the 2nd Vermont moved out, Pvt. Jerome Cutler slipped off to a spring to get water as he explained later:

> after becoming somewhat refreshed at the spring I went on after our boys who had formed in line of battle and had commenced to ascend a hill whare we wer to open fire on the enemy but got part way up and had to stop and set down again. Jona-

***Left:* Second Lieutenant Anson H. Weed, Company G. USAMHI. *Right:* First Lieutenant Jerome B. Case, Company H, wearing the original gray uniform. USAMHI.**

> than Chase had been hit on the top of the head by a piece of barn and I kneeled down with one or two others rendered what assistance we could, it however did not injure him very much.[39]

Shoulder to shoulder, the men of the 2nd Vermont and the 4th Maine started up the steep hill. As they did, Lt. Edmund Kirby, of Ricketts's battery, his face covered with blood, raced past with a team of horses pulling a caisson. The sight revealed what had happened to the battery they were supposed to support. Before reaching the crest of the hill, the 4th Maine got tangled in some underbrush, leaving the 2nd Vermont to reach the crest alone. At the top, the regiment emerged from the woods into a rough pasture. Because of the short range of their smoothbore muskets, they had to continue half way down the other side of the hill before stopping to engage the rebels. As Capt. Randall, commander of Co. F, explained, "Their fire opened on us at once, but on account of the miserable guns we carried, we were unable to respond until we gained a more advanced position." Already the rebel bullets were thick and men began to fall. The 2nd Vermont fired several volleys which drove the enemy's skirmishers, the 2nd and 8th South Carolina Infantry Regiments, 200 to 300 yards in the distance, for the cover of the woods. Finally, the 4th Maine came on line and started pouring lead into the South Carolinians. It was obvious by now that they were not going to reach Henry Hill to support Ricketts's battery. What was left of the battery could be seen off in the distance.[40]

The battle on Chinn Ridge now began in earnest, neither side giving ground. In addition to small arms fire, Howard's brigade received fire from a Confederate battery to its left. More and more men fell. Orders went unheard amidst the cacophony of artillery and the screams of the wounded. Shells hit in the midst of companies, which would scatter, then rally. Utter pandemonium reigned. The men were loading, firing, and reloading so fast that their musket barrels became so hot they could not be touched without burning their hands.[41]

As the Confederate bullets continued to pour in, Capt. Edward A. Todd, commander of the 2nd Vermont's Co. C, went down, hit by a musket ball which entered on the left side of his neck just under the jaw. The ball traveled in front of his throat where it glanced off the cartilage of his trachea and exited on the right side of his neck, almost hitting the carotid artery. The exit wound was so large that his men could see the artery pulsating with each heartbeat. Lt. Col. Stannard caught a stray horse and placed Todd on it and Todd rejoined the regiment later that evening in Centreville. With Todd down, 18-year-old 1st Lt. John S. Tyler took command of the company. "From 10 to 15 men were shot within 6 feet of me," Tyler wrote later. "Many of our Co. acted most bravely standing by me to the last minute."[42]

Another bullet took down Pvt. Victor Goodrich of Co. F, boring through his head from ear to ear killing him instantly. A premonition had come true. At age 23 he had danced his last dance.[43]

Sgt. Maj. William Guinan received a gash just above his left wrist, from a bullet or shell fragment, severing the tendons and rendering his left hand useless. Although painful, the wound did not keep him from taking a saber from a dead rebel cavalryman as he was leaving the field. He was discharged for disability the following September.[44]

Pvt. Andrew J. Noyes, an 18-year-old laborer from Bennington in Co. A, took a minié ball in the right leg two inches above the knee, shattering the thighbone. His friend, Corp. William Murphy, tended to his wound. Since Noyes could not walk, Murphy stayed with him and both were later captured and imprisoned by the rebels. Noyes would be on crutches the rest of his life.[45]

Pvt. Alonzo Kinsley, from Fletcher, in Co. H was standing by Sgt. Eli Ellenwood, a 46-year-old farmer from Cambridge, firing as fast as he could, when he was stunned by a bullet. He screamed over the roar of musketry, "Ellenwood I am hit!" Ellenwood helped him unbutton his coat to inspect the wound. It was Kinsely's lucky day; the ball was spent by the time it had hit him. It had passed through his coat sleeve, two layers of his coat, and lodged against his breastbone just above his stomach. He survived his wound with only an ugly bruise.[46]

In Company C, 22-year-old Corp. Charles B. Rice of Brattleboro was hit by a minié ball in the left leg about three inches above the ankle. The bullet traveled up his leg breaking the fibula and leaving a four-inch gash in his calf as it made its exit. His friend Corp. Royal Fife helped him off the field. Eventually, Fife was able to grab a stray horse for Rice, but both were captured during the subsequent retreat. They were finally paroled and returned to Union lines on January 16, 1862. Rice would remain in the hospital until discharged the following November. The wound, which would never heal properly, left him an invalid.[47]

First Lieutenant John S. Tyler, Company C. Pictured here as a lieutenant colonel. His tenure as the fourth commander of the 2nd Vermont would last less than an hour. USAMHI.

During the melee, Maj. Joyce watched Capt. Charles Dillingham, the 23-year-old commander of Co. D and a life-long friend, issue orders as coolly and self-possessed as when he was on the parade field. Then Dillingham fell. Joyce rushed to help, but Dillingham was already back on his feet. His cap had been pierced by a minié ball which just grazed his scalp. He put his hand to his head to check for damage but, finding no blood, he turned to his soldiers and said, "They have not killed me yet. Give it to them boys."[48]

Sgt. Ethan Allen Priest, a 24-year-old farmer from Mt. Holly in Co. I, was shot in the right thigh. Although it was only a flesh wound, he had to leave the firing line to stop the bleeding. He limped to the rear and sat down under a tree to dress his wound. His company commander, Capt. Volney S. Fulham, came to him to get his ammunition, but Priest only handed him few rounds keeping the rest for

Postwar photograph of Sergeant Ethan Allen Priest, Company I, wounded in the right thigh July 21, 1861. Dennis Devereux.

himself. As soon as he dressed his wound Priest resumed firing at the rebels from under the tree where he was sitting.[49]

Next the color bearer of the 4th Maine went down. Col. Hiram G. Berry, the regiment's commander, seized the flag and carried it himself. His horse was shot out from under him, and his clothing and the flag were riddled by enemy bullets, yet miraculously, he survived.[50]

Meanwhile, Col. Howard returned to the ravine to bring up the 3rd and what was left of 5th Maine. While Howard was positioning the first line on the top of the ridge, the 5th Maine had a stroke of bad luck. A stray artillery round hit in its midst while a retreating Federal cavalry unit came galloping through the ravine. The shaken Maine men mistook the Federal unit for Confederate cavalry. This was too much for six of the regiment's companies, and they broke for the rear. Col. Howard collected what was left of them and the 3rd and pushed them up the hill.[51]

While Howard's brigade had been moving from its morning reserve position, newly arriving Confederate units were being maneuvered about the battlefield. Brig. Gen. Kirby Smith's brigade arrived by train at about 3 P.M. and was directed to move to the Confederate left. Smith executed this order immediately with his infantry units, along with Lt. Beckham's Culpeper Artillery. Moving rapidly through fields and woods, they arrived a little before 4 P.M. As Smith stopped to confer with Col. Joseph B. Kershaw, Howard's brigade unleashed a volley, knocking Smith from his horse and severely wounding him. The next senior man, Col. Arnold Elzey, took command and formed his line in a woods a little south of Chinn Branch. At the same time, Lt. Beckham positioned his four artillery pieces and roared into action. Col. Jeb Stuart, with his 1st Virginia Cavalry Regiment, arrived shortly after Beckham opened fire and provided support to the artillery.[52]

Back on Chinn Ridge, Howard had just led the 3rd and 4th Maine to the top of the hill when an artillery round scattered the 3rd, sending the men back under the protection of the hill. When the 3rd reformed, it took a position

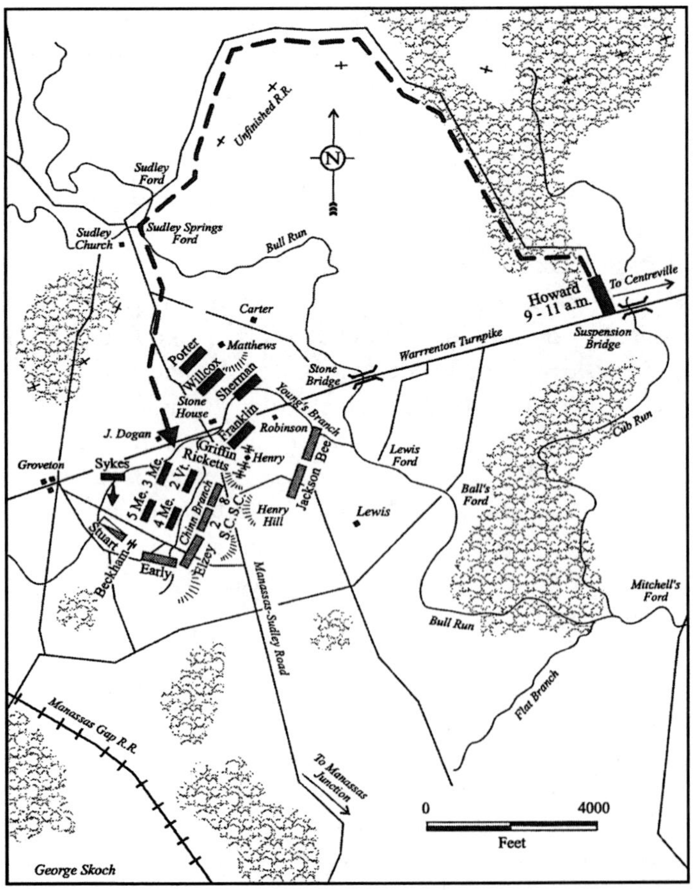

The Battle of Bull Run at 4 P.M. July 21, 1861

behind and above the 2nd Vermont. The Maine soldiers commenced firing uncomfortably close over the Green Mountain Boys' heads.[53]

Meanwhile, Capt. Walbridge, commander of the 2nd Vermont's Co. A, had seen Elzey's men moving in on the right. He asked Col. Whiting if he could take his company in that direction and engage them, and Whiting agreed. Later in the war, and with more experience, this type of maneuver would never have been allowed as massed fire was crucial to success. Lt. Col. Stannard saw Co. A moving to the right and knowing the regiment should not be splintering its force, went after Walbridge to get him back into position. When Walbridge told Stannard that he had Col. Whiting's permission, Stannard deferred. Walbridge moved his company several hundred yards to the right and started hammering away at Elzey's troops.[54]

By now the action on Chinn Ridge was intense. Rebel artillery was pounding Howard's units from both flanks and Elzey's newly arrived forces were adding greatly to the volume of small arms fire. As one Confederate officer wrote later, "the foe made a determined resistance on a rising ground in the vicinity of Chinn's House, and it looked like

Captain James H. Walbridge, commander of Company A and second commander of the 2nd Vermont. USAMHI.

an island round which flames were gathering, in all directions." Sensing trouble, Howard pulled the 2nd Vermont back to form a reserve. Col. Whiting gave the command to march to the right "by the right flank," but in all the noise, boiling smoke and dust, many of his companies either did not understand or did not hear the order and continued firing. One rebel soldier, who had gotten close to the 2nd Vermont, yelled that they were firing on friends, and the firing ceased, but in a few moments, the Vermonters saw a Confederate flag fluttering in the breeze and poured another score of rounds into the woods in front.[55]

Seeing the 2nd Vermont starting to fall back, the major of the 4th Maine asked Col. Howard if he had ordered a retreat. Howard answered "no," with a shake of his head, and the major tried to halt his men. At the same time, the commander of the 5th Maine told Howard that he could do no more. Officers tried to keep their men in formation, but as the Confederate fire increased the men started withdrawing on their own. Realizing the untenable situation they were in, Howard ordered a general retreat, intending to fall back to the ravine and reform. As the brigade moved over the ridge, company formations started to break up. Howard observed the men "continued to retire, not at first in a panicky manner, but steadily, each according to his own sweet will."[56]

Pvt. Elijah Brown, who had been on the skirmish line with Co. F, wrote: "...we had the order to retreat & we would not go. we fired some five or six rounds & had the order again to retreat ... they [their muskets] was so hot that we could not touch the barrels. I loaded my gun after the second order to retreat was givin & before I got the cap on it went off."[57]

As the Vermonters started to pull back, Oramel G. Howe, a 20-year-old five foot eleven inch tall clerk from Ludlow, now a corporal in Co. I, was helped up by his friends. A cannon ball had hit so close that it spun him around and twisted his body so severely he could hardly move.[58]

Color bearer Harrington made sure the 2nd Vermont's national colors came off the field honorably. Although his six foot, five-inch frame made an excellent target, he bravely stood his ground during the entire battle and left the field without a scratch. The flag, however, had six bullet holes in it.[59]

One of the last men in the 2nd Vermont to leave the field was Pvt. Charles Harran of Berlin, Vt., and Co. F. Harran had been out on the skirmish line firing away when he noticed his company withdrawing. As he turned to join them, he felt a pain in his left leg. He realized that some time during the battle, he had taken a bullet in the fleshy part of his left thigh. As the wound started to slow him down, his brother, Pvt. Selden B. Harran, hoisted him onto a retreating cannon and saved him from being captured. Selden later transferred his brother to an ambulance and finally to a baggage wagon which took him to a hospital in Washington.[60]

As Howard's brigade began withdrawing, Maj. George Sykes's battalion of U.S. regulars came onto the field, to Howard's right, to cover the retreat. Capt. Walbridge and his company joined with Sykes and with their rifled muskets continued firing on Elzey's men.[61]

Not long after Elzey's units had assumed position, Col. Jubal A. Early's brigade arrived on the Confederate left. It entered the line from behind the woods where Elzey's troops were deployed and took position parallel with the road leading from the Chinn House. The flanking of the Federal right was thus complete.[62]

Just as Early had gotten men on line, he saw Elzey's troops, on his right, begin charging Chinn's Ridge. Early did likewise. About half-way up the ridge one of Elzey's aides rode up to Early and told him the troops in gray uniforms they had seen on the crest of the ridge comprised the 13th Virginia and not to fire on them. Early was skeptical, but held his troops in check. He rode across the ridge and saw the troops in gray uniforms, but could not tell from their flag, drooped around its staff, if it was U.S. or Confederate. The gray clad troops were in fact the 2nd Vermont. A few shells from Beckham's battery caused them to shift position and Early could suddenly see it was the U.S. flag. He immediately ordered his troops forward again.[63]

Sykes and Walbridge kept up a hot fire as the Confederates charged, until Stuart's cavalry joined the fray. Seeing the cavalry closing, Sykes fell back and gave the order to "form square," which was rapidly accomplished. Seeing the Federals in a tight square, the cavalry started to falter, but the Confederate artillery started laying in rounds, and the order to reduce square was quickly issued by Sykes. Capt. Walbridge now felt it was time to rejoin his regiment. While moving back to the top of the ridge, Walbridge saw a body of Confederate troops at the edge of a stand of woods and could not resist giving them one last shot. He halted his men and had them loose a volley. In return he received a volley of equal measure. Only one of Walbridge's men was hit, sustaining only a minor wound in the cheek. Marching back to the top of the ridge from where he had started, Walbridge found the Federal units gone, and he hurried after the retreating masses.[64]

By the time Early and Elzey reached the crest of the ridge it was vacant, but they ordered their men to fire several volleys into the woods on the back of the ridge for good measure. After resting their men for a few minutes, the two colonels pushed them down the backside of the ridge and across the Warrenton Turnpike.[65]

Corporal Oramel G. Howe, Company I. USAMHI.

Meanwhile, several Confederate infantry regiments and a battery followed the Federal retreat. The Confederates crossed the Stone Bridge spanning Bull Run and proceeded on toward Centreville. As the rebels crested a hill, they saw, several hundred yards distant, Federals hastening back toward Cub Run. At the same time, Howard's brigade and others who had retreated by way of Sudley Springs Ford were coming down the road from the ford which joined the turnpike just before the suspension bridge. Both bodies of Federals collided at the entrance to the bridge just as the Confederates opened fire. The first round hit the middle of the bridge at the moment a wagon was crossing. The terrified horses upset the wagon on the rickety bridge, blocking all traffic. The rout became bedlam. All wagons and artillery waiting to cross were abandoned. The Confederate fired several more rounds, each one increasing the desperation of the Federals who either waded or swam across the stream. Then the guns were turned to the left and fired on the men who were still coming down from Sudley Ford.[66]

The 2nd Vermont tried to maintain its organization in the retreat, but when it crossed the Warrenton Turnpike and started for Sudley Ford, panic set in. All organization was lost as it reached a spot where a jam of ambulances, artillery, and ammunition wagons filled the road. Officers and noncommissioned officers tried to get the men to re-form, but it was a lost cause. Howard had given up trying to regain control over his units and sent word for all Maine and Vermont men to rally at their camps at Centreville.[67]

Capt. Randall recorded the scene he witnessed at the suspension bridge in a letter to the *Daily Free Press*:

> Horses and wagons were often overturned, and left piled pell-mell in the gutters. At one place we had a bridge to cross, and I never saw such confusion. There we lost most of our baggage. I counted as many as twenty dead horses, with wagons innumerable, piled in this ravine, and troops actually crossed over this mass of horse-flesh and wagons, boxes and barrels and cannon & etc. rather than over the bridge. I had thus far kept the most of my company together, and from the fact of our being last off the field, and in the rear, I was every moment expecting an attack on our retreating columns. But the delay here was so great that I rallied my men and was passed to the left into the woods, to a point above the bridge some few rods, where we crossed, by wading the creek, which was about waist deep. This carried us to about the middle of the column, and we stopped a moment to witness the dreadful scene at the bridge. I saw an ambulance in which were several wounded troops, run off the bank, killing the horses, but leaving the men alive. All sorts of horrible sights, too shocking to contemplate, were before us.[68]

In this confusion and turmoil, 28-year-old Pvt. Warren Gifford of Co. B and a Danby resident was hit in the hand by a shell fragment which took him down. He was later captured and would not rejoin his company until the following January.[69]

Another casualty here at the bridge involved the 2nd Vermont's baggage wagons. Unable to cross the bridge and with the rebels closing in, the wagon drivers fled for their lives, leaving behind all the regiment's knapsacks, equipment, and rations.[70]

July 21 was a busy day for the 2nd Vermont's surgeons. Dr. Ballou had set up his hospital in a cooper's shop near Sudley Church. Seeing the army in flight, he loaded as many wounded into an ambulance as he could and followed. Not long after getting started, the ambulance broke down. Ballou felt he had done all in his power for those in his care and left on foot to join the retreat.[71]

Assistant surgeon Carpenter had earlier in the day been assigned to a makeshift hospital in a small house along the Warrenton Turnpike. When the retreat started, Dr. Carpenter had all ambulatory patients join on foot. He flagged down passing wagons to transport the others. Carpenter used his pistol to change the mind of any driver not willing to risk his own skin to assist the patients. After clearing the hospital, he and another surgeon joined the retreat to Centreville. The men who were saved never forgot the resolute young Vermont surgeon.[72]

And what of John C. Thayer? As the regiment was being recruited, Thayer had been a student at Fairfax Theological Seminary in Fairfax, Vt. Overcome with a desire to serve, Thayer left school and tried to join the 2nd Vermont. Because of a stiff wrist, he was rejected, so, he accompanied the regiment as a cook in Co. H. The morning the regiment marched off to battle, Thayer was left in camp at Centreville. Listening to the battle during the day was more than the young man could take, so he set off on foot to join his comrades. Somewhere along the way he picked up a rifle from a wounded soldier. During the confusion of the retreat, Thayer was overtaken by troops of the 30th Virginia Cavalry. A young officer started after Thayer yelling for him to surrender. Thayer wheeled and shot the man from his saddle, killing him instantly. The Vermonter stripped the dead man of his sword, sash and field glass, then escaped unscathed except for four bullet holes in his coat and one in his cap. Thayer returned to Vermont soon after taking his trophies with him. His coat was later presented to Vermont's Senator Foote as a battle trophy.[73]

According to Col. R.C.W. Radford, commander of the 30th Virginia Cavalry, who led the pursuit along the Warrenton Turnpike, a Lt. B. L. Bowles was separated from his troop during a charge and was killed. He was probably the man Thayer shot.[74]

The losses at Bull Run for the Federals numbered 418 killed, 1,011 wounded and 1,216 missing. The Confederates lost 387 killed, 1,582 wounded and 12 missing. Surprisingly the 2nd Vermont's losses included only two enlisted men killed, one officer and 34 enlisted men wounded and one officer and 30 enlisted men captured. Of the 30 enlisted men captured, 21 were wounded, making the total loss for the regiment 68 men. Corp. Elisha L. Keables and Pvt. Edward P. Gilson, both of Co. C, Pvt. John Gowing, Co. D, and Pvt. John Leonard, Co. I, were wounded when captured and died of their wounds while imprisoned in Richmond.[75]

The officer captured was Capt. John T. Drew, a Montpelier native and commander of Co. G. Drew had been ill for several days before Bull Run, but followed the regiment to battle, with assistance of an officer of the 4th Maine, who placed him on his horse. Weak from vomiting, Drew was dropped off at the field hospital at Sudley Church. After a short rest, he started on again and soon met the Vermonters on the retreat. The men helped him for several miles until they found an ambulance. Within 10 minutes the ambulance was overtaken by rebel cavalry, and Drew was carried to Richmond to spend nearly 13 months in rebel prisons. He returned to Vermont with shattered health and resigned from the service on October 8, 1862.[76]

Pvt. Patrick F. Flaherty of Co. D, a 34-year-old farmer from Waterbury, was another of the unfortunate men nabbed by the Confederates during the retreat. Flaherty was imprisoned in Richmond, Va., July 23 and was not paroled until January 3, 1862. Upon his release he had to be discharged for disability because of "chronic diarrhea and loss of teeth rendering him unable to bite a cartridge or even eat hard food."[77]

About 7 P.M., as it was starting to get dark, Beauregard ordered his units back to the Stone Bridge, giving the Federals a chance to retreat to their camps at Centreville, at least those who would stop running.[78]

Howard's brigade reached camp at Centreville around 9 P.M. Most men dropped in their tracks and went to sleep while a few boiled coffee or tended to the wounded. "I thought a great many times [in my life] that I was tired but I never knew what it was to be tired before," wrote Lt. Leach. "When we came off the field, I could hardly stand up, but we were 8 or 10 miles from our camp." Soon rumors had the rebels closing in. Col. Howard, however, was determined to retreat no farther and sent a courier to headquarters for instructions. The answer was to continue on to Alexandria. The men were roused from sleep and the brigade shuffled out of camp toward Fairfax Court House, with the 2nd Vermont bringing up the rear.[79]

Between 3 and 4 A.M. on July 22, the brigade staggered into Fairfax Court House and collapsed for another hour's sleep. The men were up at daybreak and on the road to Alexandria. To add insult to injury, the sky unleashed a steady downpour of rain that lasted the rest of the day. Before reaching Alexandria, what was left of the brigade stopped at its old camp at Bush Hill, and the men retrieved whatever they could carry. There, Col. Howard commandeered a train for the last four miles to Alexandria.[80]

The 2nd Vermont reached Alexandria around 1 P.M. The men were soaking wet, bone weary, angry, and depressed. As Col. Howard said, "And now came the most trying period of the war to all patriotic hearts." Capt. Randall's Co. F seemed too tired to complain as he described in a letter:

> We ate some luncheon from our haversacks about eleven yesterday, just before going in the battle, and that was the last we had until some time after noon today. I have been trying to get up life enough with the boys to have them wash and improve their looks a little, but all except one or two are still sleeping in the dirt, so black [from the residue of black powder] you could not recognize them. We succeeded today in getting some bread and butter, which is all we have had to eat, but the men are so tired they all lie around me unconscious of hunger.[81]

Without most of their equipment and with only the clothing on their backs, and short of rations, the men became somewhat rebellious. On July 25 the 2nd Vermont was ordered back to the camp at Bush Hill. On that day, Col. Whiting was in Washington, and Lt. Col. Stannard was in command. It took Stannard nearly two hours to get the regiment formed to board the train.[82]

After arriving at Bush Hill, the men stacked arms and most fell to the ground. Many of the weaker ones were literally sick from exhaustion. All were without tents or overcoats, many without knapsacks or blankets. There was no uniformity of arms, many of the men having exchanged their muskets for ones picked up on the retreat. In the troubling days after the defeat at Bull Run, the 2nd Vermont, like the rest of the army, was in a shambles. As Col. Howard indicated, "the men distrusted their officers, many pleaded to go home, some mutinied, and some deserted." He went on to say, "it was almost two weeks before much reliance could be placed on the men."[83]

As soon as the army had returned from Bull Run, guards were placed on all the bridges leading to Washington and on all the wharves along the riverbank to keep boats from crossing the Potomac. Plenty of Southerners were more than willing to assist the Yankees in getting home. Three soldiers of the 2nd Vermont's Co. E fell victim to these accommodating citizens.[84]

The first, George W. Flanders, a 17-year-old private from Sharon, left the day after reaching Alexandria. According to Flanders, a barkeep invited him into his saloon and got him "pretty well beered." Flanders continued, "and then asked if I did not wish to go over into Maryland. I first said I would not go. He kept talking till at last I went. He showed me where to get a boat."[85]

The second man, Pvt. Charles C. Goodwin, from Randolph, left on July 28 after the 2nd Vermont had returned to Bush Hill. Goodwin testified:

> I went out to bathe and went down to Alexandria. Then a man sold me liquor. I bought one glass from him. Then after that he kept treating me, giving me money. I got tight, not clear down, but so I did not know much. He gave me clothes and told me I had better run away. He took a boat and carried me across the river. When I got across the river he gave me another glass of liquor. Then I went home. After I got home I was taken sick and was sick about three months. As soon as I got able to come back my father gave me money and told me to come back and give myself up. He told me it wont the way to do business to run away after I had enlisted. I came back and gave myself up to the Colonel.[86]

The third deserter, Pvt. Charles Quade, also from Randolph, could basically tell the same story as the other two. He slipped away to Alexandria on July 29. He also said he had not left camp with the intention of deserting, but, "I should not have gone away if I had not been pretty well liquored up. When I left camp I had no more idea of leaving than I do now. I staid all day in Alexandria and never started till after four P.M."[87]

Flanders and Quade were both tried by general courts-martial on October 31. They were found guilty, sentenced to forfeit all pay and allowances, and were drummed out of the service. Goodwin was tried on February 2, 1862, and sentenced to forfeit $8 of his pay for six months, and confined to hard labor for one month during which time he would wear a 24 pound ball attached with a chain to his right ankle.[88]

It was during this time of discontent that reports surfaced that Col. Whiting had hid behind a tree during the fight at Bull Run. The rumors started turning into truths as they reached home in letters and started appearing in newspapers all over Vermont. Pvt. Sanford R. Barnes of Co. H said in a letter to his wife, "Our Col. nor Capt. [Burnham] were neither of them of any practical benefit in the battle for one was not on the field & the *Col.* was behind a tree.... Our Col. did order a retreat & he was the first to *execute too.*"[89]

Sgt. William H. Bond, a 21-year-old Danby native in Co. A, wrote his parents, "Our colonel, Colonel Whiting who had command of our Reg went in the woods and hid."[90]

On August 2 the *Burlington Weekly Sentinel* reported, "I regret to say that there is dissatisfaction with Colonel Whiting, whether justly or unjustly, is not for me to say. If all reports are correct it is due to him, and to the brave sons of Vermont who have fought so gallantly, that the matter should be investigated."[91]

The *Rutland Daily Herald* stated on July 26:

> Col. Whiting, it is *positively* asserted by members of the regiment, distinguished himself in nothing except as a *poltroon and coward*, having shown the *white feather* on the first approach of danger, and secreted himself safely behind a tree or under a pile of logs. Wonderful heroism this for a "old army officer who has seen hard service!" It is said here, by those who have taken the trouble to examine his record, that he resigned his commission in the Army when ordered to Mexico.
>
> What an outrage to place such a man at the head of such a regiment. It is hoped that he will now resign, and relieve the regiment of his unwelcome presence—The conduct of the regiment, notwithstanding the incubus of a coward Col., is spoken of in the highest terms of praise.[92]

The regiment's sergeant major, while home on convalescent leave, was quoted in the *Daily Free Press* expressing the regiment's dissatisfaction with the colonel's behavior. Curtis A. Coburn, a servant in Co. D, put bluntly in a letter to a girlfriend, "P.S. *Our* Col. is a *coward.*" Coburn, however, indicated in the same letter that he was not personally on the battlefield, so was only repeating camp gossip.[93]

Sergeant William H. Bond, Company A. Pictured here as a captain and commander of Company A. USAMHI.

To counter the rumors, Col. Whiting drafted a letter with his version of his actions at Bull Run and asked the regiment's officers to sign it. Some did, but Maj. Joyce refused, explaining he could not since he had not personally witnessed all the incidents noted in the letter. Whiting was furious and threatened Joyce with discipline. Joyce wrote a rather lengthy letter on August 1 to *The Burlington Times*, chronicling the regiment's activities from its arrival in Washington through the battle at Bull Run. The letter was read by Col. Whiting on August 12. One sentence in Joyce's account laid another insult on Whiting:

> About this time Col. Howard rode up and ordered our regiment to form line of battle in a deep ravine and march up a steep bank covered with brush wood, on to an incline plain in full sight of the enemy. The order was given to Col. Whiting, who was near me at the time completely exhausted and worn out—he immediately ordered me to give the order and see that it was executed, which I did.[94]

On reading the article, Whiting blew up and ordered Joyce to report to him. When Joyce arrived at the colonel's tent, he was met by the angry colonel waving the newspaper in his face, and asking if he had written the article about the 2nd Vermont signed "Major." Being an experienced lawyer, Joyce remained silent until he could determine why he was being asked the question. The colonel then pointed to the offending sentence and asked Joyce if he wrote it. Joyce replied by asking the colonel if it was true. The colonel said he did not propose to discuss that question. There the confrontation ended. Later that day, Whiting sent for Maj. Joyce's sword and sash and placed him under arrest, charging him with violating Article 25 of Army regulations which prohibited any member of the army from discussing or publishing any censure or approbation toward his superiors.[95]

Pending trial on these charges, Maj. Joyce was placed under arrest and confined to camp. Joyce, who was quite popular with the regiment, had the sympathy of most of the line officers and enlisted men. He wrote a letter expressing his regret at having written the portions of his published letter which were in violation of army regulations, but he still remained under arrest. A letter requesting Col. Whiting's resignation was drawn up and signed by a majority of the regiment's officers, but it was never presented to him. Lt. Col. Stannard and Surgeon Ballou then sent a letter to the governor of Vermont stating that the prejudicial reports of Col. Whiting were instigated by the regiment's sergeant major whom Whiting had disciplined for getting drunk in New York City on their way to Washington. They went on to express surprise that the paper even printed the letter since a copy of Col. Howard's official battle report had been run in the newspaper containing a line that read, "Col. Whiting was at his post when I left for the second line, and I refer to his report, for notice of his field and other officers." Capt. Randall also had a letter published in a Vermont newspaper that stated, "there would have been no difficulty with Col. Whiting had he been a Vermonter." Early in the dispute the *Rutland Daily Herald* opined, "We believe that the reports unfavorable to the character of Col. Whiting of the Vermont Second, for courage, are *unfounded*, and are due to unpopularity arising from other causes." An article in the *Boston Journal* read, "a member of the brigade of which our regiment was a part, an eye witness of their share in the battle, says, 'Col. Whiting, Vermont 2d, showed great coolness and courage." While these and other such statements quieted the public clamor in Vermont for a while, the ill feelings in the regiment still existed.[96]

It would be several months before the morale of the 2nd Vermont would rebound. The humiliation of the loss at Bull Run, as well as the loss of comrades, were bitter pills to swallow. Lt. Leach summed up the campaign for the regiment when he wrote his wife, "Our boys feel almost disgusted by the battle.... It was a disgraceful affair—the whole of it."[97]

CHAPTER 3

HE DIED A HERO

After the defeat at Bull Run, President Lincoln wasted no time replacing McDowell. On July 25, 1861, Maj. Gen. George B. McClellan assumed command of the army and changed its name to the Army of the Potomac. McClellan immediately instituted three measures aimed at getting his army under control. He established boards to examine the competence of volunteer officers, and during a period of several months more than 300 were dismissed or forced to resign. Second, he established a strict system of inspection of men and arms. Last, he initiated an effective provost marshal force that quickly cleared Washington and Georgetown of the drunken and rowdy officers and enlisted men who roamed the streets day and night.[1]

With the change of commanders, the men's morale started to improve. Comrades thought killed or captured at Bull Run began to wander back to camp, and a regular supply of rations and new tents improved their health and rebuilt their worn bodies. The Green Mountain Boys got back to a normal military routine of drill and picket duty. Since they had lost most of their possessions in the retreat from Bull Run, they were short of clothing, excepting that on their backs. "Our men have not any shirts & such like yet to replace those lost at Bull Run," Lt. Leach said in a letter to his wife. "A good many have to go without any when they wash theirs, but expect they will have more soon."[2]

While the unit's morale was starting to climb, it had a minor setback on Friday, August 2 when the men were required to witness an execution. After it occurred, Lt. Leach wrote to his wife:

> Well, Ann, I have seen a sight today such as I never saw before nor ever expect to see & can't say that I ever want another of the like sort. That is, I saw a man hung. Just after I had commenced writing, orders came to camp that we must be ready at half-past one P.M. to march to Fort Ellsworth to see a man executed for the crime of murder. So, at the time we were formed in line ready to march, the Capt. & Case preferred not to go & got excused, so I took command of our company. Fort Ellsworth is situated on the main road from here to Alexandria, about three miles from here. We had a regular sweat of it going to the Fort & back, for it has been the hottest day we have had yet. We arrived at the place of execution about three o'clock. There must have from six to ten thousand soldiers to witness the execution. At 5 minutes past 4 o'clock the prisoner was led to the platform, and 5 minutes after he was dropped. He was a man between 30 & 40 years of age, of the 2nd N.H. Regt. I think, though there conflicting reports about the regiment. He marched on the platform perfectly calm, attended only by the executioner. When the rope was put over his head, he took his cap off and replaced it, & put his hands behind him to be tied. I think neither the prisoner nor the executioner spoke a word after they mounted the scaffold. A handkerchief was tied over his face & then a trap door in the platform dropped & he was done with this world. From the position we occupied, we could not see him after he dropped. He dropped about two feet. I think he did not struggle much by the looks of the rope. I don't know the particulars of his crime more than this. A woman of ill fame got his money and he shot her. Report is among our boys that he paid her before & and then she ran.[3]

Leach was fairly accurate in his relating of the incident. The man who was hanged was William F. Murray of the 2nd New Hampshire Infantry. He had shot Mary Butler, an Alexandria prostitute, in the back with his musket on July 27. He was so close to her when he fired, the muzzle flash caught her dress on fire. She died instantly. The coroner testified that when he moved her body, the exit wound in her chest was so large her heart fell out. The exact reason Murray shot her was not brought out at his court-martial.[4]

Capt. Volney S. Fullam, a 31-year-old lawyer from Ludlow and commander of Co. I, wrote to his mother of having to witness the execution and said, "it was the first sight of this kind I ever witnessed. I hope it may be the last."[5]

After his experience at Bull Run, Pvt. Oramel Howe said of having to witness the execution, "It seemed we were to see death in all its forms."[6]

Captain Volney S. Fullam, commander of Company I. He left the 2nd Vermont in January 1862 to become the lieutenant colonel of the 7th Vermont Infantry Regiment. USAMHI.

The 3rd Vermont Infantry Regiment arrived in Washington on July 26 and moved out to Georgetown to Camp Lyon at the head of the Chain Bridge. Located on the hills to the rear of the town, the camp was strategically placed to guard the Chain Bridge over the Potomac and the reservoir that supplied Washington with fresh water. The 3rd Vermont was temporarily under the command of Lt. Col. Breed N. Hyde. The regimental colonel's position was as of yet unfilled because the governor of Vermont wanted a regular army officer as the commander. Finally, Capt. William Farrar "Baldy" Smith, a native Vermonter and a regular army officer, was selected. He was promoted to colonel of volunteers and joined the 3rd Vermont shortly after its arrival at Camp Lyon. Smith, the senior officer at Camp Lyon, also had under his control the 33rd New York Infantry; 6th Maine Infantry; an artillery battery; and a cavalry company.[7]

Smith, born in St. Albans, Vt. in 1824, was an 1845 graduate of the U.S. Military Academy. He had been commissioned as a lieutenant in the Topographical Engineers and remained at the academy as a surveying and mathematics instructor for several years. In 1859, he supervised construction of a lighthouse and harbor facilities in Chicago. While there he met and became friends with Gen. McClellan, who at the time was a vice president of the Illinois Central Railroad. In 1860, Smith was transferred to Florida to do engineering work on lighthouses. While there he contracted malaria that brought him periods of weakness and depression the rest of his life. The opening hostilities of the war found Smith serving as an engineer at the U.S. Light House Board in Washington. Champing at the bit to get into the war, he applied to the governor of Vermont, Erastus Fairbanks, for command of a regiment and was selected to command the 3rd Vermont. His commission was backdated to April 27 1861, so he would out-rank Col. Whiting. Although nothing remains to explain why Smith's commission was backdated, it may have been a way to punish Col. Whiting for his performance at Bull Run. Smith would thus be eligible for promotion to brigadier general before Whiting.[8]

Smith was as a short, portly man, with a light brown shaggy mustache. Fond of controversy, Smith spent much of his time criticizing the plans of other generals, particularly those of his superiors. Although he had more hair than most men his age, Smith retained his U. S. Military Academy cadet nickname "Baldy," given because at that stage of his life, his hair was thinner than normal.[9]

Shortly after taking command, Smith suggested to McClellan that he form a Vermont brigade, in anticipation of the arrival of the 4th, 5th, and 6th Vermont Infantry Regiments, due south in a couple of months. Army policy

Brigadier General William F. Smith, first commander of the Vermont Brigade. Library of Congress.

was against brigading regiments from the same state together because serious combat losses might be bad for the morale of the soldiers and the citizens of the home state. However, McClellan consented, and Smith immediately notified Whiting to move his unit to Camp Lyon.[10]

Whiting issued orders on the morning of August 12 for the 2nd Vermont to prepare to move to Camp Lyon. Near nightfall, the regiment boarded a train to go to Alexandria, the first leg of the journey.[11]

The 2nd Vermont would see Clermont only one more time during the war, and the beautiful farm would suffer the ravages of war. The 4th Maine remained on the site and ransacked the house. Later it was used as a picket post for the 40th New York Infantry, then as a contraband (ex-slave) hospital, and finally, as a hospital for soldiers and civilians suffering from smallpox. Commodore Forrest lost Clermont in 1863, when the federal government sold the property for back taxes.[12]

The 2nd Vermont reached Alexandria just after dark and halted until about 9 P.M. Its next stop was on the Virginia side of Long Bridge where the men rested until daybreak. The next morning, they crossed the bridge into Washington, passing the Washington Monument and the White House as they marched upriver. They reached Camp Lyon around 10 A.M. very tired and hungry. The 3rd Vermont graciously provided them with a breakfast of sandwiches and hot coffee.[13]

On August 13, Col. Smith was promoted to brigadier general and Breed Hyde replaced him as colonel of the 3rd Vermont and the nucleus of the First Vermont Brigade was formed.[14]

On August 17 Lt. Tyler of Co. C had the misfortune of having his tent burn down. Tyler described the incident:

> Being the officer of the day I was obliged to make the "grand rounds" after 12 o'clock, i.e. visit the sentinels & out posts to see that they were doing their duty. During my absence I had left the light burning in my tent & when I returned lo! & behold my trunk was all on fire, the light having tumbled down under the trunk which was elevated about a foot from the ground. Two linen shirts, 2 woolen ditto, two or three pr of stockings, 1 pair of continuations are among the missing or rather burned. Currant jelly is *preserved.* The greatest loss however is the trunk itself, for which I paid $25.00.[15]

The men quickly made the camp as comfortable as they could as Pvt. Cutler noted:

> I will tell you how I got along (perhaps you will laugh but then you know I don't care) to sleep on nights. I have fixed up a sort of bedstead by driving down four little crotches in which I place two poles about my length across these I lay some short sticks. This is my bedstead. On this I lay my straw tick just large enough for myself (there was a lot sent us from Vermont) and use my blanket and overcoat for bed clothes. This keeps me off the damp ground and rest as nice as can be.[16]

Just as it was getting settled on Sunday, August 18, the 2nd Vermont received orders to relocate to Great Falls 12 miles up the Potomac for a week of picket duty. The men were up early on Monday morning and moved out at 6 A.M. in a driving rain. Two miles out of camp the column split. Because the road that led directly to Great Falls was so muddy, the baggage wagons and two artillery pieces that accompanied the regiment had to take a roundabout route increasing the march to 15 miles. The eight companies that accompanied the wagons and artillery struggled through ankle deep mud and swollen streams. They finally reached camp about 2 P.M., exhausted and soaked to the hide. The new camp was located on a strip of land between the Chesapeake and Ohio Canal and the Potomac River. The regiment's mission was twofold, to ensure that no Southern sympathizers smuggled supplies across the river to Confederate forces and to inspect canal boats for contraband.[17]

The week at Great Falls was one of the most enjoyable the Vermonters had experienced in a while. Plenty of fresh vegetables were available from the passing canal boats and from the surrounding farms. When not on duty, the men foraged for food, fished, and swam in the river. They were quartered in a large two-story building built as a barracks for workers who constructed the canal years before.[18]

The only real excitement during the week occurred on August 21, when Whiting was ordered to send a scouting party across the Potomac to find out what the Confederates were up to, and he directed Capt. Randall to take the mission. Randall, in turn, chose Pvt. George W. Doty to accompany him.

The facts that Capt. Randall was selected for this mission and that he chose Doty to accompany him were not surprising. Both were self-made men used to relying on their own resourcefulness.

Francis Voltaire Randall was born February 13, 1824, in Orange County, Vt., second of nine children. His father, Gurdon Randall, moved his family from Braintree to Northfield in 1831. Francis worked his way through college and was admitted to the Vermont bar in 1847 at the age of 23. He was a partner of Albert V. H. Carpenter for a while and then went into partnership with Charles H. Joyce. In 1857, Randall sold out and moved to Roxbury and then to Montpelier in 1860. During his residence in Montpelier, he was chosen a brigade judge advocate of the Vermont Militia. In the spring of 1861, he raised Co. F of the 2nd Vermont and was elected its captain.

Another factor possibly contributing to Randall's attitude was his recent divorce. He had married Caroline E. Andrews in 1846 while living in Northfield. In 1859, he caught her in a love affair and applied for divorce, charging her with adultery. The divorce was final November 27, 1860. Whether or not this had any bearing on his devil-may-care attitude cannot be proven, but one can only assume it had to have had some effect.[19]

George W. Doty was born February 16, 1838, in Montpelier. O. L. Metcalf of Morristown adopted him as an infant. Doty developed a fascination for the military at an early age. When he was 10 years old, he formed a company of 40 boys and drilled them every month during summer vacation for four years. At age 19, Doty left for Kansas and settled in Mapleton, where he served as constable. While in Mapleton, he joined a militia company and was involved in the bloodshed over slavery that preceded the Civil War. In 1857, Doty's company was part of the force that surrounded the Kansas State House and forced adjournment of its bogus legislature. He left Mapleton in 1860 to become a teamster hauling supplies over the Rocky Mountains to gold miners in the Pike's Peak region. He returned to Vermont in February 1861, on the eve of the Civil War. That spring, he raised a militia company, but due to some disagreements, he left the unit and enlisted in Co. F of the 2nd Vermont.[20]

Both men also shared one other common trait: Neither was shy about bragging about himself.

With the help of several other men from Co. F, Randall and Doty soon had a raft lashed together and quickly paddled across the Potomac.

The two men scouted the far bank for several miles inland, but found no rebel soldiers. Nearing nightfall, they decided to get back across the river. Two men from Co. F, Sgt. George W. Bridgeman and Pvt. Amos N. Bennett, had been sent upriver to find a rowboat with which to bring the two scouts back across the river, but when Randall and Doty reached the river bank, Bridgeman and Bennett were nowhere in sight. With darkness rapidly approaching, the two attempted to recross on their raft. Halfway over the raft started to break up. Clutching pieces of the raft, Randall and

Captain Francis V. Randall, commander of Company F. University of Vermont.

Sergeant George W. Doty, Company F. USAMHI.

Doty were carried downstream by the swift current. When they hit the rapids opposite their camp, the raft totally disintegrated, and the two men were left clinging to boulders in midstream to keep from being swept over the falls. Both finally managed to climb atop one of the larger boulders but were so far out in the river, and the raging water made so much noise, they could not raise attention in the camp. Doty, the strongest swimmer, dove in and swam from boulder to boulder, reaching the shore just before being swept over the falls. He then motioned for Randall to stay put and went to camp for help. Not only did Randall's Co. F respond, but most of the other men in the regiment did as well. A long rope was taken upstream to a small island and one end was floated down to Randall. The captain tied the rope around his waist, and with help from his men finally made it to shore. Both Randall and Doty were severely bruised and suffered from a chill, but rebounded after several days' rest. No more river crossings were attempted.[21]

The 2nd Vermont was replaced by another regiment at Great Falls on Monday, August 26, and returned to Camp Lyon.[22]

Whiting's men finally received new weapons on August 28, trading in their smoothbore muskets for newer rifled Enfield muskets. Pvt. Edwin N. Turner of Co. D stated, "We had quite a surprise the other day in the shape of bran new Enfield rifles which adds to our contentment some." Soon after that the quartermaster was also able to supply the men with much needed shirts, underwear, and shoes.[23]

The first week in September, McClellan began to occupy those portions of Virginia within sight of the capitol dome. Smith's brigade received orders September 3 to move across the Chain Bridge that evening. The 2nd Vermont moved out at about 10 P.M. Everyone thought they were going to attack the rebels at Fall's Church. Their excitement was further heightened when, after crossing the bridge, they were put into line of battle; however, after moving several miles down the Leesburg Pike the men were ordered to make camp for the night. Next morning, they quickly discovered they were not on a combat operation, but were, instead, to clear land and build fortifications. Because they had pushed out so far from Washington's defenses, their new camp was christened Camp Advance.[24]

Pvt. George W. Meigs, a Vergennes farm boy in Co. K, described the operation:

> Well one day the Capt. and his company went scouting and when we came in the regiment was ordered across Chain Bridge into Virginia. There was a good many Regiments and a good many pieces of artillery crossed that night. Well we marched up a hill and all at once we were ordered into the woods (or on a little road in the woods) and in line of battle.... After a while we started on the march over such a road it went up hill here through a gully then through bushes and finally we were stationed on the top of a hill in the bushes to cut off the Enemy's Retreat if they came that way for our troops had a body surrounded. We were without tents about a fortnight ... during that time we had nothing but an old brush Shanty which the company made. We had not been here long before they set us to work building a fort with several other Regiments. We worked pretty hard there for a week. We would shovel in the forenoon and in the afternoon we did not have anything to do unless it was some fellows that were on double duty when they miss Roll Call or cut up monkey shines or other and then they have to go to the guard house and to do double duty.[25]

Work in the fortifications was interrupted on September 10 by a surprise visit from President Lincoln, Gen. McClellan, Secretary of War Simon Cameron, and the governor of Pennsylvania and his wife. Picks and shovels were dropped and a mad rush was made toward the caravan of carriages. Three rousing cheers were given "Old Abe," who introduced the others in the entourage. The men again cheered when McClellan was introduced. It was the first time the Vermonters had seen their young commander and his hands and arms were covered by the soiled hands of the Vermont soldiers.[26]

On September 11, companies A and F, under Lt. Col. Stannard's command, accompanied a force of 2,000 men on a reconnaissance to Lewinsville, Va. The objective was to map the Lewinsville area to determine if it was suitable for a permanent camp. The force, commanded by Col. Isaac I. Stevens, commander of the 79th New York Infantry, consisted of the 79th, four companies of 65th New York Infantry, five companies of the 19th Indiana Infantry, 3rd Vermont, four guns of Capt. Charles Griffin's battery, and about 100 cavalry troopers.

The units left Camp Advance at 7:30 A.M. and reached Lewinsville, by the way of Langley (present day site of the Central Intelligence Agency headquarters), at 10 A.M. Skirmishers were thrown out beyond the village and in the process several Confederate pickets were chased away. Capt. Griffin set up his artillery pieces on several roads that led into the village and the engineer proceeded to map the area, completing his task shortly after 2 P.M. The skirmishers were then called in to prepare for the return to camp. Unbeknownst to the Federals, the Confederate pickets had reported to their headquarters. As a result, Col. Jeb Stuart with about 500 infantry, cavalry, and a section of artillery had been dispatched to attack the Yankees.

Most of the Federal skirmishers had returned when the 19th Indiana saw rebels approaching. A few shots were exchanged, alerting the whole command. The rebel infantry fell back as the Confederate artillery pieces came up and went into action. For about an hour an artillery duel ensued. The 2nd Vermont's men, assigned to support Griffin's guns, held their position ready to repel any attempt by the rebels to charge the guns. Meanwhile, the rest of the command started the return march, with the artillery protecting the rear. Although several Federals were killed and wounded, no men of the 2nd Vermont were hurt. Some did have a close call when a shell exploded, shredding several of the men's uniforms, but no one suffered more than scratches.

The command returned to Camp Advance at 5:30 P.M. While the foray was of little military consequence, it did accomplish three things. First, it raised the men's morale and confidence through their pulling off a successful operation. Second, it provided the information Smith needed to decide whether to relocate his division's camp. Last it got one Col. Jeb Stuart promoted to brigadier general.[27]

During the rest of the fall and winter, the 2nd Vermont built forts, drilled and did picket duty. Night alarms were frequent, and the men repeatedly fell into line in the darkness and stood under arms until dawn. The severe fatigue and interrupted sleep took its toll on the men.[28]

Pvt. Cutler explained what it was like on the picket line:

> I have told you that were required to keep pacing on foot, but you see we boys are astonishing ignorant we don't see the practical bead of it when we can set on one knapsack or a log or stump or perhaps at the end of our beats and talk awhile, so long as we can watch over alloted ground and have ample time to stop anyone who may be approaching, but whenever the officer of the guard rides along the line to see if all is right, of course all is alright. We are up marching back and forth with our guns on our shoulders as though nothing had happened for you see he has to go to the front one first, and whenever he is seen he is seen approaching the fact that his official dignity will soon pass along the line is managed to be telegraphed through. If it be night we manage to challenge him so boisterous loud that the three or four next posts hear all about the matter, and of course if it should happen to be cold or windy night, we are not at that particular, shielding ourselves behind an old root or stack of rails. Being behind a [*illegible*] I would not have you understand that we are curled down whare we cannot keep a good look out for midnight prowlers.[29]

Although picket duty was usually more boring than dangerous, Confederate troops occasionally probed Federal positions and sporadic firing broke out. On the night of September 19 while on picket, Pvt. William E. Snow of Co. H, a 22-year-old farmer from Fletcher, went to a nearby creek to fill his canteen. In a few minutes, the other men heard several shots. His body was never found. The exact time of his death is not clear, but his service record indicates he died of his wounds while in the hands of the rebels. For some reason, he was carried on the company rolls as a deserter. A number of years later this was corrected.[30]

On September 20, 150 recruits, enlisted by officers of the regiment who had been dispatched to Vermont soon after the battle of Bull Run, arrived at Camp Advance and were distributed among the companies, bringing the aggregate strength of the 2nd Vermont to nearly 1,000 men.[31]

There was great excitement in camp on September 23. Baldy Smith had finally had enough of the bickering between Col. Whiting and Maj. Joyce and published an order releasing Joyce from arrest.[32]

News of the order spread quickly through camp and the men found the major in Capt. Randall's tent and cheered him with a rousing "three times three." Joyce returned their gratitude, but declined to give a speech as requested. Though Maj. Joyce had been released, the matter was not cleared. A resolution was introduced in the Vermont House of Representatives on November 12, asking Whiting to tender his resignation since he had lost the confidence of officers and men, but it was never acted upon.[33]

The 2nd Vermont's camp was moved out about a mile toward Lewinsville on September 24, but the chief work of the regiment continued to be fatigue duty, specifically, the

Left: **First Lieutenant Walter A. Philips, Company F. The first officer in the 2nd Vermont to be court-martialed and dismissed from the service. University of Vermont.** ***Right:*** **Second Lieutenant Horace C. Crossman, Company F. Pictured here as a captain. USAMHI.**

construction of the fort. It was a large fort, covering six acres, and intended to mount 50 guns. Building it involved an immense amount of hard labor, the lion's share of which was born by the Vermonters. Corp. Henry L. Franklin, a 23-year-old mechanic from Brattleboro in Co. C, wrote his mother, "We are building a large Fort at this place and we have a plenty large guns here but the fort is about half done but if Old Jeff happens to come along this way we will give him a warm reception to his content." Their work was recognized by Gen. McClellan in General Order No. 18, dated September 30, 1861, naming the fort for Vermont's Revolutionary War hero Ethan Allen. In the same order, an earthwork they had built near the Georgetown reservoir was designated "Battery Vermont."[34]

Several of the 2nd Vermont's companies were on picket September 27 and 28 near Langley. They returned to camp on Saturday, September 28, around noon and went directly to their tents for some sleep. This tour of duty had been especially rough as it had rained steadily all Friday night and was extremely cool. Everyone was completely worn out and a number were sick. Rest, however, was short lived. Near 5 P.M., the order to move out was quickly passed through the regiment and within 20 minutes the men were on the road toward Fall's Church. After making about four miles they were halted and returned to camp without anyone knowing why. The regiment reached camp around 9 P.M.[35]

The men who had been on picket went immediately to their tents and dropped into bed. Around 10 P.M., the drums again beat "fall in" and everyone was told to have a day's rations in his haversack. Then the 2nd Vermont left camp with a larger column, under the command of Brig. Gen. Winfield S. Hancock. The objective was to surprise and occupy the Confederate outpost on Munson's Hill. The position had been an annoyance to the federal government for several months since its Confederate flag could be seen from the U.S. capitol.[36]

Lts. Walter Philips and Horace Crossman, both of Co. F, and some 160 enlisted men and noncommissioned officers, all of whom had been on picket the night before, had had enough of false alarms and stayed in their tents.

In the darkness, Col. Whiting and the other field grade officers failed to notice their absence.[37]

Just after the drums had sounded, Capt. Randall had gone to Philips's and Crossman's tent to get them up, and in his words:

> I went to the tents of my lieutenants, and found them both asleep, as I supposed I should, the drum not having waked them. I waked them, and Lieut. Philips was really sick. He had a high fever and I saw was not able to go, and Lieut. Crossman was not much better. Things looked pretty tough certainly, but I finally told my Lieutenants to keep their beds, and I would go out that night and they must come in the morning early and relieve me, as probably I should be worn out by that time [Randall had just returned from a three week illness] as I had walked six miles and back already that day, besides taking charge of one hundred and fifty [wood] choppers through the day. I then went for my Company and found them about as bad as the Lieutenants. I, however, got out the most of them, and excused a few that appeared the worst. Some undoubtedly were so sound asleep they did not wake up at all—things on these occasions being done in a great hurry, and a Regiment is off in ten minutes after the first beat of the drum sometimes.[38]

Pvt. Edwin M. Turner wrote to his wife about failing to turn out:

> It was Saturday the 28 of Sept. I was on picket the night before in a drenching rain and got a very bad cold and consiquently did not feel at all well and when the order came at 9 o'clock at night for every man to be ready to march in 15 minutes with 24 hours rations think I to myself Ed you and I can't go that and so he makes himself scarce till the regiment had gone and then he goes back to his tent and enjoys a good nights rest.[39]

The march started at 10 P.M. with Hancock's brigade in the lead column followed by a second column with the 2nd Vermont at its head. The command passed Vanderwerker's farm about midnight and had moved another half mile when firing was heard in the first column. While passing through thick woods, the 71st Pennsylvania Infantry, at the head of the lead column, was fired on by a portion of the 5th Pennsylvania Cavalry. The horsemen had been sent out in advance of the infantry and had lost their way in the dark. Somehow, they had circled back upon their own column, which they mistook for a Confederate ambush. The firing, yelling, and cussing alarmed the whole command, and was followed by a second collision, in which the 69th Pennsylvania Infantry fired into the 71st, which also returned fire. Adding to the confusion, a stampede of artillery horses, which in a panic had turned to the rear and broken from their pieces, dashed through some of the infantry, injuring a number of men.[40]

While the confusion reigned in the first column, Col. Whiting deployed companies A and F on the right flank of his column. As they moved into position, stretcher-bearers brought two dead and two wounded men down the road from the front column. The sight got everyone's attention. Just as companies A and F got into position, the panicked cavalry troopers bumped into their line. The 5th Pennsylvania Calvary fired into the 2nd Vermont, which returned fire, killing one and wounding another of the horsemen. Firing then ceased for the night and the officers had the men remain where they were for fear of another collision. As soon as the sun came up, everyone saw that the dead and wounded men lying in front were wearing blue. It was then obvious to all what had happened, and as Pvt. Elijah Brown wrote, "it was awful to witness our men and horses piled up in the road." A total of nine men were killed and 25 wounded. The Vermont troops escaped with nothing worse than bruises. Pvt. Hiram H. Tilly, a 16-year-old lad from St. George in Co. G, summed up the affair to his parents, "by sombodys *blunder* our men had quite a fight among themselves." After order was restored, the command remained halted in place until the next afternoon. Meanwhile, information was received that the rebels had quietly, and probably with some bewilderment, evacuated Fall's Church and Munson's and Upton's hills while the Federal troops had been killing each other.[41]

Around 5 P.M., Gen. Hancock started the command back to camp. They had just gotten started when they were met by wagons bringing them supper. The column was

Private Hiram H. Tilly, Company G. Pearce Civil War Collection, Navarro College.

quickly halted and food handed out. When the wagons left, Capt. Randall hitched a ride back to camp. Lt. Crossman had come out earlier in the afternoon to replace him as directed. Lt. Philips had stayed in camp still too sick to venture out.[42]

After supper, all units, except for the 2nd Vermont, started back to camp. The regiment bivouacked for the night on the Vanderwerker farm where it had stopped for supper. As Capt. Randall put it, "This of course left me in camp and them out." It was here that Col. Whiting discovered that a good many of his men had stayed in camp. This breech of discipline caused the largest case of mass punishment that ever occurred in the 2nd Vermont. When the regiment reached camp the next day, Col. Whiting had all the AWOL enlisted men put under arrest and thrown into the guardhouse until they could be court-martialed. Pvt. Edwin Turner confessed his predicament in a letter to his wife:

> ... by the way Addie I am a prisoner. I have been quartered in the guardhouse over a week for a crime of not going with the regt ... a great many that is in the same fix of our company there is Bill the Blade Bill Kelly, James Diamond and a number of others that you don't know and don't care about. There is 106 of the regiment under arrest and in the guardhouse so you see we have plenty of company. We have been court martialed but have not received our sentence yet.[43]

All the enlisted men had received their punishment by the last week of November; most receiving time already served. A few were fined. The noncommissioned officers were reduced to the ranks. Randall and Philips were put under arrest and charged with disobeying orders. Both were confined to their company area until they could be brought to trial. Randall was suspended from duty for 30 days. Except for this blemish, his record was excellent and in October 1862, he was chosen as colonel for the newly formed 13th Vermont Infantry.[44]

Philips, who had entered Norwich University in 1859, but had dropped out in 1861 to enlist in the 2nd Vermont, was tried on November 19. In his defense, he stated that he had been suffering from a severe cold and understood that Capt. Randall had given him permission to stay in his tent. Unfortunately, Randall was not in camp during the trial to corroborate Philips's story. Philips was found guilty and dismissed from the service. In January 1862, Philips wrote to his congressman, E. P. Walton, asking him to get the conviction overturned or allow him to be allowed to resign from the service. He indicated that with either outcome he would be able to join another unit. Walton sent two letters to McClellan pleading Philips's case, but the records do not show whether McClellan overturned the sentence. Philips did, however, enlist as a private in Randall's 13th Vermont Infantry in August, 1862 and was commissioned a first lieutenant the following June. He was mustered out with the unit on July 21, 1863, and joined the 3rd Vermont Artillery in August serving with distinction until having to resign for medical reasons in February, 1865. After the war he became a success in the furniture business in Illinois until his death on February 5, 1901.[45]

During the last week of September, the men of the 2nd Vermont were cheered by the arrival of the 4th and 5th Vermont Infantry Regiments which went into camp close by. They needed cheering partly because they were without the overcoats they had lost at Centreville in July. The cold rains beat through their old and thin tents, and their uniforms, faded by the summer sun and worn with fatigue duty, gave little warmth. Corp. Henry Franklin wrote, "I havent had a shirt to put on for five weeks but one. I mean only one to wear." About this time partial supplies of army clothing were secured from the government, and the army blue began to mingle with the gray in the ranks. The supply was insufficient because the government had more men to clothe than it had uniforms, and the sick roll grew larger before the needs of the men were supplied.[46]

Baldy Smith was selected as a division commander on October 3. He was replaced by 40-year-old William Thomas Harbaugh Brooks, previously a regular army captain in the 3rd U.S. Infantry Regiment, who had been promoted to brigadier general of volunteers on September 28. Although Brooks was an Ohio native, his father was originally from Montpelier. Unlike Col. Whiting, Brooks was admired by the men of the brigade because of his lineage and reputation. He had seen active service in the Mexican War and on the frontier and had established a reputation as a brave, experienced, and capable soldier.[47]

Smith's division consisted of three brigades. The First Brigade commanded by Brig. Gen. Winfield S. Hancock, the Second commanded by Brooks and the Third commanded by Brig. Gen. John M. Brannan.[48]

Gen. Smith soon made another short advance, deeper into Virginia on October 9. The division moved four miles nearer Lewinsville, where Smith established a camp named Camp Griffin, after the gallant commander of Griffin's Light Artillery Battery. The Vermont regiments stayed at Camp Griffin for five months, longer than they stayed anywhere else during the war. The site was in fine rolling country, with open fields and sprawling woodlands, many acres of which fell under the axes of the Vermont boys. The knolls around had been dotted with mansions, most of which were in ruins under the ruthless touch of war. The camp was located on the road from Chain Bridge to Lewinsville on and around Smoot's Hill. The 2nd Vermont's camp was just

Brigadier General William T.H. Brooks, the second commander of the Vermont Brigade. Vermont Historical Society.

south of MacKall's Hill toward Lewinsville. From the top of the hill, the camps of most of the regiments and batteries of Smith's division could be seen. The Confederate outposts were five or six miles away and the mass of the Confederate Army lay at Centreville and Manassas, 15 miles to the southwest.[49]

From Camp Griffin, the 2nd Vermont participated in many reconnaissance missions on almost a weekly basis. Although billed as a reconnaissance, its main mission was to confiscate food and animal forage from local farmers to deny its use by the Confederates.[50]

The 2nd Vermont's clothing shortage became more serious as fall wore on. On October 21 Gen. Smith telegraphed the governor of Vermont that the men of the 2nd and 3rd Vermont regiments were suffering from lack of clothing, and that 850 coats, 1,500 pairs of pants, and 100 tents were needed at once. Col. Whiting followed with a letter, signed by nearly all the officers of the regiment, to the Vermont Legislature, certifying that the men of the 2nd Vermont had insufficient clothing and tents. The Vermont quartermaster general, George F. Davis, was sent by the governor to Camp Griffin to investigate. Upon returning, he reported that the federal government had already partially supplied the regiment and would fully supply it as soon as possible. The Vermont authorities, though anxious to provide for the wants of their troops, acquiesced to the War Department. The needed supplies were gradually provided, and by the end of October, the regiment's condition was much improved. To supplement the government supplies, the Green Mountain Boys received boxes of clothing and food from Soldier's Aid Societies, formed by the women of the villages and towns of Vermont.[51]

Before new uniforms arrived, three privates in Co. C came close to being executed, due in part to their lack of adequate clothing. The two Butterfield brothers, George P. and Joel P., and Madison Cook, all farmers from the Brattleboro area, were caught sleeping while on picket. George Butterfield was found asleep on October 25 at his post. He was brought before a general court-martial on October 30. He was found guilty, but offered as an extenuating circumstance that the cold weather had caused his left side to go numb and he had lain down to get warm and fell asleep. The problem with Butterfield's side was verified by his company commander, Capt. Todd, and his platoon leader, Lt. Tyler. Regardless of the affliction, he was found guilty and sentenced to be shot. But all of the officers of the court, of which Col. Whiting was the president, signed a letter recommending that Butterfield be spared. McClellan agreed and George went on to serve honorably with the regiment and reenlisted December, 1863.[52]

Three nights later, George's brother Joel, and Madison Cook, were also found asleep on picket. Both were tried, found guilty, and sentenced to be shot. Again the officers of the court recommended the men be spared. In Cook's case they stated:

> The condemned is only eighteen years old; he was marched from his camp at three o'clock in the morning and immediately posted and remained on the same post unrelieved until he was found asleep at one o'clock on the following morning a period of twenty two hours during which time the weather was very cold and the condemned without an overcoat and without other sufficient protection against the weather entered the hut of boughs which was habitually occupied by the pickets of that post, and exhausted nature yielded to excessive fatigue and cold.
>
> In consideration of these circumstances, the youth and good character of the condemned and the entire absence of criminal intention upon his part the undersigned members of the court earnestly recommend him to the favorable consideration and clemency of the Commanding General.

Joel Butterfield received a letter of clemency almost

Top: Photograph of the 2nd Vermont's camp at Camp Griffin taken by Vermont photographer George H. Houghton. The hospital for the 2nd Vermont can be seen under construction at upper left. George Houghton Album, University of Vermont. ***Bottom:*** Houghton photograph of a foraging party preparing to leave Camp Griffin. George Houghton Album, University of Vermont.

identical to Cook's. On recommendation of the officers of the court, McClellan spared the two.[53]

As fall came and the nights grew colder, the men's efforts turned to improving their comforts. Although the officers and some of the more ambitious enlisted men built log huts, the majority of the men built structures that were a combination of logs and tents. They started by digging a two to three foot hole in the ground, the same size as the tent floor. Then they would put up a log wall two to three feet high, with their tents as the roof. At one end a fireplace was dug and a mud chimney built on the outside. The soil at Camp Griffin would get brick hard after several fires. Inside, wooden platforms were built two feet off the floor for beds under which firewood and personal belongings were stored. Pegs or nails were driven into the log walls for hanging rifles and other military equipment. Candles or oil lamps provided light. Although a bit close in the huts for three or four men, they were quite comfortable and warm.[54]

Amid the cheers of other Vermonters, the 6th Vermont arrived at Camp Griffin on October 24 completing the formation of the First Vermont Brigade.[55]

In November, the 2nd Vermont was fully supplied with blue uniforms and overcoats, but of poor quality. Pvt. Wilbur Fisk, a 22-year-old school teacher from Tunbridge in Co. E, wrote:

> Since the boys here have received their new clothes, they have been able to keep themselves tolerably comfortable. Before this they had just cause for complaint. I cannot very highly recommend some of the clothing they have given us. I have seen some of these blue pants after a fortnight's service, so far gone as to be actually indecent to wear. Some of the boys have no rubber blanket, nor bed-tick, nothing but the ground to lie on. These articles are very necessary,—almost indispensable. Many of the soldiers would gladly accept an extra woolen blanket these cold nights.[56]

Poor as the new supplies were, they did help improve the health and morale of the men. By Thanksgiving the regiment was starting to warm up to Col. Whiting somewhat, as endorsed by one of Lt. Leach's letters:

> The VT soldiers were excused from duty on Thanksgiving day after 12 O.C. except guard duty. I gave thanks by having to go on picket, making twice this week. Our Co. spent Thanksgiving day the same, most of them (on picket), but the Col. had given them today to pay for it. The Col. invited us with the rest of the officers who were on picket Thursday to take tea with him last night [November, 29]. Of course we accepted. We had supper, oysters, biscuits and butter, pie, berry sauce and tea. A very good supper.[57]

Private Doty gave a description of how the enlisted men fared:

Private Wilbur Fisk, Company E, who, in addition to being an infantryman, served as a reporter for Montpelier's *Green Mountain Freeman*. Emil Rosenblatt.

> On Thanksgiving day we had only one drill, early in the morning, and the rest of the day was given us to enjoy as we saw fit. (per Brig. Gen. Brooks) In most companies enough extra rations had been disposed of to buy potatoes, fresh pork, chickens, turkeys, and such other luxuries as could be got, and all ate their *fill*. In the evening, old acquaintances got together, cooked their oysters, drank cider and smoked a "*mild Havana*" while telling over their exploits while on picket, and rehearsing the good times they had *lost* this year at Thanksgiving. At 9 P.M. they adjourned to their own quarters, and by listening one could hear the songs, "I am glad I'm in this army," "We are all going home," "Red, White and Blue," & etc. All in all, it was a day of joy, and thanksgiving to us Vermonters.[58]

Pvt. Jerome Cutler spent Thanksgiving on the picket line and wrote:

> My thanksgiving supper consisted of bread meat, and hard crackers, and a little butter to greece them so they would not strike fire on my teeth, I tosted my bread by a fire made out

> of Vaginia rails. We Vermont boys are so naughty that we have burned up the fences for miles around. I guess Vermont farmers would make a fuss about it would they not?[59]

On December 17 all the 2nd Vermont's company officers were in the colonel's tent for mandatory tactics instruction, when about noon they heard yelling and the sound of men running. Outside they saw that lightening could strike twice. First Lt. Tyler's tent was ablaze again. Rather than dig a fireplace like the other men, Tyler had bought a stove for his tent. Tyler described the scene in a letter home:

> I was attending the regular recitation in tactics at the Colonel's tent, when "Fire!" "Fire!" cries somebody, and I rushed wildly to the scene. The fire evidently caught on the floor of the tent from the stove, & finally extended to the tent itself, which burnt like tissue paper. Everything in the tent was destroyed except the contents of my trunk, among them Various Bible & Prayer Books, pincushions & C given me by Grandmother and others. My sword was destroyed—pistols slightly injured, rubber bed and bed clothes burnt up, also one dress coat.[60]

During December, a controversy arose between Col. Whiting and the governor of Vermont. Through combat losses, sickness, and resignations, officer vacancies had occurred in the regiment. Because company grade officers sometimes found it difficult to command men who were their neighbors and equals at home, Whiting had made it a point to transfer officers from one company to another. This did not meet the approval of the governor, who wanted to retain the militia system in which the field grade officers approved the selection of company grade officers, and when transfers from one company to another were recommended, it was approved by "the subordinates" of the company. Whiting said he could neither waive his rank as commander of the regiment nor be responsible for the discipline of the regiment "if the head was to be in the tail." As a result of this impasse, Whiting's recommendations were hung up in the Vermont adjutant general's office for some time.[61]

Col. Whiting applied for and was granted a 30-day leave of absence to return home on January 4. In his haste to leave Michigan to take command of the regiment, he had sold his lumber business for $10,000 and left without receiving payment, but now he needed to return home to collect. During his absence, the acting commander, Lt. Col. Stannard, worked a compromise that satisfied both the governor and adjutant general, and the commissions were issued.[62]

The majority of vacant positions in the regiment were filled by the beginning of March. The regiment's quartermaster, Perley P. Pitkin, was promoted to captain and moved up to brigade staff. He was replaced by QM. Sgt. Lauriston L. Stone. Sgt. Maj. William Guinan was discharged for the wound he had received at Bull Run and was replaced by Bradbury W. Hight of Co. K. The commander of Co. D, Capt. Charles Dillingham, was promoted to major in the 8th Vermont Infantry and was replaced by 2nd Lt. Enoch E. Johnson, of Co. B. Capt. Edward A. Todd, commander of Co. C, was discharged for the wound he had received at Bull Run and replaced by John S. Tyler. Amasa S. Tracy replaced William T. Burnham as the commander of Co. H. Capt. Volney S. Fullam, commander of Co. I, was promoted to lieutenant colonel of the 7th Vermont Infantry and was replaced by Newton Stone.[63]

Sergeant Major Bradbury W. Hight. Pictured here as a first lieutenant and adjutant of the 2nd Vermont. Brad Limoge.

In December, the regiment lost its band. The musicians grew sick of army life, and by special order of the War Department, left Camp Griffin on December 15 just as they had enlisted, *en masse*.[64]

Later in the war, the Vermont Brigade would make a name for itself as one of the best fighting and fastest marching brigades in the Army of the Potomac, but in the winter of 1861–1862, it was better known for having the largest number of men on sick roles, hugely disproportionate to that of any other brigade. The army's medical staff was bewildered. The predominate diseases were measles, remittent and intermittent fevers, typhoid, pneumonia, and diarrhea.[65]

This phenomenon began in November and grew steadily worse as winter progressed. In a report by the medical director of the Army of the Potomac in November, the 5th Vermont had 271 men out of 1,000 sick; the 4th Vermont, 244 out of 1,047; while the 2nd Vermont had 87 out of 1,021, and the 3rd Vermont, 84 out of 900. The lower figures for the 2nd and 3rd Vermont regiments were probably the result of their having been in the field longer and thus exposed to disease in warmer weather. Why the other Vermont regiments fared worse than those from other states was never determined. Particularly curious was the case of the 5th Vermont, which lost more men than any of the other Vermont regiments. Capt. Randall wrote in November, "The 5th has suffered most. A funeral every day and sometimes twice a day."[66]

Pvt. Cutler described the funeral of one of the members in his Co. H to his fiancée Emily on November 24:

> The day has mostly spent thus far in attending to our usual Sunday morning inspection during which was read to us by the Colonel the Governors proclamation for thanksgiving and also attending the funeral of one of our comrades in our company, one Philo Runnels, [Philo Reynolds from Belvidere, who died of disease on November 22] making two that has died in our company. the procedings of the funeral were as follows. the procession was led by the band followed by eight of us with arms reversed (that is the gun under our left arm with the barrel pointing downward) then the coffin born by six. the remainder of the company in the rear without their arms. after we arrived at the grave and wen they wer lowering the coffin into the grave and the chaplain was reading a portion of scripture and offering a prayer. We stood with our guns the barrel resting upon our left foot and our heads leening upon the but, after the ceremony was over we loded and fired three salutes over the grave and returned to camp. Solemn thought to leave our comrade intered benith Vigina soil far away from home and friends, laid as a sacrifice on their countries altar.
>
> Their has but ten or twelve died out of our regiment since we left home, while some twenty have died in the 5th, twelve or more in the 4th about the same in the 3rd, we are I think the healthiest of either of the Vt. Regt's, not withstanding we came here in warm weather and have been longest in the field. The smallpox has shown itself among the troops here, had one case in our regiment, and orders have been issued that the soldiers be vaxinated immediately. I hope and pray that we shall not be visited by this awful disease.[67]

Houghton photograph of a Vermont soldier's burial at Camp Griffin. George Houghton Album, University of Vermont.

On February 6, 1862, the medical director reported that he had sent a large detachment of convalescents to Philadelphia, to make room for the Vermont Brigade sick in the hospitals. He hoped the other patients might benefit from not seeing so many sick men from one organization. The governor of Vermont sent five additional assistant surgeons to tend to the brigade. Log houses were built and the sick men were moved out of hospital tents. Unit officers attempted to ensure a good police of the camps and inspected their men's personal cleanliness. Even with the best medical care the army and the state of Vermont could provide, between July 22, 1861, and March 31, 1862, the 2nd Vermont still lost 33 men from death due to disease, 47 discharged for disabilities due to disease, and seven discharged for disabilities due to wounds received at Bull Run. Like most regiments throughout the war, the 2nd Vermont would lose more men to disease and accidents than to combat. The health of the Vermont brigade did finally improve and the depression that had set in began to lift as winter drew to a close.[68]

Although a lot of men griped about having inspections, Pvt. Hiram Tilly found them a necessity. In a letter to his parents he wrote, "We have just got through another Sunday morning inspection. things have to be in fine order. ourselves as well as guns and extra clothing have to be clean and nice. it's a good thing for we have men with us that would not wash themselves or their clothes from one week to another if they were not oblige to." In another letter home that fall Tilly answered a question his mother had asked him about the men having head lice, "oh *no* we are not troubled with head *lice.* but have plenty of the *secesh* [secessionist] as we call them in our clothes. every day or two we strip and hunt them. we have got so use to snaping them we can do it every time."[69]

As difficult as it was for the soldiers to deal with the death of friends from sickness, it was especially difficult for the families back in Vermont. For loved ones to die needlessly in a hospital hundreds of miles from home was difficult to reconcile. The following poem was published in Burlington's *Daily Free Press* on March 8, 1862. It was written in memory of Charles N. Collins from Waterbury, a 17-year-old private in Co. D of the 2nd Vermont. Collins had fought at Bull Run, only to die December 17, 1861, in a Washington, D.C., hospital of typhoid fever.

HE DIED A HERO

He died a hero, though no peal
Of cannon tolled his knell,
Nor flashing sword, nor bayonet,
Gleamed o'er him as he fell.

The battle angel passed him by
Upon Manassas' plain:
Though round him on the bloody field
The bullets fell like rain.

Not his the death a soldier craves.
Who grasps the victor's crown;
And with his heart's blood writes his name
Upon thy page, Renown.

But steadily the fever fiend
Drank up the tide of life,
That in his young and eager heart,
Was bounding for the strife.

And he who feared no mortal foe
Resigned his parting breath,
When fell upon his ear, the call
Of his Commander, Death.

He died a hero-they who fell
By southern steel, may claim
A prouder grave, yet none more worth
The hero's deathless fame.

"He died a hero," let them write
Above his place of rest;
And plant the fadeless hazel-nut tree,
Upon his marble breast.[70]

Life at Camp Griffin did have its pleasures. The winter weather made the ground too muddy for drill. About the only duty was picket and some fatigue assignments, specifically, finishing the forts. As Lt. Leach put it, "We are all well & enjoying ourselves like 'a hog in a mud hole,' at least we are in the mud, whether we enjoy it or not." In fact, life was so relaxed that many of the officer's wives joined them in camp for part of the fall and winter.[71]

To while away the hours, the men read books and newspapers, wrote letters, whittled and played games, like checkers, chess, or backgammon. Lt. Leach wrote:

> As you know, idleness is the breeder of many vices & the like, which are not strictly military. Gambling is one thing that a great many busy themselves about when not otherwise employed & not infrequently the amount of two months wages is lost in a short time after payday. The practice is not only among the men, but the Officers too & on a larger scale as their amount is larger.

Pvt. Henry Franklin confessed to his mother, "as to myself and George [Henry's older brother] we are as fat saucy and no good and full of the Devel as we used to be at home. what little [money] we get to ourselves we spend it in playing cards and other amusement to pass away time."[72]

The favorite games of chance were poker, twenty-one, euchre, and keno. Soldiers also shot craps and rolled dice in a game known as chuck-a-luck, played by rolling three dice on a board, cloth or poncho marked off into numbered squares. Pvt. Marshall Twitchell, of the 4th Vermont, was visiting the 2nd Vermont's camp one cold winter day and saw several of the men wagering on their muskets. They were loading their weapons with blank cartridges, laying them on the ground and with strings tied to the triggers, discharging them, and betting on the distance of the recoil.[73]

As usual, there was a liberal use of alcohol. Sometimes the drinking got out of hand, as in the case of Pvt. Francis Flynn, a 23-year-old farmer of Underhill and Co. K. During the evening of January 29 Flynn had too much to drink and became rowdy. Co. K's skipper, Solon Eaton, Sgt. John T. Beach, and Cpl. Bradbury W. Hight went to quell the disturbance. Flynn started cussing them and Eaton ordered his two subordinates to subdue Flynn and take him to the guardhouse. Flynn started punching and kicking the two NCOs. Finally, after much effort and several bruises, they got the drunken private to the guardhouse. Flynn was brought before a general court-martial on February 6 and found guilty of conduct prejudicial to good order and military discipline and of violation of the ninth Article of War [striking a superior]. The episode cost Flynn $10 a month for eight months and a tour of hard labor while dragging around a ball and chain. The punishment apparently had the desired effect as Flynn's records show no further infractions.[74]

Henry Franklin also had a thirst for liquor. In asking his mother to send him a box of goodies, he added, "you can put in a Bottle of Brandy to go with the rest."[75]

"There are many good and virtuous young men here," wrote Pvt. Jerome Cutler, "and to their are many vicious and here away from the society and restraint of home they give loos reins to all their wicked habits and practices."[76]

As February wore on the weather became much milder, and the ground dried up allowing the men's free time to be filled with drilling and target practice. The 2nd Vermont exchanged its Enfield rifles for Springfield rifles on February 7, and the men were thus equipped with one of the best weapons in the U.S. government's arsenal.[77]

February 24 began like a typical day at Camp Griffin until the start of a torrential downpour and gale force winds. The rain did not last too long, but the fury of the wind continued unabated for hours. When the 2nd Vermont's camp was established in the fall, it was situated on the crest of a hill in a grove of second growth pine with a few oak and chestnut trees interspersed. As winter progressed, the trees in the surrounding area were consumed for firewood and building materials. It had reached the point that even stumps were chipped off close to the ground. Since winter had started to break and in anticipation of soon leaving for the spring campaign, the officers had let the men start cutting trees within the camp. Now, confronted with gale force winds, there was little protection. More than 50 tents were flattened and others were ripped to shreds. The pines that had been left standing by the men were now downed by the wind, and some made direct hits on tents. Lt. Leach described the scene: "Many of the tents were blown down & the trees were tipped up by the roots, which made a very lively scene for a while. A tree about 8 inches through at the butt fell across our tent, but went so slow that the tent held it up. A number of other tents had trees fall across them." Surprisingly no one was hurt although the wind was strong enough to overturn an empty supply wagon.

Postwar photograph of Captain Solon Eaton, commander of Company K. Vermont Historical Society.

As night approached, the temperature dropped below freezing, but the wind did not stop. Those without tents huddled around fires to stay warm. Not until around midnight did the wind subside. Next morning an old hospital tent was raised to house the tentless men until new tents could be procured. Life got back to normal with a brigade drill in the afternoon on the frozen ground.[78]

By February, the regiment had made amends with

Col. Whiting, who had by now returned from leave. As Lt. Leach mentioned, "The Col. is liked by the Regt. Very much better than formerly. There is not much dislike now for the winter but [for] picket duty." While Whiting was at home in the early part of the month, the privates of the regiment took up a collection of nearly $400 to purchase several gifts of appreciation for him. The money was given to Lt. Col. Stannard to buy something appropriate. He purchased a sword, sword belt, sash, matching pistols, saddle, and horse equipment. The sword was inscribed, "Presented to Col. Henry Whiting by the privates of the 2d Vt. Regt., 1862, *Fiat Justitia* [Let justice be done]." At 9 A.M., March 6, the regiment was formed in front of the colonel's tent for the presentation ceremony. The gifts were presented by Pvt. Vernon D. Rood of Co. H and a 20-year-old law student from Fletcher, hero of the day for volunteering to be the spokesman. In his presentation, Rood told Col. Whiting that the men of the 2nd Vermont, "descendants of such men as Ethan Allen," were ready to follow wherever he might lead them.[79]

In his reply, Whiting noted that, "If this present had been the result of winking at violations of military discipline its reception would, in my estimation, be degrading."[80]

Now all was out in the open. Although shrouded in rhetoric, the men finally acknowledged that Whiting's strict discipline had been necessary and they were sorry for opposing him. Sgt. Francis M. Edgerton of Co. B wrote a letter to the editor of the *Rutland Daily Herald*:

> It is well known that for the first few weeks after leaving Vermont the 2d Regiment was much dissatisfied with its commanding officer. Unused as all were to the strict discipline of a military life, and accustomed to do and say what *we* thought best, it is not strange we thought our duties irksome, and the officers who insisted on their being faithfully performed a hard master and even tyrannical. But time and experience have taught us that we must part with much of our freedom and many of our privileges to render us efficient soldiers. Now we regard our duties and officers with respect and love. It is a common remark among the privates of the Regiment, "We would not exchange our field officers for any in the service."[81]

Pvt. Frank H. Carrigan of Co. B noted in a letter, "Col. Whiting has survived the troubles in the regiment, and is now loved by all."[82]

Although the regiment was making amends with Col. Whiting, trouble was starting to brew in Co. G. Toward the end of January, Pvt. Hiram Tilly, in response to his parents' question about why the company's rations were short, wrote:

> you wanted to know who was to blame that we did not get our full rations. we think its our commanding officers fault. that is old Sharply. he is drunk most of the time and pretends he is sick. he lays in his tent from one weeks end to another. so we have no commissioned officer on duty in our company. Lieut. Weed is yet under arrest. we are all in hopes he will be released before long and that *old* Sharply was in h _ _ l or some other such place as he is an old cheat. you all seem to think that Weed was put under arrest for being drunk but that is not the case. he came into camp before the Regt. did while we were at Camp Advance the time our soldiers got to fighting among themselves before daylight one morning. it was thought Weed was scared at the shooting and came to camp for safety.

On February 9 Tilly complained:

> Lieut. A. H. Weed was released from arrest yesterday so he marched us out on dress parade. when we got back to camp the *boys* gave him three harty cheers and a *tiger*. we all like Weed but dispise old Sharply for Sharply does no duty. some of the boys think he is under arrest and hopes he will always remain so for he is not fit for a private soldier in the rear rank.[83]

While McClellan's men were in their camps around Washington learning to be soldiers, Johnston's Confederates were doing the same 15 miles away at Centreville. All winter Abraham Lincoln had been pressing McClellan to attack, but, like McDowell, McClellan did not think his men ready. In addition, he falsely believed he faced 115,000 rebels at Manassas, instead of Johnston's army of 50,000. McClellan had approximately 150,000 troops. Finally on January 17, Lincoln ordered a general advance of all U.S. armies to begin on, or before, February 22. Four days later he issued an order directing McClellan to occupy a point on the Orange and Alexandria Railroad southwest of Manassas Junction and to start on February 22.[84]

McClellan rejected the plan and countered with one of his own, which called for his army to be transported down the Potomac River to the Chesapeake Bay and up the Rappahannock River to Urbanna, Va. From there he would push to West Point, at the head of the York River, then with two supply bases established, he would move on to Richmond. McClellan contended that such a plan would place his army between Johnston's army and Richmond, forcing the evacuation of Manassas without a fight. Lincoln initially opposed McClellan's plan, fearing Washington would be exposed, but by mid-February gave in to the young general.[85]

Johnston threw a monkey wrench into McClellan's designs on March 9 by moving his army from Manassas to Gordonsville behind the Rappahannock River. McClellan marched his army the next day toward Centreville. Unbeknownst to the rank and file of the Army of the Potomac, who thought they were off to meet the rebels, this was only a "shake down" to exercise the army as a whole and rid it of useless baggage in preparation for the movement south.[86]

CHAPTER 4

"A Dam Failure"

At midnight on March 9, 1862, the Army of the Potomac received orders to have two days' rations cooked and to march the next morning at 3 A.M. This news was received with cheers and rejoicing throughout the Vermont Brigade. Shortly, Camp Griffin was ablaze with bonfires of equipment and supplies which the men could not carry and would rather burn than leave. The men busily packed knapsacks, wrote letters home, and performed other preparations. At 3 A.M. the next morning, the Vermonters heard the drum beat to fall in. The men were in light marching order their knapsacks and the rest of their personal belongings would be sent later. The Vermont Brigade was marshaled with the rest of Smith's division in an open field to wait their turn to join the rest of army on its move forward.[1]

As the Vermonters stood in formation ready to take their place in the column, regiments, brigades, divisions, and miles of artillery and cavalry passed by. This procession was followed by long trains of army wagons covered with black rubber cloth, on which was printed in large white letters, "AMMUNITION," followed by a long somber-looking line of ambulances. Pvt. Henry Franklin wrote, "75 thousand soldiers have passed here today on their way to the fight. it is a splended sight to see so many men marching together." Then, as usual at the beginning of a march, it started to rain. The roads got so bad that some of the wagons returned and the men thought the affair was off and were starting to feel dejected; but excitement soared again when the command "Forward march!" was shouted. With bands playing "The Girl I Left Behind," the Green Mountain Boys marched through Lewinsville and past Vienna to the southwest. No one doubted they would soon meet the enemy, perhaps on the plains of Manassas. Not only were they glad to be on the way to battle, but also to get out of camp. One 2nd Vermont soldier wrote, "If the men had just been freed from prison their countenance would hardly have worn a more gleeful expression." Even the drizzling rain could not dampen their excitement at the thought of redeeming themselves for the disaster at Bull Run the summer before. For the most part, the march was made through the fields, since the roads were clogged with long trains of army wagons. After covering nearly a dozen miles, Smith's division stopped in the afternoon at Flint Hill, north of Fairfax Court House. Strangely, it remained there all afternoon. Apparently something had arrested the movement of the division, and toward night a rumor floated through camp that there was no enemy attack.[2]

As evening approached, the 2nd Vermont set up its new shelter tents on the soggy ground. This was the first of hundreds of times the Vermonters would sleep under these little tents. Shelter tents, very much like the ones used by our army today, were made of two cotton halves approximately five feet by five feet with metal buttons along two sides with corresponding button holes along the others. Each man was issued one panel, and two or more men had to join forces to have a complete tent. Pvt. Wilbur Fisk described the tent as more like a "hencoop with the ends open."[3]

While the men were setting up camp, the wind changed and came in from the northwest, dropping the temperature. The men used pine boughs for bedding in their tents, but the water still seeped through. Before dawn most were huddled around bonfires trying to stay warm. In the morning the camp was moved a short distance away to dryer ground.[4]

Also that morning, the rumor from the afternoon before was confirmed. Gen. Joe Johnston, with an army of fewer than 50,000 men, which for six months had kept the Confederate flag flying within sight of the nation's capitol, had evacuated Centreville.[5]

That afternoon Col. Whiting tried to nip in the bud the one thing the 2nd Vermont had gotten good at: plundering. Fisk recalled:

> The orders at dress parade gave us to understand that stealing, plundering private dwellings, house burning, and such unsoldierlike depredations would be visited by severe and speedy punishment. The limits of our encampment were drawn pretty close, and any one found beyond them, without permission, would be held to a strict account. The Colonel told us that, if necessary to enforce these restrictions, he would establish a line of pickets around the entire camp. It was evident that the lawlessness of the men, which characterized last summer's campaign, was to find no counterpart in this.[6]

McClellan reviewed Smith's division the next day and Fisk probably expressed most Vermonters' opinions when he wrote:

> As the General rode around the square formed by this Division the men everywhere cheered him as he passed them, with the intensest enthusiasm. His very looks, with his lofty and gentlemanly bearing, are sufficient to enkindle a spirit of energy and bravery in the hearts of the troops under his command. All the men place the most unbounded confidence in their General.[7]

On March 13, McClellan called a council of war to modify his Urbanna campaign plan. Since Johnston had moved to Gordonsville, debarkation at Urbanna was too risky. The plan was modified by moving the debarkation point to Fort Monroe. From there he could move up the Virginia Peninsula between the York and James Rivers toward Richmond. This plan was approved by the president the same day.[8]

With the plan approved, McClellan reorganized his army for the upcoming campaign and orders were issued to start embarking the army at Alexandria on March 17. The Army of the Potomac was reorganized into five corps. The First Corps was commanded by Maj. Gen. Irwin McDowell, the Second by Maj. Gen. Edwin V. Sumner, the Third by Maj. Gen. Samuel P. Heintzelman, the Fourth by Maj. Gen. Erasmus D. Keyes, and the Fifth by Maj. Gen. Nathaniel P. Banks. The Vermont Brigade became the Second Brigade of Smith's Second Division of the Fourth Corps. Also under Smith's command were the batteries of Captains Romeyn B. Ayres, Thaddeus P. Mott, Charles C. Wheeler, and Terrence J. Kennedy.[9]

At 6 o'clock Saturday morning, March 15, Smith's division packed up and moved toward Alexandria to board transports for Fort Monroe. Before reaching Fairfax Court House, it started to rain. From Fairfax Court House, the division took the road to Alexandria. The torrential rain made the 20-mile march very tedious. Because of its service the previous summer, the 2nd Vermont was the only Vermont regiment in the brigade that had ever made a march this tough. In the other Vermont regiments, some of the weaker men fell out of the ranks, while others threw away their knapsacks containing their blankets and all of their extra clothes. In the 2nd Vermont, the company officers assisted the men the best they could, often taking a rifle or knapsack of some lagging soldier and carrying it themselves. To Lt. Leach, it was reminiscent of the retreat from Bull Run: "It is on the same road, but the circumstances are a little different & rained some harder...." To Pvt. Charles M. Hapgood of Co. A, one of the new replacements who had arrived the previous fall after Bull Run, it was the "Hardest time we have seen."[10]

Smith's division reached the outskirts of Alexandria and set up camp in a patch of scrub pine. This time the men arranged their tents in circles around large fires. By now everyone was thoroughly drenched to the skin, and still it rained. Some of the men stood around their fires nearly all night. Others piled large quantities of pine boughs in their tents and spread their rubber blankets on them for a bed. They lay down in their wet clothes wrapped in wet blankets and tried to sleep, while directly under them water was running. The troops literally "steamed" where the warmth of their bodies made contact with their cold wet clothes. Pvt. Cutler complained, "...we wer completely drenched through, it was almost impossible to start a fire when we got here at night but we finally succeeded and it was not long before hundreds of fires were blazing all over the woods, we partialy dried ourselves and then bundled up in our blankets and laid down to sleep under small tents ... that we brought with us." It stopped raining around midnight and the next day the sun came out and started drying things out.[11]

The next morning the transports were not ready, and the brigade marched back four miles to Cloud's Mills, where it remained the rest of the week. This camp, which the men named Camp Hard Crackers, was much better. It was situated on the slope of a hill bordering a small pebbly stream of pure water, and there was plenty of oak timber for firewood. Just in front of the camp, at the top of the hill, was a level piece of ground hemmed in on all sides by thick woods. It made an excellent place for drilling. In addition to drill, bayonet exercises were added to the training schedule.[12]

Camp Hard Crackers was about two miles from the 2nd Vermont's old camp at Clermont. So many men were badgering their officers for passes to go see the old camp that Col. Whiting marched the entire regiment there on March 21. The men were disappointed by what they saw. Chester Leach wrote, "The place did not look very natural on account of the woods along the brook & railroad in front of the ground being all cut down."[13]

Smith's division, now 13,000 strong, marched on Sunday, March 23, with spirits high, bands playing and flags flying, to board the transports at Alexandria. The 2nd and part of the 3rd Vermont were loaded aboard the side wheel steamer *Vanderbilt.* In the late afternoon, the division sailed down the Potomac River, and a little after sundown, dropped anchor for the night opposite Mount Vernon. The next day it steamed on to Fort Monroe.[14]

Smith's division arrived at Fort Monroe around noon Sunday, March 24. By the time it finally debarked, it was dark and the men spent the night on the sandy beach just outside the fort.[15]

At daybreak on Monday the men of the 2nd Vermont got their first good look at Hampton Roads. The men were awed by the huge fort. Fort Monroe, the largest masonry fort in the United States, was an enormous seven-sided granite and masonry structure a third-of-a-mile across surrounded by a substantial moat. It had been completed in 1834 at Old Point Comfort, the finger of land forming the tip of the Virginia Peninsula. It had been too strongly defended for the rebels to capture at the outbreak of the war, and now it was a secure base from which the Federals could launch their advance on Richmond.[16]

The harbor was full of transports and combat ships, giving it the appearance of a forest of masts. Within sight was the famous *Monitor* that had fought the Confederate *Virginia* (previously the U.S. *Merrimack*) to a standoff on March 9. The Vermonters agreed with the Confederate newspapers' description of the *Monitor,* it did look like a cheese box on a raft.[17]

After gawking at their surroundings, the enlisted men started fires from scrap lumber and driftwood lying around the beach, boiled coffee and had breakfast from their haversacks while the officers walked over to the Hygeia Hotel for theirs.[18]

At 9 A.M., Smith formed his division and left Fort Monroe for Newport News. Not far from the fort the division crossed the Hampton River and marched through the town of Hampton. The sight of the town shocked and sickened the men. They had seen individual homes in northern Virginia ravaged by war, but this was the first time they had seen an entire town destroyed. Hampton had been burned August 7, 1861, by Confederate soldiers to keep it from becoming a safe haven for traitors and contrabands. About all that was left were the burned and blackened chimneys and crumbling brick walls of once beautiful houses. Flowers and peach trees were in bloom in deserted and fenceless gardens, and japonica and laurel covered heaps of ugly rubble. Old St. John's Church, built in 1727, had withstood British naval gunfire in 1775 and plundering by British forces in 1812, but had been consumed by the recent fire. Only its walls of scorched Flemish bond bricks were left standing. Many of the tombs and vaults had been broken into and bones scattered about. "On March 25th," wrote Capt. John Tyler, "we marched thro' Hampton which is entirely burned. It is very sad to see the beautiful buildings and churches a mass of ruins." One of the

***S.S. Vanderbilt*, the ship that brought the 2nd Vermont to Fort Monroe. This 1,700-ton side-wheeler was donated to the U.S. Navy by multi-millionaire shipping magnate Cornelius Vanderbilt. U.S. Naval Historical Center.**

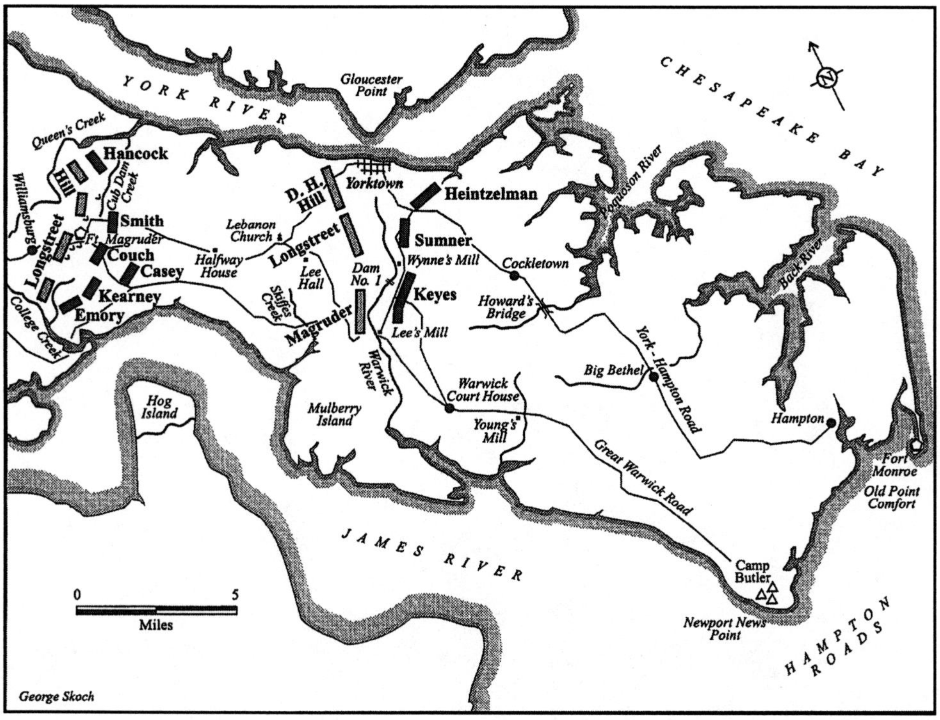

The lower Virginia Peninsula

Both divisions moved on the same road. The enemy had destroyed all the bridges on the route, but the pioneers (similar to present day combat engineers), advancing at the head of the column, quickly repaired them. After marching about five miles, Smith's division bore to the left at a "Y" in the road toward Warwick Court House, and Porter's continued on directly toward Big Bethel. After making about 10 miles, Hancock's brigade, which was leading Smith's division, ran into the enemy's pickets near Deep Creek. Smith halted his division and prepared to encounter the enemy which was supposed to be in force. The men of the 2nd Vermont thought they heard gunfire after Hancock's men were sent forward, but after they excitedly caught up to them, they found it was a false alarm. What they heard as Hancock's men knocking a board fence apart with their rifle butts which at a distance sounded like gunfire.[21]

soldiers simply said of the scene, "It was horrible." They marched three or four more miles and camped in a large field (in present day Newport News) about three-quarters of a mile from the James River. The camp was probably near Camp Butler where the 1st Vermont had been quartered the year before.[19]

On the March 26 Smith's and Maj. Gen. Fitz-John Porter's divisions were ordered to move the next day toward Big Bethel for a reconnaissance in force. March 27 dawned a beautiful day and Smith's division marched not long after sunup. The road was level, dry, and lined with locust and pine trees. The countryside was beautiful. The miles of blue clad soldiers marching with shouldered muskets glistening in the sunlight and banners waving in the warm breeze made an inspiring sight. The men of the 2nd Vermont knew this was the day they were going to meet the rebels and hasten the end of the war.[20]

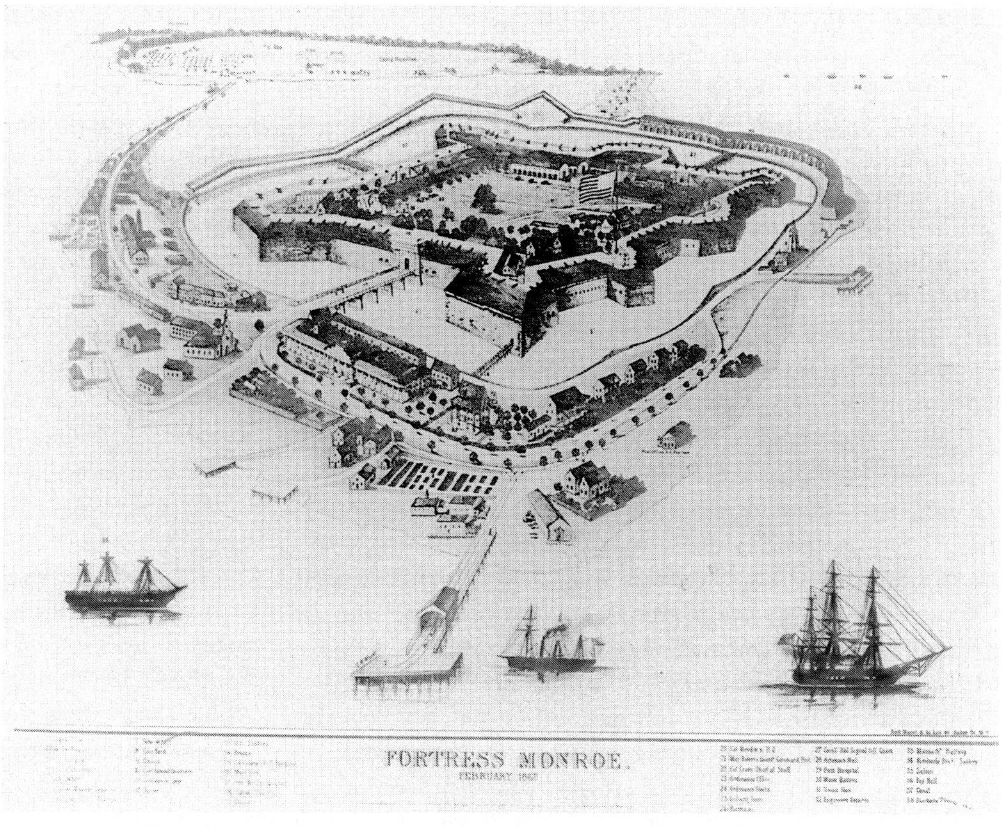

Fortress Monroe, Virginia. Casemate Museum.

The ruins of Hampton, Virginia. The town was burned by Confederate forces August 7, 1861, to deny its use by the Federals. Library of Congress.

The right wing of the 2nd Vermont, under Col. Whiting, was sent to the right to hold the road toward Big Bethel. After advancing a short distance, Whiting's men found a rebel cavalry picket's fires still burning and a bag of grain for their horses which was left behind, indicating they had just left. The left wing of the 2nd Vermont, under Lt. Col. Stannard, was sent up the Great Warwick Road as skirmishers. (This road was usually called the Lee's Mill or James River Road by the Union forces. Today it is named Warwick Boulevard, U.S. Route 60.) Both elements of the 2nd Vermont advanced for a mile, but neither met the enemy, so they returned to the division area and camped for the night.[22]

As soon as their camps were set up, the Vermonters started foraging for food to supplement their meager army rations. Although strictly forbidden, they stole and killed local farm animals. In a childish attempt to cover their misadventures, they called everything they killed a "Virginia rabbit," which they were allowed to shoot. One of the soldiers in the 5th Vermont wrote that some of the men in his regiment had killed a Virginia rabbit that was covered with wool and tasted "as fully good as Vermont mutton." He was especially complimentary of the foraging prowess of the boys in the 2nd Vermont. He recounted, "I ascertained that the Second Boys succeeded in finding and securing several kind of rabbits, some with horns, some with bristles, some with wool, and some few with wings and feathers."[23]

The next morning the division marched back down the Peninsula, and the Vermont Brigade went into camp about two miles above Newport News Point. The Vermonters were infuriated. They could not believe they had been ordered to retreat after only running into a couple of rebel pickets. Pvt. Fisk summed up the mood in the 2nd Vermont when he wrote, "Twenty thousand men drive in a few rebel pickets and then fall back! Is this war?"[24]

Smith's division remained in camp for a week. It initially camped on a low plain covered with reeds which was a good spot in dry weather, but after a day of spring rain the camp was afloat. It moved a short distance to higher ground near a brick house and set up a new camp. The Vermonters made ample use of the opportunity to bathe in the river and feast on Virginia oysters. The most exciting event of the week occurred on March 31 when the Confederate gunboat *Teazer* came downriver from Richmond and threw several shells at the men who were along the shore. No one was hurt, but they got a good scare, and the other men of the division on the shore had a good laugh watching the men under fire scramble for safety. Pvt. Cutler described the scene in a letter home: "some of the boys were down on the bank of the river gathering oysters when a rebel gun boat steamed down the river and threw some shells at them. One stuck on the side of the bank in the water and did not go off when one of the 3rd boys picked it up and started for camp when another came screaming by and burst nearly over our camp, it is all war and excitement here."[25]

McClellan arrived at Fort Monroe on April 2 and immediately launched his campaign. He planned to send two columns up the Peninsula to confront Maj. Gen. John B. Magruder, who was entrenched in and around Yorktown. The Fourth Corps was to proceed up the James River side of the Peninsula to the "Half-way House," located between Yorktown and Williamsburg and serve as a blocking force. The Second and Third Corps were to march directly from Fort Monroe to Yorktown and attack. McClellan expected the U.S. Navy to protect his left flank on the James River and, in concert with the Second and Third Corps, bombard Confederate defenses at Yorktown. With his back to the York River and his escape route blocked, Magruder would be trapped in Yorktown, as Cornwallis had been in the Revolutionary War, and be forced to surrender. If Johnston attempted to move from Gordonsville to reinforce Magruder, McDowell's First Corps, still in Alexandria, would land on the Gloucester side of the York River to intercede.[26]

Gen. McClellan's plan was sound but immediately started to unravel. The only units ready to move were the Second Division of the Second Corps, the First and Third Divisions of the Third Corps and the First and Second Divisions of the Fourth Corps, plus Brig. Gen. George Sykes's brigade of regulars, the reserve artillery, and about nine cavalry regiments. Besides the division artillery, McClellan had about 58,000 men and 100 guns in all. The Third Division of the Fourth Corps had debarked but was grounded at Fort Monroe awaiting wagons. The U.S. Navy, which had never fully bought into McClellan's plan, was getting cold feet. It feared the *Virginia* in the James River and, after second thought, felt that Yorktown, at the mouth of the York River, was too well fortified to attack. Also, prior to his leaving Alexandria, the War Department had given McClellan control of the 10,000 troops under Brig. Gen. John E. Wool's command at Fort Monroe, but on the evening of April 3, Lincoln sent a telegram denying him their use. Last, although he did not know it yet, the maps of the Peninsula he had been issued were grossly inaccurate.[27]

Regardless of his misgivings, McClellan issued orders on April 3 for his army to move early the next day. His orders directed the Fourth Corps to move up the Great Warwick Road at 6 A.M., with Smith's division in the lead. Smith was to proceed as far as Young's Mill and camp for the night.[28]

Porter's and Sedgwick's divisions were to be on the march at 6 A.M. up the New Market Bridge Road to Big Bethel, and then to Howard's Bridge before stopping. The rest of the army was to follow Porter and camp at Big Bethel.[29]

Col. Whiting read the movement order to his regiment on April 3 at evening formation. He prefaced the order by telling his men that in all probability they would see the enemy before sunset the next day. None of the men especially wanted to be maimed or killed but wanted to get the job over with and go home. Col. Whiting's talk apparently had the desired effect on the regiment. Pvt. Hapgood ended his diary entry that night with, "I want to see my dear Mother's face again, but if I do not on Earth I hope I shall in Heaven. I now bid all good bye."[30]

Promptly at 6 A.M. on April 4, the Fourth Corps, with the Vermont Brigade in the lead, started up the Peninsula. Around noon, the skirmishers met Confederate pickets at Waters Creek, but the gray-backs quickly fled. Gen. Keyes stopped the column at this point and closed up the two divisions. During the halt, he received a report from his cavalry scouts that strong fortifications had been sited at Young's Mill occupied by two enemy regiments.[31]

The corps resumed the march at a cautious pace. After proceeding two more miles, the skirmishers came upon a cleared plain about 1,000 yards across, and the column stopped. On the other side of the plain were the rebel fortifications sitting atop a 20 to 30 foot rise above Young's Mill. Below the brow of the rise, the road dropped into a ravine and crossed a millpond dam. On the right of the dam was the millpond and on the left a swamp. Where the road started to rise up the other side of the ravine, the rebels had erected a stockade wall with a large gate made of logs, four to six inches in diameter, and sharpened to a point at the top. The embankments below the fortifications were littered with felled trees.[32]

Smith threw the Vermont Brigade forward to clear the works, but all it encountered was several enemy cavalry pickets, who put up a bit of a fight before leaving, wounding one man of the 4th Vermont.[33]

The obstacle Smith had encountered was Magruder's first of three lines of defense. This line was more of a screen to slow down, rather than stop, a force as large as McClellan's. The line stretched from Young's Mill, at the head of Deep Creek, across the Peninsula to Harwood's Mill at the head of the Poquoson River. The only major fortifications were at either end blocking the two main roads running up the Peninsula.[34]

The works at Young's Mill were extensive and within its perimeter were barracks made of pine slabs that had housed several thousand rebels during the previous winter. The Vermonters found the rebels had, in making their hasty getaway, left their evening meals cooking on campfires. The Green Mountain Boys made good use of both the cooked meals and the barracks.[35]

Keyes moved the Fourth Corps at 6 A.M. on April 5 toward his day's objective, the Half-way House. The day started badly with the men awakening in a fierce thunderstorm. The roads, which McClellan had been assured were well drained and sandy, were not. They were soon transformed into a morass of deep, sticky, clay mud. Forward movement of troops and artillery was slowed to a crawl, and the supply wagons were at a virtual standstill. However, the men pressed on and passed Warwick Court House about noon. Warwick Court House, consisting of a dilapidated brick courthouse, a jail, a store, a tavern, and two houses,

Sketch by Vermont artist Larkin G. Mead of the Vermont Brigade attacking Young's Mill. George Houghton Album, University of Vermont.

would serve as the Fourth Corps headquarters for the next month.[36]

About three miles past the courthouse, Smith's division, which led the corps, halted at Lee's Mill. Facing it was the Warwick River, and on the other side, Confederate fortifications bristled with cannons and muskets. This was quite a shock for the high command. The maps the army had been given showed the Warwick River running parallel to the Peninsula, not across it. Intelligence also failed to indicate the area was fortified. Gen. Brooks wrote to his father, "Our knowledge of the country was '0.' Our maps worse than none for they were entirely wrong and served only to mislead us. We have got ourselves in a sort of hornets nest that will take all our strength and energy to work thro." Reaching the Half-way House was now out of the question.[37]

With the fortifications at Lee's Mill uncovered, Smith deployed his division with Davidson's brigade on the left and Hancock's on the right. Brooks's Vermonters were tagged as the reserve and headed to the right of the Great Warwick Road into the woods behind Hancock's men. Firing by the skirmishers began immediately. Hundreds of men in the rear brigades were brought up to corduroy the roads which Gen. Brooks described as "without bottom." Trees were cut down, trimmed, and laid side by side to form a kind of bridge over the swampy areas so the artillery could come up. By 2 P.M. artillery was in position and joined the fray. By now the thunderstorm was so violent that, at times, it drowned out the roar of the cannons.[38]

Maneuvering in this wooded terrain with its tangles and briars was difficult. It was not long before the men were scratched and bleeding. Pvt. Fisk described the scene:

> We were marched into an interminable woodland swamp, picking our way through brush, briers, and all manner of bogholes. Sometimes our knapsacks would get entangled in the thicket and bring us to a sudden halt at the imminent risk of a dangerous collision with the next man's bayonet,—but on we marched, filing right and filing left, until not one in a hundred could tell the points of compass or where we were any more than if we had fetched up in the interior of Africa.[39]

Near 3 P.M., reports from the front indicated several thousand Confederates were moving downriver. Keyes sent a brigade to investigate. A little later he sent another brigade farther to the left to the mouth of the Warwick River. Both commanders reported extensive fortifications all along the other side of the river.[40]

The Fourth Corps was facing Magruder's second and most heavily fortified line of defense. He had been working on his three lines since the previous summer, using impressed slaves and soldiers. This second line, known as the "Warwick Line," stretched across the Peninsula from Yorktown to Mulberry Island on the James River. Around the village of Yorktown, the British redoubts from the Revolutionary War had been rebuilt and just west of the village two new ones were constructed. About 2,000 yards west of the new redoubts, at the headwater of the Warwick River, the Warwick Line commenced. From its headwater to Lee's Mill, the Warwick River was no more than a sluggish creek, meandering through a swampy forest. At Lee's Mill it deepened and the banks became steep, in places rising 30 to 40 feet straight up from the water and widening to several hundred yards. Magruder had constructed three additional dams between the already existing dams at Wynne's Mill and Lee's Mill to deepen and widen the water into a series of small ponds. From Yorktown to the James River, the Confederate side of the Warwick Line was laced with a continuous network of trenches and rifle pits, fortified with redoubts at vulnerable points. Magruder had about 11,000 men to defend his line. Roughly 6,000 defended the anchors on the York and James Rivers and 5,000 were spread in between for approximately nine miles, defending its weakest points. Magruder totally misled McClellan as to his troop strength by military theatrics until he could be reinforced. At morning roll call, Confederate officers would shout orders, within earshot of the Union lines, to nonexistent units. Companies and regiments would be marched over and over again through breaks in the forest visible to McClellan's scouts causing them to believe they faced up to 100,000 Confederates.[41]

Confederate reinforcements started to trickle down the Peninsula in early April, and on April 17, Johnston arrived with the rest of his army. As the senior commander, Johnston assumed command of all Confederate forces which by now numbered about 53,000. He quickly reorganized his army into four divisions commanded by Gen. Magruder, Maj. Gen. James Longstreet, Maj. Gen. Daniel H. Hill, and Maj. Gen. Gustavus W. Smith. Magruder was assigned command of the right wing of the army, Longstreet the center, and Hill the left wing. Gustavus Smith's division was held in reserve.[42]

As afternoon of April 5 turned into evening, the Vermonters saw the wounded men from Brig. Gen. John W. Davidson's and Hancock's brigades being carried through their lines as they were evacuated rearward to the corps hospital at Young's Mill. The skirmishing and artillery duel continued until dark, when it gradually subsided, as did the rain. That night Smith's men, including Smith himself, slept on the soaking wet ground without tents wherever darkness found them. Some buildings across the Warwick River had caught fire from the shelling and burned brightly most of the night, casting an eerie glow over the battlefield. These sights along with being soaking wet, tired, hungry, and without a dry place to sleep added only to the anxiety of what tomorrow might bring.[43]

April 5 had been a day of surprises for McClellan. The weather, road conditions, and the Warwick Line had been bad enough, but that afternoon he had received a telegram informing him that the president was retaining McDowell's corps for the defense of Washington. McClellan was incensed and started a feud with Washington that would last through the entire campaign.[44]

The next day, Sunday, April 6, the men awoke before dawn to the sound of reveille in the Confederate camps across the river. After sunrise, the firing commenced again and continued throughout the day. An occasional artillery shell came crashing through the treetops, but no one in the 2nd Vermont was hurt.[45]

The troops in reserve, such as the Vermont Brigade, continued the task of corduroying the roads and constructing emplacements for the artillery pieces. In some areas the men had to carry the logs on their shoulders for over a mile. Even though the roads would be greatly improved over the next week, the artillery and ammunition trains would have priority. The wagons with rations would not be forward for several more days.[46]

Early in the morning on April 6, Smith sent Hancock's brigade upstream on a reconnaissance to find a weak spot in the Confederate line. If Hancock could find one, he was to hold it until Smith could reinforce him and then attack. Knowing Keyes was not one to take responsibility, Smith rode to Keyes's headquarters to inform him of what he had done. In the middle of their conversation, an orderly handed Keyes a message from McClellan. Keyes quickly read the order and handed it to Smith. The message directed all McClellan's commanders not to undertake any offensive operations until the line had been thoroughly examined by engineers. Smith related in his autobiography, "Very much chagrined, I rode back to my camp to find a message from Hancock that he had found a place at 'Dam Number 1' where he could cross. I had only to reply to him to come back to camp."[47]

On Monday evening, after having been under fire for two days and nights, the Vermonters were moved a little more to the rear near the Garrow Farm, where they remained for several weeks. Even the artillery pulled back, leaving wooden guns in the emplacements. These apparently fooled the rebels, explained Lt. Leach: "Earthworks were thrown up by our men, for the artillery, at their first position, but the pieces are withdrawn & wooden guns mounted in their place, which I understand the Rebs dismount occasionally & they are soon mounted again. Perhaps real guns will take their place when the time comes for action." As the Vermonters started to move, the rain began again and did not let up, day or night, until April 10.[48]

During this time four companies of the 2nd Vermont were sent forward on the line as Capt. Tyler described:

> My company with four others of our regt. has been stationed within 1000 yds. by actual measurement of their fort. The left of the picket line consisting of my company was within easy rifle shot of their sharpshooters. My men were obliged to lie behind logs and trees and on exposing any part of their bodies to view-whist!-would come a rifle ball and if we fired five or six shots in return they would compliment us with a shell. For 2 days we have remained in this interesting position, until relieved last night.[49]

By the time the rain stopped on April 10, McClellan had most of his army or at least all that Lincoln was going to give him. Heintzelman's Third Corps covered the Yorktown end of the line from the mouth of Wormley's Creek to a point little more than two miles below Yorktown toward Wynne's Mill. The Second Corps held the center with Sedgwick's division. Brig. Gen. Israel B. Richardson's First Division of the Second Corps would not get forward until April 16. The Fourth Corps held the left.[50]

During this time, because of the trouble of getting the supply wagons forward, the entire Fourth Corps had been on half rations. Foraging parties were organized, and local cattle, hogs, and sheep that were running loose were captured. A soldier in the 10th Massachusetts, in Smith's division, wrote his mother, "The inhabitants here have fled leaving everything and the woods are full of cattle, horses and hogs. Our boys have been bringing in quarters of beef all day long. They build up a fire, hang up the beef on a stake and soon are reveling in roast beef, or beef steak, or Pork or mutton as the case may be." A Confederate soldier on the other side of the Warwick River added, "Not much seasoning was required in their eating, as their flesh was so strongly impregnated with wild garlic, which formed a considerable portion of their food." Even with foraging, Pvt. Hapgood complained in his diary on April 10, "Don't have half enough to eat." In addition to the rations not getting through, neither could the sutlers. This caused even more of a problem, at least as far as the men were concerned, due to the lack of tobacco. Hapgood continued, "Can't get any tobacco anywhere." Lt. Leach also noted the dilemma, "Our sutler I guess has left us, so we can get no fixings, hardly tobacco, which every one thinks is indispensable.[51]

The Vermonters were not alone in their craving of tobacco as illustrated in a letter by Chaplain A. M. Stewart of the 120th Pennsylvania:

> The filthiest of all living animals is *man*. No brute, so called, has ever yet become so debased as to chew or smoke tobacco. Three-fourths, perhaps, of our regiment either chew or smoke—many do both, and this is a sample of all other regiments in the service.... More than ten days since, the stock of the weed on hand became small ... till finally all the treasury notes of Uncle Sam sufficed not to buy a single plug. Then what an outcry; what peevishness, what complaints and irritability! They were certainly the worst-used soldiers in the universe. Uncle Sam was a humbug; the sutlers were all a set of rascals and swindlers.... In this almost mutinous condition of affairs, our sutler, after nearly a month's absence, came up. The supply of luxuries brought along consisted principally in a limited supply of chewing and smoking tobacco. This was distributed as equitably as possible through the regiment. Then what filth and nastiness! What chewing, spitting, squirting, and whiffing! The nerves were all speedily quieted, the irritability soon gone, and a more contented set of men it was not easy to find. What strange freaks this fallen humanity of ours does exhibit![52]

By April 15 the area was starting to dry out. With dryer weather and the newly corduroyed roads, rations were finally coming forward. More importantly, the sutlers were now in camp and Pvt. Hapgood happily noted in his diary, "Got some tobacco and cookies." The majority of the 2nd Vermont was off duty for the day, and along with visiting the sutler, the men spent most of the day playing baseball. The day of rest was brought short in the evening with orders to be in light marching order the next day with two days' rations.[53]

The marching orders were the result of a directive from McClellan to make a reconnaissance at Dam No. 1 which spanned the Warwick River midway between Lee's and Wynne's Mills. On the Confederate side of the river was a small exposed redoubt with a 24-pound howitzer, known as the "one-gun battery," flanked with trenches and rifle pits. Two hundred yards to the rear near the tree line were two more redoubts, each with one gun. The redoubt on the Confederate right held a six-pound smoothbore and the one on the left a 24-pound howitzer. The artillery positions were protected by the 2nd Louisiana on the upstream side of the dam and by the 15th North Carolina on the downstream side. Intelligence reports from the pickets indicated that the Confederates were strengthening their fortifications. McClellan did not want the enemy to reinforce its positions anywhere along the line. He sent an order to Keyes to put a stop to the Confederates' work and to silence the guns. Keyes passed the order down to Baldy Smith to execute. Smith assigned the task to Brooks's Vermont Brigade.[54]

On the Federal side of the river opposite Dam No. 1 was a clearing, several hundred yards wide and 600 to 700 yards deep on the high ground just above the river. In the clearing stood three burned chimneys, the only remains of the Garrow house known as Merry Oaks. The Confederates had burned the house just before the arrival of the Federals on April 5. The spot was referred to by several names in Federal reports: "Garrow Chimneys," "Three Chimneys," and "Burnt Chimneys." The most commonly used was "Burnt Chimneys." With the exception of the several hundred yards of cleared land, known locally as Garrow's field, that bordered the Warwick River, the rest of the bank above and below the dam was covered with a fairly dense growth of woods. Smith's division had been picketing this area since its arrival on April 5.[55]

Gen. Brooks had his brigade up before daylight on April 16. He moved the 4th Vermont out at 6 A.M. followed by the 3rd, 2nd, 5th, and 6th Vermont regiments. As the 4th Vermont approached the Garrow farm, a little over a mile from camp, it veered to the right of the clearing until its skirmishers came to the river's edge where they halted. The 3rd Vermont skirted the clearing to the left and also halted in the woods at the edge of the river. The 5th was sent to the rear of the 3rd as support. The 2nd and 6th Vermont were held in the rear in an old cornfield to the right of the chimneys, out of sight of the rebels, as a reserve.[56]

Hancock's brigade, with two batteries, secured the Lee's Mill Road, and Davidson's brigade, with one battery, was held as a general reserve.[57]

Houghton photograph of Confederate earthworks at Dam No. 1. Supposedly taken while the works were still occupied by the enemy. George Houghton Album, University of Vermont.

As the Vermont regiments were getting into position, a section of Mott's artillery battery stopped in the right rear of the chimneys and unlimbered. As soon as the artillery was in position and ready to fire, the 3rd and 4th Vermont, as well as Mott's guns opened fire on the 2nd Louisiana's sector across the river at about 8 A.M. The Southerners replied in equal measure with rifle and artillery fire. As the rebel artillery returned fire, Mott brought forward his other two sections, and they quickly started pounding the Confederate positions. The Confederates' fire, although steady, was not as strong as the Federal's since the rebel's 24-pounder on the upriver side of the dam was in a position to do more damage to their own troops than the Federals' and ceased firing. Ten men were picked from each company of the 5th Vermont as sharpshooters and under rebel shell and canister fire, deployed forward in front of the chimneys where they remained the rest of the day harassing the enemy.[58]

Near 10:30 A.M., while the Vermonters and the rebels were busy banging away at each other, Gen. Smith sent one of his aides below the dam to determine if it was possible for troops to cross the stream. With the combatants concentrating on each other, the aide not only crossed the waist deep stream, but came within 50 yards of the rebel trenches and returned unscathed to make his report.[59]

The area the aide reconnoitered was guarded by the 15th North Carolina, but on this day the rebels were back from the river, just inside the tree line, working on their fortifications. Their forward rifle pits were manned by a light force of pickets, reinforced by Co. D of the 16th Georgia.[60]

A little before noon the howitzer in the forward-positioned one-gun battery was knocked out of action leaving the rebels only the six-pounder smoothbore, which the Vermont sharpshooters kept quiet. The enemy's small arms fire had also subsided, and Gen. Smith ordered a cease-fire on his side of the Warwick. The first phase of the operation was complete.[61]

Brooks's aide reported to Smith about the time the firing ceased and at the same time that Gen. McClellan arrived with a large entourage. The aide indicated that the stream was not very deep and the trenches on the other side were very lightly defended. After hearing the report, McClellan told Smith to send a force across the stream, but not to bring on a major engagement and to withdraw his troops if serious resistance developed. Smith chose two companies from the 3rd Vermont for the attack.[62]

Just before 2 P.M. Gen. Brooks ordered the 2nd Vermont back to camp to get its gear and prepare to spend the night on the line. As the 2nd was moving out Smith had his other batteries brought forward and put into action. The 2nd Vermont returned to the Garrow farm around 2:30 P.M. and went into position in the rear to the right of the artillery. Just as it got settled, Brooks ordered it to the left to support the 3rd Vermont. In the process of crossing the cleared area in the rear of their artillery, the 2nd Vermont was hit by enemy artillery fire. A fragment from one of the shells hit Pvt. William Fuller of Co. F in the head and killed him. Within minutes the 2nd was across the cleared area and in the relative safety of the woods. Pvt. Erastus Worthen of Co. B, who had fought with the 2nd Vermont at Bull

Mead sketch of the Vermont Brigade's attack at Dam No. 1. George Houghton Album, University of Vermont.

Run, wrote, "I tell you it is not very plesent to be where the bullets are flying in all directions and the shels bursting over your head it makes me think of home some times hope the time will come soon that we shall meet on the old green hills of Vermont."[63]

At 3 P.M. Col. Hyde, commander of the 3rd Vermont, ordered companies D and F across the stream to take possession of the enemy's trenches. Although Hyde had been ordered to send over two companies, many of the men of the two companies selected were out as skirmishers leaving them shorthanded. To beef up the assault, Hyde added companies E and K. As soon as the lead companies had secured a position they were to signal with a white handkerchief, and the Federal artillery fire would be shifted away from them and reinforcements would be sent over. The Vermonters started receiving fire on their left flank as soon as they entered the water, but they quickly crossed the stream and scrambled up the opposite bank and into the enemy's works. The few rebels that were encountered melted away as the Vermonters advanced 100 to 150 feet inland from the Warwick where they made a stand in the Confederate's first line of trenches.[64]

As the 3rd Vermont had been advancing, the rebels were recovering from the Yankees' surprise assault. The 15th North Carolina troops, alerted by their pickets, dropped their picks and shovels and grabbed their muskets. With his men letting out the rebel yell, Col. William McKinney led his regiment in a charge against the Vermonters. The Tar Heels ran into a wall of lead as they neared the rifle pits occupied by the 3rd Vermont. Col. McKinney was killed instantly by a minié ball through his forehead. Their commander's death threw the North Carolinians into confusion, and their charge disintegrated.[65]

With the appearance of their brigade commander, Brig. Gen. Howell Cobb, the 15th North Carolina soon recovered and renewed the attack. It was joined by elements of the 2nd and 10th Louisiana and the 7th, 8th, and 11th Georgia Infantry Regiments. The four companies of the 3rd Vermont were now in serious trouble. Not only were they outnumbered, but also part of their ammunition had gotten wet crossing the stream and their dry cartridges were nearly gone. The Vermonters signaled they had secured the position, but no reinforcements came. Eventually, a messenger was sent back across to personally tell Gen. Brooks to send reinforcements, but Brooks said later that he never received the message. They held out almost 40 minutes, but with no reinforcements forthcoming, they had no choice but to retreat. Retreating through the waist deep water was difficult in itself, but the rebels pumped so much lead into Union ranks that 2nd Lt. Erastus Buck, of the 3rd Vermont, said it "made the water boil with their bullets." It was a slaughter. Of the 192 men who made the charge across the river, only 100 returned unharmed.[66]

Seeing that the Warwick could be crossed, Smith ordered another assault. This time Brooks choose the 4th and 6th Vermont. At 5 P.M., Col. Stroughton, with three companies of the 4th, raced downstream, parallel with the river, to cross the dam. At the same time Col. Lord led four companies of the 6th Vermont across the stream where the 3rd had crossed earlier. By the time the elements of the 6th had reached the far bank and the 4th had reached the dam, the crossfire from the rebels was so intense the attack was called off. The 6th Vermont was now in the same predicament the 3rd had been in earlier. It had to retreat back across the river in full view of the rebels and suffered the same fate. It was torn to shreds by the time it reached safety. The 4th, although in a cleared area, did not have to face retreating through water and managed to cut its losses by the men jumping up and running a few steps and then throwing themselves flat to the ground again. In this manner they worked their way back to the cover of the woods. Finally, the futile battle of Dam No. 1 was over.[67]

In all, the Vermont Brigade lost 44 men killed, 21 mortally wounded and 148 wounded. Seven of the wounded were taken prisoner. The 2nd Vermont lost only the one man previously mentioned.[68]

Why had the battle of Dam No. 1, or Lee's Mill as it became known, happened? What was gained? Neither of these questions can be fully answered with the information available today. It appears that McClellan had always planned to lay siege to Richmond since he had brought a large number of siege guns to the Peninsula with him. The Warwick Line just caused the siege to develop sooner than anticipated. As events during his tenure as the commander of the Army of the Potomac would prove, McClellan also seemed reluctant to bleed his troops. Last, as an engineer, McClellan had been impressed with the siege warfare he had witnessed in the Mexican War and as a military observer for the U.S. Army in the Crimean War.[69]

The gain from the action was minimal. True, the reinforcement of the Southern fortifications at Dam No. 1 was curtailed and Smith was able to fortify closer to the water's edge, but this could have been accomplished without pushing troops across the river for no reason.

Many asked these same questions at the time. One explanation for the failure of the assault was that Smith was drunk during the action; so drunk in fact, that he fell off his horse. After a court of inquiry by McClellan and an investigation by a congressional committee which had received a letter signed by all the field grade officers of the Vermont Brigade stating that Smith was not drunk, he was cleared. Smith's explanation in his autobiography was that he was following McClellan's orders not to bring on a general engagement and after being thrown from his horse was somewhat dazed and did not realize the advantage he had gained. The reason he ordered the second assault by the 4th and 6th Vermont regiments was not addressed. The true facts of the case will probably never be known. The entire affair, however, was probably best summed up by the 3rd Vermont's Lt. Buck: "This Battle took place at Dam No. 1 in Warwick creek and was a Dam failure."[70]

As night fell over the battlefield, the Vermont regiments quickly started digging trenches and rifle pits to secure their side of the river. Rifle fire subsided and all was quiet except for a Federal cannon that lobbed a shell at random across the river every half-hour to keep the rebels awake and to prevent them from repairing their damaged works, "and darkness put an end to the fight." Wrote Capt. Tyler, "Throwing down our arms, we took up axes and shovels and by daylight Mr. MacGruder found some strong earthworks right under his nose."[71]

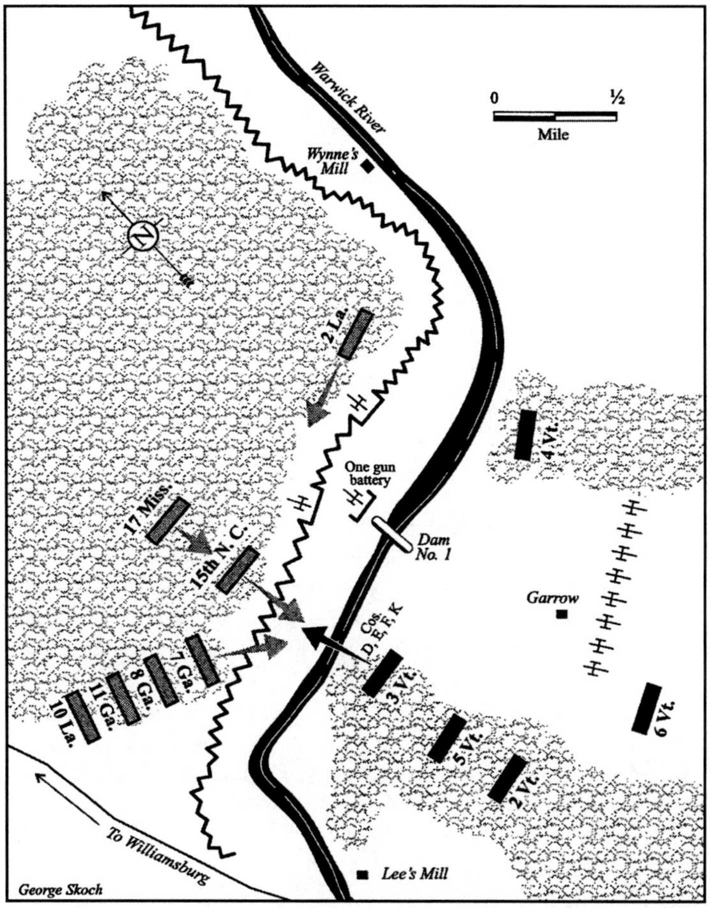

The Battle of Dam No. 1, April 16, 1862

At daybreak on April 17, rifle fire between the pickets commenced again. A number of Berdan's sharpshooters were sent over from the Yorktown end of the line to add their firepower. Some of the sharpshooters were armed with rifles with telescopic sights that were deadly accurate. They were so effective that by April 19 Magruder was complaining to Richmond about them:

> I beg leave to call attention of the commanding general to the great difficulty in carrying on the exhausting defense at the dams assigned to my command, particularly dam No. 1. Sharpshooters of the enemy have been pushing their way forward causing it to be extremely dangerous to relieve troops except in the night.... Troops at the dams are almost constantly under fire, and that though they exhibit fine spirit they must inevitably become exhausted.[72]

Capt. John Tyler:

> Our and the rebel sharpshooters blase away at each other. One old fellow sets on our earthworks, and every time he hits a rebel, he yells "Tally!" He has a rifle weighting 15 pounds. The rebels are now unable to shell us at all, for two reasons—If they get their guns mounted our artillery tips them over very quick and the minute a man show himself at the gun, a hundred bullets are showered at him by the pickets—They make *their negros* go up and load their cannon—This we can see plainly.[73]

Pvt. Edwin Turner of Co. D wrote of shooting at rebel pickets:

> We have a great deal of fun with the rebels when we are on picket being within easy rifle range of them. Our company was on picket a few days since in a pine grove each behind his tree flat on his face with rifle cocked ready to blaze away when there is any rebel in sight when we saw what we took to be a party of fatigue men fileing through the thickets. our Captain gave the word fire and we did fire and you had ought to heard the howling. Oh the d_ _ d yankee sons of bitches and the d _ _ d yankees will kill us all was all we could hear for five minutes. then crack crack went a score of rifles and whizz went as many balls but the d _ _ d yankees were behind trees about that time, but the yankees do get hit sometimes.[74]

Early morning April 18, just after sunrise, Pvt. John H. Savory, a cook in the 2nd Vermont's Co. B, took breakfast and hot coffee to the trenches for his men on picket. After dispensing the meal he could not resist the temptation to take a look at the rebel fortifications across the river that had been causing all the fuss. Savory was warned to remain behind the breastworks, but curiosity got the best of him, and he walked into the open for a better view. It was the last mistake he ever made. A rebel sharpshooter put a bullet through his heart killing him instantly. His comrades pulled his body to safety, but Savory was beyond help, and he was buried that afternoon. Eight years prior to his death, Savory became the sole provider for his parents, Ephrain and Mary Savory, and after his death they received an $8 a month pension from the government.[75]

So it went for the next several weeks, exchanging shots with the rebels during the day and digging at night. Men not employed in digging or on picket were denied a decent night's sleep by being called into line of battle several times a night, only to find it a false alarm. To add to their misery, the men were constantly assailed by insects. Lt. Charles H. Brewster, of the 10th Massachusetts, suffering as much as the Green Mountain Boys, complained:

> we get to sleep at night jump up three or four times in the night and form line of battle, find it a false alarm and lie down again, get up in the morning and strip off our clothes and go digging Wood Ticks out of our flesh, then wash all over, and likely as not have to perform the same operation again before noon. we are all covered with little sores caused by these wretches and there is no help for it. they are as thick as leaves, and thicker for every leaf is occupied by half a dozen of them. they are hard shiny backed fellows and it takes a hammer and chisel to kill one of them.[76]

A white flag of truce was hoisted on the Confederate side of the Warwick on Saturday, April 19. The rebels wanted the Vermonters to retrieve their dead left behind during the battle of April 16 and so they could gather up their dead killed by the Yankee sharpshooters. One of the Federal soldiers reported, "Our sharpshooters had shot lots of them since then [April 16] and there they had to let them lie, until they smelt very badly...." As soon as the flag of truce was acknowledged by the Vermonters, the rebels came out of their trenches and as one witness described it, "you should have seen the heads pop up over their breastworks. They looked just like the bees when they swarm on the outside of a hive." Col. William M. Levy, commander of the 2nd Louisiana, walked halfway across the dam and was met by Capt. Currie of Gen. Smith's staff and the truce was negotiated. The officers had an unusually sociable meeting and went so far as exchanging coat buttons from their uniforms. The rebels brought the dead Vermont soldiers across the dam, where their comrades received them. Due to rapid decomposition from lying in the hot sun for several days, the bodies of the dead men were unidentifiable. They were carried away and interred with the rest of the fallen Vermonters on the Garrow farm.[77]

After several hours the truce ended and the Federal sharpshooters and pickets went back to work shooting at the rebels as though the friendly visit had never happened.[78]

Fifty-three new recruits from Vermont arrived in the 2nd Vermont's camp on April 29 replenishing the regiment's ranks that had been thinned by sickness. The heat and humidity, along with rations of hardtack and rancid salt pork, were quite a shock for the new men. "they look fatter than they will in a month from now I reckon," predicted Pvt. Lucius Savage.[79]

The 2nd Vermont received orders early on April 30 to make a reconnaissance down the Warwick River below Lee's Mill to verify reports that the Confederates were erecting additional fortifications. With Col. Whiting on court-martial duty, Lt. Col. Stannard led the command. Stannard threw out companies A, B, and I as skirmishers. Co. A was on the right, Co. I in the center, and Co. B on the left. Three other companies were just behind them as support, with the rest of the regiment a little farther behind the supporting companies. In a drizzling rain, the 2nd Ver-

Houghton photograph of the 3rd Vermont's graveyard on the Garrow Farm. George Houghton Album, University of Vermont.

mont moved out and was soon picking its way through the thick underbrush. A mile below Lee's Mill the skirmish line was hit with a volley of rebel rifle fire from across the river, and as Pvt. Horace G. Ross, a Castleton boy in Co. B, wrote, "we had a pretty hot time of it." Co. A took the initial shock. Pvt. Louis Wood was the first to go down with a mortal chest wound. Pvt. Leander M. Towsley and another man rushed forward to rescue Wood. Just as they bent over to pull Wood to safety, Towsley received a mortal wound in the chest. As Lt. Col. Stannard was getting the other two companies wheeled around to pour fire into the rebels, Co. A lost yet another man, Pvt. Lucius Carpenter. Carpenter, like Towsley and Wood, was also hit in the chest, but died instantly. Neither Towsley nor Wood made it back to camp alive. From the appearance of the wounds, some of the men thought the same sniper had hit all three, but this could not be proved.[80]

Within minutes all three companies were parallel to the riverbank and pouring fire into the rebels, who were forced back from the river's edge to the protection of their rifle pits. The men remained in position on their stomachs trading shots with the enemy for almost two hours. Pvt. Ross bragged to his father, "I shot at one of the rascals seven times." He did not indicate whether or not he hit his intended target. With orders only to make a reconnaissance and not to bring on a general engagement, Stannard finally pulled the regiment back just as the rebels were being reinforced. Co. A's three men were the only casualties during the affair.[81]

Leander Towsley's body was sent back to Vermont the next day for burial. The men in Co. A built crude coffins for Carpenter and Wood that night and buried them the next day in the ever expanding Vermont Brigade graveyard on the Garrow Farm. While digging the new graves, the Vermonters dug into an old unmarked grave. The buttons and other artifacts uncovered revealed they had dug up the body of a American Revolutionary War soldier buried there during Washington's siege of Yorktown in the fall of 1781. After the war, all the soldiers buried on the Garrow Farm were reinterred in the National Cemetery at Yorktown.[82]

Being at the bottom of the chain of command, the men of the 2nd Vermont were unaware that McClellan was finally ready to commence his bombardment of the Confederate lines on May 5. Gen. Johnston, however, was. From observing the progress of the Federal's work and the intelligence gained from Union prisoners and deserters, he knew it was time to pull back from his untenable position on the Peninsula. The Confederates unleashed a furious cannonade along the Warwick line that lasted most of the night of May 3 as their troops filed into the roads toward Richmond. As the Federal observation balloons ascended in the early morning hours of May 4, they could see the rebels' tents, but there was not a soldier in sight. Scouts were sent into the rebel lines near Yorktown and found them deserted. McClellan immediately sent orders to all his commanders to pursue the retreating rebels.[83]

As the men of the 2nd Vermont were going about their daily morning routine they were unexpectedly ordered into formation and told of the rebels' departure. The 5th Vermont was immediately sent across Dam No. 1 to secure the area. After the area was secured, other Vermonters wandered over to see the forts. They were amazed at the extent of the damage they had inflicted over the past month. Destroyed equipment lay everywhere. The only thing left behind of any value were the tents used to deceive the Yankees. There was hardly a tree in the area that did not have bullet holes in it or branches torn off by artillery shells, and the ground was furrowed by cannon balls. Because of half-buried horses and mules, open latrines and rotting food, the stench was intolerable. After looking around everyone was sent back to camp to pack up and be ready to move.[84]

Baldy Smith's and Maj. Gen. Joseph Hooker's divisions were ordered as lead elements, to follow Brig. Gen. George Stoneman's cavalry in pursuit of the rebels. Smith's division pulled out at 8 A.M. with orders to take the Great Warwick Road and Hooker the road from Yorktown to Williamsburg. To get to the Great Warwick Road, on the other side of Lee's Mill, Smith had to cross the Warwick River at Dam No. 1, pass through the Confederate trenches, and then veer left. While traversing the trenches, a man in the 77th New York stepped on what appeared to be a rag laying on the ground, but it emitted a report like a pistol shot. The regiment's commander lifted the rag with his sword tip exposing a torpedo (Civil War term for a land or waterborne mine). The torpedo consisted of an artillery shell planted vertically in the ground topped with a fuse that would ignite when stepped on. Luckily, this one did not explode. This was not the case for a number of Federal soldiers on the Yorktown end of the line. Smith's men were now cautious where they stepped, avoiding any scrap material lying on the ground. Later in the day, Smith included the following line in a note to McClellan, "Our road through the fort was lined with torpedoes, but happily none went off."[85]

The torpedoes were the handiwork of Gabriel J. Rains, the officer who had mustered the 2nd Vermont regiment the year before, and now a brigadier general commanding a brigade in Maj. Gen. D. H. Hill's division. When Maj. Gen. James Longstreet was informed that Rains was planting the shells, he sent a note to Rains to cease the operation as it was beyond the bounds of legitimate warfare. Both governments decried the use of these "devilish devices." Such would not be the case later in the war.[86]

As the division reached the Great Warwick Road, Smith ordered Col. Whiting, with six of his companies, to make a reconnaissance down the road on Mulberry Island. They would not catch up with the division until the next morning. The rest of the division, with Hancock's brigade in the lead, trudged on toward Williamsburg.[87]

About noon, Hancock was stopped at Skiffes Creek where retreating rebels had set fire to the bridge. The remaining four companies of the 2nd Vermont were sent forward to put out the fire, but the bridge was too badly damaged to allow the artillery and wagons to cross. Near 3 P.M., Gen. Sumner, commanding both columns, ordered Smith to turn right, cross-country, and pick up the Yorktown Road near Lebanon Church. Smith reached the church before Hooker and without waiting, spurred his troops forward. When Hooker arrived at the church, Smith's column was still filing onto the road forcing Hooker to wait. After following Smith's division for several miles, the impatient Hooker veered to the left on a crossroad and picked up the Great Warwick Road just above Skiffes Creek.[88]

During the march, Smith's division, with the Vermont Brigade in the lead, was to make a halt at the Half-way House to allow Keyes's other two divisions to close up, but Smith pressed on. Keyes called for one of his orderlies and said, "If your horse has bottom enough to catch up with the Vermont Brigade, I want you to overtake them and order a halt. Tell them we are not going to Richmond today."[89]

The two roads the Federal troops were following came together two miles from Williamsburg. Here lay Magruder's third and final line of defense stretching seven miles from College Creek on the James River to Queen's Creek

Houghton photograph of Captain Romeyn B. Ayres's battery crossing Dam No. 1 on the morning of May 4, 1862. George Houghton Album, University of Vermont.

on the York River. The line consisted of a series of 14 redoubts. Near the center of the line, where the two roads converged, Brig. Gen. Paul J. Semmes's brigade manned redoubt No. 6, also known as Ft. Magruder.[90]

By the time Smith's division arrived on the right of the line it was nearly 5:30 P.M. Under orders from Gen. Sumner, whom McClellan had put in charge, Smith formed his command for an assault with Hancock's brigade in the lead and the Vermont Brigade in support. It was 6:30 P.M. before the lines moved forward, but as soon as this division entered woods, Smith found it too thick with underbrush, and with the increasing darkness, called off the advance. The troops bivouacked in place for the night. Around midnight it started to rain, but the men were so tired they hardly noticed. As Pvt. Hapgood noted in his diary that night, "I am almost tired to death."[91]

The next day Smith had his division up early. Although somewhat refreshed, the men were stiff and sore from the march the day before and from sleeping on the cold, wet ground. Smith had the division in line of battle early ready to assault the Confederates, but Sumner held it in place fearing an attack on his center.[92]

Hooker, however, took matters into his own hands. Without a plan of battle, and without consulting Sumner or his corps commander, he assaulted Fort Magruder at 7:30 A.M. As the battle intensified Gen. Longstreet, who along with a part of D. H. Hill's division had been left behind by Johnston to protect the Confederate retreat to Richmond, brought in three more brigades and started pushing Hooker backwards. Hooker asked Sumner for reinforcement, but was denied. His only hope now was that Brig. Gen. Philip Kearny's division of the Third Corps, slogging through the mud on the Hampton Road, would arrive in time to help him.[93]

During the morning, Baldy Smith had not been idle. He had sent his engineer to reconnoiter the rebel works in his front. The engineer returned and reported that a deep ravine that was not conducive to an assault protected the redoubts. But a black man he had met told him that two miles to the right there was a road that crossed a dam in the ravine and would allow an approach to the rear of the redoubts. Smith dispatched four companies of the 4th Vermont to verify the intelligence. The four companies returned around 10:30 A.M. with great news. Not only did the road and dam exist, but the redoubts were unoccupied. With that information in hand, the overly cautious Sumner allowed Smith to send one brigade to seize the redoubts. Smith chose Hancock's brigade for the mission. Without Sumner's knowledge he reinforced Hancock with two additional regiments from Davidson's brigade, Wheeler's battery, and a company of cavalry.[94]

Around noon Hancock started and in a short time had secured the redoubts. Now the Federals had effectively flanked the enemy. Once in position Hancock was ready to attack the two manned redoubts between him and Fort Magruder as soon as Smith could send reinforcements.[95]

While Hancock was making his end run, Sumner changed his mind about supporting Hooker and ordered Smith to send a brigade to help him. Fearing Hancock would need reinforcement more than Hooker, Smith got Sumner to change the order. The Vermont Brigade was up and formed in the road ready to move when Sumner again changed his mind and ordered the men to stay in their current position.[96]

From their position the Vermonters could see Hancock pushing the rebels back toward Fort Magruder with his skirmishers and artillery, but Hancock hesitated to occupy the works without being reinforced. They could also see Brig. Gen. Jubal Early's brigade, of D. H. Hill's division, advancing on Hancock and knew he was in trouble.[97]

Smith asked Sumner several more times to allow him to aid Hancock. Twice the Vermont Brigade was sent to the right only to be recalled. The last time it reached the dam before being recalled. As Smith said in his autobiography, he and the Vermont Brigade "turned backwards to the field of nincompoops." Brooks, apparently more upset than Smith, broke into a swearing rage.[98]

The rebels assaulted Hancock's position and were repelled with terrific losses, including Early, who was wounded twice. By 6 P.M., the rebels pulled back leaving Hancock in possession of their left flank, having lost only 100 men.[99]

Hooker was barely holding his portion of the line when Kearny finally arrived around 3 P.M., in time to reinforce him. Together, Hooker and Kearny stopped the rebel advance and regained most of the ground that Hooker had lost. The battle of Williamsburg was now over.[100]

As the firing ceased and the smoke lifted, the Vermonters could see that Hancock's command was still intact and in possession of the flank. Their pent-up emotions poured forth like water from a ruptured dam. They started cheering at the tops of their voices. The cheering, however, galled the rebels, who lobbed several shells at the Vermonters, inflicting no casualties, and causing them only to cheer louder. After dark, the Green Mountain Boys tried to get some rest the best they could, as Pvt. Kirk Rand, a Brattleboro boy in Co. C explained: "Monday night we sat on our knapsacks or leaned up against trees or any way to sleep but lay down as the mud and water was too deep to lay down."[101]

Between 10 and 11 P.M. that night, the Confederates withdrew from the Williamsburg line and continued their retreat toward Richmond. If there was a victor of the battle it would have to be the Confederates. They suffered 1,682 men killed, wounded or captured to the Federal's 2,283 and bought time for the rest of the army to continue its retreat unmolested.[102]

Tuesday, May 6, dawned clear and pleasant after a night of near torrential rain, and the scene of two days earlier was repeated. Yankee pickets edging forward at first light discovered the rebel lines deserted. Smith's division, following orders received the night before, marched around to the right to where Hancock had fought, expecting to pursue the rebels, but instead were ordered to go into camp. For the next three days, the Federal army sat idle while the rebels closed on Richmond.[103]

With nothing else to do, the men in the 2nd Vermont killed time by wandering the battlefield. They were shocked by the horrible human destruction they saw as described by Pvt. Fisk:

> I visited the battle-field where there were many of the dead still unburied. One can hardly refrain from shedding a silent tear over the last resting place of these brave men. I saw as many as a dozen buried side by side in one grave, all from one company. Perhaps in other places there were even more than that. Those that I noticed in particular were from the 1st regiment Excelsior Brigade [2nd brigade, Hooker's division]. Like a band of brothers they had fought like the heroes they were, and perished, nobly contending for the cause of humanity against armed usurpation; and now a simple shingle with their name marked on it tells the traveler where they lie. But the saddest sight of all was to see wounded still alive and uncared for. I saw a man wounded in the head, a clot of brains marking the spot where he was hit. He was leaning back against some logs, in a partially upright posture, still breathing, though apparently unconscious. I might multiply descriptions of these horrors if it were pleasant to write of them, but it is not.[104]

Lt. Leach also described the battlefield scene in a letter to his wife:

> The dead are not all buried yet, but the men are burying them as fast as possible. Our dead are mostly buried, but the ground is strewn yet with the Rebs. There is hardly a tree in the woods where they fought, however small, but has one or more bullet holes in it. The woods is full of rebel guns, which are Springfield muskets, smooth bore, which once belonged to the U.S.[105]

Pvt. Lucius Savage saw for the first time, "the long lines of trenches that had been dug, for the burial of the dead. The sight of these trenches when filled with bodies, was photographed on my mind, never to be forgotten."[106]

CHAPTER 5

"The Awfullist Thing That Ever Was"

McClellan's army started leaving Williamsburg piecemeal on May 6. Smith's division of the Fourth Corps did not leave until Friday morning May 9. The pace up the Peninsula was rather leisurely making only 10 to 12 miles a day. Smith's division camped near Burnt Ordinary on that night. On May 10 after passing through Barhamsville, it camped near Slaterville, where it stayed until May 12.[1]

On the march from Williamsburg, the supply wagons had been slowed by the muddy roads and by the time the Vermont Brigade reached Slaterville, the men's haversacks were empty. Although McClellan had issued orders to the army to respect Southern civilians and their property, the Vermonters were not going to go hungry. The Confederates had pretty much stripped the country during their retreat, but as Lt. Leach wrote, "a hen or a turkey occasionally gets picked.…" Pvt. Fisk recorded, "you will hardly blame the boys for being tempted to capture some of the 'Virginia rabbits' that were squealing about in the woods near by, apparently common property." Under these circumstances, the officers turned a blind eye to the flagrant violations of orders.[2]

On the evening of May 12 Smith's division moved to New Kent Court House. Early in the morning of Tuesday, May 13, Smith was ordered to move to Cumberland Landing. The route of march for some reason was cross-country through the woods "with only little signs of a road." Although it was only a four or five mile trek, it was difficult passage.[3]

After a couple of hours marching the column emerged from the woods on the brow of a hill overlooking the landing. The plain below was full of tens of thousands of troops, artillery parks, squadrons of cavalry, and hundreds of white canvas topped wagons. Some of the units were already encamped while others could be seen moving about in formation. The sight impressed Pvt. Kirk Rand enough that he wrote a friend, "we arrived on the ground we now occupy at 12 this noon and now at sun down as far as the eye can see there is nothing but soldiers and baggage wagons." The river beyond was filled with transport ships and gunboats. This was the only time during the war that the entire Army of the Potomac could be seen in one place at one time. Here Smith's division camped in a wheat field for two days.[4]

As dawn streaked the sky on the morning of May 14, the 2nd Vermont with the rest of Smith's division was ordered to fall in and with Franklin's and Porter's divisions moved five miles up the Pamunkey River to White House Landing. Although it was only a short distance, the muddy road slowed the movement to a crawl. McClellan noted in his report of the campaign, "So bad was the road that the [wagon] train of one of the divisions required thirty-six hours to pass over this short distance."[5]

After reaching White House Landing, Smith's division camped in a 300-acre clover field. The 2nd Vermont got its tents up around 4 P.M. just as it started to rain. Pvt. Rand indicated the men made themselves at home, "the folks that

Mead sketch of Cumberland Landing, Virginia. George Houghton Album, University of Vermont.

owned the farm here had just a fenced it with new rails but there is not a rail to be seen now." Here the Vermont Brigade remained until May 19.[6]

White House Landing was of particular strategic importance to McClellan. The York River Railroad, running from West Point to Richmond, crossed the Pamunkey River there. As the Confederates had retreated to Richmond, they had left the railroad intact except for several small bridges which the Federal engineers quickly repaired. This railroad would become the lifeline of the Army of the Potomac as it attempted to take Richmond.[7]

Virtually overnight White House Landing became an enormous supply depot. Transports soon arrived with locomotives and cars, and the railroad was put back into operation. Floating docks made of planked-over barges and canal boats protruded from the riverbank. Acres of boxes and barrels and crates of rations, ammunition, and supplies soon covered the landing. There were wagon and artillery parks and mountains of baled forage.[8]

Before continuing the advance on Richmond, McClellan reorganized his army on May 18 by forming two new corps. A Fifth Corps was formed under the command of Fitz John Porter, from Porter's First Division of the Third Corps and George Sykes's regular infantry division. A Sixth Corps was formed under the command of William B. Franklin, from Franklin's First Division and Baldy Smith's Second Division of the Fourth Corps.[9]

The days the 2nd Vermont spent at White House were very relaxing. The men had virtually no duties to perform and pretty much stayed in their tents resting and talking over the events of the day. One of the most popular topics was about Negroes as Pvt. Wilbur Fisk described:

> The inevitable negro question would of course be the subject of the most animated conversation of anything we could bring up, for that inexhaustible subject claims preeminence in camp as well as court, and there are almost as many opinions expressed in regard to it in a tent's company as there are in Congress. The boys think it *their* duty to put down rebellion and nothing more, and they view the abolition of slavery in the present time as saddling so much additional labor upon them before the present great work is accomplished. Negro prejudice is as strong here as anywhere and most of the boys would think it a humiliating compromise to the dignity of their work to have it declared that the object of their services was to free the repulsive creatures from slavery, and raise the negro to an equality with themselves. I verily believe if such a declaration was made to-day a majority would be inclined to lay down their arms and quit the service in disgust. The most cordial reception by far that we have received since we left the free states, was tendered us by this sable species of human property. As we-were passing by the premises of one of the more wealthy farmers on our way here, a group of negroes, a score or more composed of men, women and children of all ages, climbed upon the fence by the roadside and greeted us in their earnest simple way "God bress you," "I's glad to see you," "I's glad you's come," "God bress you," and many similar exclamations as they bowed, and courtesied, and waved their hands to us, attesting their childish glee at seeing so many Union soldiers. They were dirty and ragged and probably as a perfectly natural result were ignorant and degraded, but they seemed to understand, as nearly all the negroes here do, that somehow all this commotion has a connection with them and will bring about their freedom in the end. They seem conscious

of being at the bottom of all this trouble, and all the deceptions their masters could invent have failed to rob them of this knowledge.[10]

After several false starts, the 2nd Vermont along with the rest of Smith's division finally moved out of White House Landing on May 17 but only marched about five miles and camped for the night near Tunstall's Station. Two more days of marching brought the division to the vicinity of Gaines's Mill on May 22, where it stayed until May 24 when Smith moved his division forward three-quarters of a mile closer to the Chickahominy and camped on Doctor Gaines's farm.[11]

McClellan now had Franklin's Sixth Corps on the right of the Union line, three miles from New Bridge, supported by the Fifth Corps. Stoneman's cavalry was on the right of Franklin and within about a mile of New Bridge. The Second Corps occupied the center, near the Tyler House, and connected on its left with Keyes's Fourth Corps which held the left of the line near Bottom's Bridge with the Third Corps in reserve.[12]

Smith's division would remain on Gaines's farm until June 5. During this time it was kept busy with picket duty, corduroying roads, and building bridges across the Chickahominy. Some of the more mechanically minded Vermonters got Dr. Gaines's mill back into working order and were soon producing flour for the division. They also helped themselves to the doctor's tobacco that was drying in his barns.[13]

Just as darkness was nearing on May 29, the sky opened up with a terrific lighting and rainstorm. By morning the rain had

Top: Houghton photograph of camps at White House Landing, Virginia. The tents in the foreground are supposed to be those of the Vermont Brigade. George Houghton Album, University of Vermont. ***Middle:*** Houghton photograph of (left to right) Lieutenant Colonel George J. Stannard, Colonel Henry Whiting, and Assistant Surgeon Benjamin W. Carpenter. George Houghton Album, University of Vermont. ***Bottom:*** Houghton photograph of (left to right) Captain Perley P. Pitkin, Colonel Henry Whiting, and Quartermaster (first lieutenant) Lauriston L. Stone. George Houghton Album, University of Vermont.

Top: **Houghton photograph of the 2nd Second Vermont's NCO staff (left to right): Sergeant Major Bradbury W. Hight, Commissary Sergeant Augustus J. Robbins, unidentified, unidentified, and Larkin G. Mead. George Houghton Album, University of Vermont.** ***Bottom:*** **Houghton photograph of a group of 2nd Vermont officers. Standing (left to right): Larkin G. Mead; Second Lieutenant Eugene O. Cole, Company A; Second Lieutenant Charles M. Bliss, Company B; unidentified; Second Lieutenant Edward W. Appleton, Company H; Captain Newton Stone, Company I. Front row (left to right): Unidentified; Unidentified; Captain Enoch E. Johnson, Company D; Major James Walbridge; Adjutant Guilford S. Ladd. George Houghton Album, University of Vermont.**

stopped, but the Chickahominy was a wide raging river. The Army of the Potomac was now split into two pieces with no way to reunite. Gen. Johnston attacked the three Federal corps on the south side of the Chickahominy that afternoon at Seven Pines. But Keyes and Heintzelman, reinforced later by Sumner, made a good fight against superior numbers and at nightfall still held their ground. In addition to the fact that the attack by the rebels was badly handled from the beginning, they lost their commander, Gen. Johnston, who suffered a severe bullet wound in the shoulder. To the Southerners, the loss of Gen. Johnston seemed like a terrible tragedy at the time, but the selection of Gen. Robert E. Lee to replace him would change the course of the war. The battle renewed the next morning and after two or three hours ended in the withdrawal of the Confederates into their lines around Richmond.[14]

May 30 was a day of mixed emotion for the 2nd Vermont. This was the day Lt. Col. Stannard left for Vermont to take command of the newly formed 9th Vermont Infantry Regiment. The men were proud that their lieutenant colonel had been chosen for such a prestigious position but extremely sorry to see him leave. Pvt. Rand lamented Stannard's leaving in a letter to his girlfriend, "I am afraid that the 9th and 10th Regts. will fill up slow but they have got a good Col. in the 9th. he does not know the name of fear. we miss him a good deal here. I had rather they had taken the Col. and left him with us but I am glad he has got the promotion…." Maj. Joyce was selected to replace Stannard. Capt.

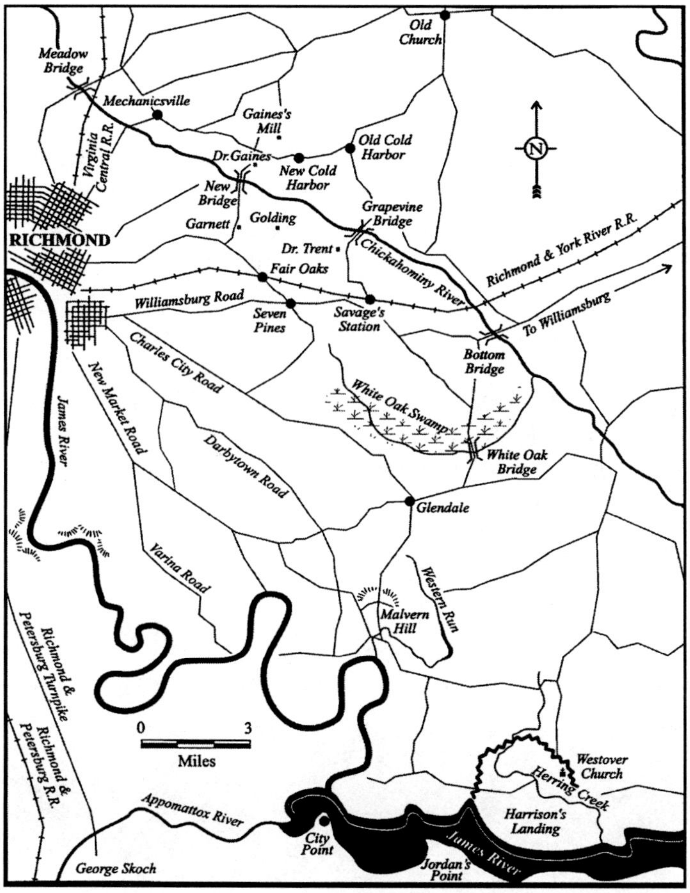

Richmond and vicinity

Top: **Captain William H. Cady, commander of Company A. USAMHI.** ***Bottom:*** **Assistant Surgeon William J. Sawin. USAMHI.**

James H. Walbridge, commander of Co. A, replaced Joyce and 1st Lt. William H. Cady replaced Walbridge as commander of Co. A.[15]

Lt. Col. Stannard selected assistant surgeon Carpenter as his chief surgeon for the 9th Vermont. Carpenter accepted the position but elected to stay with the 2nd Vermont until the current campaign was over. Dr. William J. Sawin, of Chicopee Falls, Mass., who had been serving as a private in the 3rd Vermont, was chosen to replace Carpenter. Sawin was commissioned on June 21 the same day Carpenter's promotion to the 9th Vermont was effective. Sawin was a native of Northfield and a graduate of Dartmouth College, class of 1854.[16]

The Vermonters were under orders to be ready to take arms at a moment's notice during the entire battle on May 30 but were never called upon. They nervously listened to the battle all day. Toward night, Lt. Leach reported the sound "was, a continuous roar of musketry." At 3 A.M. the men were finally ordered to move with the rest of Smith's division to the Chickahominy, but the water was still too high to allow passage. The Vermonters sat around at the bridge until about 10 A.M. when they decided the water was not going to subside and they went back to their camps. For the second day in a row, Smith's men sat and listened to someone else do the fighting.[17]

By the first week of June the rebels had set up their artillery on the other side of the Chickahominy opposite the Vermonters and had become a nuisance, as Pvt. Kirk Rand noted in a letter written on June 3:

> the Rebels are within sight of us here. we are encamped in a piece of woods on a hill and just across the Chickahominy on another hill are the Rebels. they have got a good position, but I am afraid they will leave it. there is a Battery just in front of our camp that are shelling them now. the cannon will keep pretty still for a while and then when they see anything pop will go 3 or 4 guns at them. our officers wont let us go out of the woods so that they can see us from the other side and they keep just shady. it is a good deal like playing hide and seek only they get caught the most.[18]

The Sixth Corps was ordered to the south side of the Chickahominy on June 5. It left camp at 3 A.M. and marched about five miles to the river and crossed on Sumner's upper or "Grapevine" bridge. After crossing the river it marched back upstream several miles and camped on the Golding farm.[19]

The Vermonters finally got their wish to be near the enemy. Here on the Golding farm the rebel and Yankee picket lines were only 400 to 500 feet apart and separated only by a field of oats. Sniping by the pickets and an occasional exchange of artillery fire, and building corduroy roads was the routine for the rest of the month.[20]

One night soon after arriving at Golding's farm, firing broke out on the picket line. The next morning Pvt. William Clark of Co. F, a 23-year-old farmer from Waterbury, reported in with his right thumb missing. He claimed it was shot off by the rebels. Clark was thought of as "odd" and "peculiar" by the other men in his company. He was not careful about his personal hygiene and always tented alone. He refused to go to the hospital to have his thumb tended to and chose to bandage it himself. Consequently, in several days his wound was crawling with maggots. He finally reported to the regimental hospital and was evacuated to

The Grapevine Bridge spanning the Chickahominy River. Library of Congress.

the Chesapeake General Hospital in Hampton, Va. Somewhere between Yorktown and Hampton, the ambulance in which he was being transported hit a bump and he was thrown out. He landed on his right hip doing almost as much damage as having his thumb shot off. Clark was discharged from the army January 16, 1863, for disability.[21]

According to Pvt. Lucius Savage, the pickets were not always sniping at each other as he noted in his diary on June 13: "Went on picket at 9 A.M. Rebels in view just across a small clearing. Some of the boys exchanged papers with them, meeting in the open field between the two lines." Capt. Tyler also wrote of the unofficial truce, "Our men and the rebels, whose picket lines in front of our brigade are actually no further apart than from your house to Uncle George's have, independent of the officers, agreed to have no firing at each other. Consequently both sides stand out in plain sight, no doubt longing for a social chat, but the orders wont allow it. Genl Toombs's Georgia Brigade lies in front of us."[22]

To add to the soldiers' misery, Gen. Smith instituted an order that had all his regiments up at 3 A.M. every morning in line of battle in anticipation of an enemy attack. Pvt. Savage wrote, "They have made a practice lately of getting us into line at 3 o'clock A.M. and have us remain in line till after daylight. The object I suppose is to prevent our sleeping to soundly as there is no other apparent object." This practice was abandoned toward the end of the month when the lack of sleep and the fatigue from their daily labors started putting more men in the hospital than did enemy action. Afterward, to lessen the burden, only one regiment in each brigade had to pull the daily alert duty on a rotating basis.[23]

A bit of news ran through the 2nd Vermont's camp on June 15. The word was that 1st Lt. David. L. Sharpley of Co. G had submitted his resignation. The rumor was true. His 58 years of life, rigors of the campaign, and disease had worn him down. He had been stricken with a severe case of rheumatism the previous January back at Camp Griffin. In fact, it was so bad that he had to be carried back from the picket line to camp, but after a few weeks he had bounced back. This time, however, he was too used up. He departed for his home in Burlington on June 24 leaving 2nd Lt. Anson Weed in command of the company.[24]

On the day Sharpley left, newspapers from Vermont that arrived in that day's incoming mail carried an article that the past commander of Co. H, 51-year-old William T. Burnham, had died suddenly in Montpelier on June 20. The cause of death was what doctors at the time diagnosed as inflammation of the brain. No mention can be found in any surviving documents to indicate that anyone in Co. H, or the entire regiment for that matter, shed a tear for him.[25]

In an attempt to keep his right flank open for the expected link-up with McDowell's corps, McClellan left Porter's Fifth Corps and Stoneman's cavalry on the north side of the Chickahominy. Lee decided to take advantage of this on June 26. He had intended to overpower the Yankee force at Mechanicsville with an early morning attack by Longstreet's, A. P. Hill's, D. H. Hill's divisions, and Jackson's command, which had just joined the Army of Northern Virginia after a successful campaign in the Shenandoah Valley. Through a series of misunderstandings and bad coordination, only A. P. Hill's division and one brigade of D. H. Hill's division made the disastrous late afternoon assault. The Confederates' losses for the day were between 1,300 and 1,400 to the Federals' 361. During the night McCall's division, which had taken the brunt of the day's fighting, fell back to Gaines's Mill where the rest of the Federal Fifth Corps was positioned.[26]

Lee pressed toward Gaines's Mill on June 27 where Porter had set up a solid defensive position. After encountering only light resistance in the morning, A. P. Hill pushed steadily from Mechanicsville toward Gaines's Mill, where he was stopped at about 2 P.M. Successive Confederate attacks failed to break the Federal Line. Meanwhile, Porter was reinforced by Slocum's division of Franklin's Sixth Corps, and the Federal line held. About an hour before dark, the Confederates finally brought all their forces to bear, and the Federal line fell back. The attack soon ran out of steam as the rebel units became separated and confused in the darkness, allowing Porter to get his men across the Chickahominy to safety. This ended the battle of Gaines's Mill. The Federals lost 6,837 men and the Confederates 8,751.[27]

While Lee was directing the Confederate attacks on the north side of the Chickahominy, Magruder, with only 25,000 men, was using his military theatrics again to tie up the 60,000 Federals on the south side. He could not have found a better audience. McClellan and his corps commander bought the act lock, stock, and barrel. In addition to marching his troops to and fro, Magruder would unleash sporadic artillery barrages to keep the Federal's heads down and to fool them into thinking an infantry attack was imminent.[28]

Early in the morning of June 27, Smith had pushed Hancock's pickets forward and occupied some unfinished rifle pits in a field overlooking the Garnett house and adjacent fields. They were now no more than 50 yards from the rebels' picket line. Brooks's and Davidson's brigades were held as support behind Hancock. The Vermonters remained in their camp in line of battle ready to defend the line wherever needed. Their camp came under a heavy artillery bombardment around 4 P.M., and they had to "skedaddle" to the rear for protection under a steep bank.

The bombardment lasted until almost dark. Then, as quickly as it had started, it stopped. As soon as the firing stopped, in a very badly coordinated effort, Magruder attacked with Brig. Gen. Robert Toombs's and Col. George T. Anderson's brigades. Hancock's portion of the line took the brunt of the attack, but held.[29]

The 2nd Vermont went at the double quick to help Hancock's boys, but found as it arrived, the 4th Vermont was already there and fully engaged. The 2nd Vermont stayed in the rear as a reserve, but was not needed. Darkness ended the battle that would become known as Garnett's Farm. Around 10 P.M. the 2nd Vermont marched back to its camp. The overall losses for this battle were 368 Federals and 461 Confederates.[30]

Around 11 P.M. as Porter's men were crossing to the south side of the Chickahominy, McClellan gathered his corps commanders except Keyes, who already had his men on the move, at his headquarters and informed them he intended to perform a change of base to the James River. Smith's division was selected as the rear guard for the army. Accordingly, Smith had his division up at 3 A.M. on June 28 and in line of battle ready for an early morning attack. With no attack forthcoming, the men were released at daybreak to fix their breakfast. They were also informed that right after breakfast they were to pack up and move. Smith's task was to shift his position so that instead of facing to the northwest, his line would face the enemy in a more northerly direction across the river. After the camps were moved a mile or two toward Fair Oaks Station, the men were marched back to the river to fell trees for clearer fields of fire. Around noon they were again subjected to a savage artillery bombardment. Capt. Tyler described the 2nd Vermont's only casualty:

> The rebels open on us with both infantry and artillery. We remain close to the ground, as a support to the pickets in front. Soon the rebel infantry is repulsed, but their artillery keeps up a galling fire. Then it was that Corpl. Paddleford of my company, with whom I was conversing at the time was struck in the left shoulder by a piece of shell. His wound is not dangerous, but being unable to march he had to be left to the tender mercies of the rebels.[31]

Corp. Frank G. Paddleford, from Brattleboro, survived his ordeal and was paroled by the Confederate government September 13, 1862. He would return to his company and serve honorably until discharged at the expiration of his enlistment June 29, 1864.[32]

Gen. Smith quietly got his division moving at 3 A.M. on Sunday, June 29. The thin picket line that had been left to keep up a show of strength in front of Magruder's lines was withdrawn at sunrise. The division moved to the east along the highlands skirting the Chickahominy, halting and forming in line of battle near the Trent House to cover the rear of the army's wagon trains. Then turning to the southwest, it marched toward Savage's Station.[33]

The rebels were not encountered during the morning, but the constant threat kept everyone in a state of high anxiety. En route to Savage's Station, the Vermonters passed through the camp of the 4th New Jersey Infantry. Here they stopped long enough to destroy abandoned boxes of hardtack and camp equipment to prevent them from being captured by the rebels. Cutting, slashing, or crushing, rather than burning to keep smoke from giving away their position, they destroyed everything. This was the first time the Vermonters had seen intentional destruction of Federal stores, and the gravity of the situation struck home. Pvt. Rand was rather shocked at this task: "we commenced to destroy commissary stores and every thing we could lay our hands on. it looked to bad but I suppose better to destroy than to let the Rebs have it, but we lived pretty well that night on butter, ham, sugar and so forth." This was only a precursor of what they would see later that day. As they prepared to leave the 4th New Jersey's camp, the 2nd Vermont was ordered to throw out skirmishers to the rear. For the first time, the men realized that they were the only obstacle between their army and the pursuing rebels.[34]

Smith's division arrived at Savage's Station on the Richmond and York River Railroad about 1 P.M. and got two hours rest. The scenes at the station that hot steamy afternoon would be forever burned into the men's memories. First were the endless miles of infantry, artillery trains, wagons, and several thousand head of cattle moving toward the James River. Second was the mass destruction of supplies that had been staged at the station. "at the station the work of destruction was going on," Pvt. Rand wrote several days later: "piles of crackers as big as a common house were burnt up. boxes of Ammunition, barrels of powder and shells, muskets and every thing was burnt up. a train of cars stood on the track a burning ... things looked smokey around there and the soldiers looked dirty as it was awful hot and dusty." The last horrible scene was over 2,000 wounded and sick Union soldiers clustered about the station in a makeshift hospital that was left behind to be captured by the rebels.[35]

Near 4 P.M., Smith's division, leaving Sumner's Second Corps to guard the rear, continued its retreat toward the James River. It plodded along in the hot and sultry afternoon for several miles when heavy firing was heard to the rear, and Smith was ordered back to the station. Sumner's men had been hit by Magruder's command.[36]

Smith quickly moved his men back to the station at the double quick with Brooks's Vermonters in the lead. When

The federal hospital at Savage's Station. Library of Congress.

they arrived, Smith posted Brooks on the left side of the Williamsburg Road. Hancock's brigade was sent to support Richardson's division near the station to the right of the road, and Davidson's brigade was held in the rear as a general reserve. The Federal front now consisted of, from left to right, Brooks's brigade, whose right flank was anchored on the Williamsburg Road, and then the brigades of Brig Gen. Willis A. Gorman and Brig. Gen. William W. Burns.[37]

Facing the Federals was Magruder's command. Starting on the Federal left, they consisted of Brig. Gen. Richard Griffith's brigade commanded by Col. William Barksdale, since Griffith had been mortally wounded earlier in the day, followed by the brigades of Brig. Gen. Paul J. Semmes, who was astride the Williamsburg Road, Brig. Gen. Joseph B. Kershaw, Brig. Gen. Howell Cobb, and Brig. Gen. Robert A. Toombs. To back up the center of the Confederate line was Kemper's Alexandria battery. To the far right on the railroad was a 32-pounder Brooke cannon mounted on a flat car.[38]

Smith had halted Brooks's brigade in the Williamsburg Road about a mile from where the battle would eventually take place. His orders were to advance into the woods ahead and push back the rebels who were swarming forward, threatening Gorman's left flank.[39]

Brooks formed his Green Mountain Boys in line of battle with the 6th Vermont on the left and the 5th on the right with its right flank on the Williamsburg Road. Companies A and K of the 2nd Vermont were thrown forward as skirmishers under the command of Maj. Walbridge. The rest of the 2nd Vermont filed in behind the 5th Vermont as support. The 3rd Vermont supported the 6th, and the 4th was held as a general reserve. In this order, the Vermonters entered the woods as the sun was starting to set.[40]

As Brooks's men moved forward, the enemy's artillery raked the woods with shells and canister rounds (rounds similar to small paint cans filled with cast-iron balls), taking its toll on the 2nd Vermont's skirmish line and the men in the 5th. As the brigade neared the rebels at about 7 P.M.,

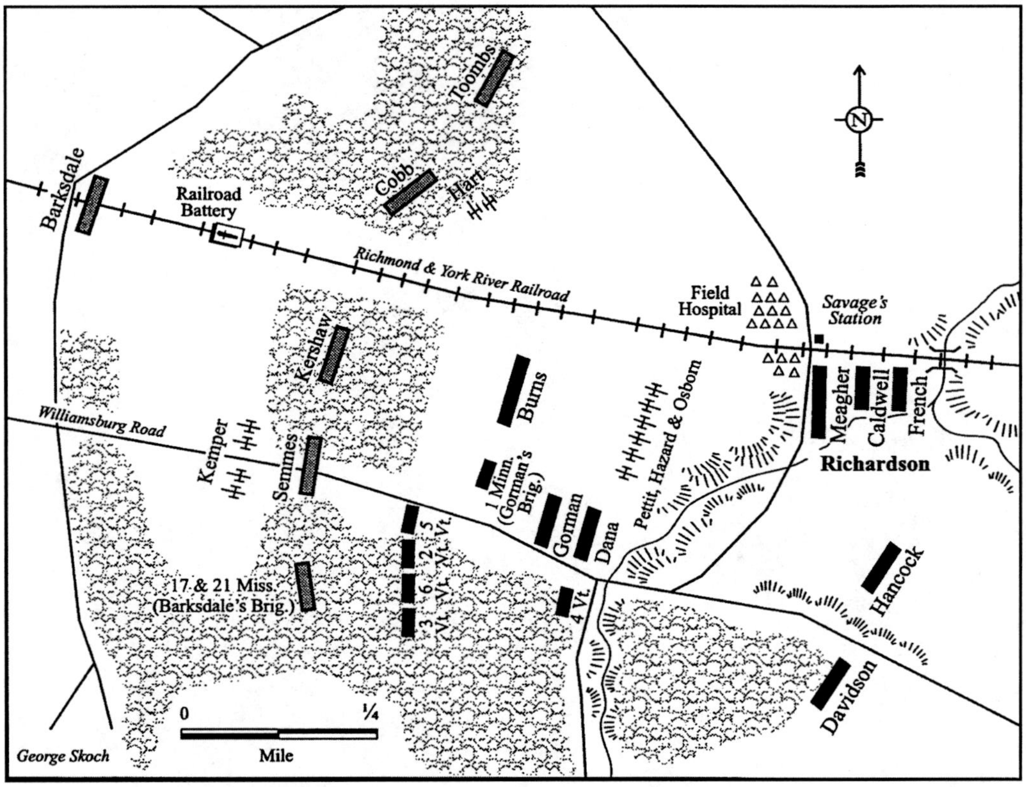

The Battle of Savage's Station, June 29, 1862

the woods gave way to an open field. The 2nd Vermont's skirmishers cleared the woods, and as they stepped into the field men started dropping.[41]

Pvt. Daniel M. Priest of Co. A and a farmer from Peru, Vt., took a minié ball in the left forearm about three inches above the wrist. The bullet fractured the radius and made a horrible wound. He was captured the next morning and his arm was amputated between the elbow and the wound. He was paroled on August 3 and discharged October 15, 1862, and lived until 1921.[42]

A minié ball struck 24-year-old Pvt. James H. Shippee of Co. A, from Searsburgh, in the left thigh. The bullet hit the bone but fortunately did not fracture it. Like Priest, Shippee was left on the field and was captured. He was paroled in August and discharged November 27, 1862.[43]

Maj. Walbridge led the 2nd Vermont's skirmish line off to the left just as the 5th Vermont was nearing the field behind them. The skirmishers were led to the rear of the brigade where during the rest of the battle they served as a rear guard to keep shirkers from sneaking to the rear. In front of the 5th Vermont was part of Semmes's brigade in a hollow that hid them from view. On a crest beyond, in a clearing on the Williamsburg Road, were Kemper's roaring guns.[44]

The 5th advanced until the enemy was clearly visible in the hollow about 200 yards in front of them. Then, Lt. Col. Lewis A. Grant, who was leading the regiment for Col. Smalley who was absent on sick leave, ordered a bayonet charge. The 5th charged at the double quick until they were within 40 to 50 yards of the rebels. The rebel line broke to the left and right, unmasking two additional Confederate regiments with rifles aimed directly at the Vermonters. Grant halted his regiment and opened fire. The rebels almost simultaneously returned two volleys in quick succession and in conjunction with Kemper's battery, caught the 5th in a deadly crossfire. The effect was catastrophic. Within minutes half of the regiment was either dead or wounded. Men lucky enough to be left unharmed found protection in a slight swell in the ground and behind what few trees were in the area. Despite their terrific losses they held their ground. Grant ordered two companies to concentrate maximum fire on the battery. This had the desired effect, and Kemper quickly limbered up his guns and left for the evening. The heavy firing with the rebel infantry continued until dark. By this time, most of the Vermonters had used up their 60 rounds taken into the battle and were using those of the dead and wounded.[45]

When the Vermont Brigade initially started its advance, the 6th Vermont was on the left and keeping up with the 5th, but the farther the 6th advanced, the more it veered to the left, eventually opening a gap between the two units. One Confederate regiment took advantage of this mistake and charged into the gap firing off a volley before retreating.[46]

Col. Whiting saw what had happened to the two leading regiments and wanted to fill the gap. Unfortunately, the 2nd Vermont was still in a column formation. Instead of stopping and forming his regiment in line of battle, he screamed over the din, "Charge bayonets!" There was no such maneuver from a column formation in the tactics books, and in the confusion, the regiment froze. Whiting admitted later that he was "at wits end." Out of shear desperation he could think of nothing else to do but to order his men to cheer which they did with a vengeance. This broke the impasse, and they were quickly deployed and charged forward to plug the hole. Col. Whiting admitted later, "That command to cheer I lay up as the best act performed by me during my service. Only soldiers can estimate what a cheer may accomplish when matters seem to be on the balance."[47]

As the 2nd Vermont got nearer the enemy, it quickly started taking casualties. Pvt. Charles C. Dodge of Co. F took multiple hits. One bullet pierced his neck just behind his right ear, as another one almost simultaneously grazed his head behind his left ear. Pvt. Elijah S. Brown, also of Co. F, helped Dodge to temporary safety. Later Brown wrote of the casualties in his company, "Charles Dodge is one of them & he is probably dead for when I left him he could not speak the ball passed through his neck he was bleeding to death & fast & the Dr. said he would not live for an hour & then I left him for the enemy was close on to me...." Dodge was left on the field to die. Although weakened from the loss of blood, he dragged himself into a ravine where he saw water trickling from a wooden spout that a local farmer had stuck into a spring. He let the water run over his head to cool his wounds until he was found and captured the next morning by Stonewall Jackson's men. He survived captivity in Libby Prison in Richmond and was paroled September 13. He was transferred to the Veteran Reserve Corps on January 15, 1863 and was discharged from the service June 20, 1863. His wound left his mouth partially paralyzed, causing a speech impediment.[48]

Not long after Pvt. Dodge was hit, Capt. Randall, commander of Co. F, saw another one of his men receive a wound. Pvt. Henry L. Harris was hit almost simultaneously in his left side and right hand but was able to keep on firing. A few minutes later another bullet hit him in the right arm finally taking him down. He had received a nasty wound in the upper arm just below the shoulder. The arm was amputated the next day. He was imprisoned in Richmond until paroled September 13, 1862 and served in the Veteran Reserve Corps until he was discharged June 20, 1864.[49]

Another one of Capt. Randall's men to get wounded was Pvt. Harlan P. Stoddard of Waitsfield. He was hit by a bullet that entered the left side of his pelvis fracturing the pelvic bone, passing through the rectum and finally exiting through his left buttocks. Stoddard was left writhing on the ground in the darkness. He was taken as a prisoner of war the next day and paroled on July 25. He spent the next year in the hospital and was discharged from the army in August 1863 on a disability.[50]

Pvt. William H. Clark of Co. E took a buck and ball round in the front of his thighs. His left thigh was hit by the round ball, and one of the buckshot hit near his right groin. For some reason neither round could be removed by the surgeons in either the Confederate hospital where he was taken after he was captured, or the Federal general hospital in Philadelphia where he was admitted after he was paroled on August 6. He would have to use a cane for the rest of his life. The shot that wounded him came from one of the three regiments of Semmes's brigade that was using smooth-bore muskets with buck and ball ammunition. In his after-action report, Semmes stated, "Much of the time the enemy were engaged at a distance of not above 40 yards. Their heavy comparative loss doubtless resulted mainly from the greater efficiency of our smooth-bore muskets with buck and ball at short range, the superior steadiness of our men, and the precision of their fire."[51]

Pvt. Vernon D. Rood, the man who made the presentation to Col. Whiting in March, was hit in the right thigh. Although the wound was not life threatening, it was bad enough that he was left behind on the battlefield with the rest of the wounded. He was paroled July 25, 1862 and was hospitalized until September 1, 1863, when he was transferred to the Veteran Reserve Corps. Rood was discharged June 27, 1864. When he returned to Vermont, he enrolled in the Burlington Medical School from which he graduated in June 1867. Despite his wartime injury he became a successful doctor in North Hyde Park, Vt.[52]

Pvt. Lucius Savage of Co., F, related later his experience in the engagement:

> I remember of taking deliberate aim at their ranks by dropping on my right knee and resting my elbow on my left knee. In this way I had fired several rounds, rising to my feet to load. While loading my gun and standing at about a half face to the right a rifle ball came from our left, passed in rear of my left knee carrying away my pant's leg in its passage and entered my right leg directly behind the knee. I fell (or swayed) over supposing at first that some comrade in falling had hit my leg with his musket, the ball causing a feeling similar to a sudden blow from some heavy instrument. But as the blood began to flow quite freely and I was not long in doubt as to the real cause of my falling. As the ball struck me I had just inserted a cartridge and was just entering the rammer with my arm extended up at full length. I soon made up my mind that I could be of no further service by remaining there. So taking my gun in one hand I crawled away towards the rear on my hands and knees, expecting every moment to be riddled with balls as they were passing like hail stones and men were lying in heaps across the road and on either side. After crawling a short distance and turning a bend in the road and being protected somewhat by trees, I arose to my feet (or foot) and taking my gun in my hands jumped along a little ways when some one called my name and asked if I was wounded. It proved to be Dan Laporte of our Co. and he soon called to his brother Julius to come and help Savage as he was wounded. I placed my arm around the neck of the Laporte boys and *used them for crutches* until they were relieved by a line of sharp-

> shooters and ordered back to the front. This line of sharpshooters were the skirmish line as we went into the fight, and they fell back and formed a line to prevent straggling. While being assisted by the Laportes, we came to where comrade H[arlan] P[age] Stoddard lay upon a stretcher. I approached him and asked him how badly he was wounded. He told me he was shot through the groin and should probably live but a few hours; said he had given his watch and other valuables to his brother Horace &c. As we left him lying there by the roadside on that stretcher I bade him goodbye supposing it would be the last time I should see him, even if I were fortunate enough to pull *through myself*. The sharpshooters helped me back to a small house near where we formed for our advance through the woods, where they left me. By this time it was night.[53]

The 3rd Vermont had started forward with the rest of the brigade just to the rear of the 6th Vermont, but marching through the dark woods, it lost sight of the other Vermont regiments. Without realizing it, the 3rd Vermont had veered too far to the left, totally losing the protection of the regiment in front. When Lt. Col. Veazey, acting commander of the 3rd, realized his predicament, he put his regiment in line of battle and continued to press forward.[54]

As the 3rd Vermont was moving forward, Semmes was moving the 5th Louisiana to the Confederate right, straight into the path of the Vermonters. When about 40 yards from the Vermonters, Semmes could hear troops moving through the underbrush in the darkness in front of him, but he could not tell if it was friend or foe. He halted the 5th Louisiana and ordered Pvt. Maddox of Co. K to go forward and challenge the unit in front of them. Maddox cautiously moved forward and yelled out, "Who are you?" The answer out of the darkness was, "Friends." Maddox then asked, "What regiment?" Someone replied, "The Third Vermont." The rebels replied immediately with a volley of musket fire, which took down about half of the 3rd Vermont's Company C. The 3rd unleashed its own volley in return and let out a cheer. The rebels, unable to see the size of the force confronting them, retreated and were out of action the rest of the night. The 3rd Vermont maintained its position until recalled an hour later.[55]

As the firing subsided after dark, Gen. Brooks and Maj. Walbridge were rounding up troops on the left when they heard rustling in the bushes in the darkness. Walbridge called out, "What troops are those?" Someone off in the darkness replied, "Who are you?" Walbridge again called out, "What regiment is that?" The reply was, "You tell!" Then out of the night Walbridge and Brooks heard the order, "Ready!" They did not wait for "Aim! Fire!" and wheeled their horses around for a quick get away. The expected spray of minié balls followed in a split second. Walbridge, who was by now lying forward on his saddle to make as small a target as possible, escaped without a scratch. Brooks was not as lucky and received a slight bullet wound just above his knee but did not leave his command. Pvt. Elijah Brown of Co. F recalled seeing Brooks after he was wounded, "Gen. wounded in the knee—his horse & saddle covered with blood ... he did not leave us in the fight ... but stayed with his men...."[56]

By 9 P.M., it was pitch dark and both the Confederate and Federal commanders were afraid to maneuver their troops any more for fear of firing into their own units and fell back. The Vermonters gathered up their wounded the best they could in the dark and dropped them off at the hospital at Savage's Station. Its patients now numbering about 2,500. Their dead, unfortunately, had to be left on the field.[57]

To assist in the care of the wounded Vermonters, Dr. William P. Russell of the 5th Vermont and Dr. Sawin of the 2nd, along with several hospital attendants, were detailed to stay behind. Dr. Sawin rejoined his regiment three weeks later after being paroled on July 22.[58]

Pvt. Savage described his experience as one of the wounded left behind in a small house near the battlefield:

> There was a lady, the wife of a major in the 88th NY Regt. Irish brigade who was doing all she could to assist the wounded that were left there. To be sure she could do but little as she had no conveniences in particular, but she had bandages with her and she used them and busied herself on our behalf until a ambulance came for her and she left us.... I spread my blanket upon the floor and laid down, determined to resume my journey in the morning towards the James River where the men of our Co, with but few exceptions supposed I had already gone.... Sleep was entirely out of the question as some of our men were terribly wounded and in their agony or oblivion would groan and yell at all times during the night.
>
> Monday morning June 30th at daylight I determined to resume my journey towards the James River. I rolled my blankets up, placed them on my knapsack, but upon attempting to arise I found that I could not raise my wounded leg from the floor for an instant. So I unrolled my blankets and laid down again, realizing for the first time that I was left with hundreds of others to be taken prisoners. As I looked out the door upon attempting to get up I saw the rear guard of our troops passing in the direction of White Oak Swamp.... About 8 o'clock A.M. the Confederates made their appearance, first indicated by a line of skirmishers emerging from the woods.
>
> During Monday I was carried on a stretcher (by some of our men who had remained to care for the wounded) back to another house nearer the battlefield of the previous night, where there was a large number of our men left that were wounded. A day or two after my arrival here I was somewhat startled after having had some conversation with some of the nurses to hear someone ask if that L. D. Savage. And upon looking in the direction of the nurse I saw E. W. Loomis with one arm gone. He had been lying under the porch of the house as it had been

raining and had just emerged from his den. And standing there with an old dirty army blanket thrown over his shoulder, I could not think from his appearance it was anyone I had ever seen, but I recognized his voice upon asking who it was. We were outdoors during our stay at this place and it rained most of the time. My wound was quite painful. My foot and leg were much discolored and I feared it was mortifying. I called the attention of Dr. Bromley of a Michigan Regt. to it and he examined it carefully and said that the blood circulated a little. He told me that the ball in passing through my leg had bruised the main artery, but did not sever it, which caused the stopping of the circulation. After a few days this discoloring disappeared and my leg resumed its natural color.... Previous to coming over to the hospital (or station) in spite of all my precaution, my wound had become maggoty and there is no describing the misery I was in, and how to remove them was a puzzle, but I obtained some turpentine after getting to the station (which others were using for the same purpose) and turning my leg in the right position, I turned in the turpentine letting it pass entirely through the wound, which had the effect of cleaning out the wound *and the maggots*. I learned while here that comrade H. P. Stoddard was living and was there at this hospital, but I could not visit him nor him me. But communication was kept up between us by another of our Co. that was shot through the neck, but could move about very slowly. This comrade's name was Charles C. Dodge. We remained here at the station about 10 days, losing large numbers of our men daily....[59]

Pvt. Savage survived captivity and was discharged from the army on November 29, 1862.[60]

The final tally of casualties for the Vermont Brigade in this action was 358. The 2nd Vermont lost five men killed and 43 wounded, three of which died later of their wounds. The 5th lost the most men with 206, followed by the 6th with 75 and the 3rd with 24. The 4th, which was never engaged, left five men sick in the hospital when they departed the station.[61]

Although the battle of Savage's Station was not a large battle, it was crucial to the safety of the retreating army and at times was quite ferocious. Pvt. Oric R. Ward, a 21-year-old from Plymouth and Co. I, related the horrors of the battle and its aftermath in a letter to a friend:

Jerome this is the awfullist thing that ever was. You can't form any idea about it to see so many young men shot down in the prime of life & others wounded arms shot off feet shot off & everything else. It is a shame to see how our wounded & sick are used.... Jerome if the boys knew how the sick and wounded men were used they wouldn't get many more to volunteer.[62]

Shortly after 10 P.M. Smith had his division pulled together and was on the road in a pouring rain to the James River some 20 miles off in the darkness.[63]

The division moved quickly to secure the bridge across White Oak Swamp before the rebels could catch up. The march was one of the most dreadful the Vermonters would ever make. The night was dark and rainy and the mud grew deeper with every mile. The men were exhausted by the day's march and the evening's battle and depressed about retreating. The road was completely filled with wagons, ambulances, and artillery mingled with horsemen and infantry, all crowding forward with utmost speed. There were also long lines of staggering sick and wounded men, leaning on their muskets or sticks for support, tottering after the retreating column desperately trying to reach safety. The teamsters and stragglers that had preceded them had made numerous cooking fires alongside the road that now produced an eerie glow and cast dancing shadows over everything in sight. "Many a poor fellow, exhausted, fell out of the ranks," wrote Capt. Tyler, "and was picked up next day by the rebel cavalry."[64]

The march continued all night. Shortly after daybreak, the lead units crossed the White Oak Swamp Bridge which was destroyed after the last unit crossed. In the meantime Gen. Smith had received an order from McClellan, "to hold that position at all hazards till relieved by an order from him." He quickly made proper disposition of his troops to hold the crossing as ordered.[65]

After several changes of position, the Vermonters were halted about a quarter of a mile above the bridge and east of the road in an open field bordered in the rear by a stand of pines. Everyone, officers and men, sank to the ground and immediately went to sleep.[66]

Sleep was not going to be allowed that morning by the rebels. Stonewall Jackson, who had been shadowing the rear of the Federal column, reached the destroyed bridge across White Oak Swamp about noon. To cover his effort to repair the bridge, he had secretly posted all his artillery, approximately 31 guns, on a wooded bluff overlooking the Yankees. Shortly before 2 P.M. he unleashed the fury of his guns. The first incoming salvo produced pandemonium. Men who only split seconds before had been sound asleep sprang to their feet, and in addition to being scared out of their wits, were totally disoriented and ran in every direction for cover. Officers were wandering about in the smoke and dust looking for their commands. Pvt. Rand related his experience during the shelling:

as we were tired most of us were asleep when the first thing we know we were greeted with a shower of shell, grape and every other missile that is used in cannons. it was awful of all the cannonading I ever saw or heard that beat the whole and to add to the scene Mott's battery which was in front of us catched it so hard that they had to cut their horses loose and leave some of their pieces and their horses and officers horses.

> [horses] that had broke loose came tearing through our ranks knocking some of us over and scattering in every direction. we were more afraid of the horses than we were the shells.[67]

Capt. John Tyler remembered, "Twas the most terrific scene I ever witnessed, and I feel entirely unequal to the task of describing it."[68]

After the bombardment started the Vermonters collected fairly quickly in the pines behind the field where they had been asleep. The coolness with which some of their officers behaved, like the 2nd Vermont's assistant surgeon Carpenter who coolly rode back and forth in the crowd, calmed the men down. Within several minutes, Gen. Brooks rode slowly among them, and the regiments fell into formation amid cheers for their general. Brooks then threw a skirmish line forward, just beyond the tree line, and waited for what might come next. "Our division having rallied from what bid fair to panic, we held our ground," stated Capt. Tyler.[69]

Within a short time the Federal artillery returned fire. The artillery duel went on sporadically all day, but Jackson never rebuilt the bridge nor forced passage of White Oak Swamp until the next day after the Federals had left.[70]

After dark the Federals withdrew and Franklin pushed his divisions hard during the night. The Sixth Corps halted in a field near Turkey Creek at sunrise where the James River was close enough that the men could see the masts of the Federal gunboats off in the distance. Everyone was absolutely exhausted. Gen. Smith in his autobiography wrote of the march:

> There is no agony I have ever experienced to compare with that of an intense desire to sleep on horseback. Accustomed to falling asleep and continually waking the seconds of sleep were filled with the most horrible nightmares in addition to intense physical pain. That march is burned into my memory.[71]

Breakfast and sleep would have to wait. Responding to the threat of the rebels closing in, the corps was ordered to backtrack a short distance and deploy on line in some woods facing Western Run. It remained in position all day, but the enemy never appeared in their front. In the afternoon and evening, as the men lay in the woods, they could hear the sounds of the fierce fighting on their left that would be known as the Battle of Malvern Hill. This battle was a Confederate disaster with 5,355 casualties compared to the Federal's 3,214.[72]

At 2 A.M., July 2, just as the rain started to pour, Smith's division was on the move again toward the James River. The road immediately turned into a sea of sticky mud. Pvt. Kirk Rand shared the miserable experience with a friend in Vermont:

> to add to the beauty of the subject it commenced to rain and oh how it rained. in the morning we started again through the rain and mud. We went about 5 miles. not far it may seem to you but it was a good ways to us traveling through the mud up to our knees, but we were laughing to see each other slipping in the mud. many a poor fellow would get his shoes stuck and his feet would come right out of them and he would go a head bare foot.[73]

With the end near, the men were throwing away everything that would impede their flight. The roadside was littered with thousands of rifles, knapsacks, and other types of military equipment. In the middle of the road were dead and dying mules and horses along with abandoned wagons mired down in the morass of mud. Physically exhausted and sick soldiers fell out by the hundreds only to be picked up later by the Confederates and imprisoned. Somewhere along the route in the pitch dark rainy night, the 2nd Vermont's Pvt. Eri S. Gunnison of Co. F was literally knocked down and run over by a troop of Union cavalry. Amazingly, his only serious injury was a severely sprained back. His buddies picked him up and helped him along. Smith's men slogged on through the miserable downpour and the mud until a little after noon when they finally reached the safety of Harrison's Landing.[74]

At Harrison's Landing, the majority of the army was clustered on what was actually Berkeley plantation. For some reason over the years, the area had become named for the landing on the James River in front of the house. Berkeley, built in 1725, was the historic home of Virginia's Harrison family, which had produced Benjamin Harrison, a signer of the Declaration of Independence, and William Henry Harrison, ninth president of the United States. It was also the site of the first official Thanksgiving service in 1619. The Harrisons' fields along the river measured roughly four miles by one mile; there McClellan had squeezed in 90,000 soldiers, 288 artillery pieces, 3,000 wagons and ambulances, 27,000 horses and mules, and 2,500 head of cattle.[75]

In no time, the soldiers had stomped the soggy fields into a sea of semi-liquid paste. After the divisions had been guided into their positions, the men sank exhausted to the ground. Those who still had them put up their tents, using the wheat in the fields as flooring. Those without tents pulled their rubber blankets over themselves and slept the sleep of the dead. Just before sundown, the 2nd Vermont was issued hardtack, salt pork and coffee. By this time the men were starving. Pvt. Rand wrote, "I eat pork enough to last a small family." The rain continued through most of the night and by morning the men who had set up tents now had wet canvas in their faces since the ground was too saturated to hold the tent pins.[76]

While the exhausted Yankees had been sleeping, Jeb Stuart, who had been following the retreating army, set up his artillery on Evelynton Heights across Herring Creek from Berkeley, near Westover Church. Evelynton Heights was about 20 feet higher than the fields around Berkeley and provided an excellent field of fire. A little after 8 A.M., Stuart let loose several rounds that fell into the sleeping Yankees' camp, causing quite a stir, but little damage. A few return rounds from the Federal gunboats quieted the rebel artillery and an infantry division was sent forward by McClellan and chased off Stuart's cavalry.[77]

Top: **Westover Church as it appears today. Sarah Zeller.** ***Bottom:*** **Present day interior view of Westover Church. Sarah Zeller.**

McClellan immediately dispersed his divisions for better defense of the area. Smith's division was moved to the area surrounding Westover Church, on the Ruffin farm, called Evelynton. The entire army was then set to work, day and night, digging an entrenchment that would, within a week, surround the entire army from Herring Creek to Kimages Creek.[78]

Westover Church had been established in 1613. The structure around which Smith's division camped was built in 1737. The quaint little church had been attended over the years by presidents Washington, Jefferson, William Henry Harrison, and Tyler. As with most property in Virginia, including churches, the Vermonters paid little respect. A private in the 2nd Vermont wrote, "We are right in front of a nice little church furnished up in good style, all carpeted and cushioned inside with two organs in it. One of them is locked up, so it cannot be got to." Lt. Leach wrote his wife a little later, "The Co.s are making ovens with the brick from the wall around the church to bake bread, but how long they will have the benefit of them is more than I can tell." Several weeks later he wrote, "The boys are feeling quite well now, on account of having soft bread to eat, which Co. makes themselves and good bread it is too. Butter is to be had too." To this day the brick wall around the church has not been replaced.[79]

The Vermonters also used the church for its intended purpose as described by Pvt. Cutler: "There is a pretty little brick church surrounded be a grove of trees about five rod [s] from our camp in which we have religious services

Adjutant Francis M. Edgerton. Vermont Historical Society.

now every sabath. I attended las Sabbath the 3rd regiment chaplain preached to us, it seemed a good deal like home to attend a meeting in a church."[80]

The 2nd Vermont's chaplain, Claudius B. Smith, resigned on July 7 and was replaced by Chaplain Durell W. Dayton, a Methodist Episcopal clergyman from Middlebury, on August 18. Adj. Guilford Ladd, beaten down by the campaign, resigned on July 17 and was replaced by Francis M. Edgerton of Co. F on August 4.[81]

President Lincoln came to confer with Gen. McClellan on Tuesday, July 8, to determine what could be done next with the Army of the Potomac. While there, the president and McClellan reviewed the army. They did not get to the Vermont Brigade until after dark, but as Lt. Leach explained, "President Lincoln made us a visit the other day or night rather, so I could not see how he looked, as I should like to have done. The firing of salutes told where he was to be found, as he rode from one point to another." Even though the Vermonters were tired from standing in formation for hours, they still had enough spirit to give the president "three cheers and a tiger" as he passed by. At least one member of the 2nd Vermont had lost his enthusiasm for standing in formations and the army as a whole, when he wrote, "Uncle Abe came and reviewed us a few days ago, so I guess he has not forgotten us, but I wish he would think enough of us, to discharge us and send us home...."[82]

The day after the review by the president was a scorcher, and a number of the Vermonters went down to Herring Creek, behind Westover Church, for a swim. A group from the 2nd Vermont's Co. E was led by Sgt. George E. Allen, a strapping 22-year-old five foot, nine inch farmer from Chelsea. The boys stripped down and jumped in. Allen had swum across the creek which was about 120 to 150 feet wide and was returning when he was sized by stomach cramps and sank. He clawed his way to the surface and yelled for help, but the man nearest him was a weak swimmer and was afraid to attempt to rescue him. Allen sank again, surfaced one more time, and then went down for good. Word was quickly relayed to camp, but by the time a rescue party arrived, it was too late. Due to the swiftness and depth of the water they could not recover his body.[83]

One of Allen's friends in Co. E, Sgt. Charles C. Morey, a young farmer from Royalton, wrote of Allen's death in his diary that night:

> It is the most severe blow this company ever sustained, he being beloved by all the members of the company both as a companion and soldier, he was always at his best in time of danger and did not fear to sell his life dearly if necessary in the cause in which he was engaged but he went with a fate little expected by any of us.[84]

The next morning a number of the boys from Co. E went back to the creek and finally found Allen's body floating face down on the surface. His body was brought to camp and a coffin was procured for his burial.[85]

The whole regiment was shocked and upset over Allen's death. Pvt. Hollis Montague, Co. H's fifer, thought not enough had been done for Allen:

> His body lay in the water overnight. They couldn't find him until his body arose the next day. What a difference between a soldier & a citizen. Should a citizen be drowned in that way, the inhabitants would turn out for miles around. But here, where hundreds were sitting around within 50 rods & none thought of going to see him, even after his body was taken out.[86]

That afternoon Allen was buried just south of the church overlooking the creek where he had drowned. Sgt. Morey recorded in his diary that night:

> Rev. D. A. Mack [3rd Vermont] presided and made a very touching prayer and appropriate remarks and many a tear stole down the cheeks of the hardy soldier; there is a little feeling

Sergeant Charles C. Morey, Company E, the last officer in the 2nd Vermont to be killed in action April 2, 1865. Ed Italo Collection.

> left in the heart although we have become accustomed to scenes of violence and blood. We buried him with military honors. He sleeps his last sleep. He has fought his last battle.[87]

By the middle of July, the fortifications surrounding Harrison's Landing were completed. Even though most of the hard fatigue duty was over, the heat, malaria and stress of the campaign were taking their toll. Lt. Leach wrote on July 20, "There were 10 to 15 excused from each Co. by the Surgeon this morning, which tells something for the health of the Regt. There were 13 in our Co. including Sawyer and myself. Some are lame and one thing and another, but the general complaint is diarrhea." Several days later he described the conditions in the field hospital:

> The tent is quite large, so that the patients lie on each side with their feet in the center. A very little straw is on the ground and their blankets spread on that, constitutes a bed. About the care they have, I know little about, except, [Sgt. Eli] Ellenwood and [Corp. Henry L.] Ballard thought they did not live as well as they did in the Co. They have ice water to drink, so there is one good thing.[88]

Pvt. Oric R. Ward wrote about the hospital in even less glowing terms than Leach: "Elbridge W. Prior [Co. I from Plymouth] is very sick with a fever. He is in the hospital. He lays on the ground and that a poorly place for a sick man to lay on the damp ground. I go & see him twice a day it seems to bad to see him lay there...."[89]

Pvt. Warren S. Leslie, a 20-year-old farmer from Plymouth in Co. I, also wrote on July 30, "It is very sickly here now and the men are dying off pretty fast. One of our Corprils died last night and the men that are on duty are nothing but skin and bones and that is the way the world goes now a days."[90]

During the month of July the Army of the Potomac reported 42,911 cases of sickness in its camps.[91]

There was depression among the troops as much as there was physical ailments as noted by Pvt. Leslie. On July 30 he penned, "O when shall war seace and peace dwell in our country again. I fear it will not in your day nor mine but hope it may for if I ever get out of this I shall know how to injoy a peaceable life after induring the horers of war."[92]

Pvt. Ward simply noted in one of his letters to his friend back home, "Jerome I haven't any faith in the Union...."[93]

The situation, both mental and physical, was just as bad in the 2nd Vermont's other companies.[94]

At the evening dress parade on July 20, Pvts. William Flanders and Henry G. Hunter, both of Co. B, were drummed out of camp. They had been sentenced by courts-martial earlier for refusing to fall in with the regiment to meet the enemy on June 1. Twenty-four year-old Pvt. Jerome Draper, a member of Co. A and a Shaftsbury native, had also been sentenced to be drummed out but deserted rather than face the humiliation. He was arrested at home on January 21, 1864, and charged with desertion.[95]

During the last two weeks of July, Maj. Joyce received word from Vermont that his wife had received an erroneous telegram informing her that he had been killed at the battle of Savage's Station. His wife apparently took the news very badly and even though she soon found out the information was a mistake, she was still quite distraught. Joyce submitted a request for a leave of absence on August 3 stating, "Leave of absence for twenty days is hereby respectfully requested to enable me to return to Vermont to visit my family who are quite ill, caused by a false telegram to them that I was killed in the fight at Savage's Station, & also to recruit my own health, which is such as to render me unfit for duty."[96]

Even though his request went all the way up the chain of command to the assistant secretary of war, Joyce did not get his leave of absence. Rather than resign to go home like Chaplain Smith, he contented himself with corresponding with his wife by mail.[97]

Maj. Gen. Henry W. Halleck, chief of staff of the army, came to Harrison's Landing on July 25 to consult with McClellan. McClellan wanted to cross the James and assault the yet unfortified city of Petersburg, a valuable Confederate railroad hub. Halleck was dead set against the idea. By the time Halleck left, McClellan was under the impression that Halleck was going to send reinforcements and order the renewal of the push against Richmond, so the army continued to sit along the banks of the James River.[98]

The four weeks without enemy action at Harrison's Landing was interrupted in the early morning on August 1. On the opposite side of the James River from Harrison's Landing was Coggin's Point jutting out into the river. Here the width of the river was reduced to a mere 1,000 yards. During the last couple of days of July the Confederates had silently and without detection positioned 43 pieces of artillery and aimed them at the Federal fleet and the camps at the landing. At 1 A.M. on August 1, they unleashed their guns. Pvt. Rand wrote of the scare the Federals got from the shelling:

> well last night it was dark and rainy and about one o'clock we were woke up by heavy and rapid cannonading. we put on our shoes pretty quick you had better believe and looked around to see what was the trouble and we soon found out the Enemy under cover of the river the darkness had got their guns placed on the bluff on the opposite side of the river and was amusing themselves by shelling our transports and camps. it wont long before our gunboats and batteries got to work and there was a pretty noisy time. Some of them big guns on the boats would sound just like thunder only quicker noise but full as loud and it was so dark we could see their shells going in every direction. it was like pictures you have seen where they have been shelling places and you could see the marks that denotes the course the shells had taken. well they kept it up an hour or so and then stoped and all was quite.[99]

The bombardment only lasted about a half an hour, and Union losses were light with 10 men killed and 15 wounded. On August 3, McClellan sent a force across the river and secured the point to preclude any further surprise attacks.[100]

Capt. Solon Eaton, commander of Co. K, left on August 3 to receive a commission as major in the newly formed 10th Vermont Infantry. He was replaced by Erastus Ballou. About the same time, Capt. Richard Smith, commander of Co. E, was discharged for disabilities and was replaced was 1st Lt. Orville Bixby from Chelsea.[101]

Captain Erastus Ballou, commander of Company K. USAMHI.

Near the end of July, intelligence reports indicated the Confederates were pulling units away from Richmond, and Halleck ordered McClellan to start a new push against Richmond. On August 5, McClellan assembled an expedition of infantry and cavalry, 17,000 men in all, led by Gen. Hooker to retake Malvern Hill. Officially, McClellan's purpose was to follow orders; privately, his motivation was to embroil himself in a contest that would forestall Halleck's evacuation order. Hooker's force drove in the enemy's pickets and he occupied the area. On the night of August 6 the Confederates closed in and McClellan's resolution evaporated. He withdrew his units to the safety of Harrison's Landing the next morning.[102]

After the Malvern Hill expedition went sour, McClellan could no longer justify maintaining his position on the James and preparations were started to move the army. Lt. Leach wrote on August 10:

> The removing of the sick and the removing of some other things have looked like a move from this point and tonight we have orders that show that a move is to be made in some direction. All surplus baggage is packed and at the quartermasters tonight including the men's knapsacks and if I am good

at guessing, we shall be farther from Richmond in a very short time than we are now. The knapsacks of the men were packed Sunday night.

He wrote later:

Thursday night before we left Harrison's Landing, Joseph Morton, Company H of Cambridge, died of a sore throat. We expected to start the next morning and we made a box and dug a grave and buried him at night. I have read of midnight burials but never attended one before. I suppose his body will rest all the same.[103]

Smith's division, again rear guard for the army, did not leave Harrison's Landing until August 16 several days after the move began. "We left camp about 4 o'clock on Saturday afternoon," remembered Lt. Leach, "and marched 5 or 6 miles and halted for the night [at Charles City Court House]. All the baggage wagons had left before we started." Part of the delay was the 25-mile-long wagon train that preceded the Sixth Corps. Col. Whiting stated, "It was forty-five hours after the first train passed, till our brigade, next to the last, passed out."[104]

Twelve miles were made on August 17 bringing Smith's men to the Chickahominy River, where they crossed a 2,000-foot pontoon bridge spanning the river and camped for the night. On Tuesday, August 19, they reached Williamsburg, passing by the College of William and Mary and the old Virginia Capitol. They camped that night near the spot where they had witnessed the battle of Williamsburg.[105]

The march down the Peninsula continued for two more days with camps at Yorktown, Big Bethel, and finally Hampton on August 22 where the Vermont Brigade remained until the next day.[106]

Being back in civilization, the Vermonters wasted no time looking for decent food, as Pvt. Kirk Rand related:

as soon as we camped we all left and after a while you could not see a soldier but what he would have a big melon, a bucket of peaches, apple pies, can of oysters and so on. every one had enough to last a small family 6 weeks. well the amount of it was most of us got sick and then we stoped eating and came to the conclusion that salt beef and Bread was as good for a mans health as anything.[107]

On Sunday morning, August 23, the 2nd Vermont marched out of Hampton to Fort Monroe where it boarded a steamer and sailed up the Chesapeake Bay to the Potomac River, leaving the Peninsula in its wake. Pvt. Rand probably expressed the feelings of everyone in the 2nd Vermont when he wrote, "got all boarded about 11 o'clock and the order was given to cast lose and we bid farewell to the Peninsula without sheding a tear."[108]

CHAPTER 6

"The Greatest Battle Yet Fought"

While McClellan's army was campaigning on the Peninsula, the federal government created a new army on June 26, 1862. Although named the Army of Virginia, it was more a collection of units than a real army. Its mission was to protect Washington and the Shenandoah Valley and to move east of the Blue Ridge Mountains to draw Confederate troops away from Richmond. It consisted of three corps with a strength of about 47,000 men.[1]

Maj. Gen. John Pope, who had a successful career with the Army of the Mississippi, reluctantly accepted command of the Army of Virginia on June 27. Unfortunately in his acceptance address, he maligned his units as well as the units of the Army of the Potomac.[2]

Robert E. Lee was now in a very tenuous position. The Army of the Potomac lay on the outskirts of Richmond. Burnside's army of 7,500 men was at Newport News, Va. Burnside was something of a wild card with the ability to march up the Peninsula to reinforce McClellan or move up the south side of the James and attack Petersburg. Finally, Pope could drive south to link with McClellan.[3]

Lee watched and waited. Then on July 12, Pope left Washington. Knowing he could not wait and withstand an attack from the combined forces of McClellan and Pope, Lee sent Jackson with two divisions to intercept Pope. The two forces clashed at Cedar Mountain on August 9. Pope's men were driving the Confederates until Ambrose P. Hill's division delivered a crushing counterattack and the Union forces fell back.[4]

By now, Lee knew that McClellan's army was being withdrawn from the Peninsula to reinforce Pope. Seeing an opportunity to strike Pope before this junction could take place, Lee moved with Longstreet's corps to join Jackson. Due to a series of Confederate blunders, Lee's anticipated attack never materialized, and Pope was allowed to escape.[5]

Finally, refusing to abandon the hope of a decisive blow against the enemy, Lee adopted a bold plan to send half his force on a wide strategic envelopment to get astride the Federal line of communication and then to follow a day later with the rest of his army. On the morning of August 25, Jackson, with Stuart's cavalry, left on his raid.[6]

Pope observed Jackson's movement on August 25 but assumed he was returning to the Shenandoah Valley and therefore did not order a pursuit. Longstreet kept up his activity on August 25, but the next day left to rejoin Jackson.[7]

Pope was content to maintain his position along the Rappahannock on August 26. Later in the evening when he learned that Jackson had raided Bristoe Station, he started withdrawing. He ordered his corps to concentrate between Jackson and Longstreet. Pope's forces, now numbering 75,000, had an excellent opportunity to hold off Longstreet's 30,000 troops and defeat Jackson's 24,000.[8]

Jackson's men destroyed the Federal depot at Manassas Junction on the evening of August 27 and then moved north of Groveton, where Jackson could hold off Pope if necessary. Pope, however, had lost track of Jackson. Pope moved to Manassas on August 28, but the Confederates were gone. Getting reports of the enemy in Centreville and assuming this was the entire Confederate force, Pope ordered all his units to converge there. Brig. Gen. Rufus King's division, moving toward Centreville, was fired on at Groveton, causing a small, inconclusive battle. Pope again thought he was up against Jackson's retreating column.[9]

On August 29, Pope, again missing an opportunity to destroy Jackson, conducted a series of piecemeal frontal attacks, all of which failed to drive Jackson's men from an unfinished railroad cut.[10]

While Pope's army was sparring with the Confederates, the 2nd Vermont arrived at Aquia Creek on the Potomac River on August 24. The Sixth Corps's initial order was to disembark there and march overland to reinforce Pope, but because the wharves were so crowded with the supplies, its destination was changed to Alexandria, which it reached at 9 A.M. the next morning. By the time it landed, the men were tired and filthy. "You better believe we were a dirty lot," wrote Chester Leach, "as our clothes were all sent on the boat before we started and we have not seen them since. A fortnight without changing and a week's march in the dust where you can hardly see does not leave one very clean."[11]

The Vermonters loafed around the wharf until their gear was unloaded in the afternoon and then moved three miles out of Alexandria, camping near Fort Ellsworth.[12]

Rather than rushing to the front to assist Gen. Pope, the Sixth Corps lay in its camps until August 29 waiting for the horses to pull its artillery and transport wagons. After their experience on the Peninsula, not everyone in the 2nd Vermont was eager to go to the front again. Eight men deserted on August 28 after orders were issued to move out the next morning. Another six would "go over the hill" between August 29 and 30. This loss of men occurred in spite of close security, as described by Pvt. Warren Leslie: "we are about two miles from the city with a guard around camp so we can't get wood enough to cook our coffee nor we can't get a drop of water without a Corp. to go with us and the men begin to feel pretty cross. Some would as quick fight for old Jeff [Davis] as for the Union but I think that times can't last all ways so."[13]

Franklin finally moved his corps on Friday, August 29 with Smith's division leading the way, as battle was raging at Manassas. He stopped at Annandale after making only seven miles. Smith had received reports that a large Confederate force was at Fairfax Court House, and being short of ammunition, he was reluctant to proceed on.[14]

During the night ammunition arrived, and the next morning the Sixth Corps marched toward the sound of the fighting. Pvt. Hapgood noted the occasion in his diary, "Start again this morning and go 14 miles to Centreville and then go out about 3 miles beyond and almost to the battlefield where we stop a little while and then come back to Centreville in the dark and stop for the night. Wounded coming in here all the time."[15]

Pvt. Wilbur Fisk thought things looked a little ominous when he wrote:

> Before we arrived at the old battle-field things began to look suspicious. The road was full of wounded, some on foot, some in ambulances, hurrying as it seemed to a place of safety. Instead of shouting Jackson is cornered, the boys now changed their tune and called it Bull run No. 2.[16]

Without firing a shot, the Sixth Corps returned to Centreville at nightfall. The regiments were drawn up in line of battle across Warrenton Turnpike to turn back stragglers and shirkers.[17]

Sunday, August 31, the Sixth Corps remained at Centreville. The scene was worse than the day before. With the battle over, thousands of stragglers and wounded wandered about in a miserable rain without knowing or caring what had become of their commands, and long columns filed past to take up new positions. The appearance of these skeletons of units bore witness to the toll the terrible long series of engagements had brought.[18]

On Monday morning, September 1, the Sixth Corps moved toward Fairfax Court House but was ordered back to Centreville for an attack that never came and it returned to Fort Ellsworth around 10 P.M.[19]

The trip back to Alexandria was completed in about seven hours, despite the muddy roads, rather than the 50 hours needed to make the trip out. Many people then, as well as now, believe the foot dragging on the part of McClellan and his cronies was intentional in retaliation for Pope's stinging insults in his acceptance address. This thought is for good reason. In McClellan's own report, he states that when asked by Lincoln what should be done to help Pope, McClellan replied, "I am clear that one of two courses should be adopted: First, to concentrate all our available forces to open communications with Pope; Second, to leave Pope to get out of his scrape, and at once use all our means to make the capital perfectly safe." It is not the intent of this work to delve into this controversy, but to illustrate why the Federal troops had a hard time understanding how the army worked.[20]

Disgusted with the army's performance, Capt. John Tyler complained, "Well! Here we are, where we were a year ago and here we shall probably be for some time longer. I am ashamed of myself & the army & feel generally disgusted with the way affairs are managed. Yet still & ever for the glorious old Union."[21]

By his own recommendation, Gen. Pope was relieved from command on September 2, and McClellan was given overall command of both armies. For the next week the whole army was busy in a reorganization. Maj. Gen. Nathaniel P. Banks was given command of three corps for the defense of Washington, and McClellan retained the other five.[22]

During this lull, Lee's army disappeared for a short while but was soon found to be heading to Maryland. Lacking sufficient resources in Northern Virginia to feed his army, both men and horses, Lee decided to take his army north. In addition to the full larder in Maryland, he hoped the invasion might cause an uprising by the already sympathetic Marylanders. If this was possible and with Washington surrounded by a large Confederate force, Lee reasoned the Federals would stay north of the Potomac, taking the pressure off Virginia. Finally, a significant victory in the North might earn diplomatic recognition from Great Britain and France and thereby garner direct military aid.[23]

From the time the Vermonters reached their camp on September 1 they had little to do except rest and recuperate. Lt. Col. Joyce, Maj. Walbridge, and Asst. Surgeon Sawin had a delightful surprise when their wives joined them in camp on September 4, and as Lt. Leach put it in his dry New England wit, "it seemed to be a happy meeting." Unfortunately this reunion was short lived as McClellan moved his army out of its camps around Washington in the pursuit of Lee on September 6.[24]

The Sixth Corps's route of march took it across Long Bridge, through Washington and Georgetown, to Tenallytown where it camped for the night. Lt. Leach thought, "It seemed almost like home to be in Washington and Georgetown." The corps did not leave Tennallytown the next day until almost dark and made six or eight more miles. It pushed on steadily for the next four days, stopping on September 11 near Barnesville, Md., where the 2nd Vermont's skirmishers exchanged shots with a small rebel rear guard.[25]

While able to feed his army in Maryland, Lee still had to bring his ammunition down the Shenandoah Valley. Harpers Ferry, garrisoned by Federal troops, was only 16 miles from this route and had to be neutralized. In one of his most audacious moves of the war, Lee split up his already outnumbered army. On September 9 he ordered the capture of Harpers Ferry. To seize the town, Maj. Gen. Lafayette McLaws with his division and Maj. Gen. Richard H. Anderson's division would cross South Mountain and approach Harpers Ferry from the northeast, taking Maryland Heights. Brig. Gen. John G. Walker was to move to Loudoun Heights southwest of Harpers Ferry, while Stonewall Jackson, with a larger force would cross the Potomac above Harpers Ferry and come down on the town from the west. In the meantime, Longstreet would move northwest from Frederick, cross South Mountain at Turner's Gap and move to Hagerstown. After the capture of Harpers Ferry, which Lee anticipated by September 12, the army would reconstitute at either Boonsboro or Hagerstown. One copy of Lee's order was lost near Frederick. A Federal soldier found it on September 13 and forwarded it up the chain of command to McClellan. McClellan now had an opportunity to destroy Lee's splintered force.[26]

The day before Lee's lost order was found, "Baldy" Smith's division passed the southern foot of Sugar Loaf Mountain and camped near the Baltimore and Ohio Railroad line. On September 13, it followed the railroad to Adamstown, Md. about eight miles from Frederick, and camped.[27]

While at Adamstown, Lt. Col. Joyce's health gave out and he was admitted to an army hospital in Frederick. Col. Whiting's health was also declining due to chronic diarrhea. On September 22, he was granted a 20 day leave of absence to go home to recuperate. Maj. Walbridge would command the 2nd Vermont during the entire Maryland Campaign. Whiting and Joyce did not rejoin the regiment until October.[28]

In addition to Whiting and Joyce, another member of the 2nd Vermont was hospitalized on the march north. Because of a hernia, Pvt. Auburn T. Patch, a member of Co. C and a native of Benson, was sent to the Harewood General Hospital in Washington. He was kept in a ward until December when he was assigned to the hospital's provost guard. In January 1863, Patch asked the surgeon what they were going to do with him. After several evasive answers, the surgeon finally told Patch they were going to operate. Patch was determined that no army sawbones was going to cut on him. On February 3, he got a pass to go downtown but instead went home to Vermont. By the end of November 1863, Patch felt well enough to go back to his unit and returned to Washington and turned himself in on December 5. He was tried by a general court-martial for desertion on December 29, 1863. The officers of the court apparently shared Patch's feelings toward army doctors and reduced his charge to absent without leave. His only punishment was a $10 a month fine for five months, he also had to make up the time he spent in Vermont after his normal expiration of service.[29]

After verifying the authenticity of Lee's lost order, McClellan issued orders to his corps commanders. He gave Franklin the picture in detail, telling him about finding Lee's lost order and explaining the positions of Lee's troops. Franklin was ordered to move at daybreak in the morning, September 14, for Crampton's Gap. Once through the gap, his first duty was to cut off, destroy or capture McLaws's command and relieve the Union troops at Harpers Ferry. After that, depending on events, he would either rejoin the main army at Boonsboro or move west to Sharpsburg to cut off Lee's retreat. To make it perfectly clear, McClellan added, "My general idea is to cut the enemy in two and beat him in detail." McClellan also gave Franklin the option to change any details of the order as he saw fit; unfortunately, he did not emphasize the sense of urgency.[30]

While the Sixth Corps was to be taking Crampton's Gap, McClellan's First and Ninth Corps were to force passage through Turner's Gap, seven miles to the north. Clearing Turner's Gap would open the way for the rest of the Army of the Potomac to attack the other half of Lee's divided army.[31]

Not a man to exceed his orders, Franklin did not move until the next morning, September 14, at 6 A.M., and at a leisurely pace crossed Catoctin Mountain at Mountville Pass and descended into the Catoctin Valley. Around 10 A.M., he halted his corps three miles west of Jefferson to wait for Maj. Gen. Darius N. Couch's division, which had been temporarily attached to his corps, but Couch never appeared. Near 11 A.M., Franklin moved on. The lead elements of Slocum's division which was spearheading the Sixth Corps bumped into Confederate pickets in the village of Burkittsville around noon and quickly cleared them away. Instead of trying to secure the gap, Franklin halted his men for lunch while he assessed the situation.[32]

Burkittsville lies at the eastern foot of the South Mountain range. Here the mountain has a gap called Crampton's Gap. West Main Street, running out of the village of Burkittsville, and the Arnoldstown Road both run in a westerly direction toward the gap. As both roads begin their climb to the gap, they are bisected at the foot of the mountain by the Mountain Church Road, which in 1862 was intermittently lined on one side or the other with rail fences and stone walls. The sides of the mountain are wooded and steep, with numerous outcroppings of rocky ledges.[33]

McLaws had placed Brig. Gen. Paul Semmes in charge of the defense of Crampton's Gap and Brownsville Pass. Brig. Gen. William Mahone's brigade, now under the command of Col. William A. Parham, reinforced Semmes's brigade. In this position of natural defense, the Confederates had stationed the 2nd and 12th Virginia Cavalry Regiments under the command of Col. Thomas T. Munford and the 16th Virginia Infantry Regiment from Mahone's brigade at the foot of the mountain below the gap. The 2nd Virginia cavalry held the Confederate right. It was ensconced behind a stone wall west of David Arnold's barn. Connecting with 2nd Virginia's left were eight companies of the 16th Virginia infantry. The 16th Virginia's other two companies manned the intersection at the summit of the pass. The 12th Virginia Cavalry held the left flank along Arnoldstown Road. Parham's other four infantry regiments were on duty on the west side of the mountain.[34]

A mile south of Crampton's Gap, Semmes's brigade, one of the brigades the Vermonters had faced at Savage's Station, and the six guns of Capt. Basil C. Manly's Battery A, 1st North Carolina Artillery battery, defended Brownsville Gap. All the other Confederate units in the immediate area were on the west side of the mountain in Pleasant Valley, in and around the villages of Brownsville and Rohrersville. From the Confederates' position on top of the mountain, the Federals had been under observation coming from Jefferson since about 9 A.M. that morning.[35]

When the Sixth Corps's advanced skirmishers came within one half mile of Burkittsville, Manly's artillery at Brownsville Pass and Chew's battery and the Portsmouth

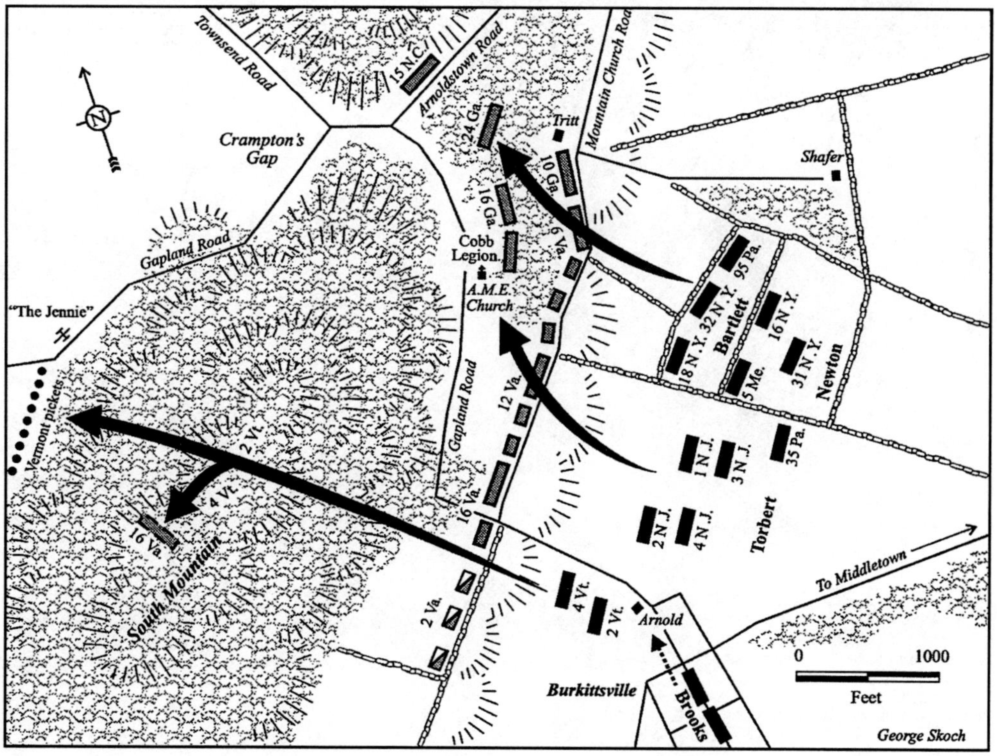

The Battle of Crampton's Gap, September 14, 1862

Light Artillery unleashed their fury. Slocum arrived around 1 P.M., got his units under cover on the right side of the village, and waited for further orders. In mid-afternoon, Col. Joseph J. Bartlett, commanding Slocum's Second Brigade, was selected to lead the attack on Crampton's Gap. Bartlett led with his brigade and was followed by Slocum's other two brigades commanded by Col. Alfred T. Torbert and Brig. Gen. John Newton. Brooks's Vermont Brigade on the left side of the village would support Slocum's division and was to protect the left flank.[36]

While Franklin got his 12,300 troops fed and determined what he was going to do next, the Confederate commanders called for reinforcements. Parham recalled his 6th and 12th Virginia Infantry Regiments from Brownsville. Semmes sent over, from his position at Brownsville Pass,

Private Alden C. Loomis, Company H, wounded at Burkittsville, Maryland, September 14, 1862. Ed Italo Collection.

the Tenth Georgia Infantry Regiment. The 12th Virginia Infantry went into position on the left flank of the 16th Virginia Infantry. The 6th Virginia Infantry fell in on the 12th Virginia's left. The 10th Georgia fell in on the 6th Virginia's left, anchoring its left flank on the Susan Tritt Farm. Capt. Roger P. Chew's Virginia artillery and a section of the Portsmouth (Va.) Light Artillery were set up opposite the Ceres Bethel African Methodist Episcopal Church on Gapland Road. Even with all the additional units, the Confederates still only had about 1,700 men with which to face Franklin's entire corps. The Confederates' fate was already sealed; they just did not know it yet.[37]

At 4 P.M., Col. Bartlett started forward. As soon as he had maneuver room, Col. Torbert moved New Jersey Brigade to the left of Bartlett with his left flank guiding on Main Street. Newton followed Bartlett's and Torbert's brigades as support. By the time the two lead brigades got on line about 300–400 yards from Mountain Church Road, they were pinned down by Confederate artillery on the mountain and rifle fire from the troops behind the stone wall in their front. For the next 20 minutes Slocum's men banged away at the rebels while final arrangements were made to charge the mountain.[38]

The Vermont Brigade had been resting to the left and rear of Burkittsville since arriving. The men were lucky enough to have been treated to refreshments as recalled later by Corp. Oramel Howe, "The patriotic ladies of this little village were very brave and kind to us, dispensing coffee and bread, even while we were being shelled from off the South Mountain by rebel guns." Lt. Leach recorded, "One man, Loomis [Alden C. Loomis], was wounded [slightly] in our Co. while we were lying down in the road just as we left the village. Others were injured in the Regt. at the same time, but I guess none mortally." Their respite was brought short with orders from Gen. Smith to support Slocum's division. Brooks selected the 4th Vermont to lead the assault with the 2nd Vermont following close behind. The other Vermont regiments were held in reserve.[39]

As Bartlett's brigade moved out on the right of the village, Brooks's Vermonters, with a loud hurrah, leaped up and headed through Burkittsville toward the Confederates. As the Green Mountain Boys passed through the village, residents who had not left their homes cheered them as they passed by. Lt. Leach recalled later:

> When you want to see joyful faces, go into a village after they have been under fire, & if you want to see anxious faces look at villagers while shot & shell are coming among them as was the case when we marched through Burkittsville on Sunday the 14th, & the Rebs shelling as some were in the street & some looking out from behind half-closed doors, some wishing every Rebel killed, some offering anything they could do,

& others offering to take care of the wounded if they would bring them there, etc.[40]

After clearing the village, the Vermonters, in one long column, poured down West Main Street toward the Arnold Farm under a plunging fire from the mountain. As the 4th and 2nd regiments entered the Arnold's barnyard they were protected from 2nd Virginia Cavalry's dismounted sharpshooters by the Arnold barn. David Arnold had recently harvested a bountiful hay crop that had been heaped into a huge stack at the barn's left or south side, ready to be hoisted into the loft. Here the 4th Vermont captured 20 rebels hidden behind the haystack. Due to the limited space, the other Vermont regiments were left spread out along West Main Street from the Arnold Farm back toward Burkittsville.[41]

As soon as the first two Vermont regiments reached the safety of the barnyard, Brooks and his staff rode up. Lt. Abel Parsons of the 4th Vermont was ordered to ride out past the left of the haystack to determine the enemy strength. Parsons cautiously rode out into the open and immediately started drawing enemy fire which fortunately was too high to hit him. He quickly returned to tell Brooks that the back side of the stone wall at the far end of the field was filled with rebels. Brooks, not one to get overly excited, turned to the lieutenant and calmly, but loud enough for the troops nearby to hear, replied, "I don't think there are quite so many as all that," and ordered his two regiments to form in line of battle.[42]

The 4th Vermont filed out from the protection of the barn and formed in an open field. John Colin of the 4th Vermont said later, "We did not let grass grow under our feet in executing this maneuver for obvious reasons." The 2nd Vermont followed suit behind the 4th. For about ten minutes both regiments were exposed to the enemy artillery fire from the mountaintop and rifle fire from behind the stone wall, both of which thankfully were generally go over their heads.[43]

At about 5:30 P.M. as Bartlett was about to move his brigade forward, the two New Jersey regiments on Torbert's far left jumped the gun and ran toward the base of the mountain. Seeing the New Jersey Brigade moving out, Brooks gave the order for the 4th and 2nd Vermont to advance. With their battle lines formed and bayonets fixed, the Vermonters charged at the double-quick simultaneously with the Jerseymen on the right, charging square into the 2nd Virginia Cavalry and 16th Virginia Infantry firing from behind their stone wall.[44]

Parham's infantry and Munford's troopers fired as fast as they could, but it was plain to every one of them that they were about to be overwhelmed by the blue wave. Companies A and B of the 16th Virginia turned and ran for the woods behind them and scrambled up the steep mountainside, dropping knapsacks and canteens and anything else that would slow them down as the Green Mountain Boys charged toward them. The other companies of the 16th Virginia on the other side of West Main Street did the same as the Jerseymen came at them taking flight up Gapland Road with the troopers of the 2nd Virginia Cavalry already well ahead of them. When the Vermonters reached the stone wall that the rebels had just vacated, they stopped for several minutes to pump lead into the fleeing gray-backs.[45]

After jumping over the stone wall, the Vermonters headed west about 400 yards and penetrated the woods along the base of the mountain. A sheer rock ledge brought them to a halt. Rather than move to the right to avoid the ledge which was already crowded with New Jersey troops, the Green Mountain Boys, who were used to steep mountainsides in their native state, climbed it with their bare hands and struggled on through the bushes to the top of the mountain.[46]

A half-hour prior to the Sixth Corps' assault at around 5 P.M., Munford requested to be reinforced by Brig. Gen. Howell Cobb's brigade. Cobb sent in the 15th North Carolina and 24th Georgia Infantry first. The 15th North Carolina was posted along the Arnoldstown Road while the 24th Georgia was situated in the woods in a ravine just below the east side of the gap. The Cobb Legion infantry followed by the 16th Georgia Infantry was sent up the mountain next and moved down the east side to a position just below the Ceres Bethel African Methodist Episcopal Church. Cobb's men had no more than reached their position when the Southern troops who had been fighting along the Mountain Church Road came clambering up the hill in retreat. Cobb's men did their best to hold back the Yankees, but they too were overwhelmed and had to give way.[47]

After the Green Mountain Boys reached the top of the mountain, Brooks ordered the 4th Vermont's 1st Lt. George Hooker to take four companies of his regiment and silence the guns near Brownsville Pass that had been tormenting them all afternoon, but Hooker never got that far. Riding ahead of his troops along a little used wagon track, Hooker ran into a group of rebels. They were 116 men from the 16th Virginia Infantry rallying on their colors and their leader, Maj. Francis D. Holladay, for withdrawal to Brownsville Pass. Hooker rode up to the group and without hesitation ordered their surrender telling them that his regiment was almost upon them. The ruse worked and Hooker ended up with Holladay's sword and the 16th Virginia's colors. Leaving two companies to guard the prisoners, Hooker and the other two companies sprinted on toward the cannons but they had already limbered up and moved out before the Vermonters could reach them.[48]

While the 4th Vermont was capturing the 16th Virginia, the Confederates continued their retreat up the mountainside. There was a brief stand at the summit, but Cobb could not rally enough of the retreating rebels to stem the tide of blue that was pouring into the gap. Col. Munford stated in his official report, "they behaved badly and did not get into position before the wildest confusion commenced, the wounded coming to the rear in numbers and more well men coming with them. Gen. Cobb attempted to rally the men, but without the least effect, and it would have been as useless to attempt to rally a flock of frightened sheep."[49]

During Cobb's attempt to halt his men at the gap, Lt. Henry Jennings's two-gun section of the Troup Artillery came rolling into the gap. One gun named "Jennie" was positioned on the left fork of the road and the other, "Sallie Craig," on the right. During the few minutes it took to unlimber and load the two guns, the Yankees popped up over the crest of the gap only to be knocked back by blasts of canister. The two guns held out for a while but were soon threatened with being overrun by the New Jersey troops. Both pieces were forced to limber up and retreat back down the west side of the mountain. By all accounts the "Jennie" had been struck by numerous bullets during her short exchange, and during her bumpy gallop down Gapland Road the axle broke, leaving the gun leaning precariously to one side as she dragged to a dead halt. The gun crew quickly cut the horses loose and rode off.[50]

While Lt. Hooker was capturing the 16th Virginia, the 2nd Vermont rolled on down the backside of the mountain looking for some rebels to fight. Finding no one to take on, they halted at the foot of the mountain. Here the men policed up gear left by the rebels to include the disabled "Jennie." One young soldier in Co. C wrote, "At the foot of the mountain they left everything, guns, knapsacks, blankets, &. Our men got the things they left and the next day we had a great time looking them over and reading their letters." Lt. Leach profited from the rebels' hasty retreat: "The Rebels left in such a hurry at this place, that they left their blankets & everything & I made out to get a good new woolen blanket & a nice one too. It is a U.S. blanket & I presume was taken at Bull Run this fall from our men. Some found revolvers & all sorts of stuff." Pvt. Hiram Tilly wrote his father, "I got a knapsack, in it was a fine two faced lap robe used I suppose for a blanket some shirts, socks, coat, vest and pants and this paper which I am writing on. some pictures and a lot of letters."[51]

By dark, figuring he had done enough for the day, Franklin had most of his troops assembled around Burkittsville, where they spent the night. Brooks's Vermonters remained on guard at the west foot of the mountain. Couch, who had finally arrived at 10 P.M., was sent to Rohrersville two miles north of the gap. The Confederate troops, after McLaws had persuaded them to stop running, were put into a defensive line across Pleasant Valley, a mile and a half south of Crampton's Gap to protect the Confederate rear.[52]

The Federal loss in the battle of Crampton's Gap was 152 men killed or mortally wounded and 420 wounded. The Vermont Brigade got off lucky, losing only one man killed and 14 wounded in the 4th Vermont, five wounded in the 2nd Vermont, and one officer and two enlisted men killed in the 6th Vermont. In addition to the captured soldiers, Franklin's men also gathered up 700 rifles, one cannon (the "Jennie"), and four stands of colors. Although no accurate figures remain for the Confederates, their loss is estimated to be 179 killed or mortally wounded, 317 wounded and 377 captured. Col. Munford wrote in March 1863, "several of my regiment sealed with their lives the love of country on that rugged mountain side."[53]

The Federal forces at Turner's Gap were not as successful as the Sixth Corps. In a desperate and costly struggle Maj. Gen. D. H. Hill held off the Yankees all day. In performing this feat, Hill lost 2,300 men to the Federal's 1,800. During the night the Confederates withdrew from the gap but had bought the time necessary for Lee to reunite his army.[54]

During the night Franklin received orders for the next day, September 15, to attack and destroy the Confederates and, if possible, to relieve the Union contingent stationed at Harpers Ferry. Franklin's only activity, however, was to move a couple miles down the valley until he ran into McLaws's troops. Fearing he was outnumbered, Franklin set up a defensive position and did nothing as the beleaguered Federal troops at Harpers Ferry surrendered. One of those regiments was Col. George J. Stannard's 9th Vermont Infantry Regiment.[55]

By late afternoon of September 15, Franklin had let McLaws's force escape and rejoin the Army of Northern Virginia at Sharpsburg, Md.[56]

The Sixth Corps continued to wait in Pleasant Valley on September 16 doing nothing but guarding McClellan's flank and listening to the booming of the artillery as Hooker's First Corps initiated an inconsequential attack on Lee's left at Sharpsburg.[57]

Franklin received orders during the night to move the next morning to Keedysville with Smith's and Slocum's divisions. Couch's division was ordered to stay and guard the vacated Harpers Ferry.[58]

The battle of Antietam opened on the Federal right at first light on Tuesday, September 17, and was fought in three separate phases. The morning phase started at dawn with

Hooker's First Corps attacking a plateau thick with rebel artillery on the Union right. If Hooker could take the plateau, he could break through and destroy the Army of Northern Virginia. Jackson's two divisions opposed him. The fighting raged mostly in and around the cornfield, to be distinguished in later years from other cornfields in the area as "The Cornfield," on the east side of the Hagerstown Pike and in the woods between it and the Dunker Church. Over this part of the field, the battle swept back and forth in waves. By 9 A.M., Hooker had been wounded in the foot and had lost nearly a third of his corps.[59]

Maj. Gen. Joseph K. F. Mansfield, commanding the Twelfth Corps which had come to Hooker's aid, now had his turn. In the next two hours, the Federal troops made some headway but eventually, like Hooker's corps, were badly cut up, and Mansfield was mortally wounded.[60]

In the second or midday phase, Gen. Sumner, commanding the Second Corps, sent Maj. Gen. John Sedgwick's division against the Confederate center. Sedgwick's division swept across the cornfield and ran squarely into Jackson and McLaws and was driven back with terrible losses.[61]

Next French's division of Sumner's corps hit Gen. D.H. Hill's division, which was entrenched in a sunken road. The road, an eighth of a mile south of Dunker Church, was a country lane running zigzag east and south from the Hagerstown Turnpike to the Boonsboro Turnpike. Through years of use and erosion, the road had been worn down several feet below ground level. Both sides of the road were lined with snake-rail fences. On the side facing the Yankees, the rebel troops had taken down the rails and piled them up in a low breastwork. The approach to this position would have to be made across open fields with no cover or concealment. Maximizing the advantage of this natural fortification, Hill had placed about 2,500 men.[62]

French's division hit the sunken road, later referred to as Bloody Lane, and was fought to a standstill, losing hundreds of men. By the end of the fruitless assault, the Federals were seriously threatened by a Confederate counterattack on their left flank, but Maj. Gen. Israel B. Richardson's division, Sumner's last uncommitted division, arrived in the nick of time to blunt the Confederate attack.[63]

The appearance of Richardson's men kicked off a chain reaction of events in the sunken road that would almost cause the Confederates to lose the battle. The sight of so many fresh blue-clad troops caused one Confederate brigade to pull out of the crowded road for a better fighting position, but the withdrawal got out of hand, and word quickly passed along the line that there was a general retreat. Panic spread to three newly arrived rebel brigades and the road was lost. Yankee troops ran down the banks of the road, clambered over the rail fence and fired into the backs of the retreating enemy.[64]

Although the Confederate line was temporarily breached, a Federal force sufficient to exploit it never materialized. McClellan let victory slip through his fingers and Lee had time to plug the hole. The battle still continued for a short time, but finally fizzled out. During the final stage of the action, Richardson, the man first offered command of the 2nd Vermont, was mortally wounded and died on November 3.[65]

The Sixth Corps moved as ordered at 5:30 A.M. on the morning of September 17 with Smith's division in the lead and arrived around 10 A.M. as the battle was raging. Franklin posted his corps in some woods in the rear of the Philip Pry House that McClellan was using as his headquarters. Smith was ordered to move his corps quickly to the center of the battlefield to reinforce Sumner.[66]

In column formation with Hancock's brigade spearheading Smith's division, the Sixth Corps forded Antietam Creek and moved south and west across the battlefield. For a while, the column was protected on its right by low undulating ground, a few trees, and an occasional house. Hancock entered the fray first and pushed back the rebel skirmishers, saving several of Sumner's threatened batteries. Hancock was then pulled by McClellan to replace Richardson. In the meantime the Vermont Brigade was dispatched to support Gen. French's weakened right flank. As the Green Mountain Boys entered the open cornfield just south of the Samuel Mumma House, Brooks swung his regiments into line of battle. Almost immediately they came under what Brooks described as "a galling fire of both artillery and sharpshooters." As the Vermont Brigade moved into the Mumma cornfield, Brooks got his men down on the ground in a swale for protection. The brigade's left connected with French's right near the lane leading to the William Roulette Farm. Their right was anchored on the Mumma's lane. Brooks's front was parallel to and about 170 yards from the sunken road.[67]

Franklin and Hancock wanted to attack, but Sumner, shaken by the violence of the morning's combat, refused to allow it. Although Franklin pleaded his case to McClellan, the overly cautious McClellan sided with Sumner. So here the Vermonters would remain for the next 48 hours being sprayed by dirt and rocks from the exploding artillery shells. One of the boys in the 2nd Vermont's Co. C apparently did not mind missing the major part of the battle when he wrote, "They took us on to the field, and as good luck would have it, it was in a place where we did not lose many men, although they shelled us for thirty-six hours, nearly all the time."[68]

Lt. Leach described his involvement in the battle in a letter to his wife:

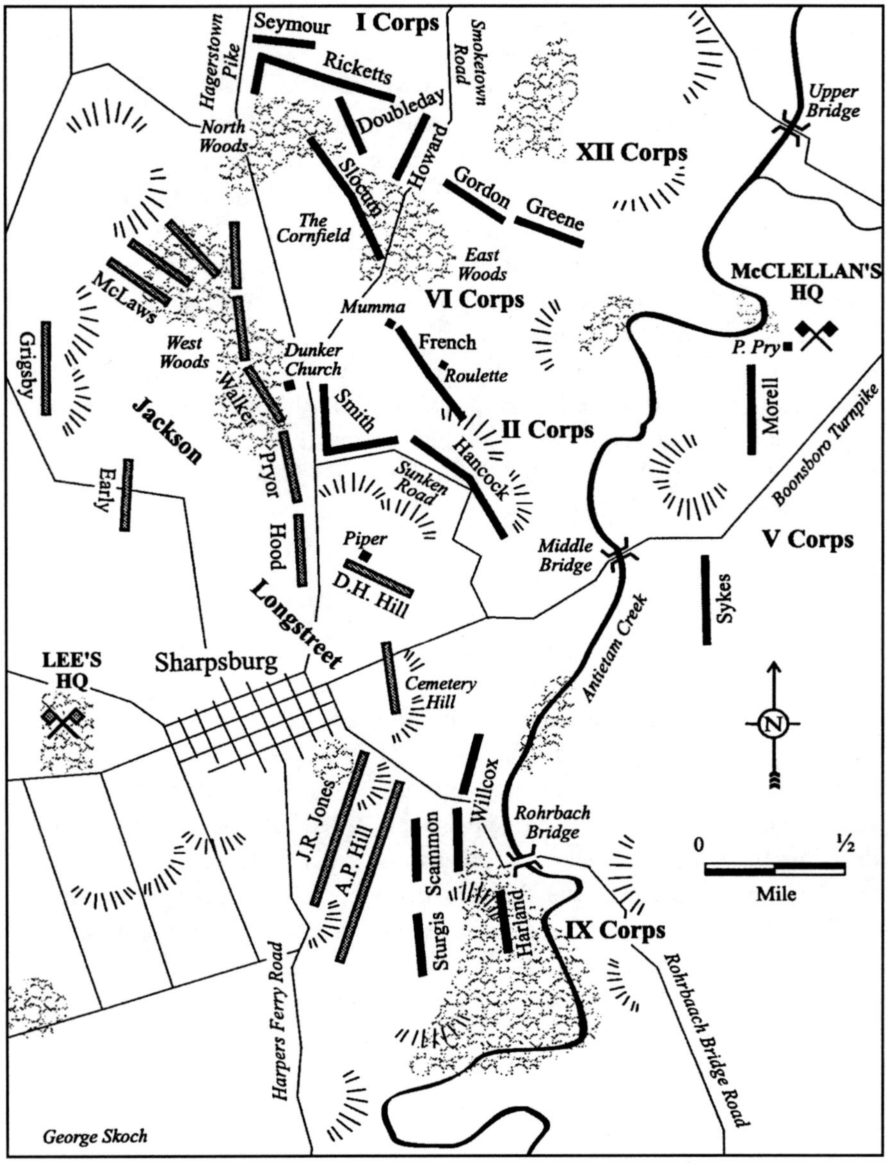

The Battle of Antietam, September 17, 1862

> We were marched to the front as far as possible without being exposed to the batteries & laid down in a corn field, skirmishers thrown out in front. There we lay the rest of the day with now & then a shell bursting over our heads & bullets fired at our skirmishers falling among us & now & then hitting a man.[69]

Brooks was able to keep his casualties to a minimum by keeping his boys flat on their stomachs behind a slight rise in the ground facing the sunken road. The 2nd Vermont had only five men wounded and none killed. While getting into position, Pvt. George W. Pierce of Co. G was hit in the right knee by a shell fragment that knocked him down. In attempting to break his fall he sprained his back and right wrist. None of his injuries were severe, but he was out of action for several weeks. Pvt. Oliver B. Drake of Co. K, a 19-year-old farmer from Bristol, was hit in the right arm by a minié ball. He could only be saved by having his arm amputated. He was discharged for disability in March of the following year. Pvt. Dorr Blood, a 24-year-old hostler from Putney, took a flesh wound in the right thigh, matching the one in his left thigh that he had sustained at Bull Run in the summer of 1861. Although the second wound would never heal properly, he lived until 1895. While lying down with the rest of the regiment, trying to keep out of harm's way, 17-year-old Pvt. Lorenzo J. Marks of Co. G was hit in the right foot by a shell fragment. The wound was minor, and he completed the rest of his enlistment to return home to Shelburne in July 1864.[70]

Brooks roamed back and forth on foot between his regiments, keeping up morale. Unfortunately, he made a handsome target for rebel sharpshooters. During the afternoon, he was hit in the mouth by a minié ball which knocked out two of his teeth. One of his men jumped up and ran to him asking if he was badly hurt. The grizzled old veteran turned to the man, while spitting out a molar, and said, "No, had a tooth pulled!" Although the wound was quite painful, Brooks did not leave his command for medical attention until after dark.[71]

Late in the afternoon there was one flare up in the Vermont Brigade's sector. The 7th Maine was ordered forward to drive some rebel sharpshooters from the buildings on the Piper Farm. The regiment reached the farmyard, chased out the rebels, but became surrounded and had to fight its way out, returning with less than half the men who had gone in. The 7th Maine's commander stated afterward that if the Vermont Brigade had been sent to his support he could have broken the rebel line.[72]

The final action of the Battle of Antietam occurred on the Union left. Gen. Burnside's Ninth Corps was to make an attack against Lee's right flank in the morning, but had been stymied at what would be forever known as "Burnside's Bridge." It was not until the middle of the afternoon that Burnside finally forced passage across the Antietam. Everything seemed to be going his way until A. P. Hill's division arrived on the field from Harpers Ferry and counterattacked, pushing the Ninth Corps back across the creek.[73]

The battle ceased at sundown, and the wounded were gathered the best as possible. All that night the Vermonters lay on their arms in the front line. They had little sleep due to the skirmishers firing at anything that moved. Corp. Oramel Howe remembered:

> After the battle that night, we were sent out on the skirmish line and remained there during the night. We were so situated, that all through the night in front and far to the right and left, the cries and shrieks of the wounded and dying, some begging for water, others to be put out of their misery, some praying and some cussing from their sufferings, were heard. Very little assistance could be given them, for upon the slightest movement on our part, brought the fire of the enemy's pickets.[74]

Under the cover of darkness, the Vermonters could hear the rattles and squeaks of Confederate ambulances as they retrieved their wounded. The men in the 2nd Vermont struggled with trying to relate to the folks back home what they saw around them after the largest and most horrible battle so far experienced in the war. Corp. Howe wrote:

> The battlefield was beyond description. The dead and mangled forms of our men in many cases lay side by side with those of the rebels; for the ground had been fought over many times. In a narrow road in our front [the Sunken Road], a rebel regiment had been posted and was most destroyed by the fire in front and enfilading batteries. In crossing this road it was impossible not to step on a dead body. Some were shot while attempting to get over the fence in their rear and their remains were hanging there.[75]

Another soldier in the 2nd Vermont related:

> In the morning I went out on the field to see the killed and wounded. Such a sight I never saw. All day and night I could hear the wounded crying for water and help, but neither side could get to them without being shot. I saw on one piece not bigger than your garden over one hundred dead rebels.[76]

Pvt. Hiram Tilly of Co. G wrote of the scene before him, "a short distance from me is a road with a rail fence on each side and for nearly ½ mile the road is so full of dead rebels that one could hardly step between the bodies. Some places one two or three deep or lying over each other. on the fence is dead men partly over when killed. the sight is awful." In the same letter, Tilly described his experience when he went to the field hospital to visit his wounded friend Lorenzo Marks: "I was just over to a large barn which is used for a hospital in the yard near the barn is a pile of legs and arms as big as large stack of hay that the surgeons have cut off in the past two days."[77]

McClellan made the biggest mistake of his military career on September 18 by not attacking Lee. Although he had lost 2,108 men killed, 9,549 wounded and 753 missing, the Fifth and Sixth Corps had not yet seen much action. Lee had lost approximately 11,172 men, but McClellan still thought he was outnumbered. He waited until the morning of September 19 to renew the attack, but Lee had already escaped.[78]

The Sixth Corps started after the rebels on September 19, over fields strewn with hundreds of bloated and blackened bodies. The air was thick with the sickening stench of rotting flesh of men as well as horses. Pvt. Tilly, relieved by the move, wrote, "we were all glad to get away from the battle field as the smell was awful. A great number of the dead had to be burned by getting them on some dry rails. There was so many dead that it was impossible to dig graves

Confederate dead in the Sunken Road on the Antietam battlefield. Library of Congress.

Bodies of Confederate dead on the Antietam battlefield. Library of Congress.

> Gen. Brooks' reign was *new* & *novel* to Hagerstown, but it did them good. There were 59 liquor bars, when he assumed control—(all public) & he closed *every one* & kept them so for his whole rule, by military guard.
>
> The people admit that they were never before so well governed or had so quiet a town. No officer or soldier (the guard excepted) were allowed to remain in town after 5 P.M. or to go without the Gen.'s pass.[83]

Life in Hagerstown was easy. The troops had sufficient army rations supplemented with as much of the local poultry and fresh vegetables as the men could buy or steal. The days of loafing and drilling were broken only by heated discussions of Lincoln's newly announced Emancipation Proclamation.[84]

Although the men were enjoying the rest, their uniforms were wearing out, as Leach described:

for them all." The streets of Sharpsburg were filled with disabled wagons and Confederate equipment. Houses were riddled by artillery shells, and structures left intact were being used as hospitals. The Sixth Corps bivouacked that night between the Potomac River and Sharpsburg.[79]

The next day Franklin marched his corps back to Sharpsburg. Corporal Howe wrote, "We followed the retreating army for a day, and we were then ordered to retrace our steps; and passing through Sharpsburg and over the battlefield, the stench was unendurable." After passing over the battlefield the column turned north and marched to Williamsport, Md.[80]

While in camp in Williamsport, Pvt. Cutler wrote to his fiancée what was probably the sentiment of most of the men of the 2nd Vermont, "War! war! war! I have got sick of it, and sick of writing about it, and dearest what shall I write about."[81]

On September 23, the Sixth Corps moved to Bakersville, Md. on the Hagerstown Turnpike and on September 26 marched another 10 miles to Hagerstown. Here it remained for a month, and Gen. Brooks was appointed as the military governor of the town of 5,000 people. The Vermont regiments pulled duty as the provost guard.[82]

Maj. Stephen M. Pingree, of the 4th Vermont, wrote of Brooks's strictness with not only the Vermont soldiers, but the civilians in Hagerstown:

> Our boys were never so destitute of clothing as now. Their knapsacks being sent when we were at Rockville about three weeks ago, & the men, having only the clothes on their backs, have got to be very ragged & a great many just about barefooted.
>
> When they wash their clothes, they have to go without the articles, till they are dry, without they dry them on their backs. The knapsacks are expected here every day, & why they are not along before this time, I can't tell.[85]

On October 8 Leach wrote:

> Our teams have gone to Harpers Ferry today after the knapsacks & baggage. It was brought from Washington to that place on [rail] cars & the teams are now after it & will be back in about three days. The men have never been so dirty as since we left Harrison's Landing, not having any change of clothing, but they have had to do as I have heard them tell about but never saw before.[86]

The men's baggage finally arrived in camp on October 10.

Pvt. Charles Tillison of Co. E and Underhill was not as interested in their lack of clothing as was Leach. His eye was more toward the women of Hagerstown as he included in a letter to a schoolmate back in Vermont, "there are some fine folks there especily of the opposite sex, some with rosy cheeks."[87]

While the Vermonters were lounging around Hagerstown, Lee decided to send Jeb Stuart on another raid around the Army of the Potomac. His objectives were to collect intelligence, destroy a key bridge on the rail line running from Pennsylvania to Hagerstown, and to gather much-needed horses. At dawn on October 10, Stuart, with 1,800 cavalrymen, crossed the Potomac River several miles upstream from Williamsport and began his raid.[88]

By nightfall the Confederates had reached Chambersburg, Pa. The commander of Chambersburg's small home guard immediately surrendered the town when confronted with the daunting force of Stuart's fabled cavalry. The rebels were unsuccessful in doing any damage to the iron railroad bridge but gathered up hundreds of horses and destroyed a quarter-million dollars worth of army supplies stored at its railroad depot, as well as a number of warehouses and a quantity of railroad track. The rebels left town at 9 A.M. the next morning and continued on their way. Stuart and his troopers recrossed the Potomac at White's Ferry near Leesburg on October 12. By the time they returned they had collected 1,200 horses and totally embarrassed McClellan.[89]

The 2nd and 5th Vermont regiments were hurriedly sent by train to Chambersburg in pursuit of Stuart on October 11, but Stuart was long gone by the time they arrived. Maj. Pingree of the 4th Vermont wrote of the operation, "the 2nd and 5th having gone to Chambersburg Penn. for the purpose of *locking* the door 'now the horse is gone' and that the failure of the pursuit was in no way the fault of Gen. Brooks."[90]

The Vermonters returned to Hagerstown around 2 P.M. on October 16. Upon their return, they learned that the 26th New Jersey Infantry had been attached to their brigade. The 26th was a nine-month regiment numbering about 1,000 men. This was the first and only time a non–Vermont unit would be assigned to the Vermont Brigade.[91]

The Green Mountain Boys who by now considered themselves crusty old veterans did not especially care for the newly formed New Jersey regiment. This feeling was reinforced later by the New Jersey regiment's lackluster performance in combat. However, the Jerseymen looked up to the seasoned Vermonters, as one of their soldiers noted, "These were the soldiers whose example became our chief teacher in the art of war."[92]

In addition to the New Jersey regiment, the Vermont Brigade had 250 new recruits join its ranks. To the surprise of Capt. John Tyler, one of the new men in the group was his 15-year-old brother Rufus. Capt. Tyler was not going to have a boy so young exposed to army life, as he wrote his father on October 18:

> I much regret his enlisting. I'll smuggle him home in spite of red tape. He is far too young. He has been quite sick, with the headache for two or three days, but today he is quite well. I think I shall succeed in getting him discharged. The doctor has already put him on the list of unqualified recruits at my special instance and request.

"I am confident of succeeding in obtaining Rufus's discharge, which accomplished I would beseech you all to use your utmost endeavors to keep him clear of the Army," Capt. Tyler wrote his uncle; "I think what little he has seen of the Service will in measure satisfy him." Tyler was successful in getting his brother discharged. In fact, he was discharged several days later without ever being officially assigned to any regiment of the Vermont Brigade.[93]

Rufus Tyler might have been better off if he had stayed in the army. In the fall of 1863 he went to sea and on May 13, 1866, he was killed in a shipwreck on Auckland Island.[94]

October 21 was a sad day for the Vermont Brigade. Their commander, Gen. Brooks, whom the officers and men feared, respected, and loved, was selected to the command of the First Division of the Sixth Corps, replacing Gen. Slocum. Gen. Slocum had been promoted to the command of the Twelfth Corps, replacing Gen. Mansfield. Col. Whiting, as the senior colonel, was put in command of the Vermont Brigade. Lt. Col. Joyce, who had just returned from the hospital, took command of the 2nd Vermont.[95]

Sgt. Charles Morey of Co. E wrote several months later of his fondness of Gen. Brooks in a letter to his mother:

> It was little more than one year ago that we were on drill at Camp Griffin and Genl. Brooks called us d_ _ _d cornstalk militia but at the battle of Fredericksburg one of his regiments broke and run and he told them he had rather have the old Vermont Brigade than that whole division, for, said he, "they will stand." Although he was very rough in his language yet every man in the brigade liked him for he is an excellent commander.[96]

As the end of October approached, the temperature started to dip. Lt. Leach wrote, "Our boys got some overcoats yesterday. They were all furnished with them last spring before going to Fortress Monroe, but they were pretty much all gone. A few from Fletcher & vicinity sent them home, but more of them were thrown away when on the march." Two days later he continued, "There was a very white frost & the ground froze a very little. Our time is pretty well taken up now in drilling. Four drills per day of one hour each, two for the whole & two for the recruits separately."[97]

In the last week of October, the Army of the Potomac finally started to move. After returning to Virginia, Lee had again split his army of approximately 90,000. Jackson was back in the Shenandoah Valley causing trouble, and Longstreet's corps, after leaving the valley to counter McClellan's movement south, was near Culpepper. McClellan's intent was to attack Longstreet before Jackson could come to his aid. At a leisurely pace, McClellan advanced his units across the Potomac River into Virginia on October 26. The Sixth Corps moved out on October 29 to Williamsport, Md., camping for the night where it had camped five weeks before. The Vermonters received two months' pay and marching orders on October 31. The next morning, Saturday, November 1, before the 2nd Vermont moved out, there was a row in Co. A. Pvt. Abel T. Wyman from Dorset decided he could not bear going back to Virginia and deserted. To make matters worse, he stole a pair of good boots from a comrade's tent, leaving his worn out ones in their place. Co. A would not see Wyman again until the next September, when he would voluntarily return to the regiment. After the excitement had subsided, the 2nd Vermont started off toward Virginia, camping that night near Boonsboro.[98]

Whiting had his men moving at first light on Sunday morning and made about 15 miles. They marched through Crampton's Gap and Burkittsville and camped for the night near Berlin [present day Brunswick], Md., to await their turn to cross the Potomac River.[99]

By now the Vermont Brigade had developed its famous marching gait that could out-distance any unit in the army, and the neophyte 26th New Jersey had trouble keeping up on the march as explained by Sgt. Amos J. Cummings:

> Acting Gen. Whiting, Colonel of a Vermont regiment in our brigade, rode at our head, and seemed bent on "bushing" us, if possible. Rests were, like angel's visits, few and far between, and many a weary Jerseyman either slung away his knapsack in toto, or distributed a portion of its contents by the roadside, which exactly suited the cormorant tastes of the Vermonters in our rear. Many an interchange of opinion concerning Col. Whiting revealed the estimation in which he was held by our panting files, and if one-half our wishes that day had been gratified he would have gone to—somewhere several thousand times. Toward night the men began to fall out of the ranks, and your correspondent, with several of Companies B, and A, formed what we called a "Starlight Brigade," and limped into camp at Berlin, on the Potomac, six miles below Harpers Ferry after nine o'clock, footsore, feverish, and altogether fit subjects for a benevolent Almshouse-keeper.[100]

At half past six on Monday morning, November 3, the Sixth Corps was on the march again. It crossed over the Potomac on a pontoon bridge into Virginia. Pvt. Kirk Rand wrote:

> Well Monday morning we crossed over into Virginia once more (and I hope for the last time). we were all feeling well singing and cheering because we had rather spoil this state than any other and I think it will be spoilt this time as the soldiers seem determined not to leave any thing whole. we are now 5 miles from Berlin and I dont believe there is a pig, chicken or a rail fence left behind us. Virginia will wish she hadn't suceeded before this Campaign is over.[101]

The Sixth Corps headed west, passing through Lovettsville, along the base of the Blue Ridge Mountains, reaching the village of White Plains on November 6 where it went into camp. Because of a storm which dropped about three inches of snow, it remained in its camp at White Plains through November 8.[102]

While at White Plains, the Green Mountain Boys went about the usual business of supplementing their rations with whatever they could forage from the surrounding countryside. One afternoon the New Jersey boys from the 26th decided to have a little fun with the Vermonters as told by the New Jersey regiment's Chaplain:

> A pretty good instance of Diamond cut Diamond, or rogue catch rogue, occurred the other night, in this wise: The Vermont Boys, with whom we are brigaded, are adepts at plundering, as I suppose all the old Regiments are, and last night they were leading off in that direction, when some Jersey boys taking some guns and one of them the Colonel's sword, went out and pretended to be the provost guard fell in with some Vt. Boys who were carrying off a yearling which they had taken and killed. They made them "stand and deliver" and ordered them to repair to their quarters, telling them if they were caught again they would at once be reported to Gen. McClellan—the Jersey boys meanwhile appropriating the plunder.[103]

On November 4 Sergeant Cummings also commented on the Vermonters' foraging, which by now they had turned into an art form:

> The Vermonters—in fact all the old regiments—pitched into the chickens and sheep in the vicinity, and soon returned laden with fresh meat, and that of the best kind, while the poor green 26th lay with hungry stomachs, with the exception of a few rabbits which they ran down in the woods and fields adjacent.

On the next day Cummings noted how the Jerseys were trying to imitate the Vermonters:

> Again your correspondent joined the "Starlight Brigade," and again found our camp on a wooded-hill. The campfires

again gleamed, and to some purpose, as the boys "began to learn the ropes" from the Vermonters, and fresh meat made its first appearance in our camp. Cabbages, potatoes, etc., were unearthed, and many a Secesh homestead, in the vicinity, found itself minus of eatables that night. Pig-headed Whiting fired at some of the boys on a foraging excursion, but we did well, nevertheless, and many an empty stomach of the previous night, lay calmly reposing in full glory on the night of Wednesday, November 5th 1862.[104]

The Vermont Brigade was up early on November 9 and marched down the Warrenton Turnpike to New Baltimore and went into camp for a week. During the march the 2nd Vermont along with several other units under the command of Brig. Gen. Francis L. Vinton, commander of Howe's Third Brigade, was detailed as the division rear guard. While slogging through the deep mud between White Plains and New Baltimore, Vinton happened along and told the Vermonters to move along more quickly. Pvt. Ralph Ditty of Co. F and a Roxbury native took exception to the order. Ditty had fallen back about six paces from the rest of his group and caught the general's attention. In Vinton's words:

> I took pains on the way to close up all stragglers.... When I first noticed the conduct of the prisoner as being insubordinate, I was urging up some stragglers belonging to the rear guard and not addressing him (the prisoner) he in an insolent tone said you can't make us go any faster than we can and you can't ride us down much or words to that effect. This called my attention to the prisoner [referring to Ditty]. I saw he was a little behind his guard, so I rushed my horse toward him and ordered him to close up. He jumped to one side, clubbed his piece and lifted it over his shoulder in a threatening attitude to strike. The moment he threatened I checked my horse and dropped the point of my sword to run him through if he did strike and at that moment with a laugh, he stepped into his guard.

Ditty was brought before a court-martial on November 19. He was charged with two specifications in violation of the ninth article of war, which, in short, authorized the execution of any officer or soldier who would strike, draw or lift a weapon, or threaten violence to a superior officer. The first specification was for speaking disrespectfully to a superior officer and the second for threatening a superior officer. At the trial, Ditty's description of the confrontation in the muddy road that day differed from Vinton's. Ditty stated:

> The first I knew of his being an officer he rode his horse close onto me and ordered me to close up. I said I was closing up as fast as I could. He kept along side, his horse pretty close to me. I had to step to one side. He drew his sword at this time and struck at me. He said close up again. I said give me a chance. I walked into the ranks as fast as I could. He ordered the Lieut. of the guard to take my name and have me court martialed. At the time I stepped out to one side of the road, I had to catch hold of my musket with both hands and at the same time, keep his horse off me. I did not attempt to strike the officer at all. My gun had a rubber cover upon it.

Witnesses for Ditty were Capt. Horace F. Crossman; 1st Lt. Elijah Wales; and Pvt. George A. Ayers of Co. F. They all corroborated Ditty's statement, but the court found him guilty of the two specifications. He was not, however, found guilty of violating the ninth article of war. He was sentenced to forfeiture a half a month's pay for three months and had to memorize the ninth article of war and repeat it verbatim to his first sergeant. Considering it was a case of a private's word against that of a general's, he got off fairly easily.[105]

While in camp at White Plains, a big shake up took place in the army, although most of the men were unaware of it for several days. Tired of trying to push McClellan into action, Lincoln relieved him of command of the Army of the Potomac on November 7. Lincoln had visited McClellan's headquarters in early October for several days but was unable to get him to set the army in motion. The officer who had brought the order to relieve McClellan had gone to Gen. Burnside's camp first. He informed Burnside that he had been selected to replace McClellan. Burnside, who was a friend and admirer of McClellan's, immediately declined the offer as he had done after the Peninsula and Maryland campaigns when Lincoln had offered him the command. Burnside was informed that if he did not accept the command it was going to be offered to Gen. Hooker. This changed Burnside's mind. He intensely disliked Hooker and did not want to serve under him and therefore accepted the offer. Burnside then persuaded McClellan to remain in command for a couple of days longer to facilitate an orderly changeover.[106]

McClellan made his farewell review of the army on November 10 at New Baltimore. Both McClellan and Burnside with a large trailing entourage galloped along in front of each corps while batteries fired salutes and bands played. The majority of the regiments cheered McClellan with a wild abandon. Several of the regiments threw down their weapons in a sign of protest of losing their beloved commander while others yelled, "Send him back! Send him back!"[107]

The next day, November 11, McClellan boarded a train at Warrenton Junction bound for his home in Trenton, N.J. That was the last the Army of the Potomac would ever see of him.[108]

CHAPTER 7

"Another Good Defeat"

Burnside wasted no time in reorganizing his army after McClellan's departure. He divided it into three Grand Divisions, as he called them. The Left Grand Division commanded by Gen. Franklin consisted of the First and Sixth Corps. The Center Grand Division commanded by Gen. Hooker consisted of the Third and Fifth Corps. The Right Grand Division commanded by Gen. Sumner was made up of the Second and Ninth Corps. Removing Franklin, Hooker, and Sumner from corps command caused a domino effect in command positions. In the Sixth Corps, Brig. Gen. Albion P. Howe replaced Smith as commander of the Second Division, and Smith replaced Franklin as the commander of the Sixth Corps.[1]

None of these changes was eagerly welcomed by most of the men of the Army of the Potomac who were still stinging from McClellan's removal. They did not know of his arguments with the Lincoln administration or of his disobeying orders. On the other hand, they had no ill feeling toward Burnside, who was well known and respected by the army.[2]

The Vermonters were leery of Howe, who had come to them from brigade command in Couch's division even though he was a New Englander. Nor were they especially happy with Col. Whiting's filling Gen. Brooks's shoes as commander of the Vermont Brigade. The officers and men generally approved of Whiting in camp, where he took good care of his men, but they felt he could not be relied upon in combat.[3]

Burnside did not like McClellan's plan of taking Richmond via the Orange and Alexandria Railroad. Having completed the reorganization of his 125,000-man army, he received reluctant permission from Lincoln on November 15 to move on Richmond by way of Fredericksburg. Burnside's plan proposed a feint toward Culpeper, then making a quick movement down the Rappahannock River and taking Fredericksburg. He figured he could cross the Rappahannock on pontoon bridges at Falmouth and take Fredericksburg before Lee could bring the two portions of his army back together and offer a serious threat. He would establish a new base of supply at Aquia Creek to keep his army fed and armed. Orders were issued for the army to move out the next morning, November 16.[4]

Howe's division moved out at first light and by day's end it had made about 18 miles and went into camp two miles after crossing the railroad at Catlett's Station. By November 18, it had covered another 20 miles and went into camp near Aquia Creek about four miles north of Stafford Court House.[5]

The 2nd Vermont was ordered to guard supply trains on Wednesday evening, November 19. Lt. Leach described the operation:

> Wednesday, just at night, as our Regt. was ordered to go to Aquia Landing as guard to a train going after provisions, so we started out & crossed to the north side of the creek & there had to wait until about nine o'clock before the wagons were collected ready for a start. The right wing of our Regt. went with our division trains & the left wing was left to go with another division's, which did not come that way, so they went back to camp the next day.
>
> We went that night to within sight of the Potomac River & halted until daylight. Then went down the river to the landing, or to the other side of the creek from the landing, for the landing is on the south side & we were on the north side.

The provisions were on boats anchored in the stream & had to be loaded on a flat-bottomed boat & poled over to the shore & something of a job to load 68 teams that were with us.

We worked all day Thursday & at night there were about 20 more to load, so we had to stay over another night. It rained all day Thursday & Thursday night, but we had a deserted house to stay in, so we got along very well. I guess the house will need some repairing before anyone lives in it again, for it furnished shelter & wood also.

We all got back to camp just at night on Friday [November 21], & glad to get back too.[6]

While the men were in this camp at Aquia Creek, trouble that had been brewing in Co. G surfaced. Toward the end of October, 31-year-old Phillips N. Chase, a native of Mt. Holly, had been selected to replace Capt. John Drew. Drew, who had been captured at the battle of Bull Run, had been released from captivity in August but due to his health had resigned. Lt. Weed, who had been commanding the company since Lt. Sharpley had resigned in June, was not happy that he had not been chosen as commander. The reason Weed was not selected may have been because of his drinking, which had also caused him to fall from favor with his men. Pvt. Tilly had noted in October that "the boys don't like Weed as well as they did as he drinks to much." Weed's not being selected for permanent command apparently elevated his consumption of alcohol as Tilly related on October 28, "We think every thing of our new Capt. Chase. Lt. Weed is trying to get out of the army. He is under arrest now for being drunk while out on drill and sassing the Major as I presume he will be sent home. They may as well for he is no good here." Weed would not be released from the service until March the following year. Capt. Chase commanded Co. G until the expiration of his service June 29, 1864.[7]

One reason the men in Co. G may have been so fond of Capt. Chase was his leniency toward their plundering. Pvt. Tilly mentions such an incident in one of his weekly letters to his parents written on November 21:

Day before yesterday our company were ordered out to guard a lot of teams that went out five or six miles in the rebel country after a lot of corn. After getting the corn and on our way back to camp at sun down our Captain "Chase" told us to help our selves to any thing we could find while on our way back to camp. we soon came to a large plantation with the usual number of farm buildings and stock with turkeys and chickens on the roost. To make this story short I will tell you that when we got into camp we had potatoes, cabbage, fresh pork, chickens and turkeys, and a little bag of dried apples. It was dark when some of us were in the hen house. so could only find the chickens by feeling on the roost for them which were higher than our heads. I reached for a chicken and got hold of its wing at the same time as some one else on the other side of the roost got hold of the same chicken. Both of us pulled for it over the roost and the next morning I found only one wing of that chicken in my sack and Sidney [Sidney N. Tilly] had the rest of it. This goes to show that we calculated to take everything we got our hands on. for dinner yesterday we had chicken. Today we had boiled potatoes, cabbage and fresh pork.[8]

Captain Phillips E. Chase commander of Company G. USAMHI.

Pvt. Kirk Rand related how while on detail down at the landing, he had foraged to provide Thanksgiving dinner for himself and several other boys in Co. C:

I brought home 1 hen, 1 good fat rabbit, 6 large turnips, 6 pounds sausage meat, a small bag of indian meal and a ten quart tin of oil. it was taken from the enemies of the Union. all but the hen which I paid for. I got it all to camp and laid it by for my Thanksgiving which was only 2 days off. the first day I worked on my house and the next day our Reg. was ordered on picket. well we came and I left my stuff in camp. Nelson Cole of your place a fellow by the name of Fox [Martin L. Fox] and myself are on post together and put up some rails for a shelter. found some boards for a floor and we have got a fire in front. our hut is on the edge of the creek on a little bluff about 10 feet from the water. it is the most pleasant post I ever had on picket. well last night about 12 Nelson and I got to talking when along came a soldier from the other end of the line and said the whole Division had orders to move at daylight. we did not like it but came morning sure enough they went and we were left on picket till they got their commissary stores along. it will give us about 3 days trip. well this afternoon I began to talk about supper so we played cards to see who should go up to the camp and get my things and Cole had to go and get them. When he came back he had all the things and a table he got in some of the camps where they had left in the morning. we had all the pots to cook them in. Fox went to a house a short distance off and got some potatoes and a hoe cake. I went to work cookin them. I put the rabbit and hen in the pot together and made some stew thickened with meal. boiled the potatoes and turnips and we got them all cooked and ready to eat just after dark. I went and got a fellow that tents with us on another post. we sat the table (it was about 2 feet long by one foot ½ wide). put a rubber blanket on for a cloth. Out with our tin plates and spoons and went to eating and I never enjoyed a supper better. We talked of the folks at home and how they was probably talking about us and wishing we were at home but it will be a long time I am afraid before we shall be at home if we get home at all.[9]

Gen. Sumner, moving at a speed unusually quick for the Army of the Potomac, led his Grand Division to Falmouth on November 17. There were only a handful of rebels on the Fredericksburg side of the river, and he could have made a quick and almost unopposed crossing, but for one thing: The pontoon boats were nowhere in sight. In fact, they were not even on their way south from Washington. So, Sumner sat idle while the rest of the army caught up and let Lee get Longstreet's corps in position on the hills behind the town. This blunder started a chain reaction of events that would make the campaign a tragic disaster.[10]

The 2nd and 5th Vermont regiments were left to guard the telegraph lines and roads above Aquia Creek while the other regiments of the Vermont Brigade moved south with the Sixth Corps on December 3 and made camp at Belle Plains. The 2nd and 5th Vermont left their camps on Aquia Creek on December 9 to rejoin the brigade as explained by Lt. Leach:

The troops all left the place but two or three Regts. soon after we went out on picket & marched to Ball [Belle] Plain, some 12 or 15 miles from our camp on Aquia Creek. We left camp as soon as we could pack up after getting in from picket, but when we had marched a few miles & crossed the railroad at Brookes Station, we found the road full of teams, & we camped for the night, it being impossible to get along.... This morning at Six we started on our march again & came up with the brigade before noon.[11]

The 2nd Vermont's quartermaster, 1st Lt. Lauriston L. Stone, was confident of the army's success in the upcoming campaign when he wrote home to a friend on December 3:

We are under marching orders now. Expect to go nearer to Fredericksburg.... We all hope to see and end to this unhappy & *unholy Rebellion*. Most of our men are in good spirits and eager to go on. The weather is pretty good. Very good for this season of the year. And unless we have long & continual storms soon their is no reason on the account of the roads why we should not proceed on our journey to Richmond. This country is the most desolate and forsaken of any land I ever saw. Every thing for man & beast is eaten. I really do not know what the women & children are going to do for substance. Oh—the *horrors* & *desolations* & mournings of *war*! The South are experiencing these things. The North are not & I hope may never. We hope to go on a campaign soon. Our army has been detained here in front of Fredericksburg. Some little time but what Gen. Burnside is ready the blow will be struck. We all felt it a strange time to remove McClellan. Amid and on a campaign. But all *may* prove for the best. We hope so. Shortly—I think you may hear *good* & *great* news from *this way*.[12]

By December 10, Burnside finally had everything in order for an attack, including the pontoon boats. That day he called his commanders together to give them their orders for the next day. Sumner was to cross the river directly across from Fredericksburg, Franklin was to cross several miles downriver from the town, and Hooker was to be held on the Falmouth side of the river as a general reserve. Burnside's plan had Franklin taking Hamilton's Crossing, outflanking Lee's right and rolling up his line. Sumner was to charge across the river and up Marye's Heights. Lee would then be forced to retreat, but that is not the way it came off. His written orders were not that succinct. Franklin thought he was to conduct a reconnaissance-in-force and Sumner assumed he was to charge a lightly defended position.[13]

Burnside's men would not be attacking lightly defended positions, nor was there any element of surprise left after the two-week delay. Lee now had both of his corps, totaling about 78,000 men, in strong positions on a seven-mile front ranging from Falmouth, north of Fredericksburg, and paralleling the Rappahannock River to Massaponax Creek to the south. Longstreet's corps was covering about five miles of the line from the Confederate extreme left to Deep Run, and Jackson covered the last two miles.[14]

At 5 A.M. in the dark and freezing morning of December 11, Franklin had both his corps up and on the move toward the Rappahannock. As they descended the hill to the river bottom, a dense fog bank blanketed the men's view of the other side of the river. The engineers had been hard at work laying the bridges, but rebel skirmishers had been a problem until a few volleys from Federal artillery chased them off. The men lounged around their crossing points until the bridges were ready. One bridge was completed at 9 A.M. and the other around 11; but when Burnside was notified of their completion, he ordered Franklin to stand fast. The problem was a hold-up in constructing the bridges in Sumner's sector.[15]

As soon as the morning fog had lifted, the engineers laying Sumner's bridges ran into a hornet's nest of Mississippi sharpshooters ensconced in the buildings across the river. Every time the engineers would run out to the end of their unfinished bridges to lay another section, the sharpshooters would send them scurrying back to shore. The Federal artillery on Stafford Heights lent a hand in the form of a 9,000-round bombardment of Fredericksburg, but when the barrage was lifted, the sharpshooters were still there. Finally, several regiments of infantry boarded pontoon boats, quickly paddled across the river, cleared the town of the rebels, and secured the bridgehead.[16]

With Sumner's bridges in place, Franklin was given the nod to send his two corps across, but the order was almost immediately countermanded. Instead, he was told only to send across a brigade to secure the bridgehead for the night. Thus ended the Sixth Corps's action for the day.[17]

The Sixth Corps was ordered back to the hills above the river and bivouacked for the night on the frozen ground. Because the men were in light marching order, tents had been left behind; consequently, they had only their overcoats and blankets for protection against the freezing night.[18]

Before dawn on Friday, December 12, the Sixth Corps was on its way back to the river. Thousands of soldiers were clustered together on the riverbank waiting for their turn to cross. Howe's division crossed at 10 A.M. followed by the First Corps which secured the left of Franklin's line.[19]

Franklin's sector of the operation was a plain that extended from Deep Run on the north to about two miles down river. About one mile in from the river on a slight rise, the Old Richmond Stage Road traversed the plain from left to right. About 600 yards in front of the road and parallel to it ran the Richmond, Fredericksburg and Potomac Railroad. On the far side of the plain was a thickly wooded range of hills that extended from Fredericksburg to Massaponax Creek, which masked Jackson's corps from the Yankees' view.[20]

Gen. Smith described the disposition of his Sixth Corps in his battle report:

> As soon as the crossing was completed and the lines formed, I pushed the command forward, General Brooks holding the Richmond Road and Deep Creek with one line in front of the creek, while General Howe occupied the crest of a hill, over which ran the Richmond Road, his right at a sharp turn of Deep Creek. These movements were all made, when the fog, which had concealed us, lifted, and our lines became visible to the enemy, who occupied the hills in front of us.
>
> The troops were as well protected as the topography would allow, and there was nothing to be done but maintain our skirmish line, which was engaged nearly all the time, and to submit quietly to the feeble and spasmodic artillery fire of the enemy, which both encircled and commanded us.[21]

The Vermont Brigade was formed into double columns and positioned at the rear of the division. Other than the 6th and 4th Vermont regiments serving as skirmishers at various times, the Vermonters lay on the ground all day and night to avoid Confederate rifle and artillery fire.[22]

Franklin had his orders by 7:30 A.M. the next morning, Saturday, December 13. He was to use one division to seize Hamilton's Crossing and be prepared to roll up Jackson's line. The First Corps with Brig. Gen. George G. Meade's division spearheading the attack moved forward at 8:30. By early afternoon it had pushed across the railroad tracks and hit the rebel's first defense line in the woods, but in a bloody counterattack by A. P. Hill's division, the Federals were pushed back.[23]

While the First Corps was engaged with the enemy, the Sixth Corps had been left in place to guard Franklin's right flank and the bridgehead. When the sun drove off the heavy fog later in the morning, Gen. Howe discovered that the enemy had been active during the night reinforcing its skirmish line and moving in additional artillery which kept up a sporadic fire on Howe's men all day.[24]

Before sunrise on December 13, after spending a miserable night on the frozen ground, the Vermonters received their knapsacks and two days' rations. At about 1 P.M. the 2nd and 3rd Vermont received orders to take over the skirmish line. Lt. Col. Joyce rushed the 2nd Vermont forward in the face of Confederate musket and artillery fire, losing several men. While making the rush forward, Corp. Oramel Howe in Co. I had the stock shot off his rifle. Then adding insult to injury, a ball cut his haversack strap spilling all the hardtack he had just received onto the ground. Without thinking, he immediately dropped to his knees and retrieved his food as bullets whizzed all around him. He was teased for years afterward by the members of his company for the ludicrous sight he made that frosty morning.[25]

Pvt. Henry P. Diamond, a 20-year-old farmer from Moretown in Company D, was down at a creek filling his canteen when he saw the regiment moving out. He picked up his knapsack and ran after his unit, unsuccessfully trying to put on his knapsack as he ran. Once he caught up with his company, he told his company commander, Capt. Enoch E. Johnson, that he wanted to stop and put on his overcoat and knapsack. Johnson told him they did not have time. Diamond sat down anyway, put on his things, then started after his company again. Before he reached his company he met one of his friends who had just been wounded. The wounded man who was bleeding badly asked Diamond if he would help him to the hospital. Diamond consented and was not seen by his unit for several days. One of the other privates of Co. D, Chauncy S. Shonio from Duxbury, also fell out of the ranks, but more about Diamond and Shonio later.[26]

As the Vermonters were filing into position on the skirmish line, an artillery round exploded in the midst of Co. A. Pvt. Henry Holden, a 20-year-old machinist from Bennington, was almost on top of the shell when it went off. A fragment of the shell hit his rifle which he was holding at shoulder arms, slamming it into his right side, breaking several ribs. In addition, the concussion threw him several feet backwards and knocked him unconscious as well as causing internal injuries. He was eventually evacuated to a general hospital in Washington where he was discharged as medically unfit for service on June 24, 1864. He would suffer from liver problems for the rest for his life.[27]

Postwar photograph of Henry Holden demonstrating to the U.S. Pension Bureau how he was holding his musket when it was hit by a shell fragment, September 13, 1862. Apparently he brought the damaged musket home as a souvenir. National Archives.

Lt. Col. Joyce got the 2nd Vermont on line and down on the ground as quickly as possible and with minimal casualties. Although being on their stomachs kept the men safe from most rifle fire, the screaming shells bursting overhead and raining down steel and lead were an ever-present danger. Pvt. George G. Center, a Waterbury man in Co. D, became one of those unfortunate casualties when a white hot shell fragment buried into his left hip. He survived the wound and was transferred to the Veteran Reserve Corps on September 1, 1863. He received a disability discharge because of his wound in April, 1864.[28]

The Vermonters continued to hug the ground in relative safety until late afternoon when troops from Brig. Gens. Evander Law's and Dorsey Pender's brigades made a desperate attack on their skirmish line, but the Vermonters held. Lt. Col. Joyce and his men were singled out in Gen. Howe's official report for their steadfastness in fending off the rebels:

> I relieved the first line (General Pratt's) by General Vinton's brigade. Soon after this the enemy, with re-enforced line of

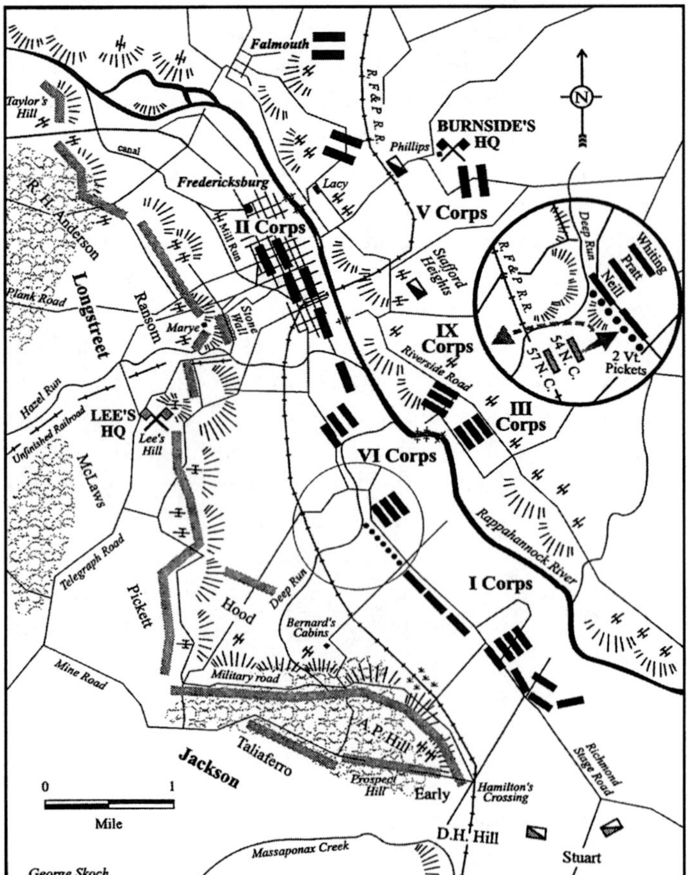

The Battle of Fredericksburg, December 13, 1862

> skirmishers, attempted to drive back our skirmish line, but they immediately came in collision with those hardy veterans of the Vermont Brigade, under Lieutenant-Colonel Joyce, of the 2nd Vermont, and were handsomely repulsed, themselves driven back.[29]

The repulse was not without heavy casualties. Pvt. Edwin M. Turner of Co. D described his wound to his wife in a letter on December 19:

> Perhaps you have heard of it that I am wounded in the right leg, the ball went in about 6 inches above the knee on the inside of my leg and came out at my hip near my pants pocket inflicting a severe flesh wound which is doing well. I am now at Harewood hospital about 2 miles northeast of Washington. I arrived here yesterday afternoon.[30]

Lying on the ground and trying to load a musket was a dangerous operation in the low-flying lead storm. The men were generally safe when pouring in the powder and dropping the minié balls into the muzzles of their rifles, but then they had to elevate the weapon to ram the bullet home. This step of the process was dangerous when the hand and arm were elevated. Pvt. Henry C. Smith of Co. B, a young teamster from Castleton, raised his rifle to ram home the ball and took the impact of a rebel "buck and ball" round. The round ball hit his right hand between the third and fourth fingers, passed through the hand and wrist, and exited out his forearm. Simultaneously one buck shot struck the back of his right hand and passed out the wrist. Another buck shot hit him in the upper right arm where it remained lodged for the rest of his life. His right hand was so mangled that his ring finger had to be amputated. Smith's soldiering days were over, and he was discharged the following May with an arm that he could never use again.[31]

Twenty-year-old Pvt. Henry G. Hemenway, a farmer from Ludlow in Co. I, was a little luckier than Smith. When he raised his left arm to load his musket, he brought down a hand with a neatly amputated little finger. Undeterred, Hemenway merely wrapped his hand and kept on firing. He survived his enlistment with no other wounds and was discharged June 29, 1864.[32]

A second soldier in Co. I, Pvt. William Sinnott, a 44-year-old Irish immigrant and a blacksmith from Duxbury, was struck in the right arm. Even though he was evacuated to Lovell General Hospital in Portsmouth Grove, R.I., the doctors were unable to remove the minié ball lodged in his elbow joint. Sinnott was discharged from the service May 18, 1863, and went home with an arm that would continue to wither. He enlisted in the Veteran Reserve Corps July 27, 1863, but did not serve long before being sent home on sick leave due to hepatitis. He died from that disease March 29, 1864, leaving a widow and three young children.[33]

The hand and arm were not the only parts of the body exposed when loading the rifle. Pvt. Cyrill Wheeler, a 34-year-old farmer from Montpelier and Co. I, had managed to get his rifle loaded without having his arm or hand perforated; however, when he raised himself up on his left elbow to put the percussion cap on his weapon, a rebel minié ball came skimming a foot or so above the ground and smacked into his forehead just above his left eyebrow. The ball penetrated his skull, shattering the bone, and passed out his left eye socket, taking the eyeball with it. He was evacuated to a general hospital and discharged on a disability May 11, 1863. The wound never completely healed and constantly discharged fluid. He also suffered from severe headaches and dizziness, not to mention disfigurement. He could not hold a job and had to live on his $8 a month government pension the rest of his life. He died March 18, 1876, in Berlin, Vt., at age 47 from complications of his wound.[34]

Once a soldier stood to fire, the rest of the body became a target for the rebels. Pvt. Alden C. Loomis of Co. H, a 23-year-old farm boy from Roxbury, stood up and was just raising his rifle when a Confederate minié ball tore through his right shoulder taking away the center part of his collarbone. His comrades stopped the bleeding, but with most of the collarbone gone, the arm was useless after it healed. Loomis spent the rest of his time in the service in the Veteran Reserve Corps until discharged April 25, 1864.[35]

Thirty-seven-year-old Pvt. Richard Dodge stood up with the rest of Co. D to fire off a volley and was hit in the right shoulder. The bullet missed the collarbone but buried itself in his shoulder and had to be dug out at the hospital. Dodge, an old man at age 37 in contrast to most of the men in the 2nd Vermont, had served in the 9th U. S. Volunteers in the Mexican War. The wound he had just received only added to his collection. In the war with Mexico, the five-foot seven and one-half inch Vermonter had been shot twice, sliced by a saber on the head and left wrist, and bayoneted in the left jaw and left foot. He was discharged March 29, 1863, on a disability and returned home to Worcester, Vt. A little over a year after he had recovered from his wound, he enlisted in the 17th Vermont. He was mustered out July 14, 1865, having received no additional wounds.[36]

Pvt. John Q. A. Ditty, a 27-year-old Roxbury man in Co. F, took a very painful wound in the right groin. The bullet did not hit the bone, but did severe damage when it tore through the nerves, veins, and muscle. He was eventually transferred to the Veteran Reserve Corps and was discharged after the war on November 13, 1865. He was left with a bad limp for the rest of his life.[37]

John Ditty's brother Ralph, the soldier who had been

court-martialed the month before for threatening Gen. Vinton, survived the battle without a scratch. Gen. Vinton on the other hand was not so lucky. Early in the battle he took a bullet in his abdomen that the surgeons had to remove by cutting through his back. It was a severe wound which he survived, but because of the wound effects, he resigned from the army May 5, 1863.[38]

Sgt. George W. Doty, the Co. F soldier who had crossed the Potomac with Capt. Randall in September 1861, was shot in the outside of his right knee. Pvt. Harry Hall, also a member of Co. F and a native of Washington, Vt., helped Doty to the rear for medical attention. Between this wound and the malaria he had contracted on the Peninsula in 1862, Doty never returned to his unit. Neither the doctors at the field hospital nor those at two general hospitals that he passed through were able to remove the bullet without doing additional damage to his knee. Doty served in the Veteran Reserve Corps during his recuperation from the wound until discharged June 29, 1864. He returned home to Morrisville where he became a very successful furniture store owner and undertaker. He died August 20, 1910.[39]

Pvt. Thomas J. Jaquith, a 29-year-old, five-foot eleven and three-quarter-inch mechanic from Londoneery of Co. I, was hit in the left thigh. The ball went on through the hip to his left buttock where it lodged in the hip joint. The bullet was removed in the hospital and after nearly a year's convalescence, he returned to duty.[40]

Another Co. I soldier was wounded soon after Jaquith. Pvt. Warren S. Leslie was hit in the left breast by a rebel minié ball that lodged near his heart. He survived the wound with the ball still lodged in his chest, but the least physical exertion sapped his strength. He was discharged from the hospital February 11, 1863 with a 100 percent disability.[41]

Pvt. Cornelius Nye of Co. D described his experience on the skirmish line:

> Found the Rebels strongly fortified on the hills. Fought them hardly and they us in the same way.... Our regiment was brought up in line of battle to within 20 rods of the enemy as skirmishers opposite the rebel skirmishers in front of the field of battle. The reserve and artillery laying in line back of us and there we laid loading rapidly as possible during the afternoon of Saturday with shot and shell flying over our heads from the heights from our guns to the rebels and from the enemy artillery to ours. Some 15 of our company was wounded, but none have died yet as I have heard of.... Charles Hartwell was wounded in the head. Slight from what I hear. Have not seen him since we first marched on the field. He stood some 3 feet from me when he was hit.[42]

Unbeknownst to Nye, Hartwell was severely injured. The bullet had smashed into his forehead, but somehow he had been able to cling to life. His battle to stay alive did not last long and he died in the hospital January 1, 1863. His young widow received a small government pension after his death which helped her make ends meet.[43]

Pvt. Storrs W. Start of Co. H wrote of what he had seen from his perspective:

> There is one thing certain. I have no desire to go into another battle, but if it is my duty I shall go and do my best. The Battle of Fredericksburg was not half so terrific a fight as the Battle of Antietam but the VT Brig. were not so fortunate. My regiment suffered severely. We lost 65 [actually 59] and only 5 were killed on the field. It was a great wonder that we did not loose five times that number. Our position being so exposed to the murderous fire of both their artillery & infantry. My Regt. were the first line of Battle. We were on a plain & it was nearly level. When we advanced in line of battle the rebels opened on us with a battery of six pieces throwing grape and canister. Their battery appeared to be about 85 rods from us in plain sight and their line of battle was much nearer firing at the same time. Well then our men had about ten pieces of artillery on a little rise of ground in the rear of us firing as lively as possible at the same time.... I reckon the shower of bullets made the dirt fly in front of me. What saved us we were deployed as skirmishers & huged the ground.[44]

Pvt. Joseph Butterfield of Co. I proudly recorded in his diary after the battle, "I fired 50 rounds."[45]

The 2nd Vermont was relieved from the skirmish line at 10 P.M., and under the cover of darkness moved to the rear. During its tour on the skirmish line, which was their only real action in the battle of Fredericksburg, the 2nd Vermont lost five men killed and 59 wounded.[46]

Several weeks later, Pvt. Tilly, in reply to his mother's inquiry as to the casualties from the battle of Fredericksburg, replied, "no we did not stay to help bury our men as we had to go back on this side and on the other side of the river in the night appeared to us that we were beaten and had to retreat in the night." In explaining his reason for not visiting his friends in the hospital, he said, "I do not see many of the wounded as they were taken to a large house on one side of the field in which we were. I have not cared to visit a field hospital since we were at Antietam. I don't think I will forget that sight and don't care to see such a one again."[47]

While Franklin's men were trying to take Hamilton's Crossing, Sumner's Grand Division assaulted Marye's Heights behind Fredericksburg. They were bordered on the left by Hazel Run and on the right by a canal. The town extended about a quarter mile back from the river. From there a 600-yard plain ran to the foot of Marye's Heights. A drainage ditch that came off the town's canal ran the length of the plain just at the edge of town and a sunken road with a stone wall lined the other side of the plain at the base of the heights. To assault the heights, the Federals had to pass through the town in column formation, cross over bridges spanning the drainage ditch, and then form into line of battle, all of this partially in view of the Confederates. Behind the stone wall, Longstreet had placed a Georgia brigade and a North Carolina regiment. The heights above were ringed with artillery and infantry units. These terrain features would funnel the Federal units directly into the Confederate's kill zone.[48]

About noon Sumner began his attack with a brigade at a time. Wave after wave, 15 in all, assaulted the heights, but none reached the impenetrable stone wall. By nightfall the slaughter finally stopped with nearly 8,000 Federal soldiers lost and nothing gained. Burnside wanted to assault the heights in one final grand charge, personally leading his old Ninth Corps, but his generals talked him out of it.[49]

The Vermonters spent their third night on the frozen ground on Saturday. On Sunday morning, December 14, Howe relieved Gen. Neill's brigade, which had been manning the front line, replacing it with the Vermont Brigade. It stayed until 5 A.M. Monday morning. In his report Howe stated:

> Early on the morning of the 14th, I relieved the first line (General Neill's) by Colonel Whiting's brigade. Soon after daylight enemy appeared on nearly the same ground as the day before, with another outfit of artillery, and opened upon our lines in a very spirited manner, but in twenty minutes from the first fire our batteries compelled them to leave the field. This was the last appearance of the enemy's artillery on our front while we held this position. Our skirmish line during the day continued active, and at night again our men rested on their arms.[50]

The rest of the day was easy according to the 2nd Vermont's Pvt. Butterfield. The day's entry in his diary read, "We are today lying as a support to a Battery, But little firing."[51]

The Army of the Potomac lay in front of the Fredericksburg heights until after dark. Gen. William F. Smith wrote in his after-action report, "On Monday night the corps was ordered to cross after the other troops, and everything was done quietly and expeditiously." The Sixth Corps marched back across the pontoon bridges (which had been covered with hay to deaden the noise to deceive the rebels) and up to the top of Falmouth Heights where it went into camp. This disastrous campaign had cost the Federals 12,600 casualties, almost two-thirds of which occurred on the few acres of ground in front of the stone wall. Lee's army lost 5,300.[52]

On December 20 Lt. Leach wrote, "We are back again where we were before we marched down to the river. We came back yesterday. So it does not look like anymore fighting just at present." This camp was at White Oak Church. Later Leach explained how they were settling in:

> We have been fixing up our tent today. Have not got it done yet quite, but enough so we can occupy it tonight. We dug a hole in the ground a little larger than the tent about 2 feet deep & log it up from the bottom with pine logs split in two, the flat side in, & then set the tent on top of that. We have ours loged up about as high as the top of the ground, but are going to put on another joint. We then have a hole cut through the logs on the back end of the tent & a fire place made in the dirt. The ground is hard enough that all it needs is to dig it out in the shape you want, & lay up a chimney of logs over where it comes out of the ground. I am in the tent with the Capt. now, & shall probably remain so.... It is very dull in camp, having such nice weather & nothing going on to stir one up. Many pass a good deal of their time in playing Bluff. A name of a game of cards of gambling, & now while writing, I can hear it going on, although it is ten O.C. I have no doubt there 25 to 50 boards going all the time in this Regt., when there are no duties to call the men out, except at night & then sometimes it is kept up pretty well. I don't know as anyone that came from Fletcher gambles or ever has except Vernon Rood, who used to "[play] at it" a good deal.... I reckon we will get a storm soon, & then it will be mud up to your a_ _ holes.

He continued in another letter a few days later about the sickness in camp:

> Another man of our Co. died last night. His name is [Oramillo W.] Doane of Bakersfield. He has been failing, but kept with the Company till yesterday morning at Surgeon's Call they took him in the hospital & just after dark he died. I think his body will be sent home.... Deaths of soldiers are very frequent at this time. I think the loss by death since we came back from over the river has been as great in this Brigade as it was killed while in the battle.[53]

The 2nd Vermont was again ordered to report to Belle Plains Landing on December 29. Capt. Pitkin had probably influenced this decision. Lt. Leach thought it "hard to leave our camp just as we had got fixed up so as to be comfortable...."[54]

After returning to the landing and settling into a daily routine, Henry Diamond and Chauncy Shonio (the two men who had fallen out of the ranks on the move to the skirmish line December 13) were brought before a court martial on January 5. Diamond was charged with misbehavior before the enemy. He explained to the court that he had, in fact, dropped out of formation to put on his overcoat and knapsack, but before reaching the company, he had helped a wounded man to the hospital. He went on to say that while he was at the hospital, the 2nd Vermont's surgeon, Dr. Ballou, told all the unwounded Vermonters to stay at the hospital to assist with the wounded. He had remained at the hospital until he was released to his company on December 15. He then played his trump card and handed the prosecutor a signed statement from Dr. Ballou verifying the facts. Diamond was found not guilty.

Pvt. Shonio's trial came next. He was also charged with misbehavior before the enemy. Unlike Diamond, he pleaded guilty but entered the following in his defense:

> The reason I left the field was, because I had been lame some weeks (three), and had not been able to march with the regiment or done no duty that length of time. When we were back on picquet at Aquia Landing, the orderly [first sergeant] told me to give my gun and accouterments to one of the recruits. I was not ordered to take new gun and accouterments until we crossed the Rappahannock. I was then so lame I could not keep up with the regiment. Lt. Bass offered to help me across the ditch in the plain on the other side of the river when we were marching into line of battle. I fell behind the regiment going up. When it arrived on the battle ground and formed in line, our company deployed as skirmishers. I thought I could not keep up with them, so I fell behind the regiment. When I was ordered to lay down, I layed down with it. I remained there some two hours. Then I came back to the road. I laid down behind the bank and remained down there until night. Then I went down and stayed with the sick until the next morning. I joined my regiment about dusk in the evening. The other reason I left was, because they gave me a gun with the bayonet broke, and one which would not crack a cap after I had tried seven times.

The court found no reason for leniency and pronounced Shonio guilty. He was sentenced to forfeit all his pay and to be confined at hard labor during the remainder of his term of enlistment.[55]

The next day, January 6, 1863, on the advice of the regiment's surgeon, Lt. Col. Joyce resigned from the service. On that same day the regiment's chaplain Durrell W. Dayton resigned to continue his career back in Vermont. The 2nd Vermont would not have another chaplain for the rest of the war.

Lt. Col. Joyce departed the landing on January 9 accompanied by his wife. Mrs. Joyce, like the wives of Maj. Walbridge and Dr. Sawin, had been visiting her husband since shortly after the battle of Fredericksburg. Maj. Walbridge took over temporary command of the regiment in Joyce's place until a replacement could be appointed.

Joyce returned to Northfield where he quickly regained his health and resumed his law practice. Within two years, he moved his practice to Rutland. In 1869 he was elected to the state house of representatives, and in 1874, he was elected to the U.S. House of Representatives where he served from 1874 to 1880. After retiring Joyce moved to Pittsfield, where he died November 22, 1916.[56]

While a lot of the Vermonters liked the easy duty at Belle Plains Landing, Capt. Tyler was not so enthusiastic about acting as stevedore as he expressed in his first letter of the new year:

> Here all the forage, hay & grain, and some Commissary stores are landed for the use of the Army, and the romantic employment of getting it off the boats and onto teams devolves upon us. Any regiment would jump at our chance, as we get rid of picket duty, occasional skirmishes, and such little amusements, but as for myself I *fail to* perceive it.[57]

The 2nd Vermont probably would have remained at the landing had other circumstances not intervened. Since the battle of Fredericksburg, the weather had been unusually warm and dry, and the roads were firm, so Burnside decided to take another crack at Robert E. Lee. Burnside's present plan was to cross the Rappahannock at Banks Ford about six miles above Fredericksburg. After crossing, he expected to turn Lee's left flank and fight a decisive battle on Salem Heights. Five bridges were to be laid across the river at the ford on the morning of January 21. Franklin and Hooker were to set their grand divisions into motion on the day before, and Sumner was to stay in place and cross at Falmouth as soon as the other two grand divisions were across the river.[58]

On the afternoon of January 20, the sky clouded over, and by the time the Sixth Corps camped for the evening near Banks Ford, it had started to rain. First, it was just a drizzle, then it turned into a downpour, and the temperature started to drop.[59]

The 2nd Vermont's order for the day was to catch up with the rest of the Vermont Brigade. This was easier said than done, as Lt. Leach explained:

> Our Regt. Left bell Plain Landing Tuesday afternoon to join the brigade on the road to Falmouth. We marched till dark, & not knowing where to find the brigade, halted in a piece of woods (or rather where there had been woods) for the night. It soon commenced to rain & rained all night & you can guess it was nice, being without tents or blankets but Hollis and John Ayers fixed up their little tents to shed off the rain & we kept alive by building a brush fire.[60]

Pvt. Tilly remembered:

> our Major was in command of the regiment and some how got on the wrong road. we marched 6 or 8 miles in a drizling rain. it got so dark that we were oblige to stop here. it was 8 o'clock before we got our tents put up. then we tried to make some fires with green pine wood so as to make coffee. It rained all night and this morning we found ourselves lying in water. This morning we got quite a good camp fire started and made tea for breakfast. The other boys are trying to dry our blankets.[61]

By morning, the entire army was thoroughly soaked, and the roads were a quagmire. As the morning wore on, the rain as well as the roads grew steadily worse. The day's march became an exhausting struggle in the knee-deep mud, and the army made very little progress. Ammunition and pontoon wagons, artillery pieces, and ambulances became completely entrapped in the mud. As many as 16 horses tugged at a single artillery piece to no avail. Men were set to corduroying roads. The Vermont Brigade, which was well to the front of the column, was given the task of helping the exhausted horses and mules in pulling artillery pieces and pontoon boat wagons through the mud. It took up to a hundred men to pull a single pontoon wagon. Gen. Burnside seemed to be everywhere encouraging his men, but it soon became clear to him, as well as to the rest of the army, that the operation which was supposed to have been concealed from the rebels was a failure.[62]

As the rest of the army was struggling through the mud, the 2nd Vermont continued its search for its brigade. Lt. Leach related:

> The next day [Wednesday, January 21] the Major sent off someone to find the Brigade & also our teams which could not find us the night before, although they passed but a short distance from us. The teams were found & came to us, but the Brigade was not found till the next day.[63]

On Thursday morning the army started the laborious trek back to its various camps. Again men were used to assist the animals in moving the wagons and artillery. To add insult to injury, as the army moved by Fredericksburg the rebel soldiers taunted and jeered the drenched and mud-covered Yankees and placed large hand-painted signs on the other side of the river that read "Burnside stuck in the mud." The Northern soldiers, not failing to see the humor in this, quickly spread the expression the entire length of the floundering column. This operation, from then on, would be known as "Burnside's Mud March." Several days after the army's return to its camps, the rebels were still laughing at the Yankees as Pvt. Tilly related, "perhaps you have read in the news paper about the army getting stuck in the mud while trying to get to the rebels. the day that we were camped near Falmouth some of us went to the river bank opposite Fredericksburg and could and did talk with the rebel soldiers that were in the city. they joked us about Burnside getting stuck in the mud."[64]

Sgt. William H. Bond of Co. A had a typical soldier's perspective of the whole mess: "the army of the Potomac got stuck in the mud and are a going back to the old camps as fast as they can.... Hope that the mud will continue the remainder of my enlistment."[65]

The 2nd Vermont stayed in camp until Friday, January 23, when it was ordered to join the Vermont Brigade in its camp at White Oak Church and thus were spared the humiliating taunts of the rebels. After arriving at White Oak Church, the Vermonters started digging in for the winter. Pvt. Cutler described the hut that he and his tentmates constructed:

> Well four of us tent together Jehiel [Bailey] and myself and two boys from Fletcher Charly Blair & Monroe Bingham, we have dug out the side of the hill a place some ten feet square and about six feet deep on the upper side, inside of this we have laid up a block house out of hewn logs over this we have put our tent for a roof, on the upperside in the bank we have dug a fireplace, and on one side we have made two bunks one above the other to sleep on.[66]

Pvt. Joseph C. Felton of Co. H, a 41-year-old five-foot five and one-half inch farmer from Fairfax, wrote: "I will describe our house as well as I can. It is 10 by 6. A place shoveled into the ground walled up with pine poles covered with cotton cloth. A fire place dug out of the side of the tent and a hole through the ground on the upper side. So you see we live very much like wood chucks."[67]

After returning from the Mud March, Gen. Burnside learned from President Lincoln that several of his corps and division commanders considered him incompetent and had lost faith in his ability to command the Army of the Potomac. With this disloyalty in mind, Burnside drafted an order dismissing Gens. Hooker, Brooks, Newton, and John Cochrane from the service. This same order also relieved Gens. Franklin, W. F. Smith, Samuel D. Sturgis, and Edward Ferrero from command. Burnside delivered the order to Lincoln for approval with the stipulation that if Lincoln did not approve the order, then he wanted to be relieved. Seeing the names of the officers in the order and considering their past performances, as contrasted to Burnside's, Lincoln elected to accept Burnside's resignation. The next day the president appointed Gen. Joseph "Fighting Joe" Hooker as the commander of the Army of the Potomac.[68]

Hooker, a handsome 49-year-old veteran of the Mexican War, had the reputation in the army as a hard fighter and a competent officer as well as a hard drinker and womanizer. In spite of his shortcomings, Hooker was a soldier's general and quickly made sweeping changes in the Army of the Potomac that greatly improved the men's quality of life, as well as the efficiency of the army. Hooker's new job was not an enviable one. The army's morale was at its lowest level ever, and the 2nd Vermont was no exception, as evidenced by the following passages from several of the men's letters written during that trying time.[69]

Pvt. Jerome Cutler tried to keep up a positive front in a February letter to his aunt and uncle:

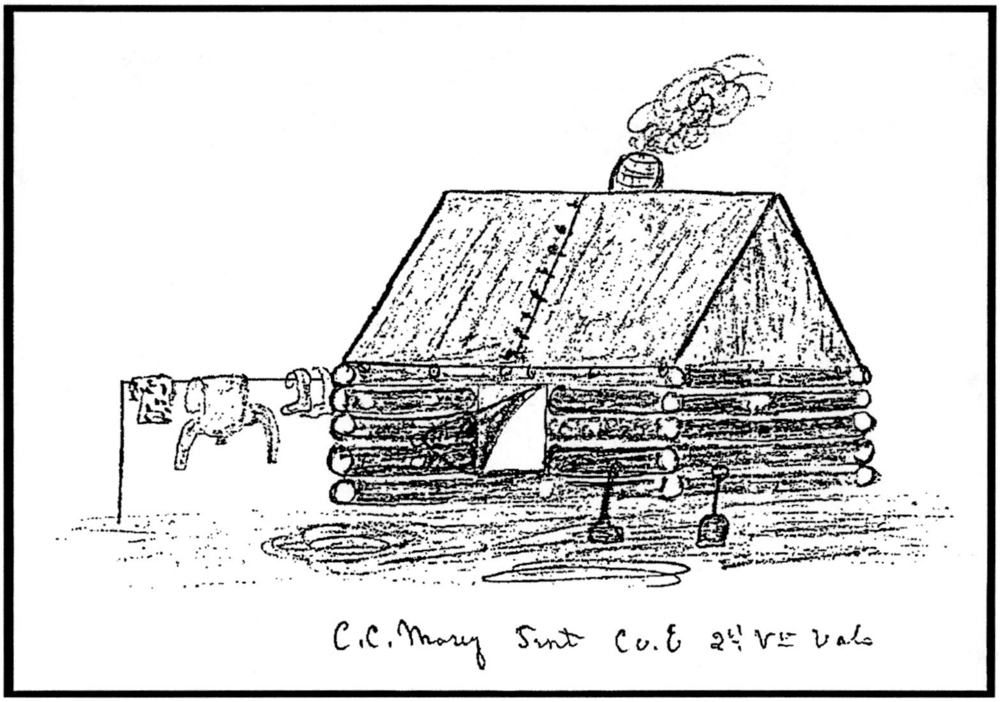

A sketch by Sergeant Charles C. Morey of his winter hut, included in a letter to his mother. USAMHI.

> Well you say you have not lost confidence in the ultimate success of our cause, neither have I and the soldiers jeneraly but nevertheless, we are getting sick of the war, and hate it, but as bad as we hate it, there is one thing we hat more, peace democrats, old foggies, and seccession sympathizers at the north.

Cutler's spirit continued downward as winter wore on. In March he responded to a letter from his Emily about the forlorn tone of his previous letter:

> you speak of my last letter being written in a rather dispending spirit, I presume it was, I have most forgotten what I did write, I presume I was in a rather gloomy mood at the time.
>
> I tell you Emily I almost believe sometimes that I was never made for a soldier. military parade and tactics seem like boys play to me, there are so many "Reards march" and "Gods may" among the officers, so much impartiality shown, and so much abominble wickedness that I sometimes grow sick of the whole thing, give me a peaceful, and quiet home among loved friends and I should be content.[70]

Pvt. Joseph Butterfield of Co. I noted in his diary on March 3, "The snow has fallen two inches and I fear the mud will be as deep as ever. I am so tired of sitting that I hope to be able to rest by making an advance into Enemy country soon and driving them from their strongholds and blotting out this stain on our country."[71]

Pvt. Bromley of Co. B seemed really down in the dumps when he wrote his brother and sister on December 25:

> we enjoyed another good defeat to Fredericksburg as usual. if we did not get whiped perhaps we would whip somebody but it is our luck to get defeated about every time but I guess that I can stand the press my time out and then the union may go to the Devil for all I care. there is somebody that is to blame a most damdly about this and who is it. I think it is the secretary of war and our Congress men and old abe. They can sit there in Washington and say go ahead and they dont have the least idea how things is comming out.[72]

Sgt. William Bond shared the blues with his mother:

> Gary Emerson came over to see me yesterday. His Reg is encamped about five miles from us. He tells me that he is the only one from Danby that is with his regiment. They are all in the general hospital. Now this general hospital is all a sham. These men who stay in there are no better than deserters. they go there and stay there. I never knew one of them to come back to their regiment. The amount of it is they are sick of this war and want to keep as far from it as they can. We have got 8 of this kind in Co. A. They are what the soldier calls played out pimps. I think that the name is appropriate for them. They ought to be drummed out of the army and have the letter D branded on their _ _ _ or some other good place.[73]

Bond mentioned the single most serious outcome of the demoralization so pervasive in the Army of the Potomac—desertion. The soldiers were deserting in droves, sometimes as many as 200 per day. After the Mud March and just before Burnside's relief from command, Sgt. Bond wrote, "The men are deserting all sorts. The army is about used up. it seems that Gen. Burnside can not do anything with the army. The army is down on him."[74]

One of the most frequent methods used to desert was for a soldier to have civilian clothes sent to him by family or friends. He would discard his uniform, don the civilian garb, slip out of camp and make his way north. In an attempt to stem this tide of departing soldiers, Hooker required the express companies that were delivering boxes by the carload to the army to verify that the boxes did not contain any civilian clothes. He explained that this measure was required because of "the pernicious practice of treasonable persons sending citizens' clothing to soldiers here to encourage or facilitate desertion."[75]

Another method of deserting was through the hospital system. Men who were wounded, sick or, as Sgt. Bond noted, were good at pretending to be sick, were evacuated back to general hospitals in their home state. Unfortunately these hospitals were under the control of the governor and reported only to the U.S. surgeon general. For all intents and purposes, the patients were out of the control of the military. Because of local politics or a lack of concern on the part of the hospital authorities, many of the men simply drifted away, some never to return.[76]

Wilbur Fisk was one of those soldiers who availed himself of the opportunity to desert while in the hospital. Fisk was hospitalized from an illness in September 1862 and by January 18, 1863 was in a general hospital in Brattleboro. From here he went home without authority and got married in February. With guilt preying on his mind, Fisk returned to the hospital in Brattleboro and turned himself in to the authorities on March 2. He was immediately tossed into the guardhouse, and two days later he was on a train back to his regiment. The only thing that saved him from a court-martial when he returned were the articles that he wrote for the *Green Mountain Freeman*. It seems that his superior officer had political aspirations and did not want to cut off the stream of good press that the regiment was getting through Fisk.[77]

Hooker also ordered guards to be posted around the camps, but Lt. Leach, now a learned veteran, doubted their effectiveness:

> There is an order ... that each Regt. shall have a camp guard, that is a chain of sentinels around the camp, something that we have not had for some time. I very much doubt a camp guard preventing a man of nerve deserting if he is bound so to do. It will make employment for fifty to one hundred men daily to each regiment & that I think will be the most it will do.[78]

In addition to Hooker's efforts, President Lincoln issued a proclamation on March 10 providing a grace period for all men who had deserted the army. There would be no retribution if they returned on or before April 1. Although desertions slowed somewhat with all the measures Hooker put in place, soldiers still continued to drift away from the army.[79]

Another measure used to stem the exodus was granting furloughs. Although these were parceled out judiciously, they did improve morale somewhat. If men were lucky enough to get furloughs but returned late, there were harsh punishments, as Leach mentioned:

> Hampton Maxfield [Co. H from Fairfax] had to lose ten dollars of his pay for not getting back when he was expected. Some boys were in the same fix and the noncommissioned officers were reduced to the ranks & have to do a few turns of extra guard duty. Military life is not lived like when one can go & come when he pleases.[80]

Congress also became involved in trying to raise men for the army. On March 3, 1863, it passed the Enrollment Act that allowed the Federal government to draft men into service. Even though volunteer enlistments had been steadily declining since the previous fall, the draft was very unpopular with the American public. To have to draft men from their congressional districts was quite embarrassing to local politicians. To preclude running a draft, local authorities added additional money to the already existing $300 bounty the Federal government was offering for three-year volunteer enlistments. Unfortunately, Congress embedded a provision in the Enrollment Act that allowed a man who was drafted to hire a substitute to take his place. This led to two types of unscrupulous men—bounty brokers and bounty jumpers. Bounty brokers were the agents who recruited men for substitutes. Those who were money hungry and wanted to make a quick buck would recruit men who were either unfit for military service or men who were unsavory characters. The latter led to bounty jumpers, who were men who would sign on as substitutes but desert as soon as they could after they were paid their bounties. Many would repeat this process time and time again from state to state. The 2nd Vermont was no exception and started receiving substitutes and draftees in the coming summer.[81]

At least one member of the 2nd Vermont thought that the draft was a good idea. Sgt. Bond expressed his view when he wrote:

> What do they think about the draft in Danby? Something has got to be done. Either another army must be raised or the rebels have gained their independence. I sometimes think that all will have to come before this war can be brought to a close. I think that some of the men of the North would like to have the rebels have their independence. they are not willing to sustain the President. they ought to be drafted and put in the front of the army and get acquainted with the rebels that they like so much.[82]

In spite of the desertions, all was not gloom and doom in the Army of the Potomac. One of Hooker's most important improvements concerned the commissary department. First, he cracked down on unscrupulous contractors supplying the army food and improved the quality of the rations being issued to the troops. Second, he ordered all regiments to establish a company level system of regular cooks. Third, he ordered bakeries to be built to supply the men with fresh soft white bread.[83]

Pvt. Cutler was one of the men in the 2nd Vermont

assigned as a cook. He wrote to his cousins in March of his new duties:

> I am writing this on the side of a hard bread box, we just got a brigade bakery a going so we got soft bread for the first time for a great while, I am cooking yet and I tell you I have got so that I can make some of the greatest stews out of fresh beef potatoes and onions, you ever heard of. We cook two and three kettles full at a time. Kettles holding some fifteen quarts apiece, and o you ought to see the beans that I stew sometimes a half bushel at a time, and occasionally we have two larg kettles full of rice. I tell you that I am getting to be quit a cook.[84]

Pvt. Joseph Felton explained what it was like to be on the receiving end of the new system: "Our food is pilot bread, and a piece of boiled beef or pork together with a cup of coffee twice a day and soup of potatoes, onions or beans with dinner ... by order of Gen. Hooker the regiment has now a bakery built and expect soft bread while we stay here."[85]

Lt. Leach gave the officer's perspective:

> Perhaps you would like to know what I had to eat for supper. It was boiled potatoes, fried ham, biscuits & butter, coffee. That is about the way we live only different sorts of meats & occasionally baked beans, or bake pudding, pancakes, & sometimes pies. There is about a dozen in our mess & when we're in camp, live in very good shape.[86]

Because of the bad weather, the troops had a lot of free time on their hands from January to April. As in the previous winter, some of their time was spent constructively and some was not. Lt. Leach described in his letters a typical day in the officers' tent in Company H:

> Perhaps you would like to know how I spend time. Well, I will tell you how it is generally. In the morning I lay abed till called to breakfast, which is generally from eight to nine, & then till noon, it is playing euchre, reading novels, (when any is to be had) & newspapers also, (smoking thrown in). Noon, dinner, & then the afternoon is spent like the forenoon, supper just at night, & the evening goes about the same as the day. Of course there are all sorts of little fixtures mixed in, but these are the bulk when I do *anything*. Labor is generally out of the question, although I helped bring poles to day to fix the tent with. Yesterday we had a regular old-fashioned snowballing scrape, & I feel some lame from it today, too.

Pvt. Wilbur Fisk recorded some of his leisure time in his diary:

> 20 Mar–Snow storm. Played checkers, read and dozed.
> 4 Apr–Cold windy day. No drill. Played backgammon.[87]

Sgt. Bond wrote of a prank played on the regiment on April 1: "The 2nd Vt. had a good April Fool played on them. There was a First Sergeants call and orders for the men to get up at 12 o'clock at night and wash their feet. Some of them did it. I did not let them catch me though."[88]

Much has been written about a number of the most famous large-scale snowball battles that took place in the Army of the Potomac during the winter of 1862–1863. Some of the battles were waged between brigades, though they were normally between regiments and below. During these battles prisoners would be taken, regimental standards captured, and even some causalities inflicted. Lt. Leach explains that snowballing seems to have been an everyday occurrence in camp, as long as there was enough snow on the ground to make a snowball: "the Officers here getting to snow balling. It is generally a perfect shower of snowballs here when the snow is in good condition. The other regiments in the Brigade turn out one against the other & go in for a regular battle." Later he wrote:

> twelve inches of snow on the ground & very damp & we had ourselves a snowballing. About noon, Capt. Tracy & myself went out & commenced throwing at Co. E Officer's tent. We threw a long time but could get none of them to come out. They kept quiet till just at dark, they sent a boy up on some errand, but to find out if we were in our tent & at the same time threw some pepper on our stove & then they commenced snowballing our tent & gave it a good pelting & asking if we would surrender. Someone held the door so we could not get out at first. After we went out, we all started and bombarded the tents & made the inmates fall into our ranks. All went well for a time but some of them saw what was coming & just got their men out & hid behind their tent & when we came up they lit into us & we had to retreat.... When there is snow on the ground, one can hardly show himself without getting a snowball after him. Capt. Tracy got one right between the eyes & could hardly see last night.[89]

As spring came and the days and nights started getting warmer, the men got out more and the amount of mischief increased. In March, the 2nd Vermont noticed it had been losing carcasses of fresh meat from its cookhouse. For some reason the men suspected the New Jersey boys as the culprits. A detail, sent out in the dark of night, captured the New Jersey regiment's mascot, a large, fat Newfoundland dog, which belonged to Col. Andrew J. Morrison, the regiment's commander. The dog was killed, dressed and hung in the 2nd Vermont's cookhouse. Sure enough the next morning the dog's carcass was missing. As the men expected, it had been stolen that night by some of the New Jersey boys who mistook it for mutton. The Vermonters tracked the dog meat into the New Jersey camp and confirmed that it had been served to the regiment's officers. Of course the Jerseymen had to be let in on the prank to make it effective and for months afterward, the Vermonters started barking anytime they spotted the Jerseys.

Pvt. Fisk noted another misadventure with the New Jersey boys in one of his *Green Mountain Freeman* articles written in April 1863:

> Our boys love to make them visits occasionally, after roll-call at night, and, as they generally come back in high glee, with a mouthful of stories to tell, it may be safely considered that the visit was a pleasant one to at least one of the parties. In one of these nocturnal visits some of our boys, for some reason or other, probably a misunderstanding, got caught, and were put into the guard-house. But the guard-house didn't hold them long. They run the guard and outrun the guard's bullets, and, though the Jerseys did their best, they couldn't imprison them again, nor tell who they were. After that our boys generously offered to stand guard for them, but our services were declined. Some time ago some officers of the Fifth [Vermont] advised the Jerseys to let the Second boys alone or they would find more than they could handle, and the Jerseys are beginning to think it best to accept this advice.[90]

As Lt. Leach noted in one of his letters, games and pranks sometimes stood aside for other entertainment: "I reckon they are having a concert in Co. F tent by the noise. The voices there are numerous & the discords well put in, accompaniment played on an accordion. I guess it is all spiced with a little whiskey. Such things are done sometimes."

In late April he again mentioned drinking in his company:

> We don't exactly keep a beer shop here, but if you had just stepped in, within the past two days, you could have had all the ale you wanted to drink. Sawyer [2nd Lt. Joshua P. Sawyer from St. Albans] bought a whole keg of it day before yesterday & run the machine for awhile. It is impossible for him to have money & not have a bust occasionally.[91]

Pvt. Fisk also mentions drinking in his diary. On April 6, he entered, "Dress parade at the usual time. Capt. Cady was too drunk to stand still and far too drunk to walk straight. He is a captain so it is all right. If he was a private he would have lodging in the guard house and perhaps worse penalties."[92]

Sometimes the activities were even worse than just drinking. One such incident took place in the Vermont Brigade on April 19. Pvt. Fisk was so disturbed by it that he included it in one of his articles in the *Green Mountain Freeman*:

> Quite a disgraceful affair occurred the other day with the 5th regiment which perhaps I ought to mention. Five or six from Co. D, of that regiment went out to a house near the picket line, for purposes too foul to mention. The guard stationed at the house was relieved, who reported his suspicions of something wrong at the nearest picket reserve. A squad of pickets was immediately sent to arrest the guilty party. They succeeded, but were fired upon and two of their number hit. I do not know the extent of the injuries received. The affair will soon undergo an investigation, and some think the death penalty will be inflicted upon one or more of the culprits.[93]

Lt. Leach was more graphic in the description of the incident in a letter to his wife:

> A bit of a row occurred night before last out a short distance from camp, in which one man got shot, so it is thought he will die if not already dead. About a dozen boys from the 5th Vt. went out to a Nigger Shanty where there were two or three wenches for the purpose of "Blacking their canes" or "dressing them in Mourning," if it is more proper.[94]

The group from the 5th Vermont's Co. D that Fisk and Leach referred to was led by Sgt. Lawson M. Perkins. The men were liquored up and determined to have sex with the two females who lived in a cabin just outside the picket line. They went out to the cabin which belonged to a black family named Frazier and chased off a New York soldier who was visiting. Perkins told the Fraziers they were guards sent by Gen. Sedgwick to protect their property. As soon as they gained entrance to the house, Perkins and another soldier dragged Mr. Frazier out of the house and started beating him. The other soldiers split into two groups of three. One group dragged Mrs. Frazier out of the house and into a gully where one of the men raped her. Two of the soldiers in the second group still in the cabin held down Mrs. Frazier's 13-year-old niece while a third soldier raped her. The women screamed so much that a contingent was sent on the run from the picket line to investigate. As the guards were rounding up the drunken rapists, one of them fired on the officer of the guard who returned fire killing the man. Perkins and the others were tried by court-martial and sent to prison.[95]

A major change took place in the Sixth Corps on February 4 with Gen. Smith being relieved from command. Although he had survived Burnside's intended purge of senior officers, he had told too many people, too many times, that he would not serve under Gen. Hooker, so Hooker accommodated Smith's desire. Smith was transferred to command the Ninth Corps only to be replaced Gen. Burnside a month later. Smith bounced around in the army in several nondescript jobs until the spring of 1864 when he was again given command corps, but was relieved again in June, 1864, for not being aggressive enough in the initial assault of Petersburg. He was placed on "special duty" for the remainder of the war, and resigned from the service in 1867.[96]

Gen. Smith's replacement to command the Sixth Corps was Gen. John Sedgwick, a Connecticut native born in 1813. He had graduated from West Point in 1837 and had seen service in the Mexican War and on the western frontier. Prior to coming to the Sixth Corps he had commanded the Second and Ninth Corps. He was one of the best-liked general officers in the army and was affectionately known to his men as "Uncle John." His penchant for wearing the coarse field uniform of a private endeared him only that much more to the enlisted men. Although loved by his men, Sedgwick was a strict disciplinarian and a highly competent corps commander. The Vermonters were at first leery of him, preferring the Vermont born Smith, but they quickly warmed up to Uncle John.[97]

Another change in the Sixth Corps quickly followed Gen. Smith's removal. On February 9, finally realizing that he would never be promoted to brigadier general, Col. Whiting resigned. As the ranking colonel of the Vermont Brigade, he had seen Gen. William F. Smith, his junior, rapidly advance from brigade to corps command. Whiting considered himself entitled to the command of the brigade when it was given to Gen. Brooks, but accepted the decision gracefully until Col. Edwin H. Stoughton, the youngest colonel in the brigade, was promoted around him. At that point Whiting thought it best to resign. At Gen. Howe's request, he postponed the action for a few weeks and then submitted his resignation, which was accepted. It read:

> Camp near the Rappahannock
> Headquarters Second Brigade, Feb. 2, 1863
>
> Sir,—Having esteemed it my duty on account of having received a military education, to offer my service in this war, and having found that though the regiment which I have had the honor to command is admitted to be one of the best in the service, it having at all times performed all that has been ask of it, as well as the Second Brigade since I have commanded it;—it is therefore believed by me that my undertaking has not been a failure, in point of a full, hearty and effectual service. Still I now find myself at that point where I have no doubt that it is my duty to resign.
>
> I do therefore hereby resign my commission as Colonel 2nd Vermont Infantry, and consequently the command of the Second Brigade. Though the first colonel mustered into service in the first five Vermont regiments, I am the only one now holding that office, and one of the field and staff of the first three Vermont regiments I am the only one. I have served an age and am entitled to an honorable discharge. I have the honor to be,
>
> Very respectfully your obedient servant,
> H. WHITING
> Lt. Col. E. Mattocks, A. A. G., 2nd Div., 6th Corps.[98]

Col. Whiting returned to his home in St. Clair, Mich., and went back into the lumber business. He died June 23, 1887.[99]

Not everyone in the Vermont Brigade was sad to see Whiting go. Maj. Stephen M. Pingree of the 4th Vermont wrote on January 6, "Col. Hyde is now in trial for cowardice at the battle of the 13th. I fear the case will be 'proven.' Another prominent officer [Col. Whiting] of our Brigade ought to be tried. He was reported shaky at the first Bull Run. I know of his cowardice I think."

Pingree wrote on February 13 after Whiting's departure:

> Henry Whiting—the *hero* of Bull Run—Savage Station and Fredericksburg—formerly Col. 2nd Vermont, after a service of 19 months & over, without promotion has *resigned*, & been discharged the Service. He was a graceless coward at Fredericksburg—and, from this, (which I know) I feel justified in presuming the truth of similar reports of his conduct at the first Bull Run. He has been in command of our Brigade—everyday since Nov. 19, except *Dec. 13 & 14*!! On the 13 [th] he was 1½ miles from the attacking line—(2nd & 4th Regts.)—and ought to have been tried for cowardice, & would have been had his conduct been properly laid before Gen. Howe.[100]

Lt. Leach put it in plain soldier language in a letter to his wife: "Col. Whiting, I understand, has tendered his resignation, & the reason for it, I believe, is that the eagle that sits on his shoulder cannot be made to shit a star...."[101]

Lt. Col. James Hicks Walbridge succeeded Whiting as commander of the 2nd Vermont. He was born July 29, 1862, in North Bennington (then known as Paper Mill Village) into a family with a long and prominent Vermont lineage. His grandfather Ebenezer Walbridge was one of the early settlers of Bennington County and an officer in Ethan Allen's Green Mountain Boys during the Revolutionary War. James's father, Stebbins D. Walbridge, farmed and owned a woolen mill in North Bennington. After completing his public education, young James worked on his father's farm until he was 16 years old. His youthful restlessness caused him to leave for the coast of Massachusetts where he went to sea for three years fishing for mackerel. He returned to his father's farm for a short while after getting his fill of fishing but went back to Massachusetts where he worked in a paper mill in Springfield. In April of 1842, he was again hit with the wanderlust and went to California to seek his fortune in gold mining. After a modest success in mining, he purchased a printing business in San Francisco. While residing there he became active in the Peace and Order Committee (also known as the "Vigilantes") who forcibly put down the "rowdies and cut throats" that were trying to take over that city. He was also active in the California Home Guard. Walbridge returned to Vermont in 1857 and purchased his grandfather Ebenezer's farm in North Bennington and settled into the life of a farmer. In May 1861, he

Major Newton Stone, later the third commander of the 2nd Vermont. USAMHI.

was chosen as the captain of the company raised in Bennington that became company A of the 2nd Vermont.[102]

Maj. Newton Stone succeeded Walbridge as lieutenant colonel. Stone, originally from Readsboro, was a 23-year-old lawyer establishing his practice in Bennington when he was commissioned as a first lieutenant in Co. A on May 14, 1861. Because of his demonstrated leadership and courage under fire, he had been selected as the commander of Co. I in January 1862, when Capt. Volney S. Fullam was promoted to lieutenant colonel in the 7th Vermont.[103]

Twenty-year-old John S. Tyler of Co. C was appointed major. Tyler was born in Brattleboro April 29, 1843, into a distinguished Vermont family. His father was the Reverend Thomas P. Tyler and his grandfather the highly regarded Judge Royall Tyler. Although Tyler's family had moved to New York during his childhood, he was in Brattleboro studying law in his grandfather's law office when the 2nd Vermont was being recruited. Because he had attended an academy several years earlier that provided military training and he knew how to drill troops, he was promoted to second lieutenant soon after enlisting in Co. C of the 2nd Vermont in May 1861. Before enlisting he had written to his father asking whether or not he should enlist. His father's response made his decision an easy one: "My Dear John:—If you do not enlist, you will be ashamed hereafter to look your children in the face." The young Tyler had worked his way up the officer ranks to captain and commander of Co. C by the time he was chosen as the regiment's major. He was well thought of by everyone in the regiment, as expressed by Pvt. Fisk, "The Major does not look like a fellow out of his teens but he fills his position with dignity and self-restraint.... I think he bears his promotion without giddiness."[104]

There were also several changes at the company level in the regiment. First Lt. Elijah Wales was promoted to captain and replaced Tyler as commander of Co. C. First Sgt. George B. Worcester of Co. G was promoted to second

Captain Elijah Wales, commander of Company C. USAMHI.

Top: **Captain Daniel S. White, commander of Company I. USAMHI. *Bottom:* Colonel Lewis A. Grant, the third and final commander of the Vermont Brigade. USAMHI.**

lieutenant and replaced John J. Bain who was promoted to first lieutenant. Ethan A. Priest, first sergeant of Co. I, was promoted to first lieutenant, replacing Charles C. Canning, who had resigned on February 8. Sgt. Oramel G. Howe of Co. I replaced Daniel S. White as second lieutenant. White was promoted to captain to command Co. I.[105]

Col. Lewis A. Grant, commander of the 5th Vermont, was selected to replace Whiting. Grant, however, was home on furlough at the time and Col. Morrison, commander of the 26th New Jersey, took temporary command until Grant returned.[106]

Lewis Addison Grant was born January 17, 1829, in Winhall, Vt. At the outbreak of the war, he was a successful attorney in Bellows Falls. He entered the service as major in the 5th Vermont. Grant had married Sarah Augusts Hartwell, March 11, 1857, but she died January 27, 1859. While in Vermont on furlough, he married Mary Helen Pierce on September 9, 1863, in Hartland.[107]

As winter turned into spring, the weather improved and the ground started to dry out. With the dry ground came a return to a more strict military camp routine.

Pvt. Fisk wrote of the increased activity in one of his newspaper articles:

> Then we were set to work cleaning up our camping grounds. Regular streets were laid out for each company in the different regiments of this brigade. To do this, tents, (I suppose it is proper to denominate them tents—we call them "shanties" or "houses" here) which in the hurry of camping here, supposing their stay to be only temporary, had been huddled together in all manner of shapes, had, many of them to be removed and made to square with the company street. We brought pine trees from the woods and planted a row on each side of these, making each street a vista, at once pleasing and beautiful. The officers had their tents encircled by a grove of pine, and many of the men did the same. Our camp now almost has the appearance of a well laid out pleasure ground. At the entrance of each street, an arch is made of poles draped with evergreens, the company letter ingeniously made of the same, suspended from the apex. The whole gives an air of beauty and refinement to the camp, that cannot be without wholesome effect.[108]

Pvt. Felton also mentioned improvements they made in his company's section of the camp:

> we turnpiked [planked] a road through our company. The camp is laid out very much like a city having streets running from North to South making in all ten streets there being ten companies in the regiment. We also set out [,]or stuck down [,] little pine trees on both sides of the road, and built a large arch of evergreens at the end of the street with the letter H in its centre.[109]

Although the outward appearance improved, Pvt. Fisk

wrote in his diary that as the ground started drying off, the camp "smelled like a dishwater drain."[110]

With the drier weather the regular military routine returned. Besides drill, the men also had target practice. Over the winter, the men had obtained little practice, as Pvt. Fisk noted:

> Had target practice in the morning. We fired 4 times a piece. I believe only three shots hit the mark out of the whole company. The distance was 300 yards. We frightened some of the pickets and a number of the picket officers came over to palaver about it. The colonel tried to convince them they were more scared than hurt, but I presume they did not see the point. The company shifted position a little and kept on firing. In coming off picket, the officer in charge would not let us go back to camp until all pickets came in. The men hissed the officer as much as they dared to. He heard them but couldn't help himself.[111]

With the improving weather came plans for the spring campaign. Gen. Hooker was determined that when the campaign started his army was not going to straggle when on the march. On March 21, he issued an order requiring the men of each corps to wear a distinctive cloth badge on the top center of their caps so stragglers could be identified and quickly returned to their units for punishment. Hooker's chief of staff, Maj. Gen. Daniel Butterfield, is credited with having designed the patches for the corps of the Army of the Potomac. The badge styles were as follows: First Corps, sphere; Second Corps, trefoil; Third Corps, lozenge; Fifth Corps, Maltese cross; Sixth Corps, St. Andrews cross; Eleventh Corps, crescent; Twelfth Corps, star. The badges of the first division of each corps were red, the second division white and the third division blue. Eventually badges were designed for the other corps in the Union army.[112]

Apparently having to sew on the badge did not seem like a chore to the men in the 2nd Vermont, since nothing about the badges is recorded in any of their letters or diaries. By the next year, however, the corps badge became a symbol of pride, and not only did the men wear it on their caps, but in most of their photographs they can be seen wearing a metal version of the badge on the breasts of their uniform coats. Hooker's order is the origin of the division and corps patches worn on the uniforms of our soldiers today.

As April wore on, the men could see the signs of the upcoming spring campaign. Sgt. Bond lamented:

> We have sent overcoats and everything that we can get along without to Washington. The furlough order was countermanded yesterday so you may give up all hopes of seeing me till next winter. You don't know how I wanted to come home but all is for the best. May God give me the strength to Battle for the right till this rebellion comes to an end.[113]

While things in the field were improving for the men in the 2nd Vermont, a tragedy occurred to one of their former comrades back home. Daniel K. Stickney, who had been a member of Co. F, died on April 7. The five-foot eight and one half-inch native of Berlin, Vt. had enlisted May 7, 1861, at the age of 18. He was captured in the retreat from Bull Run and spent six months in a Confederate prison in Richmond until paroled January 3, 1862. He had survived the rigors of the Peninsula Campaign and Lee's invasion of Maryland but was discharged February 5, 1863, for chronic diarrhea. His father had died in 1857, and Daniel had been helping to support his mother. Mrs. Stickney applied for a pension soon after Daniel's death, but the bureaucracy drew out the process for almost a year. In frustration, she cut out the middlemen and went straight to the top with a letter to President Lincoln.

> Berlin Vermont Apr 21 1864
>
> Mr. A. Lincoln President of the United States, I feel it a duty to write you concerning my son Daniel K. Stickney. he was a volunteer in the United States service, he inlisted in the Vermont 2d Company D previous to his enlistment he was part of my support. After his enlistment he gave me the seven dollars he drew from the state of Vermont but now I am deprived of him and the support he gave me. he sufered the privations of war, all this time he was brave untill sickness came upon him then he gave up after months sufering with the Chronic Direahes. he got his Discharge hoping to save his life but he was to worn out. I had all don that could be done to save his life but to no efect there was no help for him. he was enrolled on the Seventh day of May one thousand eight hundred and sixty one, he was Discharged from the service of the United States the 5th Day of February 1863, he was in the service twenty two months. I think his bounty ought to be paid to me and a pension to help me in my declining years. I was looking up to my son for support in my declining years but my hopes are all blasted. you stand at the head of government and I hope you will do all you can for me, yours with respects
>
> Cynthia Stickney
>
> I write myself to save expence

Either feeling she had not made the letter strong enough, or else having gotten her Vermont dander up, she added a P .S.:

> My son lived only eight weeks after he got home. he died the 7 day of Apr 1863. I know soldiers that was not in the service so long as my son that got their Discharge and saved thar lives and have drawn thar Bounty and have a Pension. I want justis done and I hope it will be in my case
>
> Cynthia Stickney

Whether the President himself intervened in Mrs. Stickney's case is unknown. There are no notes by him on the letter, only those of his staff; but she soon received a pension for $3 a month which was retroactive to the time of Daniel's death. In 1866 her pension was increased to $8 a month.[114]

Orders were finally issued on April 14 for the Army of the Potomac to get ready to move. Lt. Leach wrote in a letter:

> The men have nearly all packed their overcoats, & only have one woolen blanket, rubber, & tent, besides their underclothes. I fear we will have to march in the rain tomorrow if we march at all for there are strong signs of a storm. Our destination I don't undertake to guess, for I know nothing about it, only it is where the Rebels are, or where they will be. I don't think we are going to cross the river in the vicinity of Fredericksburg, but probably above. I hope wherever we may go it will prove to be a success on our part & I think I have faith that it will be, & therefore am ready & willing to go, as much so as though it were to lay here 6 months longer.[115]

Leach was correct in his prediction of the approaching storm. In fact, the rain was so bad that it delayed the army's movement for about two weeks, giving the men a short reprieve before the next round of bloodletting.[116]

CHAPTER 8

COVERED WITH GLORY

Hooker's spring campaign, which would become known as the Chancellorsville Campaign, began on April 27, 1863. Not wanting to repeat Burnside's fatal frontal assault on the Confederates on the heights above Fredericksburg, Hooker's plan called for the Fifth, Eleventh and Twelfth Corps to move rapidly around Lee's left flank via Kelly's Ford, to Chancellorsville 12 miles west of Fredericksburg. The Second Corps was to feign crossings at United States and Banks Fords to deceive the Confederates as to the movement of the other three corps. The First and Sixth Corps, under the command of Sedgwick, were to cross the Rappahannock and threaten Lee's forces that were crowning Marye's Heights to keep the pressure off the three Federal corps at Chancellorsville. Maj. Gen. Daniel E. Sickle's Third Corps, also under Sedgwick's control, would remain on the Falmouth side of the river as a general reserve.[1]

The Sixth Corps received marching orders on April 28, which quickly trickled down the chain of command to the 2nd Vermont. The Vermonters' camp was suddenly a beehive of activity. Eight days' rations were issued, and tents were pulled down. In preparation for moving out, love letters, novels, newspapers, and any other non-essential items were burned to lighten the load. All of this was done during a rainstorm that threatened to delay again the start of the campaign. But the rain stopped around noon as the Vermonters moved out of their camp to join the miles of long blue lines of soldiers marching toward the Rappahannock River. As the sun came out and started drying up the road, the men soon began singing, laughing, and joking in the ranks. Despite the humiliating defeat they had received in December, the soldiers were full of confidence that this would be a successful venture.[2]

The Sixth Corps halted for the night behind the bluffs overlooking the Rappahannock near where it had crossed the river in December. To hide their movement, the Federal soldiers were not allowed to have cooking fires that night and had to settle for a supper of cold salt pork and hardtack. Then they wrapped themselves up in their blankets and turned in for the night.[3]

During the night, pontoon boats were quietly carried down to the river, and at daybreak, a portion of Brooks's division paddled across the river, driving off the startled rebel pickets, and established a bridgehead. This crossing was made at Franklin's Crossing where the Sixth Corps had crossed in December. Three bridges were quickly laid, and the rest of Brooks's division was soon on the other side of the river.[4]

Howe's Second Division of the Sixth Corps was held on the Falmouth side of the Rappahannock with the Third Corps as part of the reserve and had nothing to do but to watch the goings on across the river. Later in the day, Hooker sent an order for the Third Corps to join him at Chancellorsville.[5]

Thursday, April 30, was pretty much a repeat of the day before for Sedgwick's troops. The rest of the corps on the Army of the Potomac's right, however, was moving, and moving fast. By Thursday afternoon with virtually no opposition, it was ensconced in and around the country crossroads of Chancellorsville behind Lee's army.[6]

Friday morning in a cold, chilly drizzle Hooker pushed his units east toward Fredericksburg. By mid-morning, his advance units were at the foot of a commanding ridge topped with a small wood-frame Baptist church known as Zoan Church. To keep Lee from moving troops from the Fredericksburg area, Hooker ordered Sedgwick to stage a demonstration against the rebels but not to bring on an actual fight. That afternoon Sedgwick had brigades put into line of battle and marched about to attract the rebels' attention.[7]

Lee was outnumbered by the Federals 130,000 to 60,000. Gen. Longstreet, with Pickett's and Hood's divisions, was in Suffolk, Va., on a foraging expedition. Lee was not fooled by Sedgwick's performance, and in one of his most daring maneuvers, he split his army, sending Jackson's Corps to attack the Federals who were then at Chancellorsville. Lee left Gen. Early with 12,000 troops at Fredericksburg to contain Sedgwick. Near noon, Jackson attacked. Thinking Hood had reinforced Lee, Hooker pulled his forward corps back to Chancellorsville. Nightfall found Hooker's men fortifying their positions in and around the crossroads.[8]

Early on Saturday, May 2, Gen. Reynolds's First Corps was ordered to proceed to Chancellorsville, leaving only the Sixth Corps to force the rebels out of Fredericksburg. Again, Howe's division lay all day along the riverbank. By now Gen. Howe was itching to get into the fight. He rode across the river and asked Gen. Brooks if he would like his exhausted division relieved by Howe's. Pvt. Fisk, undoubtedly repeating a rumor, reported that Brooks replied, "No, G_d d_ _n it, if you want a position fight for it." Fisk went on to add, "The Gen. always swears." Accordingly, Howe's division remained inactive for the fourth straight day. Just after nightfall however, Howe was finally ordered by Sedgwick to move his division across the river and into position to the rear of Newton. Pvt. Fisk related the movement from the 2nd Vermont's perspective:

> Last Saturday night, as soon as it was dark, we crossed the river and halted on the plain opposite. The whole transaction was executed very quietly, and everything was very still. We spread down our blankets in the bright light of a full moon, and sought repose, expecting on the morrow to march against the foe and measure swords with him once more.... At midnight they called us up to have us draw half a dozen more hard tack apiece; we had but eight days' rations of them in our knapsacks, which probably rendered this insignificant addition indispensable to the safety of the Union. After this we slept without interruption till the day was beginning to dawn.[9]

The rest of the Army of the Potomac was not as inactive on May 2 as Sedgwick's men were. During the night of May 1, Lee devised his most audacious scheme of the war. He decided to further split his army by sending Jackson with 26,000 men around Hooker's right flank for a surprise attack. During Jackson's movement, Lee, with 17,000 men, kept up the pressure on the Federal troops at Chancellorsville. By late afternoon, Jackson was in position. Just as the men of the Union Eleventh Corps were starting their suppers, Jackson struck. The element of surprise was overwhelming, and the Eleventh Corps crumbled and fell back in sheer panic before Jackson's screaming hoard. Only nightfall saved Hooker from total defeat. The same darkness that saved Hooker brought about one of the South's most tragic losses. While out reconnoitering for a night attack, Jackson and his escort were fired on by their own troops. Jackson received a mortal wound in his left arm that would take his life eight days later.[10]

To relieve the pressure on the Federal army at Chancellorsville, Hooker ordered Sedgwick to make a night attack on Fredericksburg on May 2 and proceed to Chancellorsville. Hooker figured that with the small number of rebel units defending the town and with the light of a full moon, Sedgwick could easily push aside any resistance in his front and hit Lee from behind the next day.[11]

Although Hooker had sent messages by telegraph and messenger, it seems nothing could overcome the army's chronic communication lapses. It was 11 P.M. before Sedgwick received the order to attack Fredericksburg. Newton's division spearheaded for the corps but was harassed and delayed by the enemy's skirmishers all the way. Next came the Light Division followed by Howe's division which did not file into the Old Richmond Stage Road until after daylight. Howe pushed his division to Hazel Run on the south side of Fredericksburg and took position in the road facing Marye's Heights. Here his men lay for four or five hours while other troops ahead were getting into position. Pvt. Fisk described the 2nd Vermont's participation in the movement:

> As soon as the morning twilight began to appear we were promptly in line, ready to move forward. We took our positions a short distance in advance, sheltering ourselves in the road. The batteries took their positions on the flats and fired over our heads at the rebel works. The enemy's shot, as well as our own, passed over our heads, and their music was quite lively and interesting. Occasionally a shot or a piece of shell would come so low as to hit some one in the road, but for all that the officers found it almost impossible to make the men obey the order, "keep down."[12]

To avoid another frontal assault of Marye's Heights, Sedgwick first ordered Maj. Gen. John Gibbon's division, which had crossed the river during the night, to probe the enemy's left to see if a flanking movement was possible. Gibbon moved his division up-river through the town to a clear area in which to maneuver, but he found a wide canal in his path. The canal was too deep to ford, and the flooring of the bridge that crossed it had been removed by the rebels. Gibbon's men tried to repair the bridge, but the Confederate rifle fire was too heavy. Sedgwick finally came to the conclusion that only a frontal assault would carry the heights and open the Orange Plank Road to Chancellorsville. Newton's and Howe's divisions were tapped for the job. Brooks's division was left in place to anchor Sedgwick's left.[13]

Although not as formidable as the force in December, Jubal Early's Confederates manning the hills behind Fredericksburg were not going to be moved without a stiff fight. If Sedgwick had attacked as he had been ordered to the previous afternoon (when Early had mistakenly been ordered to move out a large part of his men to reinforce Lee), he could have probably pushed on through without much effort. Now, the rebel troops who had left were back. Early had approximately 12,700 infantrymen and 46 guns. Sedgwick outnumbered the rebels with his 23,600 men, plus Gibbon's 3,500, but the topography was in Early's favor.[14]

The plain of Fredericksburg is encircled by hills rising in terraces to an elevation of about 130 feet in back of the town. On the edge of this plain nearest the town is the Marye house and hill. At the base of Marye's Hill is a stone wall built to face and support a terrace, forming a parapet along its front. An extension of Marye's Hill to the south is known as Cemetery Hill or Willis Hill. South of Cemetery Hill and about half a mile from Marye's Hill is a higher ridge called Lee's Hill. Between these hills run the valley and stream of Hazel Run, breaking from the heights above and running easterly to the river. To the left of Lee's Hill lies Howison Hill. In front of the hills ran the Richmond, Fredericksburg and Potomac Railroad and the Old Richmond Stage Road.[15]

From the Confederate left, Early had his troops arrayed as follows: Brig. Gen. Cadmus M. Wilcox's brigade, of Anderson's division, on Taylor's Hill; Brig. Gen. William Barksdale's brigade, of McLaws's division, on Marye's Heights and Telegraph Road, followed by the brigades of Brig. Gens. Harry T. Hayes, Robert F. Hoke, William Smith, and John B. Gordon of Early's division. Confederate infantrymen lined the infamous stone wall at the foot of Marye's Heights as well as rifle pits at the foot of the other two hills. To support the infantry, Confederate artillery crowned the summit of each hill.[16]

Sedgwick's plan called for Newton to assault Marye's Heights on the right of the Orange Plank Road and the Light Division to make a direct assault against the stone wall. At the same time, Howe's division was to move at the double quick across the plain, assist in taking Marye's Heights on the right of Hazel Run, and take Lee's and Howison's Hills to the left. This would require Howe's troops to move rapidly over three-quarters of a mile of open ground, commanded at every point by the rebel artillery. They would then have to drive the rebel infantrymen out of the railroad cut and the rifle pits at the base of the hills, scale the hills, and storm a double line of redoubts and breastworks full of infantry and artillery at the top.[17]

Just before 11 A.M., Gen. Howe received orders for the assault. He formed his units into three attacking columns as follows: first column, Gen. Neill commanding, 7th Maine, 77th New York, 33rd New York, and half of the 21st New Jersey. Col. Grant would command the second column consisting of the 2nd Vermont, 6th Vermont, and 26th New Jersey. The third column, under the command of Col. Thomas O. Seaver of the 3rd Vermont, consisted of the 3rd and 4th Vermont and the other half of the 21st New Jersey. Gens. Newton and Burnham, on the right, formed two attacking columns from their divisions in the streets of Fredericksburg.[18]

Earlier in the morning, Col. Morrison had approached Gen. Howe about the 26th New Jersey moving up a ravine and attacking a rebel battery off to their left. The New Jersey regiment's nine months of service would be up soon, and for political reasons, Morrison wanted to go home with some combat on his record. His regiment had been present at the first battle of Fredericksburg but was not engaged. Howe pointed to the heights ahead as a more worthy objective and promised Morrison a chance a little later for the Jerseys to distinguish themselves.[19]

Col. Grant put his three regiments in line of battle with the 6th Vermont on the right, the 26th New Jersey in the middle, and the 2nd Vermont on the left. As promised, the 26th New Jersey was to lead the attack. Pvt. Stowe related the preparation for the assault as seen from the ranks of the 2nd Vermont:

> The Colonel commanding this brigade called our Colonel and told him that his regiment (the 2nd Vt.) had got to charge and if possible carry the heights. The 26th NJ regiment being a larger regiment than any other in our brigade the Colonel commanding the brigade thought it best to let the 26th make the charge and have our regiment follow close behind them as a support. Our Colonel (Walbridge) came and told all our line officers what we was to do and gave us orders to take off our knapsacks and haversacks and go in the lightest possible manner. We was to carry nothing but gun and equipment. The enemy wasn't looking for us to charge on the heights from this place.[20]

The Federal artillery had kept up an almost continuous fire during the morning by long-range guns on the north bank of the Rappahannock and also by some of Sedgwick's light batteries along his line. A little after 11 A.M. the sound of Newton's first gun opened up, which was the signal to start the attack, and the order to charge was given. With a resounding "hurrah," Howe's men were up and charging across the plain without firing a shot. Neill's brigade led off, followed by Grant and then Seaver. As soon as they left the safety of the road embankment, the Confederate batteries opened on them. Pvt. Fisk felt that the rebels used "every piece they had, from a 24-pounder to a pocket pistol." Pvt. Stowe continued his description of the action:

> No sooner than our regiment advanced from our hiding place behind the road the top of the hills was lighted with a sudden flame of smoke and iron hail that cut the 26th NJ regiment badly. The very earth shook with the roaring of artillery and shot and shell fell around us like hail but on we went closing up our ranks as fast as our men fell a victim to the enemy's fire as we went.[21]

Although they were moving too fast for the Confederate artillery to get good aim on them, some men were hit. Pvt. Hampton L. Maxfield, a Fairfax native in the 2nd Vermont's Co. H, was knocked unconscious when a piece of shell struck him on the left temple. Although the shell fragment cracked his skull and cut his scalp, he rejoined his company in a few weeks.[22]

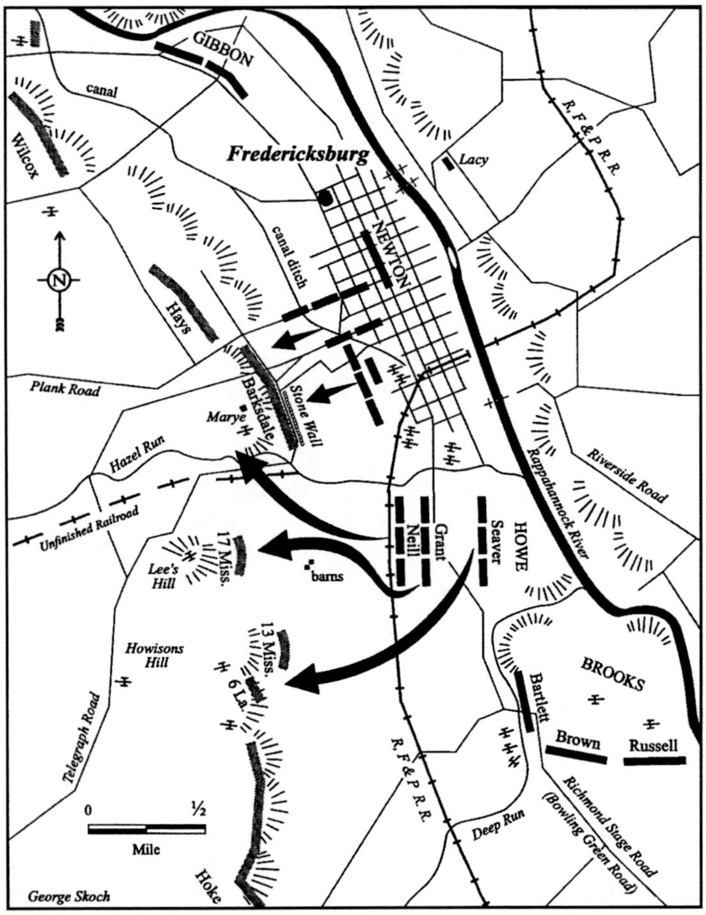

The Second Battle of Fredericksburg, May 3, 1863

Another member of Co. H was brought down just after Maxfield was hit. Pvt. LeRoy M. Bingham, a young farmer from Fletcher, was taken out with a gunshot wound in the right thigh, but like Maxfield he was back on duty in several weeks. Just after Bingham was hit, Pvt. Levi L. Munson of Co. B took an ugly wound when a shell fragment tore into his right knee. He went down with a scream from a fractured kneecap and severed muscles and tendons. Munson never returned to his company. He was transferred to the Veteran Reserve Corps where he served until discharged July 13, 1865, when he returned to farming in Poultney.[23]

The Jerseymen and Vermonters ran across the open expanse of ground as fast as they could, but their progress was slowed somewhat by a drainage ditch in their path. While the 2nd Vermont's Co. I was crossing the ditch, Pvt. Henry M. Parker, a 27-year-old farmer from Plainfield, had a shell fragment smack into the inside of his left ankle. The skin on the ankle was not broken, but nerve damage was done and Parker was down with a temporarily paralyzed leg. He lay on the field until dark when he was found and taken to the hospital. He would be away from his company for seven weeks.[24]

While jumping the same ditch, Pvt. Albert Parkhurst of Co. B landed hard on the other side and reinjured a rupture on the left side of his scrotum. Although blinded by pain, he staggered on a few more steps, but was taken out of the charge by a rebel minié ball that hit his left ankle. The latter wound was a minor, but the rupture would keep him out of action for months.[25]

As they neared the railroad cut, Pvt. Harry Hall of Co. F was shot dead. Ironically, this was the same railroad and not far from the spot where he had helped Sgt. George Doty to the rear when Doty had been shot on December 13, 1862.[26]

The Jerseys, who were ahead of the 2nd Vermont, were taking the brunt of the incoming fire, and it was affecting their nerve. As it crossed the railroad cut, the unit started to fall apart, as described by the 26th New Jersey's Sgt. Cummings:

> the boys pressed forward in fine style, clearing the first ditch, and still preserving a good line. Already the shrieks and heart-rending groans of the wounded were heard, but the cheers overbalanced the groans. The shells howled above us with a most fearful energy, and we could hardly hear the commands of our Colonel, but could see him in front, almost standing in his saddle and bravely waving us onward with his sword. The railroad was passed, but within its protecting banks numerous "dead beats" sought a shelter from the iron hail mercilessly

bursting above us. In vain Maj. Morris called them cowards, and applied his sword to their backs. Fear had in measure paralyzed them, and they lay upon their bellies like over-turned statues.[27]

Cummings continued the tale of his regiment's disintegration after clearing the railroad cut:

Once more the word was "Forward!" and once more the regiment raised a feeble shout, and again broke forward at double quick. Another ditch was crossed. Half of the plain was behind us. The men were out of breath, and becoming exhausted. The rebels obtained our range, and were doing fearful execution in our ranks. The men began to scatter, and drop upon the ground like logs of wood. "Forward, boys!" shouted the Colonel, and the command was repeated by the Major. The "dead beats" were pricked forward, and the regiment pressed to the front, first by the right and then by the left flanks.

As the 26th New Jersey was making the flanking movements that Cummings described, it was veering farther and farther to the left until it was in front of the 2nd Vermont, which caused it to lose its momentum.

Col. Grant made a corrective move as he stated in his after-action report: "Soon after passing the railroad, the 26th New Jersey broke, and in some confusion, bore to the left and in front of the 2nd Vermont. I ordered the 2nd Vermont by the right flank, and took it around by the right of the barns...."[28]

Sgt. Cummings continued his description of what happened to the 26th New Jersey after the 2nd Vermont passed them and went around the barns:

We were going at a right-oblique past an old barn and house, behind which the cowards were breathlessly ranging themselves, and among them a First Lieutenant, upon whom one of Col. Grant's aides drew a pistol and swore he would shoot him if he refused to go onward and join his men. A shell exploded beneath the Lieutenant Colonel's horse, nearly lifting him from his saddle, but his only reply was "Forward, men—act like Jerseymen!" and toward the heights the reeling human wave again surged.

Somewhere near the barns, the 6th Vermont was directed to join Neill's brigade. (Whether this was pre-planned or Grant and Neill made the decision on the run is not recorded in either of their after-action reports) Neill then veered to the right, crossed Hazel Run, and headed for a ravine that ran up Cemetery Hill just behind the last Confederate artillery position on the far right of the hill. (The ravine is just on the out-side of the brick wall of the present day National Military Cemetery and is less steep than the face or side of Cemetery Hill.) By now the 6th Vermont had outdistanced the 33rd New York and the 7th Maine and poured into the Confederate trenches at the top of Marye's Hill right behind the 77th New York. Moments before Neill's men reached the top of the hill, Burnham's men had successfully reached the top from the front of the hill. The rebels, seeing they were almost surrounded, attempted to retreat, but many were not fast enough. The Washington Artillery had 45 officers and men and six guns captured. A number of infantrymen from the 18th and 21st Mississippi, plus the 18th's colors were also captured. The whole action had taken only 15 minutes. The 33rd New York and 7th Maine, seeing that the hill was secured, went back down the slope to Hazel Run valley. The 6th Vermont was directed to take the skirmish line for Newton's division and led that division's pursuit of the retreating rebels.[29]

While Neill's units were taking Marye's Heights, the 2nd Vermont, with Col. Grant leading, finally reached the foot of Lee's Hill. As it had passed the barns, it started receiving fire from the 17th Mississippi's 330 riflemen manning the trenches at the bottom of Lee's Hill; but the sheer mass of blue and the incoming Federal artillery rounds were too much for the Mississippi boys, and they retreated up the hill and fell in with their artillery. Under the protection of the hill's steep bank, which the Confederate artillerymen could not depress their guns enough to reach, the 2nd Vermont jumped into the vacated trenches and halted for a few minutes for the men to catch their breath before continuing the assault. According to Sgt. Oramel Howe, as the men lay on the ground panting, Col. Walbridge walked among the ranks of the 2nd Vermont shouting over the din of battle, "Bully boys, bully boys, no troops could have done better. Now take a fresh breath my lads and we'll go to the top of the hill." While in this protected position the remains of the 26th New Jersey caught up with the 2nd Vermont.[30]

Unable to reach the blue troops beneath them, the rebel artillery on Lee's and Howison's Hills turned their fire on the Federal soldiers swarming over Marye's Heights.[31]

Before resuming the assault, Col. Grant sent an aide with an order for the 33rd New York to come forward and support the 2nd Vermont. At the same time, Col. Walbridge sent two companies forward as skirmishers. Then Col. Grant yelled at the top of his voice, "Up now, my brave boys and give it to them," and up the hill they charged. Col. Grant, who had led the charge across the plain on horseback, saw that the hill was too steep for his horse and went on foot. He followed behind the 2nd Vermont cheering them on as they scaled the hill.[32]

Pvt. Fisk related his account of the assault:

The hill up which we charged, was covered with brush besides being very steep and every way difficult to climb. At the

> right there was a deep ravine [Hazel Run] also filled with brush and felled trees. The right of the regiment had to make their way up through this. The rebs had set fire to the brush on the top of the hill, and the hot, suffocating smoke drifted into our faces, but we moved straight onward, regardless of everything. The air was intensely hot and sultry, the fire of the rebel musketry as we neared the top of the hill, was hot, too, but not a man flinched.[33]

As soon as the 2nd Vermont cleared the safety of the rifle pits the Mississippians, firing from the top of the hill, started picking them off. In spite of the intense rifle fire and the steepness of the hill, the Vermonters kept a steady pace until they reached the top. The rebel artillery swung its guns back around from pounding Marye's Heights in time to receive the Vermonters with several rounds of canister. The 13th Mississippi, supporting the battery, added their firepower against the oncoming Green Mountain Boys. As one of the New Jersey officers observed, "A terrible volley thinned the ranks of the Vermonters...." At this point the entire regiment started to lose its momentum.[34]

Fisk continued the scene as they crested the hill:

> For a moment our regiment wavered. A little way beyond us through the smoke, the rebels could be seen hesitating the same way. Their officers were trying to rally them. It was a critical moment. If our men would come forward now they would certainly drive them; a moment more and all might be lost. The crisis was imminent, immense consequences hung poised on a few seconds of time. Some of the rebels were panic-stricken and running, some were rallying to renew the fight. A bold attack from them just then, would certainly have driven our men, so would a bold attack from us drive them. Now was the precious moment to strike. Oh! if our boys only would rally,—thank God they did.[35]

One of the first Vermonters hit as they crested the hill was Sgt. Martin V. B. Davis, a 23-year-old six-foot farmer from Chelsea in Co. E. A minié ball slammed into his left breast knocking him back down the hill. Second Lt. Henry R. Hayward, a platoon leader in Co. E who was several yards behind, stopped Davis's tumble. At first glance Davis appeared to have a severe, if not mortal, chest wound with blood flowing out of the hole in his coat. Hayward got several men to help Davis back to the hospital where it was discovered that Davis's life would be spared. A diary that Davis carried in his breast pocket absorbed the main force of the bullet, and he had received only an ugly flesh wound and a broken rib. Although the diary was ruined, Davis would be back on duty within a few weeks.[36]

The first man to reach the rebel redoubts was the 2nd Vermont's six-foot-five-inch color sergeant, Ephriam Harrington. Although wounded, he charged up the hill and planted the 2nd Vermont's colors on top of the enemy works.

Top: **Sergeant Martin V.B. Davis, Company E, whose life was saved by a diary he was carrying in his breast pocket. Jeffery S. Jones Collection.** ***Bottom:*** **First Lieutenant Henry Hayward, Company E, who stopped Sergeant Davis's tumble down Lee's Hill. Euclid Farnham.**

The rest of the unit was only a split-second behind him. Years later Harrington would be awarded the Medal of Honor for his heroic act.[37]

The speed with which the Vermonters took the hill seemed to surprise the rebels, and one of their artillery pieces was captured before they had time to escape. The Green Mountain Boys were on them in an instant. "I must say that their artillery men was gritty," Pvt. Stowe commented, "for they did not abandon their guns until our men had shot nearly all of them down and when they was a loading it the last time our men shot the one from his gun before he could have time to fire. the rammer was left in the gun."[38]

The rebel infantry fell back on an artillery battery in its second line of defense near Telegraph Road and continued to fire away at the Vermonters. After clearing the works at the top of the hill, Col. Grant ordered Walbridge to halt the 2nd Vermont until its support could come up. Here the men fired like demons. Pvt. Stowe recalled, "I done some tall shooting till my gun got so hot that I had to throw it [to] one side and I took our first Sargts that lay close by after he was killed."[39]

The sergeant to which Stowe referred was Amos N. Bennett from Montpelier. He was not only shot, but as one man in Co. F wrote, Bennett was "badly riddled with bullets."[40]

Another sergeant in Co. F, William H. H. Camp, also of Montpelier, was wounded about the same time that Bennett was killed. Camp was hit with a minié ball that went through his upper right arm, into the right chest, through the lung and out his back. He never returned to his company. Camp was transferred to the Veteran Reserve Corps November 20, 1863, and mustered out upon the expiration of his service on June 29, 1864.[41]

Pvt. Frederick W. Chamberlin, a member of Co. E from Royalton, was hit in the neck by a minié ball that severed his jugular vein. He fell to the ground with a stream of blood spurting from his wound. Several of his friends gathered around him and told him that he did not have long to live, asking if he had any last words to send home. "Tell them that I was a good soldier," was his reply, and within five minutes he was dead. Pvt. Fisk wrote, "He had been with the regiment from the beginning, and was never excused by the surgeon but five days during the whole time, and two of those days was in consequence of a wound received at Fredericksburg before." Sgt. Charles Morey wrote of his childhood friend, "he was one of the best soldiers in the company and he came to his end in the line of duty defending that 'old flag which so proudly waves 'ore the land of the free and the home of the brave.'" [42]

Another Co. E soldier, Pvt. Andrew J. "Jack" Wills from Tunbridge, was hit about the same time as Chamberlin. Fortunately for Wills, the bullet that hit his stomach had run out of steam and did not even break the skin, but he was so badly bruised that he was hospitalized for two weeks.[43]

Private Andrew J. Wills, Company E, wounded in the stomach by a spent bullet May 3, 1863. Jeffery S. Jones Collection.

Co. I's 27-year-old Pvt. Hiland Snell, a large six-foot one-inch farmer from Ludlow, took a nasty hit in the right calf two inches below the knee. His shinbone was spared, but the bullet took out so much muscle and tendon that after he recovered from the wound he had to be transferred to the Veteran Reserve Corps. Years after the war when Snell was asked if he was ever captured, his favorite comeback was that he was never taken prisoner, but he "had the offer of it several times." He died October 20, 1904.[44]

Pvt. Norman C. Lawson of Co. H, a stone cutter from Woodbury, was shot in the left foot. Lawson had been wounded in his left leg and captured at the battle of Savage's Station the year before. He had recovered sufficiently after a month and a half's stint as a prisoner of war that he was returned to duty. This time he would not be so lucky. By May 8, he was in a general hospital where his foot was saved, but the wound was severe enough that he was transferred to the Veteran Reserve Corps for the rest of his term of service. Like many of his other comrades who were wounded that day, Lawson would have a permanent limp the rest of his life.[45]

Pvt. Hiram P. Bixby, a 29-year-old farmer from Ludlow in Co. I and a veteran of the First Vermont Infantry Regiment, was firing as fast as he could. He was just ramming home another round in his musket when he was knocked down by a Confederate minié ball. The bullet went through his right forearm midway between the wrist and elbow, then traveled through his chest and right lung and exited out his back near the spine. Somehow he miraculously survived his wound and lived until 1898, although he lost the use of his right arm.[46]

Col. Grant was hit on the inside of his left thigh, a little above the knee. The wound was not very serious, and he stayed with his men.[47]

This was the first battle in which the 2nd Vermont's officers sustained a number of casualties. First Lt. Dayton P. Clark, a painter from Montpelier and a platoon leader in Co. D, was downed by a wound in his left thigh about four inches above the knee. Although he would be out of action for a few months, he would return to the regiment and be promoted to captain of Co. F in November.

Capt. Amasa S. Tracy, Co. H's commander, was hit in the left leg, part of the fibula was torn away and the tibia fractured, leaving Lt. Chester Leach in command of the company. Tracy's leg was so badly torn open that Leach wrote home that the leg would probably have to be amputated. Fortunately his leg was saved and Tracy would return to the regiment in several months.[48]

Captain Amasa S. Tracy, commander of Company H and the fifth and final commander of the 2nd Vermont. USAMHI.

First Lieutenant Dayton P. Clark, Company D, wounded in the left thigh May 3, 1863. USAMHI.

Capt. Horace F. Crossman, commanding Co. F, was getting his men into position when a minié ball slammed into his left knee. The bullet mangled his knee, and his leg had to be amputated mid-way between the knee and thigh the next day. He never returned to his command but served in the Veteran Reserve Corps until he was discharged August 18, 1866.[49]

Company F's first sergeant, Pratt Stone from Readsboro, went down hard. A minié ball had struck him in the right shoulder and lodged just below the second rib. Unlike a lot of other men in the 2nd Vermont that day, Stone would return to the regiment and serve until the end of the war.[50]

By now the Confederate artillery and rifle fire was terrific. Lt. Leach said, "I never got into a place where the air was quite as full of lead as it was for a short time when we got on the top of those heights, & it almost seems a wonder how so many remained unhurt, & another wonder is how one Regt. stood alone as long as ours did before we had any aid."[51]

In this man-made hell, Pvt. William H. Foster, a 24-year-old farmer from Dummerston in Co. C, went down with a groan. He had just turned to his right when a bullet hit him from the left. The bullet mangled the middle and

Left: **Sergeant Pratt Stone, Company F, wounded in the right shoulder May 3, 1863. Pictured here as a captain. USAMHI.** ***Right:*** **Private Orlenzo M. George, Company F, wounded in the left jaw May 3, 1863. Kelly Dolan.**

ring fingers of his left hand before it tore through his left thigh. Unfortunately it did not stop there, but hit his penis and scrotum before passing out through his right thigh. Unbelievably he returned to his unit several months later to serve out his enlistment. The wound to his private parts must not have been too bad because he fathered five children after the war and lived until 1909.[52]

Minié balls were not the only things taking out the Green Mountain Boys. Pvt. Jerome Cutler was hit in the left thigh by a cast-iron canister ball. Fortunately, as he said, "it struck the ground before it did me...." The ball did not break the skin, but it bruised his leg bad enough that he was laid up for two weeks.[53]

Pvt. John H. Murray of Co. D was not as lucky as Cutler. Murray was hit in the right leg by a canister ball that almost took his leg off. He was taken to the hospital where within two hours his leg was amputated. He survived the amputation and was discharged on April 7, 1864.[54]

Pvt. Orlenzo M. George of Co. F received an unusual but painful wound. He was looking down to load his weapon when a minié ball hit him in the left jaw. The bullet stayed just below the skin and traveled down his neck, across his back and exited over the top of his right shoulder blade. It took many months for him to recover, and he was finally transferred to the Veteran Reserve Corps until discharged July 4, 1865. He spent the rest of his life in Albany, Vt., until he died of cancer of the bowels August 27, 1915.[55]

William Coagle, a farmer from Ira serving as a private in Co. B, was hit in the left cheek. The minié ball shattered the jawbone and lodged near the joint. The bullet was extracted on May 11 but it would cause him to be transferred to the Veteran Reserve Corps the following September. While serving in the Veteran Reserve Corps in Boston, Coagle, who was by now apparently feeling much better, contracted syphilis and was back in the hospital April and May 1865. He was finally discharged July 3, 1865.[56]

Capt. Erastus G. Ballou, a native of Boston, Mass., commanding Co. K, was one of the lucky men of the 2nd Vermont. With all the lead and iron flying about and men dropping like flies, the only wound he received was from a minié ball which came so close to his face that it ripped the skin off the bridge of his nose. The wound bled profusely, but no real damage was done.[57]

After what seemed an eternity but was probably not more than five minutes, the 33rd New York and then the 7th Maine crested Lee's Hill. The 2nd Vermont let out a cheer and went dashing forward toward the Confederate second line. The rebels opened up with a determined fury, but the Federal artillery fire from a gun that had just been set up near the Marye house and the oncoming mass of blue-clad soldiers closing in on their left flank was too much for them, and they again fell back.[58]

While the 2nd Vermont was taking Lee's Hill, Col. Seaver's regiments were carrying Howison Hill. As the 3rd Vermont charged up the hill, the Mississippi regiment that was dug in on top opened up on them. The 3rd returned fire and was almost immediately reinforced by the 4th Vermont and the 21st New Jersey. The rebels fell back, leaving the top of the hill in the hands of the Yankees.[59]

Early's men attempted to make one last stand on Lee's Hill, but his artillery ran out of ammunition, and his soldiers joined the other Confederate troops retreating down Telegraph Road. They fell back about two miles to the Cox house, where Early collected his units and formed them into line of battle awaiting an attack that would never come.[60]

As soon as the shooting had stopped and the Confederates were out of sight, the rejoicing started in the Union ranks. The air was full of shouts of joy. Hats were tossed, and backs were slapped. This was the first real success for the Vermonters since Crampton's Gap the previous September. Col. Grant wrote in his after-action report three days later, "The 2nd Vermont covered itself with glory." But for Col. Walbridge the joy did not last long. As he turned around and looked back through the smoke to the crest of the hill they had conquered only a short time before, he could see the wounded writhing on the ground and hear their screams and moans. Almost a quarter of his command was down. Overcome by this sight of human suffering and possibly touched by a tinge of guilt because he was unscathed, he sat down and broke into tears.[61]

Walbridge's time for grieving was cut short with orders to get his men in position to hold the ground they had just taken until Brooks's division could come up. Men not sent forward on picket were detailed to bury the dead and collect the wounded.[62]

Within an hour Brooks's division crested Marye's Heights on the Plank Road and Howe's division was ordered to retrace its steps back down the hill to retrieve its knapsacks and then rejoin the rest of the corps.[63]

The Sixth Corps had brilliantly executed the assault on Marye's Heights. They had stormed it so quickly that Barksdale's brigade alone lost 592 men, 327 of whom were reported missing. Early lost eight of his artillery pieces and was completely cut off from the rest of Lee's army. He could have been in an even worse position if Sedgwick had not been ordered to proceed directly to Chancellorsville as rapidly as possible.[64]

This victory cost the Federals nearly 1,100 men. The Vermont Brigade's loss was 132 killed and wounded, 105 of which were from the 2nd Vermont. The breakdown of the 2nd Vermont's losses were 11 killed and 94 wounded, of which seven would die later from their wounds. Pvt. Joseph C. Felton wrote his daughter Emily after the battle, "I hope never to see another such a Sabath as the last...."[65]

Col. Grant was awarded the Medal of Honor, April 25, 1893, for "Personal gallantry and intrepidity displayed in the management of his brigade and in leading it in the assault on Salem [Marye's] Heights, Va., May 3, 1863, in which he was wounded."[66]

When the Green Mountain Boys reached the Old Richmond Stage Road where they had left their knapsacks, they were given time to boil some coffee and gobble some hardtack and chatter about the events of the day. One topic of discussion was Col. Morrison's being sent to the rear by Col. Grant soon after taking Lee's Hill. It seems that Morrison had fortified himself with a large quantity of John Barleycorn before the charge. After a short rest, the troops strapped on their knapsacks and started off to rejoin the rest of the corps. While passing through Fredericksburg to the Orange Plank Road, Pvt. Stowe observed the condition of the town: "One brigade had bin a fighting in the citty and the streets was strewn with the dead of both armeys. The buildings was literaly riddled with both infantry and artillery shots. It was a doleful looking place inhabited by nothing but negros and a few woe begotten white people that dare not say their soul was their own."[67]

While the Sixth Corps had been hard at work in Fredericksburg, the rest of Hooker's army had been equally busy around Chancellorsville. After Jackson's wounding on the evening of May 2, Maj. Gen. Jeb Stuart took command of Jackson's Corps. At sunrise on May 3 Stuart hit Sickles's Third Corps at Hazel Grove. A vicious fight ensued, and the Federals were eventually driven back to entrenchments nearer the Chancellor House, where they held. During this action a little after 9 A.M., a pillar on the Chancellor House porch against which Hooker was leaning was hit by a cannon ball. Hooker was knocked to the floor unconscious. He soon revived but remained disoriented for several hours.[68]

Lee was about to renew the attack against the Yankees' new position when news of the disaster at Fredericksburg arrived. He quickly decided to hold Hooker's part of the army in check while he dealt with Sedgwick. McLaws's division, along with Brig. Gen. William Mahone's brigade of Maj. Gen. Richard H. Anderson's division, was ordered to rush to Early's aid.[69]

Back at Fredericksburg, Brooks's division had finally reached its position on Marye's Heights. Sedgwick's delay in moving Brooks's division out gave Hays, who had been cut off from Early when the Sixth Corps broke through at Marye's Heights, time to rejoin Early by quickly moving around the head of the Sixth Corps. Wilcox, who had also been cut off, took advantage of the delay and selected a strong position from which he opened fire with his artillery, further delaying Brooks's departure. After harassing Brooks's troops for a while, Wilcox retreated toward the River Road; but finding he was not pursued and that Brooks was advancing with great caution, Wilcox turned back and occupied a position at the Orange Plank Road's toll gate, half a mile from Salem Church. When Brooks put serious pressure on him, Wilcox fell back and joined McLaws, who was now in position at the church.[70]

McLaws formed his line at 2 P.M. in the strip of woods that ran along the low ridge at Salem Church. He had two brigades in line of battle on each side of the road. Wilcox's brigade, when driven in, was directed to occupy a position around the red brick church and adjacent log schoolhouse. The Confederates were now in a strong position with Wilcox's men barricaded in the buildings and McLaws's other troops sheltered by the woods. Brooks's men on the other hand had to form up and charge across open fields. After a brief artillery contest which ended when the rebels ran out of ammunition, Brooks's division went forward at about 4 P.M. His men made a gallant charge and after some fierce fighting captured the buildings and drove in part of Wilcox's line. Out of desperation, Wilcox personally took charge of his reserve regiment and aided by Semmes's brigade made a fierce counterattack. The fight for the schoolhouse raged with great fury. (The brick walls of Salem Church to this day are pockmarked from the Federals' bullets). Finally, the Federals were obliged to yield a portion of the crest. Their withdrawal from the schoolhouse made a gap forcing the other portions of the Federal line to retreat to avoid being flanked. Brooks was therefore driven back to the shelter of the Federal guns which had been set up at the tollhouse. With Brooks's beaten troops safe behind their own artillery, Newton's division came up and formed on his right and Howe's division on his left.[71]

When Wilcox had left the vicinity of Banks's Ford earlier in the day to aid in the defense of Fredericksburg, Union Brig. Gen. Henry W. Benham, commanding an engineer brigade on the opposite side of the Rappahannock, constructed a pontoon bridge at Scott's Ford. Located about a mile downriver from Banks Ford, this bridge enabled him to maintain communications with Sedgwick. The bridge also allowed Sedgwick a means of retreat if necessary.[72]

As night fell, Brooks's division was stretched out along the Orange Plank Road facing south. Newton's division, on Brooks's right flank, was perpendicular to the road facing west toward Chancellorsville. Howe's division, on Brooks's left flank, was also perpendicular to the road facing toward Fredericksburg and stretched toward the river.[73]

Around midnight, Pvt. Elwin K. Headle, a 22-year-old farmer from Mt. Holly, of Co. I, who was detailed to the regiment's commissary sergeant, lumbered into the 2nd Vermont's position with a wagonload of rations. After issuing his load, Headle started back down the Orange Plank Road and crossed the Rappahannock around daybreak, a mere two hours before the Confederates cut off the Sixth Corps from Fredericksburg. He related later that it was his shining moment of the war. He stated, "It was my duty to see that the boys had enough & I always done my best to get full

Private Elwin K. Headle, Company I, who resupplied his comrades with rations during the early morning hours of May 4, 1863. USAMHI.

rations for them." Now with their stomachs full, the boys in the 2nd Vermont settled down for some sleep wondering what the next day might bring.[74]

The next morning, May 4, found Sedgwick surrounded on three sides with his back to the river. Even the enlisted men in the 2nd Vermont could tell they were in trouble as evidenced by Pvt. Halpin's diary entry, "This morning found us in a tight place nearly surrounded." Newton's and Brooks's divisions were confronted by McLaws's division. Howe's division once again faced Early's soldiers who in the wee hours of the morning had reoccupied the lightly defended positions on Marye's Heights, cutting Sedgwick off from Fredericksburg.[75]

Early had been allowed to retake his old position through a mistake on Sedgwick's part. Sedgwick thought that Gibbon was going to hold the heights. Gibbon's assignment, however, was to hold the town and the pontoon bridges and he assumed that Sedgwick was to hold the heights. Because of this lack of communication, Early retook the heights virtually unopposed and cut off the Sixth Corps from Fredericksburg.[76]

On the morning of May 4, Gen. Lee reconnoitered the position held by the main body of the Federal units at Chancellorsville and, finding that it had been strengthened during the night, determined not to attack until he had his whole force reunited. He left Stuart to hold Hooker in position and turned his attention to Sedgwick. With McLaws's and Early's divisions now in position and Anderson's on its way to reinforce them, the Confederates would soon number about the same as Sedgwick's troops. Lee was determined to destroy the Sixth Corps and went in person to direct the attack. With Sedgwick out of the way, he could again turn his attention to Hooker.[77]

By mid-afternoon, Anderson was in position in front of Brooks's division. All three Confederate divisions were to attack simultaneously, but owing to the nature of the ground and a delay in reconnoitering Sedgwick's position, the attack was not ready until evening.[78]

While Lee was making his preparations to attack, Sedgwick sent a message to Hooker asking for assistance. Hooker was up and back in command but refused to send him help. Sedgwick was now alone to get out of his own scrape.[79]

For the boys in the 2nd Vermont the day started off well enough but then quickly changed as Pvt. Fisk noted:

> We were not aroused till we had had plenty of sleep, and ample time was given us to prepare and eat our breakfast. Everything seemed to be as well as heart could wish, and our anticipations rose high of an easy and glorious victory. But our hopes were quickly annihilated when a volley of rebel shells fired from the very hill we had taken Sunday, came hissing over our heads and bursting in our midst. This sounded in our ears as the death knell of all we had been toiling and hoping for, and we knew enough to know that instead of marching triumphantly on to Richmond, the prospect of having to skedaddle for our very lives was much more imminent. We packed up instanter, faced about and marched back to take up a position for defense. We marched from place to place, taking position in one spot, and then moving to another, so that to the enemy it might appear that we had a considerable force. At last we halted in an open field sheltered by a slight swell in the ground while a strong line of battle was posted in front of us.[80]

Around noon Col. Grant relieved Col. Morrison from command and put him under arrest. Morrison had hit the bottle again and was drunk. Lt. Col. Martindale assumed command of the 26th New Jersey in Morrison's stead. Morrison was later tried by court-martial and dismissed from the service in disgrace on June 11, 1863.[81]

Although Early's and McLaws's divisions skirmished with Sedgwick's troops during the day, it was not until almost 5 P.M. that everything was ready for the rebels to attack. Earlier in the day, Gen. Early had attempted to turn Howe's left flank. The rebels' two regiments hit Neill's brigade, but they were repulsed with a loss of about 200 prisoners and the 58th Virginia's battle flag.[82]

Howe, with only two brigades numbering a little fewer than 6,000 men, had a line nearly two miles long to hold. The Vermont Brigade held the right of the line, its own right resting on the Orange Plank Road and connecting with the left of Brooks's division.[83]

Lee finally decided to make his main attack on the right and center of Howe's line, intending to break through and destroy as much of the Sixth Corps as he could. A few minutes after 5 P.M., Howe's line was attacked, "with a violence," Howe stated in his after-action report, "that I had never before encountered." Early's assault was started by Hays, then followed by Hoke and finally Gordon. In preparation for the attack, Howe had formed his division in a double line. The front line consisted of Neill's brigade and the 5th Vermont, with a line of skirmishers in front, consisting in part of two companies of the 5th. The other regiments of the Vermont Brigade and an artillery battery formed the second line arranged as follows from right to left: 3rd Vermont, Capt. James H. Rigby's battery, 6th Vermont, 2nd Vermont, 26th New Jersey, and 4th Vermont.[84]

The 4th Vermont was posted well to the front in the edge of a piece of pinewoods, with a ravine and open field in front of it. The line of the other regiments extended along a slight swell of ground, the crest of which afforded partial protection to the artillery and to prone infantrymen. In this order they waited for Early's assault. As it developed, battery after battery of Confederate artillery came into position on the crests in front of Howe, and the shells began to whiz and crack along his lines.[85]

The Confederate charge began in grand style, but soon after Hoke's brigade got underway, Hoke was knocked from his horse with a minié ball in his shoulder. Hoke alone had received instructions from Early for the attack and had not shared them with his subordinates. Now his brigade was without direction and became tangled up with Hays's brigade. They kept crisscrossing each other's paths, but still continued the advance. Col. Isaac E. Avery, commander of the 6th North Carolina, took command and got the brigade back on track, but in their excitement neither command could fully get its organization back before hitting the Yankee line. Additionally, Hays's lead regiments had outdistanced the rest of the brigade and suffered for it by taking the majority of the Yankees' fire. In spite of all of this, the attack continued.[86]

Howe's men were unaware of the confusion in the rebel ranks. All they could see were heavy masses of gray infantry moving down the slopes in successive lines. As they came on, the Confederates grazed Brooks's skirmish line and then squarely hit Howe's right and center. The 5th Vermont's skirmishers received the initial impact of the Confederate skirmish line. Falling back inch by inch, they resisted the enemy's skirmishers until the gray line of battle came up. As the rebels crossed a swell in front of the 5th Vermont, they bore to their right and struck Neill's front. Seizing the opportunity now offered him, Lt. Col. Lewis at once swung forward the right of the 5th Vermont and poured a sheet of lead into the gray ranks sweeping past his front. The 5th kept this up until a second Confederate battle line came up. As this extended beyond his right and to prevent being flanked, Lewis drew his regiment off through a ravine behind him. The 5th then passed to the rear of the 3rd Vermont and took a position in the second line.[87]

In the meantime, the left of Neill's line had been hit hard and began to give way after taking heavy losses. Grant's line now had to receive the brunt of the assault. The safety of the Sixth Corps depended on his ability to hold back the rebels.[88]

Col. Grant quickly shifted his units to meet the rebel attack. He moved the 26th New Jersey to the right and a little forward. Then he moved the 2nd Vermont to the left into the place vacated by the 26th New Jersey. The 3rd Vermont filled the 2nd Vermont's void and the 6th Vermont held the extreme right of the brigade line.[89]

Fired by the success they had achieved so far, the rebels came on with their shrill "rebel yell" which could be heard over the roar of the battle. Col. Grant remembered them as "yelling like demons." The 26th New Jersey was hit first by Hoke's brigade. They gave the Confederates a flaming volley, which staggered, but did not stop them. As Hoke's men rushed in, the Jerseymen broke and ran. Pvt. Wilbur Fisk described the scene:

> At first we could see that our men were falling back, but as they approached us the woods hid them from our view. We waited in suspense for the issue of the contest, but we did not have to wait long before we could see the ground covered with our men emerging from the woods in wild disorder, completely panic-stricken. They had the same old story to tell; their regiment was all cut to pieces and there was no use fighting, the enemy were coming in five lines of battle and would surely overwhelm us. Some of these men were forced into our ranks and compelled to fight, but as a general thing, they were too thoroughly frightened to be of much use. One fellow that was forced to take his place in the rear rank a little to the right of me was so beside himself with fear that he discharged his

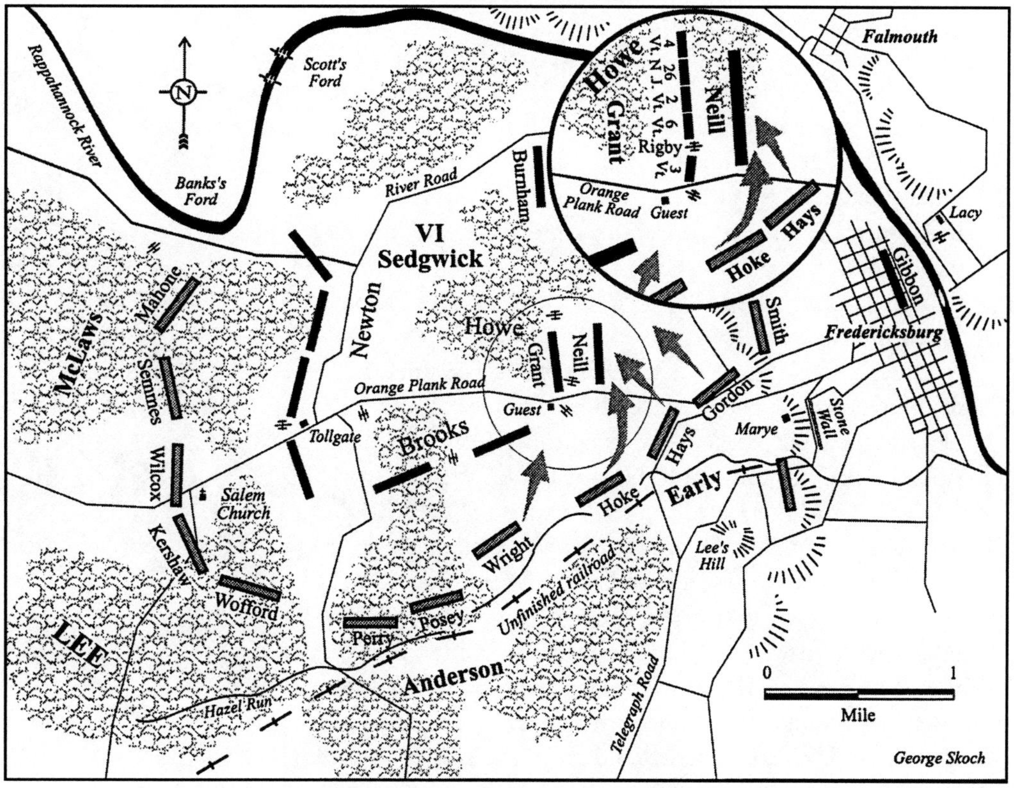

The Battle of Bank's Ford, May 4, 1863

> gun as soon as he could after getting into his place, without waiting to even raise his piece from the ground. We were lying on our faces, and it so happened that he fired directly under his file-leader in the front rank, the ball going his whole length but so close to the ground that it did him no injury. The escape was almost miraculous. The Captain concluded after that, that it would be as safe to let the skedaddlers run.[90]

The rebels next smacked into the 2nd Vermont, but after so easily tearing through the New Jersey regiment, they got a surprise. The boys in the 2nd Vermont who had up to now been kept down on the ground rose up and poured volley after volley into the oncoming Southern mass. Walbridge's men fired so fast that it sounded like one continuous volley, and the smoke from the black powder enveloped the area nearly blocking their vision. As soon as the demoralized Jerseymen got out of the way in their flight to the rear, the 3rd Vermont added their firepower to that of the 2nd and Hoke's men halted and broke. Several days later Pvt. Stowe wrote of the assault:

> the lines of battle in front of us was cut to pieces and our brigade constituted the rear line. the rebils came on at a charge bayonet expecting to take us all prisoners but they got mistaken in their plans when they ran against our brigade. their lines came so near to us that I could almost hit them with my gun. the Colonel of one of their regiments was killed within five rods of our regiment so you can see that we got close together before they run. their dead covered the ground as grey as a badger in front of us.[91]

One of the first men hit after the 2nd Vermont jumped to its feet was Pvt. Chauncey L. Church of Co. G. Chauncey, age 22, had enlisted on August 20, 1862 after completing his first year at the University of Vermont. He had bravely fought in the first and second battles of Fredericksburg. As soon as the rebel charge hit the 2nd Vermont, Church was struck in the forehead with a minié ball that killed him instantly.[92]

Pvt. Lewis M. Wilson, a Bakersfield boy in Co. G, took a rebel minié ball in the left hip that lodged in his lumbar vertebra, but he kept on firing until a shell fragment ripped out part of his skull. He was left on the field when the Union forces retreated and was captured. He was paroled May 16 and survived the ordeal. He was discharged for disability June 29, 1864, and went back to Vermont with a silver plate in his head. On August 17, 1894, Wilson became ill and while attempting to get out of bed and fell, striking the part of his skull with the silver plate on the bed post causing a blood clot. He died from a stroke caused by the clot three days later. His wound from 1863 finally killed him.[93]

Just after Wilson was hit, Pvt. David Hastelton of Co. G from Westford was hit in the forehead and like Church, hit the ground a dead man.[94]

Yet another Co. G soldier, Pvt. Hiram H. Tilly, an 18-year-old from St. George who had been standing beside Hastelton, was also hit in the head by a minié ball. It struck him on the left side of his head just above the temple. The blow was a glancing one, but the ball still crushed a small part of his skull and as Tilly said, "made me prety wild for some time." Unlike Wilson, Tilly was able to remain with his company and was eventually gotten to a hospital. The wound, although not life threatening, was troublesome. For months, small pieces of his skull kept working to the surface and had to be removed, until he had a hole in his skull, which, like Wilson's, had to be covered with a plate. Tilly served the remainder of his service in the Veteran Reserve Corps until discharged September 13, 1864, and lived until March 1, 1915.[95]

Just before Tilly was hit, the 2nd Vermont's Sgt. Maj. Henry Prouty was taken down by a bullet that went through both thighs, breaking the femur in the right one. He was quick to mend and returned to the unit several months later and was promoted to second lieutenant in Co. H in November.[96]

Co. K was taking its share of casualties. Pvt. William Wiggins, a young man from Shoreham, took a bullet in the

Sergeant Major Henry H. Prouty, who was wounded in both thighs May 4, 1863. Pictured here as a captain. USAMHI.

stomach that soon took his life. Sgt. Hiram P. Matthews, a 22-year-old farmer from Panton, was hit in the lower part of his left jaw. The bullet exited two inches behind his left ear. Matthews served the rest of his time in the Veteran Reserve Corps, but he lived to 1913. Pvt. Fayette A. Harris was spared from wounds by the rebels but was hit in the eye by a piece of percussion cap when he was firing his rifle. He would be partially blind the rest of his life.[97]

Pvt. Patrick Burgin, a 31-year-old Irish immigrant framer from Montpelier in Co. D was not so lucky. He was hit in the back by a piece of shell. He survived his wound long enough to be admitted to the general hospital that had been established at Potomac Creek but died the following Sunday, May 10.[98]

Little five foot, four inch Pvt. Truman O. Brown, a 22-year-old Pittsfield farmer in Co. E, was shot through the chest. Like Burgin, Brown survived the evacuation off the field but died three days later in the hospital. His commanding officer, Orville Bixby, wrote a letter to Brown's young wife in an attempt to console her and told her that Truman had done his "full duty." Truman and his wife Lydia were married on August 19, 1862, six days after his enlistment. They lived as man and wife for only 27 days before he was mustered into service.[99]

Hays's brigade pressed on until it ran into the 4th Vermont. The 4th let loose a volley that cleared the ravine in front of them of rebels. What was left of the gray wave passed on toward the 4th Vermont's left. To preclude being flanked, the 4th Vermont changed its front and poured in fresh volleys, holding the enemy's lines in check. Seeing that the 2nd and 3rd Vermont were holding their own, Grant sent the 5th Vermont forward to reinforce the 4th.[100]

The Confederate assault momentarily stalled but then rallied and came on again with renewed fury. The Green Mountain Boys were not to be moved and spewed forth a wall of lead.[101]

Thinking there was a gap on the right of the Vermont Brigade's line, Early tried to push in more units. The Confederate troops, sensing a weak spot, came on the run screaming and waving their battle flags. Unbeknownst to Early, the 6th Vermont had been lying down behind a slight rise in the ground waiting for the right moment to unleash its fury.[102]

Officers cautioned the men "Hold your fire, boys!" "Keep quiet there!" "Down with that rifle!" Then the right moment arrived. They let the Southerners come within about 20 feet of them, sprang up and gave them a volley straight into their faces. Feeling the volley was not enough, the 6th Vermont's commander screamed, "Charge, boys, charge!" The impromptu charge cleared their entire front of the gray-clad troops. In the process, they captured a colonel, a lieutenant colonel, a major, 17 company grade officers and 237 enlisted men. A portion of the 26th New Jersey, which had been rallied by Lt. Col. Martindale, also joined the 6th in the charge.[103]

Neill's brigade had been pushed back so far that Col. Grant feared the Vermont Brigade might be flanked. He sent the 4th Vermont and a battery, plus two regiments from Newton's division, to extend the left of the line. After quickly getting into position, the battery roared into action. An officer in the 4th Vermont noted, "Each discharge of the Napoleon battery knocked their columns open, but they gathered in and moved on. Their steadiness was the admiration of all of us." Pvt. Fisk noted in a newspaper article, "the grape [shot] could be heard rattling against the trees like throwing a handful of pebbles against the side of a building." As determined as the Confederates might have been, they were no match for the wall of lead and steel they confronted and the attack quickly petered out. Again Pvt. Stowe described the action:

> After they found they couldn't break our lines they tried to flank us but in that movement they found a bloody bath for our artillery was got into position on our left and it put the grape and canister into their ranks. They fairly melted like dew on the grass in the noon day sun. Orders came from Gen. Howe to fall back a few rods in order to call the enemy out of the woods. Our lines was again formed on an open field. The rebeils thinking we had given the field up to them came on mad with joy till the field in our front was literaly covered withm.[104]

Gen. Howe said later of this last assault:

> The enemy, apparently thinking our left was giving way, rallied and confidently advanced until they brought their flank opposite the woods in which was placed those sterling soldiers of the Vermont Brigade. At the favorable moment, this brigade opened its fire upon the flank of the enemy's columns, and immediately the batteries in front opened a direct fire. The effect of this flank and direct fire upon the enemy was most marked. In a short time not a hostile shot came into our lines. Darkness now came on, but soon the moon rose and again lighted up the field, and not a rebel could be seen between our lines and the heights of Fredericksburg[105]

The Confederate troops now pulled back, leaving the ground fairly covered with their dead and wounded. The Vermonters had captured officers and men from the 7th, 8th, and 9th Louisiana and the 6th, 21st, 24th, and 57th North Carolina infantry regiments. The Vermont men had made a good accounting of themselves and secured their portion of the line.[106]

Anderson's and McLaws's attacks fared no better than Early's. The onset of darkness ended the bloody work for the day.[107]

The rebel loss had been fearful. Col. Grant stated afterward, "The ground in front of the 2d, 3d, and 6th was literally covered with the rebel dead and wounded." Sgt. Cummings of the 26th New Jersey described the scene as "one comingled mass of rebel knapsacks, haversacks, canteens, muskets, besides the dead and dying." Early's badly coordinated assault cost him 1,200 casualties to Howe's 900. The Vermont Brigade lost 16 killed, 123 wounded, and 12 missing. The 2nd Vermont tallied 6 killed, 20 wounded, and four missing.[108]

Realizing he was not going to get any support from Hooker, Sedgwick decided the only way to save his corps was to retreat across the river at Scott's Ford, where Benham had by now laid a second bridge for just such an emergency. Howe's division covered the retrograde movement.[109]

The Green Mountain Boys were a little surprised by the order to pull back after holding their own during Early's attack, but orders were orders. At about 10:30 P.M. after the rest of the Sixth Corps had crossed the river, Howe began to withdraw his division. The Vermont Brigade was ordered to remain behind to guard the division's departure. Col. Grant arranged his regiments as follows from left to right: 5th Vermont, 6th Vermont, 26th New Jersey, 3rd Vermont, 2nd Vermont, and 4th Vermont. The left of the brigade rested on the river, and the majority of the 5th Vermont was thrown forward as skirmishers. Here the Vermont Brigade stood while the rest of the Sixth Corps moved to the river. Then the Vermonters slowly fell back over the two miles of ground. In the wee hours of the morning, they formed a new line of battle and guarded the bridgehead while the rest of the corps crossed the river.[110]

After they reached the crossing, a strong skirmish line consisting of parts of the 2nd, 3rd, and 6th Vermont regiments was sent back to the top of the bluff overlooking the ford. The skirmishers repulsed one slight attack and held their ground until the corps had crossed the river. The crossing was somewhat slowed by a Confederate battery upriver which hit the upper bridge and destroyed it. About 3 A.M. the three Vermont regiments withdrew to the river. Just before daylight in a dense fog, the skirmishers were safely brought off the hill, only to find the bridge on which they had expected to cross, the one that had been hit by Confederate artillery, cut loose from their side of the river and swinging downstream with the current. Lt. Leach mentioned to his wife the anxiety they felt when they came to the river and found the bridge gone: "You can guess of how we felt, for we were expecting every minute to have the Rebs down on our heels." Before too long they all crossed safely, some in pontoon boats at the upper bridge and others at the remaining bridge several hundred yards downstream.[111]

Lt. Leach also mentioned that Co. H had little trouble as it was crossing the river in the pontoon boats: "When we crossed back this side of the river, about a dozen of our company got tipped over into the river, but they were near the shore & no damage was done."[112]

As soon as Sedgwick had moved all his troops across the river to safety, he received a telegram from Hooker countermanding the order to cross, but by now it was too late. The rear guard caught up with the rest of the Vermont Brigade just after sunrise about a mile from the crossing. The brigade had halted for a rest, and the men in the rear guard found their respective units and dropped to the ground in exhaustion. They had just become settled when the rebels lobbed a couple of artillery rounds into the middle of the 6th Vermont, wounding several men. The brigade was quickly on its feet and moved several more miles from the river and again halted for a rest. Later in the day, the Sixth Corps moved about four miles farther toward Falmouth and bivouacked for two days, while the rest of the army marched to its old camps.[113]

Against the counsel of the majority of his corps commanders, Hooker started pulling the rest of the Army of the Potomac back across the Rappahannock late in the day on May 5. He expected to have the crossing completed before daylight on May 6, but a severe rainstorm set in that night and the army was not safely across until after daybreak.[114]

Hooker now had his army reunited on the same side of the river and safely moving back to their old camps, but the campaign was lost and he would soon pay the price.[115]

Although the Chancellorsville Campaign had been another Federal failure, the Vermonters were proud of the fighting they had done. An order from Col. Grant was read at the evening dress parade on May 7 praising them for their gallantry on May 3 and 4. The men in the 2nd Vermont thought a reward might follow, but as Pvt. Fisk noted in his diary that night, "The men expected a whisky ration at supper, but didn't get it."[116]

The Sixth Corps marched back to White Oak Church on May 8 and went into camp. The Vermont Brigade camped about a mile back of its former camp, near Belle Plains. The Sixth Corps was now on the left of the army and the Vermont Brigade on the left of the corps. Here the Vermonters remained for about a month. It was a pleasant time for the troops. The forests leafed out and the weather started getting hot, so hot that Lt. Leach complained that it "was hot enough to roast niggers." Tall pines shaded the camps and the men erected evergreen arches at the head of their company streets. They rebuilt their brigade bakery and there were plenty of rations. The health and spirits of the regiments greatly improved. The troops were now back on the normal camp routine of drill, inspections, fatigue duty, and picket.[117]

As usual, some of the men tried raising their morale by drinking. Lt. Leach wrote to his wife of his concern that his old tent-mate, Joshua P. Sawyer, would return: "Sawyer is Acting Adjutant yet, but I am afraid he will have to come back to the Co. I hope not, for I had rather be alone. Lately he keeps himself perfectly pickled with liquor all the time, & if he don't hold up, I guess he will leave the Adjutant's office."

Pvt. Fisk mentioned a little "row" in one of his newspaper articles:

> We have our "rests," when, as at recess in school-time, we can play with and plague each other as much as we please. Co. E and Co. I had one regular pitched battle. For shells they threw at each other empty-bottles. (The confiding reader will excuse me for not telling what kind of bottles they were; for as true as I live I do not know.) It was lively sport for a few minutes and one had to look sharp and dodge quick to save his head. The loss was about equal on each side, and was finally settled by compromise.[118]

Some soldiers sought more benign ways to entertain themselves. Fisk continued:

> Our boys have a swing to amuse themselves with. They have got a large pole about 30 feet from the ground between two pine trees, notched in at the ends & a swing made of old trace chains picked up around the camp, hung from that. It is just in the lower end of our Co. street. The boys pass many hours with it.[119]

On May 14 Capt. Orville Bixby, commander of Co. E, submitted a letter through the chain of command that was a little out of the ordinary. He was so impressed with Pvt. George W. Durrell's performance in the battles of May 3 and 4 that he requested Durrell's court-martial sentence be remitted. The letter read:

> Camp 2nd Regt. Vermont Vols. May 14th 1863
>
> Sir
>
> I herewithin hand you statement in case of Private George W. Durrell Co, E, 2nd Regt. Vt. Vols. who deserted from his company with others on or about the 23rd day of November 1862. He was arrested near Alexandria, Va. and confined in the slave pen forty two days and then let out to go where he pleased.
>
> He voluntarily returned to his company January 22nd 1863 while his other comrades went to Vermont. He was immediately arrested and court martialed and sentenced to forfeit ten dollars per month of his pay during his term of service. The said Durrell had always been one of the very best of soldiers up to the time of his desertion, and since he has been released a better soldier never shouldered a musket.
>
> He fought with great bravery on the 3rd and 4th Inst. his clothes being twice pierced with bullets; but it did not scare or drive him from the front rank. In this soldier I have the fullest confidence and am satisfied he would not have deserted unless he had been led away by other bad men.
>
> For this reason and for his noble conduct and great bravery in the late battle I respectfully request that his sentence be remitted.
>
> I Am Sir Very Respectfully
> Your Obedient Servant
> Orville Bixby
> Capt. Cmdg. Co. E.2nd Regt. Vt. Vols.[120]

Private George W. Durrell, Company E, cited by his company commander for heroism May 3 and 4, 1863. Jeffery S. Jones Collection.

Durrell's sentence was remitted.

While relaxing in camp and reflecting on the charge they had made on the Fredericksburg heights, 1st Lt. Eben N. Drury of Co. K wrote the following poem immortalizing the Vermonter's charge on May 3:

Charge of the Vermont Brigade

The Sabbath morning dawned bright and clear upon the third of May,
As underneath St. Marye's Heights the Corps of Sedgwick lay:
A silence, ominous and deep, was on the hillside then—
Though on the top and at the foot were hosts of hostile men.

The thunder of the rebels guns the solemn stillness broke,
And echo answered echo back, as one by one awoke;
But soon our Rifled Parrots spoke, in tones we knew so well,
and poured upon the rebel hordes a refluent storm of shell.

In quick response our well served guns their deadly missiles pour,
And through the scarp and parapet of their intrenchments tore;
But grape and shell and solid shot, though showered forth like rain,
To drive the Greybacks from their works proved impotent and in vain.

Green Mountain Boys! "Ye heroes of a dozen bloody fights,"
The call is now for men who dare to scale the dizzy heights;
And see, "advancing o'er the plain, their serried lines appear,
Unbroken by the storm of grape," unparalyzed by fear.

The 26th New Jersey, then attached to our Brigade,
Supported by the Second's Boys a master stroke essayed;
But struggling through a miry bog that stretched across their way,
They broke in wild confusion and went hopelessly astray.

Then came the long-tried Second up, and passed them on the run,
Vermont well might be proud that day of every martial son,
With volley answering volley as they climbed the shelving track,
And shouting forth their battle cry, they drove the rebels back.

Upon our right the Light Brigade dismay and carnage spread,
Far to the left our own "Brave Brooks" his troops triumphant led;
Each proudly emulous of each, were deeds of valor done,
And on the crest layed down to rest—St. Marye's heights were won.

All honor to the brave who fell, nor shed their blood in vain,
Who rested with us, "but alas!", no more to rise again,
By Rappahannock's storied stream their verdant graves were made
Who, dying, shed new luster on the "Old Vermont Brigade".[121]

By May 18, it appeared that the army was settling in for a while as Lt. Leach assured his wife:

> A large fatigue went out from our Regt. as well as others yesterday to prepare for Gen. Hooker's Headquarters. He is going to move from where he has been all winter, & establish himself about a mile from our camp. It does not look like an immediate move for him to be moving his Hd. Quarters, & laying out so much labor in preparing the ground.[122]

Lt. Leach wrote to his wife on May 19 about a silver service the Vermont officers had bought for their old commander, Gen. Brooks:

> The Officers of this Brigade have produced a set of silver plate to be presented to Gen. Brooks. The cost was $500.00 or at least that was the amount to be raised. I saw it at Col. Grant's quarters yesterday. There are eight pieces of it. A teapot, pitcher, cream pitcher, sugar bowl, "poy" or punch bowl, two goblets & a salver. Each piece has the initials of his name & also one of the engagements which he was in with the Brigade. At first a horse was to be bought with equipments, but something that would always last, suited nearly all better. I have an interest of two dollars & fifty cts. in the set. Gen. Brooks is gone at present but as soon as he returns, the presentation will take place. It is to be presented by Col. Grant.[123]

The Vermont Brigade received their new band on June 1. All of the Vermont regimental bands had been discharged by late summer of the previous year. Being newly organized, this band apparently was not as good as the 2nd Vermont's band had been, since Lt. Leach, now turned music critic, wrote his wife:

> Our Band has at last arrived, came on Sunday. Yesterday morning they officiated at picket guard mounting & last night they were present with our Regt. at Dress Parade. I guess they will be good when they have a little practice. I guess they are all good musicians, but need practice together to make all things lovely. It will be pleasant a great many times to have a band to make music.[124]

Others, such as Pvt. Fisk, had a better appreciation for the band's talents:

> We have just come in from another three days' picket sweat, ill-natured and covered with dust. Our guard mounting this time had been enlivened by the newly arrived Brigade Band. We have been for a long time eagerly expecting this Band, and it was no small satisfaction to see these musicians with us. It is getting to be quite a rare treat now-a-days, to hear good martial music, but this seemed all the better for being sent from Vermont for our special entertainment and gratification. Fifes and drums lost their charms long ago, if, indeed, they ever had any. This Band made a fine appearance, their music was excellent, and it turned off our guard mounting quite agreeably.[125]

As the camps of the Sixth Corps took on a more permanent look, many ladies, wives, and relatives of officers visited the camps. Large halls were built out of pine logs and boughs. There were balls and "sounds of revelry by night" in these rustic palaces.[126]

Pvt. William C. Jackson of Co. A was disgusted by the ball held at Howe's headquarters. He included in a letter home, "I guess that most of them got a little too drunk. About 50 ladies from Washington was down. They was sent for by the officers. They must be of low carracters of course to come here in the army to a ball … I should think this is no place for a ball here at the Battle Field."[127]

Sgt. Charles Morey, like Jackson, was equally appalled by Howe's ball. He wrote his sister:

> Last night there was a *ball* at Genl. Howe's H.Q. and I understand that Genl Hooker was there. What a disgrace for a man holding the position he does; to engage in any thing of this kind. We never knew anything of this character when Genl. McClellan was in command of the army; he knew that it was no time nor place to engage in such pursuits, he thought it best to spend his time in watching the movements of the enemy and doing something for the benefit of his army instead of seeking pleasure and then again he is not a man who seeks

> such kind of amusements. I think that this one act of Genl. Hooker's will make him more unpopular with the men than almost any other act he could have performed here in the face of the enemy.[128]

While the Army of the Potomac lay in its camps along the Rappahannock, Lee was busy reorganizing his army and developing his next objective. The loss of Jackson had left a significant void in the senior leadership of the Army of Northern Virginia. Lee's solution to this shortfall was to reorganize his two corps into three smaller, more manageable ones. Longstreet was left in command of the First Corps. Richard S. Ewell was selected to command Jackson's Second Corps and A. P. Hill was promoted to lieutenant general to head a Third Corps.[129]

Emboldened by his recent success at Chancellorsville, Lee obtained approval from the Confederate government to invade Pennsylvania. There were a number of reasons for this Northern invasion. The two most important were Lee's inability to feed his army in this portion of war-ravaged Virginia, and the notion that a successful invasion might break the will of the Northern people to sustain the war effort, thereby forcing the federal government to seek peace terms with Richmond.[130]

Gen. Lee began slipping his units away from the Rappahannock northward on June 3, and by June 5 only A. P. Hill's corps remained in the lines of Fredericksburg to mask the movement. Hooker was informed of the movement by his intelligence operatives and his men in observation balloons. On June 4, he issued orders for his army to be ready to march at a moment's notice with three days' rations. At the same time, Sedgwick was directed to move his corps to the river below Fredericksburg. For the third time, he was to cross at Franklin's Crossing to feel the enemy's lines and discover if any considerable portion of Lee's army remained. For this task, Sedgwick selected Howe's division. At noon on Friday, June 5, the division broke camp and marched to the river. As it reached the ridge above the river at about 4 P.M., several batteries were taking position along the brow of the hill overlooking the river, and the pontoon trains were moving down to the river bank.[131]

The enemy pickets on the other side of the river had a strongly entrenched picket line, which kept up an annoying fire on the engineers as they approached the river with their boats. It soon became obvious that the Confederates must be cleared out of their rifle pits if the bridges were to be laid without serious loss. Four or five batteries were quickly advanced, and cannon balls began to plow the rebel breastworks into ridges, almost hiding them in clouds of dust and smoke. The Confederates, however, hunkered down in their fortifications and took the half-hour bombardment with minimum casualties. Seeing that the artillery barrage was not going to work, Howe decided to try another tactic. He ordered Lewis Grant to send two regiments across the river in pontoon boats to drive out the rebel pickets. Grant chose the 5th Vermont and 26th New Jersey for the job.[132]

Before moving out, about 40 of the Jerseymen, seeing the assault was going to be hazardous, decided not to go. They said their nine-month obligation was about to expire. They based this argument on the date they enlisted, not the date they were mustered into service, which was September 18, 1862. Leaving the protesters behind, the New Jersey regiment reached the boats and started loading.[133]

As the Jerseymen crowded along the naked riverbank, they became easy targets for enemy sharpshooters on the opposite side of the river, and several men were hit. Three or four boats were hastily shoved into the water. Sgt. Dodd of the 26th described what happened next:

> There was a moment of desperate confusion; no one responded to the frantic but unfamiliar orders of officers to "Get into those boats!" when out of the crowd one man sprang forth, leaped to the gunwale of one of the boats and waving his gun high in the air cried, "Come on, boys!" ... Instantly the boat was filled, pushed off from the bank, and the engineers with their big oars began to row out into the stream. Another boat quickly followed, and soon a flotilla of seven of these great scows, deeply laden, bristling with bayonets, was making such speed as is possible for such awkward craft toward the opposite shore.[134]

Another Jerseyman wrote:

> When we were half way across the stream a bullet struck the oar of one of our rowers, close to his hand with sharp ping and shock. For an instant the man seemed paralysed; he stopped rowing and our boat's head swung around, threatening collision with the craft beside us. In that other boat was a red-haired captain, a fiery little Irish gamecock. Quick as thought he grasped the situation, and leaning far over the gunwale with uplifted sword, he hissed at the frightened oarsman: "Row, damn you, or I'll cut your head off!"
>
> Never can I forget the appealing glance of the poor fellow at that impending sword, nor his sudden transformation from helpless inertness to desperate energy.[135]

The Jerseymen landed on the far shore and quickly leaped out of the boats, fired one volley at the enemy above, and instead of charging, halted under the shelter of the riverbank. Just minutes later Companies G and C of the 5th Vermont hit the shore, pushed the Jerseys out of their way and dashed up the hill heading straight for the earthworks in front. The Vermonters jumped into the rifle pits, and at the command to surrender, the Confederate outpost, consisting of six officers and 84 men, threw down their arms and gave up without resistance. Lt. Col. Martindale rallied a number of the Jerseymen and assisted the 5th Vermont in collecting the prisoners and securing the bridgehead. The other companies of the 5th Vermont, as well as the 2nd, 3rd and 4th Vermont, followed as fast as boats became available. Grant remembered later, "It was an amusing scene, our men crowding the boats, and with cheers, rowing for the other side of the river, and at the same time boats returning with rebel prisoners." As fast as the troops could cross they were put into line of battle and pushed forward until the skirmish line reached the Old Richmond Stage Road in a giant arc fanning out from the bridgehead. In this "exciting and brilliant affair," as Col. Grant called it, the 26th New Jersey lost two men killed and 17 wounded. The 5th Vermont had seven men wounded during the crossing.[136]

As soon as the bridges were laid, the 6th Vermont joined the brigade. During the night, a company of the 18th Mississippi, two officers and 34 men on outpost duty near Deep Run, surrendered themselves to the Vermont pickets. They indicated that they assumed they were surrounded, and besides they had "got enough of the war."[137]

The next morning, enemy skirmishers attacked a portion of the Vermont Brigade's skirmish line held by the 6th Vermont. The firing was very sharp for two hours and continued sporadically the rest of day. Although the Vermonters were outnumbered almost two to one, they held the line. By noon a resupply of ammunition was required, many men having fired over 30 rounds apiece.[138]

During Friday night and Saturday morning, the Vermont Brigade was the only Union force on the south side of the Rappahannock. On Saturday afternoon, another brigade moved across and rifles were traded for shovels and existing rebel breastworks were converted for Federal use. Thankfully for the Vermonters, the cautious Sedgwick thought the Confederate forces crowning the heights in his front were too strong to attack, nor did Lee have any intention of bringing on an engagement at this juncture. Howe's division was relieved by another division on June 7 and returned to the north side of the river.[139]

Once the combat operation below Fredericksburg was over, everything got back to normal along the Rappahannock. The Union and Confederate pickets went back to exchanging half-amiable insults and carrying on trade across the river, in direct violation of orders. Pvt. Fisk wrote that one of the times he was on picket, the rebel pickets asked what the Vermonters were fighting for. "We told them we were fighting to save their niggers, which they seemed to resent a little."[140]

Even though trading newspapers, tobacco, and coffee across the river was forbidden, some officers like Lt. Leach turned a blind eye to the practice as he explained to his wife:

> We had a very good time on picket. The right of our line was opposite the left of our skirmish line on the other side of the Rappahannock, & extended down the river to where the 1st Corps crossed the 1st of May. The most we had to do was to keep the pickets the right side of the river, for the men would swim over to exchange papers, coffee, tobacco, etc. Two or three men of Co. H swam over & we kept posted on the news from Richmond as long as we were out.

The next morning the Vermonters and the rebels got a little more chummy. Stowe wrote about the events as they transpired:

> our boys went acrost the river last evening and got a rebil paper dated the 8th of May. at the time of my writing the boys are undressing themselves to cross over and get the morning papers from Richmond, Va. the rebils are on the other bank waiting with papers in their hand. the one is now half way over. Now he reaches the bank shakes hands with the enemy changes papers comes back agin. another one goes over with another paper in his mouth to change with them. the last one gets most tired out. calls for the former one to get a pole to help him ashore. after he gits ashore he changes papers with them. starts back. this is contrary to orders and has to be done on the sly. If our officer knew of it would be a hard job for them that went over to the rebils. One of the boys that crost the river isent a very good swimer so the rebils goes and gets a plank for him to come back on. they are a having a good time with each other talking of the different battles they have bin in during their soldier life. finally they both take to the water start back. one of them lose their plank. the rebils stand on their side of the river and watch them until they reach this side of the river and then bid them good by telling them they have got back safe. biding them good by the enemy goes on reading their papers and our men come off with their prize feeling fatigued of their plank expedition.[141]

Pvt. Fisk also mentioned the men in Co. E trading with the rebels in one of his letters to the *Green Mountain Freeman* and added, "I couldn't help thinking it a great pity that we should have to shoot such good hearted fellows." Little did Fisk realize how soon it would be before they would be trying to kill their newfound friends.[142]

CHAPTER 9

A REPRIEVE AT GETTYSBURG

The largest cavalry battle of the Civil War occurred at Brandy Station on June 9, 1863. Although the Federal cavalry under Brig. Gen. Alfred Pleasonton was forced from the field by Maj. Gen. Jeb Stuart's troopers, it was a hard-fought battle that showed the Federal cavalry had finally come of age. Besides improving the morale of the blue-clad cavalrymen, the excursion verified intelligence reports that Lee's army was on the move north. Then came the news that Lee's advance had pushed across the Blue Ridge into the Shenandoah Valley and was threatening Winchester. Hooker's plan was to attack and destroy A. P. Hill at Fredericksburg and then force Lee back southward. Hooker would place the Army of the Potomac between Lee and Richmond, cutting off Lee's lines of communications. It was a good plan, but it found no support in Washington. A plan to keep the Army of the Potomac between Lee's army and Washington was adopted, and Hooker immediately put his army in motion north.[1]

The Vermont Brigade moved out with the Sixth Corps at 9 P.M., Saturday, June 13. The night was dark, and the roads, made slippery by thundershowers, snaked for miles through thick woods. The troops stumbled along in the darkness, a long invisible procession of laughing, singing, swearing soldiers. Pvt. Fisk said, "we made the best of it we could, and when some unlucky fellow fell headlong into the mud, gun, knapsack and all, we considered it a rich joke, and immensely aggravating as it might be to the victim, it was lively sport for the rest."[2]

At 2 A.M. the next morning, the corps halted north of Potomac Creek and remained there the rest of the day, while other troops, baggage wagons, ambulances and artillery moved by. Toward evening, while waiting for marching orders, the boys in the 2nd Vermont grew bored and started a little action of their own as Pvt. Fisk described:

> They got up a spirited battle on their hook, just as the heat of the day was passing off, throwing socks, with the toes filled with dirt, for shells, and one needed the agility of a cat to keep clear of the fast flying missels. Advantages were rapidly gained and lost on either side. Charges were boldly made and boldly repulsed. Victory alternated from side to side, but capriciously refused to crown either. Men were literally knocked down, but with a cheer they jumped to their feet again and pitched into the melee with more enthusiasm than before. It was exciting sport. The General and his officers enjoyed it immensely. A spectator from a distance, hearing the cheering, and seeing the dust we kicked up, ... might have thought a battle was actually in progress.[3]

Starting at 9 P.M. that evening, the Sixth Corps was off on another night march. After a short rest at Stafford Court House at daylight, the column moved on toward Dumfries. The day was terribly hot, and the dust, stirred by tens of thousands of hooves and feet, rolled up from the road in thick suffocating clouds. Hundreds of men fell out by the roadside, many with sunstroke. Some of them died, but the column pushed on. Pvt. Fisk said that "A Bible full of general orders couldn't have prevented straggling that day." Pvt. Jerome Cutler of Co. H also complained of the hard march, but calling upon his Vermont grit said, "I made out to stand it through, but it seemed as if I could hardly pull one foot after another." They finally reached Dumfries at 3 P.M. Here the exhausted men were allowed to throw themselves down in the fields, rest their blistered feet, boil some coffee, and eat whatever remained in their haversacks.[4]

Later in the evening, the Vermont Brigade was drawn up in hollow square to hear the sentences imposed on the 40 men in the 26th New Jersey who had been court-martialed for refusing to cross the Rappahannock on June 5. The culprits were drummed out of camp to the tune of the "Rogue's March." On June 18, to the relief of the Vermonters, the 26th New Jersey left for home. Never again would a regiment from another state be assigned to the Vermont Brigade.[5]

Sedgwick had his men up at 2 A.M. on June 16, and by four, the corps was on the march again. By afternoon, it forded the Occoquan River at Wolf Run Shoals where it entered the outer lines protecting Washington. This portion of the line was held by the 2nd Vermont Brigade which consisted of the 12th through 16th Vermont Infantry Regiments. All were nine month regiments commanded by the 2nd Vermont's previous lieutenant colonel, now a brigadier general, George J. Stannard. A two-hour rest gave the men a chance to take a cooling dip in the river and visit with the 14th Vermont, whose camp happened to be near the shoals. Lt. Leach wrote his wife about the reunion, "I guess they thought we were a tough lot of men for whiskey was plenty & a great many drunk." Refreshed, the First Vermont Brigade moved on another six miles to Fairfax Station. Here the Sixth Corps halted for a day and the men of the First Vermont Brigade got to visit with the other regiments of the 2nd Vermont Brigade and First Vermont Cavalry.[6]

The Sixth Corps moved on to Fairfax Court House on June 18, and on June 20 it was sent by the way of Centreville, Bull Run and Manassas Junction to Bristoe Station. Here it lay picketing along the Occoquan for three days. In a driving rain on the night of June 25, the Vermont Brigade returned with the rest of the Sixth Corps to Centreville, where it found the 2nd Vermont Brigade, which had been assigned to the Army of the Potomac. Passing through Drainsville on June 27, the Sixth Corps crossed the Potomac on pontoon bridges at Edwards Ferry and bivouacked for the night in Maryland.[7]

The army was doing some pretty hard marching during this time, and the Sixth Corps continued making its 20 miles a day, passing through Poolesville, New Market and Westminster. By June 30 it reached Manchester, Md., 30 miles southeast of Gettysburg. Lt. Leach wrote that "We have never done such marching before, but our men have stood it first rate, only it makes their feet sore."[8]

As the Army of the Potomac was moving rapidly north, it once more got a change of commanders. On June 27 Hooker, provoked by the refusal by Gen. Halleck to permit the garrison of Harpers Ferry to be attached to his army, resigned his command. The next day Maj. Gen. George G. Meade was placed at the head of the Army of the Potomac.[9]

During July 1, the first day of the battle of Gettysburg, the Sixth Corps lay quietly at Manchester, unaware that the great battle had already begun. Early that morning, a chance meeting took place between Union and Confederate forces at Gettysburg. Brig. Gen. John Buford's Federal cavalry division, scouting ahead of the Army of the Potomac, ran into Brig. Gen. James J. Archer's Confederate brigade of Maj. Gen. Henry Heth's division, allegedly in search of shoes reported to be in the town. Buford knew the importance of Gettysburg as a transportation hub and quickly formed his troopers to defend the town on its western outskirts. Archer was soon reinforced by the rest of Heth's division and Maj. Gen. William D. Pender's division. Buford's troopers were saved from annihilation by the timely arrival of the First and Eleventh Corps around 10:30 A.M., but by day's end the Federal forces had been pushed back through the town to Culp's and Cemetery Hills, where they finally rallied and made a stand. The Federals had taken heavy losses in the first day of fighting with the Eleventh Corps alone losing 4,000 men captured in addition to combat losses, and the First Corps commander, Maj. Gen. John F. Reynolds, had been killed by a rebel sharpshooter.[10]

By evening, the Sixth Corps had orders to move to Gettysburg immediately. Howe's division started at once but was delayed by other columns of troops and made only about five miles before daylight. Then it struck the Baltimore and Gettysburg Turnpike and moved off on the longest and most rapid march in its history. It was 30 miles to Gettysburg, and it was on this march that Gen. Sedgwick paid the Vermont Brigade its supreme compliment by his famous order: "Put the Vermonters ahead and keep the column well closed up."[11]

The second day of the battle of Gettysburg dawned with Federal forces posted on Culp's Hill on the north and spread south along Cemetery Hill and Cemetery Ridge ending in the south at two hills called Little Round Top and Big Round Top, forming the shape of a fishhook. The Twelfth, Eleventh, and First Corps held Culp's Hill and part of Cemetery Hill. The Second Corps held the center of the line, and the Third Corps held the southern end. The Fifth Corps, which had come up during the night, was held behind Cemetery Hill as a reserve. Lee's units stretched around the outside of the fishhook with Lt. Gen. Richard S. Ewell's corps on the north, A. P. Hill's corps in the center, and Longstreet's corps on the south. After numerous delays, the Confederates opened the second day's battle about 4 P.M. with Longstreet's corps, minus Pickett's division which had not yet arrived, hitting the southern end of the Federal line.[12]

Maj. Gen. John B. Hood's division was the first Confederate unit to advance. Hood successfully, although not without bloody losses to including Hood himself, pushed through a strongly held position known as the Devil's Den and started up the steep slopes of the Round Tops. Securing the summits of the Round Tops would open the Federal left flank and almost guarantee the destruction of the Army of the Potomac. While Hood had been making his advance, Union Brig. Gen. Gouverneur K. Warren, posted on the summit of the yet defended Little Round Top, ordered up Col. Strong Vincent's brigade of the Fifth Corps. Once in position, the 20th Maine Infantry Regiment would have the dubious honor of being the southernmost unit of the Federal army. The responsibility for securing the left flank fell heavily on it. After several furious rebel attacks, the 20th Maine, which was almost completely out of ammunition, made a bayonet charge down the face of the hill straight at the rebels. The audacity and surprise of the charge cleared away the Confederate units and permanently secured Meade's left flank.[13]

Meanwhile, Longstreet's other division and a division from Hill's Corps hit the Third Corps which was about a half-mile out in front of the rest of the Federal army. Although the Third Corps put up a valiant struggle, it was pushed back to Cemetery Ridge in disorder, leaving a hole in the Federal line. Meade rushed divisions from other corps to plug the hole and the line held.[14]

The Vermont Brigade crossed the state line into Pennsylvania near 11 A.M. on July 2. At Littletown, Pa., ten miles from Gettysburg, the signs of a great battle were unmistakable. Flowing opposite the Vermont Brigade's direction of travel were ambulances and carriages full of wounded and dying men and soldiers moving on foot and covered with bloody bandages. As the Vermonters came closer to Gettysburg, they could hear the sound of battle and see clouds of dust rising in the distance. White puffs of smoke from bursting shells hung high in the air. One Vermont soldier remembered:

> Already the corps was meeting the tide of wounded hastening with desperate energy to the rear—that most demoralizing experience to a body of troops approaching a battlefield. With scarcely any exception the tale they told was one of disaster to the Federal army. "You fellows will catch it, the whole army is smashed to pieces !" said more than one brawny fugitive with a bleeding arm or a bandaged head, glancing over his shoulder as though fearing the pursuit of a rebel column.[15]

The sun was scalding hot, and the men had already made more than a long day's march, but on they hurried. Farmers' wives and daughters along the way brought water for the thirsty men as they trudged by. The number of stragglers left along the way started to multiply, but on the column pushed, every man knowing that he was needed ahead.[16]

The Sixth Corps halted about a mile to the rear of Gen. Meade's headquarters between 5 and 6 P.M. As the sunburned and weary men threw themselves to the ground, they could hear the roar of muskets as Hood's men were futilely trying to dislodge the 20th Maine from Little Round Top.[17]

The men were not allowed to rest long after their 30-mile forced march before the order to fall in came, and even though they thought they were headed off to battle, they quickly obeyed. "The dashing readiness," wrote Gen. Howe, "with which the division went on to the field, on the evening of the 2d, after its long and continuous march of the previous day and night, and the handsome way it bore itself during the engagement, was worthy of its former reputation." Sedgwick divided Howe's division in half. Neill's brigade was sent to the right to reinforce Gen. Slocum's Twelfth Corps, while the First Vermont Brigade and the rest of the Sixth Corps were moved a mile-and-a-half to the left near Big Round Top to protect the army's extreme left flank. The Vermonters quickly assumed position and prepared for action. Pvt. Fisk wrote:

> We have constructed us a sort of breastwork on our own hook, of rails and dirt, that we fancy will help us some, though I dare say it is not very formidable. I noticed the General smiled as he rode by and saw it a minute ago. At any rate it will stop the minniés; but if the rebels place a battery in the woods yonder and throw some solid shot they will poke the rails on to us and make the splinters fly so that our engineering will be worse than nothing. Perhaps they won't attack here at all.[18]

Near 6 P.M. as the Vermont Brigade was getting into position, Ewell attacked the Federal units on Culp's Hill. He succeeded in getting a foothold on the hill, where the line had been weakened by Meade pulling out units to plug the hole on his left, but was unable to hold it. The second day of fighting at Gettysburg was over.

The third and final day of the battle of Gettysburg dawned sultry and became oppressively hot as the sun burned through the haze about noon. The Federal troops had worked feverishly through the night to improve their defenses. Although hot, the morning started off uneventfully. Meade used the time to continue to move his units

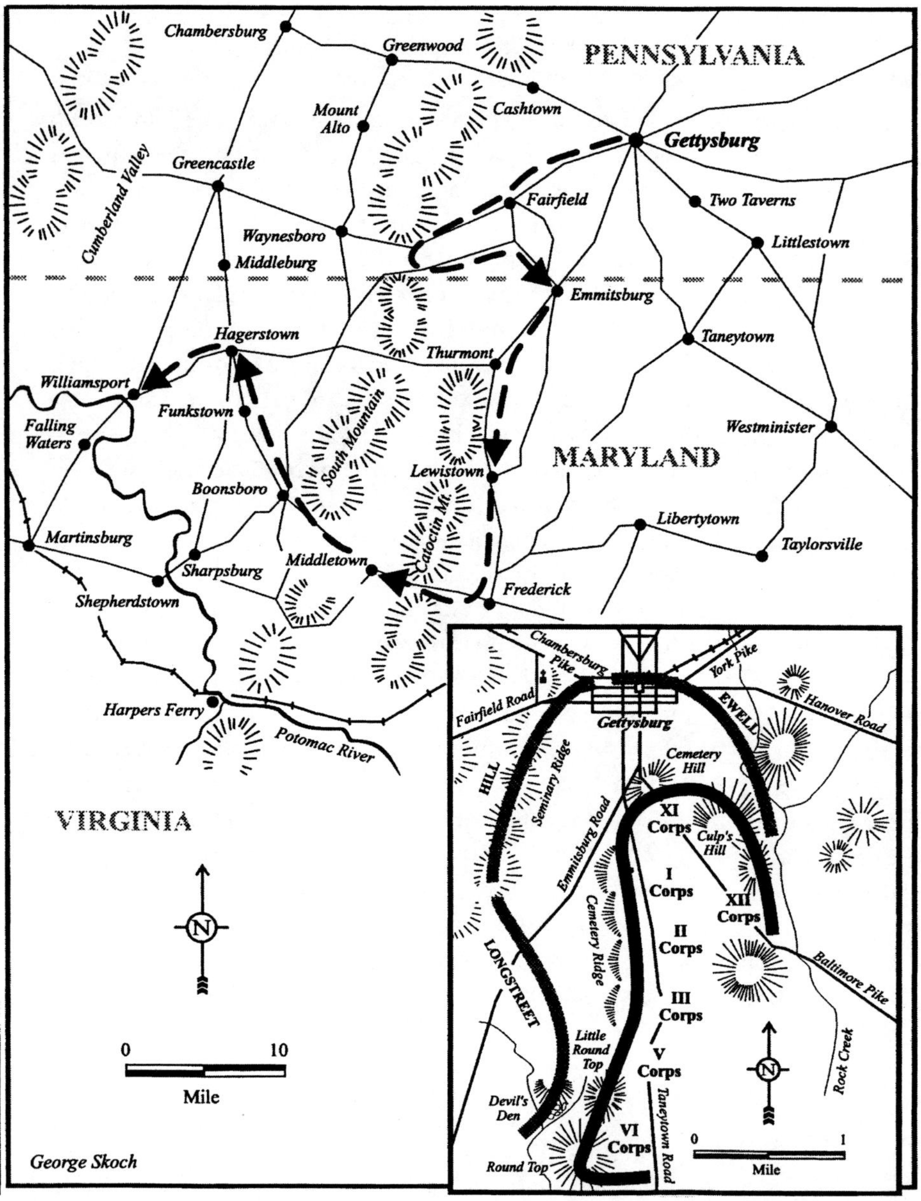

The route taken by the Sixth Corps in pursuit of the Army of Northern Virginia. The insert depicts the opening of the third day of the Battle of Gettysburg, July 3, 1863.

to reinforce his center. He guessed that since Lee's attack on the Federal right had failed the first day and the attack on the left had not succeeded on the second, the third day he would try the center.[19]

The main Confederate attack would be delivered by Longstreet with Pickett's division, Heth's division commanded by Brig. Gen. James J. Pettigrew, and two of Pender's brigades under the command of Maj. Gen. Isaac R. Trimble. Following a heavy preparatory artillery bombardment, the 15,000-man Confederate force started over the half mile of open field toward the Federal line atop Cemetery Ridge at 1: 45 P.M. The Federal artillery opened up on them at long range as soon as they moved out, tearing holes in their ranks, but without firing a shot, the gray ranks continued to press forward. As they came closer, the Yankee riflemen protected by a stone wall started pouring lead into them as the Federal artillery went to canister. The carnage was awful, but on they came until Pickett's men hit the Federal infantry at the stone wall and fighting became hand to hand. The Confederate left began to falter under the terrific fire of a Union regiment. Meanwhile, Gen. Stannard, with three regiments from his 2nd Vermont Brigade, hit the Confederate right. The Federal resistance was too much and the Confederates fell back. Thus ended the last day of the battle of Gettysburg. The losses on both sides had been enormous over the three days. Lee's army lost 3,903 killed, 18,735 wounded and 5,425 missing. The Army of the Potomac came out the victor, but still had staggering losses with 3,155 killed, 14,529 wounded and 5,365 missing.[20]

Pvt. Fisk got his wish on the last day of the battle. The Vermont Brigade was not engaged. It moved a short distance and took a position with its right resting on Big Round Top and its left on the Tanytown Road. A few stray shells did fall into its lines and spattered some of the men with earth, but it saw little of the fighting which shook the solid ground beneath the men's feet, and suffered no loss.[21]

On the July 4, the two great armies sat glaring at each other, each daring the other to attack. Except for a small skirmish the 4th Vermont picket line had with the rebels, the First Vermont Brigade remained inactive.[22]

During the night, Lee began his retreat to Virginia. The next morning, Sunday, July 5, the Sixth Corps was sent in pursuit. It passed around Big Round Top and across the battlefield to the Fairfield Road. As the men moved along, they came across parts of the battlefield where the bodies had not yet been buried. Pvt. Fisk described the scene:

> Further on through another belt of woods the dead were still unburied. Here the troops halted for a short time, and those that wished to had an opportunity of looking over the field. I

saw but a small portion of it, but I saw all I wished to. The rebel dead and ours lay thickly together, their thirst for blood forever quenched. Their bodies were swollen, black, and hideously unnatural. Their eyes glared from their sockets, their tongues protruded from their mouths, and in almost every case, clots of blood and mangled flesh showed how they had died, and rendered a sight ghastly beyond description. My God, could be it possible that such were lively and active like other people so shortly previous, with friends, parents, brothers and sisters to lament their loss.... I thought I had become hardened to almost anything, but I cannot say I ever wish to see another sight like that I saw on the battle-field of Gettysburg.[23]

"Harvest of Death," Gettysburg, July 1863. Library of Congress.

After marching over the battlefield, the Sixth Corps proceeded on for another ten miles. Lt. Leach noted, "Every house and barn for three or four miles from the battlefield was filled with their wounded which they had to leave behind."[24]

A mile or two beyond the village of Fairfield at Fairfield Pass, Lee left a rear guard so strongly posted that Sedgwick decided not to try to force passage without orders from Meade. Gen. Meade concluded that he could make a more effective pursuit by a flank route and the Sixth Corps was withdrawn, except for Neill's brigade of Howe's division that was left to harass the enemy's rear. On July 6, Sedgwick marched his corps due south to Emmittsburg. As it neared Frederick, Md., on Tuesday, July 7, it turned west and crossed the Catoctin mountain range, reaching Middletown, Md., the next morning.[25]

Crossing over the Catoctin Mountains was difficult. The corps had to travel over a narrow rocky road in the dark of night and in a heavy rain. Lt. Leach told his wife in a letter, "Tuesday we marched toward Frederick City, but before we got there turned to the right & took a kind of a cow path & marched over a mountain. The like of which we never did before. It was rough, dark & muddy & rained hard. One could not see a man four feet from him." Pvt. Jerome Cutler wrote:

We had to pass through narrow defiles and up places whare it was most as steep as chamber stairs and to cap the whole it was very rainy and dark as pitch, I played out before we reached the top, and turned out into the bushes threw my rubber blanket over me and lay down and sacked until morning.

At daylight I started for the top and I was suprised to find all the way up the path lined with soldiers, officers, horses, pack mules, and two or three division flags showing that some of the Generals had slept, and all were soaking in the wett and rain, when I got up to the top whare the regt. or what was of it had stopped I got a cup of coffee when we had to paddle on again in the mud and rain, who wouldn't be a soldier![26]

The Vermonters were glad to halt and rest near Middletown the next morning where the rest of Meade's army was concentrated. The next day the Green Mountain Boys marched across South Mountain to Boonsboro. Then turning to the North, they moved up the Antietam Valley toward Hagerstown where a large part of Lee's army lay. The rest of the Army of Northern Virginia was stretched out along the road from Hagerstown to Williamsport on the Potomac, waiting for the river to subside and a pontoon bridge to be built.[27]

Preceded by Buford's cavalry, Howe's division headed the Sixth Corps's column on July 10. Early in the morning, while moving up the National Road to Funkstown, Buford found Jeb Stuart's force dug in on a crescent shaped line east of the town with Antietam Creek to its back. The Confederate left flank was toward Hagerstown while the right flank was anchored on Antietam Creek and the National Road south of Funkstown. Southern cavalry protected both flanks, and the infantry brigades of Brig. Gen. Paul J. Semmes and Brig. Gen. George T. Anderson, with Manly's artillery, held the center. Chew's Battery supported the Confederate flank from a hill west of the National Road. Large stone barns were located on each flank and served as fortresses for rebel sharpshooters.[28]

Buford's attack began at 8 A.M. and by afternoon his men were running low on ammunition. While his men were holding the enemy in check, Buford rode back a mile-and-a-half to where Howe put his division into camp and asked him to come forward and relieve him. Howe indicated that Sedgwick had instructed him not to bring on an engagement with the enemy and he could not advance without authority from Sedgwick. Communicating with Sedgwick took a while, but finally Howe obtained permission to help Buford. Near 3 P.M., just as Buford's troopers were starting to pull out, Howe's men arrived to replace the played-out horsemen. Gen. Howe quickly ordered Col. Grant to occupy Buford's position with the Vermont Brigade.[29]

Grant could see there was no time to lose and immediately moved his men forward. He deployed the 5th and 6th Vermont as skirmishers and hurried them to the wooded crest from which the cavalry had just retired. It was a race with the enemy's skirmishers to gain the crest, but the Vermonters won. It was an excellent position with a fair amount of cover. The Vermont Brigade's skirmish line stretched nearly two miles along the crest. The 5th Vermont was on the left and the 6th was on the right. The line was too long for two regiments and a gap soon developed between the left of the 5th and Antietam Creek. Two companies of the 2nd Vermont were quickly sent forward to plug the hole. The rest of the 2nd Vermont was held in reserve and the 3rd and 4th Vermont supported the 3rd New York Artillery.[30]

It was clear to Grant that the enemy was in strong force and that the position was important to them. In fact, Lee's entire army, which was two or three miles away, was in a precarious position with the swollen Potomac trapping it on the Maryland side of the river. It was of utmost importance to Lee to guard the approach from Funkstown while he deployed his troops and dug hasty fortifications.[31]

Col. Grant saw that the enemy wanted the crest and accordingly decided to hold it. The Vermont Brigade came under a severe fire for several minutes from Confederate batteries near Funkstown and knew it meant that an infantry attack was not far behind.[32]

In an attempt to reinforce his line, Grant sent the 3rd Vermont forward to support the 6th, and the 4th Vermont was sent to support the 5th. The eight remaining companies of the 2nd Vermont not on the skirmish line stayed in place in support of the battery. Grant's orders to his regimental commanders were to hold at all costs.[33]

The Confederates advanced in full line of battle against the center of Grant's line. They apparently thought that the skirmishers in their front were still Buford's dismounted cavalry and expected to easily brush them aside. The Vermonters, however, did not budge an inch and met the gray line with a fire so deadly the Confederates recoiled and fell back. Reforming their line, the rebels advanced again. This time, they sent one regiment across Antietam Creek to take Grant's line from the left. To meet this threat, Col. Walbridge sent five additional companies of the 2nd Vermont to repulse the flanking movement, driving the enemy well back from the stream and extending the Vermont Brigade's skirmish line.[34]

As the 2nd Vermont was pushing the rebels back from the stream, Pvt. John Comstock of Co. K and Salisbury was hit. A rebel minié ball tore into his left knee, leaving a wound so severe that he would have to be discharged with a dis-

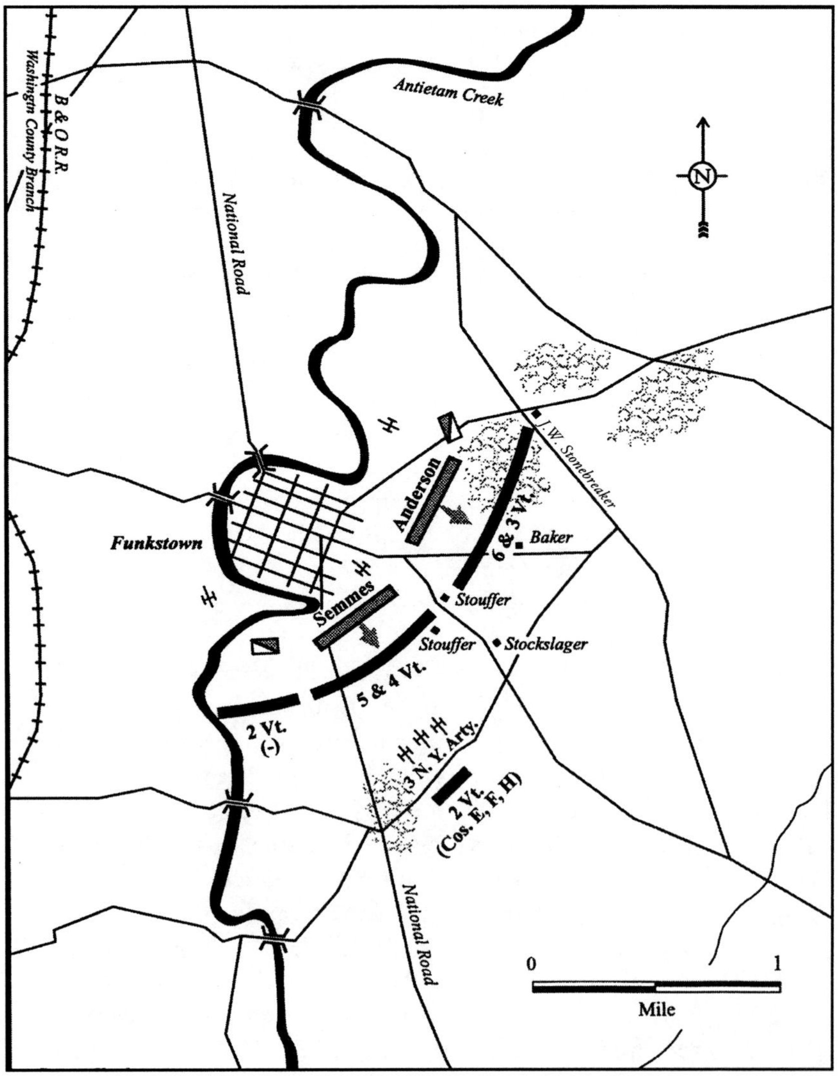

The Battle of Funkstown, July 10, 1863

ability. He was never again able to walk without the aid of a cane.[35]

Co. C had just taken a firing position when Pvt. George M. Colt, from Brattleboro, had a minié ball pass cleanly through the front of his left thigh. The wound, which did not get infected, healed quickly and Colt was back with his company in a couple of months, only to be wounded again the next year.[36]

The Vermont Brigade's skirmish line was now nearly three miles long. It stretched in an arc from the Stonebreaker Farm on the right to Baker's Farm, through Stouffer's Woods and to the Antietam on the Federal left. The only support within a mile-and-a-half were companies E, F, and H of the 2nd Vermont left supporting the artillery. Undaunted, the men took advantage of what protection they could get from the rail fences and timber and prepared for the next assault. When the Confederate battle line advanced for the third time, it was again met with a ferocious fire and was soundly repulsed. Pvt. Fisk proudly wrote:

> "Mr. Johnny Rebs" thought he was going to crush our thin picket line, but the whistling Minniés from our accurate rifles came most too thick and close for their courage to stand. They hesitated. Their officers tried to urge them on; they shamed and threatened them; they told them that there were but few of us, and we could easily be captured. Some turned on their heels and run, some rallied again to the charge. They came on a few rods further, when their ranks broke, and the whole battalion, officers and all, skedaddled for their very lives. They had discovered that they were blundering on to a nest of Vermonters. No wonder it was difficult to restrain the boys from rushing after them. With a few more Vermonters we could have annihilated the whole crew.[37]

Col. Grant stated in his after-action report, "as the center of the enemy's lines went back in confusion, some of our men jumped upon a fence, and, tauntingly calling them cowards, told them to come back, that there was nothing there but militia." But the beaten Confederates did not return.[38]

Although the battle of Funkstown paled in comparison to the battle of Gettysburg, it was intense, and it took raw courage on the part of the Green Mountain Boys to stand their ground over such an extended front. Most of the men used up their 60 rounds of ammunition, and a resupply had to be brought forward on stretchers during the fight. During the night, the men tried to improve their positions as Pvt. Cutler explained: "we dug holes out with our bayonets and piled dirt up in front of us to cover ourselves for we expected as soon as daylight came they would commence to pop away at us but they did not so we got up and walked around in sight of them and their batteries. at noon we were relived by the 3rd division." In praise of his men Col. Grant wrote, "It is believed that another instance of a skirmish line, necessarily extended over so great a distance, repeatedly repelling the assaults of strong lines of infantry at different points, cannot be found in the history of any war."[39]

The accolades that Col. Grant bestowed upon his men were not without cost. The Vermont Brigade lost nine men killed and 59 wounded, of which seven died later from their wounds. The 2nd Vermont lost one man killed and six wounded. Grant estimated the Confederates lost somewhere between 30 to 50 men killed and 100 to 150 wounded.[40]

On July 12, the Sixth Corps moved on through Funkstown. The Confederates fell back toward Williamsport as the Federals advanced and formed in line of battle along the hills in front of Lee's main force. Lee's strongly dug defenses stretched from a point northwest of Hagerstown along a crest of hills about nine miles to Falling Waters. The rebels could barely be seen through the dim light of the rainy day. Meade held a council of war on July 12, but the majority of his corps commanders advised against attacking the rebels. That was all the time Lee needed, and during the dark and foggy night of July 13, Lee finally succeeded in getting his army across the Potomac to safety.[41]

The Sixth Corps remained in the vicinity of Williamsport for another two days. Lt. Leach wrote to his wife of a horrible sight he had witnessed there:

> I saw a sight yesterday that beats all I ever saw. A Negro boy that the Rebels left in a barn, entirely naked. His breast cut & bowels were scratched or cut & the Dr. said turpentine had been put on him & also his privates had been cut off. I went in the barn to see him, but it was rather dark. He lay on his back, his legs bent, knees up & grinding his teeth & foaming at the mouth & seemed to take no notice of anything & breast & bowels looked as if they had been cut & burned all over. I understand the reason of the act to be because he would not go over the river with them.[42]

Countermarching on July 15, the Sixth Corps moved back to Boonsboro and camped. The next day it crossed South Mountain and moved down the valley via Middletown to the Potomac River at Berlin. Several other corps were ahead of them waiting their turn to cross the river on the pontoon bridge, so the Sixth Corps went into camp for several days. With the bands playing "O, carry me back to Old Virginny," the Sixth Corps crossed the Potomac on Sunday, July 19.[43]

The march south took the Sixth Corps through the now familiar Virginia villages of Lovettsville, Philmont, Uniontown, White Plains, and Orleans. Marching at a more leisurely pace than the one northward three weeks before, the Vermonters had ample opportunity to fall out and pick blackberries and steal chickens and livestock. They finally went into camp on July 25 near Warrenton. The Vermont Brigade's camp was situated on a prominent hilltop near an old log church in a grove of lush timber. Here the Green Mountain Boys had five days' rest. The weather was hot and muggy, but they had nothing more strenuous to do than picket duty and daily drill. The rest of the time was consumed in foraging.[44]

On August 1, Howe's division moved to Waterloo where it remained for five days. Then on August 6, it marched back toward Warrenton and camped near Warrenton Springs. In the meantime, Gen. Lee withdrew his army to the south bank of the Rapidan River.[45]

While near Warrenton Springs, Pvt. Wilbur Fisk and a comrade left camp looking for milk. They finally bought a canteen full from an old black man. The experience caused Fisk to reflect on how his feelings, and probably those of other men in the 2nd Vermont, toward blacks were softening:

> We made our purchase of a respectable colored man, who, with his able partner, occupy a very substantial two story house of the better sort, but which has felt the effects of war in its most practical form, it having been pierced in several places with solid cannon shot and an almost endless number of bullets. Everything within this house had the appearance of scrupulous neatness. The walls, chairs, ceilings, and whatever furniture I noticed was cleanly kept and tidily arranged, evincing considerable taste, and refinement even, on the part of the occupants, "niggers" though they were; that was apparent to the most casual observer. Yet this dwelling was occupied by two Africans, well advanced in years, belonging to a race whose title to respectability we are loth to recognize, and who are excluded from the pale of the proud Caucasian's society. I couldn't help wondering, as I talked with this man—had I ought to say nigger?—so respectful and gentlemanly in his demeanor, and thought how universally he was avoided and despised, whether He who made his skin black and mine white, would endorse my title to exclusiveness in that other world where we conclude there are no such visible distinctions made, and where he was evidently much more fitted to enter than my humble self. I found him well informed in regard to the war, as well as the citizens generally. He was conscientious in his religious beliefs, as almost all of his race are, and, as is their nature, would rather suffer wrong, than wrong another.
>
> This man had never been a slave, and has consequently possessed many advantages that are denied to slaves; but if his superiority to the common negro is attributable mainly to freedom, it only furnishes an argument against this institution of bondage that all the sophistry of the infernal regions cannot overthrow. If the soul of the African has sufficient elasticity to rise to such a height, when released from the pressure of slavery, it must be a fearful responsibility for a nation to keep them down. This nation has run the risk, and is reaping the consequences. It is of no use to speak of the prejudice against that race; but when this prejudice leads to the revolting scenes that were enacted in New York during the late bloody riots, it throws off its mask and shows its hideous deformity. A hatred that leads men to murder women and children, burn orphan asylums, and makes it dangerous for a colored person, however innocent, to be seen abroad anywhere—and all this from no provocation whatever, except the crime of color—must be wholly wrong, unnatural and unjustifiable. What if Jehovah should espouse the cause of this despised race, and shift the inequality to the other side, where then, my negro-hating friend, would your arguments and your boasting be? Should Omnipotence punish our insolent pride in that way, we must not lay it all to "radical" teachings, nor make the Republican party responsible for our damages.[46]

The riots Fisk referred to were the New York draft riots. The implementation of the Enrollment Act of March 3, 1863, had started the riots. The governor of New York challenged the constitutional right of the federal government to enforce a draft but lost. On Saturday, July 11, the provost marshal drew the first names for the draft, which were published in the newspapers the next day. That afternoon mobs started gathering and on July 13 when the drawing was resumed, rioting began which the local government was unable to control. The mob, which soon numbered 50,000, burned a Negro church and orphanage and black men were hanged from trees and lampposts. They also sacked and burned armories, draft stations, the office of the New York *Tribune*, and the home of the provost marshal. In all, they did about $1,500,00 worth of property damage and killed more than a dozen people. Working class Irishmen made up the majority of the mob and their main victims were Negroes on whom they blamed the war.[47]

The Vermonters' life of leisure came to an end on August 14 when they received orders to report to Alexandria the next day. The Vermont Brigade, along with several other units, had been selected to assist the state of New York in quelling the draft riots. The brigade was on the road at first light making a fast march over the 16-mile distance to Warrenton Junction. The day was extremely hot, and many men fell by the roadside. The brigade finally reached the junction near sundown where it was to take the train the rest of the way to Alexandria. The men boarded freight cars outfitted with wooden planks for seats at 10 P.M., and after a very uncomfortable ride, they reached Alexandria at 1 A.M. on July 15.[48]

The Vermonters remained in Alexandria until July 19 awaiting the ships to transport them to New York. Duty was light and the appearance of the pay master with two months pay improved everybody's morale. With money in their pockets, some of the men sneaked out of camp and made for downtown Alexandria. Maj. Tyler had not placed guards around the camp, telling the troops they would be sorry if they left without permission. On August 17, William S. Foster, Jr., Henry H. Osgood, and James A. Walcott, all natives of Royalton and corporals in Company E, were caught out of camp. True to his word, Maj. Tyler had them busted on the spot. Walcott must have set a unit record for holding a rank for the shortest amount of time. He had just been promoted to corporal on August 7.[49]

When the transport ships finally arrived on July 19, the 2nd Vermont was up at daylight and, along with the 5th and part of the 4th Vermont, boarded at 6 A.M. The steamer with the 2nd Vermont on board sailed down the Potomac as far as Belle Plain and anchored for the night. The next day, at 5 A.M., the ship was off again and sailed straight for the open sea. Once it left shore, the vessel pitched and heaved furiously and many of the Green Mountain Boys, who had withstood many a battle, were brought to their knees by seasickness. Pvt. Fisk sarcastically wrote:

> We had quite a pleasant voyage from Alexandria, as pleasant as could be expected with a disabled engine, a strong head wind, and a sufficient admixture of sea-sickness with our sensations of pleasure, to maintain a natural equilibrium. We were four days coming from Alexandria to New York. We were packed into the boat from the hold to the upper deck, in a manner very similar, I take it, to that adopted by slave pirates of their cargo. Every available spot on the floor was a soldier's bed, and at night we were obliged to lie in rows, with our heads apart, and our feet and legs locked together in dove-tail fashion, to make room.[50]

Pvt. Cutler also complained of the rough trip, "by the way Jehiel and I had the fun of being seasick on the way for about 24 hours. you ought to have seen us heave up Jonah on deck. the sea was what I call pretty rough. part of the way the boat rocked and tipped so that we could hardly stand up."[51]

With great relief the Vermonters finally sailed into New York harbor on the night of August 24. The troops stayed aboard until noon the next day, while the officer went into the city to get their orders.[52]

Without fanfare, the Vermonters disembarked and marched to their designated camping areas. The 2nd and 4th Vermont, along with a regiment of regulars, went into bivouac on Washington Square. Their principal mission for the present was to guard their own camps to keep the men from running amok in the city. Pvt. Joseph Felton in Co. H wrote, "I have been for the last week in the heart of N. York City as much confined and more so that we were in [the] front. I realize only one advantage we have better food." Since the Vermont Brigade was so close to home, many wives, friends, and families came down from Vermont to see their loved ones. To assist in getting the citizens from Vermont to New York City the railroad offered special discount fares. Camping on the grassy ground of the square was not unusual, but the stone sidewalks and the "Keep off from this grass" signs were something the soldiers had not seen for a long time. Lt. Leach gave a description of the park to his wife:

> we marched to this place & a very nice place it is too. The grounds contain 5 or 6 acres, crossed all over in all directions with paved walks & having shade trees set all over the grounds. In the center is a pool of water & when the water is let on it will rise from the pipe to the height of 30 feet. The ground is enclosed by an iron fence, & the only fault I find with the place for a camping ground is that it is not large enough for the numbers of troops here encamped.[53]

Pvt. Cutler wrote to his wife about the New Yorkers who would come to see them:

> Ladies and gentlemen flock in to the park to see us some of them bring apples and peaches, and are eager to hear the war stories the old Veterans as they call us have to tell—we all have to keep looking neet and trim boots blacked white gloves when on duty ha ha—so you see soldering is a very fine thing in New York.[54]

Children also flooded the camp as Pvt. Fisk noted:

> We have had to skirmish through the camp occasionally, to drive out the juvenile population, but in these operations we are not always so brilliantly successful, for the ubiquitous rascals will either flank us, or spring up spontaneous in our rear. Getting rid of them is out of the question. After all, it is quite convenient to have these youngsters around, for some are the most accommodating fellows you ever saw. They are always on hand to run errands, such as filling canteens, purchasing kincknacks, whatever we may want, always, of course, expecting a respectable commission.[55]

During the first week of September, the 2nd, 3rd, 5th, and 6th Vermont regiments were sent to other cities in New York where drafts were going to be held. The 2nd Vermont's destination was Poughkeepsie. After a leisurely ride on a steamboat up the Hudson River, the regiment arrived in Poughkeepsie at 12 A.M., September 6. The Poughkeepsie *Daily Eagle* reported, "The appearance of the rank and file of these scarred veterans as they marched up the street with heavy tread in the dead of night was grand and imposing. Not a word was heard save now and then the usual order."[56]

With the regiment being nearer to Vermont, even more friends and relatives were able to come down from Vermont by train to visit the regiment as the *Daily Eagle* noted: "A number of officers and members, taking advantage of their close proximity to their native state, have telegraphed to their wives and families to come to this city. Quite a number have arrived here already, and happiness beams from the countenance of each of them."[57]

The draft in Poughkeepsie went off without a hitch, and the services of the Vermonters were never needed. In fact, the townfolk and the men of the 2nd Vermont seemed to get along quite well as the *Daily Eagle* reported on September 10, "A number of our citizens have taken different members of this regiment to their residences on various occasions to enjoy their thrilling tales of the war over a hearty dinner." In addition to visiting with families and the citizens of Poughkeepsie they men were kept occupied with drills, as Pvt. Fisk explained:

> The boys take pride in drilling before so respectable an audience of spectators, and I know Col. Walbridge was not dissatisfied with our drilling on the last occasion; his smiles of approval told us plainly that he was not. It has been some time since we have drilled any before, but we believe we have not quite forgotten how. We gave our audience some practical illustrations of a few of the manoeuvers on a battle-field. The Colonel deployed one Company as skirmishers in front of the regiment and ordered them to lie down and load and fire. They went through with all the motions as we have been instructed in such things except actually firing—loading on their backs, then turning on their faces, fire, and immediately reload. The skirmishers being sorely pressed, he ordered them to fire in retreat, while the regiment behind supporting them pitched in a few volleys and then charged. With a shout, not quite so full of energy perhaps as one we gave on a certain day near the city of Fredericksburg, but something like it, we rushed forward double quick, when at the command "down," we were prostrate in an instant. As soon as the enemy's volley of shot and shell sent to annihilate our charge was supposed to be fairly over, we got up and resumed operations once more. The ladies laughed and the children shouted with delight. It was fun for them, and for us too on this occasion, but we have seen manoeuvers performed when the attending circumstances made the operation a little less pleasing.[58]

To the regret of the boys in the 2nd Vermont, the regiment was relieved of duty on September 12. They loaded aboard a steamer at 9 A.M., September 13, and sailed back to New York City where they joined the rest of the Vermont Brigade and took another vessel to South Amboy, N.J.

At least one member of the 2nd Vermont was extremely sad to leave Poughkeepsie. Pvt. Stephen M. Taylor, a young mechanic from Plainfield in Co. F, had met and fallen in love with a young lady named Mary Jane Board. After he was mustered out of service July 15, 1865, Stephen went back to Poughkeepsie. On August 8, he and Mary Jane were married and moved to Vermont where Taylor became a farmer.[59]

At South Amboy, the brigade boarded a train and followed the same route south it had taken on its way to war in the summer of 1861. The train was not fitted with passenger and sleeper cars as it had been on their first trip. Instead, the men were unceremoniously packed into boxcars like cattle, as Pvt. Fisk complained:

> The latest style for soldiers are simply freight cars with boards propped up for seats. For windows, we had the benefit of two side doors to begin with, but long before our journey concluded we had plenty of ventilation, owing principally to the energetic use of the butt end of somebody's gun-stock on the boards at different places on the sides of the car. Each car was filled as full it would hold of men, knapsacks and rations, huddled in together promiscuously.[60]

After stopping in Philadelphia for a midnight supper, the Green Mountain Boys arrived in Havre de Grace, Md. just at daybreak, September 15. While the engine and cars were being ferried across the Susquehanna River, the men took the opportunity to stretch their legs and see what food they could buy in Havre de Grace. The town's merchants quickly took advantage of their captive audience. Fisk continued:

> At this place we stopped long enough to buy us a breakfast all around at the groceries near by. It is curious how quickly the prices of eatables advance in a small place at the advent of a regiment of soldiers. The moment we stopped I stepped into a bakery and bought a loaf of bread for five cents. Handling this to a friend, I returned to the same place and found bread selling rapidly at two loaves for fifteen cents. A few minutes later and the price was ten cents a loaf, and still going up. The price of cheese went up to 25 cents a pound, and that of butter was more than doubled.[61]

The men reached Washington by evening and were quartered at the Soldiers Retreat. The next morning they moved on and camped near Fort Ellsworth. After its two-year occupation by Union troops, Alexandria had lost its quaint appearance as Lt. Leach noted: "Wednesday we took boat for Alexandria, where, according to my mind, you find the most miserable place at this time."[62]

On September 18 in a torrential downpour, the Vermont Brigade left Alexandria for the front. On this march, it had to guard a wagon train, making for a comfortable pace. The route was a familiar one, taking it through Fairfax Court House, Centreville and along the Orange and Alexandria Railroad.[63]

The brigade crossed the Rappahannock River on September 21 and the next day marched to Culpeper Court House, around which the Army of the Potomac was camped. The march past the camps of the various corps from Brandy

Station to Culpeper was quite an unusual experience for the Vermont boys. The troops of the other corps lined the roadside and cheered them as they passed. Three miles south of the village of Culpeper, the brigade passed the camp of the 10th Vermont Infantry, now part of the Third Corps, and halted for a rest and a chance to visit with friends and relatives. Two miles more brought the brigade to the camp of the Sixth Corps, where it was met by a large contingent of corps, division, and brigade staff officers. As it passed Gen. Howe's headquarters, Neill's brigade received it with band music and military salutes.[64]

During the last week of September, the Vermont Brigade started receiving its first replacements consisting of conscripts and substitutes. By the middle of October, it would have nearly 600. None of the veterans were particularly fond of them since these new men had not volunteered. The 2nd Vermont received 200 of the new men, bringing its strength up to a little over 900. For some reason, the 2nd Vermont seems to have received the worst of the lot, as Lieut. Col. Samuel M. Pingree, of the 3rd Vermont, observed on October 2:

> The 2nd Regt. has received 200 men mostly substitutes—and 58 have deserted. The 3d has received about 200, and lost several. We have received 190 and two only have deserted.
>
> The men we got by this process are superior to any lot of volunteer recruits ever sent to this Regt.
>
> The same is not true of the Second Regt. as I understand their men are "scallawags."[65]

Lt. Leach noted:

> We have had about 50 more recruits for our Regt. this week, five to a company. Brush of Cambridge is one of them in our Co., Dr. Brush's son. I hope he may get a better place than serving in the ranks before long. They were a good lot of men, much better than the first lot we got, they being mostly foreigners, of every distinction.[66]

The man Leach referred to was Pvt. Edwin R. Brush, a 27-year-old draftee from Cambridge, Vt.. Like his father, Edwin was also a doctor. Leach got his wish; Brush became the 2nd Vermont's assistant surgeon on October 15 and served in that position for the remainder of the war.[67]

When the 2nd Vermont returned from Poughkeepsie, not all its men had made the trip back with it. Some had taken advantage of the proximity of Vermont and went home on "French leave." Toward the end of September, most of them were back to face the music. Lt. Leach: "Yesterday [September 28] about 20 of our Regt. were tried & fined 10 dollars each for being absent since we left New York, only getting back day before yesterday."[68]

Lt. Leach mentioned on September 29 that for some

Assistant Surgeon Edwin R. Brush. USAMHI.

reason, probably because the the new recruits were deserting, the security in the camps had been tightened. Chafing against the reins of authority as usual, the boys in the 2nd Vermont had their fun with the guards.

> After Taps at night, the Provost Guard visits all the camps to arrest all breakers of the peace, & I will tell you a trick the boys of our regt. played on the guard in our camp. They bent down a tree & attached a snare to it some way so that when the guard came along, it caught two of them by the legs & swung them up so they could but just touch their fingers to the ground. The boys, of course, were all asleep about that time, but made out to wake up to help them down after a while.[69]

After two weeks of relative quiet, the Sixth Corps was ordered to relieve the Second Corps, which was on picket duty along a two-mile stretch of the Rapidan River, and moved out on October 5. The rest they had enjoyed since leaving for New York had made the men soft, and the veterans complained of being "made pack-mules to carry wormy bread," and the new men whined about the day's 14-mile march. The corps reached the Rapidan about sundown, and within several days, the men stopped carping and got into the routine of talking and trading with the rebels as Lt. Leach explained to his wife:

> Our Corps are the only troops here & our duty is to do picket duty along the Rapidan & Robertsons Creek, which

> runs in to the Rapidan from the north. Our pickets are in sight of the Rebels, & in shooting distance, but all have kept quiet thus far, talking to each other & occasionally meeting & exchanging papers.[70]

During the month of August, Gen. Lee, through recruitment and the return of stragglers and those who had been hospitalized, brought up the strength of the Army of Northern Virginia from 58,000 to nearly 61,000. Fearing a defeat in the West, President Jefferson Davis ordered Longstreet's corps shipped to Chattanooga.[71]

In late September Lee received reports that the Federal Eleventh and Twelfth Corps had also been sent to the western theater. For nearly two months, Lee had been bluffing the Army of the Potomac, but now knowing they had been reduced by 12,000 men, he decided to retake the initiative.[72]

Lee's plan was to drive around Meade's right and get between him and Washington and force him into battle on ground favorable to the Army of Northern Virginia. As soon as Meade learned of Lee's movement, he slowly fell back. The movements became a race for Centreville Heights, the best ground in the area.[73]

The 2nd Vermont, as well as the rest of the Sixth Corps, moved out on October 10 and did a lot of marching and countermarching but saw little action.[74]

The only significant encounter occurred on October 14. A. P. Hill's corps approached Bristoe Station in the late morning, and without waiting for support, attacked what Hill believed to be only the Federal Third Corps. In his haste to attack, Hill had overlooked the Second Corps, which was hidden out of sight in a railroad cut on his right flank. When two Confederate brigades advanced, they were surprised by a devastating fire from the Second Corps's three infantry divisions and artillery. Caught in a withering flanking fire, the rebel commanders had two choices—retreat or charge. They decided to charge, but neither brigade reached the railroad cut. Both commanders were seriously wounded and their commands cut to pieces and had to fall back. In fact, they fell back so quickly they left a Confederate battery uncovered, and a unit from the Second Corps came screaming out of the cut and captured four of the guns. In addition to the four guns, Hill lost about 1,900 men to 548 from the Second Corps.[75]

Meade won the race for the Centreville Heights. Lee knew better than to fight on ground so favorable to his enemy and retired behind the Rappahannock River. The only loss sustained by the Sixth Corps in this campaign was from Maj. John S. Mosby's guerrillas, who infested the region. On October 16, Mosby hit part of Gen. Howe's headquarters trains.[76]

One of the men captured was Pvt. John B. Miller of the 2nd Vermont's Co. F. Miller was one of the new recruits who had arrived just two weeks before. He was imprisoned in Richmond where he died of disease February 27, 1864. Also captured in the raid was the 2nd Vermont's 1st Lt. Eugene O. Cole of Co. A, and Shaftsbury, who was serving on Howe's staff as the acting provost marshal. Cole was much luckier than Miller. After being disarmed and placed with the rest of the prisoners, he found a moment when the guards were not looking and made good his escape. He returned to his own lines later that day. Cole would serve out the rest of his term of service without incident.[77]

The Sixth Corps started back south on October 18. Howe's division moved over the old Bull Run battlefield to Gainesville on the Warrenton Turnpike where, at about 5 P.M. on the next afternoon, it met Maj. Gen. George A. Custer's cavalry. A short time before, Custer had been attacked by Stuart and Brig. Gen. Fitz Hugh Lee at Buckland's Mills and was driven back. Lee was pressing Custer's rear, and the Union infantry column was a welcome sight. Letting Custer's men pass through their lines, the infantry quickly fell into line of battle to receive the rebels. A skirmish line consisting of the 6th Vermont and 7th Maine was thrown forward and had barely deployed when the Confederate horsemen appeared. As they emerged from a piece of woods, the rebels dashed out into the open in front of the Union skirmishers. They were received by a volley of musket fire that brought them to an abrupt halt.[78]

The next morning with the Vermont Brigade leading, Howe's division, was on the road again. The march ended at Warrenton on October 20 where the army started building its winter quarters.[79]

Because Lee had destroyed the railroad from Bristoe Station south, the Army of the Potomac had to be resupplied by wagon train. This was a dangerous proposition since the route was through Mosby's territory. In fact, the area between Brandy Station and Alexandria was commonly known as "Mosby's Confederacy." On October 26 a wagon train containing some of the 2nd Vermont's wagons was hit near New Baltimore. The 2nd Vermont's quartermaster, Lauriston L. Stone, Stone's brother, J. P. Stone, and three other men were captured. One of the teamsters captured was Pvt. Eugene C. Sleeper, a young man from Strafford and a member of the 2nd Vermont's Co. H. Mosby and about 70 of his guerrillas dressed in Federal uniforms approached the column without arousing suspicion. At first they represented themselves as a squadron of the 18th Pennsylvania Cavalry. After Mosby spread his men alongside the wagons, they made their true identity known and took the Federals prisoner. After gathering the prisoners, Mosby's men ran off the mules, plundered the wagons, and set them on fire. In addition to looting the supplies, Mosby confiscated a large sum of government funds that Stone was carrying plus Stone's own personal money.[80]

The captured Yankees were marched nearly all night to Thoroughfare Gap where they bivouacked until noon. Then they were marched to Gen. Jeb Stuart's headquarters where they remained a few hours and then to Culpeper Court House. On October 28, they were sent to Richmond and imprisoned. During his captivity Stone was incarcerated in Richmond, Danville, Va., Macon, Ga., Charleston, S.C., and Columbia, S.C. He was eventually exchanged and arrived in Washington December 17, 1864, having been a prisoner almost 14 months.[81]

Lt. Stone was mustered out April 16, 1865, but he continued to petition the War Department for reimbursement of $82.72 that Mosby had stolen from him. The records do not indicate if he ever collected. The fate of Stone's brother, who was not a member of the Vermont Brigade, is unclear. One can only assume that he was paroled at the same time as his brother. Pvt. Sleeper was paroled November 26, 1864 and was mustered out of service February 4, 1865.[82]

A tragedy occurred in the 2nd Vermont's camp on November 4. The sun had just come up and the men were falling into company formations when a shot rang out in the camp. Simultaneously with the sound of the shot, Pvt. Lewis F. Goodell, a 23-year-old draftee from Woodbury, Vt. in Company C, slumped to the ground with a moan. The lower part of his left leg had been shattered by a minié ball. Minutes after Goodell fell, 17-year-old Pvt. Charles S. Wheeler of Company K, who had only been with the regiment about two months, came hobbling into Company C's camp with blood running out of a hole in the toe of his left boot crying for someone to cut his boot off. When asked what had happened he said that he had been trying to uncap a musket in his hut and had accidentally fired it.

Goodell was taken to the hospital where his leg had to be amputated just below the knee. Because Wheeler had entered the service as a substitute, he was immediately suspected of having intentionally shot off his toe to get a medical discharge. About an hour after the incident, 2nd Lt. Bradbury W. Height of Company C examined the musket Wheeler had fired and found it to be in perfect working order. With this information in mind, along with Wheeler's reputation for being a bad soldier, Wheeler's company commander, Capt. Erastus G. Ballou, preferred charges against him for shooting himself on purpose.

Wheeler was found guilty of intentionally shooting himself and was sentenced to forfeit $10 a month of his pay for the rest of his term of service. This seemed like a very light sentence considering the severity of Goodell's injury. One of the witnesses in the court-martial said, "Some of the Co. C boys said it ought to have been through his head instead of his toes." If Wheeler's intention was to get a medical discharge, it did not work. He was sent back to duty as soon as his toe healed. Little did anyone know that a greater tragedy lay ahead. Pvt. Goodell, who appeared to be recovering from his wound, succumbed to complications of the amputation on June 6, 1864, without ever having fired a shot in combat.[83]

For almost three weeks the Vermont Brigade remained in its camp at Warrenton. Because the temperature was starting to dip, off duty time was used to lug in firewood and build winter quarters. While the army was settling in for the winter, Meade was developing plans for his next campaign. Knowing that he only had about two more months of good weather left, his plan called for quick movement. His initial plan was to move the Army of the Potomac rapidly to the heights of Fredericksburg, but Gen. Halleck disapproved it. He then decided that if he would not be allowed to maneuver Lee out into the open to bring on battle, he could at least push him farther south.[84]

His second plan, which Halleck approved, was to divide his army into two columns, cross the Rappahannock, reunite his army and push on to Brandy Station. The first column, consisting of the Third Corps, was to cross the Rappahannock at Kelly's Ford and the second, consisting of the Fifth and Sixth Corps, was to cross at Rappahannock Station.[85]

Any thoughts of completing their winter quarters were dashed on Friday November 6, when orders were issued to the Vermonters to pack six days' rations in their haversacks and be ready to move out early the next morning. The Vermont Brigade was up at 4 A.M. on Saturday morning, and by daybreak the men had strapped on their knapsacks, shouldered their muskets, and were on the road moving south. By noon the brigade had made about 12 miles and pulled off the road for lunch. During lunch the men could hear skirmish fire and knew they would soon be in action.[86]

Due to an oversight by several senior Confederate officers in the placement of some key units, the Third Corps was able to force a crossing at Kelley's Ford without much difficulty. Sedgwick, on the other hand, had a tougher job at Rappahannock Station. At that point, Early's division occupied the south bank of the Rappahannock where it was strongly entrenched. On the north bank (the Federal side), Hays's brigade was dug in, guarding a pontoon bridge that stretched between the two banks. A dam below Early's position made the river unfordable. The position was naturally strong and the redoubts and rifle pits, supported by artillery on the south bank, made them even more foreboding. Hays was reinforced by Hoke's brigade as soon as Sedgwick's troops came in sight.[87]

At 1 P.M., the Sixth Corps formed for the assault. The First Division was placed on the left and Howe's Second Division on the right. The Third Division was held in reserve. The First and Second Divisions each formed in two lines. The Vermont Brigade was the second line of Howe's division. A portion of the 5th Vermont was thrown forward as skirmishers. At 2 P.M., the corps advanced to higher ground in front where it came within range of the enemy's artillery and was halted while the Union batteries were brought up. For three hours, a heavy artillery duel ensued while the Vermont Brigade lay behind the crest of the hill from which the Union batteries were firing.[88]

Joseph C. Felton of Co. H wrote, "got at last in shooting distance of the Enemy at Rapahonnc Station or should have had to fought had they not thought best to leave. But being the rear line of battle we fired nary a gun."[89]

The Fifth Corps gradually advanced, but nothing decisive took place until dusk when six regiments of the First Division stormed the Confederate works, capturing four guns, 103 commissioned officers, 1,200 enlisted men, 1,225 stand of small arms and seven Confederate battle flags. In all, Early lost 1,700 men killed, wounded or missing, out of the 2,000 men of Hoke's and Hays's brigades. The First Division's loss was only 336. The only casualty in the Vermont Brigade was one man wounded in the 4th Vermont.[90]

What was left of Hays's and Hoke's brigades retreated across the river, burning the end of the pontoon bridge on the south side of the river as they left. The next day Sedgwick threw a new pontoon bridge across the river and advanced his two corps. With both of its flanks breached, the Army of Northern Virginia was forced to retreat to the south side of the Rapidan. Thus ended the battles of Rappahannock Station and Kelley's Ford. This was a major embarrassment to Lee's army. One of Lee's staff officers called it "the saddest chapter in the history of this army."[91]

Still in line of battle, the Sixth Corps pushed on to Brandy Station and went into camp on November 8 on John Minor Botts's plantation one mile east of the station, where it would remain the rest of the winter. When the Vermonters first arrived, Mr. Botts boasted that he had 600 miles of rail fence, but within a week the Sixth Corps had burned it for firewood for which the U.S. government had to reimburse Botts. By the time the Vermonters left in the spring the Botts property was nearly devoid of trees, and one of his daughters was pregnant by a Yankee soldier.[92]

There was a shuffling of personnel in key positions in the 2nd Vermont during the month of November. First Lt. Dayton P. Clark, from Montpelier, who had been the regiment's acting adjutant, was promoted to captain to replace Horace F. Crossman as commander of Co. F. Second Lt. Joshua P. Sawyer, Chester Leach's tentmate in Co. H, replaced Clark. Henry H. Prouty, the regiment's sergeant major, who had been convalescing after his wound at Banks Ford, returned and was promoted to second lieutenant in Co. H and replaced Sawyer. Zadock Ufford, from Fairfax, who had been acting sergeant major in Prouty's absence, was officially promoted to the rank of regimental sergeant major, December 6.[93]

Howe's division was drawn up in a hollow square formation on both November 17 and 23 to hear the sentences read of men who had been court-martialed for desertion. Two men were sentenced on each of the days. The sentences, which included time in prison and a dishonorable discharge, were not uncommon, but what followed was. On November 17 after the sentences were read, a mobile artillery forge was driven into the center of the formation to where the prisoners were standing. Then a branding iron was taken from the firebox of the forge. On the end of the iron was affixed the letter "D" and was glowing cherry red. One prisoner was forced to lower his pants and his right hip was branded. The other man was branded on the right shoulder. On November 23 the same process was repeated on two deserters, except this time both men were branded on the palm of their right hands.[94]

Meade, who was being pressured to move against Lee, devised a plan of attack. Lee at this time was still entrenched behind the Rapidan River. His right flank rested along the left bank of the muddy little stream known as Mine Run, which runs at a right angle to the Rapidan and empties into it 10 miles south of Brandy Station. This line was held by Ewell's corps. Meade decided to throw his army across the Rapidan in three columns below the mouth of Mine Run, turn to the right of Ewell's position, and attack him from the rear. By November 25, the railroad had been rebuilt as far as Brandy Station, and sufficient supplies were brought in to resupply the army. Meade issued orders to his army to be ready to move the next day.[95]

On the night of November 25, almost as an omen of bad things to come, there was an eclipse of the moon. The Sixth Corps was up before daylight and on the road as the sun first appeared on the horizon. It was to follow the Third Corps on the march to the Rapidan. This was where the first blunder of the new campaign happened. When the Sixth Corps reached the camp of the Third Corps, the Third Corps was not ready to move. In fact, some of its units were still asleep. The Sixth Corps had to stand in the mud for hours while the Third Corps got ready to move.[96]

Finally, near 11 A.M., the Third Corps was up and on the road. The march was slow and tedious and instead of reaching the river at noon as the plan called for, the men did not arrive at Jacob's Ford until after dark. Here the second blunder occurred. The engineer unit that was to bridge the river had not brought enough pontoon boats to reach across the river, and the engineers had to use poles to complete the span. This poor preparation caused more hours of delay. Instead of being at Robertson's Tavern in the rear of Lee's right before nightfall according to the plan, the Third Corps did not even begin to cross the Rapidan until after dark. The Sixth Corps marched on a road that was not more than a narrow cut through a forest. The corps moved slowly, advancing only several yards, then standing still for several minutes before moving again. The men became tired and aggravated. They had not eaten or rested for hours. Finally, they could take no more, and from one end of the Sixth Corps's column to the other, the men started shouting "coffee!" "coffee!" As much as the officers tried to keep the troops quiet and get them moving, it was no use. Near 11 P.M. the leadership gave in, and the order "ten minutes rest for coffee" was issued. Instantly the roadside was ablaze with small cooking fires with men huddled over them boiling coffee.[97]

Sedgwick got his men back on the road after they had finished their coffee and crossed the river at about midnight. They moved on until nearly 1 A.M. and then halted for the night. The night was cold, the ground wet, and the soldiers' sleep was brief and restless. In three hours just before sunrise, they were awakened, and the slow stop-and-go march resumed. The Fifth and First Corps had crossed at Culpeper Ford and the Second Corps at Germana Ford around noon and were in their assigned positions.[98]

On Friday morning, November 27, the Sixth Corps was back on the march. Not long after getting back on the road, the men heard scattered shots of the skirmishers and an occasional discharge of artillery from the Third Corps ahead. Here a third blunder occurred. Leading his corps too far to the west, French prematurely bumped into Ewell. Confronted by only a division of Ewell's corps, French allowed himself to be held in check the rest of the day by a force not a third as large as his own. By the middle of the afternoon, he received an order from Meade to push on and prepared to force his way forward, but was himself attacked. The First and Second Divisions of the Sixth Corps were hurried forward to support the Third Corps which was now seriously engaged. The two divisions quickly took their position between the embattled Third Corps and the Second Corps which was now on line. The Vermont Brigade and another brigade were held in reserve. The rebels made repeated charges against the Second Corps but were held off. French lost nearly 500 men.[99]

During the night, the Third and Sixth Corps moved on to Robertson's Tavern where they should have been 20 hours earlier.[100]

Upon moving the next morning, November 28, toward Orange Court House, Meade found Lee's whole army posted along Mine Run. The Army of the Potomac was brought up to the north bank of the run, and in the midst of a freezing rain spent the rest of the day getting into position. As darkness fell over the two armies, neither was yet prepared to bring on battle. That night and the next day were spent by both parties building earthworks.[101]

The night of November 29 was stormy and bitterly cold, and to keep their positions secret, the troops were not allowed to light fires. The men in the 2nd Vermont made up their own way to stay warm as Pvt. Fisk explained, "By scuffling, knocking off hats, and running around in a ring that we made a path for in the woods, we managed to keep from freezing." Men in other units on picket that night were not afforded the opportunity the Vermonters had and a number of them froze to death at their posts.[102]

Toward daylight, Monday, November 30, the entire 2nd Vermont was thrown out as skirmishers to lead in the assault. All the officers and men knew that dawn would bring desperate work. Gen. Howe described the feeling of his troops: "We placed the men where we could look right into the enemy's camp, which was but a little distance from us. There seemed to be entire confidence throughout my division, that it was an easy as well as a sure thing to carry the enemy's left." Howe stated that Gen. Neill said, "I believe I can carry that with my brigade." Col. Grant piped up, "I believe there is one regiment in the Vermont Brigade that can take the key of that position." Howe continued, "They were under some excitement, and were pretty sanguine. The men were fired up and all seemed eager for the order to attack." Finally daylight came and time wore on, but the order to attack did not come. At last, at 8 A.M., the artillery opened, the men fell into line and shouldered muskets with beating hearts, waiting the word "forward!" when suddenly an aide dashed up to Gen. Howe with an order canceling the attack.[103]

In the early morning light, Gen. Warren, who was to open the assault on the extreme left, found that during the night Lee had strengthened his lines, and to attack would be a repeat of the first battle at Fredericksburg. After personally looking over the situation, Meade agreed, and the attack was suspended. Nothing could be gained by fresh maneuvering. The weather was getting colder, the six days' rations brought by the men were nearly exhausted, and Meade abandoned the effort. The morning of December 1 came and went with no further sign on the part of the Federals to press the offensive. Lee now wanted to take the initiative and said, "They must be attacked; they must be attacked." Before daybreak on December 2, Lee was ready for the attack, but Meade had withdrawn during the night. Expressing his disappointment Lee said grimly, "I am too old to command this army, we should never have permitted those people to get away."[104]

The Sixth Corps retired by way of Germana Ford, leaving the 3rd Vermont, the 77th New York, and an artillery battery to guard the ford, while the rest of the army continued its march to its former camps. Howe's division halted in the woods on the night of the December 2, approximately 10 miles from the ford, where a wagon train met them with hardtack and fresh meat. The men were grateful to be resupplied since they had been marching for the last 24 hours on nothing but coffee. Resuming the march the next morning, the Sixth Corps marched past Brandy Station and filed into the old camps on the afternoon of December 3. The Vermonters wasted no time building their winter huts.[105]

During the second week of December as the Army of the Potomac was settling in for the winter, the government started a push to persuade the original "three year volunteers" whose enlistements would be up in the late spring to reenlist. Incentives such as a $400 bounty and a 35-day furlough were offered. Whether to reenlist or not was the buzz around the camps as Pvt. Fisk noted:

> The great topic of interest in camp just now is that of reenlisting. The Vermont boys are as anxious as any troops in the field, to turn "veterans" and they are enlisting to an extent quite unexpected. Probably, before this letter is printed and read, there will be in Vermont quite a respectable representation of "veterans," from the Old Brigade, enjoying their furloughs which were given them for re-enlisting.
>
> About a week ago, at our dress parade, our Colonel talked the matter over with us, and he told us of a plan that General Howe was confident he could get approved at the War Department, which would allow all, except conscripts, to enlist. His plan was to have those who joined the regiment at Yorktown, on the Peninsula, and those who joined us at Hagerstown, Maryland, in the fall of '62, re-enlist now, and when two years of their term of service has expired, they should commence to receive bounties in regular installments from that time, the same as the others that enlist now. This plan General Howe had great confidence would succeed. He took measures to ascertain how many would reenlist, providing they could have this matter arranged as he proposed, and the whole Division get a chance to go home to recruit and have a good time generally. This was fully explained to us to the minutest particular. We had several dress parades, in which the exercises were limited to hearing a full explanation of all the advantages that might be expected from re-enlisting, and at one time we had a brigade dress parade, when Col. Grant took the stump, or the saddle, rather, to explain a great many mistakes that he supposed we might be possibly laboring under. He was very anxious, he said, to have the whole brigade go home as a brigade, and claim all the dignity of veteran soldiers. He told us of the probabilities of a speedy close of the war.... Col. Walbridge ventured the expression at another time, that if we went home as a regiment or brigade, we might never be called back.[106]

Two weeks later Fisk wrote:

> Reenlisting here goes bravely on. The Fifth regiment left for home last Monday. They go as a body. I hear that they met with a serious accident ... three killed and several injured. The reenlisted men from the sixth regiment, except one company that goes as a whole, started this morning. The other regiments are waiting for the paymaster that they may settle with the Government for their old term, to commence again anew, and then they will be ready to start too. This regiment will turn out about a hundred "veterans," the noblest and best the country affords. Cos. E and I will produce fifteen each, C produces thirteen, and the other companies a still less number, but all are represented. The furloughs were made out for the "veterans" in this regiment day before yesterday, and those that preferred going home then, to waiting for their pay, had that privilege, and quite a number accepted it. The majority however, are now waiting for the dilatory paymaster.... The furloughs are for thirty-five days, and this must cover all the time that the soldier is away from camp.[107]

Lt. Eben Drury of Co. K wrote the commander of Co. H, Amasa Tracy, who was still in Vermont convalescing from his wound of May 3, "Co. H *wont* re-enlist,—there is no use talking. Co. C is much more likely to. I reckon there is not much show of getting the division home, which is what Genl. Howe is working for. I heartily wish he may succeed."[108]

The 2nd Vermont did not get enough men to reenlist to be able go home as a unit, but 96 men reenlisted in December 1863, 58 in January 1864; 7 in March 1864, and 14 in April for a total of 175 men. The Vermont Brigade altogether had 1,030 men reenlist. In the train wreck that Fisk referred to which occurred on December 14 between Brandy Station and Alexandria, the 2nd Vermont lost one man. Pvt. Lafavor C. Perkins, an Essex native in Co. H, was on the train on his way back to Vermont on reenlistment furlough when he was crushed in the wreck. He survived the evacuation to the hospital but died on February 6, 1864. Lt. Leach wrote his wife, "Perkins, poor fellow, has gone up, after passing through many dangers of battle was killed through the carelessness of someone. So the world goes."[109]

Howe's division had a most distasteful duty to perform on December 18. In an attempt to stop the flow of deserters leaving the army, the entire division was required to witness the execution of two Vermonters who had been convicted of desertion. The two men were Pvt. John Tague of Co. A, 5th Vermont, and Pvt. George E. Blowers, Co. A, 2nd Vermont. George Blowers and his older brother William had been born in Washington, N.Y., but were living in Arlington, Vt., when they enlisted in the 2nd Vermont on August 14, 1862. Both brothers had been assigned to the 2nd Vermont's Co. A. William had deserted in route to the regiment in Alexandria, Va., on September 20, 1862. George deserted on the march to Gettysburg at Manchester, Md., in the early morning hours of July 2, 1863.[110]

Exactly how the brothers were apprehended is not clear, but William was arrested in Hadely, N.Y., on October 19, 1863. George resisted arrest and ran but was captured later in Day, N.Y. Regardless of how they were caught, someone was paid a $30 reward for each brother. They were turned over to military authorities at the U.S. barracks in Brattleboro, Vt., October 26, 1863. While in confinement in Brattleboro, the authorities complained that the brothers were "Grossly insulting to people visiting the place," and that both were "desperate characters."[111]

The Blowers brothers were sent back under guard to the regiment for court-martial and arrived in camp on November 13. George was tried on November 19. Under questioning, his company commander, Capt. William H. Cady, stated:

> I was in command of the march. Left near Manchester, MD about 7 o'clock in the evening. Marched about four or five miles that night. Halted frequently. On the morning of the 2nd the prisoner was gone. Next saw him I think the 13th inst. He was returned to the regiment as a deserter. I think his wife has an influence in getting him away from what I have seen. I guess she is not very patriotic.[112]

When asked if he had anything to present in his own defense, George lamely stated, "I had been drinking a good deal. A man that was with me induced me to go. I told him we had better not but he persuaded me to go. I am sorry I left now. There is nothing for me to say." With little deliberation, the court found George guilty of desertion and sentenced him to be shot to death.[113]

William Blowers was tried on November 23 and also convicted of desertion, but for some unexplained reason, he was not sentenced to be executed. His sentence consisted of remaining in the army after his normal term of enlistment to make up time lost and after that to be dishonorably discharged.[114]

On December 18 in a little hollow just outside of camp, Howe's division was formed in a three-sided square to witness George Blowers's and John Tague's executions. The Vermont Brigade made up the right side of the formation and Neill's brigade the left side. On the open side of the formation a hole had been dug in the ground large enough to hold two coffins. Each of the condemned men arrived in a separate ambulance at three P.M., accompanied by his coffin. A 24-man guard escorted the procession, which would serve as the firing squad. Both men sprang nimbly from their ambulances as though they did not have a care in the world. Two chaplains joined the men and the division assistant adjutant general read the condemned men's sentences. As his sentence was being read, Tague threw his cap to the ground in a final act of defiance. After that each man knelt, and the chaplain standing beside him said a prayer for him. A band then played a slow mournful funeral dirge as the men were escorted to their coffins. Tague and Blowers then got up on top of their coffins and knelt down facing the firing squad. The sergeant of the firing squad put a circle of string around each man's neck, from which was suspended a white paper heart to be used by the firing squads as a target.

The prisoners were not blindfolded but looked straight into the eyes of their executioners who stood 30 to 40 feet away. The guard was divided into two squads of 12 riflemen a piece. Blowers asked to see his brother, but William, who could not bear to see his brother shot to death, had been excused from the formation. Then came the commands, Ready! Aim! Fire! At the command fire, 24 muskets unleashed their deadly lead missiles that slammed into the men's chests. Tague instantly dropped dead with his face on the ground and his feet still on his coffin. Blowers, who was hit at the same time as Tague, lived long enough to throw back his head and exclaim, "Oh! Dear me." He struggled for a moment, and then he too was dead. With that, it was over. The regiments of the division were formed into columns, and each was marched past the dead bodies, which were still lying where they had fallen.[115]

Pvt. Fisk probably summed up the feelings of everyone who had to witness the tragic event when he wrote:

> I have seen men shot down by scores and hundreds in the field of battle, and have stood within arm's reach of comrades that were shot dead; but I believe I never witnessed that from which any soul shrunk with such horror, as to see those two soldiers shot dead in cold blood at the iron decree of military law.... God grant that another such punishment may never be needed in the Potomac Army.[116]

The day before Blowers was executed, three other men from the 2nd Vermont were tried for desertion. Pvts. Joseph Solie of Co. K, John Rapalle of Co. H, and Giovanni Arbatraca of Co. B, all three Italian immigrants who had joined the army as substitutes, deserted together on October 25 while the unit was encamped at Warrenton. At their courts-martial, Corp. Augustus A. Decelle of Co. K had to serve as interpreter, since all three men spoke very little English. All three swore to the same story. They stated they had left camp to try to buy a meal at a house that was supposed to be in the area. En route they were captured by two rebel scouts who, posing as Union cavalrymen, forced them to march several miles from camp and then robbed them. Not knowing the way back and not knowing enough English to ask directions, they took the wrong road. Two days later they were picked up by real Union cavalrymen and eventually taken to Cumberland, Md., where they were thrown into the guardhouse. They were eventually returned under guard to their unit.[117]

These same three men had gone AWOL when the Vermont Brigade was at Culpeper and had been fined $10 a month for three months. The court did not buy their story and they were all found guilty. Their sentences were read on December 22, and all three received the same punishment. They had to forfeit $10 a month for 10 months and had to carry 20-pound knapsacks while marching in a circle for three hours in the morning and three hours in the afternoon for 10 successive days. Even with this punishment and the execution of Blowers as an example, both Solie and Rapalle deserted later in the war. Giovanni Arbatraca was captured by the enemy May 12, 1864 at the battle of Spotsylvania and was not paroled until November 18 the following fall. The records do not indicate whether he deserted after his release or if he was mustered out.[118]

CHAPTER 10

"A Wilderness of Woe"

By January 1864 the men of the 2nd Vermont had settled into their camp routine as they had the previous two winters, except this year there was a greater amount of alcohol being consumed. "I can see a change in one respect since I left last fall, & that is in drinking," wrote Lt. Leach on February 21 after returning from two months recruiting duty in Vermont. "Much more of it is done than when I left, both in the officers & men. It used to be that liquor could only occasionally be got, but now, it seems all that is needed is the will & the money to pay for it, & any amount can be had, & it is got & used every day, & pretty free too." A week later he complained,

> Yesterday [February 26] was kind of a Holiday here if possible to make it more so than all days, by it being Washington's birthday, & serenades, oyster suppers, & almost everything you can think, was in order last night, to say nothing of getting rather drunk to top off with. I reckon Sawyer runs the thing about the hardest of any Officer in this Regiment, but his money will soon be gone, & then he will have to drive slower, but as long as his money last, the price of anything is of no account, come it must.[1]

Maj. Tyler ended one of his February letters, "But tattoo has beaten, and there is considerable noise about camp, with which the contents of several express boxes, arrived this P.M., may not be remotely connected. Consequently I've got to go out and have a quarrel—So I'll close while in good humor."[2]

Charles H. Richardson, a private from Barre in Co. D, made the following entries in his diary at the end of March:

> 26 Mar, Sat—Sam Morey [a private in Company D from Waterbury] got a box of 28 bottles of rum somewhere and the boys got drunk.
>
> 27 Mar, Sun—The boys are still drunk. Officers and all are drunk. A lot of fighting.

In April the story was still the same:

> 2 Apr, Sat—Heavy rain and snow. No fighting in the company today because one half of the company is dead drunk.
>
> 3 Apr, Sun—All drunk again. W. Clark [Private William Clark, Company D, from Woodstock] and Crane [Private Vernon F. Crane, Company D, from Moretown] got into a fight and the captain put them in the guard house.
>
> 19 Apr, Tue—After roll call the band serenaded to officers. Band, officers and men all got drunk.[3]

The excessive drinking was a contributing factor in a group of seven men who deserted from the 2nd Vermont in April. Pvts. John Casey, Charles Coe, Arthur Devine, James Fitzgerald, and Samuel Glover of Co. C, Alvah H. Miles of Co. F, and Walter Massey of Co. G had been sitting around drinking all day Saturday, April 9. All of the men except Miles were substitutes. As they drank they began complaining about how they had been hoodwinked into joining the army and how angry they were that the state of Vermont had stopped paying the extra seven dollars a month supplement to their pay. The drunker they got, the angrier they grew at the army, the state of Vermont, and life in general, and decided to leave. In the dark of night and under the veil of a heavy downpour of rain, they sneaked out of camp. Unfortunately, the rainstorm was so heavy that the

Rappahannock River had risen high enough that they could not get across to make their way to Alexandria where they could obtain transportation north.[4]

The next morning the seven were missed at roll call and were reported to headquarters as deserters. A cavalry patrol rounded up the fugitives the next evening about eight miles from camp. They all gave up peacefully, except for Pvt. Alvah Miles who resisted arrest. The men were returned and thrown into the guardhouse. They were tried by courts-martial between April 21 and 23. Each man presented what he thought was a justifiable reason for deserting.[5]

Postwar photograph of Private Timothy S. Hoyt, Company E, and his wife Cate. Douglas L. Williams.

The officers of the court were not impressed with any of the defenses presented and sentenced each but Devine and Miles "To be dishonorably discharged from the service, to forfeit all pay, bounty and allowances that are or may become due him, and to be imprisoned at hard labor for ten years, with a ball weighing twenty-four pounds attached to his leg by a chain four feet long, in such prison or fortification as the proper authorities may direct." Pvt. Devine, no doubt because he was only 18 years old, received a five year prison sentence.[6]

Although the record of Pvt. Alvah Miles's defense no longer exists, the court looked upon his desertion and resisting arrest so unfavorably that they sentenced him to be shot to death. Fortunately for Miles, the sentence was later commuted. His lesser sentence required a dishonorable discharge, forfeiture of all pay and allowances, and confinement at Dry Tortugas, Fla., for the duration of the war.[7]

Not all the men in the 2nd Vermont spent their time carousing. Pvt. Timothy S. Hoyt, a draftee from Craftsbury in Co. E, was trying to behave himself, as he wrote in a letter to his wife, Cate: "i havn't swor since I left home Cate. Tell mother so."[8]

Another difference between this winter's camp and the two previous ones was the amount of women in camp. The 77th New York's surgeon wrote, "One agreeable feature of this encampment was the great numbers of ladies, wives of officers, who spent the winter with their husbands. On every fine day, great numbers of ladies might be seen riding about the camps and over desolate fields, and their presence added greatly to the brilliancy of the frequent reviews."[9]

Pvt. Fisk noted the ladies' presence at a review in his diary February 20:

> At 11 o'clock we had a corps review by GEN. Sedgwick on the same ground where we have had so many before. There were a large number of ladies there this time which gave the ceremonies a very pleasing look of course. I suppose the ladies liked our appearance very much. They ought to; we liked theirs.[10]

Lt. Leach wrote a month later: "Col. Grant had a Brigade review at 10 & did not have the guard relieved till after review. I expect the review was on the purpose that his wife might see how grand an appearance his Brigade could make. They were married this winter, & she has been here but a short time." Finally on March 17 Leach wrote with some relief, "The women from our regt. & I guess from the Brigade all left for home yesterday. So much encumberance gone."[11]

During January, Brig. Gen. Judson Kilpatrick, commander of the Third Division of the Army of the Potomac's Cavalry Corps, devised a plan to make a lightning raid on

Richmond. Recent intelligence incorrectly indicated that Richmond was protected by only 3,000 militia. The objectives of the raid were to penetrate the defenses of Richmond, free all the Union prisoners of war, and distribute thousands of copies of President Lincoln's recent proclamation granting amnesty to any citizen of the Confederacy who would return to his old allegiance to the Federal government.[12]

To accomplish this raid Kilpatrick directed a three-pronged attack. He would attack the Richmond defenses with the main body of the force while Col. Ulric Dahlgren with 500 troopers was to attack from the west. In the meantime, Brig. Gen. George A. Custer with his division of cavalry would make a diversionary raid toward Charlottesville. Sedgwick's Sixth Corps would follow Custer's column as support.[13]

The 2nd Vermont troops received their marching orders for the raid on Friday night, February 26. They were to leave the next morning with five days' rations. No one had any idea of their destination.[14]

The Sixth Corps marched early the next morning, and by the end of the day it camped about six miles from the Robertson River, making a distance of 12 to 15 miles. The march had been long and hard. It had been especially rough on the new recruits as Pvt. Fisk noted:

> The boys began to "play out" pretty fast towards the middle of the afternoon, though the distance marched was less than twenty miles. But our knapsacks were unusually heavy, besides we hadn't yet got accustomed to such marching this season. It made us sore and lame. I saw one fellow marching along with one boot in one hand, and the other stuck on his gun, while his stockings were nearly worn off his feet by the dirt and hard traveling. His feet were swelled and he had several large blisters on them. He was a new recruit, and one of the veterans asked him how much of his town bounty he had paid for that day. Well, he said, they might knock off about a ten spot for that, but he didn't care a damn; he should soon get toughened to it. He is a courageous fellow,—a Vermonter clear to the bone,—and his friends needn't worry but that he will be able to endure a soldier's life. Such men are not frightened to death by trifles.[15]

Pvt. Norman W. Johnson, a Marshfield boy in Co. F, noted in his diary that night, "Stragglers came in all night."[16]

The Vermont Brigade was up and on the road by 8 A.M. the next morning, February 28. It had not been on the march half an hour when Companies G and H of the 2nd Vermont were detached from the regiment and sent to guard a signal station that had been established at the top of nearby Thoroughfare Mountain. No sooner had the two companies departed than the division reversed course and headed back to its previous campsite. The cooking fires the men had left burning had started a forest fire. The Vermont Brigade was able to get the fire in their sector under control, but other units were not as fortunate and the endeavor was soon abandoned.[17]

After giving up on the fire, the corps continued its march toward Madison Court House. By the middle of the afternoon, the head of the Sixth Corps reached the town. The Vermont Brigade, which was much farther back in the column, halted near the Robertson River where it went into camp. Pvt. Fisk wrote in a letter to the *Green Mountain Freeman*:

> A couple of sheep got frightened into the crowd and captured, for somebody a fine supper of mutton. The poor sheep made a sad error when they dodged in between our regiment and the Fourth. They appeared conscious of their mistake, and if nimble feet could have saved them, they would have got away. They run first in one direction, and then in another, but were everywhere headed off by an inexhaustible multitude of soldiers. The boys cheered and shouted as the sheep escaped like lightning from one crowd into another, or dodged a dozen boys at once. But they were conquered at last by force of numbers. The Vermont Brigade is more than a match for two sheep. They had to surrender to their cruel captors, though they had earned a better fate. But the boys that got them were too mutton-loving to admit of any hopes of mercy.[18]

The Sixth Corps remained in camp until March 1 when it returned to Brandy Station, arriving late the next evening. The march back was as grueling as the one out due to an ice storm. "The morning was clear and bright," Fisk noted in his diary; "The ice hung on the branches and twigs of the trees and looked very beautiful as they glistened in the morning sun so bright and clear. Got back to camp that evening. Many had fallen out."[19]

The Vermonters would not learn of the particulars of the raid until later, but the entire operation had been a disaster. Kilpatrick and Dahlgren had gotten lost and were behind schedule when they reached Richmond. They both ran into a stiffer defense than expected and gave up the operation. Kilpatrick's group made its way to Fort Monroe and finally got back to the Army of the Potomac. Dahlgren did not fare as well. In working his way toward Fort Monroe, his detachment was ambushed near Stevensville, in King and Queen County, Va., and scattered. Dahlgren himself was killed and most of his men were either killed, wounded, or captured. Custer's diversionary foray to Charlottesville also accomplished very little.[20]

That was the only military action for the Vermonters for the rest of the winter. They were now free to snuggle down and get back into routine camp life.

The biggest snowfall of the winter covered the ground eight inches deep on the morning of March 23. The storm had started early the day before when all activity had ceased in the camps and everyone had taken to their huts to wait it out. By 9 A.M. the snow clouds parted and the sun shimmered on the new white covering. Bored with having been trapped inside for 24 hours, a group of men in the 2nd Vermont's Co. E decided to go outside for a snowball fight. Once they got started, they found that their group was not large enough to satisfy them and they tried to get the boys in Co. C to come out to join the fun. Not getting enough men from Co. C, they proceeded to Co. D. Here they found the same story—not many wanted to play. Determined to satisfy their lust, the Co. E boys, along with the few men from companies C and D who had joined their ranks, proceeded to the camp of the 6th Vermont. Here they found a willing and worthy foe.[21]

As the sounds of battle rang through the camps, more and more men turned out to reinforce their respective regiments. "Snowballs flew thick and fast," wrote Pvt. Fisk, "some of the foremost on each side getting completely plastered over with them, head, ears, neck and all." Improvised regimental flags were brought out and officers mounted their horses to lead their men. The 20-year-old Maj. Tyler, displaying his usual courage under fire, was at the front leading the 2nd Vermont.[22]

By noon the 2nd Vermont had pushed the 6th back to a knoll near its camp, where the 6th made a stubborn stand. The battle raged into the afternoon. When the snow was consumed in some areas, Orrin T. Leach of the 6th Vermont said the men "used mud." By 2:30 everyone was worn out and the battle ended with handshakes. Some said it was a draw while others were positive their respective regiments had won the field.[23]

Pvt. Fisk finished his chronicle of the event with this observation:

> It was lively sport "charging" and snowballing, capturing and recapturing officers, though it was ruinous for army coats, and the wear and tear of clothing in some of our encounters was immense. I haven't had the time to get a complete list of the killed and wounded, but as our surgeon was on the ground, I am confident that all the wounded were well cared for.[24]

The same day the Vermonters were entertaining themselves with the snowball battle, the War Department issued orders consolidating the Army of the Potomac. The First and Third Corps were disbanded and their regiments and brigades distributed to the remaining three corps. The three remaining corps were the Second, Gen. Hancock; the Fifth, Gen. Warren; and the Sixth, Gen. Sedgwick. The division commanders of the Sixth Corps were First Division, Brig. Gen. Horatio. G. Wright; Second Division, Brig. Gen. George W. Getty; and Third Division, Brig. Gen. James B. Ricketts. The brigades in Getty's division were First Brigade, Brig. Gen. Frank Wheaton; Second Brigade, Col. Lewis A. Grant; Third Brigade, Brig. Gen. Thomas H. Neill; and Fourth Brigade, Brig. Gen. Henry L. Eustis. The Cavalry Corps had a shake-up in commanders. Maj. Gen. Alfred Pleasonton was relieved on March 25 and replaced by Maj. Gen. Philip H. Sheridan. Gen. Burnside's Ninth Corps was to "act with" the Army of the Potomac operationally but was not officially assigned to it.[25]

In April after the snows had stopped and the ground dried up, the boys in the 2nd Vermont entertained themselves with sports as Assistant Surgeon Melvin J. Hyde related to his wife:

> The boys are all out playing foot-ball, the officers all join them in this play, Col., Major, Captains and privates, all mingling without distinction of rank in this exciting sport—Sometimes three or four privates will have an officer down draging him around, each trying to get the ball from him in order to kick it again into the air.[26]

Due to his failing health Col. Walbridge resigned from the army effective April 1. His resignation caused the inevitable domino effect in the 2nd Vermont's command structure. Newton Stone was promoted to command of the regiment and John Tyler replaced Stone as second in command. Amasa S. Tracy, commander of Co. H, was chosen to fill Tyler's position as major. Chester Leach filled Tracy's spot as commander of Co. H, but he could not be promoted to captain due to Tracy's convalescence leave.[27]

Amasa S. Tracy was born March 16, 1829, in Diver, Me. Shortly after his 16 birthday, he left home and moved to Uxbridge, Mass., where he worked in a cotton factory. Several years later, he moved to Middlebury, Vt., and became a carpenter, his occupation when he volunteered for the war. Tracy had just returned from convalescence leave for his wound of May 3, 1863, and had suffered a very serious accident on April 21. As he was returning to camp from sitting on a court-martial board, he was thrown from his horse. He fell face down and landed on the stump of a small pine tree. The stump tore open his leg just below the groin "breaking the flesh some six or seven inches across the thigh and shoving the flesh downward and inward making a complete pocket about 4 inches deep at the bottom." Tracy was carried to the brigade hospital where the surgeons stitched up his wound. Within a few days he was in a general hospital in Washington, and on May 26, he was furloughed to go home to recuperate. Tracy would not rejoin the regiment until later that summer.[28]

Another personnel change occurred in the Vermont Brigade toward the end of the month. The star that had for so long eluded Henry Whiting was finally bestowed upon Col. Lewis Addison Grant on April 27. Brig. Gen. Grant would remain in command of the Vermont Brigade for the rest of the war.[29]

During the middle of April the Army of the Potomac was busy with preparations for the upcoming spring campaign. Lt. Leach wrote his wife on April 16:

> Our Sutler left yesterday, as did all the Sutlers around that had not gone before. After today, their goods were to be confiscated & their employees put at hard labor, so I guess you will not find many of the sort here now. I don't know what we are going to do for some things that are necessary, but I suppose we shall get along some way.

On April 19 Leach wrote:

> Today an order came around, to send away all [men] that would not be able to march.... Our Regt. just now is being inspected to see the men have not got more clothing & other stuff than they ought to carry, one woolen blanket, one rubber blanket, change of under clothing, & shelter half is all that they are to carry. Rations will have to be carried in their knapsacks, so says the order, but don't tell how many days they will have to carry.[30]

In early March Ulysses. S. Grant was summoned to Washington, commissioned lieutenant general, and given command of all Federal armies. On March 10 in a driving rainstorm, Grant arrived at Brandy Station to confer with Meade and decided to stay with the Army of the Potomac.[31]

At the strategic level Grant planned three separate but coordinated advances against the Confederacy. The first was a push by Maj. Gen. William T. Sherman's army into Georgia to Atlanta. The second was an advance by Maj. Gen. Benjamin F. Butler up the south side of the James River to Petersburg and eventually Richmond. The third was a march by the Army of the Potomac from its winter camps in and around Culpeper Court House to Richmond. These simultaneous advances would preclude any of the Confederate armies from reinforcing each other.[32]

At the operational level, Grant had two options for the Army of the Potomac to pry Lee's Army of Northern Virginia out of its entrenchments on the other side of the Rapidan River. One was to move by his right flank, sliding along the lines of the Orange and Alexandria Railroad and swing past Lee to the west, thereby forcing him to fight in open country. The other was to go by his left flank, slipping quickly through the Wilderness and head for a position behind Lee's right where he could fight him in open terrain. Although he had to traverse the Wilderness, Grant chose the second option, which would become known as the Overland Campaign, because it was easier to logistically support. It would also allow him to keep in communication with Butler's army.[33]

The Wilderness was a man-made jungle that was almost impenetrable. It was a tangle of scrub pines, thickets, vines, and miscellaneous thin hardwood trees that covered a sparsely populated region approximately a dozen miles wide and half a dozen deep. The original hardwood forest had been cut to supply charcoal for the iron furnaces in the area and to supply planks for the Orange Plank Road. The topsoil had eroded to a point that it could support only blackjack oak, pines, and chinquapin, most of which rarely exceeded 30 feet high.[34]

In this region there were many small streams that never saw the light of day. The streams, some of which had steep banks, had cut shallow ravines through the area. Their courses wandered and twisted through the darkness turning some of the land into brush-covered swamps. Occasionally there was a small, dreary farmhouse in a clearing surrounded by the thick tangled vegetation.[35]

To provide passage through the Wilderness, there were two east-west highways, the Orange Turnpike and the Orange Plank Road. The Orange Turnpike was a crushed stone road that ran from Orange Court House through Chancellorsville to Fredericksburg. About three miles to the south and nearly parallel to it ran the Orange Plank Road, which was wide enough for two wagons to pass. Running south from Germanna Ford was the Germanna Plank Road, which intersected the Orange Turnpike at a weedy clearing dominated by the Wilderness Tavern.[36]

To expedite crossing the Rapidan River, Grant would split his army in two. The right wing consisting of the Fifth and Sixth Corps would cross at Germanna Ford and proceed south to the Wilderness Tavern. The left wing consisting of the Second Corps would meanwhile splash across the river a few miles east at Ely's Ford and then drop south to Chancellorsville. When the two segments reached their destinations, they would be about four miles apart but connected by the Orange Turnpike. Sheridan's Cavalry Corps would spearhead the operation. Brig. Gen. James H. Wilson's Division would lead the right wing and Brig. Gen. David McM. Gregg's the left.[37]

On the afternoon of May 3, the 2nd Vermont finally received marching orders. The orders directed that the regiment move out the next morning at 4 A.M. with six days' rations (three in the men's haversacks and three in their knapsacks) and 50 rounds of ammunition per man.[38]

During all the hustle and bustle of getting his company ready to move out, Capt. Orville Bixby, a Royalton native and commander of Co. E, took a few hurried moments to jot his wife a few lines:

Captain Orville Bixby, commander of Company E, killed in action May 6, 1864. USAMHI.

> My Dear Francis
>
> Yours of the 28th rec. last night and thought I would just write a note to let you know that we move tomorrow morning at 4 o'clock so you musent think it strange if you do not hear from me again for some time. I wrote you Sunday. No news here excepting the move. My health is good. Cant write any more. Good by with the true love of your Orville.
>
> To my own
> Dear wife
> Love bless you

As an afterthought or maybe because of a premonition, he included a lock of his hair in the letter.[39]

Sgt. Charles Morey wrote his mother of his hope of a successful campaign:

> I am confident of success for Genl. Grant has been very busy arranging his plans and I hope and pray that we will not meet with a disaster.
>
> Let us trust the event in the hands of Him who rules the raging battle as well as the quiet sunshine and let us pray that God may grant that this campaign may end this Hydra headed rebellion and cause the people of the south to see the error of their ways and return to their allegiance.[40]

As ordered, the Sixth Corps left its camps at 4 A.M. on May 4 following the Fifth Corps south. Getty's division led, followed by Wright and Ricketts. At this time, the 2nd Vermont numbered 941 men. Roughly 150 would not make the march owing to being on convalescence leave, in the hospital, on various details, or in prison, having deserted. This left a little over 790 men in the ranks that morning to shoulder a musket. Pvt. Fisk noted the first day's march in his diary:

> The air was clear and cool and we marched very rapidly to Germania [Germanna] Ford, a distance of about 12 miles. The boys were in good spirits and went on merrily although we well knew that we were about to undertake one of the most perilous campaigns of the war. Many of us in all probability would fall in the coming battles but it was wisely hidden from us to know who these victims should be and every one could hope that he would escape.[41]

Wilson's cavalry division had departed camp shortly after midnight on May 4 and by 4 A.M. had reached Germanna Ford. The Confederates on the other side offered little resistance, and by 6 A.M., Wilson's whole division was across and waiting for the engineers to lay the pontoon bridges for the infantry to cross. These were completed a short time later enabling the Fifth Corps to cross. Gregg had an equally easy time at Ely's Ford, so, shortly after 9 A.M., the Second Corps was crossing.[42]

The day's operations proceeded according to the plan's timetable without incident. Around 11 A.M., Meade received the first intelligence report that Lee was responding to the Federal advance. From the Confederates' movements Meade assumed Lee's forces were gathering behind their fortifications along Mine Run.[43]

The Fifth Corps reached its day's objective, Wilderness Tavern, by late afternoon, pulled off the road, and went into bivouac. The Sixth Corps crossed the Rapidan River in the late afternoon and marched a little over two more miles before bedding down on Flat Run. Wright's men spread their blankets behind Getty's division, and Rickett's division covered the remaining stretch back to the Rapidan.[44]

Wilbur Fisk remembered:

> We halted that night about three miles from the river on the rebel side. It was late in the afternoon and we were all tired and some were foot sore and nearly exhausted. We spread down our blankets for our night out in the open air, very few thinking it worth while to put up any tents as the weather was clear and fair.[45]

Lee had been aware for several days that the Army of the Potomac was going to move but had not been sure which route it would take. By 10 A.M. May 3, he had collected enough intelligence to settle on a course of action. He decided to march east and hit Grant head-on in the Wilderness. The thick vegetation there would give Lee an advantage since Grant would not be able effectively to use his cavalry or artillery. The Federal infantry which would be on the offensive would not be able to maneuver easily, again diminishing Grant's numerical superiority. The only real risk for Lee was not having Longstreet's corps, but if he could hold out until Longstreet arrived, he would only be outnumbered two to one. Ewell was ordered to move his corps by the Orange Turnpike and to camp for the night on May 4 a few miles past Mine Run. A. P. Hill was directed to move by the Orange Plank Road and camp near New Verdiersville, just short of Mine Run. The two Confederate corps would be within supporting distance of each other and would have only a short march the next morning before hitting the Federals. Longstreet's corps, in camp much farther southwest, therefore a day's march behind, was to follow behind Ewell and Hill on the Catharpin Road just below the headwaters of Mine Run.[46]

By 5 A.M. May 5, Warren's corps was moving south on a wagon track from the Wilderness Tavern toward Parker's Store. Sedgwick prepared his corps to continue south on the Germanna Plank Road as soon as Warren's men cleared the road. Hancock's Second Corps advanced from Chancellorsville on the Catharpin Road toward Todd's Tavern.[47]

The Sixth Corps was on the road at 7 A.M. and moving deeper into what the Vermonters later called "a wilderness of woe."[48]

Warren's rear guard, stationed a mile or so from the intersection of the wagon track and the Orange Turnpike, reported a considerable Confederate force moving toward it from the west on the Turnpike at about 7:15 A.M. The Fifth Corps formed a line of battle stretching from the Orange Turnpike south about one mile from the Orange Plank Road. Strung out in this fashion, Warren prepared to take on not a division, as he suspected, but Ewell's entire corps.[49]

When Ewell reported to Lee that he had bumped into the Yankees, he was ordered not to bring on a general engagement until Longstreet could come up. Gen. Ulysses S. Grant, impatient with the waiting game, ordered Warren to attack, which he did at 1 P.M. In the meantime Wright's division of the Sixth Corps was sent to support Warren.[50]

At 10:30 A.M. a courier from Warren arrived at Meade's headquarters notifying him that rebels were also moving east on the Orange Plank Road. Grant's plan for a quick push through the Wilderness was coming to an end. Rather than seeking the safety of their entrenchments behind Mine Run, Lee's soldiers were charging up the turnpike and the Orange Plank Road in force. They were wrapping around Warren's flanks and threatening to interdict Hancock's link up with the rest of the army.[51]

The intersection of the Brock Road and the Orange Plank Road was pivotal in the army maintaining connection with Hancock's corps. Sometime around 10:30 A.M. Getty's Division, which had been lounging around the Wilderness Tavern since 7:30 A.M., was ordered south to the key intersection and told, "To hold this crossing at all hazards until the arrival of the Second Corps." Simultaneously orders went to Hancock to link with Getty. Once united they were to push west toward A. P. Hill's troops on the plank road. Unfortunately Hancock did not receive his orders until nearly 11:40 A.M. and it would take some time to reroute his units.[52]

Getty quickly put his men back on the road, and in no time they were rapidly moving south. It was going to be a close race. Getty and his staff were ahead of the column and cleared the two-and-a-half miles to the intersection in a short time. They reached the crossroads just ahead of the gray-clad troops and just as the 5th New York Cavalry, which had been trying to hold back the rebel troops, were leaving. Getty assembled his staff around the division flag in the middle of the intersection to trick the rebels into thinking a much larger force was at hand. Although minié balls started flying around their heads, Getty and his staff stood their ground, and the Confederate line slowed to a halt. By then it was almost noon.[53]

Several minutes later Brig. Gen. Frank Wheaton's Pennsylvania brigade arrived, rapidly deployed a strong front, and poured a volley into the rebels, driving them back. Within minutes the rest of the division arrived. Later, dead Southern soldiers were found as close as 30 yards from the intersection.[54]

Getty ordered his division into two lines at right angles to the Orange Plank Road. Wheaton's brigade straddled the Orange Plank Road, Gen. Eustis's brigade filed to the north, and L. A. Grant's Vermonters occupied the south side. After securing the intersection, Getty was ordered to probe north in an effort to connect with Warren, but the distance between the two organizations was too great.[55]

Grant formed his Vermont Brigade in two lines of battle. The 4th regiment on the right and the 3rd on the left constituted the first line. The 2nd regiment fell in behind the 4th and the 6th behind the 3rd. Companies D and K of the 5th Vermont were thrown out as skirmishers and the rest of the 5th was held in reserve. The Green Mountain Boys erected hasty breastworks of fence rails, logs, and what little dirt they could scrape up.[56]

For the next two hours there was little action at the intersection except for the opposing skirmishers popping away at each other. Riding ahead of his troops, Hancock reached Getty's location a little after noon. Being senior in rank, Hancock took command of the situation. At 3:30 P.M., units of his lead division, Maj. Gen. David B. Birney's, arrived on Getty's left. This allowed Getty to shorten his line a bit. Wheaton moved his regiments to the north side of the Orange Plank Road and connected with Eustis's men in the woods along the Brock Road. The Vermonters filed into Wheaton's old position until their right flank rested on the plank road. Around 3:45 P.M., before all of Hancock's units could arrive, Meade ordered Getty to attack with or without Hancock's support and drive the rebels back to Parker's Store. Getty launched his attack a half-hour later.[57]

As soon as Getty's three brigades moved out, the Vermont Brigade ran into trouble. The left of the skirmish line faltered because the officer in charge was attending to matters on the right of the line. The ground was covered with brush and small timber so dense that the left side of the skirmish line could not see the right side as it moved forward. The brigade had advanced just 100 to 200 yards (accounts vary due to the lack of visibility) when the skirmish line ran smack into the main Confederate battle line. The rebels had already pulled in their skirmishers, and a wall of lead hit the Vermonters from point-blank range. The 5th Vermont's skirmishers took the brunt of the volley, but within a split second the 4th Vermont was also hit. The 3rd Vermont moved obliquely to the left, passing over the left side of the skirmish line that had not moved, and became engaged within seconds. "After passing the skirmish line for about 200 yards," wrote the 3rd Vermont's commander, "we met the enemy, who gave the first indications of his presence by delivering a full volley in our front...." About the same, time the artillery in the intersection opened up and there was soon a general engagement along the front of all three of Getty's brigades. Unfortunately, the Vermont Brigade was farther forward than the other two brigades and sustained proportionately higher casualties.[58]

Getty was facing Maj. Gen. Henry "Harry" Heth's division of A. P. Hill's corps. Heth had deployed three of his four brigades holding one in reserve. From left to right they were as follows: Brig. Gen. Joseph R. Davis's brigade, Brig. Gen. John R. Cooke (whose brigade was straddling the Orange Plank Road), and Brig. Gen. Henry H. Walker's brigade on the right. Brig. Gen. William W. Kirkland's brigade was held in reserve. All told they numbered about 6,500 men. The Vermont Brigade was tangling with Cooke's and Walker's brigades. Although neither side could see much through the underbrush, they both kept up a steady rate of fire. The Vermonters were caught in a living hell. They returned fire on the Confederates and hit the ground.[59]

As the combat intensified, the 2nd Vermont crawled forward and plugged the gap that had developed between the 4th and 3rd regiments. The 6th Vermont did likewise in support of the 3rd, and the 5th moved to the left flank. The Green Mountain Boys hugged the ground as closely as possible and kept up a rapid fire. The enemy did the same. The rebels had the advantage of position since their line was protected by a slight swell of ground; the Vermont Brigade, by contrast, was on nearly level ground.[60]

Finally, Lewis Grant ordered a charge in an attempt to dislodge the rebels from their position, but as he explained later, "the moment

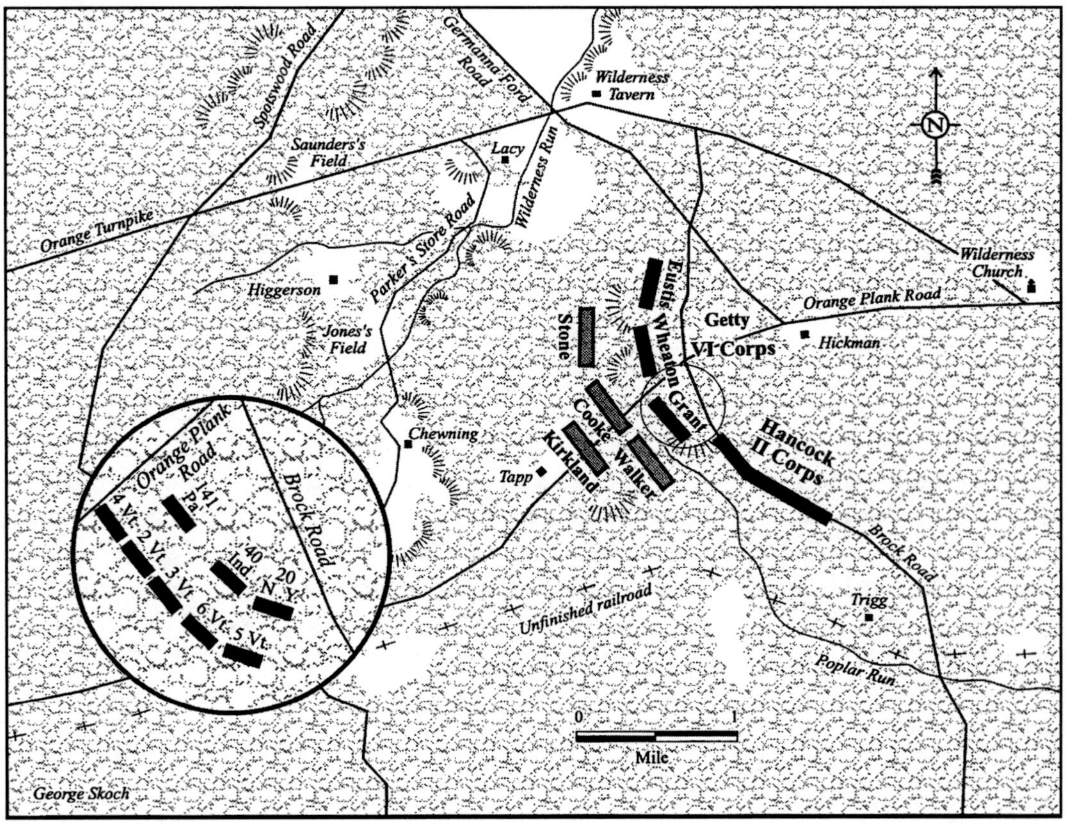

The position of the Vermont Brigade in late afternoon in the Wilderness, May 5, 1864

our men rose to advance the rapid and constant fire of musketry cut them down with such slaughter that it was found impracticable to do more than maintain our then present position."[61]

The 2nd Vermont had no more than begun fighting when it started losing men.

As Co. D was rushing forward, Pvt. George W. Colby, a 21-year-old farmer from Stowe, tripped on the underbrush and fell to the ground twisting his right knee. A man next to him helped him to his feet, and Colby limped on after his company. He got on line with his comrades and started firing. He had fired three rounds when a rebel bullet slammed into his left forearm, breaking the radius. With blood dripping from his wound, he made his way to the rear to the hospital. Colby stated later, "On my way to the rear my knee was swelled as full as the pants leg would hold and was very troublesome and I had to be assisted to walk." He spent the next eight months in the hospital until discharged. Despite his wounds, he lived until March 28, 1921, when he died from complications of a broken hip. Colby rests today in Montpelier's Green Mount Cemetery.[62]

While the regiment was moving forward, Pvt. Henry M. Parker from Plymouth, serving in Co. I, was hit in the right shoulder. The ball struck him about one-half inch from his neck and took out a piece of the collarbone as it passed on through his body. He was sent from the field to Fredericksburg where he stayed about four weeks. He then had a choice to go the Convalescent Camp at Alexandria or rejoin his company. Parker stated later, "I chose to go to my company & remained with them until I could do duty again."[63]

Pvt. Daniel D. Hemenway, a 24-year-old laborer from Ludlow serving in Co. I, took a nasty wound in the right hip. The ball lodged in his hip joint but he was able to make it to the rear, from which he was finally evacuated to the hospital. The doctors were unable to remove the bullet, and Hemenway was discharged on June 29, 1864. He had a limp the rest of his life. By the late 1880s, he had lost most of his hearing due to an explosion near him at the battle of Bank's Ford. It was not until 1900 that the ball was finally removed from his hip.[64]

About the same time Hemenway was wounded, Pvt. Azariah A. Grant of Co. A was hit in the left leg. The minié ball entered just above the knee shattering the femur. He was taken back to the division hospital where the bleeding was stopped and he was stabilized. He was evacuated to Armory Square Hospital in Washington where his leg was amputated. He was eventually transferred to Sloan Hospital in Burlington. By December 2, 1864, he was up and about on an artificial leg. He was discharged from the service May 29, 1865.[65]

Private Daniel D. Hemenway, Company I, wounded in the right hip May 5, 1864. Alan Poor.

Pvt. Theodore Wood, a 34-year-old, five-foot-ten and one-half-inch farmer from Duxbury in Co. D, apparently made an excellent target as three rebel soldiers fired at him simultaneously. All three bullets hit their mark, and Wood fell to the ground dead. His wife Eliza M. Wood was only one of many hundreds of women who became widows as a result of the fighting in the Wilderness.[66]

As 1st Lt. Eben N. Drury, a 43-year-old Vergennes merchant in Co. K, stood up and turned to yell the command "forward" to his men, a rebel minié ball slammed into his back just below the right shoulder blade. The ball tore through his body, exiting through the front of his chest. Drury's soldiering days were over, and he was mustered out June 29, 1864. He suffered from bouts of depression for years afterward which he and his wife thought were connected to his wound, but his family doctor diagnosed it as chronic cerebra-meningitis. Drury died of a cerebral hemorrhage March 25, 1875.[67]

Little five-foot four-inch Francis P. Ellsworth, a 24-year-old farmer from Tunbridge and private in Co. E, was killed outright in the short-lived charge.[68]

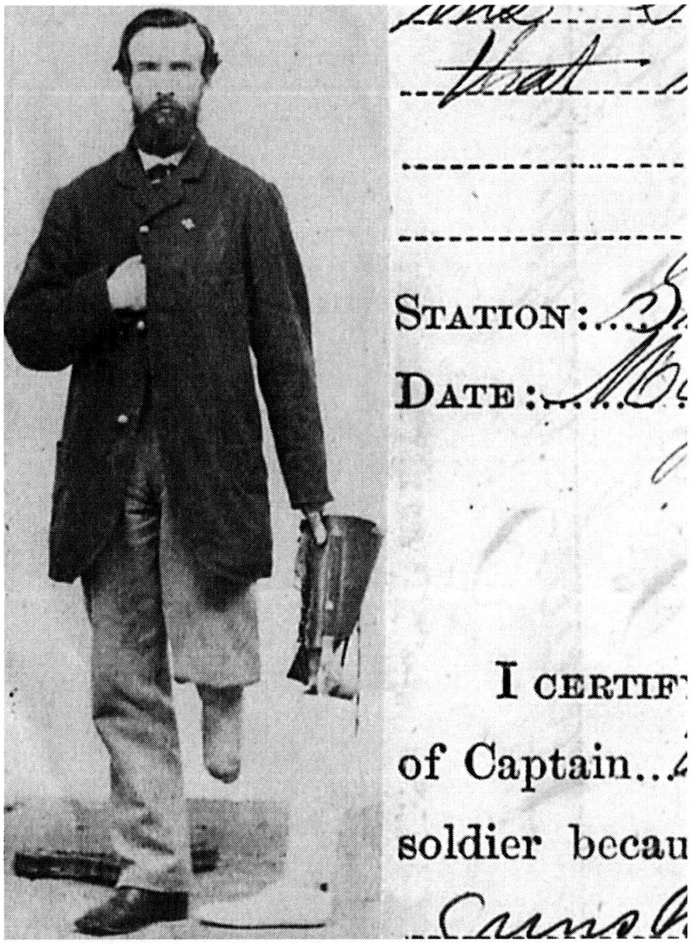

Left: **Private Theodore Wood, Company D, killed May 5, 1864. Susan Hunziker. *Right:* Photograph from Dr. Henry L. Janes's journal of Private Azariah A. Grant, Company A, exhibiting the stump of his amputated left leg. National Archives.**

Seeing a charge was impossible, the Vermonters went back to ground. Within minutes the air was thick with smoke from the black powder, further limiting their visibility. The men's faces grew powder-stained and their mouths became black from biting open paper cartridges. Between the smoke from the black powder and the thick vegetation, neither side could really see at whom it was firing. The men simply pointed their muskets into the smoke and fired blindly. The contact with the rebels seemed to go on forever. To make matters worse, the dry underbrush caught fire. The crackle of flames mingled with the wild yelling and cursing of the men and the roar of musket fire. Wounded men were seen to load and cap their muskets so that they could shoot themselves if the fire reached them. It was the most horrible combat the Vermonters had ever experienced.[69]

The 2nd Vermont, like the other regiments of the brigade, was losing men more rapidly than it had in any previous battle. Pvt. Fisk wrote:

> Just a little to the rear of where our line was formed, where the bullets swept close to the ground, every bush and twig was cut and splintered by the leaden balls. The woods was a dense thicket of small trees about the size of hop poles, and they stood three times as numerous as they are usually set in a hop yard; but along the whole length of the line I doubt if a single tree could have been found that had not been pierced several times with bullets, and all were hit about breast high. Had the rebels fired a little lower, they would have annihilated the whole line; they nearly did as it was.[70]

To stand up to fire meant almost instant death as Fisk noted:

> One ball grazed the top of my head splitting the crown of my cap completely in two and knocking it from my head. I had been standing up firing and had just got down on one knee to cap my piece as the balls were flying over our heads so plentifully and hitting so many that I deemed it best to be cautious. That simple act saved my life.[71]

Even with Fisk's caution, he was still grazed on both the left and right side of his rib cage.[72]

In a matter of minutes Fisk saw four of his best boyhood friends killed: William H. Sanborn, Francis P.

Ellsworth, William M. Noyes, and George W. Durrell. One of the platoon leaders in Fisk's company, 1st Lt. James Allen, a farmer from Tunbridge, took a minié ball in the right shoulder. The ball exited just under his shoulder blade close to the spine, causing partial paralysis of the right hand and arm. He was discharged for disability June 29, 1864, but the damage caused by the wound continued to worsen. By 1879 his doctor stated that, "He can scarcely feed himself at the table." He died April 26, 1890.[73]

Capt. Phillips E. Chase, commander of Co. G and a 37-year-old manufacturer from Mt. Holly, got his men down and into firing position. Pvt. John Farrell yelled over the din for the captain to stop exposing himself to the fire and get down with everyone else, but before Farrell finished his sentence, Chase was hit in the left wrist. A split second later, he was hit again by a ball that went through part of the outer fabric of his coat and struck his right groin, knocking him down. Pvt. Farrell helped his captain back to the hospital where Chase quickly pulled down his trousers to check the damage. To his surprise, he found that the ball had hit a metal object in his pants pocket, and that the wound was only a nasty bruise. The bullet was found still lodged in the lining of his coat. He was discharged the following month without ever returning to his unit.[74]

First Lieutenant James Allen, Company E, severely wounded in the right shoulder May 5, 1864. USAMHI.

Corp. George M. Colt, a Brattleboro resident in Co. C, was lying down trying to stay out of harm's way, but when he raised his right arm to ram home a bullet in his musket, his arm was hit. The minié ball entered his forearm three inches below the elbow, shattering the ulna. To add insult to injury, several days later while he was walking from Fredericksburg to Aquia to board a hospital boat for evacuation to Washington, he was knocked down by a horse which stepped on his chest, inflicting an additional injury. Colt never left the hospital before being discharged from the service June 29, 1864.[75]

Another Co. C soldier, Pvt. Kirk Rand, was one of the foolhardy men who stood to fire and paid the price. He was hit by a minié ball in the lower part of his left leg. His friends applied a tourniquet to stop the bleeding but had to leave him where he lay.[76]

Like Rand, Pvt. Alfred Guyett, also of Co. C, was hit in the left leg. The 27-year-old carpenter from Burlington was down with a compound fracture of the femur. He lived long enough to be evacuated to a hospital in Washington but died on June 7. He was buried in the Arlington National Cemetery on June 9.[77]

Pvt. Lyman Hulett in Co. A. received an excruciating wound in the left elbow joint that put him out of combat for good. He was transferred to the Veteran Reserve Corps November 25, 1864, and discharged September 14, 1865.[78]

Corp. Erastus Worthen was struck by a minié ball that shattered the top of his right femur. He was carried back to Fredericksburg and then to the First Division Hospital in Alexandria and eventually to Sloan General Hospital in Montpelier. He was discharged from the hospital on June 24, 1865, with a right leg that was three inches shorter than the left. The wound continued to seep pus the rest of his short life. Worthen died from an infection October 25, 1870, that a surgeon certified as "the result of breaking out anew of a wound on the right thigh."[79]

Although the Vermont Brigade's charge did not break the Confederate line, it did cause Heth to engage Kirkland's brigade that was being held in reserve, adding to the intensity of the firing. The battle seemed to go on without end. Minutes seemed like hours. Men were falling nearly as fast as the leaves from the shot-up trees.

Capt. Elijah Wales, commander of Co. C, went down with a moan as a minié ball hit him in the chest under his left arm. The ball traveled through his lungs and exited out his right shoulder, chipping his spine as it passed through. Sgt. Nelson S. Cole yelled for some men to help him carry the captain to the rear, but Wales refused saying "...it was no use for he was a dead man."[80]

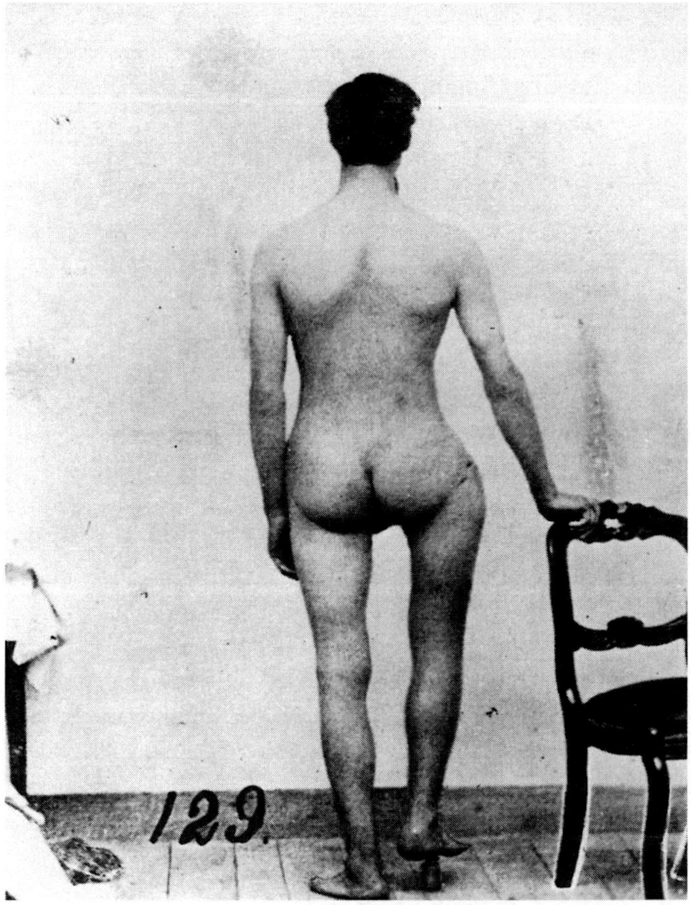

Left: **Photograph from Dr. Henry L. Janes's journal of Private Lyman Hulett, Company A, exhibiting the healed wound in his left arm. University of Vermont.** ***Right:*** **Corporal Erastus Worthen, Company B, displaying his wound for the U.S. Pension Bureau. He had an entrance and exit wound at the hip joint and a third opening at mid-thigh to discharge pus. Armed Forces Institute of Pathology.**

Just after Capt. Wales was hit, one of his lieutenants, Joshua P. Sawyer from St. Albans, went down as a minié ball ripped through his left forearm fracturing both bones. His arm was useless after it healed, and he never returned to his platoon.[81]

A rebel bullet nipped the index finger of Sgt. George W. Flagg's left hand. Flagg, a 25-year-old, six-foot farmer from Braintree in Co. F, did not think the wound was very bad at first, but he was in the hospital for several months; and when healed, the finger was permanently folded over the palm of his hand. Before the war, Flagg had left his family's Braintree farm to become the wrestling champion of Champlain Valley and was now reigning champion of the Army of the Potomac. Flagg would return to his company in a month. He survived the war, mustering out as a first lieutenant. After the war he traveled throughout the U.S. giving wrestling exhibitions. When asked about his prowess as a fighter, he would claim he was "brought up on salt pork, corned beef, boiled potatoes and maple sugar and seasoned by four years service in the Civil War." At age 48, he settled down on his farm in Braintree where he died of heart disease September 14, 1919. He is buried in East Braintree Cemetery.[82]

Pvt. L. Fay Bowker in Co. C, a young farm boy from Wilmington, had his second narrow brush with death. Bowker, who had taken a buckshot in the right knee at Bull Run in 1861, was hit in the head with a minié ball. His luck held again. The ball hit a glancing blow, penetrating the skin on his forehead near the hairline, and stayed between the skull and scalp until exiting out the back of his head. Although the wound looked terrible, he was back on duty within a few weeks.[83]

While many of the men of the 2nd Vermont were dying or receiving horrible, traumatic wounds that knocked them out of action, others with lesser wounds kept on fighting. Pvt. Warren Clough of Co. A, a 20-year-old farmer from Stamford, had the middle finger of his right hand shot off. Pvt. Joseph Slattery of Co. D had half of the middle finger of his right hand instantaneously removed. Pvt. Henry H. Bushy of Co. A, a substitute from Essex County,

Sergeant George W. Flagg, Company F, the champion wrestler of the Army of the Potomac. USAMHI.

Corporal Elbridge W. Prior, Company I, did not let having a toe shot off May 5, 1864,, keep him from looking after his men. USAMHI.

N.Y., lost the index finger of his right hand. Amos C. Humphrey, a 23-year-old shoemaker from Underhill in Co. G, lost the little finger of his left hand. Hampton "Ham" L. Maxfield in Co. H had the end of his left thumb shot off. Corp. Elbridge W. Prior, a 25-year-old farmer in Co. I from Plymouth, had the little toe of his right foot shot off, but he never slowed down. He had to look after his men so did not let his wound interfere.[84]

The hours of horror in the smoke and shadows dragged on, and still the 2nd Vermont's losses continued to mount. Pvt. Joseph E. Butterfield of Co. I, a 25-year-old, five foot, six-inch blue-eyed farm boy from Winhall, failed to hit the ground soon enough. He died instantly with a rebel bullet through his heart. After enlisting in May 1861, Butterfield had bought his parents Jesse and Harriet Butterfield a 56-acre farm. His parents, who had been dependant on Joseph for support received a meager pension from the government after his death.[85]

Pvt. William H. Stowe of Co. F was also killed outright. His body was recovered after the battle and sent home to Calais where he was buried June 5. A large congregation assembled to testify its respect to his memory.[86]

Pvt. Ira M. Carpenter, a 21-year-old farmer in Co. F, was luckier than Stowe. Carpenter was lying down firing as fast as he could when he was struck square on the bridge of his nose by either a buckshot or a pistol ball. The ball shattered his nasal bones, passed downward through his face bones, and lodged two inches below the right ear. For some reason, the ball was never removed. After several months in the hospital, Carpenter returned to his unit and served out the rest of the war. His life after the Army grew progressively worse due to the effects of his wound. His right nasal passage was completely obstructed after the wound healed, making it difficult for him to breath when lying down.[87]

Isaac Howard, a 52-year-old Co. H. private from Burlington was hit on the right side of his head by a bullet that left a one inch diameter indentation that was about one quarter inch deep. Isaac and his son, Ansel H. Howard, had enlisted in the 2nd Vermont in the summer of 1861. The

Left: **Private James G. Howard, Company A, wounded in the left arm May 5, 1864. Pictured here as a first lieutenant. USAMHI.** ***Right:*** **Private Norman J. Nichols, Company G, displaying the wound to the right side of his face to the U.S. Pension Bureau. National Archives.**

men in the company said he was a "white-haired, oldish man at that time and not fitted for the duties of a soldier." Because of his age and physical condition, he was made a company cook, but on this day, he was on the firing line and paid the price. He was discharged from the hospital September 13 and went home to recuperate. He enlisted in the army again January 30, 1865, and served until Jan 29, 1866.[88]

Brattleboro native Pvt. James G. Howard of Co. A was hit in the left arm. The ball struck him in the back of his upper arm and exited through the biceps. After the wound healed, he could not fully extend the arm; however, he returned to the regiment and was promoted to 1st Lt. by war's end.[89]

Pvt. Norman J. Nichols of Co. G, a 28-year-old carpenter from Essex, was loading his weapon when he was hit on the right side of the head. The bullet struck him one-half inch from the corner of the right eye, fracturing the cheekbone. The ball then entered the eye socket nearly destroying the eyeball and exited on the lower side of his right jaw. After the wound healed, he could only distinguish light from dark with his right eye. He was discharged for disability May 27, 1865. After the war, he became a civil engineer and was the chief engineer for the La Dorado Railroad in Honda, Colombia.[90]

Another Nichols in Co. G was hit. Pvt. LeRoy B. Nichols from Williston was struck on the right side of his head by a minié ball. The ball did not penetrate his skull but crushed it, doing internal damage. For the rest of Nichols's life, he suffered from partial blindness in his right eye, deafness in his right ear, and epilepsy.[91]

Pvt. George B. Ordway of Co. E and from Chelsea was hit by a ball that entered his right forearm just above the wrist, breaking the ulna. The wound healed fast, and he was back with his unit in several months.[92]

As the condition of affairs worsened for the Vermonters, L. A. Grant asked Gen. Getty for support. The 20th Indiana, 141st Pennsylvania, and 40th New York were cut from Birney's division and sent to Grant's aid. The 141st Pennsylvania filed in behind the 2nd and 4th Vermont

Private George B. Ordway, Company E, wounded in the right arm May 5, 1864. Ed Italo Collection.

regiments and the 20th Indiana and 40th New York went in support of the 5th Vermont.[93]

Grant went to Maj. Dudley, who was commanding the 5th Vermont (Lt. Col. Lewis having been severely wounded), and called his attention to the fact that the enemy in his front was less protected than those in front of the rest of the brigade. He asked Dudley if he thought his regiment, along with the two fresh regiments to his rear, could break the enemy's line. "I think we can," replied the major. Grant then addressed the two rear regiments and asked them if they could support the 5th Vermont in its advance. The men rose to their feet with a cheer and shouted over the din of battle, "We will." With that Grant ordered the three regiments forward. The surprised rebels partially gave way but then rallied and poured a volley into the oncoming Yankees. The two regiments supporting the 5th Vermont were thrown into confusion, halted, and threw themselves to the ground. Maj. Dudley, finding his regiment now far in advance of the rest of the brigade, also had his men lie down. One of Dudley's officers explained later, "When the charge was being made, we suddenly found ourselves 40 or 50 yards in advance of the remainder of the line, wholly unsupported and exposed, not only to a front fire of unprecedented severity, but also to a raking fire on both flanks of the most galling description."[94]

The charge was not a total loss however; the 20th Indiana captured the battle flag of the 55th Virginia Infantry along with a large number of prisoners.[95]

Then the rebels attempted a counter-charge. "The enemy charged and forced back our lines some 50 yards," wrote Gen. Getty, " when they were checked and repulsed." Pvt. Peter S. Chase, a 20-year-old farmer from Jamaica, Vt. in Co. I, described the action in the 2nd Vermont:

> Company I was the ninth in line, while Company A was on the left. There was a wood road at nearly right angles with the line of battle. The right of Company A and the left of Company I lay in this road, and it was here that the former was so badly cut up. That company soon fell in with Company I, or on the same side of the road with Company I, and fought till the regiment fell back to the Brock road.
>
> The only man on the left side of this wood road was Martin H. Harewood [sic] of Company A who was wounded [in the right leg just above the ankle] just before the fighting ceased. He fought as bravely and as quietly as he used to read his bible. The writer lay on the other side of the road, and on my right was William Slater, who had the honor of holding the left of the regiment at the close of the fighting. During the progress of the fight, Lieut. Col. John S. Tyler came down this road. He stopped at my side, shook his head, and made no attempt to cross this death-line. The rebels were now swinging round on our flank. Col. Tyler ordered Capt. D. S. White to send a corporal and 16 men to deploy on the left of the road, and Corporal Albert A. May started with the men. The corporal was the only man to cross the road, and he fell across wounded; all the rest were either killed or wounded before they could get over the road.[96]

Corp. Albert A. May, a 20-year-old printer from Ludlow in Co. I, was hit in the right leg. The ball passed through his lower leg breaking the tibia, but after several months in the hospital he was back with his company and served out the rest of the war.[97]

Not long after Capt. Daniel S. White had ordered Corp. May and his men across the road, a minié ball tore through his right leg just below the knee. He never returned to his company and was discharged for disability the following October.[98]

Near 5 P.M., while Corp. May had been trying to get his men across the wagon path, the 2nd Vermont's commander, Col. Newton Stone, was moving along his regiment's line encouraging his men and issuing orders when he received a flesh wound in his leg. Several of his men took him back to the field hospital where his wound was attended. As soon as his wound was dressed, he mounted his

Corporal Albert A. May, Company I, wounded in the right leg May 5, 1864. USAMHI.

horse and returned to his unit. He stopped behind one company and shouted, "Well, boys this is rough work; but I have done as I told you I wished you to do, not to leave for a slight wound, but to remain just as long as you can do any good. I am here to stay as long as I can do any good." He moved on down the line and stopped behind Company B to cheer on the men, when he was struck in the head by a rebel minié ball that knocked him off his horse. He was dead by the time he hit the ground. Brig. Gen. Grant wrote of Stone, "He was a good officer, gallant by nature, prompt in his duties, and urbane in his manner. He was beloved by his command and all who knew him."[99]

Lt. Col. Tyler assumed command of the regiment after Stone's death. Tyler was in command less than an hour when he was hit in the thigh by what he assumed was a minié ball. It nicked the femoral artery, and his boot quickly filled with blood. Several of his men ran to his aid, but he ordered them back to their posts in the line. It was only later, when he was weak from the loss of blood, that he would allow them to help him to the rear for medical attention. L. A. Grant wrote that Tyler "was a young officer of great promise. Always cool, especially in battle, he could be relied upon." Capt. Orville Bixby, commander of Co. E and senior captain in the regiment, became the temporary commander after Tyler left the field.[100]

For some unknown reason, Tyler decided to return to Vermont to recover. Accompanied by his father and uncle, he made it as far as the Metropolitan Hotel in New York City where a doctor discovered the projectile in Tyler's leg was not a minié ball but a single buckshot. Tyler died from his wound on Saturday night, May 22, in the hotel. His body was taken to Brattleboro, where he was buried with full military honors in Prospect Hill Cemetery. The governor of Vermont posthumously commissioned him colonel of the 2nd Vermont, effective May 6, 1864.[101]

In that same hour, the Vermont Brigade lost three of its other regimental commanders. Col. Barney of the 6th Vermont was hit in the head early in the action. He survived his wound for several days before dying. Lt. Col. Lewis, commanding the 4th Vermont, was hit in the left arm, which had to be amputated later. Col. Foster of the 4th Vermont took a minié ball in the thigh and was taken to the rear.[102]

"Our ammunition soon became well nigh exhausted, and a force from the Second Corps was sent in to relieve us," L. A. Grant wrote later in his after-action report:

> The regiments on the right were relieved first. As soon as the 2nd and 4th were relieved and ordered to retire, the enemy pressed forward and occupied the ground. So sudden was the enemy's advance that the staff officer who was sent to order back the 5th fell into the hands of the enemy. The 5th finding itself flanked judiciously retired. The brigade fell back to its former position on the Brock Road. The Second Corps now held the front; darkness soon came on and the firing ceased.[103]

The pullback by the Vermont Brigade was not quite as smooth as Lewis Grant intended. A little after 5 P.M., Col. Robert McAllister's brigade, of Brig. Gen. Gershom Mott's Second Corps division, came in on Grant's left. Slanting northward, a portion of McAllister's line slipped in behind the Vermonters. This put his rightmost regiment, the 8th New Jersey, to the 5th Vermont's rear. Bullets were flying thickly, forcing the New Jersey men to lie down. The Vermonters assumed that their desperately awaited help had arrived, and they retired, leaving the prostrate New Jersey troops all alone.[104]

Just as the Vermonters were pulling back to safety, Pvt. Charles H. Richardson of the 2nd Vermont's Co. D, a 23-year-old native of Barre, who had already had the top part of his left boot torn to pieces, was struck in the right hand with a piece of tree torn off by a shell. He then took a bullet that finally brought him down. He was hit in the right breast between the nipple and breastbone by a minié ball that passed on into his lung. His doctor stated later, "There is no scar or any place of exit of the ball, he carries the same in his body somewhere lodged near the spine I think." As though a bullet in his lung was not enough, the wagon train in which Richardson and about 300 other patients were being transported was attacked by 20 rebel guerrillas. Among the 300 patients, there were only about 10 muskets, but they managed to scare away the guerillas. Richardson had little use of his right arm after his wound healed. He was transferred to the Veteran Reserve Corps April 26, 1865. After the war he moved to Hinesdale, N.H. where he did mechanical work until he died June 1, 1904.[105]

Years later Pvt. Chase remembered his experience as the Vermont Brigade was pulling back:

> During this time I had received three wounds—a slight one in the neck, a flesh wound in the right leg and a compound fracture of the left thigh bone. I was compelled to cease firing to attend to the wound, from which blood was running freely. Sergeant Fred A. Fish, better known as "Uncle Ben," bound up my wounds to stop the flow of blood, after which he would load and fire his musket, and at each discharge his benediction followed the little messenger of death. The pet names he used would not read well in print, and are therefore omitted. Our men soon began to fall back. About this time, as I began to look about me, I saw many a fellow soldier on the ground as helpless as myself. The sergeant stopped long enough to fix me the best he could under the circumstances, speaking words of cheer as he bade me goodby, at the same time saying, "keep a stiff upper lip." My lip quivered like an autumn leaf in the wind, and as I tried to say goodby there was a strange bunch in my throat and I could not speak. The rebels were now within a stone's throw of us, so there was no time for him to stay. Those who have parted with a friend at such a time can imagine my feelings. I now lay between both lines of Battle. The firing on both sides being fearful. I was in more danger from shots of our own men than those of the rebels. Oh! the horrors. "Great God," I cried, "save me, a wounded soldier, from being slain by my own friends." The rebels, with a small line of battle, had passed over me. What! a prisoner? Yes and on the field of battle among the dead and wounded friends who, but an hour before, stood with me in the line of battle in the full vigor of manhood, now lay bleeding. The groans, the cries for help, and the prayers, may they never pierce the ears of any of the young men of this fair land again. Almost instantly the rebels were pursuing our men with that peculiar yell which was no music to those of us who were compelled to stay behind. Words cannot tell the agonizing thoughts which pass through one's mind at such a time.[106]

As Company C started to pull back, Sgt. Cole went to where Capt. Wales was lying and found that he was still alive. Cole yelled for Corp. George B. Prouty to give him a hand in carrying the captain. Cole had no more than called to Prouty when a bullet smacked into his knapsack spinning him around and knocking him to the ground beside Wales. Prouty came over, and the two men quickly moved Wales onto a blanket and started for the rear. Cole almost did not make it. As he was carrying the captain, a rebel minié ball ripped through the pocket of his blouse tearing open a bunch of cartridges. Then a bullet zipped through his pants leg but did not draw blood. Cole and Prouty finally got Wales safely to the field hospital. Amazingly Wales survived his wound and was back in command of Company C in two months, although pieces of bone worked their way out of the wound for years.[107]

The Vermont Brigade fell back to its former position on the Brock Road leaving the Second Corps to hold the front. The Vermonters began improving the intrenchments they had started earlier that morning as Pvt. Fisk mentioned, "we threw up breastworks as best we could, considering that we had to dig among roots and stumps with but few tools and poor ones at that. The firing stopped at dark without our having gained an inch on the enemy."[108]

Although the musket fire was not as heavy as it had been in the forest, the 2nd Vermont was still losing men. Pvt. Isaac C. Osgood, a Milton man in Co. H, had the left side of his skull fractured by a minié ball. Years later he wrote, "Our men were laying behind logs and being hit when they rose to fire."[109]

As soon as it was dark, stretcher-bearers and burial parties from both sides went out and tried to collect their fallen comrades. This was risky business, as Pvt. Chase, who was still lying in the woods between the lines, observed:

> It was about an hour before the rebels were compelled to retreat, passing over me the second time. They did not disturb me at all. Just before dark a new line of battle was sent in and formed on nearly the same place that we were driven from. During this time I had seen both sides advance as victors, and also retreat as a beaten foe. The grandest thought to me at this time was that victory was on our side, and that I was once more inside the Union lines.
>
> I was now where my friends could find me, and it was not long before I heard the voice of Corporal E. W. Prior, who came in with others looking after the wounded. If ever a boy was glad to see his friends I was one. They were friends in time of need. As soon as they could go back and procure a detail they returned, and took those of us who were unable to get back without help. Corporal E. W. Prior, with his men [Elmer G. Holmes, George A. French, and Ira D. Clark], took me on half a tent to carry me back to where the Brock road crosses the plank road. This was the commencement of my journey to the hospital. I was eager to bid adieu to the scenes of the battlefield. Think of four men carrying a man with a broken

> leg for half or three-quarters of a mile through thick brush, in the dark. The Corporal had a short piece of candle which he lit to help on the way, but as soon as the rebels saw the light they began to fire on it. The balls whistled so near us that it made us feel rather uncomfortable, and he was obliged to conceal the light under his coat. They soon had me on the plank road, where the ambulances were taking the wounded back. There they laid me down and bade me goodby. During the night I was taken in an ambulance and carried back to the old mining mill.[110]

Corporal E. Payson Gibbs of Co. G, who had a minié ball pass through both of his thighs, was not a lucky as Chase. Gibbs's friends could not get to him in the darkness and he bled to death during the night. His father had not been able to work since 1858 so he and Gibbs's mother were totally dependent on their son for support. They received a monthly $6 pension from the government starting in 1866.[111]

Col. Stone's body was also recovered under the cover of darkness. Pvt. John Kelly, from Rutland and a member of Co. B, noted in his diary that night that "Col. Stone was buried about 9 P.M."[112]

Sgt. Nelson Cole and Corp. George Prouty had just returned from taking Capt. Wales to the field hospital and found their company when someone called out in the darkness for Company C. Cole, who had not yet fallen asleep, responded. The man in the darkness said a wounded man named Kirk Rand, who had been left on the battlefield, was alive and wanted to be brought in. Cole woke up three men lying beside him, and they started after Rand. As they reached the picket line, they were told not to speak above a whisper since both sides were shooting at any sound or movement. The four men crawled on into the darkness as silently as they could. Cole remembered where Rand had fallen, and before long they were in the general vicinity. Telling the three other men to lie low, Cole called out Rand's name. Out of the darkness came Rand's reply, and a shower of rebel bullets. The men crawled over to Rand and placed him on a blanket, but as they tried to move him, he screamed out in pain which brought another shower of bullets. Rand told the men he would rather lie there in the bushes and take his chances than to get shot again. Cole could not leave one of his men behind and told the other three to go back and get a stretcher. Although the men were gone for less than an hour, Cole thought it "seemed a week." As Cole lay there in the dark with Rand, he could hear the wounded and dying in all directions crying for water. The only reply was bullets from the rebel pickets. The three men finally returned with the stretcher, and they started back with Rand. Two men carried the stretcher while Cole and the other man pulled aside the bushes and limbs to hold down the noise. They got Rand back to Brock Road where there were ambulances, and Rand was taken to a field hospital.[113]

Although Rand was finally at a hospital, he was not seen by a surgeon for four days, during which time the tourniquet remained on his leg. Within four weeks, his wound developed gangrene, and on June 25, his leg had to be amputated just above the knee.[114]

Lewis A. Grant said later, "One engaged in that terrible conflict may well pause to reflect upon the horrors of that night. Officers and men lay down to rest amid the groans of the wounded and dying and the dead bodies of their comrades as they were brought to the rear. One thousand brave officers and men of the Vermont Brigade fell on that bloody field."[115]

While the Second Corps and Getty's division had been slugging it out with A. P. Hill's men, the Fifth and the Sixth Corps tangled with Ewell's troops. The battle astride the Orange Turnpike swayed one way and then the other. By

Photograph from Dr. Henry L. Janes's journal of Private Kirk Rand, Company C; exhibiting the healed stump of his amputated left leg. University of Vermont.

dark, after hours of bloody fighting, the Fifth and Sixth Corps, like the Second Corps, were in about the same position as when their attack started.[116]

Later in the evening after the fighting had subsided, Hill's division commanders approached him about dressing up their shattered lines and digging in, but Hill told them to let their men rest. Longstreet would be up relieving them before long. As of 1 A.M., May 6, Longstreet was still miles away. The Vermonters got what sleep they could that night despite the random shots of the skirmishers and the moans and shrieks of the wounded. All night long both Grant and Lee hurried reinforcements to the front. Longstreet was moving in from Richard's Shop as Burnside's Ninth Corps was making a forced march to plug the gap between Warren's left and Hancock's right. Longstreet was to join Hill's corps on the Orange Plank Road.[117]

Unlike previous commanders of the Army of the Potomac, U. S. Grant did not shrink from heavy losses. Instead, he ordered Hancock, Warren, and Sedgwick to attack at 5 A.M. the next morning.[118]

Brig. Gen. Lewis Grant was somewhat shaken when he received the order for the attack. He wrote later, "To me, personally, the order came like a death-warrant. If the struggle of the day before was to [be] repeated, it evidently meant death to many of us. I felt as I never felt at any other time." Grant's feeling of doom was so strong that he left his personal possessions with some noncombatant staying behind with instructions for their disposition, to include his horses in case he did not return.[119]

Pvt. Fisk overheard the attack order being passed on to Capt. Bixby by one of L. A. Grant's aides:

> Before light the next morning I heard an aide tell Captain Bixby who now was ranking captain and had charge of the regiment that we were to advance down into the same place again and meet the enemy once more on the same ground. I am willing to admit that I dreaded it. The officers, too, thought that they were asking us to do more than our share of the bloody work. We were connected with Hancock's Corps and Hancock seemed determined to make us work while we stayed with him. But not a man flinched. There was no skedaddling to the rear.[120]

Fisk continued his narrative as the 2nd Vermont waited in the darkness to move out, "None of us had eaten anything that morning and if all felt like me none cared to eat a great deal. I found a piece of corn cake in a rebel haversack which I made out to eat with something of a relish as it was a change from hardtack though hardly for the better."[121]

Just before daylight and before the brigade moved out, L. A. Grant placed Lt. Col. Samuel E. Pingree of the 3rd Vermont in temporary command of the 2nd Vermont.[122]

Samuel Everett Pingree was born in Salisbury, N.H., August 2, 1832, and graduated from Dartmouth College in 1857. Soon after graduating he relocated in Hartford, Vt., to start a law practice with his brother Stephen. Both brothers enlisted at the beginning of the war. Samuel, as a first lieutenant in Co. F, 3rd Vermont, and Stephen, as a first lieutenant in Co. E, 4th Vermont. Samuel, showing great courage, was severely wounded in the Battle of Dam No. 1 in 1862, for which later in life he was awarded the Medal of Honor. He was well liked and respected in the Old Vermont Brigade. After the war, he became a successful lawyer and was elected governor of Vermont in 1884.[123]

As Hancock's men were getting into position for the morning's attack, they heard the battle open unexpectedly

Lieutenant Colonel Samuel E. Pingree, acting commander of the 2nd Vermont from the Wilderness to Petersburg. USAMHI.

to the north. Ewell had attacked at 4:45 A.M. Finding the Federals still in force to their front, the Confederates fell back to their works, closely pursued by Sedgwick's men. Ewell tenaciously held his ground as Warren and Sedgwick hammered away at him. On the other hand, Hill, who had expected to be relieved and had not straightened up his position from the day's fight, was left vulnerable.[124]

Birney's division which would spearhead the Second Corps's attack, advanced in two lines, at 5 A.M. followed by Getty's division. The Vermont Brigade, one of the units in the rear, straddled the Orange Plank Road with two regiments on the right and three on the left.[125]

Wrote Fisk:

> At half past four o'clock we were ordered to advance into the same place again. There were pale and anxious faces in our regiment when that order was given. We had insufficient rest for the two nights previous, and the terrible nervous exhaustion of fighting had left us in hardly a fit condition to endure another such an ordeal so soon. There were so many men missing from our number that it hardly seemed like the same regiment. But the order was forward, and I do not know that a single man failed to take his place.[126]

The Vermonters' luck held for a while as Lewis Grant noted later:

> At the command, all the lines moved steadily forward. We passed over the scenes of yesterday's conflict, but the enemy was not there. As we advanced, two lines from Wadsworth's Division. on our right, moved obliquely in to our front, so that there were then four lines of battle in our front. When the enemy was met these lines drove all before them. There was some sharp resistance, but the lines moved forward and pressed enemy back. We of the rear line didn't get a shot or a sight at them, and we were in no danger except from the bullets and shells that came to the rear, and these were not many, as the most of them were stopped by intervening trees.[127]

After a half an hour, Hill's lines broke, and his men were driven back through the woods. Cooke's, Kirkland's, and fragments of several other Confederate units braced for the oncoming blue wave. Getty's division soon smashed into their position. The rebel infantry and artillery put up a stiff fight, but the effort was only temporary. Getty's troops flanked their position, and the Confederates had to fall back to avoid being overrun.[128]

In the confusion of the advance, the Vermont Brigade was crowded to the south. By the time the rebel retreat slowed down, all the Vermont regiments were on the left side of the plank road. The Union advance slowed to a crawl as it neared the open fields of the Widow Tapp's farm and ran into Confederate artillery fire. The situation for Lee was critical and desperate. It looked as though he and Hill's corps were about to be gobbled up; however, in the nick of time, Lee's "Old War Horse" Longstreet arrived and immediately threw his men forward.[129]

Longstreet's two divisions formed a strong front across the plank road with Brig. Gen. Joseph B. Kershaw's division on the south side and Maj. Gen. Charles W. Field's on the north. Kershaw and Field opened holes in their lines to allow what was left of Hill's corps to slide through. With his front clear of friendly troops, Longstreet prepared to counter-attack.[130]

Hancock was also having troubles. In the excitement of the chase, his units had become disorganized, and he decided to stop and reform his lines before continuing his advance. It was now nearly 8:30 A.M.[131]

About 10 A.M., before Hancock could get his scattered troops back into some semblance of order, Longstreet attacked. The Confederate assault on the south side of the plank road caught Hancock's men by complete surprise. As Longstreet's troops poured heavy fire into the Union ranks, Birney's lead units disintegrated, leaving the Vermont Brigade to bear the brunt of the rebel onslaught. Getty went down with a bullet wound in his shoulder. Bleeding profusely, he was led to the rear, and Brig. Gen. Frank Wheaton, Getty's senior brigade commander, took command.[132]

"In less than half an hour," wrote Brig. Gen. Lewis Grant, "the four lines in our front were swept away, and heavy lines of the advancing enemy came upon us with great force."[133]

The Vermonters did have a bit of luck. They were on a slight rise the Confederates had vacated earlier in the morning, leaving hastily constructed fortifications made of logs and decayed timbers. The Green Mountain Boys quickly rearranged the logs to their advantage and prepared to take on the rebels. They did not have to wait long.[134]

Brig. Gen. Lewis Grant continued his description as the rebels hit his brigade:

> They were received with a bold front and galling fire, and their advance was completely checked and thrown back in confusion. Still determined, the enemy reformed his lines, and again advanced to the attack, and again went back. The attack was many times repeated, and as many times repulsed. The repulse, however, was complete only in front of this brigade.[135]

The units on the Vermont Brigade's flanks were not standing up to the pressure of the Confederate attack and were slowly falling back, especially on the right. Grant hurriedly faced the 4th Vermont to his unprotected right flank. As soon as it reached position, the 4th unleashed a volley on the Confederates who were approaching them from the other side of the plank road. Another Federal brigade was soon sent in to relieve the 4th Vermont and to protect the Vermonters' right flank.[136]

The 2nd Vermont's losses were starting to mount. Capt. Orville Bixby, commander of Co. E and the regiment's senior officer, was shot in the head. He was taken to the rear by several of his men where he lingered until dying that evening.[137]

The two Tatro brothers in Co. K were hit at about the same time. Pvt. Joseph Tatro was hit in the middle of the right thigh with a minié ball that fractured his femur. When the wound healed, the right leg was several inches shorter than the left. He was mustered out May 22, 1865 for disability. He died August 19, 1880 at Montgomery, Vt. from the effects of his wound. Abraham Tatro was hit in the right ankle where the bullet lodged.[138]

Sgt. William H. Foster, of Co. C and Dummerston, was hit by a minié ball that injured his penis and scrotum and exited near his rectum. Afterward his penis was slightly deformed and there was a large scar on his scrotum. He was mustered out June 29, 1864.[139]

L. A. Grant continued his narrative of the battle:

> Perhaps the valor of Vermont troops and the steadiness and unbroken front of those noble regiments were never more signally displayed. They stood out in the very midst of the enemy, unyieldingly, dealing death and slaughter in front and flank. Only the day before one-third of their number and many of their beloved leaders had fallen, but not disheartened the brave men living seemed determined to avenge the fallen, and most effectually they did it. For more than three hours did the brigade hold this advanced position, repelling every attack.[140]

Unable to gain any advantage by attacking head-on, the rebels tried flanking Hancock from the left around 11 A.M. Lewis Grant:

> Foiled in every attempt at this point, the enemy massed forces, about one-fourth of a mile to our left, and made a vigorous attack. Our lines at that point suddenly gave way and came in confusion past our rear. I immediately ordered two regiments to face to the left, but before the order could be executed the enemy rushed through the breach and opened fire into our rear, and at the same time made another attack in front. Perceiving that it was worse than useless to attempt further resistance there, I ordered the regiments to rally behind the breast-works on the Brock road, at which point we had been ordered to rally in case of disaster.[141]

Wilbur Fisk put it in simpler words: "We were then in a most exposed position and of course had to run or be taken prisoners."[142]

Just as they were about to pull back, Pvt. Nathan Franklin Smith, a Tunbridge boy in Co. E, was killed as Wilbur Fisk described:

> Frank Smith was shot through the body near the heart and died almost instantly. When he was hit he exclaimed, "Oh! I am killed," and attempted to step to the rear. A great many speak in that way when they are severely wounded and I did not notice him particularly till he fell on to me and then I looked around and saw that he was dying. I told Charles Morey that he ought to examine his pockets and if he had anything valuable to send it home to his folks. The orderly [Morey] was just about to do so when we were ordered to fall back.[143]

In the process of pulling back, 2nd Lt. Henry Carroll of Co. K was captured. He remained a prisoner of war until he escaped from prison in Columbia, S.C., November 1, 1864. He was on the run for two months, finally reaching the Union lines at Nashville, Tenn.[144]

Brig. Gen. Lewis Grant:

> Our entire lines at this part of the army went back in disorder. All organization and control seemed to have been lost. But out of that disorder the Vermont Brigade quietly and deliberately took its position in the front works on the Brock road, and awaited the enemy's advance. Other troops were rallied and placed on the right and left and rear, though thousands went beyond reach or immediate control. The lines of the left of the Second Corps were unbroken, and now took position on the Brock road. Other troops came up from the right and our position was made strong again, and here we awaited the enemy's attack.

Following up the success of his flank attack, Longstreet brought the rest of his corps up the Orange Plank Road. Riding ahead of the main body of his infantry, Longstreet and his staff were mistakenly fired on by their own troops. Longstreet was severely wounded and taken from the field. Ironically, his wounding occurred just three miles from where Stonewall Jackson had been wounded by friendly fire one year and four days earlier. Maj. Gen. Richard H. Anderson was appointed as Longstreet's replacement the next day.[145]

The Vermont Brigade waited behind their barricades along the Brock Road for the expected Confederate attack. "It came late in the afternoon; a vigorous, determined, and desperate attack," remembered Lewis Grant. "The heaviest part fell upon the troops on our immediate left, but a portion of it fell upon this brigade, and was handsomely repulsed."[146]

Lt. Col. Samuel Pingree wrote:

> At 4 P.M they had shown no disposition to attack us and another general advance is ordered by Gen. Grant to take place at 6 P.M—However, the enemy was intent upon assaulting our works and moved upon us at about 5 P.M while we were in full preparation to move into the woods upon him again. This was our streak of good luck—for being in readiness to

Second Lieutenant Henry Carroll, Company K. Captured May 5, 1864. Escaped from a Confederate prisoner of war camp in Columbia, South Carolina, November 1, 1864, and two months later entered Union lines at Nashville, Tennessee. USAMHI.

leave our line of works on the road and go out to fight the enemy how much stronger we must be to meet him behind a line of earth pits which we had been two hours in building the night before ... massed in deep lines of battle were hurled desperately against our Corps (2d) center and for twenty or thirty minutes the battle raged with intensest fury—not a gun was used—all was musketry—there was but one rolling sound and that lasted till the last enemy was driven out of sight & heading back into the woods or left dead or wounded under the murderous fire of our men. Our lines immediately advance & reestablish our morning line.[147]

Pvt. Peter Chase, who had been wounded the day before, continued his story of his stay in the field hospital on May 6:

The sun was just rising when I was being laid on the damp ground, without a blanket over or under me. Hundreds of others about me were no better cared for than myself. In the next ambulance that was being laid down was a young soldier. His sighs and groans were dreadful. His thigh was badly shattered, and his hair and face were all covered with dry blood, for he had a bad wound in his head. I did not know him until I heard his voice. I looked at him and exclaimed, "My God! is that you, Dan Schofield?" One of my own company boys. I tried to cheer him up by telling him we were all right and would soon be taken to a hospital. "Oh, my leg is nothing," he said, "but my head." The next day, all battle-stained and battle-taken, on southern field, the patriot died, and his friends know not his resting place.

During the forenoon I was taken into the surgeon's tent and laid on the amputating table. I had expected to lose one of my legs. If I had ever been brave or shown any nerve, the sight of the large pile of amputated limbs, which lay just outside and in sight, and the thought that I had to give one of my legs to that ghastly heap took the courage all out of me and I begged them to spare my leg. "We will not take a hair more than we are obliged to," said the doctor. I took chloroform and they removed the musket ball and some pieces of bone. I was then taken to a large tent, where I remained during the day.[148]

The slaughter in the Wilderness was finally over. The Vermont losses had been horrendous. The brigade lost 191 men killed, 947 wounded, and 96 missing. The 2nd Vermont suffered the heaviest losses in the brigade with 48 men killed, 220 wounded, of which 32 would die later, and 29 missing, most of whom were dead but could not be found or identified. In two days the 2nd Vermont lost almost one half of the men it had taken into battle.[149]

The total casualties in the Army of the Potomac for May 5and 6 were 2,246 killed, 12,037 wounded, and 3,383 captured. Lee lost approximately 11,000 men. Although Lee's losses were less than Grant's, they were men who could not easily be replaced.[150]

After the battle of the Wilderness nothing in the 2nd Vermont would ever be the same again. Letters which used to be written in abundance and full of tales of boyish antics would now be less in number and without as much frivolity. Nor were the details of the battles included as often. The glory of war was gone forever along with the soldiers' innocence.

CHAPTER 11

"The Slaughter Pen"

The Vermonters were up at daylight on Saturday, May 7, ready for whatever the day might bring; but as the sun came up, the only action was an occasional shot exchanged between pickets. Parties of men were soon sent out to look for the wounded and collect and bury the dead. The Vermont Brigade was ordered to send a skirmish line out ahead of the burial parties to determine the location and strength of the rebel lines. As the Vermonters moved out, they traveled over ground covered with corpses clad in both gray and blue uniforms, and wounded soldiers called for help with pathetic groans and pleas. Pvt. Wilbur Fisk, who was on picket that morning, remembered:

> We kept our post there awhile and then had orders to advance. I can hardly say that I liked to hear that order. We were advancing on the enemy a feeble line of pickets without support. The enemy were there, we could hear them talk. I would have liked to go in there with a good strong line of battle but to go in depending on our legs for a safe return was not so pleasant. We kept advancing occasionally giving and receiving a shot from the enemy. We halted just under the crest of a hill for some sharpshooters to take up their position. As they advanced one of them was shot dead. The rest turned like cowards and run. Pretty soon the order came to us "Forward." Some of the men hesitated. They hated to advance up that hill ... and very likely share the fate of the man just killed. I am sure if I had acted just as I felt I should have gone in the opposite direction from the crest of that hill but I wouldn't act the coward. Lyndon George shouted "Come on boys" and I wasn't going to be behind Lyndon. I clenched my musket and pushed ahead, determined to die if die I must, in my place and like a man. They fired but didn't hit us and we fired back and they retreated. We kept on advancing until we came to their works when they opened on us with grape and of course we had to fall back.[1]

The Vermonters withdrew to where they had earlier discovered a large number of muskets the rebels had gathered from the battlefield but had not had time to remove. Wagons were sent out, and the cache of weapons was recovered. The rest of the morning and afternoon was uneventful. Brig. Gen. Grant wrote later: "We had an opportunity to rest and look over the battlefield. Where the Vermont Brigade charged and fought May 5 the trees were cut and bruised by bullets; they were very thick, most of them quite small, but nearly every tree and sapling bore marks of the terrible conflict."[2]

By early morning, May 7, U. S. Grant decided on his next course of action. Determined not to retreat or slam headlong into Lee again, he would, under the cover of darkness, slide his army around Lee's right flank and occupy the area around Spotsylvania Court House, thereby placing his army between Lee and Richmond. Lee would then have no choice but to attack.[3]

The Fifth Corps was to move out first followed by the Second. The Fifth Corps was scheduled to reach Spotsylvania Court House by morning. Meanwhile, the Sixth and Ninth Corps, with the Sixth in the lead, would take a more easterly course through Chancellorsville.[4]

At 3 P.M., Getty's division was ordered to rejoin the Sixth Corps in preparation for the move to Spotsylvania Court House, leaving several hundred wounded men in the field hospitals. Dr. Melvin J. Hyde, the 2nd Vermont's surgeon and an Isle LaMotte native, wrote to his daughter of being left behind:

Surgeon Melvin J. Hyde. USAMHI.

O Alice we have had one of the most bloody battles this world ever saw lasting several days.... I went with my regiment till it made the charge with the rest of the Brigade, and then was ordered back to the field division hospital where I had to operate all that day and nearly all night. We put up 30 large hospital tents, which were crowded with the wounded while 1500 men lay on the ground around suffering the most heart-rending cries of agony. We numbered but 5 or 6 surgeons and it took us about 3 days to attend them and then many had to be moved in army wagons and ambulances without having their wounds dressed at all! All this time the ambulances continued to bring in the wounded of our Division and the cannonading and musketry was almost deafening. O, it was terrible to hear the poor fellows cry for water or in piteous tones cry out to any surgeon that chanced to pass near him for help. The third night we left this place and moved on about 9 miles and established our hospital on the "Old Chancellorsville" battleground, called Cherry Grove, 3 miles from Chancellorsville. We stayed here one day and a night with about 200 wounded on our hands and Dr. Allen, the Division Director, detailed me to furnish food and shelter for the wounded of the whole division—besides having to perform operations. In the night all our wounded but 300 were sent on to Fredericksburg and all the surgeons were sent on with them but I refused to go, declaring that I would never leave 300 wounded men behind without food or medical aid, to perish, for there were many Vermonters among them. I accordingly remained and rode all night around the field to keep straggling horsemen from trampling on the wounded who lay all over the field without shelter or even a blanket. In the morning I cooked them some coffee which had been left with me for them and passed it around with some hard tack. I then detailed some of the stragglers to carry 33 of them on stretchers to a house about a quarter of a mile off, as the poor fellows lay with the hot sun streaming into their faces, many of them half naked, their clothes having been torn off to dress their wounds which were now covered with matter and smelled horribly. At this moment about noon some army wagons were sent back for them but could not carry all, about 40 still remaining, including 13 Vermonters. With these I resolved to stay and starve if necessary. Just then Gen. Grant of our Brigade passed in the rear of the 6th Corps and I begged a beef of him which I butchered and kept the men alive 4 days on beef tea.[5]

Pvt. Peter Chase of Co. I described his experience as a patient as the hospital moved out:

The next day, the 7th, was quite hot, and as I had nothing to shade me from the sun it was very unpleasant. During the day a soldier from one of the other regiments brought me a canteen of water, and then sat down beside me and told me of his troubles. "There were three of us brothers, in one company," he said, "and we all went into the battle together and we were all wounded the first day. I received the slightest wound. One of my brothers died last night. I went out and dug his grave and buried him alone. Since then I have been out and buried the foot of my other brother in the same grave."

They were hurrying the wounded back toward Fredericksburg. During the afternoon it became known that all of the wounded could not be moved, so that those who could stand the journey best would be moved first. I was very anxious to undertake the journey, for there was a report that those left behind would be taken prisoner. It was just before dark that an officer rode up to the surgeon in charge and said, "There are 13 ambulances; do the best you can with them; there is not another empty in the whole army to be had." It was not until the 12th one drove in that my long watched for chance came. I rode all that night over a very rough road and did not get any sleep or rest.

Chase and the other Vermonters received only mediocre care until Governor Smith arrived at Fredericksburg on May 20 with a contingent of Vermont surgeons to treat their own. Chase's leg had been allowed to start mending without ever being set. With the bones overlapping his wounded leg was 4 inches shorter than the other. To remedy this problem one of the Vermont surgeons had to set it. Chase described the ordeal:

My bunk was just the right height, and as I lay under an open window I threw my arms over my head and clasped my

> fingers under the window sill outside. The doctor took hold of my ankle, put his foot firmly against the end of my bunk, and with one strong pull brought the bones together into place. A shock passed through me that caused me to loosen my grip, but the job was done. The pain that shook my whole frame was severe. Could I have given vent to my feelings in sighs and tears it would have been a great relief to me, but my boyish pride would not permit me to do so. I must be a soldier, and it was not manly for a soldier to do either.

Chase survived the treatment and on the morning of May 26 was evacuated north. He was discharged with a disability on May 16, 1865.[6]

Correctly anticipating Grant's next move, Lee also determined to make his next stand at Spotsylvania Court House. At 7:30 P.M., May 7, he ordered Anderson to move Longstreet's corps out just after dark at almost the same time as the Yankees. Ewell's corps was to follow and then A. P. Hill. Because of the smoke and the stench from the rotting bodies in his sector, Anderson pulled his troops out five hours early, and without either side knowing it, the race for Spotsylvania Court House was on.[7]

With the Vermonters guarding the rear, the Sixth Corps started at 10 P.M. and marched all night, arriving at Chancellorsville late in the morning of May 8. Here the Vermont Brigade guarded the Sixth Corps's trains. The trains went into camp about 4 P.M., and the Green Mountain Boys stopped to cook their suppers and get some rest. Shortly after supper, Brig. Gen. L. A. Grant received an order directing him to hurry his brigade forward to join the corps four miles ahead to support an anticipated attack.[8]

The attack was due to Anderson's corps reaching Spotsylvania before the Yankees. When Warren's corps arrived at Laurel Hill, more than one mile from Spotsylvania, he discovered he was facing a cavalry division and two of Anderson's infantry divisions. The Confederates had won the race. Warren reported his predicament to Meade, who ordered Sedgwick's Sixth Corps forward, but due to artillery and ambulances clogging the roads, it was hours getting there. As the Sixth Corps neared Laurel Hill, Sedgwick seemed distraught by the absence of his favorite unit. "Where is the Vermont Brigade?" he fretted. "Not up yet. Just when I wanted it. Everything unlucky." By the time Sedgwick joined Warren and both commanders got their troops into position, it was too dark to attack.[9]

The Vermont Brigade did not catch up with the Sixth Corps until after the attack was called off. It was soon led off in the darkness through a ravine and up a wooded hill to a new position. Here, Lewis Grant discovered that his command was far in front of the Federal lines and even in advance of the skirmish lines. He heard scattered shots by the skirmishers on his flank and rear, and without orders decided to move his brigade back to a safer location where he would know the enemy was in his front. After several hours of reconnoitering and wandering about in the darkness, the brigade finally ran into a portion of the skirmish line of the Sixth Corps and took a position behind it, which proved to be where Gen. Sedgwick had wanted it in the first place. In the process of finding a new position, the brigade had a couple of brushes with the Confederates, losing several men, but none in the 2nd Vermont. By the time the brigade got into position, the men were exhausted and dropped to the ground and fell asleep.[10]

By Monday morning, May 9, Lee had both Anderson's and Ewell's corps dug in around Spotsylvania Court House. The undulating terrain, largely covered with forests with occasional patches of cleared land and the marshy valleys of the Ny and Po Rivers, afforded excellent natural advantages for defense. To this, Lee added extensive earthworks and abatis (obstacle formed of trees felled toward the enemy). Anderson's corps stretched from the Po River to Laurel Hill. Ewell's corps continued from Laurel Hill eastward. Because of the terrain, Ewell's right formed a salient—or huge bulge—in the line, later called the Muleshoe. The Confederate line, surrounding the Court House, covered all the roads converging there from the north and east.[11]

Warren's Fifth Corps faced Anderson, and Sedgwick's troops glared at Ewell's gray-clad troops. The distance between the opposing corps was in some places no more than a few hundred yards. All day the skirmishers and artillery traded shots and sharpshooters searched for targets.[12]

Getty's division, commanded in Getty's absence by Brig. Gen. Thomas H. Neill, was in position in a clearing on a hillside a mile-and-a-half north of the Court House. In front of the clearing was a strip of woods, and beyond was a rise of open ground, along the crest of which ran the enemy's earthworks.[13]

The Green Mountain Boys spent Monday, May 9, building fortifications and pulling picket duty, a welcome change after the past three days, but it was a sad day for the Sixth Corps. Early that morning Gen. Sedgwick was killed by a rebel sharpshooter. "'Johnny Sedgwick,' as the boys call him was a favorite General with the boys of his corps," wrote Wilbur Fisk, "and they had unbounded confidence in his prudence and judgment. But he died with his armor on, and we cherish his memory, emulate his bravery so that, though dead, he still lives with us."[14]

Maj. Gen. Horatio G. Wright replaced Sedgwick. He was a native of Connecticut, and had graduated from West Point in 1841. He had been Heintzelman's chief engineer at Bull Run and was now a major general commanding the First Division of the Sixth Corps. He had attended Vermont's Norwich University from 1832 to 1836 before entering the U.S. Military Academy.[15]

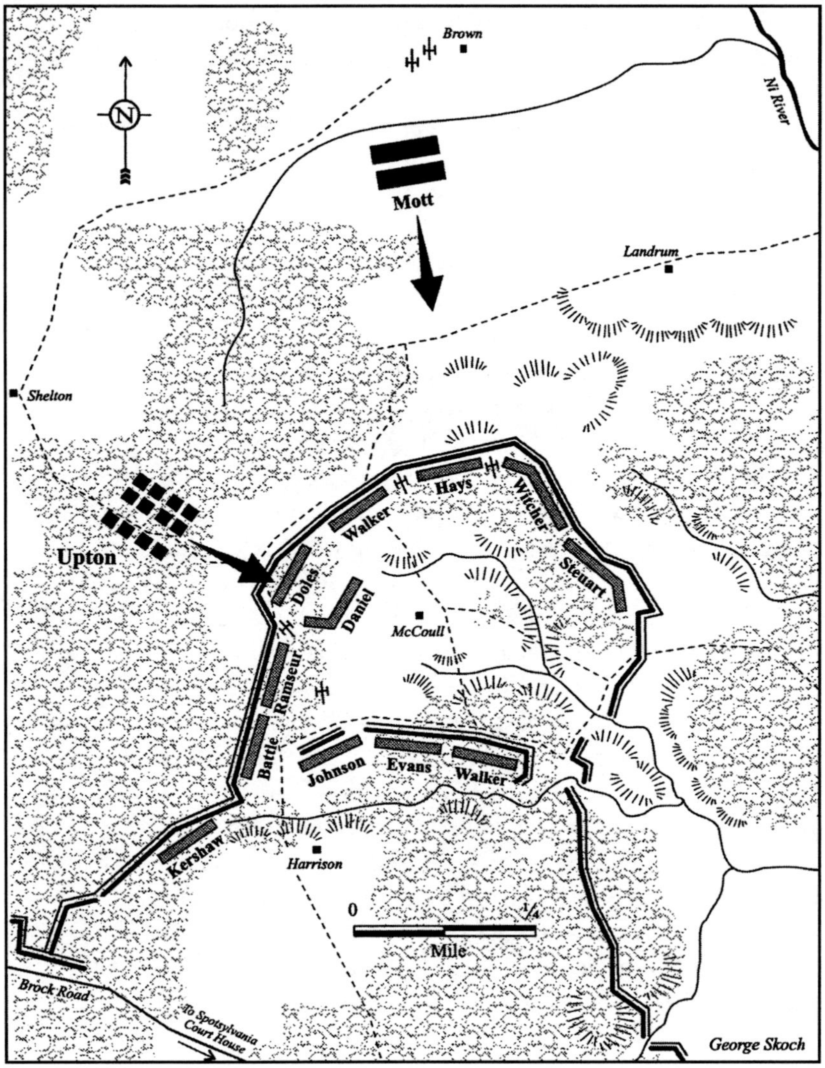

Colonel Emory Upton's assault on the Salient, May 10, 1864

The major action on Tuesday, May 10, did not occur until late afternoon. Grant's plan was to make an assault all along the Confederate line. The Second and Fifth Corps were to hit the rebels again at Laurel Hill. Burnside's Ninth Corps was to hit the Confederate left and push on to Spotsylvania Court House. The main thrust of the attack would be made by a force of 12 of the best regiments from the Sixth Corps. Under the command of Col. Emory Upton, these regiments were to penetrate the center, forcing an opening that would be exploited by Brig. Gen. Gershom Mott's division. The 2nd, 5th, and 6th Vermont regiments, under the command of Col. Thomas Seaver, were among the 12 units chosen for the assault. The point of Upton's attack was a weak spot halfway up the west side of the salient, along the brow of a hill near the McCoull house. Opposing Upton was Brig. Gen. George P. Doles's brigade of Ewell's corps. Two lines of works guarded the position. The first was especially strong with the top of the breastwork faced with heavy logs, pierced with loopholes from which Doles's Georgia infantrymen could fire in relative safety.[16]

Before the 2nd Vermont had a chance to assemble with the rest of the regiments chosen for the attack, they had a man wounded. Pvt. Albert Perry from Co. K and Panton, Vt., was on the skirmish line and took a nasty flesh wound in the right thigh. Perry seems to have had a run of bad luck. He had gone AWOL July 21, 1863, and did not return for a month. During his absence, he apparently had a wild time. By mid-September, he was in the hospital being treated for syphilis. He had only been back with his company for several months before he was shot, but his luck seemed to have changed, and he was back on duty by October and was never wounded again.[17]

During the afternoon, Upton assembled his command in the woods near his objective. The enemy works were up a little dirt road through the trees and then about 200 yards across an open field. Upton ordered the men to stack their knapsacks and haversacks and go in light. He formed the regiments in four lines of battle. The three Vermont regiments constituted the fourth line. The first line was instructed to load its muskets for the charge but not to fire until it penetrated the rebel line. Then the men were to fan out to the left and right and drive the rebels down the line. The second line would charge the gap in the rampart opened by the first line. The Vermont regiments were to follow the third line into the salient when called forward.[18]

Prior to the assault, the Sixth Corps artillery, on a crest behind Upton's troops, opened a tremendous fire on the salient. Then at 6 P.M., the artillery ceased as suddenly as it had begun, and Upton yelled, "Attention battalions! Forward, double quick!, Charge!" The men sprang to their feet and with a roar sprinted across the open ground. Quickly a sheet of flame burst forth from the rebel line as hundreds of rifles fired and cannons pumped cast-iron canister balls into the oncoming Yankees. "The rebels mowed down the men with awful effect," wrote Pvt. Fisk, "but the advancing line was not checked." They had a difficult time getting through the abatis but kept up the momentum. Within minutes, they were at the opposing breastworks where they engaged the Confederates in a hand-to-hand fight. The rebels were sitting in their trenches with their bayonets tipped, loaded muskets held upright, ready to impale or shoot the first Yankee to leap over. The first Union troops who tried were shot in the head. Seeing the fate of their comrades, some of the men held their rifles over their heads and fired down into the waiting enemy. Others hurled their rifles, with the bayonet affixed, over the parapet like a javelin, pinning the rebels to the ground and jumped over after them. The rebels retaliated with the bayonet, pinning one private in the 96th Pennsylvania to the log parapet. But the rebel resistance only lasted for a few seconds before the blue wave rolled over into the Confederate position, bagging nearly 1,000 prisoners. Without halting to take a breath, the Yankees pressed on and captured a second line of works, nearly 100 yards inside the Muleshoe, and a rebel artillery battery. Ewell, who was with Doles at the time of the attack, was himself almost captured.[19]

The Vermonters, waiting at the edge of the woods to be called forward, could not stand the wait, wrote Pvt. Wilbur Fisk:

> At the signal, Col. Upton with his three lines of infantry jumped to their feet, and rushed ahead across the open field, to the enemy's works, while we cheered as lustily as we could to heighten the effect, and help create a panic among the enemy. How terribly the bullets swept that plain, and rattled like hailstones among the trees over our heads. The boys could not be restrained in their wild excitement, and without waiting for orders (for I certainly heard no order but "halt," and I know of no one that did) they rushed in after the other brigade, and we drove the enemy from his first line of works.[20]

As the Vermonters were running toward the Confederate fortifications, they came under artillery fire. A piece of bursting shell hit Pvt. Benjamin Jerough of Co. G, a carpenter from Hinesburgh, on the right side of his head just above his ear. He was carried to the rear to the regimental hospital and was later evacuated to a general hospital. He returned to his company the following September, but the wound had caused brain damage and he acted somewhat retarded. His company commander felt Jerough was not competent enough to put back into combat and assigned him as a cook.[21]

Just as Jerough went down, 1st Lt. Ethan Allen Priest in Co. I. was hit in the left groin by a rebel canister ball. In addition to being badly hurt, he had to lie on the field for several hours before being rescued and taken to the hospital. This was Priest's third wound of the war. He had been hit in the right thigh at Bull Run in 1861 and had been hit in the head by a minié ball at the battle at Golding's Farm on June 27, 1862. He survived his wound, but his soldiering days were over, and he was mustered out at the expiration of his service June 29, 1864. Priest returned to Mt. Holly and went back to farming. He died on August 28, 1893.[22]

With the Confederate line opened, Mott led his division forward, but the rebel artillery had a murderous direct fire on the Yankees, and Mott's division broke almost as soon as it got started. Upton was on his own.[23]

The 2nd Vermont had no more than reached the Confederate trenches when Capt. Rollin C. Ward, commander of Co. B from Castleton, was dropped. A rebel minié ball had slammed into his left thigh, severely damaging the muscles and nerves, and then passed on through and out of his right thigh. Several of his men dragged him back to the safety of the woods from where they had started their assault and then to a field hospital. Ward would be hospitalized until his discharge July 15, 1865.[24]

As the Vermonters approached the rebel works, they threw themselves against the outside walls of the trenches for protection. It was here that Pvt. Egerton Hood, a Chelsea man in Co. E, ran into trouble. He was hugging the ground with his musket at his side. He was holding his musket by the base of the bayonet with his left hand covering the muzzle. In the commotion of trying to get under cover, one of his comrades kicked the hammer of Hood's musket, causing it to discharge. The ball went through Hood's hand between the bones of his index and middle fingers, mangling the index finger.[25]

Not long after Upton's men penetrated the salient, Ewell got enough of his troops organized to stop the Union onslaught. Brig. Gen. Cullen Battle's brigade blocked Upton's forward movement, while Brig. Gen. Junius Daniel's brigade hit Upton's right flank. Upton rode back to bring the Vermonters into the fray, but as he stated, "they had already mingled in the contest and were fighting with a heroism which has ever characterized that elite brigade." Finally, Ewell got Brig. Gen. John B. Gordon's brigade, led by Col. Clement A. Evens, forward, and Gordon's Georgians hit Upton head-on, stopping the blue surge.[26]

Although they had gained some of the Confederate entrenchments, there was little protection from small arms fire. Pvt. John Miller of Co. F, a 22-year-old substitute from White Hall, N.Y., was hit in the left arm near his elbow. The bones in his lower arm were completely shattered. He was carried back to the hospital where his left arm was amputated just above the elbow. He recuperated in the Lincoln General Hospital in Washington and was discharged from the service May 2, 1865.[27]

Pvt. Joseph N. Goron, an East Montpelier native in Co. F, and Corp. James M. Worthing from Bakersfield in Co. H were both firing over the parapet at the rebels as fast as they could pull their triggers and reload. Ironically, both men were hit on their foreheads just above the left eye. Goron was partially paralyzed for several days after he was hit but finally regained full use of his limbs. He returned to his unit the following fall and served until discharged July 10, 1865.

The wound left him deaf in his left ear, and he had headaches and a "prickling sensation" on the back of his neck for the rest of his life. Worthing's wound was more severe than Goron's, the bullet taking out pieces of his skull allowing the brain to protrude. Worthing was transferred to the Veteran Reserve Corps December 10, 1864, and mustered out June 29, 1865. His wound left him with a permanent case of vertigo and a large ugly scar over his left eye.[28]

Seeing that the charge had ground to a standstill, Upton was ordered to retreat. Most of the column fell back promptly after the men filled the cannons they had captured with dirt to prevent them from being used against them as they retreated across no man's land. Fisk wrote, "The left of the line had been repulsed, and we must now fall back too, or be captured. It was too bad. Had we succeeded there, it would have saved us that bloody fighting two days later." But a number of the men in the 2nd Vermont as well as a few in the other two Vermont regiments failed to get the order to withdraw. Once they realized they were alone, they still refused to go back, insisting that they could hold the works they were in, and that, in fact, it was safer to stay than to go. Col. Upton rode back and ordered them away; but they answered, "We don't want to go. Send us ammunition and rations, and we can stay here six months." Stay they did for two hours after the other Federals had retreated. During this time, Gen. Wright rode up to Lt. Gen. U. S. Grant and reported that some of the Vermonters were still in the salient and would not come away. "What shall I do?" he asked. "Pile in the men and hold it," Grant replied. Wright went back to do as ordered, but in the meantime, under orders from Gen. Russell, the Vermonters had withdrawn. Other attacks on the Confederate line fared no better than Upton's.[29]

Not all of the Vermonters were able to make it to safety. Eight men in the 2nd Vermont were captured and sent to the Confederate prisoner of war camp at Andersonville, Ga. Those men were Pvt. John P. Abbot of Co. A; Pvt. David P. Bateman and Sgt. John A. Freelove of Co. B; and Pvts. Oren Beckley, Jr., John C. Clough, James Dion, Winslow C. Rollins, and Sgt. Nelson E. Dodge of Co. D.

David Bateman, from Poultney, Oren Beckley and Nelson Dodge, both from Barre, never made it out of Andersonville. All three died from disease.[30]

John Abbot, an 18-year-old printer from Rockingham, was slightly wounded when he was captured. He survived Andersonville and was transferred to another prison camp in Charleston, S.C., where he escaped February 18, 1865. He was discharged May 24, 1865, and lived until 1914 when he died of heart disease in Somerville, Mass.[31]

Bateman's comrade Corp. Freelove was transferred from Andersonville to a camp in Orangeburg, S.C. where

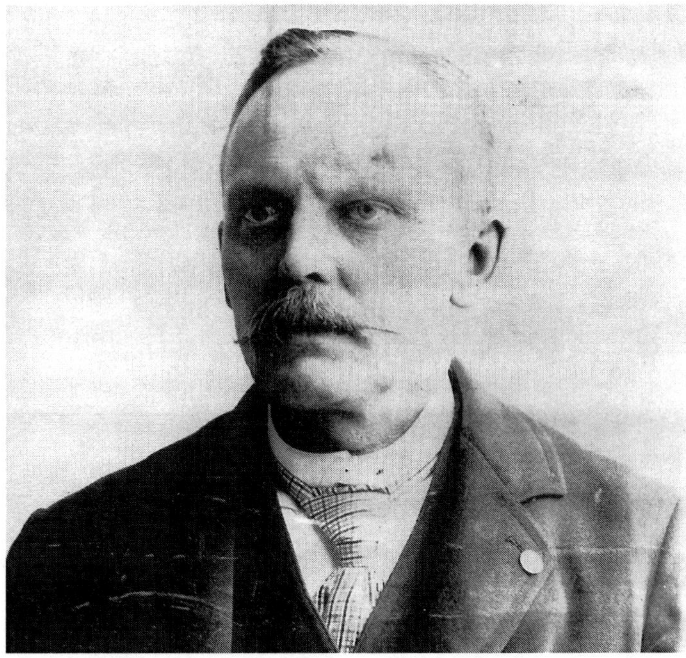

Corporal James M. Worthing, Company H, displaying the wound to his left forehead to the U.S. Pension Bureau. National Archives.

he escaped September 14, 1864. He made it safely back to Union lines and was discharged October 27, 1864.[32]

John Clough, a Williamstown resident who had a finger shot off at the battle of Savage's Station, escaped from Andersonville on January 10, 1865, and was mustered out the following July. He returned to Vermont after his discharge, married in 1873, and settled in Montpelier, where he became a stone mason. Unfortunately, he often drank to excess, and at such times he "abused his wife, striking her, and otherwise tormenting her." His wife finally tired of his abusive behavior, left him sometime around 1900, and spent the rest of her life with one of her daughters. Clough, in 1924, at the age of 83, cut his own throat and bled to death alone in his home. One can only wonder if he had been haunted by the memories of the hellish experiences he had in combat and during his time in Andersonville.[33]

James Dion from Pownal was wounded in the right arm and left leg before he was captured. The Confederate authorities paroled him in Charleston, S.C., December 11, 1864. He was mustered out April 21, 1865.[34]

Winslow Rollins, a 20-year-old young man from Middlebury, had been downed with a wound in his right leg when he was nabbed by the rebels. By the time he was released from captivity February 23, 1865, his wound had healed, but he suffered from sores on his hands and legs and the effects of scurvy. He also had "fits" on a weekly basis the rest of his life.[35]

Lt. Col. Pingree wrote of the frustration he and the

boys in the 2nd Vermont felt at not being reinforced and having to relinquish the ground they had taken:

> This I assure you was galling to the pride of brave men—When I got by myself where I would not be ashamed of it I cried like a whipped spanniel—I saw many soldiers cry like girls, and many who took things less to heart, gave vent to their mortification at having lost all they had gained so nobly—by the fault of others, by letting of unnumbered salvos of profanity.—I believed while there, & believe still that the only true way to save us was to send a column to take the enfilading work on our left. It might have cost 500 men that night. I do not think it would have cost a man more. The next day it cost us over ten times that number.[36]

In this attack, Upton's command lost approximately 1,000 men. The Vermont Brigade lost six men killed, 66 wounded and 16 missing. Of that total, the 2nd Vermont only lost three men killed, 12 wounded and captured. While there was no tactical gain in the assault, there were two personal ones. Col. Upton was soon afterwards promoted to brigadier general, and years later, Col. Seaver was awarded the Medal of Honor.[37]

The Confederate loss was roughly 1,500 men, of which 954 were taken as prisoners of war. A more significant loss for the Confederates occurred about 40 miles south of Spotsylvania Court House. In the late afternoon of May 10, Maj. Gen. Jeb Stuart's and Maj. Gen. Philip H. Sheridan's cavalry tangled at Yellow Tavern and Stuart was mortally wounded.[38]

The Vermont Brigade lay behind its entrenchments during the night of May 10 and all the next day. The fighting was confined to skirmishing and heavy artillery fire. At dusk on May 11, the Vermonters were relieved from the trenches and allowed to bivouac about a mile to the rear to get some rest. Even though it rained hard all night, the Green Mountain Boys were too exhausted to complain.[39]

Although Upton's charge against the Muleshoe had failed, it did show there was a weakness in the Confederate line. U. S. Grant spent May 11 developing a plan to attack the Muleshoe again the next day. He reasoned that if Upton's force could penetrate as far as it had, a larger force could go even deeper. His plan called for Hancock's 20,000-man Second Corps to strike the Muleshoe at its apex. Burnside's Ninth Corps would hit the east side while the Fifth Corps attacked the west. The Sixth Corps was to stand fast to send support wherever needed. The troops were to attack as silently as possible without firing a shot. To attack as the plan directed, Hancock had to move his corps from the Union right to the center.[40]

Lee, anticipating Grant's next assault, had Ewell strengthen his position and distribute a new supply of ammunition. By late afternoon however, he received reports that some of the Federals were leaving his front—Hancock's movement. Accordingly, he ordered Ewell to pull his corps out of the Muleshoe early the next morning and move closer to the courthouse. During the night, Nelson's and Page's artillery was moved from the salient ahead of Ewell's infantry[41]

The Army of the Potomac awoke on Thursday, May 12, to a day that would be filled with fog, rain, and death. On the previous night, Hancock's corps had completed its relocation to the Union center. At 4:35 A.M., just as the rain stopped and the sun came up enough for the men to see, Hancock unleashed his corps. The Second Corps moved silently out of the woods and into the fog-shrouded fields toward the salient. The Confederates' outer picket line, which could not see the blue-clad soldiers approaching was quickly pushed aside, and with a cheer the Federal soldiers cleared away the abatis in front of the fortifications. Maj. Gen. Edward Johnson's division opened fire on the Yankees, but his men's ammunition had become wet during the rainy night and many of their muskets misfired. The blue wave started to pour over the parapets near the apex of the salient. The Second Corps pushed nearly a quarter of a mile into the interior of the Muleshoe and captured some 3,000 prisoners and 20 pieces of artillery. Gen. Johnson and one of his brigade commanders, Brig. Gen. George H. Stewart, were among the prisoners. With disaster imminent, Lee threw Gordon's, Mahone's and Wilcox's divisions against Hancock's horde checking, its forward progress.[42]

As successful as the Federal push had been, it was completely stalled by 6 A.M. The Second Corps was still engaged with Gordon's troops and had lost all but a couple of hundred yards of its earlier gain. Burnside's Ninth Corps was completely pinned down by Confederate artillery fire.[43]

To break the impasse, Grant ordered the Sixth Corps to support Hancock's right flank, and taking Russell's and Getty's divisions, Gen. Wright advanced promptly up to the east angle of the salient around 8 A.M. to support Brig. Gen. Francis C. Barlow's division. Formed in two lines of battle, the Vermont Brigade moved up the slope and came under severe artillery and small arms fire on its right and lost a number of men.[44]

As the 2nd Vermont was moving forward, Corp. Charles F. Greenleaf, a 21-year-old farmer from Salisbury in Co. K, was knocked down by a minié ball that hit him in the right shoulder. He was left lying on the ground as the regiment charged forward. He soon picked himself up and started to the rear for medical attention. In his words:

> No field or regimental hospitals had been established, as I could not find any, so I made my way with hundreds of others

who were wounded, and able to walk to Belle Plain Landing on the Potomac, where I was treated for the wound on the hospital boat Maine ... and came to Washington and was placed in Carver Hospital on 14th street, where I remained until about August 8th, when I returned to my regiment.[45]

A short time after arriving at the salient, Gen. Hancock ordered Brig. Gen. Lewis Grant to send the regiments in his second line to Gen. Russell's assistance. Russell's division was holding the west face of the salient near the apex. Additionally, Hancock told Grant that the rest of the Vermont regiments would be sent as soon as he could move in some of his own Second Corps units to replace the Green Mountain Boys.[46]

Leaving Col. Seaver in command of the other three regiments, Grant took the Fourth and 5th Vermont regiments to the western angle of the salient. Here, Wheaton's brigade was supporting Russell and attempting to advance through a thick growth of bushes in face of severe fire. The two Vermont regiments quickly moved forward. The Fourth took and held a portion of the front line of breastworks to the right of the angle. Col. Seaver soon arrived with the rest of the Vermont Brigade. With his brigade again united, Lewis Grant left the 4th regiment with Wheaton and put the 2nd under the command of Capt. Dayton P. Clarke, Lt. Col. Pingree being in charge of the picket line on the right. Clark's performance in leading the 2nd Vermont during this battle would earn him the Medal of Honor. The 3rd and 5th Vermont regiments were along the outer face of the west side of the angle which was in imminent danger of recapture. The 6th Vermont was held in reserve. By about 9 A.M., Brig. Gen. Samuel McGowan's brigade of South Carolina troops of Wilcox's division regained the trenches on the inner face of the breastwork, opposite the Vermonters, from the apex down along the west side. Now began one of the most desperate struggles of the war.[47]

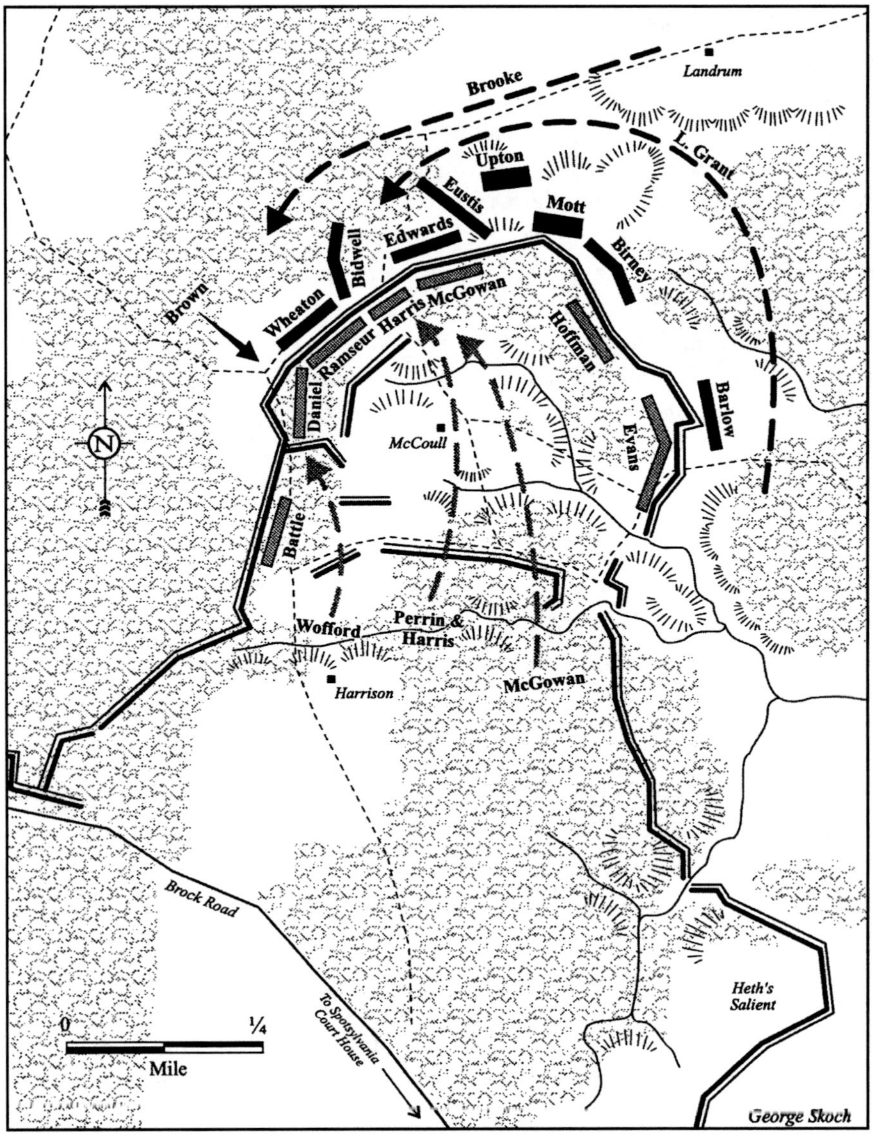

The Bloody Angle, May 12, 1864

Lewis A. Grant described what happened when his men made contact with the rebels at the parapet:

> It was emphatically a hand-to-hand fight. Scores were shot down within a few feet of the death-dealing muskets. A breast-work of logs and earth separated the combatants. Our men would reach over the breast-works and discharge their muskets in the very face of the enemy. Some men clubbed their muskets and in some instances used clubs and rails. Several times during the engagement those who occupied the other side of the works, finding escape impossible, would raise the white flag, and when our fire slackened would jump over the works and give themselves up. About 200 prisoners were taken in this way, and each time a batch came in the enemy would rush forward others in their place who, in turn, would soon show a disposition to come over. In this way the brigade was engaged for about eight hours....[48]

Pvt. Charles M. Hapgood of Co. A, a 21-year-old native of Peru, Vt., received a deep scalp wound that, in his words, made him "senseless." He was taken to a field hospital and then to Fairfax Seminary Hospital in Alexandria where he remained until the expiration of his service, October 31, 1864.[49]

Sgt. LeRoy B. Nichols, a 31-year-old farmer from Williston in Co. G, was hit on the right side of his head, causing him partial blindness in his right eye, partial deafness in his right ear, and epilepsy. He was unable to farm again after he was discharged June 29, 1864, and received a $17 a month government pension.[50]

Pvt. Rufus H. Marsh of Co. D and Moretown had just raised his rifle to fire when a rebel minié hit his left forearm. The ball tore through his arm fracturing his ulna. He was mustered out the next month. He returned to Vermont, married, and started farming. In 1890, he deserted his wife and six children and was never heard from again.[51]

Pvt. Franklin M. Cook of Co. G and Shelburne, who had sustained a slight wound at Bank's Ford in 1863, was shot in the left knee. He survived the wound long enough to be evacuated to the Armory General Hospital in Washington, where he died from complications of the wound June 2.[52]

Fighting in the trenches at the Bloody Angle May 12, 1864. *Battles and Leaders.*

Over in the portion of the trench where Company A was fighting, Corp. Giles J. Burgess, of Burlington, was firing as rapidly as he could. As he was looking down to reload his rifle, a rebel soldier leaned over the parapet and fired down at him. The ball went through his left boot, passed directly through his foot, and buried itself in the mud. He was discharged from the service the next month. In his later years he was so disabled from his wound and old age that he was admitted to the Vermont Soldier's Home in Bennington where he died December 1, 1930.[53]

Jeheil S. Bailey, Jr., a corporal from Waterville in Co. H, was hit in the left breast with a ball that passed cleanly through his lung and out his back. Although he survived the wound and was discharged the following July, he continued to suffer from a choking sensation the rest of his life. He died April 4, 1912 in Johnson, Vt.[54]

During the hand-to-hand fight across the parapet, Brig. Gen. Grant needed to shift one of his regiments, but all of his aides had been either killed or wounded. Second Lt. Augustus J. Robbins, a hotel keeper from Northfield, of the 2nd Vermont's Co. B, happened to be standing near Grant, and volunteered to go to the regiment that needed to be relocated and lead it to where Grant wanted. Grant gratefully accepted Robbins's offer. The area through which the regiment would have to pass was swept with heavy rifle fire. Robbins reached the unit without a scratch and started leading it when he had the top of his left foot laid wide open. He led the Vermonters to their objective, and was then carried to the rear. Robbins was mustered out the next month. Years later, Lewis Grant nominated Robbins for the Medal of Honor, which was awarded March 24, 1892. The citation read, "While voluntarily serving as a staff officer successfully withdrew a regiment across and around a severely exposed position to the rest of the command; was severely wounded.[55]

On several occasions, the rebels used white flags as decoys to get the Federal troops to lower their muskets, and then fired into them. One such incident happened to the 2nd Vermont as related by Pvt. Wallace William Noyes [mistakenly referred to as William Wallace Noyes in his military records], a 20-year-old farmer from Montpelier in Co. F:

> Suddenly, right near where I was lying, one of the Confederates raised a white rag or handkerchief fastened to the end of his musket. Some of our men took it for a flag of truce and one of them raised his head over the breastwork, when with a cheer the Johnnies emptied their muskets into the poor fellow, killing him instantly.
>
> Infuriated beyond control by such treachery and determined upon revenge, I called on the men near me to load their pieces as rapidly as possible and hand them up to me. Then I jumped to the top of the breastworks and killed the rebel nearest to me in such short order that the others became, for a moment, completely bewildered, and were unable to use their weapons. My comrades handed up their guns so rapidly that I was con-

Left: **Second Lieutenant August J. Robbins, Company B. Awarded the Medal of Honor for heroism May 12, 1864. USAMHI.** ***Right:*** **Private Wallace W. Noyes, Company F, awarded the Medal of Honor for heroism May 12, 1864. University of Vermont.**

> stantly kept busy. The enemy did not seem to regain their wits until I had fired five or six shots. They then began shooting at me, but for some reason they proved to be poor marksmen, and I continued to fire at them until a bullet knocked my hat off, when I jumped back to my former position. John Grant, one of my comrades, then mounted the embankment and fired a shot, but was immediately killed by a Confederate bullet which pierced his heart. Upon counting afterward we found that fifteen guns had been emptied during this brief and peculiar assault.[56]

Other than having his hat shot off, Noyes did not get a scratch during the entire affair. For his courageous act, Noyes was awarded the Medal of Honor.[57]

Sgt. Charles Morey related to his sister a close call he had just after Co. C got into position against the rebel parapet:

> soon after we arrived on the ground we were firing and just after I had discharged my piece at a Johnnies head I turned to reload and while in the act of charging cartridge I saw a Reb who had got sight of me across his musket, and I can assure you my legs grew very short in a very short space of time or else there was a joint in them, that is to say I dropped down out of his sight just in time to hear his bullet whistle over my head. Then knowing the danger had passed I straightened up and finished loading.[58]

Thirty-six-year-old Pvt. Francis A. Bush, a farmer from Castleton in Co. B, was not as lucky as Morey. He did not see the rebel who was taking aim at him and was shot in the head. The bullet struck his head with a terrific glancing blow that crushed his skull, leaving a deep indentation. He was discharged with a disability for insanity June 29, 1864.[59]

Another rebel stuck his musket through a chink in the logs and fired blindly into the mass of blue on the other side. The ball hit Pvt. Charles S. Wheeler of Co. I on the inside of his left thigh near his knee. Wheeler was the man who had shot off his own toe and mortally wounded Lewis Goodell the previous fall. He survived the wound and was evacuated to a general hospital. As the wound started to heal, Wheeler feared he would be sent back to the regiment and deserted from the hospital on September 23, 1864. Several years later he married. Over the years, Wheeler became a mean drunk and often abused his wife. He finally left her in 1907. In the 1890s, he fraudulently applied for and received a disability pension, claiming he had been honorably discharged from the First Vermont Infantry. After his death, the Pension Bureau discovered the deception and cancelled the pension that his wife was then collecting as his widow, leaving her destitute. Even in death, Wheeler was an evil man.[60]

Another Co. I man was wounded near where Wheeler was downed. Pvt. Darius D. Priest, a 37-year-old five foot nine-and-one-half inch mechanic from Mt. Holly, was hit by a rebel minié ball in the left arm. He was fortunate enough to make his way out of the hell in the trenches and make it back to the division hospital. He wrote several days later from a general hospital in Washington:

> I left Allen, Will and Stephen at Fredericksburg. I can't tell when they will get away from thare. I shall never do any more soldiering in my term of service. Fifty one of our company have been shot since the fifth of May so there is but ten left in the company now.... But I don't think we owe the Rebs anything for I think that we have killed a thousand of them. I have shot eight of the devils and killed one with my bayonet. Some of our boys have knocked out their brains with the buts of their guns. I believe we have lost all human feelings whatever, for to step on a dead man or to kneel in pools of blood and lean over the dead bodyes of our own men and [a] man will get used to it after a while. It is hard yet honest in our cause.

By May 22, Priest was in the McClellan General Hospital in Philadelphia and wrote his wife:

> This is to let you know that I am still in the land of the living.... My arm is doing well, the damned thing stinks so that I can't sleep nights, that is the worst thing now.... Tell the folks that I am not agoing to die this time no fear of that. The lead isn't out yet but that isn't going to kill me.

Darius Priest did survive his wound and was discharged June 29, 1864, the same day as his younger brother Ethan Allen Priest, who had been wounded on May 10 during the first assault on the angle.[61]

As the battle at close quarters went on, the dead and wounded on both sides were trampled under the writhing mass of soldiers, mashing them into the mud. The fallen men's flesh was torn from their bones and then the bones shattered under the heels of their comrade's boots. The rainwater collecting in the trenches was turned red with blood.[62]

Attesting to the intensity of the combat, Confederate Brig. Gen. Samuel McGowan stated later:

> Our men lay on one side of the breastwork, the enemy on the other; and in many instances men were pulled over. The trenches on the right, in the angle, ran with blood, and had to be cleared of the dead more than once. An oak tree, twenty-two inches in diameter, in the rear of the brigade, was cut down by the constant scaling of musket balls, and fell about twelve o'clock Thursday night, injuring several men in the First South Carolina regiment.[63]

Finally, with its ammunition nearly exhausted, the Vermont Brigade was relieved from the front line at dark. Feeling their way in the darkness through dense woods, the tired Vermonters were finally permitted to halt and rest for the night. In spite of the heavy rain, the fight at the angle continued with great fury until after dark. The firing started to die down during the night, but did not completely cease until 3 A.M. the next morning. During the night, the Confederate troops completed a new defensive line across the base of the Muleshoe, and Ewell's men pulled back. The fight for the salient was finally over. Although the site of the battle of May 12 would forever be called the "Bloody Angle," Pvt. Wilbur Fisk said the Vermonters referred to it as "the slaughter pen."[64]

In all, the Army of the Potomac lost 9,000 men killed, wounded, and missing. The Vermont Brigade losses totaled 42 men killed, 186 wounded and 26 missing. The 2nd Vermont again topped the brigade in casualties with 19 killed, 76 wounded and six missing. The Confederate loss is not fully known but is estimated to have been around 8,000. U. S. Grant's cumulative loss, since starting his Overland Campaign, was now around 33,000, or 28 percent of his combat force.[65]

The next day the Vermont Brigade moved back to the Federal left and was idle for several days. With the rebels now at the base of the salient, the Vermonters had an opportunity to explore the ground over which they had fought. What they saw was more horrible than the aftermath of any battle in which they had participated. Pvt. John Kelly of Co. B noted in his diary, "went on the field at 8 A.M. the mud is very deep the dead are still unburied." Pvt. Wilbur Fisk's description of what he saw was a bit more graphic: "Their pit was full of dead men. It was a horrid sight on either side of the breastwork. The dead men lay in piles. On our side they were half covered with mud and one could hardly think that they ever were human beings." Later he added, "I have sometimes hoped, that if I must die while I am a soldier, I should prefer to die on the battle-field, but after looking at such a scene, one cannot help turning away and saying, any death but that."[66]

Brig. Gen. Grant stated:

> The sight the next day was repulsive and sickening, indeed. Behind their traverses, and in the pits and holes they had dug for protection, the rebel dead were found piled upon each other.

> Some of the wounded were almost entirely buried by the dead bodies of their companions that had fallen upon them. Many of the dead men were horribly mangled, and the logs, trees, and brush exhibited unmistakable signs of a fearful conflict.[67]

Pvt. Jerome Cutler, in Co. H, lamenting the loss of his comrades wrote, "God speed the time when this awful war shall cease!"[68]

"We have still much fighting in store for us," penned Lt. Col. Samuel Pingree. "If I survive I shall consider myself a man of singular luck."[69]

Lt. Chester Leach best summed up the situation in the 2nd Vermont the day after the battle of Spotsylvania when he wrote, "It is impossible to tell how long the fighting will last, but if we keep at it much longer as we have, there will be nobody left to fight." Leach's company had gone into the Wilderness with 63 men; after Spotsylvania it had but 19. Company E was down to 16 men. The other companies of the 2nd Vermont were in equally bad shape.[70]

At 2:30 A.M. on Saturday, May 14, the Sixth Corps moved two miles to the south and was posted on the left of the corps near the Anderson House on the Ny River.[71]

The big event of Sunday, May 15, was the arrival of the 11th Vermont Infantry Regiment commanded by Col. James M. Warner. The 11th Vermont had been mustered in the summer of 1862, but after coming south, it was ordered to man the large guns in Forts Slocum, Stevens, and Totten on the outskirts of Washington and was redesignated as the First Artillery, 11th Vermont Volunteers. After the Battle of the Wilderness, Lt. Gen. Grant ordered all available troops to reinforce the Army of the Potomac, and the 11th Vermont traded in its cannons for rifles and again became an infantry outfit. On this day, it was larger than the entire Vermont Brigade, numbering 1,500 officers and men. It would be a permanent part of the brigade through the rest of the war. The brigade received on the same day 150 badly needed recruits.[72]

On May 16, Lt. Gen. U. S. Grant decided to try Lee's left one more time. The assault was to be launched on May 18 by the Second and Sixth Corps. During the night of May 17, both corps moved back to the vicinity of the Bloody Angle. Starting after dark, the troops marched all night through the mud, brush, and swamps, reaching their jump-off positions just before daybreak.[73]

With the Second Corps on the left and the Sixth on the right, the Yankees moved out at 4 A.M. toward the base of the salient. The Vermont Brigade was in two lines of battle, the old regiments in front and the 11thVermont in the rear. The troops of the Second Corps, being nearest to the point of attack, reached it first. They found that the rebels were still entrenched in force and protected by formidable fortifications fronted by a double line of abatis. Confederate artillery and rifle fire swept the ground in front. The troops reached the abatis, but they could get no farther and fell back.[74]

The Vermont regiments moved through the woods, with hostile shells crashing and cracking through the branches over their heads, and then out into open ground where the Vermont Brigade was halted to dress its lines for the charge. Starting with three brigades in front of it, the Vermont Brigade soon overtook the front line and was kindly permitted to take the lead. Here it awaited the order to advance. The enemy's batteries to the right got the Vermonters' range and started dropping rounds on them. L. A. Grant ordered his men flat on the ground as quickly as possible to get what little protection they could. In addition to the artillery fire, rebel sharpshooters in the treetops fired at anything that moved. The expected charge, however, was not ordered. In view of the strength of the enemy and their elaborate fortifications, Gen. Meade called off the attack, and about noon the troops of both corps were withdrawn. The Vermont Brigade marched back to its former position south of the Ny River on the extreme left of the army on the Anderson farm. The Vermont Brigade lost 37 men in the failed assault, almost all of whom were in the 2nd, 3rd, and 11th Vermont regiments.[75]

The majority of the 2nd Vermont's casualties came from one artillery round that landed in the midst of Co. G, killing two men outright and wounding seven others. The two men killed were Pvts. Hadley P. Ford of Brandon and Joseph Kehoe of Charlotte. One of the wounded, Pvt. Henry Amblow of Burlington, lay on the field with a shattered ankle for eight days before he was found. During that time, he sustained himself with what little food he had in his haversack. By the time he was found by the enemy troops, gangrene had set in. Confederate surgeons tried to save him by amputating his leg, but he died on June 2, 1864. Another shell exploded in Co. C, literally tearing Pvt. Israel S. Scott to pieces. A fragment from the same shell hit 20-year-old Pvt. George Dow in the head. The wound was not too serious, and he was back with his company by the following September.[76]

After two days and nights near the Anderson farm, the Sixth Corps advanced about a mile to the left. Just at dark on May 21, the rebels hit the Vermont Brigade's picket line but could not penetrate it. Somehow in the confusion of the confrontation the rebels snatched Pvt. William Ryan of Co. H and Pvt. Myron Palmer of Co. G. Ryan would remain a prisoner of war until paroled April 28, 1865. Palmer was sent to the infamous Andersonville Prison and survived until all the healthy prisoners were sent elsewhere in September 1864. He was sent to a prisoner of war camp in Savannah, Ga., where he died November 1, 1864, leaving a widow and two young daughters grieving for him in Hinesburg, Vt.[77]

After the skirmishing stopped, the Sixth Corps moved south. It halted on the night of May 22 near Guiney Station on the Richmond, Fredericksburg and Potomac Railroad. The next day, under a scorching sun, it was off again. Pvt. Wilbur Fisk remembered:

> The last part of the march ... was made very rapidly. Heavy firing was going on in our front, and we hurried along as fast as possible. We seldom march in the road, as that has to be given to the artillery, but across fields, brooks, ditches and fences, through woods that are almost impenetrable, and through mud holes that are very penetrable indeed, making a mile's marching with a heavy knapsack on one's back, and a pair of tired legs under his body, not the easiest thing in the world to accomplish.[78]

The Vermonters reached the North Anna River at Jericho Mills where the army was concentrating on May 23 and camped for the night. The Army of Northern Virginia, marching by the most direct route, had again blocked Grant's movement south. The Fifth Corps, which had preceded the Sixth Corps, had crossed the river and had been attacked by A. P. Hill's corps but had repulsed the Confederates.[79]

The Sixth Corps crossed the North Anna on the morning of May 24, but Lee had formed his army on the south side of the river and was so strongly fortified that Grant withdrew his army and resumed his flanking movement on the north side. He pushed his army on to Hanovertown on the Pamunkey River, 15 miles north of Richmond, stopping there on the night of May 26.[80]

The Vermont Brigade crossed the Pamunkey River about 9 A.M. Friday, May 27, three miles above Hanovertown. It then turned toward Hanover Court House. The next day it marched six miles south and took up a position along Totopotomoy Creek, where it guarded the right flank of the army.[81]

During the night of May 31, the Sixth Corps was ordered forward to occupy Cold Harbor near where Grant had decided to force the passage of the Chickahominy River. Cold Harbor was a key area where five roads converged leading to the Chickahominy River crossings and then to Richmond and also to White House Landing, the Army of the Potomac's new supply base. Maj. Gen. Philip H. Sheridan's cavalry had occupied Cold Harbor during the day of May 31, and after a sharp fight was holding it against heavy pressure from the rebels. At noon on Wednesday, June 1, the Sixth Corps arrived to relieve Sheridan's beleaguered force. The day was extremely hot and humid, and the dust on the road was ankle deep. The march had been exhausting and the men were glad to halt, even if it was to fight.[82]

No sooner had the Sixth Corps been dispatched on its hasty march than Gen. Lee dispatched Anderson's corps to occupy Cold Harbor and protect the Chickahominy crossings. Anderson was not able to do the first but accomplished the latter, taking a position between the Chickahominy and Cold Harbor. Here the Southern infantry dug in and awaited Grant's next move.[83]

The Vermont Brigade, marching in the lead of the Sixth Corps, moved down the road leading from Old Cold Harbor to New Cold Harbor and formed into line of battle on the south side of the road. It was on the extreme left of the army. Open ground in front extended to the enemy's intrenchments which ran along the edge of some woods, about half a mile away. The ground between the Federal and Confederate lines was mainly open fields. Gen. Wright had been ordered to attack upon arrival, but as usual, delays precluded the action.[84]

By 2 P.M., the Sixth Corps was at Cold Harbor and was being reinforced by the Eighteenth Corps commanded by the Sixth Corps's former commander, Maj. Gen. William F. Smith. The Vermonter's old brigade commander, Maj. Gen. W. H. T. Brooks, commanded one of Smith's divisions. Smith's command was from Maj. Gen. Benjamin F. Butler's Army of the James, which had been bottled up since early May on a small peninsula, Bermuda Hundred, north of Petersburg.[85]

The Vermont Brigade was placed in the front line of the Second Division with the 3rd Vermont thrown forward as skirmishers. At about 5 P.M., 50 Union guns opened up on the Confederates. As the advance was about to be made, a rebel battery fired on the Second Division, with a stiff fire from the Confederate skirmishers. One of the rebel shells burst directly over the 2nd Vermont. Pvt. Thomas L. Casavaint, a Moretown resident in Co. H, told what happened next:

> As we were preparing to make a charge the enemy opened on us with several pieces of artillery and one shell burst over our heads wounding a number of our men among them was Harrison A. Morgan my tentmate. I saw him fall and thought he was killed. I went to him found he was alive. He got up and with both hands on his head and was moaning bitterly. I tried to have him go to the hospital but he would not go.

Morgan was not hit by the shell's shrapnel but had his left eardrum ruptured by the explosion. He would soon lose most of the hearing in his right ear also. Within days his hearing was so bad that he said, "to tell the direction of a musket shot or any other sound of like magnitude even at short distance and while in the Military service I depended

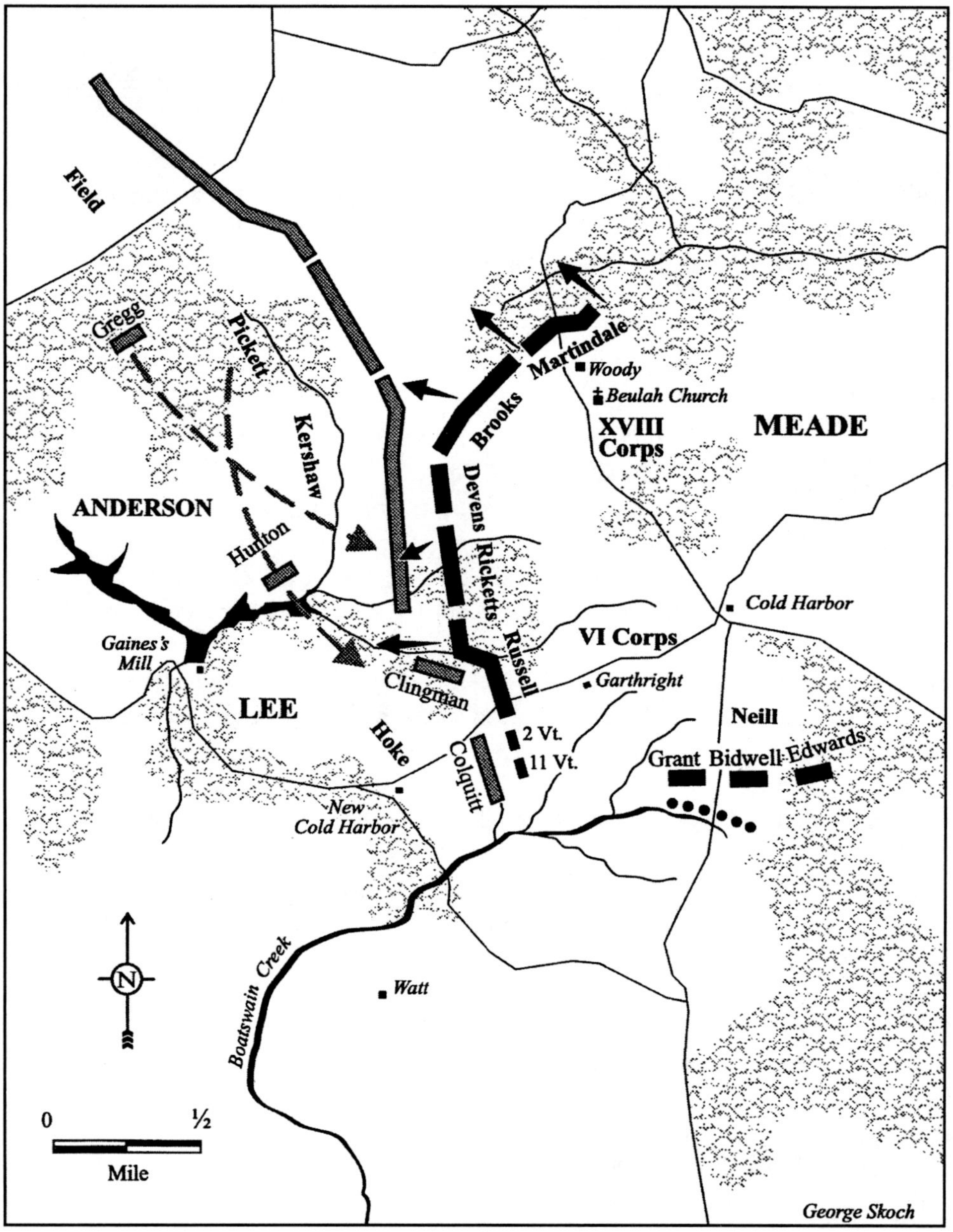

Cold Harbor, June 1, 1864

on a comrade." Later when explaining why he had not gone to the hospital, Morgan stated, "I had a dread of a government hospital and had no desire to become an inmate of one."[86]

Gen. Neill, commanding the division, ordered L. A. Grant to refuse the left of his line. Grant accordingly fronted the 4th and 6th Vermont regiments and a battalion of the 11th Vermont to the left while the 5th was detached to support a nearby battery. Due to this arrangement, these regiments did not participate in the main assault. The 2nd Vermont and the rest of the 11th Vermont went forward with Russell's division which made a simultaneous charge with Ricketts's division.[87]

Pvt. Fisk recorded the 2nd Vermont's participation in the charge:

> Our regiment was formed into the front line, skirmishers were ahead firing continually. Our batteries got into position and soon we had a furious fight with artillery. By and by the order came to advance. A charge was begun on the right. We moved slowly to the crest of the hill, then double quick. Our regiment went altogether too fast. The ground was rough and we became more broken than we needed to. The rebs poured a terrible fire into us of grape and canister besides a line of rifle pits filled with infantry that rained their bullets among us in a perfect shower.[88]

A portion of the area the 2nd Vermont had to traverse during the assault was through a peach orchard which the rebels were riddling with canister fire. Just as Co. E was in the middle of the peach orchard, one of the peach trees was cut down by the heavy cannon fire and fell on Pvt. Wallace "Wall" E. Williams. At the company's reunion in 1887, the men were still laughing at the sight Williams made fussing and struggling to get out from under the downed tree.[89]

About the same time Williams was downed by the peach tree, Pvt. Leander E. Shippee, of Co. A and Wilmington, Vt., was hit by a piece of shell which took off most of his left heel. He never returned from the hospital and was discharged from the army May 13, 1865.[90]

The enemy soldiers were well dug in and their lines were covered and concealed by woods while the Federal troops had to move over open ground. Being worn out from the day's march in the blistering heat, the Federal troops started at a moderate pace and quickly ran into horrific artillery and small arms fire. In 20 minutes' time nearly a quarter of the assaulting force was down, but on it charged.[91]

At the center, Gen. Ricketts's division struck the enemy's main line, taking 600 prisoners. The brigade on the right of the Vermont regiments did not reach the works at all, halting about 300 yards from them.[92]

Fisk continued his narrative: "Our flank gave away and we had to retreat back over the crest of the hill to a place near where we started from, when we rallied and advanced once more. Both in making the charge and retreating we were under severe fire for about 300 yards or more."[93]

It was here that 21-year-old Pvt. Henry C. Page, a farmer from Cambridge in Co. G, was hit for the second time in just shy of a month's time. He had been slightly wounded in the right leg on May 5, but was able to stay with his unit. This time his wound was not so light. A rebel minié ball struck and lodged in his right knee. He was discharged for disability 28 days later.[94]

During the assault, Pvt. Nahum C. Baker of Co. E from Royalton was captured. He was taken to Libby Prison in Richmond, but within two weeks he was shipped to Andersonville. He was sent from Andersonville on September 22, 1864 to a prisoner of war camp at Millen, Ga. On December 10 he escaped from Millen. The guards turned bloodhounds lose on him, but he killed several of them and eluded the others. Eight days later, pretending to be a Confederate soldier, he reported to the Confederate Provost Marshall at Macon, Ga., and was admitted to a hospital in Augusta, where he remained for a month. He was discharged in January 1865 and was sent by train to his fictitious Confederate unit, the 38th Tennessee Infantry Regiment, which was stationed in Tupelo, Miss. When the train neared Vernon, Ga., Baker jumped off and took to the woods. Later he was picked up by a Confederate patrol near Holly Springs, Miss., but escaped during the night and made his way to the Federal lines in Memphis Tenn., where he reported to the Provost Marshall. He was mustered out of the service March, 15, 1865.[95]

The battalion from the 11th Vermont pressed on to within 100 yards of the enemy's breastwork, when, discovering that it was advancing alone without support on either flank, it halted and withdrew a short distance. Here the men of the 2nd and 11th Vermont threw themselves flat on the ground and started digging shallow trenches with their bayonets, tin plates, cups, or anything else they had, and held their ground until nightfall.[96]

As dusk came on, stretcher-bearers could be seen through the smoke busily bringing the wounded in from the two-mile wide battlefield. The enemy continued its efforts to regain the captured works until nearly 9 P.M. During the night, Wright and Smith entrenched the positions they had gained. In this assault, Grant had consolidated the position he wanted at Old Cold Harbor, captured 750 prisoners, and bowed in the Confederate line, but had lost 2,800 men in the process. In the Vermont Brigade, the 2nd Vermont had nine men wounded.[97]

The next day, Thursday, June 2, was occupied by the high command making plans for another assault. Meanwhile, near 10 A.M., the Second Division of the Sixth Corps was pulled out and replaced by a division of the Second Corps.[98]

Pvt. Fisk wrote of the 2nd Vermont's precarious position in his diary:

> This was a rather a ticklish place for a timid person to be in. Bullets were flying continually. A man must keep his head down or he would be sure to get it hit. Only that bank of dirt was between us and death. Our rifles made the rebels' predicament but little better. When the Second Corps came to relieve they came along with their heads up as if nothing was the matter. But when the bullets began to "Zip" "Zip" amongst them pretty lively they curled down and got up to the works in their respective places as quickly as was possible. Several were hit as they were relieving us. We filed carefully out so that a building would cover us and none of our men were hit.[99]

The Second Division was placed on the far right of the Sixth Corps. Brig. Gen. Lewis Grant wrote:

> This position was a very unpleasant one. A part of the enemy's works had been carried at this point, and was now held by us under a very destructive front and flank fire. We occupied but a very short front and most of the troops were considerably to the rear, but every part of the ground for a great distance to the rear was exposed to the enemy's fire and the command found safety only by throwing up defenses.[100]

Gens. Grant and Meade had intended to make an assault at 4 P.M., but various delays and a severe thunder storm caused Grant to postpone the attack to the next day.[101]

Friday, June 3, the Federal soldiers were up before daylight. The sound of musket fire on the skirmish line announced the beginning of the new assault. The Second, Sixth and Eighteenth Corps rushed forward toward the enemy's breastworks while a storm of lead and iron pelted them. As they came closer to the Confederate works, they were caught in a crossfire of artillery and rifle fire and were cut to pieces.[102]

Hancock's corps alone lost a thousand men in 15 minutes, and though it forced its way into the enemy's works at two points, taking three guns and several hundred prisoners, it could not hold its position and was forced back a little where it dug in.[103]

In the Sixth Corps, the Second Division was formed for the attack in three lines, the Vermont Brigade forming the second line. The front line, composed of two regiments of Wheaton's brigade, drove the enemy's skirmishers from a line of rifle pits and advanced to the edge of a piece of woods, about 200 yards from the enemy's main line.

Again Pvt. Wilbur Fisk records the action:

> Shot and shell and bullets were flying as in a regular engagement. The Sixth Regiment was ahead of us. As fast as they

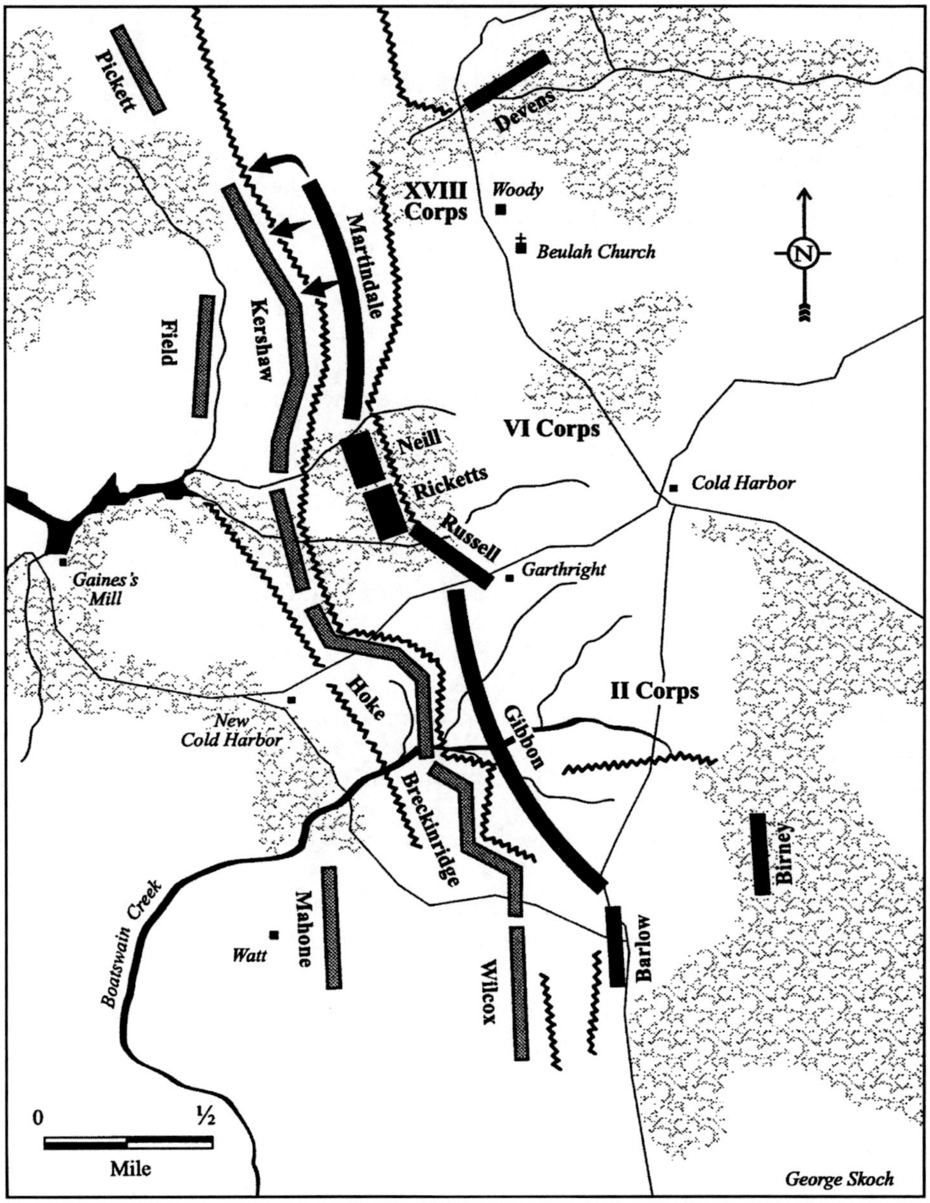

Cold Harbor, June 3, 1864

> advanced we were to follow. They were in the work just ahead of us. Pretty soon we saw them leap over their breastwork and advance to the next one. We advanced and took the one they left. Their Lieut. Bailey [Hiram Bailey in Co. B from Brandon] was killed. A piece of shell hit him in his forehead. He lived till nearly night when he was buried. The Sixth Regiment advanced to another line and we followed them as before. Everything indicated that a regular engagement was going to take place.[104]

None of the Federal units on either side were making much headway, so Wheaton halted his brigade. The Vermont Brigade moved up behind Wheaton and at Wheaton's request relieved his unit. Lewis Grant plugged the hole with the 3rd and 5th Vermont regiments.[105]

The other divisions on the Vermont Brigade's left had made a slight gain, coming within 40 yards of the enemy's works in some places, but no further advance was ordered. The assault by the Sixth Corps lasted no longer than 10 minutes. With all the death and destruction incurred, no advantage was gained at any point, and in one half hour U. S. Grant had lost 7,000 men. The loss in the Vermont Brigade was 104 men. The 2nd Vermont lost only two men killed and one wounded.[106]

Preparations were made by the corps commanders to renew the attack at noon. The Vermont Brigade, now in the front line, was to lead the Second Division. The chance of success looked slim to everyone. The men were maintaining their position in the open timber by hugging the ground. The skirmishers of the 3rd and 5th Vermont regiments in the edge of the woods were sharply engaged and losing a good many men. With a stern resolve, the men awaited the order, but it never came.[107]

Fisk remembered:

> Lt. Colonel Pingree came around and told the company commanders to instruct the men to keep closed up and maintain as straight a line as possible in going through the woods. We were going to make another charge as soon as the 18 Corps advanced on our right. Well we could make another charge and do it bravely but after so much hard fighting we did not feel that enthusiasm that we did at first. At least it was so with me. I dreaded the contest. If there had been an honorable way for me to get out of it I should have done so. But duty said go forward and trust in God and so I was determined to do. But the order to advance was not given. They discovered the enemy had too strong a position for us to carry. So we remained there all day. We were not in the front line but it was full as dangerous a place.[108]

Unlike in other battles, neither side withdrew but stayed where it was, anywhere from 40 to 200 yards apart. The fighting continued all day. There was a short but very sharp clash on the picket lines to left of the Sixth Corps at 8 P.M. in which the rebels made a short-lived charge but were repulsed.[109]

Lt. Gen. Grant now changed his strategy and decided

to hold the Army of Northern Virginia in place and concentrate on its supply lines. On June 3, he directed Sheridan to march his cavalry corps to Charlottesville, meet and join Maj. Gen. David Hunter there, and return to the Army of the Potomac, destroying the Virginia Central Railroad along the way. Grant would then be free to cross the James River, attack Petersburg, and let Richmond starve. By June 7 Sheridan was on his way. In carrying out Grant's instructions, the Federal troops at Cold Harbor would spend the next 10 days digging at night and sniping at the rebels during the day.[110]

During this time, the weather was extremely hot and humid and would stay that way for 47 days, and the dead bodies lying between the lines started to putrefy. The wounded from the June 3 assault continued to remain between the lines until a short truce was agreed upon by Grant and Lee on June 7. Brig. Gen. Grant wrote in his battle report:

> During all this time we were under fire; musketry, artillery, and mortar practice was the order of each day. There was no cessation of hostilities except a few hours one day under a flag of truce. In the night time we advanced and strengthened our lines, and during the day no man could move about with safety. The front line was constantly engaged and the enemy's guns commanded nearly every rod of ground for one-half mile to the rear. The regiments occupied the front line by turns, a change being made every night.[111]

Lt. Chester Leach wrote :

> For the last three days we have been where one could not stand on his feet unless he had a wish of getting a bullet through him.... The Reb's works, in front of ours, are about 80 or so rods distant, across an open field. So, you can see, it would not be very safe for a man to show himself a great while at a time. A few get hit occasionally by getting above the works, or by a ball glancing & falling close by the pits. Co. A lost two yesterday.[112]

One of the two men referred to by Leach was Pvt. Hiland A. Fuller from Brattleboro. While on picket duty in one of the advanced positions, Fuller was shot by a sniper, but because of the intensity of the sniper fire his comrades could not reach him and had to watch as he bled to death.[113]

While digging in the trenches one night Wilbur Fisk observed:

> Some of the operations here are quite amusing. A few minutes ago there was a lull in the firing, and the boys halloed, "Wake up there Johnnies! It is getting dull here." A half dozen shots was the reply. The other night after it was safely dark, the rebels were as "bold as sheep." They jumped upon their breastworks, and invited the "Yankee sons of b______" to come on. They said it would take a long time for us to *dig* into Richmond. Our boys replied that we should dig them into hell and *walk* into Richmond.[114]

Pvt. Jerome Cutler, who was again cooking for Co. H, wrote his wife to be on Tuesday, June 7:

> I have had to be up a good deal of the time night and day cooking and carrying rations to the company. who have been lying most of the time in the rifle pits within forty rods of the enemy line. I have had to go out most of the time to avoid their sharpshooters, and I don't get much peace in the rear whare I am cooking for their shells ar flying over more or less of the time.
>
> yesterday a ten lb. shell tore off a cornor of my tent and sent one of my camp kettles skiting. although this is serious business it is laughable sometimes to see the freak shots will cup up, another shell struck right beside Burnside's headquarters tent.[115]

The same day the 1st Sgt. of Co. G, Morey L. Aldrich from Burlington, wrote:

> We crossed the Rapidan with 64 men, armed and equipped. I report this morning *ten*. Several of those slightly wounded have been returned to duty, while two or three have been wounded the second time. The end is not yet. Fighting still continues; and while I am trying to pen you a few lines the shells are bursting around my head altogether too near to be agreeable.[116]

For over 30 days, the Vermonters had been fighting and marching in Virginia's heat, mud, and dust, and were now filthy, smelly, and ragged. Lt. Leach wrote on June 8:

> I had to borrow a shirt & drawers to wear while I got mine washed.... I never saw the men much more ragged than they are now, but some clothing is expected in a day or two. I am about as ragged as the men, but will have a pair of pants when the clothing comes. I wear yet my light blue ones that I had when at home, & my old dress coat, & they are both about played out with rags & dirty.[117]

New clothing was issued on the same day that Leach wrote home. Sgt. Morey penned, "Just before dark we drew new clothing and as soon as that was issued we went out to the front and relieved the 6th Regt."[118]

Leach wrote on Saturday, June 11:

> I wrote you a line on the 6th , & that night our Regt. was sent to the front, & occupied the second line of rifle pits, & at night on the 9th, went into the front line, & remain there yet, making three days that we have had to lay in the dust & dirt to keep our heads free from Rebel bullets. The first three nights, the Rebels fired a shell about every half hour during the night. A piece of one killing Joseph C. Felton of our Co.

from Fairfax, & and wounding Henry Shonian, a Frenchman, (substitute). Felton had been back from home but two days, having been home on a reenlistment furlough.[119]

While en route to the regiment from leave, Felton wrote in his last letter to his wife, May 31:

> The farther I get from home Mary the nearer you seem to My heart & my thoughts linger fondly on my pleasant visit with you & my Dear children & other friends. May God be with you & protect you from all harm. I havent herd from you since you since I left home but shall continue to write until I do. I expect I am writing the last that I can at present as its said that writing is not allowed from the army for a while yet. We get encouraging news. Lee is said to be in Richmond Just where Grant wants him. we hope its true. [May our] trust be in God who alon is [able to] subdue our Enemies under us ... tell Emily [Felton's eldest daughter] I have just been looking at her little presents. Often think of her takeing care of Dear Sweet little Clarry & Charley [his other two children]. Dear Mary don't work to hard. I feel very anxious about your health. Do be careful of it ... we expect to move soon. May God be with you & Comfort you.[120]

Attesting to Felton's character Wilbur Fisk wrote:

> It is a pleasure to bear testimony to his sterling integrity and Christian character. I believe he would rather have died than to have done a wrong act or neglected a single duty. I first became acquainted with him at the Convalescent Camp, where we were both detailed a short time for guard, and I remember his anxiety to get back to his regiment as soon as he thought he was well enough to do duty there. Some of the boys told him to stay where he was as long as he could; it was easier than doing duty in the field. But Mr. Felton was no shirk. He thought it his duty to go to his regiment as soon as he was able, and no argument would avail anything against his convictions of duty.[121]

It appeared to the Vermonters as though this siege at Cold Harbor would continue until they were all picked off as Pvt. Charles H. Reed of Co. E, 3rd Vermont wrote in a letter home:

> Our captin and lutinent was wounded and they detald a nother lutenent to command our compney and the 3 of June day before yesterday he was hit so he dided yestday so all the oficers we have gote now is two coprels 12 privtes in Co. E. 14 in all that is with the Co. The[re] is about 140 men in the regiment. 14 men in Co. E for duty. thank god that I am one. one or two days more will fix the rest of us.[122]

Seeing no hope of success in the siege at Cold Harbor, Lt. Gen. U. S. Grant issued the order for the movement of his army to the James River on June 11. The Sixth Corps was to withdraw as soon as possible on the evening of June 12 to a line in its rear, extending from Allen's pond to Elder's Swamp. In conjunction with the Second Corps they were to hold that line until the Fifth Corps cleared roads and then they were to move out.[123]

The Sixth Corps was to move by way of Emman's Church, crossing the Chickahominy River at Jones's Bridge (present day Providence Forge) and proceeding on to Charles City Court House.[124]

Brig. Gen. Lewis Grant started collecting his regiments together during the evening of June 11. On the bright moonlit night of June 12, the Vermont Brigade silently moved out with the rest of the Sixth Corps for the James River. The march picked up speed around midnight, and the next morning there was an hour's halt for breakfast near Dispatch Station. Then, fighting the choking dust and the oppressive heat, the column moved on steadily all day, passing Olivet Church by mid-afternoon and crossing the Chickahominy River at Jones's Bridge near sundown. After crossing the river, the Sixth Corps moved on approximately four miles before halting for the night. "Monday crossed the Chickahominy at James [Jones] Ford, having marched nearly all the time for 24 hours," remembered Chester Leach, "& if ever I was about played out, it was then."[125]

The Green Mountain Boys were on the march again at 4 A.M. the next morning. "We marched toward Charles City Court House on the James River," wrote Wilbur Fisk. "We marched only about half a dozen miles that morning when we went into camp for the remainder of the day." On the morning of June 15, the Sixth Corps moved a mile closer to the river near Wilcox's Landing, where it lay for two days guarding the bridgehead while the rest of the army passed by.[126]

In the evening of June 16, the First and Third divisions of the Sixth Corps were ferried across the James River in steamboats. The Vermont Brigade and the rest of the Second Division crossed the river on a 2,100-foot pontoon bridge. The bridge's planks were laid over 101 pontoon boats. The structure was quite sophisticated, and the engineers had constructed a draw in mid-stream to allow passage of other vessels. Under the tramp of the soldiers' boots the bridge swayed and tossed with the river's tide, but the contraption held fast until the army had crossed.[127]

The same night Grant started his army moving to the James, Lee discovered that Sheridan had left to join Hunter, and ordered Early's corps to the Valley after them. Lee instructed Early to join Maj. Gen. John C. Breckinridge and defeat Hunter, then move on up the Valley and threaten Washington. Lee hoped this move might take some of the pressure off the Army of Northern Virginia. As Early started his corps toward the Shenandoah Valley, Sheridan discovered that Hunter had disregarded Grant's orders and was heading for Lexington instead of Charlottesville. Sheridan, cornered by Confederates, had no choice but to retreat to White House Landing.[128]

On June 15, Gen. Smith was hurried forward with his Eighteenth Corps from Bermuda Hundred to Petersburg. The Eighteenth Corps, which had taken steamers from White House Landing, had debarked at Bermuda Hundred the night before. Smith reached the defenses of the city before noon; but still smarting from the defeat he had suffered against the strongly defended position at Cold Harbor, he was reluctant to attack the fortifications in front of Petersburg until he could complete a thorough reconnaissance, which took most of the afternoon. It was not until 7 P.M., after being reinforced by Hancock's Second Corps, that he attacked. The attack was successful, and before dark he carried a mile and a half of the outer intrenchments, including seven redoubts, and captured 300 prisoners and 16 guns. Then Smith's initiative fizzled out, and he did not follow up his success and force his way into Petersburg. This would be the biggest mistake of his military career.[129]

At the time Smith assaulted the works in front of Petersburg, Gen. P. G. T. Beauregard manned the defenses of Petersburg with fewer than 3,000 men, most of whom were merely remnants of units, and civilians. As thin as the manning was, Beauregard held off Smith's corps, and by 9 P.M., troops from Lee's army began to arrive. Now both Grant and Lee hurried forward all available troops.[130]

On June 16, the Second Corps, with two brigades of Brooks's division, carried three more redoubts. At daylight, June 17, Gen. Potter's division of the Ninth Corps carried about a mile of works on a ridge, east of the city, taking four guns and 600 prisoners.[131]

After crossing the James River on June 16, the Second Division marched all night toward Petersburg, where it caught up with the other two divisions of the Sixth Corps. Upon reaching the Federal lines the next day, the Second Division was posted in some captured works on the right of the line near Redoubt No. 4.[132]

Brig. Gen. Grant immediately sent the 2nd and part of the 5th Vermont forward as pickets while the rest of the Vermont troops lay on their arms for the rest of night. During the night Beauregard withdrew his forces from a large portion of his front line back to a shorter but much stronger position. The next afternoon, June 18, Gen. Meade ordered a general assault by all the corps of the army. While some ground was gained in this effort, the biggest gain was the knowledge that the Petersburg defenses were now strongly manned by the Army of Northern Virginia. During the first four days at Petersburg, Grant lost over 7,000 men killed and wounded, most of whom were lost on June 18. For one of the few times in weeks the Vermonters were not ordered to take part in the slaughter and had the rare opportunity of watching others do the fighting.[133]

In the assault of June 18 the black soldiers of the United States Colored Troops were used and made a good showing of themselves. By now, many of the men in the 2nd Vermont had overcome their prejudice against Negroes, as Sgt. Charles Morey illustrated in one of his letters: "The negro troops were engaged yesterday and did splendid service. They are just as good soldiers as we have in the field. They are well disciplined and make a good appearance and command the respect of the white soldiers."[134]

Wilbur Fisk included a mention of the injustice to Negro troops in one of his letters to the *Green Mountain Freeman*:

> Burnside's negroes claim a large share of credit in taking these works. They made a splendid charge, capturing the whole line of works, thirteen guns, and some prisoners. The negroes were remarkably well pleased with their prowess on this occasion. It was a glorious day for them. They won great favor in the eyes of white soldiers by their courage and bravery. I am sure I never looked upon negroes with more respect than I did upon those soldiers, and I did not hear a word of disrespect towards them from any of the boys. Yesterday they made another charge here, and it was done in excellent style. The best military critic could hardly find fault with it. In a steady straight line they advanced right over the crest of the hill and right up to the enemy's works, under a terrible fire, but without wavering or faltering, compelling the enemy to leave his works in the hands of the blacks. The stream of wounded that came pouring back, some leaning on a comrade and some carried on stretchers, told of the bloody work they had done.... Notwithstanding the negroes fight so well and show so much bravery, they have hitherto been allowed but the bare pittance of seven dollars a month.... And Congress has wrangled over that question all winter trying to settle it. It seems strange that a question where justice and injustice, right and wrong, are so plainly apparent, should require any wrangling or debate at all. They seem to think that it is degrading to the white soldiers to pay the blacks equally as well. Do they think we are afraid of fair competition with blacks? If negroes can fight as well as we, can we not have magnanimity enough to acknowledge it. Certainly to propose especial legislation to keep our status ahead of the blacks is acknowledging them our superiors and in a most humiliating way. Whether it suits our tastes or not, it is doubtless true that the golden rule applies to colored as well as to white people, and Congress as well as everybody else will do well to bear this in mind and act accordingly.[135]

On June 19, the men in the 2nd Vermont that had not reenlisted were pulled off the line to be mustered out the next day and return to Vermont, their three-year obligation now over. Of the 199 men who were to be mustered out, only about 50 were in the ranks shouldering a musket. With their departure and with the men wounded and sick in the hospital, the 2nd Vermont would number only 165 men in the field. Initially, the remnants of the 10 companies were going to be consolidated into six, but the men did not want their companies broken up. It was then decided to organize the 10 companies into four divisions, each under the command of a sergeant acting as a lieutenant, since only two officers remained. Companies D, B, and H formed the First Division under the command of Sgt. Fayette Stone of Co. A (the brother of the late Col. Newton Stone); F, and E, the second, under Sgt. Charles C. Morey of Co. E; C, I, and G, the third under Sgt. Horatio F. Taylor of Co. I; and companies H and A, the fourth under Sgt. Ephriam W. Harrington of Co. G. Capt. Enoch E. Johnson of Co. D commanded the regiment. Pvt. Wilbur Fisk described Johnson as "Tall, good looking, good-natured, strict and impartial, he is just the man for us." He also said, "The boys call him a 'bully officer' and all like him. If he leads us into another engagement we will show him that there is some Green Mountain pluck left in the regiment yet."[136]

On the day the men returned to Vermont, Brig. Gen. Neill issued the following order thanking the Green Mountain Boys for their service:

> *Headquarters Second Division, Sixth Corps*
> June 20th, 1864
>
> General Order No. 36—It is not necessary that any regiment of the Vermont brigade should have their deeds recounted, or their praises sung in general orders. How many well fought and bloody fields bear witness to their bravery! Least of all do you, the soldiers of the 2nd Vermont, the veterans of the brigade, who have shed your blood on almost every field from the first Bull Run, need a panegyrist. Your deeds speak for themselves, and will keep your memory green, while courage, steadiness and devotion to duty are honored among men. But that you may know how your general and your comrades regret and mourn your departure, and to bid you farewell and Godspeed, this order is written. Again farewell, brave and noble men. For three years you have borne the brunt of battle, and now returning home with scarce a tithe of your original numbers, with just pride you can proclaim that you have done your duty. You have fulfilled your compact. History will record your services. Let this order express the feelings of those you leave behind.
>
> By order of Brig. General Neill
> Hazard Stevens, A. A. G.[137]

Watching the men leave for home caused Pvt. Fisk to lament:

> For the first time I regretted most bitterly having reenlisted. This terrible campaign with its ill proportioned results I confess has discouraged me considerably and the more I look at it the more I feel a misgiving about the final issue. Men that fight as these Southerners do are not to be easily beaten. God forbid that the war should last three years longer.[138]

The Vermont Brigade remained in the trenches on June 20, and as Sgt. Morey noted in his diary, "They shelled us vigorously but hit only one man in the regiment and one wounded in the P.M. by a rifle ball."[139]

The man that Morey referred to was Pvt. Benjamin P. Wheeler of Co. B. Wheeler, a 33-year-old farmer from Pawlet, was hit in the left thigh, but the bullet did not stop until it had passed through his left buttocks and then the right buttocks where it lodged. The minié ball was removed while Wheeler was in the hospital, and he returned to duty several months later. In applying for a pension years later, he filed an affidavit that was quite descriptive of the shape his company was in at the time he was wounded. He explained he had no officer or noncommissioned officer to corroborate his being wounded in the line of duty because:

> 1st the Col. was killed at the battle of the Wilderness. Leiut. Col. was wounded in same battle and died soon after. The Capt was wounded in the Wilderness and was relieved from duty and did not return. Lieutenant commanding company was killed at Cold Harbor. Orderly Sergeant was wounded at Battle of Wilderness and soon after discharged.

Wheeler got his pension is spite of not being able to produce eyewitness verification of his being wounded in the line of duty. He lived until July 4, 1918.[140]

Lorenzo A. Dodge, a private from Ludlow in Co. I, was also wounded. He was hit by a buckshot or pistol ball that went in his leg about an inch below his left knee. He was evacuated to a general hospital in Washington and returned to his company the following October.[141]

The Union assaults at Petersburg had thus far been directed against the lines on the east and southeast of the city. Realizing he was not going to make any headway by frontal assaults, Lt. Gen. Grant had his men dig in and began extending his lines to envelop Petersburg on the south. He also began a campaign to cut the railroads entering the city from the south and southwest, which were the main arteries of communication and supply between the Confederate capital and the rest of the southern states.[142]

On the evening of June 21, the Sixth Corps was relieved by the Eighteenth Corps after having taken another day of shelling by the rebels in which the 2nd Vermont had one man wounded. Moving out at midnight, the Sixth Corps marched all night, halting the next morning near the Williams House, just west of the Jerusalem Plank Road. Gen. Wright's orders were to move on the next day some two miles to the Weldon Railroad south of Petersburg. It was then to seize the railroad and dig in until the Second Corps arrived to fill in the hole between the Sixth Corps and the rest of the army. However, the Second Corps did not thoroughly fill the void, and the Confederates quickly took advantage of it. During the afternoon, Gen. A. P. Hill, who had been sent out by Gen. Lee to protect the railroad, breached the gap left between the two Union corps. Making a quick penetration, he got in behind the Second Corps and with little opposition captured 1,600 men before returning to the safety of his own lines.[143]

Resolutions were at once made to avenge the disaster to the Second Corps. At dusk, that corps was again thrown forward, and Gen. Wright also advanced, driving in a skirmish line of the enemy for a mile through thick brush, while the Vermont Brigade guarded the left flank of the corps. It was nearly midnight when the Sixth Corps halted, about a mile from the Weldon Railroad. In this movement, the picket line composed of the 3rd Vermont and a battalion of the Eleventh was strengthened by the Fourth regiment. The night passed quietly on that portion of the Sixth Corps's line, and in the morning no enemy was visible in its front.[144]

On June 23, the Vermonters were roused before daylight expecting to advance, but no movement took place. During the morning, Capt. Beattie of the 3rd Vermont was sent out with a detail of 90 men to reconnoiter. He reached the Weldon railroad unopposed and sent back word that he had found the road unguarded and had cut the telegraph line. A party of pioneers was then sent forward to tear up and destroy the track. To protect the pioneers, Brig. Gen. L. A. Grant sent out a guard force of 200 men from the 11th Vermont.[145]

Brig. Gen. Grant was then ordered by Brig. Gen. Wheaton, commanding the Second Division, to furnish another detail to support the skirmish line. Grant sent more troops from the 11th Vermont. This detachment was stationed by an officer of Gen. Wheaton's staff about half a mile or more in front of the brigade.[146]

In front of the line of the Vermont Brigade was a swell of ground that commanded the entire open area toward the railroad. Infantrymen supported by artillery could protect the entire area. The advantage of occupying this crest was obvious to Lewis Grant. After waiting for someone else to take the initiative to occupy it, he ordered the Vermont Brigade forward. He then asked the brigade commanders to his left and right to move forward and reconnect with his flanks. The one on the left did, but the one on his right refused and Grant was forced to move his Vermonters back to their original position. Frustrated, Grant went in person to Wheaton and asked him to advance the division line to occupy the crest, but his pleas fell on deaf ears. Receiving no satisfaction from Wheaton, Grant went up the chain of command to Maj. Gen. Wright. Wright rode with Grant to see the crest for himself, but by the time they arrived, heavy skirmishing was in progress in front. Rebels could be seen coming from the direction of the railroad, apparently aiming for the left and rear of the Vermont detachments on the skirmish line. Gen. Wright told Grant that it was now too late to advance the division line to the crest. When Grant expressed his concern for the safety of his skirmish line, Wright told him that if attacked the Vermont boys could fall back into the woods on their right behind Ricketts's picket line. Wright was under the impression that Ricketts's line had advanced nearly to the railroad; however, this was not the case. Beyond advancing the skirmishers of the 4th Vermont to cover the left flank of the men from the 11th Vermont, the deployed Vermonters were left to fend for themselves.[147]

The Green Mountain Boys near the railroad never stood a chance. Before they could react to the threat, they were surrounded. They put up a brief fight, but soon saw it was hopeless and surrendered. In one fell swoop the rebels nabbed 400 men from the 4th and 11th Vermont regiments.[148]

The rest of the Vermont Brigade could not leave its position to help and during the horrible episode was ordered to dig in where it was. Later that evening, the 2nd Vermont was sent forward to the main skirmish line and had a brush with the Confederates, losing one man wounded. Near midnight, the Vermont Brigade was withdrawn from the line and sent to its old position near the Williams House. In the action at Weldon Railroad, the Vermont Brigade lost 13 men killed, 45 wounded, and 401 captured. Of the men captured, 232 would die in Confederate prisoner of war camps. The only loss in the 2nd Vermont was the one man previously mentioned.[149]

Except for one short expedition, the Vermont Brigade remained in its works near the Williams House for two weeks. At noon on June 29, Gen. Meade learned that Gen. Wilson's cavalry command, which had been on a 10-day raid against the Richmond and Danville Railroad and the South Side Railroad, had been ambushed on its return at Reams's Station, 10 miles south of Petersburg. The Sixth Corps was sent to the station to open a corridor for Wilson's safe return into the Union lines. Leading the corps, the Vermont Brigade moved out at 2 P.M. Arriving within half a mile of the station at 6 P.M., the 3rd Vermont was deployed as skirmishers and engaged the rebel skirmish line, driving it from the field. Earlier in the morning, Wilson had been surrounded at that point by Gens. Fitzhugh Lee and Mahone's infantry and after a disastrous fight in which he suffered heavy loses had retreated south. The enemy, having driven off Wilson's small force, made no attempt to tangle with the Sixth Corps. The Vermont Brigade bivouacked at Reams's Station that night. The next day, according to Sgt. Morey, "They destroyed a large machine shop, tore up the track and burned the ties and bent the rails and inflicted all the damage we could on the Johnnies." Then it returned with the corps to the lines in front of Petersburg. Wilson, in the meantime, made a detour to the south and east and came in two days later.[150]

CHAPTER 12

DUTY IN THE SHENANDOAH VALLEY

As the Army of the Potomac lay in its trenches in front of Petersburg there was action going on in the Shenandoah Valley. Gen. David Hunter, who had sacked Lexington, headed up the Valley to Lynchburg where Jubal Early confronted him. Outnumbered and low on ammunition, Hunter withdrew on Sunday, June 19, to the Kanawha Valley in West Virginia. Lee, seeing the Shenandoah Valley empty of Federals, ordered Early to push his corps rapidly toward Washington, hoping to pull troops away from the Army of the Potomac. Early's approach caused considerable panic in the nation's capital. Maj. Gen. Lew Wallace, commanding the troops in Maryland and Delaware, scraped together 2,800 soldiers, mainly new recruits and 100-day militia, to stop Early. Wallace rushed his force from Baltimore to make a stand five miles south of Frederick at Monocacy Junction. At the same time, Ricketts's Third Division of the Sixth Corps was dispatched from Petersburg to reinforce Wallace. Ricketts arrived just in time on July 8. Early, reinforced by Maj. Gen. John C. Breckinridge's division, attacked the next day, and in spite of the addition of Ricketts's troops, the Federal force was defeated.[1]

Wallace's losses were heavy, but he had managed to delay Early's advance on Washington for two days. In the meantime, the rest of the Sixth Corps was ordered north. The Vermont Brigade received its movement order late Saturday evening, July 9, and by midnight, along with the rest of the Sixth Corps, it was on the march to City Point, which it reached by 6 A.M. the next morning. On Sunday, July 10, the two divisions, preceded by Getty and his staff, loaded aboard transports for Washington, and by noon they were steaming down the James River. The 2nd Vermont steamed past now familiar places such as Harrison's Landing, Fort Monroe, and Aquia Creek. It was a welcome change of pace for the men who had spent the last two months marching, fighting, digging and living in trenches.[2]

A few weeks prior to being ordered to Washington, Gen. Getty, who had recovered from the wound he had received in the Wilderness, was back in command of the Second Division. Lt. Col. Amasa S. Tracy was also back after recuperating from the injury he had received in April, and was in command of the 2nd Vermont. The Vermont Brigade now barely numbered 2,600 officers and men. With the sick and wounded who had returned from the hospitals, the 2nd Vermont had approximately 180 men present for duty.[3]

Gen. Getty and his staff landed in Washington a little before 2 P.M. on Monday, July 11. President Lincoln and Secretary of War Edwin M. Stanton were standing on the Sixth Street wharf as Getty and his staff made their way down the gangplank. "What troops does this steamer bring?" asked the president of the first men he saw. "It brings Maj. Gen. Getty and his staff, but no troops," the man replied. President Lincoln was reported to have turned away muttering in disappointment, "I do not care to see any major generals, I came here to see the Vermont Brigade."[4]

The vessels with the remaining two divisions of the Sixth Corps arrived later that day. As the troops disembarked, the president was on the wharf nibbling a piece of hardtack and chatting with the soldiers. He appeared to be relieved that the Sixth Corps was finally at hand. All of Washington shared his feeling. Early, who had marched straight for Washington after the battle of the Monocacy, was only five miles from the capitol. The sound of the Confederate cannons and the skirmishing in front of the forts just outside the city the day before had everyone on edge.[5]

The fortifications north of the city were hurriedly manned with a few regiments of 100-day troops called out by the president for this emergency, with a few companies of heavy artillery, some detachments from the Veteran Reserve Corps, and several battalions of civilian government clerks and laborers. The Sixth Corps reached Washington none too soon. As the columns of troops in their faded blue uniforms marched up Seventh Street to the front, there was wild cheering by the Washington citizens for the battle-worn veterans who had come to save them. The citizens ran through the lines with buckets of ice water for the troops suffering from the summer heat. Newspapers and snacks were passed from the sidewalks into the blue column. This was a far cry from the reception the 2nd Vermont had received from the Washingtonians when it had arrived in June of 1861.[6]

Early had halted the previous afternoon in front of Fort Stevens with approximately 10,000 to 12,000 very tired soldiers and 50 pieces of artillery. His skirmish line was about 500 yards from the fort, and his sharpshooters were ensconced in dwellings on both sides of the turnpike leading to Silver Spring and Rockville. A portion of Wheaton's brigade, the first Sixth Corps unit to reach the front, was deployed as skirmishers in front of the works. When the Vermont Brigade arrived, the 2nd and 3rd regiments were sent forward to man the rifle pits to the left of the fort. The rest of the Green Mountain Boys were massed in a piece of woods west of the fort where they camped for the night.[7]

Tuesday morning, July 12, after looking at the rebels facing them, Pvt. Hulburd wrote, "In five days the Rebs got nearer Washington than our men to Richmond." But he confidently added, "Guess we can hold them." Before starting an attack Wright sent a brigade to feel out Early's position and relieve the Union line from the harassing fire of the rebel sharpshooters, whose bullets were flying thick and fast in and around the fort.[8]

Shortly after 4 P.M., Getty's Third Brigade filed out into the road in front of Fort Stevens. The forts opened a vigorous supporting fire with their heavy guns, and the brigade moved forward. The Federals moved up a slight rise to a house from which the Confederate sharpshooters were speedily driven and then to a crest beyond where the main rebel force was posted. Here Early's troops had thrown up a breastwork of rails and earth and made a stout resistance. Every regimental commander in the Third Brigade was either killed or wounded, but the advance did not stop. The Federals cleared the crest, driving Early's line back for nearly a mile. The Third Brigade was relieved at sundown by the Vermont Brigade as the hostilities ended.[9]

Determining that the Sixth Corps had reinforced the Federal position, Jubal Early decided to withdraw, and that night he fell back through Rockville. He marched all night to the northwest toward the fords of the Potomac.[10]

At noon, July 13, Getty's and Russell's divisions started in pursuit of the rebels, followed by Emory's division of the Nineteenth Corps, which had just arrived from New Orleans, all under command of Gen. Wright. The Vermont Brigade, selected as the rear guard for the corps, left later in the afternoon. The men were already weary after a night and day of picket duty. To make matters worse, the roads were narrow and obstructed with army wagon trains, making for an exhausting march. The Green Mountain Boys had made about 20 miles when they halted for breakfast the next morning. After a short rest, they were off again making Poolesville by days end.[11]

The Sixth Corps remained at rest in Poolesville during Friday, July 15. The only excitement while the men were in this camp was the execution of a captured spy. Pvt. Wilbur Fisk noted the incident in his diary:

> I suffered my curiosity to take me to the fatal spot. The miserable man was conducted to the gallows by a squad of cavalry with drawn sabers, he walking afoot in their midst. He looked pale and a restless, nervous anxiety which he struggled to master told of the agony of his soul at that time. He took no notice of the people around him apparently, his mind was absorbed in things beyond sight. When everything was ready he was conducted to the scaffold and the rope placed around his neck. He was blindfolded, his feet tied together and his hands tied behind him. He spent a few moments in silent prayer when the platform was dropped from under him and he was suspended from the neck until dead.[12]

At daylight on July 16, the Sixth Corps crossed the Potomac. The Vermonters forded at Conrad's Ferry where the water was about four feet deep. Maj. Aldace F. Walker of the 11th Vermont wrote of the experience:

> The scene at the ford was new and exhilarating; the river is quite wide at this point and about thigh deep; the horses were loaded double or treble, and most of the footmen, not having the fear of women before their eyes, carried their clothing upon

their shoulders; brigades were crossing in several places for a mile up and down the river; every one greeted the unusual sensation of the slippery rocks and the gurgling water with shouts and laughter; the burdened men were here and there overthrown by the swift current, and occasionally one would slip from a staggering horse and be buried for an instant in the stream, to the intense amusement of all but the unfortunate; in such a gleeful humor we re-entered Virginia, and laid ourselves out to dry upon her sacred soil.[13]

Now back in Virginia, the Sixth Corps moved on through Leesburg to the Catoctin Mountains. Brig. Gen. George Crook, with the two divisions of Hunter's command (referred to as both the Army of West Virginia as well as the Eighth Corps) reached the Shenandoah river at Snicker's Ferry just in time to attack Early, but was defeated. Early then withdrew before Crook's and Wright's forces had a chance to unite and escaped to Fisher's Hill south of Strasburg.[14]

Supposing that Early was on his way back to rejoin the Army of Northern Virginia, and believing that his own mission was accomplished, Wright decided to return to Washington. Crook's Eighth Corps headed to Winchester. Wright rested his weary troops on July 20 and the next day faced them about, recrossed the Shenandoah River (or the "Shining Door" River as the Vermonters jokingly called it), and headed toward Washington. Getty pushed his men on across Loudoun County with only brief halts for coffee. They recrossed the Catoctins the next morning and marched on without halting to Leesburg. At Leesburg, the Sixth Corps hit the turnpike, picked up speed, and moved on through Drainsville. On July 23, it marched through Lewinsville, past Camp Griffin, crossed Chain Bridge and went into camp near Tenallytown.[15]

The Sixth Corps remained at Tenallytown for three days. In that time the men of the 2nd Vermont received four months back pay, new uniforms and shoes, and plenty of needed rest. Pvt. Hulburd wrote from this camp, "There are lots of sutlers round camp now. I have paid them but 50 cents yet—for cheese cakes and raisins, but am going out soon and see if I can't get a good drink of cider or strong beer."[16]

The corps expected to return to Petersburg, but when orders finally arrived on July 25, it was directed back to the Shenandoah Valley. When Gen. Early learned that the Sixth Corps had vacated the valley leaving only Crook's small, tired corps behind, he advanced from Fisher's Hill and defeated the Federals at Kernstown and forced them out of the Shenandoah Valley. Early then proceeded to break up the Baltimore and Ohio Railroad at Martinsburg and dispatched his cavalry, under Brig. Gen. John McCausland, into Pennsylvania. When the news of Crook's defeat reached Washington, U. S. Grant ordered the Sixth Corps at once to assist Hunter and Crook, who were guarding the South Mountain gaps in Maryland. The Sixth Corps started before noon on July 27 and moved north through Rockville, forded the Monocacy and marched to Jefferson, Md., where it camped about 8 P. M.[17]

On July 29 after crossing the Potomac River, Wright pushed his men past Harpers Ferry to Halltown, W.Va. Here Hunter's and Wright's forces were united, with Hunter taking overall command.[18]

As the Sixth Corps was crossing the Potomac, McCausland started on his raid. The electrifying news quickly hit Washington, and the War Department ordered Hunter to move his forces to repel the invasion. Despite Hunter's reply to Washington that Wright's troops were too tired and scattered to move immediately, he was ordered to move them anyway. The day was a scorcher as the Federals filed into the valley at Harpers Ferry. The army was backed up for hours in the ungodly heat as the troops re-crossed the Potomac River. Getty's division finally crossed during the night and barely made five miles by morning, due to the bunching up of troops, horses, guns, and wagons. The next day, however, the foot race was on again and the Sixth Corps made 20 miles. Marching that kind of distance in the sweltering heat had its cost. Hundreds of men were downed by sunstroke, and thousands more fell out by the roadside. By dark the corps, or what was left of it, marched into Frederick, Md.[19]

The 2nd Vermont's Surgeon, Melvin Hyde, wrote his wife about the horrible march:

Yesterday was the most severe march that the 6th Corps ever had—I never experienced so hot a day—the heat was dreadful—The boys fell out of the ranks in every direction at every step and several of them died with sunstroke and exhaustion—Even some of the Officers who rode on horseback were obliged to give up—Dr. Porter of the 11th Vt. fell from his horse completely overcome by the heat and it was some time before we could restore him—Officers and men were straggling along the road for miles—Scarcely a regiment in our corps came into camp last night with ¼ of its command—some had not more than a dozen men but they are all in this morning except those who died on the way or rode in the ambulances.[20]

Pvt. Wallace W. Noyes of Co. F mentioned grueling marching they had completed in a letter home and added, "The men are not low spirited or homesick–but they have little respect for the judgment of Gen. Wright—our corps commander–in handling men."[21]

The Sixth Corps remained at Frederick for a day and night during which time most of the stragglers came in. On August 3, it moved south and went into camp near Monocacy Junction. Here the corps camped along the hillsides of a pleasant valley. Other than the usual picket duty, the men were allowed to lounge in the shade, bathe in the river, and regain their strength after all the hard marching they had done.[22]

During this week of comparative quiet for the Sixth Corps, Early's cavalry was foraging in Pennsylvania and Maryland. On July 30, McCausland reached Chambersburg, Pa., and demanded $500,000 in cash or $100,000 in gold or else he would burn the town. The townspeople could not come up with the money, and McCausland torched the town. He withdrew south pursued by Brig. Gen. William W. Averell's cavalry. Averell attacked McCausland at Moorefield, W.Va. and defeated him.[23]

About this time, both President Lincoln and Lt. Gen. Grant agreed that something had to be done to reenergize the operations in the Shenandoah Valley. Since the beginning of the war, the Shenandoah Valley had been troublesome for the Federals. The Valley was of great military importance because it was a corridor through which the Confederate armies could move rapidly over well-maintained roads. Even when the roads were blocked with wagons, the land was so neatly cleared and cultivated that soldiers could march unimpeded through the fields. As important as its strategic transportation network was, the Shenandoah Valley was also known as the granary of Virginia. Not only did it provide the Confederacy with needed foodstuffs, but it was also a favorite place for Confederate armies to rest and rebuild after hard fought campaigns. Grant meant to deny the Confederates the Valley's resources.[24]

Finally, and probably just as important, a victory in the valley was needed for political reasons. The national election was only three months away, and Lincoln required victories to garner needed votes from a populace that was rapidly growing tired of the protracted war.[25]

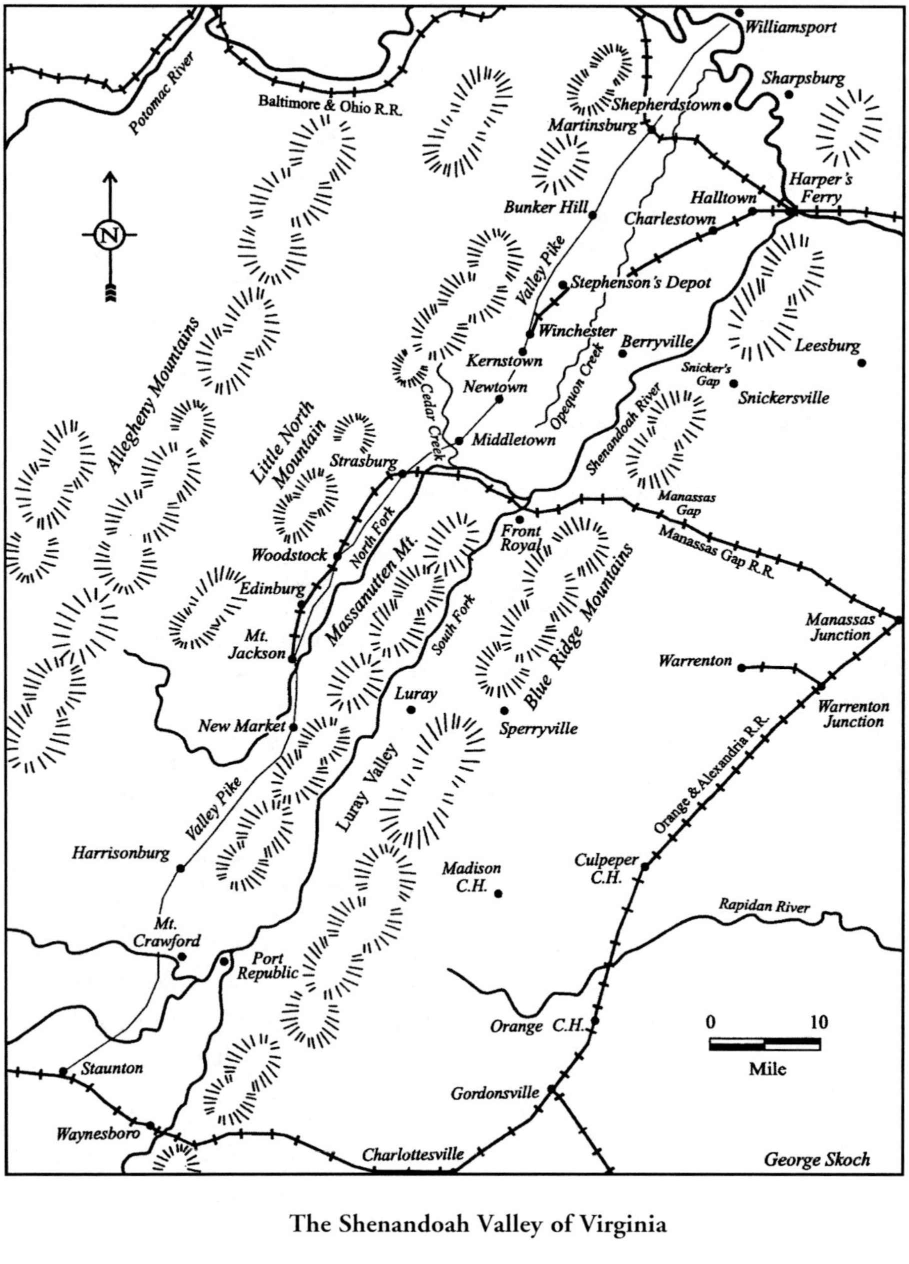

The Shenandoah Valley of Virginia

To take the Valley, Grant chose 34-year-old Maj. Gen. Philip H. Sheridan. Although many in Washington thought Sheridan was too young to command such a large independent force, Grant got his way. Grant's friend, Maj. Gen. William T. Sherman, telegraphed his support of the decision, stating, "I am glad you have given Sheridan the command of the forces to defend Washington. He will worry Early to death." On August 7, Sheridan assumed command of the Army of the Shenandoah and made his headquarters at Halltown, W.Va. His orders were to follow Early's corps "to the death." Later in an order to Sheridan, Grant wrote that "He should make all the Valley south of the Baltimore and Ohio Railroad a desert as high up as possible. I do not mean that houses should be burned but all provisions and stock should be removed and the people notified to get out." Sheridan would follow this order to the letter and maybe a little more. It was imperative that Early's army be defeated so that he could not rejoin Lee at Petersburg.[26]

By August 9, Sheridan concentrated his army in the vicinity of Halltown. It consisted of the Sixth Corps, reduced to less than 12,000 men by its hard campaigning; a division of the Nineteenth Corps, to which its other division was soon added; Crook's Eighth Corps; and a three division cavalry corps. With his artillery, this gave him about 35,000 men.[27]

The Sixth Corps came by rail from Monocacy Junction on August 5; and as it once more passed through Harpers Ferry, the men started calling the little town by the title of the most popular tabloid of the day "Harper's Weekly."[28]

Gen. Early's headquarters at this time was at Bunker Hill, W.Va., 10 miles west of Halltown. His small army of consisted of only 13,000 to 14,000 men. He was waiting to be reinforced by a part of Lt. Gen. Richard H. Anderson's corps consisting of Maj. Gen. Joseph B. Kershaw's division, part of Maj. Gen. Fitz Lee's cavalry division, and Cutshaw's battalion of artillery, which would add approximately 15, 000 troops.[29]

Three days after assuming command, Sheridan put his army into motion south. Because Early was awaiting reinforcements and was not ready to fight, he withdrew up the Valley. On August 13, Early made a stand at Fisher's Hill two miles south of Strasburg. Here he dug in to await Anderson's troops and repel the Federals.[30]

The Sixth Corps moved on August 10 and by the end of the day had reached Clifton, a large plantation north of Berryville, where it camped. Newtown was reached on August 11, and the next day Sheridan's lead units reached Cedar Creek, where they had a small brush with Early's skirmishers, but by the next morning, the rebels were gone. On Saturday morning, August 13, the Federals crossed Cedar Creek and proceeded to Strasburg, where they found Early strongly fortified on Fisher's Hill. Concluding he had no chance to successfully take on Early, Sheridan fell back to Cedar Creek.[31]

On the way to Cedar Creek, the men in the 2nd Vermont took to heart the order to lay waste to the valley as Dr. Hyde noted in a letter written on August 14:

> Our Boys have been out foraging and have come in with their horses loaded with grain, hams, chickens, mutton, lambs, green corn, Turkeys, and everything else you can think of, butter and cheese included—yes and lots of milk.... The Colonel's boys have come in too with all kinds of plunder—The boys rob the secesh farmers here with good grace.[32]

On August 14, the Vermonters lay in camp until 6 P.M., when they were ordered to advance as part of the skirmish line and got into a fire fight with Early's skirmishers at Hupp's Hill north of Strasburg. The 2nd Vermont had two men wounded. Dr. Hyde described the action:

> We had a little skirmish with the rebs after I wrote you yesterday evening—It commenced about 4 in the afternoon and lasted till dark. Capt. Wales of our regiment was shot in the forehead but is doing well—you recollect he was shot through the lungs in the wilderness on the 5th of May and recovered so as to join the reg't about the same time I returned—a young man named Morgan from Cambridge, MA also was shot through the lungs day before yesterday but is still alive. Our regiment was out on the skirmish line and were ordered to charge by Gen. Russell which they did in grand style driving the rebs on a double quick clear through the town of Strasburg but had to return to their old position one mile this side of the town.[33]

Capt. Elijah Wales, the commander of Co. C, had his wound dressed but refused to leave his company. Pvt. Harrison A. Morgan, of Co. H, was hit in the right side of his chest. The minié ball passed upward through his lung and came out at the edge of his right shoulder blade. Morgan survived his wound but remained in a general hospital until being transferred to the Veteran Reserve Corps February 21, 1865. Surprisingly, he lived until December 16, 1902.[34]

By August 16, Sheridan had decided that Cedar Creek was not a defensible position. His men's rations were running low, and there was no prospect of being resupplied any time soon since Mosby had attacked his resupply train that morning at Berryville and captured 75 of his heavily laden wagons. Also that same morning, Kershaw's division attacked a Federal cavalry patrol at Front Royal, confirming reports that Early was being reinforced. Not knowing Early's total strength, Grant told Sheridan to take a defensive posture until Early's reinforcements returned to the Army of Northern Virginia. That night Sheridan withdrew to Winchester, and the next day he pushed on to a position near Berryville. Following his orders, Sheridan burned all the wheat and hay south of Berryville and Winchester and drove off all the cattle.[35]

The Vermont Brigade started out a little after midnight August 17 in the Federal retrograde movement, and reach their old camp at Clifton at noon the next day. Here the men made quick work of what remained of their rations, which had been in short supply for the past several days. Resuming the march, they moved on toward Charlestown, where Sheridan was concentrating his army, and went into camp about two miles out of town in an area known as Welch's Spring or Flowing Spring. Here the Green Mountain Boys finally met their resupply wagons and were issued badly needed rations.[36]

Meanwhile, Early, who was following close behind the Federals, went into his old camp at Bunker Hill, leaving Kershaw's division at Winchester. Early remained quiet for two days while he and Anderson planned an attack on Sheridan.[37]

The Green Mountain Boys spent the two days of quiet

in their camp in the woods near Charlestown resting and foraging off the countryside. Sunday morning, August 21, started as peacefully as the previous two mornings. The men had been up since daybreak and were getting ready for their usual Sunday morning inspection. Then, at 9 A.M., firing broke out on the Sixth Corps picket line, which was just outside their camp. Before long the pickets fell back across the fields, followed closely by an angry rebel skirmish line. The Vermonters' camp immediately became a beehive of activity. Horses were hastily saddled, tents struck, knapsacks packed, and regiments formed. The Eighth Corps came up on the Sixth Corps's left and the Nineteenth Corps on its right, but the Confederate attack by Maj. Gens. Robert E. Rodes's and Stephen D. Ramseur's divisions was directed at the Sixth Corps, specifically Getty's division. Gen. Getty and his staff rode into the Vermont Brigade's camp and ordered Lewis Grant to move his regiments at once and reestablish the picket line. The picket line stretched in a semicircle of nearly a mile from the Winchester turnpike around to the left of the Vermont Brigade's camp. Dr. Melvin Hyde noted that by now, "their infantry were within pistol shot of us." Grant threw out the 3rd, 4th, and 6th regiments as skirmishers. The 2nd, 5th, and 11th regiments fell in behind as support.[38]

As soon as battle lines were formed the Vermont Brigade moved out. Surgeon Stevens of the 77th New York remembered, "The charge was executed with the usual brilliancy and fighting joy of that brigade." Directly beyond the field in which they had formed was a hill that sloped toward them and was covered by a large cornfield. The corn was so high that it almost entirely hid the advancing rebels, but without regard to the numbers they faced, the Vermonters fired a volley into the green mass and plowed blindly ahead. Just as the men entered the cornfield, Pvt. Jonathan Camp, a 44-year-old farmer from Pownal in the 2nd Vermont's Co. A, went down mortally wounded. He left a wife and seven children at home in Vermont.[39]

Sgt. James C. Hutchinson was another 2nd Vermont boy who would never emerge from that hateful cornfield. Hutchinson, a young man from Roxbury, joined Co. H in the fall of 1861. He was a good soldier and once boasted in a letter to his mother while at Camp Griffin, "Our oficers are good to us as eny oficers could be. They are as good as eny oficers on the ground I believe but they have to be cross meny times. They aint cross to me." He continued to be a good soldier throughout his short military career, and was promoted to corporal and then to sergeant. His widowed mother and his little sister Betsy, who depended on him for support, received a small government pension after his death.[40]

Hamilton Ovitt, a private in Co. F, was luckier than Hutchinson. The bullet that found him did not produce a mortal wound. Ovitt had been troubled with intestinal problems ever since joining his company in July 1863. The problem was so bad that he could not even wear his equipments belt, and his commander had permanently detailed him as a company cook, but this day everyone was needed on the skirmish line. A minié ball passed through his left leg just above the knee, cutting away muscle and tendons. The damage was so severe that he could not walk and had to be carried off the field.[41]

Sergeant James C. Hutchinson, Company H, killed in action August 21, 1864. National Archives.

Within minutes after the Vermonters charged into the cornfield, the gray-backs could be seen clambering over the fence on the other side of the field. With their adrenaline pumping, the Green Mountain Boys charged after the retreating rebels until they reached the hill that had been

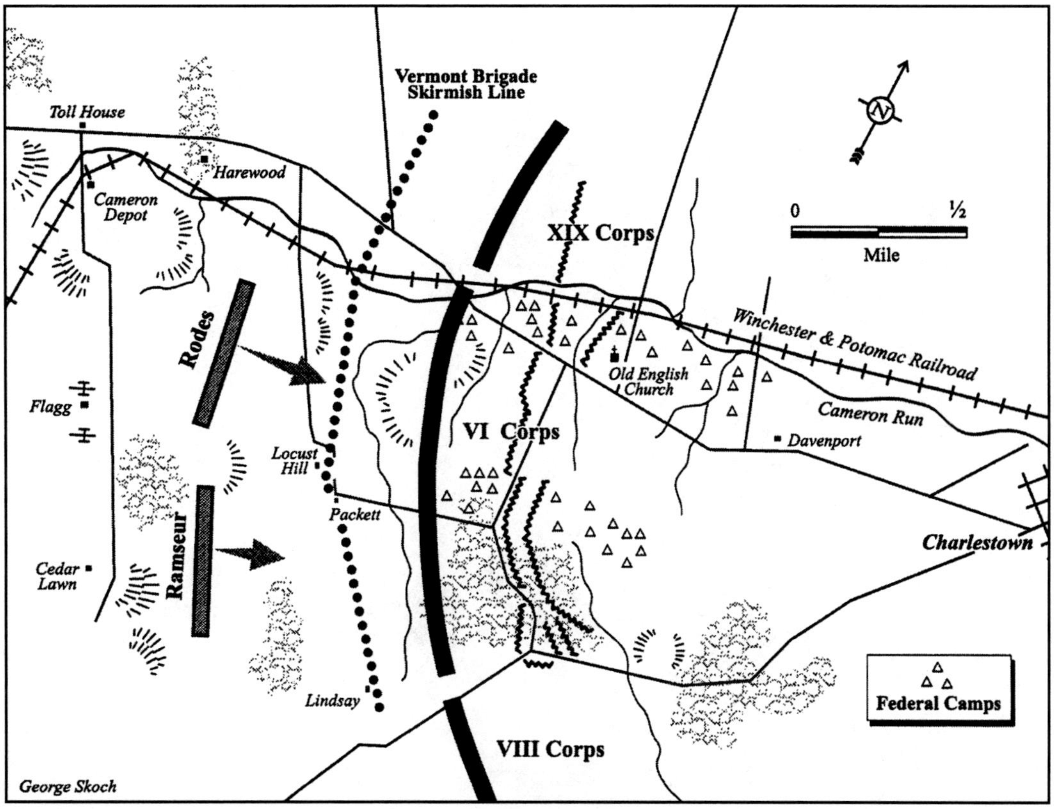

The Battle of Charlestown, August 21, 1864

vacated earlier by the Federal pickets. Here the right of the line halted, but the men in the 11th Vermont, on the left, were so excited that they kept running forward even though they could see the rebels regrouping on the next hill. Gen. Getty, who had been following the Vermonters on horseback, finally stopped the men and brought them back into position with the rest of the line.[42]

The rebels did not take long in counterattacking. From the shelter of ridges, fences, and stone walls, the Southerners hit the Yankees with heavy rifle fire. The Vermonters likewise piled rails into hasty breastworks or dug rifle pits in the sandy soil and held their ground. The firing was intense, and to expose oneself meant death or a wound. Pvt. Abraham Sherman, a 39-year-old Readsboro farmer in Co. A., raised his right hand holding his ramrod to ram home a bullet when a rebel minié ball hit his hand, mangling it and taking off his ring finger. A doctor said later that the wound caused "a total disability of that hand to nearly the same extent as if the hand were gone." Sherman never returned to the regiment and was transferred to the Veteran Reserve Corps the following December.[43]

First Lt. Charles Morey of Co. C, who had narrowly escaped death at Spotsylvania, had his luck hold again. Although he was hit in the left leg, the wound was not as bad as it might have been. Morey wrote his parents of his experience from his hospital bed in Camden Street General Hospital in Baltimore, Md.:

> at nearly 3 o'clock P.M. a stray ball came along and hit my left leg just above the knee. The ball struck butt end first but was not going with enough force to enter the flesh it merely bruised it so you see that it is very slight and I will be able to return to my regiment in a very few days. Walcott [Corp. James A. Walcott from Royalton] of E company was mortally wounded through the head. When I saw him last he was just breathing, he would not live long.[44]

Corporal James A. Walcott, Company E, killed in action August 21, 1864. Ed Italo Collection.

Pvt. William O'Brian of Co. A was hit about the same time as Morey. O'Brian, a 31-year-old farmer from Sears-

Private William O'Brian, Company A, wounded August 21, 1864. O'Brian was killed in a fight in 1881. Frank Pulaski.

burg who had also been wounded charging up Marye's Heights in 1863, was hit in the upper left thigh and spent time in Camden Street General Hospital with Morey. He was back with his company in November and on December 1 was promoted to corporal, and before the war's end he was promoted to sergeant.[45]

Pvt. Charles Hammond, also of Co. B and a 37-year-old blacksmith from Poultney, was hit in the left forearm near the elbow joint. He recovered from the wound, but his left hand was paralyzed, and he lost the use of his left arm. He was discharged April 20, 1865 with a 100 percent disability.[46]

Pvt. Alba Royce, a 26-year-old joiner from Windsor in Co. I, tried to stay behind cover, but his left leg stuck out and he was shot in the ankle. Within a few days he was recuperating in the Patterson Park General Hospital in Baltimore. Before being transferred to the Governor Smith General Hospital in Brattleboro, October 20, he was well enough to get about and contracted syphilis. He was returned to his company February 22, 1865, when apparently both his ankle was healed and his venereal disease was cured.[47]

The 2nd Vermont's Surgeon, Dr. Melvin Hyde, was on the front line during this battle and gave the following account:

> I went up to see our Col and the rest of our boys who were laying on the crest of a ridge a little way off popping away at the rebs—I staid there about two hours waiting for the fire of the enemy to slacken so that I could get back to the woods where our reserve line of battle were—But seeing no prospect of that and the place getting pretty hot where the Col and I lay—two soldiers and a Lieut getting hit close beside me I started back—My course lay through a corn-field where a part of the 11th lay flat on their faces the corn being literally cut off about three feet from the ground by the minnie balls. They told me I had better lay low and go no farther which I should have done had not my stretcher bearers just at that moment came along with a wounded man—I started on after them to direct them to our Hospital (which had moved back to a safer distance) when a ball carried away nearly half of my hat—and about three minutes after as we passed out of the cornfield I ordered a man by the name of Curtis to relieve the bearer in the rear of the stretcher—he had just done so and had not proceeded ten paces when he fell headlong over the stretcher pushing down the man carrying the front of the stretcher and upsetting the wounded man—I was just about to curse him for what I supposed to be his awkward stumbling when I perceived that he was shot through the head, his brains being spattered all over the stretcher—I thought I would take him on to the Hospital and bury him, so I placed him on one of the boy's blankets and with the assistance of two other men who I had met on the way I carried him ½ mile further into the woods.[48]

By sundown, the fighting ended with the combatants still in place. The two mules that had been carrying ammunition to the Vermonters delivered approximately 56,000 rounds during the battle. In the battle of Charlestown the Federals lost 250 men. The Vermont Brigade suffered the most losses with 24 men killed and 100 wounded. The 2nd Vermont lost a total of five men killed and 13 wounded. The Confederate casualties numbered approximately 160.[49]

That night, Sheridan, feeling he could not adequately defend his position at Charlestown, withdrew his army to Halltown. The Vermont Brigade, selected as rear guard, held the line in front of Charlestown until 3 A.M. the next morning, when it quietly withdrew and marched to Halltown where the rest of the army was entrenched.[50]

For the next three days Sheridan's men remained in their fortifications at Halltown and were busy skirmishing with the rebels. For one of the few times during its tenure in the Shenandoah Valley the Vermont Brigade was not on the front lines and had several days of comparative quiet in its camp at Clifton.[51]

Realizing that Sheridan's position at Halltown was too strong to be attacked and not daring to undertake another invasion northward, Early moved back to his old position at Bunker Hill on August 26. Sheridan followed him on August 28, taking his former position in front of Charlestown.[52]

After a run-in with Sheridan's cavalry, Early finally retired to a position on the high ground west of the Opequon Creek, between Winchester and Martinsburg. Meanwhile, Sheridan consolidated his army at Clifton facing west, with his left near Berryville.[53]

For the next two weeks Sheridan's men were able to rest with only picket and fatigue duty to contend with. One exception was a reconnaissance to Opequon Creek by Getty's division on Tuesday, September 13. The Vermont Brigade led the advance. Both Sheridan and Wright accompanied the column. At 10 A.M., the skirmishers reached the creek and crossed it, meeting the rebel pickets. Shortly afterward, a Union artillery battery went into position on the far side of the creek in front of the Vermont Brigade and opened fire. The intent was to persuade Early's artillery to open fire so Sheridan could determine the enemy's positions, but for a while, the Confederate would not cooperate.[54]

While the Federal battery probed for enemy positions, the rest of the division massed in some woods a quarter of a mile behind the artillery. The woods were clear and shady with an occasional open space. The infantrymen had stacked arms and were lounging around in small groups. The 2nd Vermont's Dr. Hyde was lying behind a split rail fence with his clothes off, picking lice, or, as he put it, "skirmishing for grey-backs." The rebels finally had enough and returned fire. Dr. Hyde tells what happened next:

> We were all taken by surprise when they commenced shelling us in the woods.... We had been shelling all day, to draw *their* fire and had not succeeded up to 3 o'clock, and we of course were lulled into a feeling of entire security—Some were playing cards, some were cooking, some were resting, some were sleeping, and *one* was skirmishing for lice! I never saw such concentrated and terrific shelling. They came upon us like a thunder clap, and in such quick succession that one had hardly time to collect his senses—I know I had hardly time to *collect my "rags"*—It was, "which one" "which one" whiz, whiz, bang, every moment—five and six coming in at a time—Every man "cut" for a tree, but as I was in a ploughed field outside of the woods, behind a fence, I had no alternative but to lie quietly on the ground (in a complete state of nudity) till I found that instead of going over me, many of them struck the ground and burst before reaching me, while others ploughed the ground on each side of me—I could not stand this long, and so made for the hay-stack—I never felt before while under fire, that I should not come out alive—but this time I had a presentiment that I should *loose* my life, and was expecting to get hit every moment—What prevented it, God only knows![55]

Even though the enemy fire was vicious, it only lasted a short time. Armed with the information he needed, Sheridan and his troops returned at nightfall.[56]

Following Grant's orders not to attack Early until Anderson's units left the valley, Sheridan's men continued to remain inactive. Lee had in fact requested the return of Anderson with Kershaw's division and the artillery battalion about September 1, and Anderson had started for Petersburg on September 3, but his movement was prevented by an unexpected encounter with the Eighth Corps at Berryville. On September 14, he started again, and this time found his route clear. His departure was Sheridan's signal for action.[57]

Lt. Gen. U. S. Grant met with Sheridan on September 16 at Charlestown to lay out a plan of battle for him. Sheridan had already drawn up a plan of his own and presented it to Grant. Grant liked what he saw and gave his subordinate the go ahead. He simply told him to "Go in!"[58]

The Army of the Shenandoah was up and on the move at 1 A.M. on September 19. The Vermont Brigade, bringing up the rear of Getty's division, was on the road at 3 A.M. from its camp near Clifton. Missing this march was Brig. Gen. Lewis A. Grant, who was home on furlough, leaving Col. James M. Warner, commander of the 11th Vermont, in temporary command.[59]

Sheridan's original plan was to move behind Early at Newtown, south of Winchester, and attack him, but upon learning that Rodes's and Gordon's divisions had moved toward Martinsburg, he changed his plan. He decided to move directly on Winchester and strike before Rodes and Gordon could return.[60]

Sheridan's new plan of attack called for Wilson's cavalry division to lead the army, followed by the Sixth and Nineteenth Corps. The infantry, with the Sixth Corps on the left and the Nineteenth Corps on the right, was to engage the enemy while one cavalry division was to work its way around to the left flank. The Eighth Corps would be held in reserve and then move to the left to support the cavalry. While this action was taking place, Sheridan's other two cavalry divisions were to charge down the Valley Pike and hit Early's left flank. The plan was complicated and called for near perfect timing.[61]

Marching through the darkness, the Sixth Corps crossed Opequon Creek at 6 A.M. At this point, Opequon Creek is in a valley with the road running from it to the west forming a long tortuous wooded ravine known as the Berryville Canyon. After a hard fought advance, Wilson's Cavalry division had cleared the narrow gorge of rebels and was holding a small earthwork on the high ground west of the canyon on Early's right that commanded the Berryville Road into Winchester, but Sheridan's plan was falling behind schedule.[62]

As the Sixth Corps took position, it immediately started receiving heavy artillery fire. Getty's division relieved the cavalry troopers and quickly formed in line of battle facing west. The Third Brigade went to the extreme left with its left flank resting on Abram's Creek. The First Brigade took a position on the right. The Vermont Brigade filled the space between the other two brigades. The Vermonters halted at the edge of a narrow fringe of woods that concealed it from the Confederates' view.[63]

With the Sixth Corps in position, Sheridan was ready for the Nineteenth Corps to come up, but an hour or so ticked by and still it did not arrive. Losing his patience, Sheridan went rearward to investigate. To his dismay, he found that Gen. Wright had brought his wagons with him, and they were blocking the narrow road and were holding up the Nineteenth Corps. In a rage, Sheridan had the wagons pushed off the road and moved Brig. Gen. Cuvier Grover's division forward. During this delay, both Gordon and Rodes returned to reinforce Early.[64]

For nearly two more hours, the men in the Sixth Corps sat resting and trying to keep out of harm's way, but with shells bursting overhead, that was hard to do. Pvt. Hulburd was one of the unfortunate men in the 2nd Vermont to get hit. Hulburd related his story in a letter to his wife: "I was just grazed by a ball from a "spherical case" which is a round shell filled with little balls about the size of a musket ball. The shell explodes and sends its contents in every direction. Just drawed blood but I did not *feel it.*" Pvt. William S. Foster, Jr., a Royalton native in Co. E, was not as fortunate as Hulburd. Foster had a shell fragment tear through his body that killed him on the spot.[65]

Finally, without waiting for the Nineteenth Corps's other division to arrive, Sheridan ordered an advance. As the Green Mountain Boys cleared the woods they were taken aback by what they saw ahead. The hill sloped gradually downward before them for about a quarter of a mile to a long winding ravine. The hill on the opposite side of the ravine was steep with its crest lined with fortifications that bristled with rebel muskets. Seeing what lay ahead, Getty's entire line hit the ground. After several minutes of waiting, the commander of the brigade to the right of the Vermont Brigade came over and asked Col. Warner to move his brigade forward. He felt that with the Green Mountain Boys on the move the rest of the division would follow. Their only hope was to get into the ravine a quickly as possible, where the far embankment was so steep the enemy fire could not reach them.[66]

The Vermont Brigade charged into the ravine as fast as it could. It moved so quickly that it lost contact with the units on its left and right. As soon as the men reached the safety of the bottom of the ravine, they were surprised by a Confederate regiment, probably some of Pegram's men, on their right flank within "short pistol range." They had stumbled into a perfect ambush. The rebels immediately started firing into the surprised Vermonters as fast as they could. The initial blast mainly hit the 5th and 11th regiments, but the other regiments in the brigade took their share. For a few minutes, it was pure slaughter. The boys in the 2nd Vermont were square in the middle of it.[67]

Private William S. Foster, Jr., Company E, killed in action September 19, 1864. Jeffery S. Jones Collection.

Pvt. Laroy Wyman in Co. A from Peru, Vt., who had been slightly wounded May 10, was hit in the right arm and right hip. The minié ball that hit his hip also fractured the femur. He died from his wound 21 days later.[68] Pvt. William Reed from Tunbridge in Co. E also died in the hospital, but unlike Wyman he only survived a few hours.[69] Pvt. Charles F. Powers, a Milton resident in Co. H, took a flesh wound in the upper right arm but was able to keep up with his company—for a while.[70]

Their only chance to get out of this living hell was to scramble up the far bank as quickly as they could. Once out of the ravine and shielded from the fire from the top of the hill as well as the bottom, the Green Mountain Boys started returning fire on the gray-clad troops who had ambushed them. Just as they started firing, the Third Division charged into the ravine and chased the rebels off.[71]

Safely extricated from the ambush, the Vermonters continued the charge. As they crossed the area above the ravine, the landscape leveled off somewhat, and they could see the foreboding breastworks in front of them. To advance seemed like a suicide mission, but the Vermont Brigade charged straight up the hill as many of the rebels behind the breastworks lost their nerve and fled. With the enemy fire starting to subside, the Vermonters threw themselves over the parapets and captured hundreds of prisoners. The prisoners, however, were soon left behind as the men, fired up by their success, continued the chase on toward Winchester.[72]

About three fourths of a mile beyond the captured confederate entrenchments, the Vermonters ran out of steam and halted to catch their breath. Just then Early unleashed a vicious counterattack that hit the point where the flanks of the Sixth and Nineteenth Corps were supposed to meet, but where a gap had developed. Led by Gen. Rodes himself, the counterattack smashed through Ricketts's division, costing Rodes his life when his skull was struck by a Federal shell. With its flank unprotected, the Vermont Brigade was forced to fall back.[73]

It appeared that Rodes's men were headed almost unopposed for Sheridan's rear, but the 1st New York Independent Battery and Battery E, 5th Maine Light Artillery, stood in the way. The Federal artillerymen poured such a devastating fire of canister into the charging rebels that the counterattack slowed to a crawl. Then Russell's division poured a flanking fire into Rodes's men, and the counterattack was broken. Sheridan followed up with a counterattack of his own with Russell's division, which pushed the rebels back, and the engagement became a stalemate. Nearly two hours passed with only heavy skirmishing between the two opposing lines while units were repositioned and a resupply of ammunition was issued.[74]

Sheridan now changed his plans for the Eighth Corps, and instead of sending it to the left of the Sixth Corps, he moved it in behind the Nineteenth Corps. At about 4 P.M., the Eighth Corps attacked Early's left flank as the Sixth and Nineteenth Corps charged forward. The three Corps, anchored on the Sixth Corps's left, swung on the Confederate line like a garden gate. Just as the gate was swinging in on him, Early was hit by Sheridan's two cavalry divisions charging down the Valley Pike and the Confederate line broke.[75]

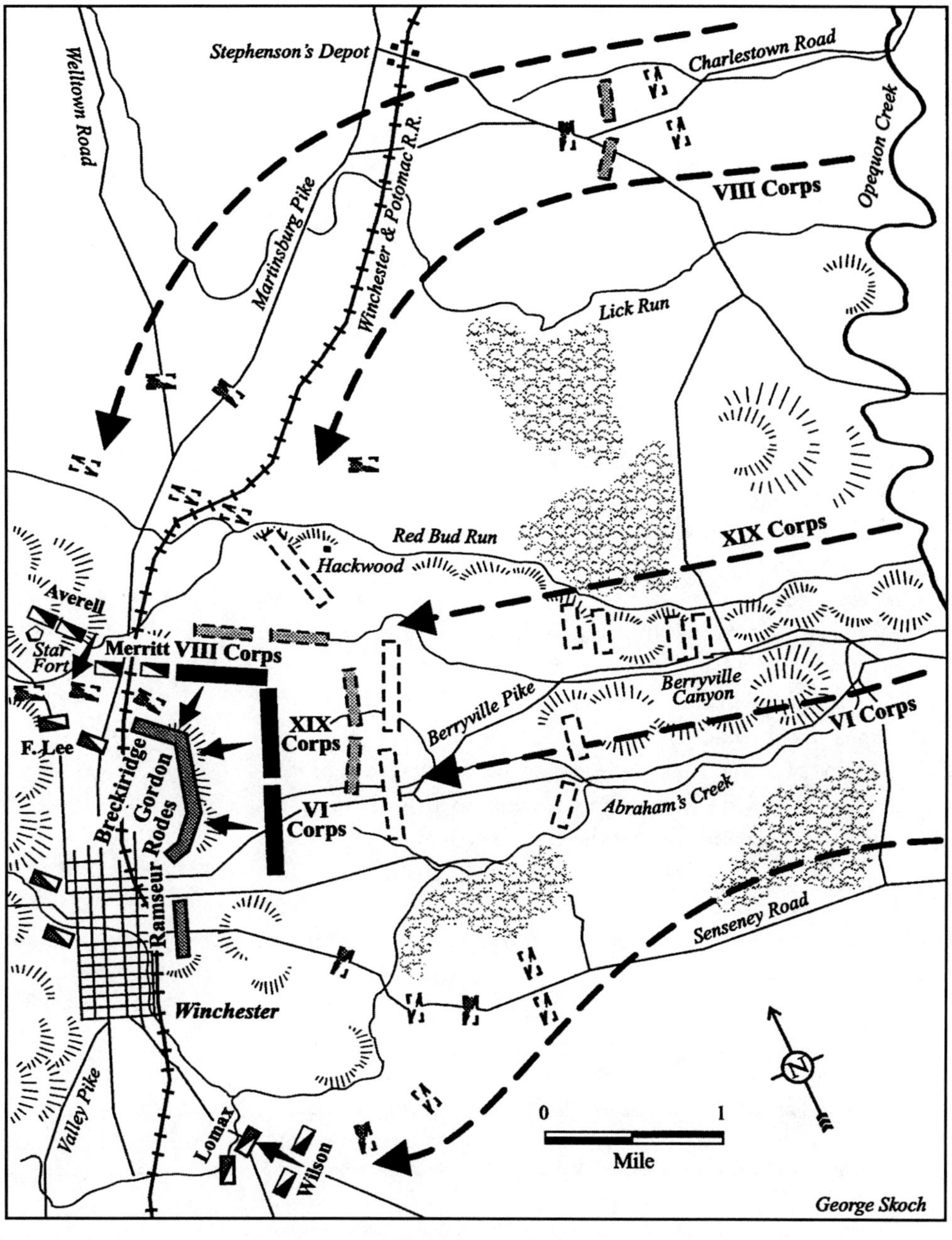

The Third Battle of Winchester, September 19, 1864

Maj. Walker described the Vermont Brigade's part of the assault:

> On this second advance it again fell to the lot of the Vermont Brigade to be thrown forward beyond the rest of the line of battle of which it formed a part. We entered a corn field with stalks full ten feet high, and could do nothing of use until

> we reached its further limit, where it was bounded by a tomato garden, at the further side of which was a strong paling fence. Behind this fence we had halted when we opened fire. The enemy was in plain sight but a short distance before us and the men worked at their guns with the diligence of desperation. We were still enfiladed by the battery at our left, and we saw the Brigade on our right withdraw a short distance for better shelter behind the crest of a little hill. It seemed to us less dangerous to remain, and we clung to our position though losing rapidly.

The rebel battery was taking its toll on the 2nd Vermont. Pvt. Oliver Lucia from Jericho in Co. E was hit by a shell fragment in the right thigh. The fragment not only laid open the thigh, but removed part of the femur, creating what the doctors called an "ununited fracture." Several of his friends carried him back to the regimental hospital.[76]

Another Co. E soldier, John A. Cilly, a private in Co. E from Royalton, was hit by a shell fragment in the right foot. His tentmate John Gravlin helped him back to the hospital, where Cilly made a pretty quick recovery from his wound, but died four years after the war from chronic diarrhea that he had contracted while in the army.[77]

Pvt. George Seger, a German immigrant from Stamford, Vt., in Co. F, was spared a wound from shell fragments, but was injured by the concussion of an exploding shell. The force of the concussion injured his lower abdomen, causing him "difficulty when passing water." He had earlier been shot in the head at Spotsylvania and was quite hard of hearing.[78]

Maj. Walker describes the scene:

> The Brigade rose as one man, rushed at the fence that had partially protected us, and as it fell, passed over it into the open plain. The whole army was seized with the same impulse and strode joyfully forward, a huge crescent, with waving flags and wild hurrahs. The scene was wonderful. The infantry kept a rapid march and the alignment seemed complete.... And in that joyful mood, conscious of strength and of victory, we closed upon the city as the evening fell.[79]

From a vantage point in the rear, Surgeon Hyde described the Vermont Brigade's charge:

> I never saw such a complete rout of an enemy, nor read of such an one—I left the wounded in good hands, during both charges made by our lines that I might obtain a fair view of one of the most sublime spectacles that I ever before witnessed—The confederates fell like grass before the sythe—Our shells and minnies made dreadful havoc among them—I held my breath in suspense when our boys made the last charge on their batteries, for I expected to see them swept away in one mangled mass or utterly annihilated by the terrible shower of grape and canister, Shells, and canon balls that were hurled upon their columns, but the noble fellows, though terribly cut up, came out all right.[80]

The 2nd Vermont indeed did get cut up. Pvt. Charles Powers, who had been slightly wounded in the ambush in the ravine, was hit in the left side of his chest, but survived. He was transferred to the Veteran Reserve Corps February 21, 1865. He died from complications of his wound March 23, 1876.[81]

Seventeen-year-old Pvt. George Crown from Grand Isle in Co. H was shot in the lower left leg. The mangled leg was amputated several hours later. Crown was discharged on disability June 6, 1865.[82]

Company K's Pvt. Oliver Clair from Cornwall had a rebel minié ball neatly amputate the ring finger from his left hand.[83]

The Union troops thought the Confederate retreat was glorious. One Vermonter remembered, "Gen. Sheridan came by, and was saluted with the wildest cheers." As Sheridan put in a telegram to Washington, the rebels were sent "whirling through Winchester." Pvt. Hulburd noted, "the way the Rebs cut was a caution." The town was now in Federal hands. The Confederates fled too rapidly to be overtaken by Sheridan's infantry but his cavalry followed them to Kernstown, where, under the cover of darkness, Early was able to retreat to Strasburg.[84]

The fighting at the Third Battle of Winchester was brutal. Sheridan lost 697 men killed, 3,983 wounded, and 338 captured. The Vermont Brigade, again in the thick of the battle, lost 23 men killed, 223 wounded, and 10 missing. Of that number the 2nd Vermont's casualties were three men killed and 29 wounded. Early reported his loss, excluding his cavalry, as 199 men killed, 1,505 wounded, and 1,818 missing.[85]

After the battle, Pvt. Wilbur Fisk, who had been on detail guarding the division's wagon train during the action, went looking for his wounded comrade Oliver Lucia. Fisk noted in his diary:

> My old friend and pupil Oliver Lucia was severely wounded. He was wounded in the leg by a piece of shell which broke his thigh and for a time it was feared that he would have to lose his leg. When I heard that he was wounded I went up to see him. The guards stopped me but I managed to get in by going around to the back of the hospital. He was lying there without having any care taken of him. Several others were there in the same condition. Dr. Content was having a world of trouble about it. He wanted I should go up to the brigade hospital and speak to Dr. Hyde about it. It was a mile or more up there. I knew it would do but little good but on Lucia's account I was willing to go.... I found Dr. Hyde busy at work with his bloody hands doing all he could to alleviate the sufferings of the wounded that were being continually brought in.

I found Mr. Hyde a very pleasant man and I was much pleased with his manners and apparent kind heartedness. He was very sorry that any from the 2nd Vt. should be suffering needlessly from neglect. He thought he had provided against that. He did not mean he said to have any case for amputation down there to Division hospital. He would go down there immediately he said; and he did.

It was a sad sight to see the wounded men as they were brought to either hospital. Some were not attended to at all, their wounds being pronounced mortal, it was a waste of precious time to dress them and they were left to die. Many were already dead, many were dying.

I went back and found Lucia just where he was before and I had been gone over two hours. It was nearly night and they told me he was brought in about noon. His leg was broken but it had not been set or amputated ... we moved him into or under a fly. There he remained till he could be moved to a general hospital.[86]

Pvt. Lucia did survive as Fisk had hoped, but died at home from complications of his wound on September 12, 1865. His mother and father, who were dependent on him for support, received a small government pension after his death.[87]

Attesting to the intensity of the combat, Dr. Hyde described the horrible aftermath that he saw on the battlefield the next day:

As I came to Winchester this morning I rode over the battle field and O! what a wreck! Army wagons in pieces, broken gun carriages, canon balls, shells, muskets, bayonets, swords, haversacks, knapsacks, blankets, coats, caps, cartridge boxes, and all other infernal paraphanalia of *war!* The ground as far as could be seen is thoroughly plowed by shot and shell—Especially that part of the field where our Division charged the foe—The rebel dead and ours lay strewn all over the hills and in the ravines in many places where shells had burst—I saw from five to eight lying in one spot Though but the day after the battle, many had begun to putrify.... I dismounted several times thinking I recognized some familiar face, but was invariably disappointed—Some of the rebel dead had papers pined on their clothes with name and rank &—I saw one poor fellow (a reb) with his skull and brains all blown out nothing remaining but his scalp—another with his head entirely cut off by a round shot, or a shell—Another man torn entirely in pieces, his legs, arms, head entrails and other portions of his body were scattered some distance—I found one of his arms and a part of a leg over four rods from the place where the shell struck him—Over the crest where our boys made the charge the dead of both armies lay in lines or rows in every position that can be imagined just as they fell—Some lay with their faces upturned and their eyes staring wide open.[88]

Not one to rest on his laurels, Sheridan had his army on the move early the next morning, September 20, chasing after the rebels with the Sixth Corps leading the way. By evening his army was in front of Early's position on Fisher's Hill.[89]

Fisher's Hill is two miles south of Strasburg in an area where the Shenandoah Valley narrows to a width of about five miles. The North Fork of the Shenandoah River winds along the eastern base of the hill. A small mountain stream called Tumbling Run borders the north side. Across the North Fork to the east of Fisher's Hill stood a Confederate signal station on Three Top Mountain which had full view of the approaches to Fisher's Hill and of the Valley to the north. The position was selected and fortified by Stonewall Jackson two years before and had been a stronghold for the Confederates in previous operations in the valley. Early strengthened the existing entrenchments and arrayed his units from right to left, with Brig. Gen. Gabriel C. Wharton, Maj. Gen. John B. Gordon, Maj. Gen. Stephen D. Ramseur (commanding Rodes's former division), and Maj. Gen. Lunsford L. Lomax's dismounted cavalry.[90]

During the afternoon of September 20, the Army of the Shenandoah arrived at Cedar Creek, and after crossing, went into position on the heights fronting Strasburg with the Sixth Corps on the right and the Nineteenth Corps on the left. The Eighth Corps was held concealed in the woods behind Hupp's Hill for another flanking movement like the one it had performed at Winchester. Averell's cavalry moved around to the right to feel out the Confederates. The rest of the Union cavalry moved up the Page valley toward Luray and New Market to threaten Early's rear and cut off his retreat. By evening, the Union pickets occupied the northern part of Strasburg and the Confederate pickets the southern.[91]

As the sun rose the next morning, Sheridan was busy making a thorough reconnaissance of the Confederate positions on the heights and repositioning his units in preparation for an attack. The Vermont Brigade was situated on the left of the Sixth Corps. The Vermonters took shelter behind fences and stone walls, and although occasionally an artillery shell screamed overhead and rebel sharpshooters shot at anything that moved, there was only one casualty. During the afternoon, as Col. Foster, now commanding the Vermont Brigade (Col. Warner having been given command of the First Brigade of Getty's division), was passing along the lines, a rebel sharpshooter squeezed off a round. Corp. Thomas J. Miller of Co. K, 3rd Vermont, serving as the brigade's color bearer, was shot through the body and killed instantly. Whether the intended target was Foster or Miller will never be known.[92]

The 6th Vermont's assistant surgeon had been standing nearby when Miller was killed and was quite shaken up by the experience. Surgeon Hyde recalled later:

> Dr. Curtis 6th Vt. just came in looking pale, he was over at Brig. Headquarters standing near the color bearer when a ball pierced the color-sergeant's heart and he fell dead at the Doctor's feet—I had just told him to stay where he belonged—Well he got pretty well frightened at all events—it will do him good too—He is always gading about.[93]

During the afternoon, the Vermonters could hear heavy musket fire toward the village of Fisher's Hill to their right. It was on the highest ground on the Federal side of Tumbling Run, and the Confederates had not yet given it up. Sheridan ordered Wright to clear the enemy off the hill, and Wright sent in two regiments from Ricketts's divisions and one from Getty's, but they had been repulsed twice. Wright then ordered Col. Warner forward with his brigade. This time the hill was cleared of rebels, and Warner was soon after promoted to brigadier general for his success. Toward evening, the Vermont Brigade reinforced Warner and spent the rest of the night digging in.[94]

Thursday, September 22, dawned clear and warm. In the morning's light, the Vermonters could see the rebels continuing to strengthen their lines on Fisher's Hill. The face of the far slope was steep and was covered with abatis.[95]

Not long after sunrise, Gens. Sheridan, Wright, Emory, and Crook rode into the Vermont Brigade's area and set up a telescope and studied the enemy's positions. Sheridan was heard to say, "I'll get a twist on 'em, damn 'em!" Soon afterward Crook left and started the Eighth Corps on its flanking movement around the Confederate left. It would be a tricky operation to get his command in position without the rebel signal station on Three Top Mountain seeing it. To assist in making a quick and invisible march, Crook had his men leave their knapsacks behind and wrap their rifles with rags to keep them from shimmering in the sunlight. The Sixth and Nineteenth Corps also helped keep peering eyes off Crook by keeping up a lively fire along the skirmish line.[96]

By 4 P.M., Crook was in position, and his West Virginians came screaming down the side of Little North Mountain and overran the cavalry on the Confederate left. Then they hit Ramseur's and Pegram's divisions which also started falling apart. Pvt. Wilbur Fisk wrote that the Confederates "left their guns and run pell mell across the field through a woods out of sight like frightened sheep."[97]

Gen. Sheridan ordered all his troops to advance and kept shouting "Forward! Forward everything!" Getty pushed his division across Tumbling Run under heavy fire from the batteries on the opposite side. The Federal guns roared into action, and the rebel artillery was soon silenced. Ricketts swung his line around and joined Crook, who was hotly pressing Early's men. Then Early's whole army broke for the rear in an utter rout. It was a dead run over fields, stone walls, and creeks. As the Federals chased the fleeing rebels, the Vermont Brigade started forward and immediately hit a shallow millpond but somehow floundered through and rushed up the hill to the rebel works. Then, as Maj. Walker noted, "in a confused delirious mass, hurried on as best it might after the scattered enemy." Sheridan's advance cleared Fisher's Hill of rebels, who took to the woods or raced up the Valley pike toward Woodstock. The Sixth and Eighth Corps were eventually halted to allow commanders time to reorganize their commands. Meanwhile, Sheridan with the Nineteenth Corps pressed on after Early. The Sixth Corps soon followed, marching 12 miles that night to Woodstock.[98]

Unbelievably, Sheridan's loss was only 36 men killed, 414 wounded and six missing. The loss of the Vermont Brigade, like that of the corps and the army, was "absurdly small." The 2nd Vermont lost only three men wounded. Early reported 30 men killed, 210

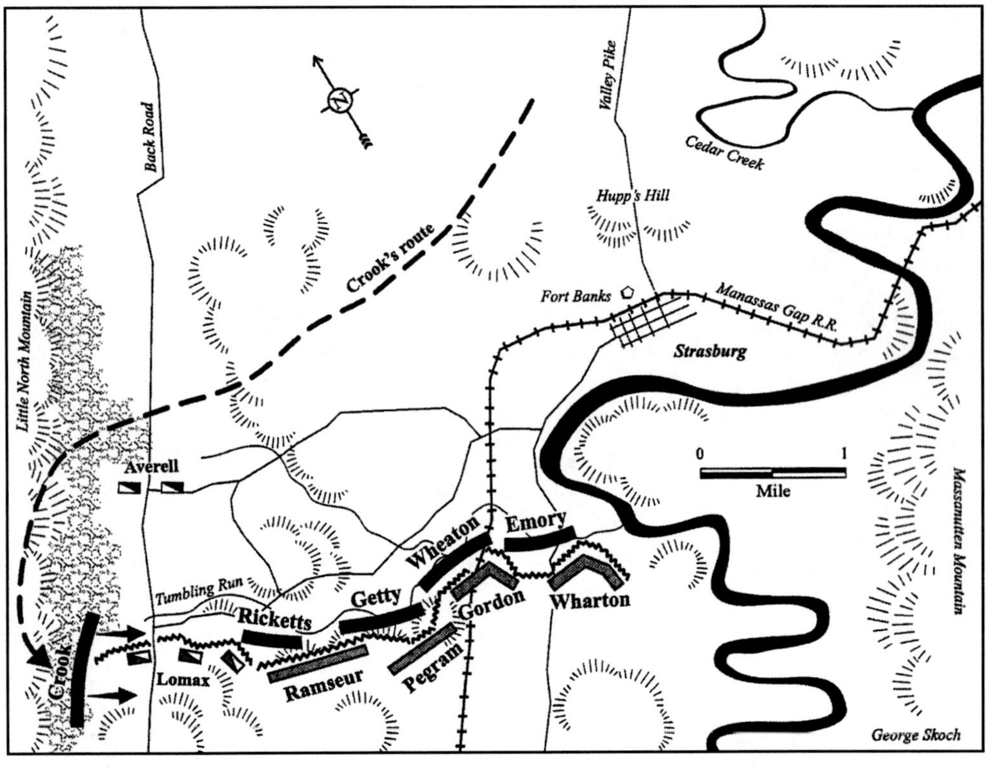

The Battle of Fisher's Hill, September 22, 1864

wounded, and 995 missing, of which he estimated about half were captured. He also lost 14 cannons to the Federals.[99]

Writing his wife Juliana about their victories at Winchester and Fisher's Hill, Pvt. Benjamin Hulburd boasted, "We have driven old Early from the valley of the Shenandoah have gained two of the greatest and most decisive victories of the war and *ain't you* proud to think that *I* had a hand in it?"[100]

Early's demoralized troops fled in disorder all night, but Sheridan's victory was shy of being complete. The Federal cavalry that was sent behind the rebels to cut them off had been stopped by a small Confederate cavalry force, allowing Early to escape.[101]

Sheridan regained contact with Early on the morning of September 24, three miles south of Mount Jackson at Rudes Hill, but Early declined to accept battle and retreated another 20 miles up the Valley, using his artillery to keep his pursuers at bay. Early finally halted his corps 60 miles south of Fisher's Hill at Brown's Gap, east of Port Republic. Sheridan pursued Early through Harrisonburg to Mount Crawford, but decided that the rebel leader was no longer a threat, reversed course, and for the next two weeks concentrated on his campaign of ravaging the Valley.[102]

From September 25 to October 5, the Vermont Brigade camped with the rest of the Sixth Corps at Harrisonburg, getting a well-earned rest. The only work was picket duty and foraging raids. The rest of the time the men lounged around camp and discussed the upcoming presidential election, which had Lincoln pitted against the Army of the Potomac's old commander, George B. McClellan, running as a "peace at any cost" Democrat.[103]

On Thursday, October 6, the Army of the Shenandoah began moving back down the Valley. The Vermont Brigade broke camp at Harrisonburg and made a forced march to Mount Jackson, where it camped for the night. As the Vermonters were passing through New Market, Brig. Gen. Lewis Grant rejoined his brigade and was glad to be back. Wilbur Fisk talked to Grant's aide, who had accompanied Grant on his leave of absence, and noted in his diary, "Lieut. Sessions said they had a pretty good time only they hurried back because we were having such glorious success here in the valley that he wanted to be back here and have a hand in it. He said he only stayed in Vermont seven days."[104]

The march continued on October 7, with a vengeance, and the troops cleared the Valley of anything that could be used by the rebels. Under strict orders from Sheridan, private dwellings and household stores were to be spared, but anything else the rebels could use was to be burned. In those two days, 70 mills and over 2,000 barns filled with wheat and hay were torched. Great pillars of smoke could be seen reaching for the sky for miles around. More than 7,000 head of livestock were confiscated and driven along with the army for its use. According to Pvt. Hulburd, not all the troops followed Sheridan's orders:

> We have been doing a great business of late in this valley but O what a destruction of property. Millions and millions would not and time never can restore to this valley what this season has cost it. There are some connected with this army whose only object is *plunder* they will enter the houses of old defenceless women and strip it of everything they take a fancy too—things that is of no sort of use to themselves they will bring away and destroy. But I thank God I can say that I up to this time have touched nothing that did not belong to me if I except occasionally a sheep or fat pig that came in our way, and fruit and green corn may have suffered some, but that is all.[105]

In another letter concerning the men's disregard of orders, Hulburd wrote, "Such acts are not allowed by the army regulations but the officers 'wink' at them if they are favorably remembered in the *division of the spoils.*"

Like Hulburd, Surgeon Melvin Hyde did not mind eating the spoils of the Valley, but did not feel good about the wanton destruction, as he expressed in a letter to his wife "Our army has burned everything in the valley. Barns, hay, grain, houses, &c. It is heart-rending to see the women, children, and Old grey headed people turned into the street without a home to shelter them."[106]

By October 8, the army was back in the area north of Cedar Creek between Middletown and Strasburg where it went into camp.[107]

While at Brown's Gap, Early was again reinforced by Kershaw's division and a battalion of artillery which came close to making up the losses he had suffered at Winchester and Fisher's Hill. On October 5, Brig. Gen. Thomas L. Rosser's cavalry brigade further reinforced him. Three days later Rosser, who was being touted as "The Savior of the Valley," attacked Custer's cavalry division, which was covering the rear of Sheridan's army. A running fight lasted the better part of the day. The next day Merritt's and Custer's cavalry divisions jumped Rosser's and Lomax's commands at Tom's Brook, southwest of Strasburg, and gave them a thorough whipping.[108]

By now Sheridan figured the fight had been taken out of Early and that the campaign in the Shenandoah was about over and ordered the Sixth Corps to return to Petersburg. On Monday, October 10, Wright moved his corps to Front Royal, where it was to be transported east on the Manassas Gap Railroad to Alexandria. After a two-day wait for the railroad to be repaired, Wright grew impatient and moved his men out on foot on October 13. The corps made 15 miles by afternoon and started fording the Shenandoah

River near Ashby's Gap. Gens. Wright and Getty were sitting on their horses in the middle of the river directing the crossing when a messenger from Sheridan came splashing up to them with orders for the Sixth Corps to return to Cedar Creek.[109]

Sheridan had assumed Early had slipped away from Brown's Gap in the Blue Ridge and to points farther south, but "Old Jube," seeing Sheridan starting to disband his army, moved part of his corps back to Fisher's Hill. Unsure of Early's intentions, Sheridan thought it better not to be too hasty in whittling down his force. The Sixth Corps camped for the night on the north shore of the river and before daylight the next day headed back, reaching Cedar Creek by that afternoon.[110]

The Army of the Shenandoah had several days of comparative rest with only rebel scouts occasionally probing its picket lines. Having been ordered to Washington for consultation, Sheridan reluctantly departed, leaving Wright in command. Starting October 13, Early came a little closer by moving a brigade to Hupp's Hill to observe the Yankees, and then withdrew it. A federal reconnaissance mistook this to mean Early's whole army had withdrawn, and the Army of the Shenandoah let its guard down. Even the daily pre-dawn formations used to guard against a Confederate surprise attack were called off.[111]

The Army of the Shenandoah in fact did occupy a strong position. The Eighth Corps lay on the east of the turnpike in two division camps almost a mile apart. It occupied several hills that overlooked the junction of Cedar Creek and the North Fork of the Shenandoah and the Valley Pike crossing of Cedar Creek. The Nineteenth Corps was in trenches on the west of the turnpike and formed the center of the line. The Sixth Corps was camped west of the Nineteenth Corps with Getty's division being the westernmost infantry unit, about two miles from Cedar Creek. Custer's and Merritt's cavalry divisions were camped on to the right of Getty's division. The other Federal cavalry division, Powell's, was stationed 12 miles away at Front Royal. The army's weak spot was the wide gap between the Eighth Corps's left and Powell's cavalry division. No security had been provided for, and the unprotected infantry line was completely in the air.[112]

With a force that now numbered a little over 21,000 men, Early decided to try to salvage his reputation and attack Sheridan on October 19. His plan of attack called for Gordon, with his own division as well as Ramseur's and Pegram's, to ford the North Fork of the Shenandoah and hit the weak spot on the left flank of the Eighth Corps. Early himself would take a column consisting of Kershaw's and Wharton's divisions, with all his artillery, down the turnpike through Strasburg to fords along Cedar Creek and attack Sheridan's center as soon as Gordon engaged the federal left flank and rear. Meanwhile, Rosser was to attack Custer's cavalry on the Federal right flank.[113]

Just after dark on October 18, Gordon left camp with his three divisions. At about the same time Early, with Kershaw's and Wharton's divisions, moved down the turnpike. Since the success of this attack depended on approaching the Yankees as silently as possible, the troops left behind anything that would make noise, and the Confederate artillery remained at Fisher's Hill to be called forward later.[114]

After passing through Strasburg, Early sent Wharton's division down the pike to the Cedar Creek Bridge while he led Kershaw's to the right to strike about two miles below the bridge at Bowman's Mill Ford. By 4:30 A.M., Kershaw's men had waded across Cedar Creek, and with virtually no resistance captured the Federal pickets. About the same time, Gordon's lead elements forded the North Fork and took position without being detected. At 5 A.M. Kershaw's men fired into the camp of the First Division of the Eighth Corps. The result was pandemonium among the unsuspecting Union soldiers.[115]

The Eighth Corps was caught totally by surprise. The rebels captured some of the men while they were still in bed. Others fled in their nightclothes or partially clothed. Many left without taking their weapons. Within minutes Kershaw's men had 500 prisoners and seven pieces of artillery which they turned on the fleeing Yankees. The Eighth Corps's Second Division made a stand, but within a few minutes it was hit by Gordon's 9,000 screaming troops and any meaningful resistance from the Eighth Corps collapsed.[116]

Having but a few minutes' warning, units of the Nineteenth Corps manned their trenches overlooking Cedar Creek and soon started taking fire from Early's guns set up on the other side. But with the Eighth Corps dissolved, Gordon and Kershaw hit the Nineteenth Corps's flank around 6:30 A.M. The Nineteenth Corps, with remnants of the Eighth, held its ground for a while but slowly had to give way as brigade after brigade dissolved.[117]

In the 2nd Vermont's camp, Lt. Col. Amasa Tracy, who had not been able to sleep, was sitting by a fire in front of his tent when he first heard the disturbance on the picket line, and like everyone else thought it was just a small Confederate probe. Within a few minutes the sound of artillery was added to the musketry fire, and he immediately knew it was more than a probe and roused his regiment. No sooner had the regiment formed than men from the Eighth Corps started streaming by to the rear shouting such remarks as, "If you don't want to be captured, better get out of this," and "The Johnnies have licked Hell out of us."

Tracy recalled later:

Although met every moment with such remarks, not a man moved, out of the ranks, but as daylight began to make faces distinguishable, I cast my eyes along the lines, and this is what I saw—500 faces, pale in the dim light of early morning, but stern and determined. No sign of cowardice along that line! My heart swelled with pride; pride that I had the good fortune to command a regiment of Vermont soldiers, men that I knew would not flinch in any place where their officers would stay, and officers who would stay with their men until the last one fell, if necessary.[118]

As the Nineteenth Corps unsuccessfully tried to form a line, Wright ordered Ricketts, who was commanding the Sixth Corps in Wright's absence, to move the Sixth Corps to the left near the turnpike and try to get in front of the Confederate attack. The Sixth Corps's three divisions quickly moved from their camps. The First and Third Divisions formed on high ground west of Meadow Mill Brook. The Second Division moved across an open field to some higher ground southwest of Middletown and closer to the turnpike.[119]

Maj. Walker of the 11th Vermont recalled the scene as the Second Division moved across the plain:

I am utterly unable to describe the universal confusion and dismay that we encountered. Wagons and ambulances lumbering hither and thither in disorder; pack horse led by frightened bummers, or wandering at their own free will; crowds of officers and men, some shod and some barefoot, many of them coatless and hatless, few without their rifles, but all rushing wildly to the rear; oaths and blows alike powerless to halt them; a cavalry regiment stretched across the field, unable to stem the torrent; and added to the confusion and consternation the frequent sight of blood, ambulances, wagons, men, stained and dripping, with here and there a corpse; while the whistling bullets and the shrieking shell told that the enemy knew their advantage and their ground.[120]

Before the Nineteenth Corps could position itself to the right of the Sixth Corps and before Getty's division, which had the longest distance to march, could get into position, Kershaw and Gordon struck the First and Third Divisions of the Sixth Corps. The two lone divisions held the Confederates at bay for nearly 40 minutes.[121]

Abandoning the idea of reaching the turnpike, Gen. Getty moved his division to high ground west of Middletown, where the town cemetery was located. Gen. Bidwell's Third Brigade held the left, the Vermont Brigade the center, and Warner's First Brigade the right. As he was positioning his division, Getty ordered Gen. Grant to clear the enemy's skirmishers from the woods between the cemetery hill and the turnpike. Grant sent the 5th and 6th Vermont regiments and part of the 11th. The Green Mountain Boys promptly deployed as skirmishers and cleared the rebels out of the strip of woods where they then halted. They were now so far out in front that they were in fear of receiving rounds from their own batteries emplaced behind the division. For the first time during the attack, the enemy was opposed by the regular formation of a skirmish line, masking a line of battle. Before long a scattered rebel skirmisher line was seen approaching through the mist and was given a volley by the Vermonters. The enemy skirmishers were stopped for a short while. Pegram's division, in two lines of battle, then came rolling out of the mist, and the Vermont skirmish line was forced to fall back, leaving several of their wounded on the field. The Vermonters, however, had bought Getty enough time to get his division formed and ready to meet the rebel attack.[122]

By now the First and Third Divisions had completely broken contact and were shielded by Getty's force. As they fell back, they took Gen. Ricketts with them. He had been severely wounded by a bullet in his chest, his sixth and final wound of the war. The Second Division was now alone on the field.[123]

The crest that the Second Division occupied was actually the southern end of a half-mile wide plateau that rose just west of Middletown and on top of which was the town cemetery. Lewis Grant stated later, "The crest was not a high one, but it was sufficiently elevated to be clear of the fog, which existed only in the low grounds." Getty reluctantly backed the Second Division a couple of hundred yards up the ridge and took a position on its southeastern crest. He positioned Warner's First Brigade on the right, the Vermont Brigade in the center, and Bidwell's Third Brigade on the left. Col. Alpheus S. Moore's cavalry brigade later pulled in on Bidwell's left and Battery M of the 5th U.S. Artillery set up in front between the Vermont and Bidwell's Brigades south of the cemetery. Both the First and Third Brigades had some cover by woods in their sectors, but the Vermont Brigade was completely exposed in an open field.[124]

As soon as Getty got his men into position, he was hit by both Pegram's and Ramseur's divisions. The skirmishers barely had time to take their places before the rebels were on them, and had to fall back to their line of battle. The brunt of the attack was on Warner's left and the Vermont Brigade's front. Warner and Grant had their men hold their fire until the gray-clad troops were within several hundred feet of the crest of the hill and then they unleashed a withering volley.[125]

Lt. Col. Tracy wrote later of the first Confederate onslaught:

The fog began to lift a little from the ground it had been hugging so closely, and a long line of legs came to view, and a spectral line of bodies above the legs, not more than 200 or

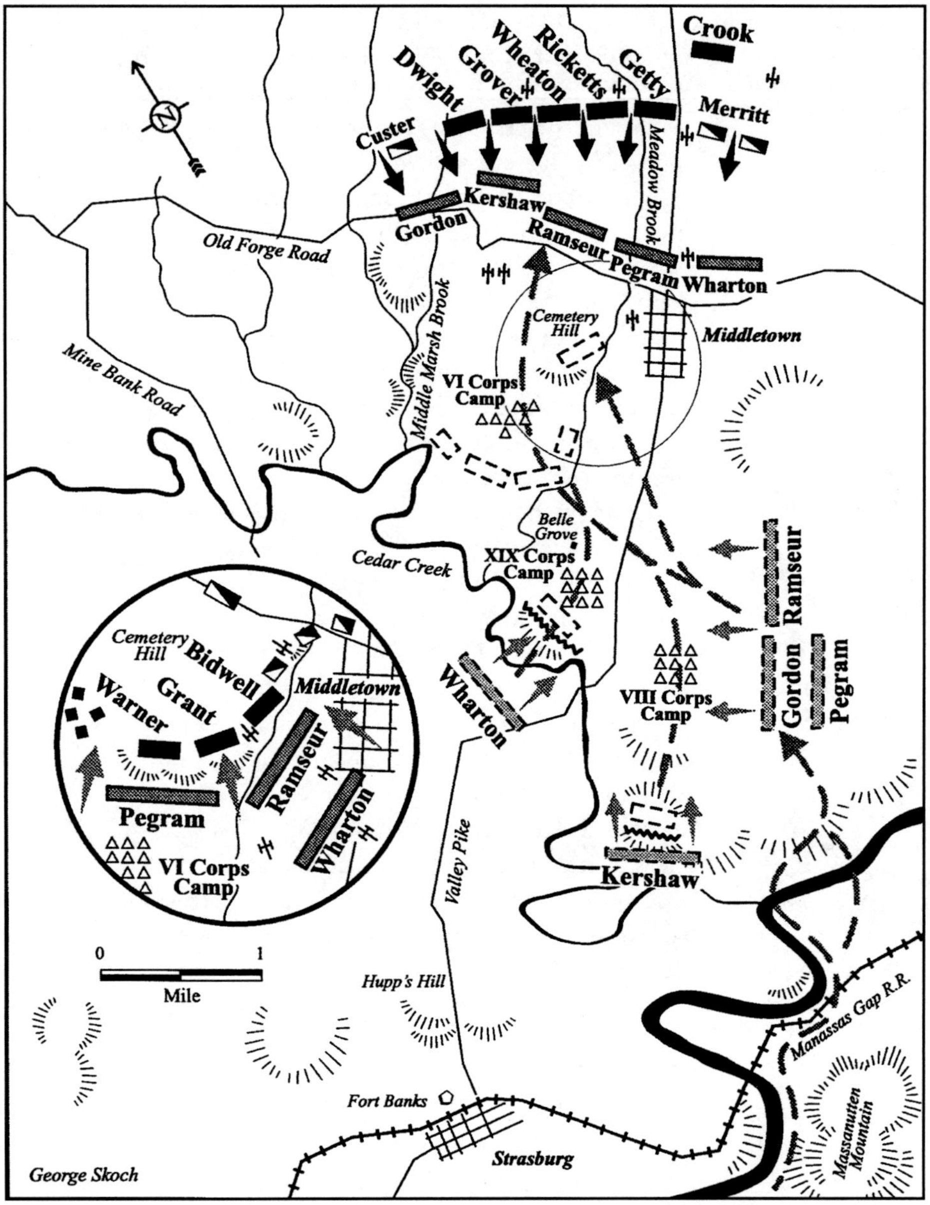

The Battle of Cedar Creek, October 19, 1864

> 300 feet in our front. Now was the moment. Fire! Then came a simultaneous flash both right and left: a crashing report: the old Vermont Brigade had spoken. For a long time it was comparatively quiet in our front: no legs, no misty bodies in the fog and smoke. All that could be heard was the grating of the iron rods as they pushed home the powder and ball in the death-dealing tubes of the Vermonters.[126]

Although the contact was short-lived, it was quite intense, and the 2nd Vermont took its share of casualties. Pvt. Albert G. Leach (Lt. Chester K. Leach's brother) of Co. H was hit in the right eye. The rebel minié ball entered the eye socket, destroyed the eyeball, glanced off his nasal bones, went through his soft palate, and into his mouth. In a state of shock, Leach spit the bullet out. He lost all sight in his right eye, and the right side of his face remained numb. For the rest of his life, the eye socket continually drained fluid into his mouth. His doctors seemed to think that the wound also caused him to become a bit mentally unbalanced. He was awarded a 100 percent disability after he was discharged May 12, 1865, and was unable to work the rest of his life.[127]

Another man in Co. H was downed just after Leach. Pvt. Wells Howard from Jamaica, Vt., was hit in the left hand, but the bullet did not stop there. After passing through his hand, it came to rest in his left lung. He was evacuated to Patterson Park General Hospital in Baltimore where it appeared he was going to recover, but the 32-year-old soldier died November 1, 1864. His mother Martha received a small government pension in return for her son's life.[128]

Pvt. Hollis L. Rich, a 28-year-old draftee from Northfield Falls in Co. D, who had been wounded in the left leg in the wilderness, took a painful hit in the right thigh. The ball traveled down through his thigh, breaking the femur and lodging just beneath the skin about four inches above his knee. The ball was extracted in the hospital, but after the wound healed, he could not straighten out his leg and it was partially paralyzed. He remained in the hospital until October 3, 1865. Once he returned home, his disabled leg apparently did not keep him from getting around. His wife divorced him for adultery in 1874 and was awarded the custody of their young son.[129]

The fusillade of lead the Second Division spewed out caused the Southerners to recoil and fall back to the far side of the stream. Realizing they could not dislodge the Union troops by an unsupported frontal assault, the Confederates brought up their batteries and pounded away at the Federal defenders for about a half an hour. As Maj. Walker noted, "The rebels now concentrated a terrible fire of artillery upon our position, and shell from thirty guns flew, screaming devilishly, over and among us. The men hugged the ground, being somewhat covered by the hill, and owing to the cover thus obtained, the loss, as Gen. Getty says, 'was lighter than could be expected.'"[130]

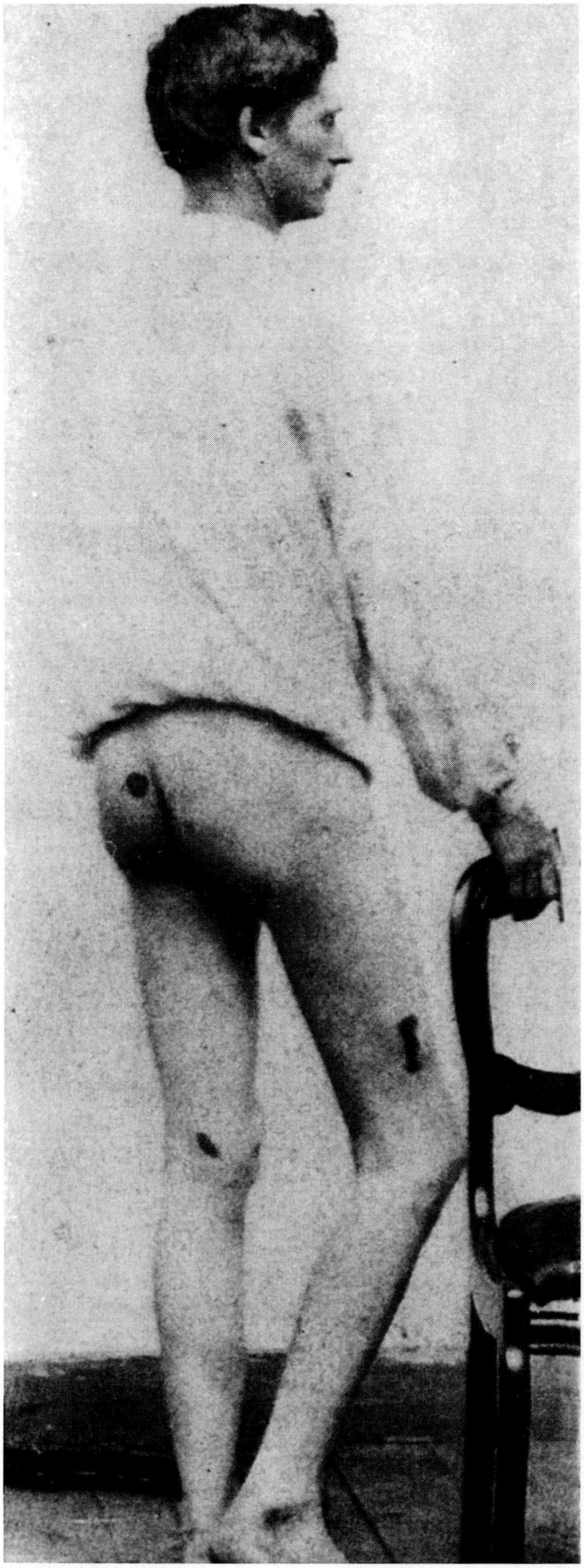

Lt. Col. Tracy remembered that the air was "full of deadly missiles, shells, grape, and cannister, shrapnel and solid shot falling all around us; but not a man moved from his place in the line." Sgt. George L. Crozier, a 24-year-old cooper from Stamford in Co. A, was tending to his men when one of the rebel shells passed so close to his head that it knocked him down. Before he hit the ground another shell burst near him, and he was hit in both knees with shell fragments. He landed with such a force that it caused a rupture on the left side of his navel. The unconscious, bleeding sergeant had to be carried off the field by several of his men.[131]

After softening up the Union line with artillery, Early tried the Second Division again. The Vermont Brigade, along with the Third and the artillery, was hit for a second time, and the Confederates came so close that hand to hand fighting ensued. But again the rebels were repulsed. It was during this attack that Getty learned that Ricketts was down and that he now had command of the corps. He immediately put Lewis Grant in command of the Second Division. Grant in turn put Amasa Tracy in command of the Vermont Brigade.[132]

During this second assault, Pvt. William L. Kinsley of the 2nd Vermont's Co. H was hit in the left arm. The 21-year-old farmer from Fletcher had only been with the regiment since August. He was hit in the arm by either a pistol ball or a buckshot. The small ball hit him about mid-forearm, traveled up the arm and lodged in his elbow joint. The ball was never removed, but he would survive his wound and would be back with his company by the following January.[133]

Pvt. William B. Nichols of Co. A, who had been with the regiment even less time than Kinsley, having arrived in September, was hit in the right thigh. Nichols must have been one of the luckiest men in his company. Not only did a spent ball hit him, but it hit a wallet he was carrying in his right pants pocket, resulting in nothing more than a bad bruise.[134]

Pvt. Alonzo Goodenough from Readsboro, also in Co. A, was not as lucky as Kinsley. He had been slightly wounded in the left thigh the year before charging up Lee's Hill at Fredericksburg, and now he was hit in the right armpit. The ball traveled just under the skin and came out just above his elbow. As bad as the wound seemed the doctors considered him only "slightly wounded." He returned to his unit after several months of recuperation in the hospital and served out the rest of the war without being wounded again. After the war he returned to Vermont, married in 1866 and by the time he died at age 74, he had fathered nine children.[135]

Left: **Private Hollis L. Rich, Company D, displaying his leg wounds to the U.S. Pension Bureau. National Archives.**

Seeing that Pegram's and Ramseur's men were becoming worn out, Early sent in men from Wharton's division who had not yet been engaged and were still full of fight. Wharton hit the Second Division line between Bidwell's Brigade and the Vermonters. Finally Bidwell's men could no longer hold out and started to fall back slowly. Then, as Gen. Bidwell was rallying his men, he was hit by a shell fragment that tore open his chest and knocked him from his horse mortally wounded. Lt. Col. Winsor B. French of the 77th New York assumed command of the Third Brigade. For a moment it appeared as though the men were going to panic at the wounding of their beloved leader, but before that could happen, French shouted to the men, "Don't run till the Vermonters do!" With a cheer that Maj. Walker described as "a cheer of desperation," the Third Brigade troops sprang forward and regained their position on the crest and pushed the astonished rebels back down the hill.[136]

Like the two preceding attacks, this one was also vicious. Pvt. John Rappallo of Co. H, the Italian immigrant who had deserted the previous spring, was shot in the right knee. The wound was severe enough that he mustered out of the service when his wound healed. He lived until 1920.[137]

A rebel minié ball slammed into the leg of Pvt. Michael Lynch of Co. E, shattering the femur. One of the men in his company applied a tourniquet, and Lynch was carried to the rear. His leg was amputated later in the day at a field hospital in Winchester. He died from complications of his wound December 1, 1864, leaving a young widow back home in Shaftsbury, Vt.[138]

By now Early had gotten most of his units up and was hammering away at the Federals. Over the course of an hour, the Second Division stood alone and repelled three separate attacks, but now Confederate units were starting to overlap both of its flanks. Gen. Getty sent word to Grant that he could withdraw the division.[139]

Grant slowly withdrew the division about a half mile to the north until he came to the Old Forge Road just to the west of Middletown, where he halted. Here the division had a chance to dress its lines and replenish its ammunition. He threw the 2nd Vermont, now commanded by Capt. Elijah Wales, forward as skirmishers. Just in case it was needed, Lt. Col. Tracy sent the 3rd Vermont in support of the 2nd. The Second Division remained at Old Forge Road for about 20 minutes, then, not finding any other troops in the vicinity, Grant decided to continue to withdraw to a better position nearer the turnpike, about three quarters of a mile north of Middletown. In open defiance of the enemy, he coolly marched the Second Division in line of battle farther to the rear where he found Gen. Getty and what was left of the army.[140]

When the 2nd Vermont finally left its position to catch up with the brigade, 24-year-old Sgt. William R. Farrington, a carpenter from Rutland in Co. K, became separated from his unit and was captured. He was sent to Richmond and imprisoned. Later he was sent to a prisoner of war camp in Lynchburg, where he was paroled February 15, 1865. He returned to his company and safely finished the rest of the war.[141]

The new position selected by Gen. Getty was behind a long fence, part of which was a stone wall, stretching west a mile or two from the turnpike. In this new position, the men felt confident that they could hold off Early's men. The Second Division's left flank, the Third Brigade, stretched from the turnpike and across Meadow Run, followed by the Vermont Brigade and then the First Brigade. Gen. Getty rounded up the First and Third Divisions of the Sixth Corps, while Gen. Wright organized the two divisions of the Nineteenth Corps and what he could find of the Eighth Corps. As the units came on line, the men hurriedly beefed up their positions to prepare for the expected attack. Wright left the Sixth Corps's Second Division where it was. To its right, he placed the Sixth Corps's Third Division and then its First Division, and last the Nineteenth Corps. To the left of the turnpike were two divisions of cavalry and what little remained of Crook's corps. A strong skirmish line was thrown out across the entire front.[142]

It was now between 10 and 10:30 A.M. The Army of the Shenandoah stood waiting for the next Confederate onslaught and, according to Maj. Walker, feeling "a little proud of what we had already done." But Early's attack had bogged down. After their repeated assaults, his units were exhausted, disorganized, and a number of the men had dropped out of the ranks to pillage the abandoned Federal camps. Early was forced to stop to reorganize.[143]

As the Federal troops stood in line wondering what would come next, they heard cheering from the stragglers and wounded who stretched along the turnpike toward Winchester. The reason soon came to light as Gen. Sheridan rode onto the field astride his black charger Rienzi. Sheridan had returned to the Valley the day before, but due to delays in his progress to the front, he stayed overnight in Winchester. After the exhausting trip, he decided to sleep in on the morning of October 19, but at 6 A.M., he was awakened by an aide and told there was the sound of heavy firing coming from the direction of Cedar Creek. Sheridan temporarily convinced himself it was only a reconnaissance and went back to bed. But the firing gnawed at him and by 9 A.M., he was on the road with his staff and a 300-man cavalry escort heading for Cedar Creek.[144]

Lt. Col. Tracy remembered later:

At length a solitary horseman is seen at the head of that dust-cloud, like a comet at the head of its trail. He is riding as though life depended upon the speed of his horse. And now he leaves the turnpike, but does not slacken his speed. The horse is washed clean by his own sweat. He is heading directly to where I am sitting on my horse. I am filled with anxiety and hope. Am I awake? Do I see aright? I rub my eyes to clear them. By all that's good, it's Sheridan. Phil Sheridan, who we all supposed was in Washington, while his army was being cut to pieces? [145]

As Sheridan rode up, Tracy took off his hat and saluted and said, "By God, I am glad to see you, General."

Sheridan replied, "By God, I am glad to be here." Then he glanced along the line and roared, "What troops are these?"

"The Vermont Brigade, 2nd Division, 6th Corps," Tracy replied while simultaneously several hundred Vermonters yelled "Vermont Brigade! Vermont Brigade!"

"I thought so," Sheridan shouted, "We're all right; we'll whip Early now before night." Then he rode through the line telling the men, "We'll have our old camps to-night, boys," and like a whirlwind, off he dashed to the right.

Tracy continued:

Cheers telegraphed to us his progress along the line, and in our hearts echoed and re-echoed his words, "We are all right": we felt it; we knew it! We felt that his words were prophetic, no more downcast looks, no more faint hearts, no more doubts as to the final result. We knew that there was to be hard fighting, and that many of our number would be mustered out. But what of that? Defeat was worse than death! not a Vermonter in that whole line but was willing to take his chance. We all felt, yes, all knew the day would end in victory for the Army of the Shenandoah, and that was sufficient for us.[146]

It was now about noon, and Sheridan spent the next hour riding through the army checking on positions and inspiring the troops. With Sheridan again at the head of the army, Wright, Getty, and Grant returned to their respective commands. Custer's cavalry moved from the left around the back of the army and repositioned on the right, or west, flank. About 1 P.M., Sheridan saw the enemy line advance and thought it was the attack he had been anticipating. The Vermont Brigade was hastily taken through the woods to the rear of the Nineteenth Corps to help repel the enemy probe, but by the time it arrived, the rebels had been beaten back. The Vermont Brigade then moved to a spot where it was concealed from the enemy's view but from which it could quickly return to its old position if needed. For the next several hours, the Army of the Shenandoah stayed in position and waited. Maj. Walker wrote that "In ten minutes half the men, with genuine soldier nonchalance, were fast asleep."[147]

While the Vermont Brigade lay hidden in the woods, the 2nd and 3rd regiments were sent out on the skirmish line. Shortly after the two regiments went forward, Lt. Col. Tracy received an order relieving him from command of the brigade and assigning him command of the skirmish line. Tracy later wrote in his recollections:

I found that the Rebel skirmishers and sharpshooters were trying to drive back the 2nd Regiment, but that was a little too big a job for the force that had been sent to do it. The skirmishers of the 2nd were under cover of a stone wall, and were making it hot for any gray-back that showed his head. I rode up to the reserve force (the 3rd Vermont), Capt. Kennedy ... was in command. I said to him, "Where is Col. Floyd?" "I don't know where he is. Have not seen him since we fell back. I am in command." At that moment a ball passed close to my head, "You had better dismount," said the Captain, "That ball was meant for you." I made no reply to this, but asked him what connection our line had on the left. He did not know of any. Of course that would not do. Another ball at that instant grazed my hat. "I tell you, Colonel, they mean you. Those sharpshooters in that point of woods are shooting close; they have hit several of my men who have ventured to show their heads above that wall." Now I must know whether my left was thrown into the air or not. In order to do this it was necessary for me to ride in plain sight and easy range of a point of woods that concealed the Rebel marksmen, for about forty rods, but I must know how it was. That forty rods was level or nearly so; beyond was a short, steep hill. Now if I was not hit before I reached that hill, I would be at least partly under cover from their fire.

I found, on reaching the left of my line, that a New York Regiment of the 1st Division had made connection with my left, so that was safe. Now to get back to my reserve (the 3rd Vermont) I had two ways. One was to take the same road and chances that I had just done; I did not like that at all. The other way was by going a little to the rear, through the point of a piece of woods on the north side of the road, down the hill through a depression in the open field and reach the reserve from the rear, with only a few rods exposed to the sharpshooters. I determined on this route in going back. The Rebels had now plenty of cannon, and were throwing their shot and shell in all directions where they thought there might possibly be a Yankee soldier, apparently without any regard to the cost of the compliments bestowed upon us so freely. I had passed through the wooded point, and was about to commence the descent of the hill, but in casting my eyes in the direction of the enemy. I could see them just beyond the hill. In the rear of their skirmishers a heavy line of battle was forming.

I dismounted ... put my field-glass to my eyes to see what their strength and object was, when a shell exploded a short distance to my left, a piece striking me in the hip.

For the third time, Tracy was wounded in the left leg. The shell fragment made a deep gash on the outside of his hip. Within a week, he was back home again recuperating.

He would not rejoin the regiment until the following February. Years later Tracy would be awarded the Medal of Honor for his courage and leadership during this battle. In his absence, Maj. Enoch E. Johnson commanded the 2nd Vermont.[148]

In his plan for a counterattack, Sheridan ordered the Sixth and Nineteenth Corps to swing in toward the turnpike. On the left or east side of the turnpike, the decimated Eighth Corps served as reserve. Union cavalry anchored both flanks.[149]

By the time Sheridan had all his units in place and had rounded up as many stragglers as he could find, it was nearly 4 P.M. Then the few guns that remained in Federal hands opened up, and the Union lines moved forward. Getty's Division was hurled against Ramseur's division ensconced behind a series of stone walls and in and around Miller's mill and the surrounding outbuildings one-half mile north of Middletown.[150]

French's brigade on the Vermonters' left crossed a long open field and into heavy fire from the rebels behind a stone wall. Under orders to move slowly as the pivot of the army, the brigade staggered and fell back to its starting place. Warner's troops on the right disappeared over the crest of a hill. The 11th Vermont was forced to halt behind a low stone wall to cover the brigade and opened fire on the rebels. The only way forward was along a narrow road by the side of a little millpond.[151]

Seeing the Green Mountain Boys refusing to fall back, French's brigade soon rallied and charged. When they were nearly abreast of the Vermont Brigade, the Vermonters joined the charge, and both brigades rushed toward the mill. Ramseur withdrew his men several hundred yards to another stone wall. The Vermonters quickly filled the buildings vacated by the Confederate troops. Those who could not get protection from the buildings hid behind haystacks, trees, and stone walls. Then, along with French's brigade, the Vermonters started firing into the rebel ranks. Grant was still unable to see any friendly troops on his right and sent several officers to investigate. What they found was another battle line of rebels. Grant decided to stay put and try to hold what ground he had gained.[152]

The enemy fire for the next half-hour was so severe that the Vermonters could not even carry off their wounded or send for more ammunition. Around 5 P.M., the Confederate right started to crumble. Then Gen. Ramseur was mortally wounded, and his division collapsed. Seeing it had the advantage, the entire Federal line started to charge. Maj. Walker wrote:

> The enemy faced our advance but for a moment and then fled in confusion; we pursued faster and faster, only stopping to hastily fill our cartridge-boxes with captured ammunition; the retreat became a stampede, the pursuit became a reckless chase, and with tumultuous cheers and throbbing hearts we crowded the motley mob before us, on and on over the miles of hill and plain to the banks of Cedar Creek.[153]

One of the men in the 2nd Vermont to get hit in this charge was Pvt. Francis S. Martin of Co. F. Martin, a 31-year-old substitute from Randolph, was struck two inches above the ankle of his left leg. Because the bones were so badly broken, his leg was amputated several days later. He

Photograph from Dr. Henry L. Janes's journal of Private Francis Martin, Company F exhibiting the healed stump of his amputated left leg. University of Vermont.

was not discharged from the hospital until August 25, 1865. He returned home on a wooden leg and went back to farming. On October 13, 1865, while digging a hole in which to move a large boulder, he was crushed to death when the boulder rolled over on him.[154]

Sheridan's infantry was halted at Cedar Creek, but his cavalry continued to chase Early's shattered army beyond Strasburg to Fisher's Hill. In the counterattack, the Federals recaptured all of their artillery lost in the early morning plus most of the enemy's artillery and trains. The Army of the Shenandoah then went back to its ravaged camps that had been abandoned at daybreak. Thus ended the Battle of Cedar Creek.[155]

The Federal loss had been heavy. Sheridan had lost 644 men killed, 3,430 wounded and 1,591 missing. The 2nd Vermont's losses was four men killed, 33 wounded, six of whom would die later, and three missing. The Confederate loss was roughly 320 men killed, 1,540 wounded and 1,050 missing.[156]

CHAPTER 13

THE END IN SIGHT

For two days after the battle of Cedar Creek, the Army of the Shenandoah remained on the field burying the dead and policing up arms and equipment. On October 21, Getty's division moved to Strasburg and established picket posts as far out as Fisher's Hill. Here the Vermont Brigade remained for two weeks.[1]

Voting in the presidential election took place in the Vermont Brigade's camps on November 8. Because of the number of veterans remaining, the majority of 2nd and 4th regiment's votes were cast for their old commander George B. McClellan. But as a whole, the majority of the brigade voted for Lincoln.[2]

The day after the election, Sheridan began to move his army to Kernstown. The railroad that ran from Harpers Ferry to Stephenson's Depot, six miles from Winchester, had been repaired and Stephenson's Depot became the army's new base of supply.[3]

The Vermont Brigade marched with the army from Strasburg November 9, to Newtown, and then to the Kernstown-Bartonsville area on November 10. Thinking that Sheridan's movement indicated the detachment of troops to Petersburg, Early followed him. On November 11, Sheridan prepared for battle, but only the cavalry was engaged. Both Rosser and McCausland were defeated and Early withdrew. Although Jubal Early's army remained in the Valley, it no longer posed a threat, and over a period of several months, Lee siphoned off most of Early's units for use at Petersburg. On March 30 of the next year, Gen. Lee ordered Early to go home and sit out the rest of the war.[4]

The Sixth Corps remained in camp south of Kernstown for a month. The troops settled into a garrison routine with formal guard mounts and brigade dress parades in the evenings. The men busied themselves with building comfortable quarters. The paymaster made his rounds, and the sutlers rejoined the army with their endless supply of goodies. Thanksgiving Day, November 24, brought barrels of turkeys and mince pies from Vermont for the boys to feast on. The weather was fine, the sick lists were short; generally the Green Mountain Boys enjoyed themselves in their new camp, which they named Camp Russell.[5]

The easy life at Kernstown came to an abrupt halt when Lt. Gen. Grant ordered the Sixth Corps back to Petersburg. The units left piecemeal, with Getty's division leaving last. On December 9, the Vermont Brigade broke camp and marched to Stephenson's Depot. The men stacked arms, and as usual the train was not ready and they had to wait. Finally, at noon, everyone was loaded aboard open flat cars, but again for some reason, the train was not ready; and during the hour wait, the men grew bored. To entertain themselves, a number of the Vermonters got off the rail cars and mobbed a nearby sutler's tent and stole his goods. They were about to raid another when Lt. Col. Foster came along and broke up the fun, and the men got back on the cars.[6]

At 3 P.M. the whistle blew and the train began to lumber down the track. It reached Harpers Ferry just at dark, when it began to snow. The trip became the most miserable the Vermonters experienced in their time in the army. Lt. Charles Morey recorded the dreadful affair in his diary: "We were on open cars, 5 of us put a wool blanket over our heads and sat up all night but the suffering was very severe and many froze their feet." By the time they reached Washington around 5 P.M., there were eight inches of snow on the ground. The men were half frozen and covered with coal dust, mud, and soot. Instead of getting a hot meal and a place to thaw out as the men had hoped, they were immediately marched to the Potomac River where they boarded the steamer *Massachusetts* for the final leg of their journey. The brigade reached City Point at noon on December 12. Here the men boarded a train on the U.S. Military Railroad and rode to Parke Station, where they camped in the woods for the night. The next day the brigade moved to the east side of Squirrel Level Road, where the Sixth Corps relieved the Second Corps which moved farther to the Union left. The Sixth Corps occupied about two miles of the Federal works extending west from the Weldon Railroad to within three miles of the South Side Railroad. This portion of the line faced to the northeast toward Petersburg. To the left of the Sixth Corps, the Union lines bent to the south, almost at a right angle, extending southwest for three miles parallel with the Confederate lines.[7]

During the Sixth Corps's absence, many changes had taken place around Petersburg. For months Lee and Grant had been lengthening their lines, and by the end of the winter, they extended them for more than 35 miles. They began north of the James River at White Oak Swamp and curved and twisted for eight miles to the north bank of the James River. Along the river itself, there was a four-mile stretch where Confederate artillery, at Drury's Bluff along the southern shore, barred the river approach to Richmond. Then the trenches began again, running for five miles across Bermuda Hundred to the Appomattox River. At Petersburg, they followed the battle lines that had been fixed the previous June and led south and west almost to Hatcher's Run. The Confederate works were virtually impregnable by a frontal assault. They consisted of an outer line of earthworks connected by breastworks reverted with logs with deep ditches in front. The front of the works was covered with lines of abatis and other obstructions. Forts for artillery were built at frequent intervals to sweep the approaches with a crossfire, and rifle pits protected the picket lines in front. Inside the main works was a second line of forts and redans, connected by breastworks, surrounding Petersburg in a line from one to two miles from the city. The winter had been particularly severe and the trenches and bombproofs that protected the soldiers were cold, wet, muddy, and miserable.[8]

After the failure of the attack at the Crater on July 30 and several other efforts to carry Petersburg by direct assault had been abandoned, Grant decided that he had no other choice but to lay siege to Petersburg. To supply the Union troops manning the ever-expanding trenches, Grant built a military railroad that passed along the rear of the Union lines.[9]

The Vermont Brigade manned the portion of the works between Forts Tracy and Urmston. The regiments were stationed from right to left in the following order: 2nd, 11th, 5th, 6th, 3rd, and 4th. A picket line was established about half a mile in front and close to the rebel pickets. The Vermonters faced a part of Gen. A. P. Hill's Corps.[10]

The Green Mountain Boys quickly made themselves comfortable by building warm huts of split logs. Their camps were located between the trenches and Patrick Station on the military railroad. Details for picket duty were large, and because of the unusually cold winter weather, duty on the picket lines was severe.[11]

On February 6, the Fifth Corps extended the Union lines to the left, to Hatcher's Run, after a hard fight. The left of the line of the Sixth Corps also advanced, taking the enemy's entrenchments at Fort Fisher and the signal tower on a height to the left of the Vermont Brigade. The Vermonters remained in their works to the left of Fort Tracy through February and March. By mutual consent however, there was little or no firing on the picket lines most of the time. The opposing pickets often met to trade coffee and tobacco and sometimes played cards together. This was especially true along the front of the Sixth Corps. The friendly understanding between the Confederate and Union pickets continued, and chopping parties of the two armies, cutting wood for the campfires, sometimes mingled freely. As the winter wore on, Confederate deserters came in increasing numbers. One night an entire company of 34 men from a North Carolina regiment, leaving their captain asleep at their outpost, came in and gave themselves up. One day in February, no fewer than 79 deserters crossed over to the Sixth Corps's lines; one group even brought a mule team with it.[12]

On February 7, Henry L. Franklin, who by now had worked his way up to first sergeant of Co. C, was promoted to first lieutenant. He replaced 1st Lt. Charles C. Morey, a young carpenter from Royalton, who was promoted to captain and given command of the 2nd Vermont's company E in which he had enlisted in 1861. Sixteen days later, on February 23, Franklin was in charge of a portion of the picket line near Fort Fisher. During the morning, he went out beyond the picket line with a canteen full of whiskey. Pvt. Josiah Rusherbeger of the 93rd Pennsylvania, told what happened next:

> I saw him on the enemy's side of the line, when I went out to exchange some soap for a little tobacco; and saw him walking beyond the woods near the enemy's sentinels, and thought he was a rebel officer, until he came through the woods towards our line I was quite near him, when he treated either four or five rebels. When the cork was taken out of the canteen I could smell it distinctly. I heard him tell the rebels to take a good drink; and they said it was very strong.[13]

Several hours later when the officer of the guard, Capt. Frank Baker, also of the 93rd Pennsylvania, made his rounds, he couldn't find Franklin. He went out to the picket line and asked Pvt. Rusherberger where Lt. Franklin was. Rusherberger told him there was an officer lying out between the lines drunk. Baker sent three men out to bring Franklin in, and according to Baker:

> when the men were about to take him up, some of the rebels told them to let him remain; but at last the men got him up; and when he came in I saw that it was Lt. Franklin. I asked what was the matter with him, and he replied, nothing, but I could see that he had drunk some liquor. He then went up to his post, and about an hour afterwards I went around to see where he was, and found him lying at the fire sleeping. The field officer of the day soon came around, and I told him about it and by his order I got the accused relieved.[14]

Franklin was charged with drunkenness on duty and conduct unbecoming an officer and a gentleman and was court-martialed on March 2. Although he pleaded not guilty to both charges, the court disagreed and sentenced him to be cashiered from the service, to forfeit all pay and allowances, and to be confined at hard labor for two years. Thankfully for Franklin the judge adjutant general overturned the two-year confinement portion of the sentence, and he was dismissed from the service May 18, 1865, and without ever having received a scratch in combat, returned to Vermont.[15]

On February 10, Capt. Charles Morey wrote to his mother of another incident that happened between the pickets:

> The other day one of our pickets and one of the Johnnies agreed to meet between the lines and cut down a tree for wood. Accordingly they met under the tree and concluded that the "Yank" should have the butt and the Reb the top, so they cut it down and then the Reb was not satisfied with his trade so they thought it best to settle the dispute by a fist fight but one was equally as good as the other and after fighting a while they thought it best to divide the whole tree equally so it was done and they both went off with his wood satisfied. While this was going on the pickets came out on both sides to see the sport go on and enjoyed it greatly.[16]

As the year of 1865 wore on, Confederate morale rapidly declined. Beyond doubt, it was a gloomy time behind the Confederate lines. Gen. Sherman had made his march across Georgia, capturing Atlanta and Savannah, then had turned north and captured Columbia and Charleston, S.C., and by March was in North Carolina. Sheridan, starting from the valley with 10,000 troopers, had swept around the west and north of Richmond, destroyed the James River Canal, and, after breaking up all the railroad tracks and bridges along his route, had rejoined the Army of the Potomac. Maj. Gen. George H. Thomas was organizing important offensive operations in East Tennessee. Maj. Gen. Edward R. S. Canby was moving against Mobile, Ala. Maj. Gen. John Pope was organizing a spring campaign west of the Mississippi River.[17]

It was becoming clear to both sides that the end was approaching. On March 2, Gen. Lee addressed a letter to Gen. Grant, proposing to meet him to discuss an "adjustment of the present unhappy difficulties," and a method of closing the war, by means of "military conventions." Under orders from President Lincoln, Grant declined the meeting stating that he could consider nothing less than the surrender of the Army of Northern Virginia. Nothing remained for Lee but to continue to fight. He still had 70,000 men around Richmond. If he could abandon the Confederate capital, he could possibly join Gen. Johnston. Johnson, with an army of 25,000 men, was opposing Sherman's march north. Between the two of them they might be able to slow down Sherman and prolong the war. In anxious consultations with President Davis, it was determined that as soon as the condition of the roads would permit, the Army of Northern Virginia would make a push for Danville, Va. There it would unite with Johnston attack and destroy Sherman, and then turn to confront Grant.[18]

Gen. Gordon, commanding Lee's Second Corps, came up with a plan to pull Grant's units off the right of the Confederate line to facilitate the army's move south to link with Johnston. Gordon proposed an attack on Fort Stedman. Then three special teams were to attack three additional batteries behind Fort Stedman. After breaching the Federal lines, Confederate cavalry would pour through and destroy Grant's supply base at City Point and if lucky capture Grant himself.[19]

Lee approved the plan, and at 4 A.M., March 25, Gordon gave the order to advance. The predawn attack was successful, and the Confederates penetrated the Federal lines and took Fort Stedman from the rear. Shortly afterward they captured Batteries No. XI and XII, but here the Confederates started losing momentum. Many of the starving rebel soldiers stopped to plunder the captured Federal bombproofs, and the troops who continued the advance ran into the Ninth Corps reserve. As the attack ground to a halt the Confederates were caught in a crossfire from the Federal batteries on either side of the breached line. Realizing the attack had stalled, Gordon withdrew, leaving almost 2,000 of his men in the hands of the Ninth Corps. By 8:30 A.M. it was all over.[20]

Assuming Lee had weakened his right by pulling enough troops to make the attack on Fort Stedman, Grant attacked that afternoon.

The firing at Fort Stedman had aroused the troops all along the Federal line. The Vermont Brigade, seven miles to the left of Fort Stedman, stood in formation, ready to repel an attack. When word came that the Ninth Corps had reestablished its line, the men stacked arms but remained in line. Around noon, orders came to be ready to move. Tents were quickly struck and knapsacks packed. At about 3 P.M., the picket line of the Third Division of the Sixth Corps advanced against the opposing picket line, nearly a mile long. The Union skirmishers met heavy fire from the rebel rifle pits in front and from the Confederate artillery in forts and batteries farther back. They reached the enemy's riflepits at several points, but the attack failed, and the division retreated. Next, Gen. Getty was directed to attack with his division, supported by Keifer's brigade of the Third Division. Getty's command filed out of the works and formed rapidly in front and to the left of Fort Fisher. The Vermont Brigade formed the left of the Second Division line arrayed in three lines of battle. The first line consisted of the 2nd and 6th regiments, the second line of the 11th regiment and the third line of the 3rd, 4th, and 5th regiments.[21]

At 4 P.M., the signal to advance came, and the lines moved forward. The enemy's artillery increased in intensity and the fire from Maj. Gen. Cadmus M. Wilcox's picket line in front doubled, but dashing forward with a cheer, the Vermont Brigade swept over the breastworks, planted its colors in the enemy trenches and captured most of the enemy's pickets. Just as the 2nd Vermont started in the charge, Company A's 1st Sgt. Burr T. Cole, from Shaftsbury, crumpled to the ground. His men thought he was dead, but this was Cole's lucky day. The bullet had struck his belt plat and knocked him out. Although he was out of the charge, he was up and about in a few hours.[22]

One of Cole's men, Pvt. Antoine Gravlin, a 26-year-old farmer from Underhill, was also hit during the charge. Gravlin was struck in the left hand by a minié ball which destroyed part of his knuckle. Gravlin was hospitalized for a little over a month before rejoining his unit.[23]

Twenty-five-year-old Pvt. James Kavanaugh, an Irish immigrant who had enlisted as a substitute in August 1863, was shot in the right foot and had to have his big toe amputated. After the war, he settled in Tunbridge, where he died of cancer April 18, 1908.[24]

George L. Lawrence, a private in Co. D from Berlin, Vt., received an excruciating wound when a rebel minié ball mangled the middle finger of his left hand. What was left of the finger was amputated in the hospital. Lawrence received a disability discharge on July 19.[25]

The rest of the division was just as successful as the Vermonters, and ensconced in their new position, the Yankees hunkered down behind the captured breastworks to obtain cover from the enemy's artillery.[26]

Private George L. Lawrence, Company D, displaying his missing middle finger to the U.S. Pension Bureau. National Archives.

The 2nd Vermont, with a company of the 11th Vermont, pushed on down Church Road another quarter of a mile to the Jones House, but since the rest of the brigade had halted at the breastworks, Lt. Col. Tracy brought his men back to cover. The enemy's sharpshooters soon afterward occupied the Jones House. Tracy sent companies D, H, and F of the 2nd Vermont forward under the command of Capt. Ward B. Hurlburt, the commander of Co. D from Weybridge. They drove out the Confederates and burned the house. "It was just getting dusk when we saw some figures moving stealthily about the house," one Confederate soldier wrote later "We opened fire, but were unable to drive them away. Presently a bright flame shot up, then another. In a few minutes the house was one huge flame of fire, lighting up the fields for a great distance around." The next morning Wilcox sent an official protest through the lines demanding Wright investigate this act of vandalism. When the necessity of burning the house was explained to Wright, he dropped the matter.[27]

Gen. A. P. Hill made several counterattacks in an attempt to regain the captured works, but was repulsed each time. Grant's Second Corps carried about half a mile of rifle pits on the left of those taken by Getty.[28]

Of the 905 Confederate soldiers taken in the rifle pits that afternoon, 547, a large share of whom surrendered to the Vermonters, were captured by Getty's division. In this advance the Vermont Brigade lost four men killed and 33 wounded. Of that total, the 2nd Vermont lost two men killed and eight wounded.[29]

Although it is difficult to determine the exact amount of Lee's casualties, he probably lost as many as 1,600 men. Wright's casualties numbered 479, with Getty's division losing 280 of that number. The Second Corps lost a total of 690, and the Ninth Corps about 1,000.[30]

During the attack, Brig. Gen. Lewis Grant thought he saw an opening in the enemy's works, but due to the exploding artillery shells and the black powder smoke, he could not be sure. The next morning he went back to the outer works to examine the rebel position again. Sure enough there was an opening a little to the right of Fort Welch. A ravine carrying one of the minor tributaries of Arthur's Swamp split the Confederate fortifications opposite Fort Welch. It was between 50 to 60 feet wide where it passed through the rebel works, but broadened into a flat marsh as it approached the Union picket line. It was evident that in the construction of the fortification the Confederates did not think it necessary to build fortifications across the ravine, which was swampy and filled with trees which during the winter had been cut, leaving behind a tangled carpet of stumps. A little to the right of the ravine the abatis had been cut away for wagons to pass in and out and had never been closed. Lewis Grant remembered, "It seemed quite certain to me that this was a weak point in the enemy's lines and that a column could be sent through them before any considerable force could be rallied to oppose it."[31]

Grant mentioned the opening to Gen. Getty, who went out and took a look for himself. Gens. Wright and Meade also came out and took a look and decided to have the Sixth Corps's Second Division exploit the weak spot, but in the meantime, another major push on the Federal left flank was being developed, and the attack was deferred for a few days.[32]

On March 26, strict orders were issued to the Union pickets to stay alert, and no sleep was permitted in the picket reserve camp. With the advance of the day before, the Yankees inherited a stand of trees that had survived the winter between the picket lines. The ax-wielding troops descended on the trees early in the morning and started stripping the expanse between Wright's Sixth Corps and the rebel lines. During the day, the rebels raised a flag of truce in front of Getty's division, requesting and receiving permission to recover the bodies of several officers killed the day before. Even though he consented to the rebels' request, Wright suspected that they would try to reclaim their picket line lost the previous day. That evening he issued orders for the entire Sixth Corps to be under arms the next morning at 4 A.M. and to remain on the alert until an hour after daylight. He also directed two regiments from each division to reinforce their picket post at 4 A.M., the hour the Confederates would likely attack.[33]

While the Federal troops were cutting timber, Gen. Lee held a council of war and decided that the portion of the captured picket line crossing a knoll called McIlwaine's Hill had to be recaptured to prevent Union artillery pounding key portions of the Confederate defenses. Wright's suspicions were well founded. At about 6 P.M. Confederate troops from Wilcox's division hit Getty's Third Brigade, commanded by Col. Thomas W. Hyde, and the Vermont Brigade. The Confederates scattered Hyde's and Lewis Grant's pickets. Hyde's brigade, near the crest of McIlwaine's Hill, took the initial brunt of the assault, which quickly spread to the Vermont Brigade on its left. Just after the Confederate attack started, the regiments that Wright had ordered to reinforce the picket line arrived. Not knowing the intentions of the newly arriving troops, the Confederate assault ground to a halt. In this short-lived action, the rebels captured four men of the 4th Vermont and 22 of the 11th. A total of 23 Green Mountain Boys, five of whom were in the 2nd Vermont, were wounded in this affair.[34]

Lt. Gen. Grant launched his final campaign against Petersburg early in the morning of March 29. Maj. Gen. Phil Sheridan was ordered to move his cavalry corps to Dinwiddie Court House on the extreme Federal left. If the Confederates left their fortifications to attack him, he was to use his entire force to defeat them. If they did not attack, he was ordered to destroy the Richmond and Danville Railroad and the South Side Railroad.[35]

On March 31, Sheridan clashed with Pickett's infantry division and Confederate cavalry at Dinwiddie Court House, with Pickett gaining the upper hand. The next day, the two forces battled again at a strategic crossroads called Five Forks. Five Forks was crucial to Lee's ability to hold his last supply line into Petersburg—the South Side Railroad. Sheridan saw the opportunity to cut off and capture Pickett's division, but he would need infantry. First he asked Lt. Gen. Grant for the Sixth Corps, but Grant informed him he was holding it for an attack on the weak spot in the Confederate line. So, Sheridan took the Fifth Corps, and with that and his cavalry, at 4 P.M. on April 1, he attacked the Confederate forces at Five Forks. Pickett was routed, losing a number of his guns and about half of his forces captured. The rest of his command, cut off from Petersburg, fled to the west, pursued until nightfall by the Union forces, but slipped away in the darkness. Lee's last supply line had been cut.[36]

With Sheridan's success on the Union left, Lt. Gen. Grant was ready to attempt to crack the Confederate line. Four A.M. on April 2 was chosen as the time to launch the assault. The Sixth Corps was to lead the attack in a wedge-shaped formation with the Ninth Corps on the right and the Fifth and Second Corps on the left. Gen. Wright was eager to exploit the weak spot that Brig Gen. Lewis Grant had discovered, and promised Meade that he "would make the fur fly" when he received the word to attack.[37]

Gen. Wright selected Getty's Second Division for the assaulting column and Getty selected the Vermont Brigade as the point of the spear that would pierce the Confederate line.[38]

The Sixth Corps occupied the lines just east of Fort Wadsworth on the Petersburg Railroad to Fort Sampson, near Peeble's Farm, a front of more than two miles. The portion of the enemy's line to be breached was an area between the left of the corps at a latitude of Forts Cummings and Sampson and the ruins of the Jones House on Church Road. The Vermont Brigade was to penetrate the Confederate line up the ravine that Brig. Gen. Grant had found. The Confederate line at that point was held by Brig. Gen. James H. Lane's brigade of Wilcox's division of A. P. Hill's corps.[39]

Lewis Grant received his attack orders about 5 P.M. on April 1. He went out again and examined the weak spot in the enemy's works and selected the position for his brigade to await the attack. Returning to the brigade, he called together all of his regimental and company commanders and explained what was expected of them. Then breaking with normal military procedures and taking a chance that security might be violated, he instructed that each company be formed and the men fully informed of the details of the attack.[40]

Brig. Gen. Grant stated later:

> Officers and men received the information and accepted the responsibility with evident satisfaction. All seemed glad of the opportunity of thus bringing the war to a speedy end. All knew that bloody work was before us, and that some would fall, yet there was activity and hilarity in camp.[41]

Moving silently, the Vermont Brigade left camp at midnight and worked its way over the breastworks to the right of Fort Welch and through openings that had been made in their abatis. The men were ordered to leave their knapsacks behind, and to preclude any accidental firing, they were not to cap their muskets. A heavy mist and the moonless night made the short trek difficult. As soon as the brigade was in position, Lewis Grant ordered his command to hug the ground and maintain silence until the order was given to advance. The men, shrouded in clouds of acrid artillery smoke, did as ordered and lay shivering on the cold damp ground waiting for daybreak. The other two brigades of the division followed and took position on the right of Grant. Seymour's division was in support to the left and rear of the Vermont Brigade.[42]

The Vermont Brigade was formed in a column with the 5th Vermont leading, followed by the 2nd, 6th, 4th, and 3rd Vermont regiments and then the two battalions of 11th Vermont. The 5th Vermont was to pass through the ravine and remain as a rallying point for the rest of the brigade. The 2nd Vermont was to follow the 5th and then bear right at the Confederate lines, and capture the artillery battery known to be just northeast of the ravine. The 6th Vermont had orders to move left of the ravine at the Confederate line and attack the batteries in that direction. The 4th and 3rd regiments were to move left and right respectively from their positions. The 11th Vermont was to bring up the rear and act as supports for the brigade as needed. Pioneers, armed with axes, were to lead the way to cut through the rebel abatis. Artillerymen with rammers and primers were with the Green Mountain Boys to man captured cannons. The regiments of the brigade were directed not to stop after gaining the enemy's works, but to proceed to the crest of a hill just beyond the works to stop any rebel counterattack. Strict orders were issued to all of the troops not to fire during the charge, and once on the crest beyond the enemy works, they were to halt, reform and await further orders.[43]

About 2 A.M., while some of the other brigades were moving into position, an order was mistakenly given for the pickets to open fire. This brought a violent return of fire from the rebels. A number of the Vermonters were killed or wounded before the firing was halted. Brig. Gen. Grant was one of the first men hit. While he lay on his stomach with his staff in the rear of the brigade, a rebel minié ball ricocheted off the left side of his head, leaving a nasty gash and temporarily stunning him. He was quickly carried to the rear for treatment. Lt. Col. Tracy assumed command of the brigade in his absence. In the 2nd Vermont's Co. G, Pvt. Baptise Lessor, a French-Canadian farmer from Pawlet, Vt., was shot in the right shoulder. The ball entered just above his collarbone, traveled through the shoulder and exited from his armpit. After the wound healed he was unable to close his right hand. He was discharged June 2, 1865, with a disability.[44]

The Sixth Corps officers finally got their men to stop firing and the Yankees yelled across the lines, "April Fool,

Johnnies," in an attempt to cover up their mistake. The Confederates also stopped firing, and the men of the Sixth Corps continued to wait for the signal to advance. The only sound breaking the silence was the Ninth Corps artillery firing to their distant right.[45]

At 4 A.M., the time for the assault, it was still too dark for the men to see, and the advance was delayed for half an hour. Finally the signal gun in Fort Fisher fired, but because of the noise of the Ninth Corps artillery, no one was sure it was the signal. Within 10 minutes, however, Lt. Col. Tracy learned that the signal had been fired and promptly gave the order to advance. The Green Mountain Boys sprang to their feet and started forward. The brigades on right and left started as soon as the Vermont Brigade got under way. The other two divisions of the Sixth Corps, farther back, followed, together forming a wedge of 14,000 men. Steadily and silently the columns moved toward the rebel trenches. "For several moments nothing was heard but the tramp and rustle of the advancing columns," wrote Maj. Gen. Getty, "but just as the enemy's picket-line was gained the silence was broken by a scattering volley." Since the element of surprise was now lost, the Sixth Corps let out a cheer and pushed on toward the trenches. The enemy artillery also opened up and rained canister balls into the charging column. The wall of lead and steel halted the Vermonters for a moment, but only for a moment. Realizing their best defense lay in the charge, and cheered on by their officers, the men started forward again. With Sgt. Thomas H. McCauley of the 2nd Vermont's Co. F, who was serving as the brigade color bearer in the lead, the Vermont Brigade charged into the ravine.[46]

In those few minutes of the charge, the 2nd Vermont incurred most of the casualties it would receive in this battle. Pvt. William W. Noyes of Co. F, the soldier who had won the Medal of Honor at Spotsylvania, was struck in the right leg just above the ankle. The bullet took a good portion of the calf muscle, leaving the ankle stiff. He was not released from the hospital until October 21, 1865, about three months after his regiment had mustered out of service. On July 1, 1910, Noyes was working on the roof of a house in Montpelier and fell off. He fractured his skull and died the same day. He rests today in the Cutler Cemetery in East Montpelier.[47]

Company A took three casualties at about the same time. Pvt. Norman H. Ryan, a 19-year-old lad from Stamford, was slightly wounded in the left groin. Pvt. Henry G. Seger, a German immigrant farmer also from Stamford, took a ball in the left shoulder. It went through the muscle just above the collarbone and exited from his back. His wound put him in the hospital for two months. Pvt. William W. Beals, a 23-year-old laborer from Manchester, had a rebel minié ball take off part of the little finger of his left hand and then bore into his wrist. He was discharged from the hospital July 15, 1865. By the turn of the century, Beals was so crippled by rheumatism in his hips and legs that he entered the Vermont Veteran's Home in Bennington April 23, 1902. He died October 27, 1904 and was buried at the Home's cemetery.[48]

Pvt. Horace G. Ross, of Co. B and Castleton, was killed instantly by a bullet that tore through his head. His wife Maria was awarded an $8 monthly pension in exchange for her husband's sacrifice.[49]

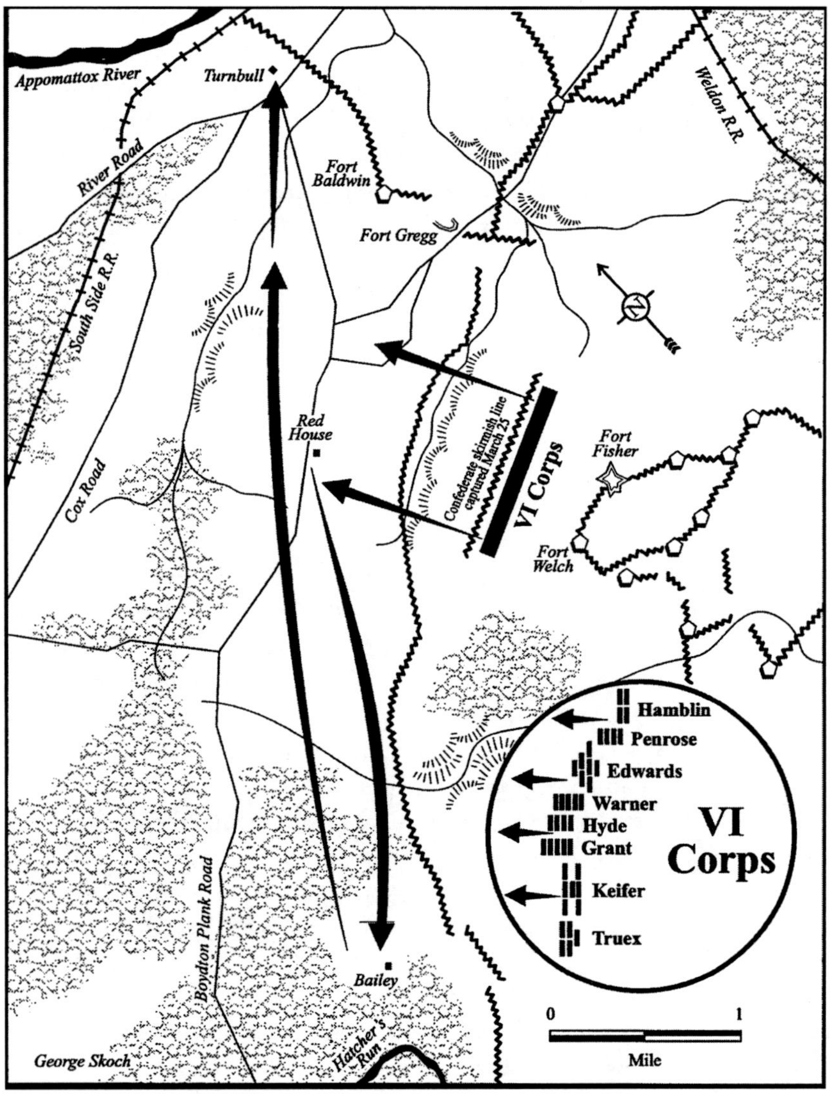

The final breakthrough at Petersburg on April 2, 1865

Pvt. Martin Hale, a Connecticut farmer from Co. H, went down with a moan. He had been slightly wounded in the left knee at Winchester, but this time he was not as lucky. He was hit by a spent ball that smacked into the right side of his head two inches above his ear. He would not be released from the hospital until the following August.[50]

Another 2nd Vermont man who did not reach the Confederate trenches was Pvt. William W. Vose of Co. K. Vose had been wounded in the right arm on May 5 in the Wilderness. The bullet had struck him several inches below the elbow and had to be dug out in the hospital. Now he had been hit again in the same arm, only this time the bullet struck him just above the elbow. Lt. Augustus A. Decelle had Vose carried back to the division hospital. Although he recovered from the wound, he never returned to the company and was discharged from the hospital May 13 with a disability.[51]

Just as the regiment started again Pvt. Joseph S. Lavake of Co. K from Burlington was knocked out of the charge by a bullet that hit him in the left groin and exited from his left buttock. He was discharged from the hospital June 8, 1865, and sent home.[52]

The Confederate abatis were brushed away like cobwebs, and the men, cheering madly, rolled over the rebel works to the right of the ravine like a blue wave. Sgt. Hoxxey C. Rogers of Co. I and Pvt. Ira Pierce of Co. F were the first two men from the 2nd Vermont to enter the enemy's works. Just behind them was the regiment's color bearer Sgt. George B. Ordway, who was the first to plant Vermont colors in enemy territory.[53]

Now operating on pure adrenaline, the Vermonters forgot to halt and reform after penetrating the enemy works as they had been ordered. Instead, they pushed on after the running Confederates, trying to kill every one of them who did not surrender, and the whole time cheering in uncontrollable excitement. The officers finally got their men to stop and reorganized their commands. Wright turned the Sixth Corps to face southwest to roll up the rest of Hill's line. The Third division formed the corps's left, aligning on the Confederate trenches, then Getty's Second Division in the center and finally the First Division with its right guiding along the Boydton Plank Road. The Second Brigade of the First Division was left behind to protect the area of the breakthrough. Just prior to moving out, Getty sent his assistant adjutant general, Lt. Col. Charles Mundee, to guide the Vermont Brigade. Unbeknownst to Getty, Mundee was drunk. When Mundee reached the Vermont Brigade, he exceeded his authority and took command from Tracy. Lt. Col. Tracy must have been surprised at his unwarranted and unexplained removal but realized now was not the time to debate the issue.[54]

Sergeant Hoxxey C. Rogers, Company I. The first man in the 2nd Vermont to penetrate the Confederate line on April 2, 1865. Vermont Historical Society.

As the Sixth Corps moved forward, the Confederates unleashed their batteries, but the Yankees could not be checked, and the rebels had to retreat. The Vermonters followed them, firing their muskets as fast as they could. The 2nd Vermont's company C, led by Capt. Elijah Wales, took one of the redoubts containing four guns. Wales turned the cannons around and within minutes was hammering the fleeing rebels with their own artillery. A group from the 6th Vermont followed Capt. Wales's lead and jumped into a redoubt containing two cannons and several of the Confederate artillerymen. The Confederates who had escaped had taken the cannon primers with them to keep the guns from being fired, but Yankee ingenuity prevailed as the Vermonters fired blanks from their muskets into the cannon's vent hole to fire them. In this manner, they got off 12 rounds before Federal artillerymen relieved them. As the 2nd and 6th Vermont's men worked the enemy's guns, the rest of the brigade continued chasing the rebels. Some of the fleet-footed gray-backs scattered into the woods and the open country in the rear of the works, but a large number were surrounded in the movement and had to surrender. The Sixth Corps did not stop until it had reached Hatcher's Run.[55]

In this grand chase, the 2nd Vermont's Corp. William L. Kinsley of Co. H, a 21-year-old farmer from Fletcher, who had just returned January 6 from recuperating from a wound in the left arm he had received at Cedar Creek, was hit just above the left eye, blinding that eye for the rest of his life. To make matters worse, Kinsley, Sgt. Orson C. Westman, also of Co. H, and another man were separated from the brigade during the charge and had to remain in enemy territory all night and did not rejoin the regiment until the next morning. Kinsley returned to his company from the hospital on May 4, but remained on light duty until he was mustered out the following July.[56]

Corp. Merritt P. Maranville, a 20-year-old, five foot seven inch farmer from Poultney, was struck in the left forearm. Maranville had been previously wounded on May 3, 1863 at Marye's Heights, May 5, 1864 in the Wilderness, and September 19, 1864 at Winchester. All were minor wounds that allowed him to return to his company. This wound, however, ended his military service. The bullet tore through his left forearm, taking about three inches of the radius with it, leaving his arm very distorted when it healed. He was discharged for disability July 27, 1865, and lived until March 12, 1917.[57]

The Sixth Corps halted about 9 A.M. to give its men a rest. During the halt Wright was informed that the Second and Fifth Corps were carrying the lines to the west, so he faced the Sixth Corps about to reverse course back on the Boydton Plank Road toward Petersburg. Brig. Gen. Robert S. Foster's division of the Twenty-Fourth Corps, which had been sent to support Wright, led the way. Its route of march lead to the rear of the spot where the Vermont Brigade had broken through the Confederate line at daybreak.[58]

While the Sixth Corps was rolling up the Confederates toward Hatcher's Run, the Confederates were trying to cobble together a counterattack to buy time until units from north of the James River could man the inner fortifications surrounding Petersburg. A small force of about 600 men from several Confederate units was formed under the command of Gen. Wilcox, and pushed back the Sixth Corps's lone brigade and recaptured a small portion of their works. Wilcox then made his stand at Forts Gregg and Whitworth and sent a skirmish line forward.[59]

As Foster's division moved up the Boydton Plank Road, it made contact with Wilcox's skirmish line, which rapidly retreated to the safety of the forts. Foster's lead units quickly pitched into the barricaded rebels. While Foster was engaged with Wilcox, Wright moved the Sixth Corps, which was on Foster's left, northward toward Petersburg. Gen. Getty's division was the first to move out, and seeing the enemy posting artillery on the Cox Road, he ordered his division forward without waiting for Wheaton, who was to join him on his left. The rebels withdrew, leaving Lt. Col. William T. Poague's Mississippi artillery battalion near the Turnbull house on Cox Road. The Turnbull house, known as "Edge Hill," had been Gen. Lee's headquarters during the previous winter and had been evacuated by him only minutes before the charge.[60]

Before reaching the Turnbull House, Wheaton caught up, and he and Getty stopped and repositioned their five brigades to establish a line from just south of Cox Road. Getty's division formed most of the Sixth Corps front opposite the Turnbull House with the Vermont Brigade deployed on the right, with Warner's men in the center, and Hyde's brigade occupying the left. Although a few shallow swales offered limited cover and the counter battery fire from Union artillery provided some relief from Poague's relentless barrage, Getty knew that standing still made little sense.[61]

The Vermont Brigade was formed in single line front with the 11th Vermont on the right, followed by the 2nd, 3rd, 5th, 6th, and the 4th on the extreme left. Several companies of the 11th Vermont were thrown forward as skirmishers. In this formation, the Vermonters rapidly moved forward. As the Green Mountain Boys neared the Turnbull house, Poague's artillerymen poured canister and shells into their left flank.[62]

As the brigade charged up the ravine toward the house, men in the 2nd Vermont started to fall. Capt. Charles Morey, who was out in front leading his company, was hit in the right shoulder by one of the cast iron canister balls; it tore through his body, taking out tissue and bone as it passed through. Capt. Ephraim Harrington, commanding Co. G, who was a few feet away, went to his friend's aid, but it was too late. Harrington wrote to Morey's father the next day:

> He lived about twenty minutes after he was hit. I stayed with him until he breathed his last. He never spoke after he was hit but he knew me about one minute. I closed his eyes and saw him carried off the field by some of the men of his own company and they buryed him with as much respect as possible.

In an attempt to ease the shock and pain of the letter, Harrington added:

> There was a Chaplain with the men when he was buryed and he made a Prayer at his grave. He is buryed where he can easly be found by any one if it is your wish to get his Body. His name written on a board and nailed on a tree by his head. I have all of his effects which I will keep untill you give me directions what to do with them. We had a very hard fight yesterday and was successful, and gained a great Victory for the Union.

Captain Morey is buried in the Poplar Grove National Cemetery on the outskirts of Petersburg.[63]

Pvt. Isaiah Piper from Braintree in Co. D had a piece of shrapnel take off the middle finger of his right hand and had another piece fracture his right collarbone while yet a third piece injured his right side. He was mustered out two months later.[64]

Corp. John S. Woodward from Holland, Vt., in Co. K, had a shell fragment hit his left hand, nearly taking off his thumb and damaging his fingers. When his hand healed, his fingers were permanently contracted over the palm of his hand. He also sustained minor wounds in his head and neck.[65]

First Sgt. Daniel B. George, of Co. F from Hardwick, was dropped by a shell fragment that ripped through his left thigh, but luckily he was well enough to be released from the hospital in July.[66]

Finally the commander of the 3rd Vermont was ordered to send some men forward on the double quick and shoot the rebel battery's horses to prevent its being removed. This daring feat was "accomplished with perfect success." In the meantime, the brigade wheeled to the left and rapidly closed on the guns. Finding it impossible to escape with his guns, the commander of the battery raised a white flag, and the firing ceased. Just as the rebel cannoneers were surrendering, a skirmish line from the First Brigade of Getty's division came up on the left, and not noticing the rebel's white flag, opened fire on the battery. The screams of the wounded rebels, mingled with the Vermonters screaming for a cease-fire, caused enough confusion that what few rebels that were not wounded made good their escape.[67]

As the enemy gunners went down, the 2nd Vermont came charging up the hill. First Sgt. Orlando S. Turner of Co. D, leading the brigade, was the first man to lay a hand on the one of the rebel cannons.[68]

After subduing the Confederate artillery at the Turnbull house, Getty's division moved on to the bank of Indiantown Creek, about a mile outside of the suburbs of Petersburg, the whole time under an enfilading fire from batteries nearer the city. Additionally, the men were being peppered by sporadic fire from Confederate sharpshooters posted in the inner defenses. A few of the sharpshooters of the 4th Vermont crossed the creek on a fallen tree, crept up the steep bank on the opposite side, and soon silenced the battery on their left. Skirmishers from other units did the same to the batteries on the right and chased off the rebel sharpshooters.[69]

The men of the Sixth Corps were by now completely worn out from the lack of sleep and the day of fighting and marching. It had also been nearly 18 hours since they had eaten. They were finally withdrawn to the safety of a ravine to the right of Cox Road, where the Vermont Brigade moved off to the left of the Nottingham house where it built hasty entrenchments and went into camp for the night. About this time, Brig. Gen. Grant returned to the brigade and in his words, "disliking the movements of an ambulance over corduroy roads, I abandoned the hospital, and went to the front." That night, as a sign of victory, Lewis Grant made his headquarters in the Turnbull house.[70]

First Sergeant Orlando S. Turner, Company D. The first man in the 2nd Vermont to reach the cannons at the Turnbull House in the Confederates' last stand at Petersburg, April 2, 1865. USAMHI.

The main lines surrounding Petersburg had finally been broken, but not without cost. The Sixth Corps lost about 1,100 men killed and wounded. The Vermont Brigade's share of the carnage was 25 men killed and 161 wounded. The 2nd Vermont's losses were seven men killed and 33 wounded, one of whom died later of his wounds. Lee's losses were not reported, but were very heavy. One of his most costly losses was Lt. Gen. A. P. Hill, who was killed in the morning by one of the Sixth Corps's skirmishers near the Boydton Plank Road close to where Getty's division had broken through the Confederate lines. The Sixth Corps alone took had captured 3,000 Confederate prisoners before 10 A.M. Lt. Gen. Grant telegraphed President Lincoln at 4 P.M. that day informing him that, "The whole captured since the army started out gunning, will not amount to less than 12,000 men and probably 50 pieces of artillery."[71]

Earlier in the morning as the Union breakthrough progressed, Gen. Lee sent a telegram to the Confederate secretary of war stating,

> I see no prospect of doing more than holding our position here until night. I am not certain I can do that. If I can I shall withdraw to-night north of the Appomattox, and, if possible, it will be better to withdraw the whole line to-night from James River. I advise that all preparations be made for leaving Richmond tonight. I will advise you later according to circumstances.

Shortly after the secretary of war received Lee's telegram, it was passed on to Confederate President Jefferson Davis, and preparations began to evacuate the government from Richmond.[72]

Shortly after the Sixth Corps forced Lee from his headquarters at the Turnbull house, he sent his last telegram informing the Confederate authorities, "It is absolutely necessary that we abandon our position tonight, or run the risk of being cut off in the morning." Lee's immediate destination was Amelia Court House located 36 miles northwest of Petersburg House on the Richmond and Danville Railroad.[73]

Under the cover of darkness Lee got his troops on the road. At 11 P.M. Jefferson Davis and his cabinet left Richmond on a train heading south. Their destination was Danville, Va. There Davis could stay in contact with both Lee's and Johnston's armies.[74]

When the Union skirmishers advanced at daybreak on April 3, the inner defense lines of Petersburg were found empty. During that day and the next, Lee continued collecting his army, still numbering between 30 and 40 thousand men, at Amelia Court House. Grant and Meade were doing their utmost to intercept him. The most logical place to cut off Lee was Burkeville Junction, where the South Side and the Richmond and Danville Railroads crossed. From Petersburg via Amelia Court House to Burkeville, which would be Lee's eventual route, was 55 miles. Grant's intended course, by way of Sutherland Station and the Namozine Road, was 36 miles. Grant had a 19-mile advantage if he could pull it off.[75]

The Army of the Potomac was on the road early on the morning of April 3. Sheridan was pushing his cavalry hard after the retreating rebels. The cavalry was followed closely by the Fifth Corps, then the Second Corps, followed by the Sixth Corps, which Getty's division was leading. The mud was deep, and there were numerous delays while waiting for other troops to get out of the way. When the column was moving, the marching was hard, but the thought that they were chasing a beaten enemy and were winding up the war exhilarated the Union soldiers, and there was virtually no straggling.[76]

Getty's division made 14 miles on April 3 and bivouacked for the night around the Mount Pleasant Church. During the day, there had been running skirmishes between the Union cavalry and the Confederate rear guard. At 4:10 P.M., Sheridan reported, "up to this hour we have taken about 1,200 prisoners mostly of A. P. Hill's corps, and all accounts report that woods filled with deserters and stragglers, principally of this corps."[77]

The next day, Tuesday, April 4, the Sixth Corps marched 12 miles nearly to Deep Creek, and bivouacked on the Featherston Farm, just behind the Second Corps. The Fifth Corps and Sheridan's cavalry were encamped at Jetersville.[78]

Lee reached Amelia Court House on April 4 and found the train carrying his badly needed rations, but when the boxcars on the siding were opened, they contained ammunition instead. Lee immediately issued a proclamation to the local populace requesting assistance, but by the next day, very little food had been procured. Lee ordered 200,000 rations to be shipped from Danville. By 1 P.M. on the afternoon of April 5, Lee had his army on the move to Jetersville, the next station on the railroad where he expected to meet his rations.[79]

Between 2:30 and 3:30 P.M. that same day, the Second Corps reached Jetersville and went into position on the left of the Fifth Corps. Wright's corps arrived around 6 P.M. and dug in on the Fifth Corps's right. The three corps were now firmly entrenched on a four-mile front awaiting the Army of Northern Virginia.[80]

Not long after leaving Amelia Court House, Lee's lead cavalry units ran into the Federals at Jetersville. Lee decided his army was in no shape to attack an entrenched enemy and decided to make a forced night march around the Union left flank that would bring him to Farmville, 23 miles away on the South Side Railroad. At Farmville he could meet the train carrying his rations and feed his starving army. Then he could head south to Keysville and follow the railroad on to Danville.[81]

Grant got his army up at 4 A.M. on April 6, and by daybreak it was on the road again chasing Lee. The Fifth Corps moved down the Richmond and Danville Railroad accompanied by the Second Corps on its left and the Sixth Corps on the right.[82]

After leaving Petersburg, the Vermonters saw signs that the Army of Northern Virginia was defeated and was disintegrating. The countryside was littered with broken wagons, ambulances, cannons with broken wheels, discarded muskets, and other such military equipment. Half-starved and exhausted Confederate soldiers were captured while bedded down in fence corners or found stumbling listlessly through the woods. The 2nd Vermont's Surgeon, Dr. Melvin Hyde wrote:

> The ground in many instances was strewn with loaded muskets which were thrown away in their hasty flight and in many instances discharged by our horses trampling upon them as we passed along—My cook was shot through the foot in this manner—In one place we passed over 90 guns, (all loaded, and laying one upon another) in going five rods—the enemy retreated in such haste that they did not stop to "fire them off."[83]

As Lee's army was struggling toward Farmville, Brig. Gen. George Custer's cavalry division charged into a gap in the column and cut off Anderson's, Ewell's, and Gordon's corps, plus the army's wagon train. Ewell sent the wagon train on a northerly route to avoid capture. Gordon, who was being pressed by the Union Second Corps, followed the wagons. While Ewell and Anderson were deciding on a strategy to extricate themselves from the situation, the Sixth Corps came up on Ewell's rear. Now began the last action of the war for the Sixth Corps—the battle of Sailor's Creek. This battle was in fact three separate battles between Ewell's corps and the Sixth Corps, Anderson's corps and Sheridan's Cavalry Corps, and Gordon's corps and the Union Second Corps.[84]

Ewell quickly formed his men on a ridge on the southwest side of Little Sailor's Creek overlooking the Hillsman Farm. Gen. Wright brought up the Sixth Corps artillery and opened up Ewell's line at 5 P.M. After a half-hour's pounding, the Federal artillery ceased, and without waiting for Getty's Second Division to catch up, Wright charged Ewell with the First and Third Divisions. Ewell's tired and hungry infantrymen gave Wright's men a volley that caused them to fall back. Then part of Ewell's line counterattacked, but were themselves forced to fall back. Wright then reformed his troops and charged the Confederates again. This time, the Sixth Corps overwhelmed Ewell and captured more than 3,000 men, including Gens. Ewell, G. W. Custis Lee (Robert E. Lee's eldest son), Seth M. Barton, Joseph Kershaw, Dudley M. DuBose, and James P. Simms. Only a little over 1,400 Confederates escaped capture. Wright lost 440 men killed and wounded. Gordon's and Anderson's losses were not as severe as Ewell's, but between them they lost over 3,000 men and were forced to retreat.[85]

By the time Ewell's corps was captured, Getty's division caught up and took the lead as the Sixth Corps pressed on after the retreating rebels. The 2nd Vermont was sent out in front of the division as skirmishers and had made about two miles when they ran into Maj. Gen. William Mahone's division. The 2nd Vermont skirmished through a piece of woods to the bank of Big Sailor's Creek. From the other side of the creek the enemy opened a sharp fire, but was soon silenced by the Green Mountain Boys.[86]

Everyone in the 2nd Vermont went unscathed in this short action except Pvt. Thomas F. Broughton. Broughton, a 25-year-old farmer from Tunbridge, was one of the unluckiest men in the regiment. He had been wounded at the first battle at Bull Run in 1861, where he had taken a rebel minié ball in his right leg just above the knee. He bound up his wound with his handkerchief and was able to keep up with his comrades on the retreat, thus avoiding capture. The wound, however, left him with varicose veins. He was so disabled that his company commander had put him on permanent detail as the company cook. Broughton was a good soldier and was allowed to reenlist in December of 1863. In October of that year, he was assigned as a cook for the regiment's hospital. On the evening of April 6, he donned the hospital knapsack with medical instruments and medicine and accompanied Assistant Surgeon Brush to the skirmish line to tend to any men who might get wounded. Fortunately, no one in the 2nd Vermont was wounded, but before Broughton and Brush could get to the rear, Broughton was hit in the right foot by a stray rebel bullet. The bullet entered his foot between the first and second toe and exited near the ankle joint, "exploding and shattering the bones of the foot." Assistant Surgeon Brush leaned over and pulled Broughton up onto his horse and took him to the division hospital. Thomas Broughton was the last man in the 2nd Vermont to be wounded in the war. He was evacuated back to a hospital in Vermont, where he remained until discharged with a 50 percent disability on September 6, 1865, five months after Lee surrendered. He returned to Tunbridge where he married Julia Diana Johnson Jan. 27, 1864. Broughton lived until October 3, 1901.[87]

This skirmish of April 6th was the last hostile action for the Sixth Corps, and the last volley fired by it appears to have been fired by the men of the 2nd Vermont.[88]

The next morning, Friday, April 7, the Sixth Corps pushed on and after a 14-mile march reached Farmville, where it crossed the Appomattox River and bivouacked. On April 8, the Vermont Brigade was detached from the corps and sent back to Farmville to guard the supply trains that were arriving with the army's rations. It remained there that day and the next.[89]

On April 9, while the Vermont Brigade guarded the railroad station at Farmville, Gen. Robert E. Lee surrendered the Army of Northern Virginia to Lt. Gen. Ulysses S. Grant at Appomattox Court House.[90]

The Vermont Brigade left Farmville on the morning of April 10 with orders to rejoin the Sixth Corps. Halfway to Appomattox Court House, Brig. Gen. L. A. Grant received word that Lee had surrendered and that the Sixth Corps was moving back. The Vermonters halted where they were and bivouacked for the night. The next day the brigade moved back to Burkeville Junction, where the Sixth Corps was concentrated. Here the Green Mountain Boys remained for 12 days while Maj. Gen. Sherman negotiated the surrender of Gen. Johnston's army near Raleigh, N.C. The seat of what remained of the Confederate government was on a railroad sidetrack at Greensboro, N.C., in a freight car which was also the residence of Jefferson Davis. On April 15, the Vermonters received the horrible news of the assassination of President Lincoln. This was a hard blow for the Vermont men considering the president's fondness for them. They mourned for him with a deep personal sorrow.[91]

The war was now over, and the troops awaited the formal proclamation. In the meantime they rejoiced that their days of fighting and hard marching were over. For most of the soldiers of the Union, that was the case, but not for the Sixth Corps.[92]

On April 23, orders came to break camp and move out. Unfortunately, the direction was south rather that north. The terms in the surrender negotiated between Sherman and Johnston did not suit the Federal administration, and U. S. Grant was sent to Raleigh with orders to terminate the existing armistice and to move at once against Johnston. Before departing on April 22, Grant had ordered Sheridan to take his cavalry and a corps of infantry and push for Greensboro as quickly as possible to cut off Johnston's escape. Sheridan, of course, selected the Sixth Corps. It was something of a damper for the men to find that they were headed for Danville, Va., instead of Washington; but in their usual style, they obeyed the order and made the best of the situation. Over the next four days, Vermonters did some of the hardest marching of their military service, making about 25 miles a day. Even though they would have rather been heading back to Vermont, the Green Mountain Boys maintained their reputation as the fastest marchers in the Sixth Corps during this four-day trek.[93]

At 9:45 A.M. on April 27, Mayor James M. Walker met Gen. Wright on the eastern outskirts of Danville and surrendered the city. During the afternoon, the Sixth Corps marched through Danville with colors flying and bands playing and camped two miles south of the city. Young Pvt. James A. Cilley, from Co. E and Royalton, expressed the mood of the Vermonters when they arrived:

> We were cursed tired when we got here and then when we got rested we had to clean up and fix up our camp and then drill and then go on picket. Our old Col. is right on his red tape now the bullets have got done flying but we think it wont last only a month or two longer. We have got a pleasant camp near the town with good water near by and a pleasant and fertile country all around us which is all right and so is everything now but the blue clothes. We all want to get on some checked pants. The boys say the time never seemed so long as it has since we got done fighting, not that we like to fight, but they say the war is done and they expect to go home soon and they don't want to wait any longer, but we cannot have our own way you know.[94]

As the men were getting their camp set up, they learned that Johnston had surrendered on April 18 and their services would not be needed. Unfortunately, the surrender did not mean a rapid return north. The Sixth Corps would remain in Danville for a month.[95]

During its stay in Danville, some of the men in the Sixth Corps's First Division rented the *Danville Register* facilities and printed their own newspaper that they named *The Sixth Corps*. Seventeen issues of this 11 × 16 inch tabloid were published at 25 cents a copy. One issue contained an order from Gen. Wright congratulating the Sixth Corps for the expeditious march that it had made to Danville. One sentence read, "In four days and four hours not less than one hundred miles have been traveled—a march almost unprecedented in this or any other war, even under the most favorable auspices." Pvt. Cilley was apparently proud of the feat. He sent several copies of *The Sixth Corps* to his father, asking him to "please keep the one that has got Genl. Wright's order congratulating the Corps."[96]

While in Danville, the Sixth Corps's principal mission was to guard the railroad between Richmond and Greensboro, N.C.; it was broken up into detachments for that purpose. The Vermont Brigade had the good luck to remain in Danville. Pvt. Cilley wrote his father about how the Southerners were accepting the surrender:

> Father you cant begin to think how these people are whipt. They cant bear to hear a word about the war. They don't say they are whipt but they are outnumbered. They say they staked everything in the war to beat the Yankees and have had a fair trial and are satisified. Will except peace on the best terms. On being asked what they think about G (I don't know how to spell it) [guerrilla] war the citizens say that every man in the South will turn out to put down such kind of outlaws. They say that there wont be any such thing started. They say every man is satisified, have got enough, are willing to go home and go to work under the best terms that they can get from the Yankees.[97]

Also during the 2nd Vermont's stay, at least one of its members learned that the days of foraging ended with Lee's surrender. On April 29 Corp. Samuel Crown, a 22-year-old laborer from Fletcher, left the picket line without orders and stole several hams and sides of bacon from the smokehouse of a Robert Wilson near Wilson's Ferry. Crown was caught with the goods in his possession, and this time his officers did not turn a blind eye to the act as they had during the past four years. Crown was charged with being AWOL and violating a standing order not to steal from the local populace and was court-martialed on May 9. His sentence for the crime is not recorded, but it must have caught the attention of the rest of the men in the regiment, since there is no record of any other such offense.[98]

Units of the Sixth Corps began leaving Danville on May 16. The Vermont Brigade left by train on May 18 and arrived the next day at Manchester, just across the James River from Richmond. Here the corps remained for four days awaiting transportation to Washington. During this time, the men were given passes to visit the city which they had for so long tried to conquer. Failing to obtain transportation for his corps to Washington, Gen. Wright decided to make the trip on foot. There was much grousing among the men that they would not be as well treated as the rebels who had been transported by the government to the points nearest to their homes; but they knew the route and knew they were going home. The Sixth Corps started from Richmond on May 24 on its last march. The trip lasted 10 days and was made in easy stages, averaging about a dozen miles a day. The weather was rainy and the mud was thick, but at least when the men went into camp in the evenings, picket duty was a thing of the past and their sleep was not disturbed by the drummer's "long roll" or the sounds of combat. The march was made by way of Hanover Court House, Fredericksburg, and Aquia Creek, and ended on June 2 in Arlington, Va. The spot assigned for the last camp of the Sixth Corps was between Munson's Hill and Ball's Crossroads. The Vermont Brigade's camp was in Arlington along the Loudon and Alexandria Railroad near Falls Church, not far from Camp Griffin. "We appear to be simply camped here without order or system," wrote Pvt. Wilbur Fisk, "just to stay till some proper disposal is made of us."[99]

The Vermont units, including the 8th and 10th Vermont Infantry Regiments and the 1st Vermont Cavalry Regiment, were reviewed in their camp on June 7 by Governor Smith and other dignitaries from Vermont. While the Sixth Corps was in Danville, the rest of the armies enjoyed a grand review in Washington on May 23–24. The Sixth Corps's moment in the sun came on June 8. The day was one of the hottest on record in Washington, and the parade and march back to camp made an experience almost as trying as the ordeals of combat. Many men staggered from the heat while passing the reviewing stand, and hundreds of others fell out from exhaustion and sunstroke, but the Vermonters took it well even though they had been reviewed the day before. They withstood the heat the best they could, and the officers and men all wore the Green Mountain Boys' badge, the evergreen sprig, in their caps.[100]

On Monday, June 19, 660 men of the five original regiments of the old brigade (168 from the 2nd Vermont, of which only 115 were present), whose three years' terms of service were to expire before October, were mustered out of service and left camp at once for home. Those who wished were allowed to take their rifles home with them, provided they allowed the government to deduct $6 from their pay, but not many took the offer, stating, "They never wanted to see one again." Several days later Lewis A. Grant, who was now a brevet major general, received orders to disband the Vermont Brigade and issued the following farewell address:

HEADQUARTERS VERMONT BRIGADE,
Second division, Sixth corps, June 24, 1865.

Officers and Soldiers of the Vermont brigade:

Our battles are over, victory is ours, and Peace smiles upon our fair land. The principles of Republicanism are established. The rights of man are vindicated, and the power of the Federal Government is settled, it is hoped, for all time. Your patriotism, your severe toils, your patient endurance of hardships, and your gallant heroism have contributed largely, to these glorious results. You are soon to visit the homes you have protected and the friends who have anxiously watched your career, and our official and social relations in the field are to cease. Having been connected with the brigade from its organization, and in command for more than two years, I cannot leave without a parting word.

Soldiers! For your good conduct, your noble bearing, your obedience to orders, and your unsurpassed gallantry in action, I thank you. The thanks of your State and a grateful nation are yours. Your record is a proud one. History records no braver deeds. Yet it is a record of blood, and many a well fought field is stained with the life blood of brave comrades. We mourn their loss, and while we cherish their memories, let us emulate their virtues.

Having successfully fought for the preservation of our common country, let us become good citizens, perpetuate its free and liberal institutions, and strive in all the arts of peace to make it, under the blessing of God, truly the wonder and admiration of the world.

L. A. GRANT,
Brevet Major General U. S. A.[101]

After the 115 men from the 2nd Vermont went home, only 197 remained present for duty. With virtually nothing to do in camp, the men found plenty of time to complain about not being able to go home. Before long this got out of hand when the 5th, 6th, 8th, and 11th Vermont regiments were mustered before the 2nd. On the same day that

Lewis Grant issued his farewell address, 1st Lt. Augustus "Duke" A. Decelle, a 20-year-old French-Canadian printer from Burlington in Co. K, wrote his mother that the veterans of the 2nd Vermont were an unhappy lot because of the men who had served the least amount of time got to go home first: "Our regiment came near rebelling as they thought injustice was done by retaining them. I tried my best to prevent trouble. Several have been arrested, charged with mutiny. My opinion is that we will be in Burlington inside of four weeks."[102]

On July 10 Lt. Duke Decell wrote:

> Happy are we to night. Orders have been received to proceed at once to make muster rolls. Am going to Washington to the War Department in the morning to procure original Muster in Rolls. We will be in old Vermont inside of two weeks. Our regiment goes to Burlington. Hope you all will be there to welcome me home from the war.[103]

The 2nd Vermont finally departed Washington on July 16 and arrived in Burlington at 6:30 A.M. on July 19 with 20 officers and 213 men. Vermont Militia cannons were fired to announce their arrival. The regiment was met at the railroad station by a committee of citizens with the Vermont Brigade's band, that had long since mustered out of service but reorganized for the occasion. At city hall, the veterans were received by Mayor Albert L. Catlin and welcomed home by Hon. George F. Edmunds in an eloquent address. Col. Tracy responded on behalf of his regiment, and then the regiment filed into city hall where the ladies of Burlington had prepared it a delicious breakfast. After breakfast the regiment marched to its quarters at the U. S. Marine Hospital, where on July 25 and 26 the men were paid for the last time, were mustered out and sent home.[104]

After the war the veterans tried to get on with their lives, but as has been illustrated by this work, that was sometimes difficult for many because of physical or mental disabilities. To memorialize what they had accomplished and to provide an association in which common tragic wartime experiences could be shared with others who understood what they had gone through, the veterans of the U.S. armies organized a fraternal order named the Grand Army of the Republic (GAR), which was similar to today's Veterans of Foreign Wars organization. Virtually every city, town, and village across the northern states had a post. Vermont had 116 GAR posts where the old veterans could meet and reminisce about the war and, as they grew older, complain about their aches and pains. It seems the Vermonters did not talk much of the war outside of their GAR meetings, according to George G. Benedict, author of *Vermont in the Civil War*. In the preface of his two volume work he complained, "As a class, it must be said, the Vermonter soldiers have not been eager to recite their deeds. This fact was noticeable during the war, especially so far as the members of the First Brigade were concerned; and their reluctance to tell their own story seems not to have lessened much as time has gone on." Of course, as time wore on and the members died off, the GAR posts eventually faded away. The following two photographs illustrate the slow and sad demise of the GAR. The first photograph, taken on a Memorial Day sometime prior to 1919, pictures the remaining members of Tunbridge, Vermont's Whitney GAR Post. In the second photograph, taken on Memorial Day 1924 at the dedication of the Tunbridge's Civil War monument, two members, Gideon Avery and Henry Hayward, are missing. Gideon Avery had died October 26, 1919, and Henry Hayward was too sick to

Second Lieutenant Augustus A. Decelle, Company K. Vermont Historical Society.

attend and died the following July. The last remaining member of the Whitney Post, George Durkee, died August 13, 1931.[105]

The last surviving member of the 2nd Vermont was Henry A. Horton of Co. A. Horton, born in Windsor, Mass., December 28, 1846, enlisted in Co. E, 31st Massachusetts Infantry on December 23, 1861, five days shy of his 15th birthday. He reenlisted in that regiment February 8, 1864. In August of that year he received a reenlistment furlough and went home. While home, he deserted the 31st and enlisted in the 2nd Vermont September 6 in Stamford, Vt. Although a deserter, Horton served honorably in the 2nd Vermont. He was slightly wounded May 5, 1864, in the battle of the Wilderness and was promoted to corporal May 15, 1865. He was honorably discharged June 19, 1865. After his discharge, he returned to Stamford, where he resided from 1865 to 1871. In 1871, he moved to North Adams, Vt., and in 1874 he married Emily Whitney. After several year's marriage, Emily died and in 1897 Horton married Ida A. Hennings and fathered four children. By 1915 Horton's second wife had died, and he moved in with one of his daughters in Troy, N.Y., where he died July 1, 1948 at the age of 101 years, six months and three days.[106]

EPILOGUE

Henry L. Franklin returned to Vermont after he was cashiered from the army on May 18, 1865. For a while he

Top: **Members of Tunbridge's Whitney GAR Post photographed on a Memorial Day prior to 1919. From left to right: Gideon H. Avery (Company D, 9th Vermont Infantry and 17th U.S. Infantry), Henry Hayward (Company E, 2nd Vermont Infantry), Charles B. Smith (Company D, 12th Vermont Infantry), Edson "Bert" B. Osborn (Company H, 2nd U.S. Sharpshooters), Charles Durkee (Company D, 9th Vermont Infantry), Elihu Tuller (Company E, 2nd Vermont Infantry), and George W. Durkee (Company D, 9th Vermont Infantry). Euclid Farnham.** ***Bottom:*** **Surviving members of Tunbridge's Whitney GAR Post photographed Memorial Day 1924. Left to right: Edson "Bert" B. Osborn, Elihu Tuller, Henry, Charles B. Smith, George W. Durkee, and Charles Durkee. The last surviving member of the Whitney Post was George Durkee who died August 13, 1931. Euclide Farnham.**

lived with his mother in Brattleboro and worked in Eugene Clark's sewing machine shop until 1886. In that year the sewing machine shop moved to Nashua, N.H. Henry followed the shop and worked in Nashua until 1869.

Sometime during 1869, Henry returned to Brattleboro, and on September 9 he married Helen Sophia Wood, the daughter of Charles and Elizabeth Knight Wood. After their marriage they lived in Brattleboro, where Henry worked as a miller in a gristmill owned by Buddington and Morris. He remained in this job for almost three years. During that time, September 7, 1870, Helen gave birth to a son who unfortunately was stillborn. Henry left the Buddington and Morris mill in 1870 and worked in several other mills until 1891. On June 30, 1877, Helen Franklin successfully delivered a baby boy, which they named Guy R. Franklin. Helen died of tuberculosis on March 8, 1879 at age 30. She was buried in Prospect Hill Cemetery in Brattleboro.

After his wife's death, Henry moved to Centreville, Vt., where he worked as a miller, but because of varicose veins in his legs caused by all the marching he had done in the army, and stomach problems, he was not able to hold a job. In the mid–1880s, after not being able to work full time, he applied for and received a government disability pension of $4 a month (later raised to $8), but it was not enough to take care of both him and his son. After leaving his job in Centerville, according to his deposition in his military pension file, Henry stated, "I became insane and remained in the Asylum [in Brattleboro] until July 1891." On August 3, 1891, Henry entered the Vermont Soldier's Home in Bennington. Who took guardianship of his son is not recorded, but it may have been his in-laws since Mr. and Mrs. Wood did not die until after the turn of the century.

Henry died in the Soldier's Home in Bennington at 8:30 P.M. on May 2, 1913, of stomach cancer. His son, by then 36 years old, brought his father's body back to Brattleboro on the train the next day. Henry was buried beside his wife and father-in-law in Prospect Hill Cemetery on May 4.

In 1999 while I was doing research at the Vermont Historical Society Library, I mistakenly ordered the diaries of a man named Horace E. Clough, whom I thought was one of the Cloughs in the 2nd Vermont. When I started reading the diaries I discovered the man was in the 3rd Vermont, but I noticed in his papers he, like Henry Franklin, had spent his remaining days in the Vermont Soldier's Home. Although I was pressed for time, I couldn't resist the temptation and quickly flipped through the 1913 diary and lo and behold, there, under May 2 was this entry, "Very warm. Went to theater with J. Sent letter to M. don't hear from her. Lt. Franklin died today age 74. Trees are leafing out." And so it is, life goes on.

APPENDIX A

ACRONYMS AND ABBREVIATIONS

Adj.—Adjutant
AWOL—Absent without leave
Brig. Gen.—Brigadier General
Bvt.—Brevet
Co.—Company
Col.—Colonel
Corp.—Corporal
Capt.—Captain
G. C. M.—General courts martial
GAR—Grand Army of the Republic
KIA—Killed in action
Lt.—Lieutenant
Lt. Col.—Lieutenant Colonel
Lt. Gen.—Lieutenant General
Maj.—Major
Maj. Gen.—Major General
MIA—Missing in action
NCO—Noncommissioned officer
N. F. R.—No further record
POW—Prisoner of war
Pvt.—Private
QM.—Quartermaster
QM. Sgt.—Quartermaster Sergeant
Sgt. Maj.—Sergeant Major
Sgt.—Sergeant
USAMHI—U.S. Army Military History Institute
V. R. C.—Veteran Reserve Corps

APPENDIX B

SECOND VERMONT VOLUNTEER INFANTRY REGIMENT ROSTER

This roster is extracted from the *Revised Roster of Vermont Volunteers and Lists of Vermonters Who Served in the Army and Navy of the United States During the War of the Rebellion*, Theodore S. Peck, Montpelier: Watchman Co., 1892, pages 30–66. Where possible information has been updated or corrected from the individual's military service records, pension, and court-martial records at the National Archives, Washington, DC.

The Second Vermont mustered into service of the United States June 20, 1861. Original Members, not veterans, mustered out of service June 29, 1864. Recruits for one year and recruits whose term of service would expire previous to October 1, 1865, mustered out of service June 19, 1865. Remaining officers and men mustered out of service July 15, 1865.

Field and Staff

Name and Rank	Residence	Date of commission	Date of Issue	Remarks
Colonels				
Whiting, Henry	St. Clair, Mich.	Jun 6, 61	Jun 6, 61	Resigned Feb 9, 63.
Walbridge, James H.	Bennington	Feb 9, 63	Feb 23, 63	Capt. Co. A; Promoted to Maj. May 21, 62; to Lt. Col. Jan 8, 63; Resigned Apr 1, 64.
Stone, Newton	Bennington	Apr 2, 64	Apr 21, 64	First Lt. Co. A; Promoted to Capt. Co. I Jan 22, 62; to Maj. Jan 8, 63; to Lt. Col. Feb 9, 63; KIA May 5, 64.
Tyler, John S.	Brattleboro	May 6, 64	May 30, 64	First Lt. Co. C; Promoted to Capt. Co. C Jan 23, 62; to Maj. Feb 9, 63; to Lt. Col. Apr 2, 64; Died May 23, 64 of wounds received May 5, 64.
Tracy, Amasa S.	Middlebury	Jun 7, 65	Jun 17, 65	First Lt. Co. K; Promoted to Capt. Co. H Jan 24, 62; to Maj. Apr 2, 64; to Lt. Col. Jun 17, 64;

				Bvt. Col. Apr 2, 65 for gallantry at Petersburg Apr 2, 65; Wounded May 3, 63 and Oct 19, 64; Mustered out as Lt. Col. Jul 15, 65.
Lieutenant Colonels				
Stannard, George J.	St. Albans	Jun 6, 61	June 6, 61	Promoted to Col. 9th Vt. May 21, 62.
Joyce, Charles H.	Northfield	May 21, 62	May 21, 62	Maj.; Resigned Jan 6, 63.
Stone, Newton	Bennington	Feb 9, 63	Feb 23, 63	See Col.
Tyler, John S.	Brattleboro	Apr 2, 64	Apr 21, 64	See Col.
Tracy, Amasa S.	Middlebury	Jun 17, 64	Jun 20, 64	See Col.
Johnson, Enoch E.	Castleton	Jun 7, 65	Jun 17, 65	Second Lt. Co. B; Promoted to First Lt. Co. B Sep 2, 61; to Capt. Co. D Jan 25, 62; to Maj. Jun 17, 64; Bvt. Lt. Col. Oct 19, 64 for gallantry in all the actions since Cold Harbor, and especially at Cedar Creek; Mustered out as Maj. Jul 15, 65.
Majors				
Joyce, Charles H.	Northfield	Jun 6, 61	Jun 6, 61	See Lt. Col.
Walbridge, James H.	Bennington	May 21, 62	May 21, 62	See Col.
Stone, Newton	Bennington	Jan 8, 63	Jan 20, 63	See Col.
Tyler, John S.	Brattleboro	Feb 9, 63	Feb 23, 63	See Col.
Tracy, Amasa S.	Middlebury	Apr 2, 64	Apr 21, 64	See Col.
Johnson, Enoch E.	Castleton	Jun 17, 64	Jun 20, 64	See Lt. Col.
Ballou, Erastus G.	Boston, Mass.	Jun 6, 65	Jun 17, 65	First Sgt. Co. I; Promoted to Sgt. Maj. Oct 14, 61; to First Lt. Co. K Jan 27, 62; to Capt. Co. K Aug 4, 62; Bvt. Maj. Aug 1, 64 for gallantry in the Wilderness and subsequent engagements; Wounded May 3, 63, Jul 10, 63, May 5, 64, and Apr 2, 65; Mustered out Capt. Co. K Jul 15, 65.
Adjutants				
Ladd, Guilford S.	Bennington	Jun 11, 61	Jun 11, 61	Resigned Jul 17 62.
Edgerton, Francis M.	Poultney	Aug 4, 62	Aug 16, 62	Sgt. Co. B; Promoted to Second Lt. Co. F Jan 25, 62; Mustered out 29 Jun 64.
Ray, Orman P.	Essex	Dec 24, 64	Jan 31, 65	Pvt. Co. G; Promoted to Sgt. Maj. Nov 1, 64; Mustered out 19 Jun 65.
Quartermasters				
Pitkin, Perley P.	Montpelier	Jun 6, 61	Jun 6, 61	Promoted to Capt. and A. Q. M., U.S. Vols. Feb 19, 62; to Lt. Col. Q. M. Aug 2 64; Resigned Nov 7, 64.
Stone, Lauriston L.	Stowe	Apr 3, 62	Apr 3, 62	Commissary Sgt.; Promoted to QM. Sgt. Jan 16, 62; Taken prisoner Oct 26, 63; Paroled Dec 10, 64; Mustered out Apr 16, 65.
Surgeons				
Ballou, Newton H.	Burlington	Jun 11, 61	Jun 11, 61	Resigned Dec 18, 62.
Sawin, William J.	Chicopee Falls	Dec 18, 62	Dec 27, 62	Transferred from 10th Mass. Inf. Regt. as Pvt. to Co. E, 3rd Vt.; Promoted to Asst. Surgeon 2nd Vt. Jun 21, 62; Taken prisoner Jun 29, 62; Paroled Jul 22, 62; Mustered out Jun 29, 64.
Hyde, Melvin J.	Isle La Mott	Aug 1, 64	Aug 23, 64	Asst. Surgeon; Mustered out Jul 15, 65.
Assistant Surgeons				
Carpenter, Benjamin W.	Burlington	Jun 11, 61	Jun 11, 61	Promoted to Surgeon 9th Vt. Jun 21, 62.
Sawin, William J.	Chicopee Falls, Mass.	Jun 21, 62	Jun 21, 62	See Surgeon.
Atwood, Augustus A.	Sharon	Sep 22, 62	Oct 7, 62	Resigned Jun 25, 63.
Noyes, Luman A.	Tunbridge	Apr 14, 63	Apr 14, 63	Resigned May 27, 63.
Hyde, Melvin J.	Isle La Mott	Sep 12, 63	Sep 12, 63	See Surgeon.
Brush, Edwin R.	Cambridge	Oct 15, 63	Oct 27, 63	Drafted; Pvt. Co. H; Mustered out 15 Jul 65.

Chaplains

Smith, Claudius B.	Brandon	Jun 6, 61	Jun 6, 61	Resigned Jul 8, 62.
Dayton, Durrell W.	Middlebury	Aug 18, 62	Aug 18, 62	Resigned Jan 6, 63; Commissioned again as Chaplain Mar 10, 63 and Oct 9, 63, but neither commission accepted.

Noncommissioned Officer Staff

Name and Rank	Residence	Date of Enlistment	Date of Muster	Remarks
Sergeants Major				
Guinan, William	Montpelier	June 6, 61	Jun 20, 61	Discharged Sep 21, 61 for wounds received Jul 21, 61.
Ballou, Erastus G.	Boston, Mass.	May 7, 61	Jun 20, 61	See Maj.
Hight, Bradbury W.	Burlington	May 20, 61	Jun 20, 61	See Second Lt. Co. C.
Prouty, Henry H.	Brattleboro	May 1, 61	Jun 20, 61	See Capt. Co. B.
Ufford, Zadock	Fairfax	May 18, 61	Jun 20, 61	Corp. Co. H; Promoted to Sgt.; to Sgt. Maj. Dec 1, 63; Reenlisted Dec 21, 63; KIA May 5, 64.
Stiles, Henry	Peru	Oct 16, 61	Oct 31, 61	Pvt. Co. A; Promoted to Corp. Jun 30, 62; to Sgt. Sep 24, 63; to Sgt. Maj. May 7, 64; Mustered out Oct 31, 64.
Ray, Orman P.	Essex	Aug 30, 62	Sep 15, 62	See Adjutant.
Fisk, Russell	Bennington	Dec 1, 63	Jan 7, 64	See Second Lt. Co. K.
Quartermaster Sergeants				
Cain, William J.	Rutland	Jun 6, 61	Jun 20, 61	Discharged Jan 12, 62 for disability.
Stone, Lauriston L.	Stowe	Jun 6, 61	Jun 20, 61	See regimental QM.
Fifield, Edson H.	Poultney	May 17, 61	Jun 20, 61	See First Lt. Co. B.
Dunham, Dennis C.	Tunbridge	May 1, 61	Jun 20, 61	See Capt. Co. E.
Fassett, Nelson	Jericho	Feb 26, 62	Apr 12, 62	See First Lt. Co. E.
Fisk, Wilbur	Tunbridge	Sep 5, 61	Sep 7, 61	Pvt. Co. E; Reenlisted Dec 21, 63; Promoted to QM. Sgt. Jul 1, 65; Mustered out Jul 15, 65.
Commissary Sergeants				
Stone, Lauriston L.	Stowe	Jun 6, 61	Jun 20, 61	See regimental QM.
Guyett, Cerel G.	Montpelier	May 7, 61	Jun 20, 61	Pvt. Co. F; Promoted to Commissary Sgt.; Reenlisted Dec 21, 63; Mustered out Jul 15, 65.
Robbins, Augustus J.	Grafton	May 7, 61	Jun 20, 61	See Second Lt. Co. B.
Hospital Stewards				
Stearns, Eli Z.	Burlington	Jun 6, 61	Jun 20, 61	Discharged Dec 10, 61 for disability.
Aubry, William	Burlington	Jun 1, 61		Discharged Jan 15, 63 for disability.
Sherry, John W.	Lowell	Jun 1, 61	Jul 16, 61	Pvt. Co. B, 3rd Vt.; Transferred to Co. H, 2nd Vt. Feb 1, 63; Promoted to Hospital Steward Feb 1, 63; Mustered out 29 Jun 64.
Merriam, Dudly C.	Westford	May 7, 61	Jun 20, 61	Pvt. Co. G; Reenlisted Dec 21, 63; Promoted to Corp.; Reduced Mar 5, 64; Promoted to Hospital Steward Aug 1, 64; Mustered out Jul 15, 65.
Principle Musician				
Remick, Charles E.	Hardwick	Jun 6, 61	Jun 20, 61	Discharged Oct 28, 62, by S. O. of War dept.
Stone, James E.	Northfield	Jun 6, 61	Jun 20, 61	See Second Lt. Co. I.
Sharpley, David T.	Burlington	May 7, 61	Jun 20, 61	Musician Co. G; Reenlisted Jan 31, 64; Promoted Principle Musician Apr 7, 64; Mustered out Jul 15, 65.

Band

Name and Rank	Residence	Date of Enlistment	Date of Muster	Remarks
Leader				
Crossett, Franklin M.	Bennington	Jun 15, 61	Jun 20, 61	Discharged Dec 19, 61 by order of War Dept.
Musicians				
Abell, Durrane O.	Bennington	Jun 15, 61	Jun 20, 61	Discharged Dec 19, 61 by order of War Dept.
Cotton, Willard S.	Bennington	Jun 15, 61	Jun 20, 61	Discharged Dec 19, 61 by order of War Dept.
Cross, Daniel H.	Bennington	Jun 15, 61	Jun 20, 61	Discharged Dec 19, 61 by order of War Dept.
Childs, Barnard F.	Wilmington	Jun 15, 61	Jun 20, 61	Discharged Dec 19, 61 by order of War Dept.
Chapman, J. Dow	Bennington	Jun 15, 61	Jun 20, 61	Discharged Dec 19, 61 by order of War Dept.
Foster, Gustavus	Whitingham	Jun 15, 61	Jun 20, 61	Discharged Dec 19, 61 by order of War Dept.
Fisk, George W.	Bennington	Jun 15, 61	Jun 20, 61	Discharged Dec 19, 61 by order of War Dept.
Holbrook, Rufus C.	Whitingham	Jun 15, 61	Jun 20, 61	Discharged Dec 19, 61 by order of War Dept.
Hutchins, Thomas A.	Bennington	Jun 15, 61	Jun 20, 61	Discharged Dec 19, 61 by order of War Dept.
Kehoe, John	Bennington	Jun 15, 61	Jun 20, 61	Discharged Dec 19, 61 by order of War Dept.
Lottridge, Joseph H.	Bennington	Jun 15, 61	Jun 20, 61	Discharged Dec 19, 61 by order of War Dept.
Monroe, Gordon	Bennington	Jun 15, 61	Jun 20, 61	Discharged Dec 19, 61 by order of War Dept.
Marsh, Chauncey R.	Bennington	Jun 15, 61	Jun 20, 61	Discharged Dec 19, 61 by order of War Dept.
Marsh, George M.	Bennington	Jun 15, 61	Jun 20, 61	Discharged Dec 19, 61 by order of War Dept.
Moon, Richard	Bennington	Jun 15, 61	Jun 20, 61	Discharged Dec 19, 61 by order of War Dept.
Norton, Edward	Bennington	Jun 15, 61	Jun 20, 61	Discharged Dec 19, 61 by order of War Dept.
Peters, Martin V.	Bennington	Jun 15, 61	Jun 20, 61	Discharged Dec 19, 61 by order of War Dept.
Puffer, Norman	Bennington	Jun 15, 61	Jun 20, 61	Discharged Dec 19, 61 by order of War Dept.
Puffer, Wales W.	Bennington	Jun 15, 61	Jun 20, 61	Discharged Dec 19, 61 by order of War Dept.
Shaw, William B.	Bennington	Jun 15, 61	Jun 20, 61	Discharged Dec 19, 61 by order of War Dept.
White, Charles	Bennington	Jun 15, 61	Jun 20, 61	Discharged Dec 19, 61 by order of War Dept.
Warren, Charles	Whitingham	Jun 15, 61	Jun 20, 61	Discharged Dec 19, 61 by order of War Dept.

Company A

Name and Rank	Residence	Date of Commission	Date of Issue	Remarks
Captains				
Walbridge, James H.	Bennington	May 16, 61	May 16, 61	See Col.
Cady, William H.	Bennington	May 21, 62	May 21, 62	Second Lt. Co. A; Promoted to First Lt. Co. A Jan 22, 62; Wounded 5 May 64; Mustered out Jun 29, 64.
Bond, William H.	Danby	Dec 24, 64	Jan 31, 65	Pvt. Co. A; Reenlisted Dec 21, 63; Promoted to Corp. Jan 16, 62; to Sgt. Nov 19, 62; to First Sgt. Aug 6, 64; to First Lt. Co. A Sep 15, 64; Wounded Aug 21, 64; Mustered out Jul 15, 65.
First Lieutenants				
Stone, Newton	Bennington	May 16, 61	May 16, 61	See Col.
Cady, William H.	Bennington	Jan 22, 62	Jan 22, 62	See Capt. Co. A.
Chase, Phillips E.	Mt. Holly	May 21, 62	May 21,62	See Capt. Co. G.
Cole, Eugene O.	Shaftsbury	Oct 17, 62	Nov 5, 62	Sgt. Co. A; Promoted to First Sgt. Sep 14, 61; to Second Lt. Co. A May 21, 62; Mustered out Jun 29, 64.
Bond, William H.	Danby	Sep 15, 64	Sep 29, 64	See Capt. Co. A.
Howard, James G.	Brattleboro	Dec 24, 64	Jan 31, 65	Pvt. Co. A; Reenlisted Dec 21, 63; Promoted to Sgt. Oct 17, 64; to First Sgt. Nov 1, 64; Wounded May 5, 64; Mustered out Jul 15, 65.

Second Lieutenants				
Cady, William H.	Bennington	May 16, 61	May 16, 61	See Capt. Co. A.
Chase, Phillips E.	Mt. Holly	Jan 24, 62	Jan 24, 62	See Capt. Co. G.
Cole, Eugene O.	Shaftsbury	May 21, 62	May 21, 62	See First Lt. Co. A.
Estes, Otis V.	Bennington	Oct 17, 62	Nov 5, 62	Sgt. Co. A; Promoted to First Sgt. May 21, 62; Wounded May 12, 64; Mustered out Jun 29, 64.
Cole, Burr T.	Shaftsbury	Jun 7, 65	Jun 17, 65	Pvt. Co. A; Promoted to Corp. Dec 1, 64; To First Sgt. Feb 7, 65; Wounded May 6, 64; Mustered out as First Sgt. Jul 21, 65.

Name and Rank	Residence	Date of Enlistment	Date of Muster	Remarks
Sergeants				
Appleton, Edward W.	Bennington	May 7, 61	Jun 20, 61	See First Lt. Co. B.
Bliss, Charles M.	Woodford	May 7, 61	Jun 20, 61	See Second Lt. Co. B.
Cole, Eugene O.	Shaftsbury	May 7, 61	Jun 20, 61	See First Lt. Co. A.
Harwood, John P.	Bennington	May 7, 61	Jun 20, 61	Transferred to V.R.C. Sep 1, 63; Discharged Jun 20, 64.
Estes, Otis V.	Bennington	May 7, 61	Jun 20, 61	See Second Lt. Co. A.
Corporals				
Robbins, Augustus J.	Grafton	May 7, 61	Jun 20, 61	See Second Lt. Co. B.
Reay, John M.	Bennington	May 7, 61	Jun 20, 61	Deserted Aug 28, 62; arrested Jun 10, 64; Deserted from arrest.
Burgess, Giles J.	Bennington	May 8, 61	Jun 20, 61	Wounded May 12, 64; Mustered out Jun 29, 64.
Wyman, Warren M.	Manchester	May 7, 61	Jun 20, 61	Wounded Dec 13, 62, May 3, 63, and May 5, 64; Mustered out Jun 29, 64.
Williams, James A. N.	Bennington	May 7, 61	Jun 20, 61	Promoted to Sgt. Jun 30, 62; Mustered out 29 Jun 64.
Secor, William	Bennington	May 7, 61	Jun 20, 61	KIA Sept 14, 62
Welch, Edwin R.	Pownal	May 8, 61	Jun 20, 61	Discharged Jul 31, 62 for disability.
Murphy, William E.	Bennington	May 7, 61	Jun 20, 61	Taken prisoner Jul 21, 61; Paroled Jan 3, 62; Wounded May 6, 64; Mustered out Jun 29, 64.
Musicians				
Gates, Horace	Shaftsbury	May 7, 61	Jun 20, 61	Discharged Mar 31, 63 for disability.
Norton, Lucius	Bennington	May 13, 61	Jun 20, 61	Mustered out Jun 29, 64.
Wagoner				
Ladd, Alfred	Dorset	May 11, 61	Jun 20, 61	Taken prisoner Jun 29, 62; Paroled Jul 22, 62; Discharged Mar 31, 63 for disability.
Privates				
Abbott, John P.	Rockingham	Jul 13, 63	Jul 13, 63	Drafted; Wounded and taken prisoner May 10, 64; escaped Feb 18, 65; Mustered out May 24, 65.
Abby, Daniel	Coventry	Jul 28, 63	Jul 28, 63	Drafted; Wounded May 5, 64; Mustered out Jul 15, 65
Adams, Everett E.	Peru	Oct 16, 61	Oct 31, 61	Deserted Aug 17, 62; returned; Discharged Nov 5, 62 for disability.
Allen, Ira	Substitute	Aug 4, 63	Aug 4, 63	Substitute for Benjamin F. Sutton, Stowe; Died May 12, 64 of wounds received May 5, 64.
Allen, James	Substitute	Sep 5, 63	Sep 5, 63	Substitute for F. E. Proctor, Brighton; Deserted Oct 10, 63.
Alsop, Joseph	Bennington	May 14, 61	Jun 20, 61	KIA May 6, 64.
Amidon, Albert	Shaftsbury	Aug 26, 62	Sep 15, 62	Promoted Corp. May 15, 65; Mustered out Jun 19, 65.
Amidon, Truman	Shaftsbury	Aug 26, 62	Sep 15, 62	Died Feb 12, 64 of disease.
Anderson, John	Substitute	Sep 5, 63	Sep 5, 63	Substitute for C. A. Ingalls, Brighton; Deserted Oct 10, 63.
Angier, Jacob B.	Substitute	Aug 12, 63	Aug 12, 63	Substitute for Ira C. Morrill, Randolph; Mustered out Jul 15, 65.

Austin, William H.	Substitute	Jul 30, 63	Jul 30, 63	Substitute for George E. Dana, Cornwall; Deserted Jul 24, 64.
Bailey, James	Substitute	Aug 7, 63	Aug 7, 63	Substitute for Marcellus Bryant, Reading; Taken prisoner May 5, 64 and died at Andersonville, Ga. Jul 11, 64.
Balch, Eliphalet E.	Shaftsbury	Aug 30, 62	Sep 15, 62	KIA Dec 13, 62.
Barnard, Benjamin S.	Peru	Oct 16, 61	Oct 31, 61	Wounded and taken prisoner Jun 29, 62; Paroled Jul 25, 62; Discharged Nov 2, 62 for wounds received Jun 29, 62.
Barrows, Waldo E.	Dorset	May 10, 61	Jun 20, 61	Promoted to Corp. Nov 19, 62; KIA May 5, 64.
Batchelder, Harlan E.	Peru	Oct 16, 61	Oct 31, 61	Mustered out Oct 31, 64.
Beals, William W.	Manchester	Dec 16, 63	Jan 5, 64	Deserted Mar 28, 64; Returned Oct 26, 64; Wounded Apr 2, 65; Mustered out Jul 15, 65.
Benjamin, George W.	Woodford	May 7, 61	Jun 20, 61	Deserted Dec 21, 62.
Blair, Enos	Substitute	Aug 1, 63	Aug 1, 63	Substitute for Albert Morse, Leicester; Taken prisoner May 21, 64 and supposed to have died while a prisoner.
Blake, Frederick H.	Bennington	May 8, 61	Jun 20, 61	Discharged Jan 4, 62 for disability.
Blowers, George E.	Arlington	Aug 14, 62	Sept 15, 62	Deserted Jul 1, 63; Returned Oct 63; Shot by sentence of G. C. M. Dec 18, 63.
Blowers, William	Arlington	Aug 14, 62	Sept 15, 62	Deserted Sep 30, 62; Returned Nov 29, 63; G. C. M. Nov 23, 63; Wounded Jun 5, 64; Deserted Sep 19, 64.
Bond, William H.	Danby	May 7, 61	Jun 20, 61	See Capt. Co. A.
Bradford, Nelson C.	Bennington	May 8, 61	Jun 20, 61	Dishonorable discharge for cowardice Jul 18, 62, by sentence of G. C. M.
Brown, Amos J.	Stamford	May 13, 61	Jun 20, 61	Discharged Mar 14, 63 for disability.
Brown, Charles N.	Stamford	Aug 30, 64	Aug 30, 64	Mustered out Jun 19, 65.
Bryant, Burton E.	Readsboro	May 13, 61	Jun 20, 61	Wounded May 4, 64; Mustered out Jun 29, 64.
Bryant, Clark R.	Peru	Oct 16, 61	Oct 31, 61	Mustered out Oct 31, 64.
Bryant, Cornelius	Substitute	Aug 7, 63	Aug 7, 63	Substitute for Henry T. Russell, Windsor; Deserted Oct 10, 63.
Bryant, Warren S.	Peru	Oct 16, 61	Oct 31, 61	Dishonorable discharge by sentence of G. C. M. Dec 7, 64 for cowardice.
Burrett, James	Essex	Aug 21, 62	Sep 15, 62	Wounded Jun 8, 64; Mustered out Jun 19, 65.
Bushey, Henry H.	Substitute	Aug 3, 63	Aug 3, 63	Substitute for Otis P. Lee, Bridport; Wounded May 5, 64; Deserted Sep 13, 64.
Camp, Jonathan	Pownal	Nov 12, 63	Nov 12, 63	KIA Aug 21, 64.
Card, Alfred	Pownal	Feb 20, 65	Feb 20, 65	Discharged Jun 13, 65 for disability.
Carpenter, Lucius	Burlington	Jun 2, 61	Jun 20, 61	KIA Apr 31, 62.
Carpenter, Samuel	Readsboro	Aug 22, 64	Aug 22, 64	KIA Mar 25, 65.
Chaffee, Ransom	Waterbury	Jul 14, 63	Jul 14, 63	Drafted; Mustered out Jul 15, 65.
Clough, Charles E.	Readsboro	Aug 16, 62	Sep 15, 62	Died Jul 9, 63 of disease.
Clough, John	Stamford	Oct 15, 61	Oct 31, 61	Died Dec 9, 61 of disease.
Clough, Marcus M.	Readsboro	Aug 16, 62	Sep 15, 62	Wounded May 12, 64; KIA Aug 21, 64.
Clough, Warren	Stamford	Aug 16, 62	Sep 15, 62	Wounded May 12, 64; Transferred to V. R. C. Nov 25, 64; Mustered out Jun 19, 65.
Cole, Burr T.	Shaftsbury	Sep 15, 64	Sep 15, 64	See Second Lt. Co. A.
Conant, Samuel G.	Stratton	Aug 30, 64	Sep 15, 64	Discharged Dec 29, 64 for wounds received May 5, 64.
Cone, Charles Jr.	Bennington	Aug 17, 62	Aug 17, 62	Wounded Oct 19, 64; Mustered out May 25, 65.
Cone, Hugh E.	Bennington	Aug 18, 62	Aug 18, 62	Mustered out Jul 15, 65.
Cooledge, Daniel F.	Ludlow	Oct 16, 61	Oct 31, 61	Wounded and taken prisoner Jun 29, 62; Paroled Jul 22, 62; Discharged Sep 16, 62 for wounds received Jun 29, 62.
Crozier, George L.	Stamford	Oct 15, 61	Oct 31, 61	Reenlisted Jan 23, 64; Promoted to Sgt. Sep 1, 64; Reduced May 15, 65; Wounded Oct 19, 64; Mustered out Jul 15, 65.
Curtice, Clark R.	Shaftsbury	Aug 26, 62	Sep 15, 62	KIA Aug 21, 64.
Davis, Curtis	Readsboro	Aug 30, 64	Aug 30, 64	Mustered out Jul 15, 65.
Davis, Laroy G.	Peru	Sep 5, 64	Sep 5, 64	Mustered out 9 Jun, 65.

Dempsey, Thomas	Bennington	May 7, 61	Jun 20, 61	Promoted to Corp. Nov 19, 62; Discharged Apr 16, 64 for wounds received May 3, 63.
Downs, Andrew J.	Bennington	May 8, 61	Jun 20, 61	Detailed to QM. Dept. to work for Col. Pitkin; Mustered Jun 29, 64.
Downs, Henry W.	Pownal	Feb 20, 65	Feb 20, 65	Joined regt. Mar 19, 65 at Petersburg; Wounded 25 Mar, 65; Mustered out May 22, 65.
Draper, Jerome	Shaftsbury	May 30, 61	Jun 20, 61	Dishonorable discharge for cowardice Jul 18, 62, by sentence G. C. M.
Dunn, Charles	Bennington	May 7, 61	Jun 20, 61	Mustered out Jun 29, 64.
Dunn, Myron	Shaftsbury	May 14, 61	Jun 20, 61	Deserted Sep 25, 63.
Edwards, Abiathar P.	Whitingham	May 10, 61	Jun 20, 61	Mustered out Jun 29, 64.
Ellsworth, Cyrus J.	Cambridge	Mar 25, 65	Mar 25, 65	Mustered out Jul 15, 65.
Ellsworth, Josephus	Underhill	Aug 31, 64	Aug 31, 64	Mustered out Jun 19, 65.
Elmer, Chester B.	Shaftsbury	Aug 18, 63	Aug 18, 63	Drafted; Wounded Jun 4, 64; Died Aug 18, 64, of wounds.
Ferguson, Myron S.	Bennington	May 7, 61	Jun 20, 61	Wounded and taken prisoner Jun 29, 62; Paroled Jul 25, 62; Transferred to V. R. C. Jul 1, 63; Discharged Nov 24, 65.
Fisk, Russell	Bennington	Dec 1, 63	Jan 7, 64	See Second Lt. Co. K.
Fox, John B.	Shaftsbury	May 7, 61	Jun 20, 61	Reenlisted Jan 25, 64; Wagoner; Mustered out Jul 5, 65.
Fuller, Hiland A.	Brattleboro	Oct 26, 61	Oct 31, 61	KIA Jun 5, 64.
Gage, William C.	Bennington	May 7, 61	Jun 20, 61	Deserted Aug 29, 62; Returned Sep 6, 62; Transferred to Signal Corps Dec 15, 63; Discharged Aug 19, 65.
Gilmore, Joseph L.	Bennington	May 7, 61	Jun 20, 61	Deserted 28, 62.
Goodenough, Alonzo	Readsboro	May 27, 61	Jun 20, 61	Promoted to Corp. Feb 6, 63; Wounded May 3, 63; Mustered out Jun 29, 64
Goodenough, Alonzo	Readsboro	Aug 25, 64	Aug 25, 64	Promoted to Corp. Oct 17, 64; to Sgt. Nov 1, 64; Wounded Oct 19, 64; Mustered out Jul 15, 65.
Goldsmith, Fletcher B.	Dorset	May 9, 61	Jun 20, 61	Transferred to V. R. C. Sep 1, 63; Discharged Nov 15, 65.
Goldsmith, Orsemus B.	Pownal	May 13, 61	Jun 20, 61	Deserted Oct 17, 62.
Grace, Edward	Bennington	May 7, 61	Jun 20, 61	KIA May 5, 64.
Grant, Azariah A.	Shaftsbury	Aug 26, 62	Sep 15, 62	Discharged May 29, 65 for wounds received May 5, 64.
Gravlin, Antoine	Underhill	Aug 15, 64	Aug 15, 64	Wounded Mar 27, 65; Mustered out Jun 19, 65.
Green, Seymour	Shaftsbury	Sep 2, 62	Sep 15, 62	Wounded May 12, 64; deserted Jul 1, 64.
Griffin, Edward	Bennington	May 7, 61	Jun 20, 61	Wounded May 6, 64; Mustered out Jun 29, 64.
Griffin, John	Bennington	Sep 2, 64	Sep 2, 64	Wounded Mar 27, 65; Mustered out Jul 15, 65.
Griffis, Sirenus	Arlington	Aug 15, 62	Sep 15, 62	Discharged Jan 2, 63 for disability.
Grousbeck, Foster	Searsburg	Aug 15, 62	Sep 15, 62	Wounded Nov 27, 63 and Jun 3, 64; Discharged May 20, 65 for wounds.
Hapgood, Charles M.	Peru	Oct 16, 61	Oct 31, 61	Wounded May 5, 64 and May 12, 64; Mustered out Oct 31, 64.
Harrington, Hiram H.	Dorset	May 9, 61	Jun 20, 61	Deserted Jun 18, 64.
Harris, Charles C.	Bennington	May 7, 61	Jun 20, 61	Mustered out Jun 29, 64.
Harris, Henry M.	Bennington	May 7, 61	Jun 20, 61	Deserted Aug 31, 62.
Harwood, H. Martyn	Bennington	May 7, 61	Jun 20, 61	Wounded May 5, 64; Mustered out Jun 29, 64.
Haskins, Henry	Readsboro	Aug 31, 64	Aug 31, 64	Promoted to Corp. May 15, 65; Mustered out Jun 19, 65.
Hathaway, Calvin	Bennington	Jul 15, 62	Sep 15, 62	Died Nov 23, 62 of disease.
Hathaway, Thomas S.	Bennington	May 7, 61	Jun 20, 61	Discharged Feb 17, 63 for disability.
Hicks, James	Manchester	May, 13, 61	Jun 20, 61	Died Nov 29, 61 of disease.
Hill, Charles H.	Manchester	May, 13, 61	Jun 20, 61	Deserted Oct 17, 62; returned Sep 23, 63; Mustered out Jun 29, 64.
Hill, Horace S.	Dorset	May 9, 61	Jun 20, 61	Promoted to Corp. Nov 19, 62; KIA May 5, 64.
Hill, William	Substitute	Aug 4, 63	Aug 4, 63	Substitute for Richabel Fisher, Highgate; Promoted to Corp. Oct 17, 64; Mustered out Jul 15, 65.

Holbrook, Selah H.	Whitingham	May 10, 61	Jun 20, 61	Wounded and taken prisoner Jun 29, 62; Paroled Sep 13, 62, Discharged Dec 27, 62, for disability.
Holden, Henry	Bennington	May 8, 61	Jun 20, 61	Promoted to Corp. Jun 30, 62; to Sgt. Feb 6, 63; wounded Dec 13, 62; discharged Jun 24, 64 for disability.
Holden, Orin A.	Bennington	May 7, 61	Jun 20, 61	Transferred to V. R. C. Sep 1, 63; Discharged Nov 15, 65.
Horton, C. Eugene	Stamford	Sep 6, 64	Sep 6, 64	Mustered out Jun 19, 65
Horton, George	Stamford	Sep 6, 64	Sep 6, 64	Mustered out Jun 19, 65.
Horton, Henry	Stamford	Sep 6, 64	Sep 6, 64	Promoted to Corp. May 15, 65; Mustered out Jun 19, 65.
Howard, James G.	Brattleboro	Oct 26, 61	Oct 31, 61	See First Lieutenants Co. A.
Hulett, Lyman	Shaftsbury	Aug 26, 62	Sep 15, 62	Wounded May 5, 64; Transferred to V. R. C. Nov 25, 64; Discharged Sep 14, 65.
Hulett, Moses	Shaftsbury	Aug 26, 62	Sep 15, 62	Mustered out Jun 29, 64.
Hupf, Charles V.	Bennington	Feb 15, 62	Apr 12, 62	Deserted Aug 8, 62; Returned; Wounded May 3; Reenlisted Apr 13, 64; Deserted May 18, 64; Returned; Deserted Aug 15, 64.
Hurlburt, Jerry	Bennington	May 8, 61	Jun 20, 61	Discharged Sep 23, 62 for disability.
Hurley, Cornelius	Bennington	May 7, 61	Jun 20, 61	Deserted Sep 3, 62.
Jackson, Albert C.	Underhill	Dec 7, 63	Dec 18, 63	Mustered out Jul 10, 65.
Jackson, John W.	Underhill	Aug 25, 64	Aug 25, 64	Mustered out Jun 19, 65.
Jackson, Lisander L.	Underhill	Dec 7, 63	Dec 18, 63	Promoted to Corp. Sep 1, 64; to Sgt. ; KIA Apr 2, 65.
Jackson, Sidney E.	Underhill	Aug 15, 64	Aug 15, 64	Promoted to Corp. May 15, 65; Mustered out Jun 19, 65.
Jackson, William C.	Underhill	Mar 4, 62	Mar 28, 62	KIA May 5, 64.
Johnson, William J.	Pownal	Dec 9, 63	Dec 9, 63	Wounded May 10, 64; Transferred to V. R. C. Nov 25, 64.
Kelley, Charles	Bennington	May 8, 61	Jun 20, 61	Wounded May 5, 64; Mustered out Jun 29, 64.
Kellogg, Joseph P.	Shaftsbury	Aug 18, 62	Sep 15, 62	Transferred to V. R. C Mar 15, 64; Discharged May 8, 65.
Lanfair, Henry C.	Stamford	Aug 16, 62	Sep 15, 62	Wounded May 5, 64; Transferred to V. R. C. Jan 28, 65; Mustered out Jun 25, 65.
Larabee, Hollis S.	Underhill	Mar 9, 65	Mar 9, 65	Mustered out Jul 15, 65.
Larabee, Lyman H.	Underhill	Mar 8, 65	Mar 8, 65	Mustered out Jul 15, 65.
Lasor, Vetal	Pawlet	Sep 1, 64	Sep 1, 64	Mustered out Jul 19, 65.
Lavine, John	Essex	Mar 20, 62	Apr 12, 62	Reenlisted Apr 13, 64; Deserted May 19, 64.
Leen, Thomas	Bennington	Dec 14, 63	Dec 24, 63	Wounded May 5, 64; Deserted Sep 23, 64.
Lesure, Russell E.	Stamford	Aug 15, 62	Sep 15, 62	Wounded May 6, 64; Mustered out Jun 19, 65.
Lord, Henry	Substitute	Jul 27, 63	Jul 27, 63	Substitute for Ray F. Livermore, Starksboro; Deserted Sep 29, 63.
Lyon, Albert	Landgrove	Oct 16, 61	Oct 31, 61	Died Feb 23, 62 of disease.
Mallett, Julius	Stamford	Aug 15, 62	Sep 15, 62	Died Dec 25, 62 of disease.
Mariner, Lewis	Substitute	Jul 24, 63	Jul 24, 63	Substitute for Nathan Foster, Berlin; Discharged Apr 5, 64.
Matteson, Albert N.	Stamford	Oct 12, 61	Oct 31, 61	Deserted Sep 28, 62.
Matteson, Oscar J.	Stamford	Oct 12, 61	Oct 31, 61	Wounded Sep 14, 62; Transferred to V. R. C. Jan 23, 64; Discharged Oct 31, 64.
Mattison, Alonzo	Shaftsbury	May 7, 61	Jun 20, 61	Deserted Sep 3, 62.
Mattison, Solomon	Shaftsbury	Aug 26, 62	Sep 15, 62	Died May 12, 64 of wounds received May 5, 64.
Mead, Ezra L.	Underhill	Jun 20, 61	Jun 20, 61	Deserted Sep 18, 62.
Millard, Henry	Substitute	Aug 5, 63	Aug 5, 63	Substitute for Charles Coleman, Rutland; Deserted Sep 17, 63.
Mooney, Charles R.	Arlington	Aug 14, 62	Sep 15, 62	Discharged Apr 5, 63 for disability.
Morrisey, Thomas	Bennington	May 8, 61	Jun 20, 61	Discharged Mar 26, 63 for wounds received Jun 29, 62.
Morrison, George	Sunderland	May 7, 61	Jun 20, 61	Mustered out Jun 29, 64.
Nelson, George M.	Arlington	Aug 14, 62	Sep 15, 62	Deserted Jul 1, 63.
Nichols, William B.	Stamford	Sep 3, 64	Sep 3, 64	Wounded Oct 19, 64; Mustered out Jun 19, 65.

Niles, Brownal	Stamford	Sep 2, 64	Sep 2, 64	Mustered out Jun 19, 65.
Niles, Johnson W.	Pownal	May 8, 61	Jun 20, 61	Died May 15, 64 of wounds received May 12, 64.
Norcross, Josiah W.	Stamford	Aug 16, 62	Sep 15, 62	KIA May 3, 63.
North, Elihu	Pownal	Feb 20, 65	Feb 20, 65	Mustered out Jul 15, 65.
Norton, Henry D.	Bennington	May 7, 61	Jun 20, 61	Deserted Sep 8, 62; Returned Feb 25, 64; Wounded May 5, 64 and May 12, 64; Mustered out Jul 15, 65.
Noyes, Andrew J.	Bennington	May 7, 61	Jun 20, 61	Wounded and taken prisoner Jul 21, 61; Paroled Jan 17, 62; Discharged Apr 3, 62 for wounds received Jul 21, 61.
O'Brian, William	Searsburgh	Aug 15, 62	Sep 15, 62	Promoted to Corp. Dec 1, 64; to Sgt. May 15, 65; Wounded May 3, 63 and Aug 21, 64; Mustered out Jun 19, 65.
Palmer, Simeon M.	Underhill	Aug 18, 64	Aug 18, 64	Mustered out Jun 19, 65.
Parento,. Gideon	Plainfield	Feb 20, 62	Apr 12, 62	Died Jun 17, 62 of disease.
Percey, Hiland	Bennington	May 7, 61	Jun 20, 61	Mustered out Jun 29, 64.
Perkins, George M.	Pownal	Feb 20, 65	Feb 20, 65	Mustered out Jul 22, 65.
Plumb, George E.	Stamford	Aug 30, 64	Aug 30, 64	Mustered out Jun 19, 65.
Potter, Benajah S.	Bennington	Oct 15, 61	Oct 31, 61	Discharged Apr 3, 62 for disability.
Powers, John	Shaftsbury	May 14, 61	Jun 20, 61	KIA May 5, 64.
Priest, Daniel M.	Peru	Oct 16, 61	Oct 31, 61	Wounded and taken prisoner Jun 29, 62; Paroled Aug 3, 62; Discharged Oct 15, 62 for wounds received Jun 29, 62.
Rice, Willard J.	Shaftsbury	Aug 26, 62	Sep 15, 62	Died Dec 19, 62 of disease.
Richardson, Henry A.	Stamford	Aug 19, 62	Sep 15, 62	KIA May 5, 64.
Richardson, Silas W.	Stamford	Aug 16, 62	Sep 15, 62	Transferred to V. R. C. May 1, 64; Mustered out Jul 1, 65.
Robbins, Charles D.	Peru	Oct 16, 61	Oct 31, 61	Discharged Feb 14, 63 for disability.
Robinson, James L.	Dorset	May 9, 61	Jun 20, 61	Wounded May 5, 64; Mustered out Jun 29, 62.
Ryan, Daniel	Shaftsbury	Sep 1, 62	Sep 15, 62	KIA May 5, 64.
Ryan, Norman H.	Stamford	Sep 2, 64	Sep 2, 64	Wounded Apr 2, 65; Mustered out Jun 19, 65.
Sanborn, Melvin W.	Bennington	May 14, 61	Jun 20, 61	Mustered out Jun 29, 64.
Samson, Chauncey S.	Shaftsbury	Aug 26, 62	Sep 15, 62	Died May 4, 63 of wounds received May 3, 63.
Schumacher, George A.	Bennington	Nov 12, 63	Nov 12, 63	Taken prisoner May 27, 64 and committed to Libby Prison Jun 15, 64; N. F. R.
Sears, William H.	Bennington	May 11, 61	Jun 20, 61	Promoted to Corp. Sep 24, 63; Wounded May 5, 64; Mustered out Oct 3, 64 to date Jun 29, 64.
Seger, Henry G.	Stamford	Aug 19, 62	Sep 15, 62	Promoted to Corp. Oct 17, 64; to Sgt. May 11, 65; Wounded Apr 2, 65; Mustered out Jun 12, 65.
Seldon, Edward A.	Bennington	Mar 22, 62	Apr 12, 62	Died Aug 4, 62 of disease.
Sherman, Abraham	Readsboro	Aug 16, 62	Sep 15, 62	Wounded Aug 21, 64; Transferred to V. R. C. Dec 20, 64; Mustered out Jul 1, 65.
Shippee, George C.	Searsburgh	Aug 15, 62	Sep 15, 62	Wounded May 3, 63; Mustered out Jun 19, 65.
Shippee, James H.	Wilmington	May 11, 61	Jun 20, 61	Wounded and taken prisoner Jun 29, 62; Paroled Aug 3, 62; Discharged Nov 27, 62 for wounds.
Shippee, Leander E.	Wilmington	Dec 8, 63	Jan 2, 64	Wounded Jun 1, 64; Mustered out May 13, 65.
Shippee, William E.	Searsburgh	Aug 15, 62	Sep 15, 62	Wounded May 3, 63 and May 5, 64; Mustered out Jul 12, 65.
Shufelt, William W.	Readsboro	Aug 29, 64	Aug 29, 64	Discharged Mar 10, 65 for disability.
Smith, Chandler T.	Bennington	May 20, 61	Jun 20, 61	Wounded Dec 13, 62; Transferred to V. R. C. Apr 15, 64; Discharged Jun 28, 64.
Smith, Francis E.	Bennington	May 7, 61	Jun 20, 61	Promoted to Sgt. Nov 19, 62; KIA Dec 13, 62.
Squires, Frederick C.	Shaftsbury	Nov 25, 63	Dec 10, 63	Promoted to Corp. Nov 1, 64; Mustered out Jul 10, 65.
Stafford, Albert	Pownal	May 20, 61	Jun 20, 61	Died Feb 8, 63 of disease.
Stafford, Emerson	Readsboro	Aug 29, 64	Aug 29, 64	Mustered out Jun 19, 65.
Stiles, Henry	Peru	Oct 16, 61	Oct 31, 61	See Sgt. Maj.
Stone, Fayette	Shaftsbury	Oct 28, 61	Oct 31, 61	Reenlisted Dec 21, 63; Deserted Feb 6, 64; Returned Mar 3, 64; Wounded Oct 19, 64; Mustered out Jul 15, 65.

Stone, Pratt	Readsboro	May 20, 61	Jun 20, 61	See Capt. Co. F.
Summers, Patrick	Shaftsbury	Dec 11, 63	Dec 24, 63	Wounded May 5, 64; Mustered out May 13, 65.
Sweet, Sylvester	Arlington	Dec 24, 63	Dec 24, 63	Discharged Apr 19, 64 for disability.
Taylor, Frank L.	Essex	Jun 20, 61	Jun 20, 61	Discharged Apr 4, 64 for disability.
Towsley, Leander M.	Shaftsbury	May 7, 61	Jun 20, 61	Deserted Aug 28, 62; returned Nov 17, 63; Deserted Jun 19, 64.
Towsley, Linus M.	Bennington	May 7, 61	Jun 20, 61	KIA Apr 30, 62.
Tracy, Nathan J.	Sunderland	May 11, 61	Jun 20, 61	Promoted to Sgt. Sep 14, 61; Discharged Dec 15, 62 for disability.
Tyler, George E.	Readsboro	May 27, 61	Jun 20, 61	Wounded Sep 17, 62; Discharged Aug 26, 63 for wounds.
Vorce, Andrew J.	Wilmington	Dec 8, 63	Jan 2, 64	KIA May 5, 64.
Westcott, Solomon H.	Manchester	May 7, 61	Jun 20, 61	Transferred to V. R. C. Oct 5, 63; Discharged Jun 20, 64.
Weymouth, William S.	Peru	Oct 16, 61	Oct 31, 61	Died Dec 14, 61 of disease.
Wilcox, Jabez F.	Pownal	May 8, 61	Jun 20, 61	Mustered out Jun 29, 64.
Wilson, Horatio K.	Searsburgh	Aug 15, 62	Sep 15, 62	Promoted to Corp. Sep 1, 64; to Sgt. Oct 17, 64; Wounded May 3, 63; Mustered out Jun 19, 65.
Wood, Louis	Readsboro	May 13, 61	Jun 20, 61	KIA Apr 30, 62.
Wyman, Abel T.	Dorset	May 8, 61	Jun 20, 61	Deserted Nov 1, 62; Returned Sep 24, 63; Reenlisted Mar 30, 64; Deserted Jan 13, 65; in Co. Apr 30, 65; Mustered out Jul 15, 65.
Wyman, Laroy	Peru	Dec 9, 63	Dec 24, 63	Wounded May 10, 64 and Sep 19, 64; Died Oct 14, 64 of wounds received Oct 19, 64.

Company B

Name and Rank	Residence	Date of Commission	Date of Issue	Remarks
Captains				
Hope, James	Castleton	May 16, 61	May 16, 61	Resigned Dec 20, 62.
Ward, Rollin C.	Castleton	Dec 20, 62	Jan 6, 63	Sgt. Co. B; Promoted to First Sgt.; to First Lt. Co. B Oct 1, 62; Wounded May 10, 64; Resigned Sep 14, 64.
Prouty, Henry H.	Brattleboro	Dec 24, 64	Jan 31, 65	Sgt. Co. C; Promoted to Sgt. Maj. Apr 14, 63; to Second Lt. Nov 2, 63 Co. H; to First Lt. Co. H Apr 24, 64; Wounded May 4, 63; Mustered out Jul 15, 65.
First Lieutenants				
Howe, John	Castleton	May 16, 61	May 16, 61	Resigned Aug 14, 61.
Johnson, Enoch E.	Castleton	Sep 2, 61	Sep 2, 61	See Lt. Col.
Appleton, Edward W.	Bennington	Jan 25, 62	Jan 25, 62	First Sgt. Co. A; Promoted to Second Lt. Co. H Sep 14, 61; Discharged Sep 25, 62 for disability.
Ward, Rollin C.	Castleton	Oct 1, 62	Oct 13, 62	See Capt. Co. A.
Bailey, Hiram	Brandon	Dec 20, 62	Jan 6, 63	Corp. Co. B.; Promoted to Sgt. Mar 7, 62; to Second Lt. Co. B Nov 24, 62; KIA Jun 3, 64.
Fifield, Edson H.	Poultney	Jun 20, 64	Jul 11, 64	Corp. Co. B.; Promoted to Sgt. Mar 7, 62; to QM. Sgt. Apr 26, 62; Reenlisted Jan 30, 64; Mustered out Jul 15, 65
Second Lieutenants				
Johnson, Enoch E.	Castleton	May 16, 61	May 16, 61	See Lt. Col.
Bliss, Charles M.	Woodford	Sep 21, 61	Sep 21, 61	Sgt. Co. A; Discharged Oct 4, 62 by special order of the War Department.
Bailey, Hiram	Brandon	Nov 24, 62	Nov 24, 62	See First Lt. Co. B.
Robbins, Augustus J.	Grafton	Dec 20, 62	Jan 8, 63	Corp. Co. A.; Promoted to Commissary Sgt. Jan 16, 62; Wounded May 12, 64; Mustered out Jun 29, 64.

Name and Rank	Residence	Date of Enlistment	Date of Muster	Remarks
Harrington, Eph. W.	Kirby	Jun 20, 64	Jul 11, 64	See Capt. Co. G.
Tenney, Marquis E.	Mendon	Jun 7, 65	Jun 17, 65	Pvt. Co. B; Promoted to Sgt. Aug 22, 64; to First Sgt. Dec 26, 64; Wounded May 3, 63; Mustered out as First Sgt. Jun 19, 65.

Name and Rank	Residence	Date of Enlistment	Date of Muster	Remarks
Sergeants				
Howard, Abial G.	Castleton	May 8, 61	Jun 20, 61	Wounded Jul 21, 61; Discharged Mar 7, 62 for disability.
Potter, Asa A.	Castleton	May 8, 61	Jun 20, 61	Reduced; AWOL from Sep 9, 62 to Jun 12, 63; Mustered out Jun 29, 64.
Edgerton, Francis M.	Poultney	May 9, 61	Jun 20, 61	See Adjutant.
Freelove, John A.	Castleton	May 8, 61	Jun 20, 61	Taken prisoner May 10, 64; Escaped Sep 14, 64; Discharged Oct 27, 64.
Ward, Rollin C.	Castleton	May 17, 61	Jun 20, 61	See Capt. Co. B.
Corporals				
Eddly, George	Rutland	May 8, 61	Jun 20, 61	Reduced Oct 13, 61; Discharged Oct 31, 62 for disability.
Potter, George W.	Castleton	May 8, 61	Jun 20, 61	Promoted to Sgt.; Wounded May 5, 64; Mustered out Jun 29, 64.
Fifield, Edson H.	Poultney	May 8, 61	Jun 20, 61	See First Lt. Co. B.
Clifton, Joseph A.	Rutland	May 9, 61	Jun 20, 61	Reduced Oct 13, 61; Mustered out Sep 8, 65.
Benedict, Jasper A.	Castleton	May 16, 61	Jun 20, 61	Promoted to Sgt. Apr 28, 62; Wounded May 4, 63 and May 6, 64; Mustered out Jun 29, 64.
Parkhurst, William	Castleton	May 8, 61	Jun 20, 61	Deserted Nov 13, 62.
Bailey, Hiram	Brandon	May 17, 61	Jun 20, 61	See First Lt. Co. B.
Parkhurst, Leonard R.	Castleton	May 12, 61	Jun 20, 61	Deserted Oct 26, 62; Returned Nov 1, 63; Reduced; Mustered out Jul 19, 65.
Musicians				
Hart, James E.	Pittsford	May 15, 61	Jun 20, 61	Deserted Oct 17, 62.
Wilson, James R.	Shrewsbury	Jun 1, 61	Jun 20, 61	Wounded and taken prisoner Jun 29, 62; Mustered out Jun 29, 64.
Wagoner				
Shaw, John M.	Castleton	May 10, 61	Jun 20, 61	Discharged Apr 3, 62 for disability.
Privates				
Andrus, Joseph	Castleton	Aug 24, 64	Aug 24, 64	Mustered out Jun 19, 65.
Arbatraca, Giovanni	Substitute	Aug 5, 63	Aug 5, 63	Substitute for Rockwood Barrett, Rutland; Deserted Sep 27, 63; Returned Oct 9, 63; Taken prisoner May 21, 64; Paroled Nov 18, 64; N. F. R.
Bailey, Alvin C.	Rutland	Jun 15, 61	Jun 20, 61	Reenlisted Jan 4, 64; Mustered out Jul 15, 65.
Bailey, Charles	Rutland	May 9, 61	Jun 20, 61	Died Jun 18, 64 of wounds received May 6, 64.
Ballard, George	Clarendon	May 8, 61	Jun 20, 61	KIA Jun 29, 62.
Ballard, George W.	Poultney	May 9, 61	Jun 20, 61	Discharged Mar 6, 62 for disability.
Barber, Charles S.	Poultney	Aug 12, 62	Sep 15, 62	Wounded May 5, 64; KIA May 12, 64.
Barber, W. Alanson	Poultney	May 9, 61	Jun 20, 61	Discharged Mar 8, 63 for disability.
Barry, Francis	Substitute	Jul 29, 63	Jul 29, 63	Substitute for Alfred Percival, Jericho; Deserted Sep 17, 63.
Bateman, David P.	Poultney	Aug 22, 62	Sep 15, 62	Wounded May 3, 63 and May 10, 64; Taken prisoner May 10, 64 and died at Andersonville, Ga. Jul 15, 64.
Bateman, John S.	Poultney	Aug 22, 62	Sep 15, 62	Promoted to Corp. Feb 7, 65; Wounded May 5, 64 and Apr 2, 65; Mustered out Jun 19, 65.
Bateman, Lewis L.	Poultney	May 8, 61	Jun 20, 61	Reenlisted Dec 21, 63; Wounded May 5, 64 and Mar 25, 65; Mustered out Jul 19, 65.
Bates, George	Essex	Jul 14, 63	Jul 17, 63	Drafted; Deserted Apr 5, 65.

Bean, Joseph	Hartford	Jul 22, 63	Jul 22, 63	Drafted; Mustered out Jul 15, 65.
Blair, James W.	Pittsford	Sep 11, 61	Oct 19, 61	Discharged Apr 23, 62.
Bolton, Jeremiah	Castleton	May 8, 61	Jun 20, 61	Wounded and taken prisoner Jul 21, 61; Paroled May 11, 62; Mustered out May 22, 62.
Bover, David	Rutland	May 9, 61	Jun 20, 61	Wounded Jul 21, 61; Discharged May 5, 63 for disability.
Brainard, Samuel	Castleton	Oct 2, 61	Oct 18, 61	Deserted Sep 5, 62; Returned Jun 10, 63; Mustered out Oct 18, 64.
Brockenraid, H. L.	Rutland	May 9, 61	Jun 20, 61	Promoted to Corp. May 7, 62; Wounded and taken prisoner Jul 21, 61; Paroled Jan 3, 62; Wounded May 5, 64; Mustered out Jun 29, 64.
Bromley, James W.	Danby	May 8, 61	Jun 20, 61	Reenlisted Dec 21, 63; Promoted to Corp.; to Sgt. Feb 7, 65; KIA Apr 2, 65.
Brown, Chauncey W.	Poultney	Aug 16, 62	Sep 15, 62	Wounded May 3, 63; Transferred to V. R. C. Feb 8, 64; Discharged Jul 13, 65.
Bryant, James G.	Substitute	Aug 4, 63	Aug 4, 63	Substitute for Samuel N. Seaver, Williamstown; Wounded Sep 19, 64; Mustered out Jul 15, 65.
Bryant, Jonathan	Holland	Jul 31, 63	Jul 31, 63	Drafted; Discharged Jan 25, 64.
Bush, Francis A.	Castleton	May 10, 61	Jun 20, 61	Wounded May 3, 63 and May 12, 64; Discharged Jun 29, 64.
Butler, Eben	Poultney	May 10, 61	Jun 20, 61	Deserted Nov 8, 62.
Butterfly, George	Weybridge	Sep 9, 64	Sep 9, 64	Mustered out Jun 19, 65.
Butterfly, James	Rutland	Oct 16, 61	Oct 18, 61	Mustered out Oct 18, 64.
Caldwell, Robert	Poultney	May 9, 61	Jun 20, 61	Promoted to Corp.; Wounded May 5, 64; Mustered out Jun 29, 64.
Cargill, Benjamin	Substitute	Jul 22, 63	Jul 22, 63	Substitute for Nathaniel C. Sawyer, Brattleboro; Died Aug 8, 64 of wounds received May 12, 64.
Carrigan, Frank H.	Poultney	May 8, 61	Jun 20, 61	Deserted May 16, 62.
Carrigan, James B.	Poultney	May 8, 61	Jun 20, 61	Promoted to Corp. Jan 29, 64; Wounded May 3, 63 and May 5, 64; Mustered out Jun 29, 64.
Castle, Charles D.	Wells	Aug 16, 62	Sep 15, 62	Died Jan 4, 63 of disease.
Clair, John	Substitute	Aug 3, 63	Aug 3, 63	Substitute for Fred H. Wilson, Putney; Transferred to Navy Apr 19, 64; Discharged Aug 1, 65.
Clark, Henry M.	Woodstock	Aug 12, 64	Aug 12, 64	KIA Oct 19, 64.
Clark, Joseph, S.	Montgomery	Jan 1, 64	Jan 1, 64	Wounded May 12, 64; Transferred to V. R. C. Dec 14, 64; Discharged Jan 27, 65.
Coagle, William	Ira	Aug 14, 62	Sep 15, 62	Wounded May 3, 63; Transferred to V. R. C. Oct 8, 63; Discharged Jul 3, 65.
Cole, Obadiah	Poultney	Aug 22, 62	Sep 15, 62	Wounded May 12, 64 and Oct 19; Transferred to V. R. C. Mar 16, 65; Mustered out Jun 29, 65.
Cone, Charles W.	Substitute	Sep 14, 63	Sep 14, 63	Substitute for Seth Meacham, Guildhall; Died Aug 2, 64 of disease.
Corse, Wells	Duxbury	Jul 14, 63	Jul 14, 63	Drafted; Mustered out Jul 15, 65.
Dickinson, Chanuncey	Georgia	Jun 15, 61	Jun 20, 61	Deserted Jul 4, 61.
Donnivan, Timothy	Brattleboro	Dec 29, 63	Dec 31, 63	Wounded May 5, 64, Sep 22, 64 and Oct 19, 64; Mustered out Jul 15, 65.
Donohue, Nicholas	Substitute	Aug 4, 63	Aug 4, 63	Substitute for Horace H. Dyer, Rutland; Transferred to V. R. C. Apr 15, 64; Discharged Nov 4, 65 for disability.
Durham, Thomas P.	Castleton	Oct 6, 61	Oct 18, 61	Wounded May 3, 63; KIA May 12, 64.
Durham, William	Castleton	May 9, 61	Jun 20, 61	Deserted Sep 5, 62; Returned ; Transferred to V. R. C. Jul 1, 63; Discharged Jul 27, 64.
Eaton, Marcus	Hubbardton	Oct 2, 61	Oct 19, 61	Died Nov 30, 61 of disease.
Flanders, William	Clarendon	May 8, 61	Jun 20, 61	Dishonorable discharge Jul 20, 62.
Gary, George W. L.	Rutland	Aug 13, 62	Sep 15, 62	Deserted Jul 4, 63.
Gibbs, Leonard S.	Benson	May 8, 61	Jun 20, 61	Discharged Feb 12, 63 for wounds accidentally received.
Gifford, Warren	Danby	May 8, 61	Jun 20, 61	Reenlisted Dec 21, 63; Promoted to Corp. Apr 1, 65; to Sgt. Jun 19, 65; Wounded and taken prisoner Jul 21, 61; Paroled Jan 3, 62; Mustered out Jul 15, 65.

Griswold, George K.	Castleton	Feb 27, 62	Apr 12, 62	Died Jun 25, 62.
Hall, John M.	Hubbardton	May 8, 61	Jun 20, 61	Promoted to Sgt. Oct 21, 62; Mustered out Jun 29, 64.
Hammond, Charles	Poultney	Aug 18, 62	Sep 15, 62	Discharged Apr 20, 65 for wounds received Aug 21, 64.
Harrington, Wm. W.	Clarendon	May 8, 61	Jun 20, 61	Mustered out Jun 29, 64.
Hart, Silas L.	Hubbardton	May 8, 61	Jun 20, 61	Deserted Aug 25, 62; Returned Oct 9, 63; Wounded and taken prisoner May 5, 64; Died at Andersonville, Ga. Oct 13, 64
Hawkins, Gideon	Castleton	May 10, 61	Jun 20, 61	Wounded May 5, 64; Mustered out Jun 29, 64.
Hewitt, James H.	Rutland	Aug 16, 62	Sep 15, 62	Mustered out Jun 19, 65
Hewitt, John	Rutland	Nov 27, 63	Dec 12, 63	Wounded May 5, 64; Mustered out Jul 15, 65.
Hinckley, James	Rutland	Aug 13, 62	Sep 15, 62	Mustered out Jun 19, 65.
Hines, Michael	Castleton	Jun 1, 61	Jun 20, 61	Wounded May 5, 64; Mustered out Jun 29, 64.
Hodges, Alonzo D.	Rutland	May 8, 61	Jun 20, 61	Transferred to V. R. C. Jul 1, 63; Transferred back to Co. Feb 19, 64; Reenlisted Mar 20, 64; Promoted to Corp. Jun 19, 65; Wounded Sep 19, 64 and Apr 2, 65; Mustered out Jul 15, 65.
Howard, Adin E.	Poultney	Aug 15, 62	Sep 15, 62	Mustered out Jun 19, 65.
Humphrey, Willard S.	Pittsford	May 9, 61	Jun 20, 61	Discharged Oct 14, 62 for disability.
Hunter, Henry, G.	Poultney	May 9, 61	Jun 20, 61	Dishonorable discharge Jul 20, 62.
Hyde, William H.	Poultney	Aug 18, 62	Sep 15, 62	Wounded May 4, 63; Transferred to V. R. C. Sep 1, 63; Discharged Jun 12, 65.
Ingleston, Frederick A.	Castleton	May 9, 61	Jun 20, 61	Deserted Sep 5, 62; Returned Sep 30, 62; Wounded May 4, 63; Mustered out Jun 29, 64.
Johnson, Endearing D.	Castleton	Oct 4, 61	Oct 18, 61	Mustered out Oct 18, 64.
Johnson, George M.	Pittsford	May 10, 61	Jun 20, 61	Promoted to Corp.; Wounded May 5, 64; Mustered out Jun 19, 65.
Johnson, Henry	Rutland	May 8, 61	Jun 20, 61	Wounded May 5, 64; Mustered out Jun 29, 64.
Jordon, Frank A.	Manchester	May 8, 61	Jun 20, 61	Discharged Apr 14, 64.
Kelley, John T.	Rutland	Aug 16, 62	Sep 15, 62	Mustered out Jun 29, 64.
King, Theodore	Castleton	Oct 4, 61	Oct 18, 61	Mustered out Oct 18, 64.
Knox, Edward	Benson	May 8, 61	Jun 20, 61	Wounded Jul 21, 61 and May 5, 64; Mustered out Jun 29, 64.
Labell, Charles	St. Albans	Dec 30, 63	Dec 30, 63	Deserted Sep 24, 64.
Lewis, William G.	Poultney	Aug 15, 62	Sep 15, 62	Discharged Feb 20, 63 for disability.
Lloyd, Patrick	Rutland	May 10, 61	Jun 20, 61	Wounded Jul 21, 61; Deserted Sep 14, 63.
Mahar, Thomas	Poultney	Aug 18, 62	Sep 15, 62	Deserted Aug 30, 63.
Mahony, William	Dorset	May 10, 61	Jun 20, 61	Discharged Jun 4, 62.
Mango, Abraham	Rutland	Aug 12, 62	Sep 15, 62	Mustered out Jun 19, 65.
Maranville, Albert E.	Poultney	May 9, 61	Jun 20, 61	Reenlisted Dec 21, 63; Promoted to Corp. Aug 23, 64; to Sgt. Feb 7, 65; to First Sgt. Jun 19, 65; Mustered out Jul 15, 65.
Maranville, Egbert L.	Poultney	Dec 19, 63	Dec 19, 63	Wounded Mar 27, 65; Mustered out Jul 15, 65.
Maranville, Merritt P.	Poultney	Aug 13, 62	Sep 15, 62	Promoted to Corp. Feb 7, 65; Wounded May 3, 63, May 5, 64, Sep 19, 64 and Apr 2, 65; Discharged Jul 29, 65.
McHolland, Neely	Rutland	Oct 16, 61	Oct 19, 61	Deserted Dec 23, 62.
McKean, John	Castleton	May 8, 61	Jun 20, 61	Promoted to Sgt.; Wounded Jul 21, 61; KIA May 5, 64.
McKean, John H.	Castleton	Oct 14, 61	Oct 20, 61	Mustered out Oct 18, 64.
McKeand, William	Rutland	Jun 15, 61	Jun 20, 61	Deserted May 16, 62; Returned Aug 21, 62; Reenlisted Dec 21, 63; Deserted Feb 12, 64.
McQuain, Peter T.	Castleton	Oct 16, 61	Oct 20, 61	Reenlisted Dec 21, 63; Mustered out Jul 15, 65.
Merrill, William	Substitute	Jul 31, 63	Jul 31, 63	Substitute for C. L. Thorp, St. Albans; Sentenced by G. C. M. Oct 10, 63 to five years hard labor on public works.
Miller, John S.	Rutland	May 8, 61	Jun 20, 61	Mustered out Jun 29, 64.
Miller, William	Poultney	May 9, 61	Jun 20, 61	Mustered out Jun 29, 64.
Morgan, Martin A.	Bennington	Feb 17, 62	Apr 12, 62	Promoted to Corp. Feb 7, 65; Mustered out Apr 20, 65.

Morrill, Charles W.	Castleton	May 8, 61	Jun 20, 61	Sentenced by G. C. M. to confinement at Rip Raps during the war for desertion; Discharged by order of War Dept. Dec 27, 65.
Munson, Jonas H.	Poultney	Aug 16, 62	Sep 15, 62	Discharged Feb 5, 63 for disability.
Munson, Levi L.	Poultney	Aug 16, 62	Sep 15, 62	Wounded May 3, 63; Transferred to V. R. C. Apr 20, 64; Discharged Jul 13, 65.
O'Brain, Michael	Poultney	Aug 23, 62	Sep 15, 62	Promoted to Sgt. May 4, 64; Wounded Aug 21, 64; Discharged May 13, 65 for disability.
O'Connor, Richard	Substitute	Aug 7, 63	Aug 7, 63	Substitute for John Whitney, Enosburgh; Deserted Jan 26, 64.
Ovitt, Henry	Substitute	Jul 28, 63	Jul 28, 63	Substitute for Henry Martin, Montgomery; Taken prisoner May 3, 64; Returned; Deserted Jan 17, 65.
Page, Jacob	Rutland	Aug 16, 62	Sep 15, 62	Wounded Apr 2, 65; Mustered out Jun 19, 65.
Parkhurst, Albert	Castleton	May 12, 61	Jun 20, 61	Promoted to Corp. May 7, 62; Wounded May 3, 63; Discharged Jun 20, 64.
Patch, Auburn T.	Benson	Sep 19, 61	Sep 20, 61	Deserted Feb 3, 63; Returned Dec 5, 63; Wounded May 5, 64; Mustered out Jul 15, 65.
Patch, David A.	Fairhaven	Jun 1, 61	Jun 20, 61	Promoted to Corp. Oct 22, 61; KIA May 12, 64.
Pearsons, Wallace D.	Castleton	Aug 24, 64	Aug 24, 64	Wounded Apr 2, 65; Discharged Aug 11, 65.
Peino, Robert	Mendon	May 8, 61	Jun 20, 61	Reenlisted Dec 21, 63; Wounded May 5, 64; Mustered out Jul 15, 65.
Perkins, Charles	Rutland	Aug 15, 62	Sep 15, 62	Wounded May 5, 64; Discharged May 13, 65 for disability.
Perry, Francis	Burlington	Jul 29, 63	Jul 29, 63	Deserted to the enemy Sep 19, 63.
Pollard, Patrick	Castleton	Oct 12, 61	Oct 19, 61	Discharged Oct 21, 62 for disability.
Potter, Ethan A.	Castleton	Oct 4, 61	Oct 20, 61	Mustered out Oct 18, 64.
Potter, Willie A.	Castleton	Jan 21, 65	Jan 21, 65	Mustered out Jul 15, 65.
Read, Gustavus	Danby	Mar 10, 62	Apr 12, 62	Discharged Sep 2, 62 for disability.
Remington, James H.	Castleton	Oct 1, 61	Oct 19, 61	Promoted to Corp. Oct 22, 61; Died Dec 24, 61 of disease.
Rice, Joseph	Rutland	May 17, 61	Jun 20, 61	Discharged Aug 3, 62 for disability.
Rockwell, Cyrus S.	Brandon	Sep 9, 61	Sep 20, 61	Mustered out Sep 20, 64.
Rodney, Louis	Montpelier	Mar 20, 62	Apr 12, 62	Mustered out Apr 24, 65.
Rondeau, Victor	Substitute	Aug 3, 63	Aug 3, 63	Substitute for Walter S. Langworthy, Middlebury; Deserted Sep 19, 63.
Ross, George W.	Castleton	Oct 3, 61	Oct 20, 61	Reenlisted Dec 21, 63; Wounded May 5, 64 and Oct 19, 64; Transferred to V. R. C. Apr 26, 65; Mustered out Jul 20, 65.
Ross, Horace G.	Castleton	May 8, 61	Jun 20, 61	Reenlisted, Jan 31, 64; Wounded May 5, 64; KIA Apr 2, 65.
Russell, James	Castleton	May 8, 61	Jun 20, 61	Discharged Oct 23, 62 for disability.
Russell, Rollin	Ira	May 8, 61	Jun 20, 61	Discharged Dec 11, 63 for disability.
Russell, Thomas	Castleton	May 8, 61	Jun 20, 61	Deserted Oct 26, 62.
Russell, Wallace	Castleton	Jan 18, 65	Jan 18, 65	Mustered out Jul 15, 65.
Ryan, Patrick	Castleton	May 8, 61	Jun 20, 61	Discharged Jun 20, 62 for disability.
St. John, Ezekiel H.	Hubbardton	Mar 5, 62	Apr 20, 62	Discharged Nov 29, 62 for disability.
Savory, John H.	Clarendon	May 8, 61	Jun 20, 61	KIA Apr 18, 62.
Sawyer, Alphonso	Ludlow	Mar 10, 62	Apr 12, 62	Mustered out Apr 20, 65.
Sheldon, Josephus	Fairhaven	May 17, 61	Jun 20, 61	Discharged Apr 24, 62 for disability.
Smith, Henry C.	Castleton	May 19, 61	Jun 20, 61	Discharged May 22, 63 for wounds received Dec 13, 62.
Smith, Lawrence	Rutland	Aug 13, 62	Sep 15, 62	Mustered out Jun 19, 65.
Smith, Timothy J.	Brattleboro	Dec 29, 63	Dec 31, 63	Died May 22, 64 of wounds received May 12, 64.
Sprague, Durham	Castleton	May 10, 61	Jun 20, 61	Mustered out Jun 29, 64.
Sprague, Ozro	Wells	May 10, 61	Jun 20, 61	Discharged Mar 16, 63 for disability.
Streeter, John	Castleton	May 8, 61	Jun 20, 61	Wounded Jul 21, 61; Discharged Nov 29, 62 for disability.
Taylor, Edwin A.	Tinmouth	May 8, 61	Jun 20, 61	Died Aug 1, 62.
Taylor, George W.	Pawlet	May 8, 61	Jun 20, 61	Died Sep 17, 61 of disease.
Tenney, Marquis E.	Mendon	Aug 13, 62	Sep 15, 62	See Second Lt. Co. B.

Titus, Abel E.	Clarendon	Aug 14, 62	Sep 15, 62	Promoted to Corp. Apr 1, 65; Wounded Dec 13, 62; Mustered out Jun 19, 65.
Tower, Horace	Clarendon	May 8, 61	Jun 20, 61	Mustered out Jun 29, 64.
Trainor, Lawrence	Castleton	May 8, 61	Jun 20, 61	Wounded Dec 13, 62; Transferred to V. R. C.; Discharged Jun 21, 64.
Wheeler, Benjamin P.	Pawlet	Aug 13, 62	Sep 15, 62	Wounded May 5, 64 and Jun 20, 64; Mustered out Jun 19, 65.
Wheeler, Jacob	Castleton	Oct 2, 61	Oct 20, 61	Mustered out Oct 18, 64.
Wheeler, John D.	Castleton	Oct 16, 61	Oct 20, 61	Mustered out Oct 18, 64.
Wheeler, Nicholas	Castleton	Oct 2, 61	Oct 20, 61	Reenlisted Jan 21, 64; Wagoner; Mustered out Jul 15, 65.
Willard, Henry C.	Castleton	Aug 24, 64	Aug 24, 64	Mustered out Jun 19, 65.
Williams, Griffith	Fairhaven	May 12, 61	Jun 20, 61	Wounded; Deserted Oct 24, 62.
Williams, Reuben H.	Pawlet	Aug 28, 62	Mar 4, 63	Mustered out Jun 19, 65.
Wilson, James	Shrewsbury	Sep 9, 64	Sep 9, 64	Musician; Mustered out Jun 19, 65.
Wood, Henry C.	Pawlet	May 9, 61	Jun 20, 61	Deserted Oct 20, 62; Returned Jan 20, 64; Mustered out Jun 29, 64.
Wood, Martin P.	Pawlet	Aug 16, 62	Sep 15, 62	KIA May 12, 64.
Woodard, Joseph C.	Poultney	Aug 12, 62	Sep 15, 62	Mustered out Jun 27, 65.
Worthen, Erastus	Rutland	May 8, 61	Jun 20, 61	Reenlisted Dec 21, 63; Promoted to Corp.; Wounded May 6, 64; Discharged Jun 23, 65.
Worthen, John	Rutland	May 10, 61	Jun 20, 61	Promoted to Corp. Aug 28, 62; Discharged Apr 16, 63 for disability.
Young, James	Benson	Oct 4, 61	Oct 20, 61	Wounded May 3, 63; Mustered out Oct 18, 64.

Company C

Name and Rank	Residence	Date of Commission	Date of Issue	Remarks
Captains				
Todd, Edward A.	Brattleboro	May 17, 61	May 17, 61	Wounded Jul 21, 61; Resigned Jan 8, 62.
Tyler, John S.	Brattleboro	Jan 23, 62	Jan 23, 62	See Col.
Wales, Elijah	Brattleboro	Mar 1, 63	Mar 17, 63	First Sgt. Co. C.; Promoted to Second Lt. Co. C Jan 23, 62; to First Lt. Co. C Oct 20, 62; Bvt. Maj. Aug 1, 64 for gallantry in the Wilderness and subsequent engagements; Wounded May 5, 64 and Aug 14, 64; Mustered out Jul 15, 65.
First Lieutenants				
Tyler, John S.	Brattleboro	May 17, 61	May 17, 61	See Col.
Campbell, Henry C.	Putney	Jan 23, 62	Jan 23, 62	Second Lt. Co. C; Resigned Oct 19, 62.
Wales, Elijah	Brattleboro	Oct 20, 62	Nov 5, 62	See Capt. Co. C.
Sawyer, Joshua P.	St. Albans	Sep 26, 63	Oct 3, 63	Sgt. Co. H; Promoted to Second Lt. Co. H Jan 25, 62; Wounded May 5, 64; Mustered out Jun 29, 64.
Gleason, Francis A.	Brattleboro	Mar 1, 63	Mar 17, 63	Sgt. Co. C; Promoted to First Sgt. Jan 23, 62; to Second Lt. Co. C Oct 20, 62; Died May 30 of wounds received May 4, 63.
Morey, Charles C.	Royalton	Jun 20, 64	Jul 11, 64	See Capt. Co. E.
Franklin, Henry L.	Brattleboro	Dec 24, 64	Jan 31, 65	Corp. Co. C; Reenlisted Dec 21, 63; Promoted to First Sgt. Co. C Jul 1, 64; Dismissed from the service by sentence of G. C. M. May 18, 65.
Second Lieutenants				
Campbell, Henry C.	Putney	Jun 11, 61	Jun 11, 61	See First Lt. Co. C.
Wales, Elijah	Brattleboro	Jan 23, 62	Jan 23, 62	See Capt. Co. C.
Gleason, Francis A.	Brattleboro	Oct 20, 62	Nov 5, 62	See First Lt. Co. C.
Hight, Bradbury W.	Albany, Vt.	Mar 17, 63	Apr 16, 63	Corp. Co. K; Promoted to Sgt. Maj. Feb 22, 62; Mustered out Jun 29, 64.

Name and Rank	Residence	Date of Enlistment	Date of Muster	Remarks
Emerson, Rufus	Brattleboro	Jun 7, 65	Jun 17, 65	Pvt. Co. C.; Reenlisted Dec 21, 63; Promoted to Corp.; to Sgt. Jul 1, 64; to First Sgt. Feb 6, 65; Wounded May 6, 64 and May 12, 64; Mustered out Jul 15, 65.

Name and Rank	Residence	Date of Enlistment	Date of Muster	Remarks
Sergeants				
Wales, Elijah	Brattleboro	May 1, 61	Jun 20, 61	See Capt. Co. C.
Gleason, Francis A.	Brattleboro	May 1, 61	Jun 20, 61	See First Lt. Co. C.
Knight, Levi E.	Brattleboro	May 1, 61	Jun 20, 61	Reduced; Mustered out Jun 29, 64.
Prouty, Henry H.	Brattleboro	May 1, 61	Jun 20, 61	See Capt. Co. B.
Cole, Nelson S.	Brattleboro	May 1, 61	Jun 20, 61	Reduced; Promoted to Corp.; Mustered out Jun 29, 64.
Corporals				
Benjamin, Russell H.	Brattleboro	May 1, 61	Jun 20, 61	KIA Jul 21, 61.
Rice, Charles B.	Brattleboro	May 1, 61	Jun 20, 61	Wounded and taken prisoner Jul 21, 61; Paroled Jan 16, 62; Discharged Nov 29, 62 for wounds.
Miller, Frederick F.	Newfane	May 1, 61	Jun 20, 61	Promoted to Sgt. Mar 63; to First Sgt. Apr 3, 63; KIA May 10, 64.
Gould, Charles S.	Brattleboro	May 1, 61	Jun 20, 61	Reduced; Discharged Jun 20, 64 for Wounds received May 5, 64.
Franklin, Henry L.	Brattleboro	May 1, 61	Jun 20, 61	See First Lt. Co. C.
Briggs, Charles R.	Brattleboro	May 1, 61	Jun 20, 61	Transferred to V. R. C. Oct 13, 63; Discharged Feb 6, 65.
Keables, Elisha L.	Brattleboro	May 1, 61	Jun 20, 61	Wounded and taken prisoner Jul 21, 61; Died in Richmond, Va. Aug 6, 61 of wounds received Jul 21, 61.
Fife, Royal O.	Halifax	May 1, 61	Jun 20, 61	Taken prisoner Jul 21, 61; Paroled Jan 3, 62; Discharged Apr 2, 63 for disability.
Musician				
Simonds, Frederick W.	Brattleboro	May 1, 61	Jun 20, 61	Mustered out Jun 29, 64.
Wagoner				
Mead, Darwin	Underhill	May 1, 61	Jun 20, 61	Mustered out Jun 29, 64.
Privates				
Adams, Edgar E.	Brattleboro	May 1, 61	Jun 20, 61	Taken prisoner Jun 29, 62; Paroled Aug 3, 62; Discharged Oct 15, 62 for disability.
Ash, Antoine	Hinesburgh	Aug 26, 62	Sep 15, 62	Died Jul 13, 63 of disease.
Baldwin, Edward P.	Marlboro	May 1, 61	Jun 20, 61	Wounded Jul 21, 61; Died Jan 22, 62 of disease.
Baldwin, Eri G.	Brattleboro	May 1, 61	Jun 20, 61	Detached on Western Gunboat Flotilla Feb 15, 62; Discharged Apr 14, 62.
Barclay, Walter S.	Brattleboro	May 1, 61	Jun 20, 61	Transferred to 5th U.S. Cavalry Oct 20, 62.
Barrett, Harvey D.	Guilford	Dec 19, 63	Dec 26, 63	Promoted Corp.; to Sgt. Feb 6, 65; Wounded May 12, 64 and Oct 19, 64; Mustered out Jul 15, 65.
Barrett, John W.	Brattleboro	Mar 24, 62	Apr 12, 62	Discharged Jan 14, 63 for disability.
Bascom, John T.	Milton	May 1, 61	Jun 20, 61	Promoted to Second Lt. Co. F 9th Vt. Jun 25, 62.
Bassett, Hiram	Hinesburgh	Aug 23, 62	Sep 15, 62	Mustered out Jun 19, 65.
Beckwith, Charles	Pownal	Nov 20, 63	Nov 20, 63	Deserted Apr 19, 64.
Beckwith, George A.	Weston	Jul 22, 63	Jul 22, 63	Drafted; Died May 14, 64 of wounds received May 5, 64.
Bennett, James W.	Brattleboro	May 1, 61	Jun 20, 61	Taken prisoner Jun 30, 62; Paroled Sep 13, 62; Discharged Dec 28, 63 for disability.
Blood, Dorr	Putney	May 1, 61	Jun 20, 61	Wounded Jul 21, 61; Transferred to V. R. C. Sep 1, 63; Discharged Apr 1, 64 for disability.

Blossom, Hiram	Pawlet	Oct 8, 61	Oct 18, 61	Reenlisted Dec 21, 63; Promoted to Corp.; to Sgt. Feb 6, 63; Wounded May 5, 64; Discharged May 13. 65.
Bowker, L. Fay	Wilmington	May 1, 61	Jun 20, 61	Reenlisted Jan 31, 64; Promoted to Corp. Feb 6, 65; Wounded Jul 21, 61, May 5, 64 and Sep 19, 64; Mustered out Jul 15, 65.
Bradley, Robert	Brattleboro	May 1, 61	Jun 20, 61	Deserted Aug 30, 62.
Brent, Frederick	Substitute	Aug 5, 63	Aug 5, 63	Substitute for Nathaniel Grout, Hartland; Deserted Dec 26, 63.
Brown, Charles W.	Brattleboro	May 1, 61	Jun 20, 61	Discharged Jun 2, 62 for disability.
Bugbee, Danford A.	Dover	May 1, 61	Jun 20, 61	Wounded Jun 29, 62 and captured; Paroled Jul 25, 62; Discharged Jan 5, 63 for wounds.
Bugbee, Edwin W.	Dover	May 1, 61	Jun 20, 61	Discharged Nov 12, 61 for disability.
Butterfield, George P.	Brattleboro	May 1, 61	Jun 20, 61	Reenlisted Jan 31, 64; Wounded May 12, 64; Mustered out Jul 15, 65.
Butterfield, Joel P.	Brattleboro	May 1, 61	Jun 20, 61	Discharged Nov 19, 62 for disability.
Caderit, Joseph	Substitute	Aug 3, 63	Aug 3, 63	Substitute for Charles Hyde, North Hero; Wounded May 5, 64 and May 12, 64; Mustered out Jul 15, 65.
Carlos, Michael	Substitute	Aug 21, 63	Aug 23, 63	Substitute for George Rice, Burlington; Promoted to Corp. Feb 6, 65; Wounded May 5, 64; Mustered out Jul 15, 65.
Carpenter, Chauncey	Brattleboro	May 1, 61	Jun 20, 61	Reenlisted Dec 21, 63; Wounded Jun 29, 62; Deserted Aug 62; Returned Oct 62; Mustered out Jul 15, 65.
Carpenter, Edward J.	Newfane	Aug 10, 61	Sep 15, 61	Wounded and taken prisoner Jun 29, 62; Paroled Jul 22, 62; Discharged Feb 13, 63 for wounds.
Carpenter, Joseph	Substitute	Aug 7, 63	Aug 7, 63	Substitute for Enoch Howe, Essex; Mustered out Jul 15, 65.
Casey, John	Substitute	Aug 21, 63	Aug 21, 63	Substitute for unknown person; Discharged by sentence of G. C. M. May 1, 64.
Chapleau, Alphonso	Substitute	Jul 31, 63	Jul 31, 63	Substitute for James R. Hickok, Burlington; Mustered out Jul 15, 65.
Charter, King D.	Marlboro	Aug 11, 62	Sep 15, 62	Wagoner; Mustered out Jun 19, 65.
Chase, Dennis	Townshend	May 1, 61	Jun 20, 61	Died Sep 22, 61 of disease.
Clair, Harrison	St. Albans	Aug 25, 64	Aug 25, 64	Deserted; Never joined Co.
Clancey, Thomas	Substitute	Jul 31, 63	Jul 31, 63	Substitute for Henry H. Laughton, Putney; Taken prisoner Oct 11, 63; Confined at Andersonville, Ga. Mar 8, 64; N. F. R.
Clark, Francis	Substitute	Jul 24, 62	Jul 24, 63	Substitute for Edwin Whitcomb, Bolton; Discharged Feb 22, 65 for wounds received May 12, 64.
Clark, Samuel O.	Substitute	Jul 28, 63	Jul 28, 63	Substitute for George W. Flanegan, Hinesburgh; Deserted Feb 20, 64; Enlisted in the 40th NY Feb 10, 65 and caught as a deserter from the 2nd Vt.
Clark, Smith	Tunbridge	Dec 10, 63	Dec 30, 63	Discharged Feb 2, 64 for disability.
Clark, William W.	Brattleboro	May 1, 61	Jun 20, 61	KIA Jun 29, 62.
Clindinning, Charles	Substitute	Sep 12, 63	Sep 12, 63	Substitute for William F. Staples, Brighton; Taken prisoner Jun 19, 64; Paroled Dec 13, 64; Deserted Jan 31, 65.
Coe, Charles	Substitute	Aug 7, 63	Aug 7, 63	Substitute for Joseph B. Kingsbury, Jericho; Discharged by sentence of G. C. M. May 1, 64; Real name Charles Howard.
Cole, William	Substitute	Sep 15, 63	Sep 15, 63	Substitute for C. D. R. Meacham, Newport; Died May 4, 64 of wounds received same day.
Colt, George M.	Brattleboro	May 1, 61	Jun 20, 61	Promoted to Corp.; Wounded Jul 10, 63 and May 5, 64; Mustered out Jun 29, 64.
Combs, Benjamin E.	Rutland	Aug 30, 62	Sep 15, 62	Wounded May 3, 63; Transferred to V. R. C. Mar 27, 64; Discharged Jun 12, 65.

Conklin, John	Substitute	Jul 31, 63	Jul 31, 63	Substitute for Henry M. Hall, Hinesburgh; Wounded May 5, 64; Deserted Aug 12, 64.
Cook, Madison	Brattleboro	May 1, 61	Jun 20, 61	KIA May 4, 63.
Cooley, Henry L.	Brattleboro	May 1, 61	Jun 20, 61	Died Jan 11, 63 of disease.
Cross, Thomas	Hardwick	Nov 27, 63	Dec 19, 63	Transferred to V. R. C. Jun 15, 64; deserted Nov 21, 64.
Dalpe, Michael	Substitute	Jul 31, 63	Jul 31, 63	Substitute for Orange Stokes, Lincoln; Wounded Oct 19, 64; Transferred to V. R. C. Feb 21, 65; Mustered out Jul 20, 65.
Davis, David	Substitute	Aug 4, 63	Aug 4, 63	Substitute for S. J. Sweat, St. Albans; Wounded May 5, 64; Deserted Aug 12, 64.
Day, Louis	Substitute	Aug 5, 63	Aug 5, 63	Substitute for Benjamin F. French, Rutland; Wounded May 12, 64; Deserted Aug 10, 64; Returned Dec 13, 64; Mustered out Jul 15, 65.
Devoid, Matthias	Substitute	Jul 21, 63	Jul 21, 63	Substitute for Smith N. Pease, Burlington; Wounded May 5, 64; Deserted Aug 12, 64.
Divine, Arthur	Substitute	Sep 12, 63	Sep 12, 63	Substitute for Hiram T. Springer, Brighton; Mustered out Jul 15, 65.
Donohue, Jerry	Substitute	Aug 1, 63	Aug 1, 63	Substitute for William J. Edgecomb, Burlington; Died May 12, 64 of wounds received May 5, 64.
Dow, George	Substitute	Jul 18, 63	Jul 18, 63	Substitute for Charles M. Fisher, Cabot; Wounded May 18, 64; Mustered out May 13, 65.
Doyon, Azro R.	Substitute	Aug 4, 63	Aug 4, 63	Substitute for Edwin P. Stephens, Enosburgh; Died Jul 5, 64 of wounds received May 12, 64.
Dueter, Francis	Substitute	Aug 1, 63	Aug 1, 63	Substitute for Warren Hall, Bolton; Mustered out Jul 15, 65.
Dugan, William H.	Substitute	Jul 31, 63	Jul 31, 63	Substitute for John P. Sergeant, Brattleboro; Deserted Aug 10, 64.
Dwyer, Patrick	Hartford	May 4, 63	May 23, 63	Taken prisoner Jun 19, 64; Paroled Dec 6, 64; N. F. R.
Edwards, George	Substitute	Aug 3, 63	Aug 3, 63	Substitute for Latham F. Truman, Burlington; Transferred to V. R. C. Jul 26, 64; Died Mar 7, 65.
Emerson, Elbridge	Brattleboro	May 1, 61	Jun 20, 61	Discharged Apr 4, 62 for wounds accidentally received.
Emerson, Rufus	Brattleboro	May 1, 61	Jun 20, 61	See Second Lt. Co. C.
Fannef, Joseph	Substitute	Jul 22, 63	Jul 22, 63	Substitute for John S. Jones, Shoreham; KIA May 12, 64.
Felton, Frederick B.	Townshend	May 1, 61	Jun 20, 61	Discharged Jan 25, 63 for disability.
Fisher, Elijah B.	Marlboro			Taken prisoner Jun 13, 62; Paroled Sep 13, 62; KIA May 5, 64.
Fitzgerald, James	Substitute	Aug 7, 63	Aug 7, 63	Substitute for Charles Carty, Essex; Discharged by order of G. C. M. May 1, 64.
Foster, William	Brattleboro	May 1, 61	Jun 20, 61	Transferred to V. R. C. Nov 20, 63; Discharged Jun 29, 64.
Foster William H.	Dummerston	May 1, 61	Jun 20, 61	Promoted to Sgt.; Wounded May 3, 63 and May 6, 64; Mustered out Jun 29, 64.
Fox, Martin L.	Wilmington	May 1, 61	Jun 20, 61	Mustered out Jun 29, 64.
Francis, William	Substitute	Jul 23, 63	Jul 23, 63	Substitute for Charles C. Laduke, Burlington; Wounded May 5, 64; Mustered out Jul 15, 65.
Franklin, Daniel H.	Brattleboro	May 1, 61	Jun 20, 61	Deserted Sep 14, 63.
Franklin, George A.	Brattleboro	May 1, 61	Jun 20, 61	Discharged Nov 8, 62 for disability.
Gibson, Edward P.	Brattleboro	May 1, 61	Jun 20, 61	Wounded and taken prisoner Jul 21; Died in Richmond, Va. Aug 13, 61.
Glover, Lemuel	Substitute	Jul 22, 63	Jul 22, 63	Substitute for John C. Tyler, Brattleboro; Discharged by sentence of G. C. M. May 1, 64.
Goodell, Lewis	Woodbury	Jul 21, 63	Jul 21, 63	Drafted; Died Jun 6, 64 of accidental wound.
Goodrich, Thomas	Hinesburgh	Aug 23, 62	Sep 15, 62	Died Mar 4, 64 of disease.
Gore, William	Brattleboro	May 1, 61	Jun 20, 61	Deserted Sep 23, 62.

Gould, Joseph	Substitute	Aug 4, 63	Aug 4, 63	Substitute for R. W. Drew, Fairfax; Deserted Aug 10, 64; Returned Dec 13, 64; Discharged May 13, 65 for wounds received Apr 2, 65.
Graham, Arthur	Burlington	May 1, 61	May 25, 63	Deserted Jun 30, 63.
Graves, Albert L.	Vernon	May 1, 61	Jun 20, 61	Taken prisoner Jul 21, 61; Paroled Jan 3, 62; Deserted Sep 29, 62.
Gray, George S.	E. Montpelier	Jul 13, 63	Jul 13, 63	Drafted; KIA May 12, 64.
Griffin, James	Brattleboro	Aug 10, 61	Oct 18, 61	Reenlisted Dec 21, 63; Mustered out Jul 15, 65.
Guyette, Alfred	Substitute	Aug 5, 63	Aug 5, 63	Substitute for J. G. Abell, Fairfield; Died Jun 7, 64 of wounds received May 5, 64.
Hall, Amos	Hinesburgh	Aug 27, 62	Sep 15, 62	Mustered out Jun 19, 65.
Harrington, Samuel E.	Wardsboro	May 1, 61	Jun 20, 61	Discharged Sep 17, 62 for disability.
Harwood, Justin W.	Pawlet	Oct 6, 61	Oct 18, 61	Reenlisted Dec 21, 63; Promoted to Corp. Feb 6, 65; Wounded May 6, 64; Mustered out Jul 15, 65.
Haven, Prescott R.	Ludlow	Feb 24, 62	Apr 12, 62	Discharged Jan 2, 63 for disability.
Hescock, Rinaldo N.	Brattleboro	May 1, 61	Jun 20, 61	Taken Prisoner Jun 29, 62; Paroled Aug 5, 62; Wounded Sep 14, 62; Transferred to V. R. C. Sep 1, 63; Discharged Jun 20, 64.
Hesselton, Abner C.	Ludlow	Feb 28, 62	Apr 12, 62	Discharged Jan 14, 63 for disability.
Holbrook, James E.	Brattleboro	May 1, 61	Jun 20, 61	Discharged Jan 20, 63 for disability.
Hood, Charles	Albany	Aug 17, 64	Aug 17, 64	Transferred from Co. F, 9th Vt.; Mustered out Jun 19, 65.
Hopkins, Henry W.	Brattleboro	Aug 10, 61	Oct 18, 61	Discharged Nov 8, 62 for disability.
Houghton, Warren V.	Putney	May 1, 61	Jun 20, 61	Promoted to Corp.; KIA May 4, 63.
Howe, Edmund P.	Newfane	May 1, 61	Jun 20, 61	Promoted Sgt.; Wounded Jun 29, 62; Mustered out Jun 29, 64.
Jerd, Peter	Braintree	Dec 8, 63	Dec 19, 63	Discharged May 3, 64.
Jones, John E.	Randolph	Aug 30, 64	Aug 30, 64	Transferred from Co. F 9th Vt.; Wounded Apr 2, 65; Mustered out Jul 15, 65.
Kellogg, Charles H.	Castleton	Oct 5, 61	Oct 18, 61	Died Dec 31, 62 of disease.
Kendall, Albert D.	Brattleboro	May 1, 61	Jun 20, 61	Mustered out Jun 29, 64.
Knight, George H.	Dummerston	Aug 16, 62	Sep 15, 62	Wounded May 3, 63 and May 5, 64; Discharged May 3, 65.
Ladd, Frank V.	Brattleboro	May 1, 61	Jun 20, 61	Discharged Jan 25, 63 for disability.
Lamb, Henry L.	Newfane	May 1, 61	Jun 20, 61	Taken prisoner Jun 29, 62; Paroled Jul 27, 62; Deserted Oct 19, 62.
Lamson, Franklin A.	————	Mar 30, 63	Apr 6, 63	Mustered out Jul 15, 65.
Lanphere, John M.	Brattleboro	May 1, 61	Jun 20, 61	Taken prisoner Jun 29, 62; Paroled Sep 13, 62; KIA May 4, 63.
Learned, Thomas J.	Whitingham	May 1, 61	Jun 20, 61	Deserted Oct 19, 62.
Lord, Robert P.	Brattleboro	May 1, 61	Jun 20, 61	KIA May 3, 63.
Lynch, Michael	Shaftsbury	Aug 10, 61	Oct 18, 61	Reenlisted Dec 21, 63; Promoted to Sgt. Jul 1, 64; Wounded May 5, 64; Died Dec 14, 64 of wounds received Oct 19, 64.
Martell, Noah	South Hero	Dec 24, 63	Dec 30, 63	Wounded May 12, 64 and Oct 19, 64; Discharged Feb 6, 65 for wounds.
Mason, Albert	Newfane	May 1, 61	Jun 20, 61	Taken prisoner May 21, 64; Paroled Nov 19, 64; Discharged Dec 26, 64.
Matteson, William S.	Shaftsbury	Oct 23, 61	Oct 30, 61	Wounded Dec 13, 62; Transferred to V. R. C. Aug 1, 63; Deserted Aug 5, 65.
McDonald, William	St. Albans	Aug 25, 64	Aug 25, 64	Deserted; Never joined company.
Mesick, Hudson	Bennington	Mar 18, 62	Apr 12, 62	Reenlisted Apr 13, 64; Deserted Aug 10, 64; Returned Mar 24, 65; Wounded Apr 2, 65; Mustered out Jul 15, 65.
Metcalf, Albert W.	Westminster	May 1, 61	Jun 20, 61	Discharged Dec 8, 61 for accidental wounds.
Miller, Morris G.	Newfane	May 1, 61	Jun 20, 61	Discharged Jun 2, 63 for disability.
Mulhulm, William	Fairfield	Dec 28, 63	Dec 30, 63	Wounded May 6, 64 and May 12, 64; Deserted Dec 64.
Norris, Ward J.	Albany	Aug 22, 64	Aug 22, 64	Transferred from Co. E 9th Vt.; Mustered out Jun 19, 65.

Paddleford, Frank G.	Brattleboro	May 1, 61	Jun 20, 61	Promoted to Sgt.; Wounded and taken prisoner Jun 28, 62; Paroled Sep 13, 62; Wounded May 10, 64; Mustered out Jun 29, 64.
Pearce, Franklin C.	Putney	Aug 10, 61	Oct 18, 61	Transferred to V. R. C. Jul 27, 63; Discharged Nov 14, 65.
Peck, Noah A.	Castleton	Oct 6, 61	Oct 18, 61	Reenlisted Dec 21, 63; KIA May 5, 64.
Perham, Merritt	Middletown	Oct 2, 61	Oct 18, 61	Reenlisted Dec 21, 63; Promoted to Corp.; Wounded May 6, 64; Transferred to V. R. C. Dec 14, 64; Mustered out Jul 19, 65.
Pettengill, Almon L.	Substitute	Sep 15, 63	Sep 15, 63	Substitute for Levi Tute, Newport; Wounded May 12, 64; Discharged Aug 7, 64.
Phillips, Eben W.	Substitute	Aug 4, 63	Aug 4, 63	Substitute for Osborn T. Atwater, Burlington; Wounded May 5, 64; Mustered out Jun 23, 65.
Pierce, George W.	Brattleboro	May 1, 61	Jun 20, 61	Reenlisted Dec 21, 63; Promoted to Corp. Feb 6, 65; Wounded May 5, 64; Discharged Jun 13, 65.
Place, Robert Sumner	Hinesburgh	Sep 10, 62	Sep 15, 62	Died Sep 15, 63 of disease.
Pratt, R. Morton	Newfane	May 1, 61	Jun 20, 61	Wounded and taken prisoner Jul 21, 61; Paroled Oct 5, 61; Discharged Nov 1, 61 for wounds.
Prouty, George B.	Brattleboro	May 1, 61	Jun 20, 61	Promoted to Corp.; Mustered out Jun 29, 64.
Rand, Kirk	Brattleboro	May 1, 61	Jun 20, 61	Reenlisted Jan 30, 64; Promoted to Corp.; to Sgt. Jul 1, 64; Wounded Dec 13 and May 5, 64; Discharged Oct 28, 65 for wounds.
Rice, George A.	Wilmington	May 1, 61	Jun 20, 61	KIA May 3, 63.
Richardson, Henry A.	Brattleboro	May 1, 61	Jun 20, 61	Promoted to Sgt. Aug 24, 63; Wounded May 12, 64 and Jun 10, 64; Mustered out Jun 29, 64.
Ripley, James C.	Brattleboro	May 1, 61	Jun 20, 61	Mustered out Jun 29, 64.
Ripley, John P.	Brattleboro	May 1, 61	Jun 20, 61	Promoted to Corp.; Mustered out Jun 29, 64.
Ripley, Willard L.	Tunbridge	Feb 13, 65	Feb 13, 65	Deserted Apr 2, 65; Returned May 12, 65; Mustered out Jun 27, 65.
Robbins, Eugene W.	Grafton	Dec 23, 63	Dec 29, 63	Mustered out Jul 15, 65.
Ross, Alexander N.	Substitute	Aug 3, 63	Aug 3, 63	Substitute for George R. Bennett, Dummerston; Deserted Sep 7, 63.
Ross, Edgar	Castleton	Oct 6, 61	Oct 20, 61	Died Dec 15, 61 of disease.
Russell, Waldo D.	Brattleboro	May 1, 61	Jun 20, 61	Deserted Sep 29, 62.
Samson, Arby N.	Putney	May 1, 61	Jun 20, 61	Mustered out Jun 29, 64.
Sawyer, George M.	Ludlow	Feb 24, 62	Apr 12, 62	Discharged Jan 13, 63 for disability.
Scott, Israel S.	Newport	Aug 10, 61	Oct 18, 61	Reenlisted Dec 21, 63; KIA May 18, 64.
Shambo, Francis H.	Montpelier	Mar 6, 62	Apr 12, 62	Mustered out Mar 28, 65.
Shields, John	Substitute	Jul 28, 63	Jul 28, 63	Substitute for Jason Young, Alburgh; N. F. R.
Sleeper, Curtis C.	Waterbury	Feb 24, 62	Mar 28, 62	Wounded and taken prisoner Jun 29, 62; Paroled Aug 3, 62; Discharged Nov 1, 63.
Sleeper, John N.	Chelsea	Aug 16, 64	Aug 16, 64	Transferred from Co. F 9th Vt.; Mustered out Jun 12, 65.
Spaulding, Amos P.	Cavendish	Sep 12, 61	Oct 20, 61	Deserted Oct 19, 62; Returned; Transferred to V. R. C. Sep 1, 63; Transferred back to Co. Jan 9, 64; Wounded May 5, 64; Mustered out Jul 15, 65.
Stearns, Edward A.	Brattleboro	May 1, 61	Jun 20, 61	Discharged Jun 12, 62 for disability.
Stockwell, Charles J.	Brattleboro	May 1, 61	Jun 20, 61	Reenlisted Jan 26, 64; Mustered out Jul 15, 65.
Stoddard, Frederick A.	Townshend	May 1, 61	Jun 20, 61	Died Jul 9, 61 of disease.
Streeter, Philander A.	Vernon	May 1, 61	Jun 20, 61	Taken prisoner Jul 21, 61; Paroled Jan 3, 62; Mustered out Jun 29, 64.
Thomas, William B.	Brattleboro	May 1, 61	Jun 20, 61	Discharged Mar 16, 65 for disability.
Titus, Carlo	Vershire	Aug 27, 64	Aug 27, 64	Transferred from Co. G 9th Vt.; Mustered out Jul 15, 65.
Warren, Amos	Fairfield	Dec 23, 63	Dec 30, 63	Discharged Mar 21, 64 for disability.
Webber, Joshua C.	Brattleboro	Aug 10, 61	Oct 18, 61	Deserted Sep 24, 62.
Wheeler, Joseph R.	Brattleboro	May 1, 61	Jun 20, 61	Taken prisoner Jul 21, 61; Paroled Jan 3, 62; Wounded Dec 13, 62; Discharged Apr 22, 64 for wounds.

Whitney, Ransom	Tunbridge	Aug 27, 64	Aug 27, 64	Transferred from Co. D 9th Vt.; Mustered out Jun 19, 65.
Willard, William F.	Putney	May 1, 61	Jun 20, 61	Reenlisted Dec 21, 63; Drummer; Mustered out Jul 15, 65.
Willis, Charles	Bennington	Dec 23, 63	Dec 30, 63	Wounded May 12, 64; Mustered out Jul 15, 65.
Wilson, William	Bradford	Dec 6, 62	Jan 1, 62	Transferred to V. R. C. Oct 12, 63; Discharged Jul 29, 65.
Wood, William	Brattleboro	May 1, 61	Jun 20, 61	Promoted to Corp.; Mustered out Jun 29, 64.
Woodbury, William	Castleton	Oct 6, 61	Oct 18, 61	Reenlisted Dec 21, 63; Mustered out Jul 15, 65.

Company D

Name and Rank	Residence	Date of Commission	Date of Issue	Remarks
Captains				
Dillingham, Charles	Waterbury	May 20, 61	May 20, 61	Promoted to Maj. in 8th Vt. Jan 18, 62.
Johnson, Enoch E.	Castleton	Jan 25, 62	Jan 25, 62	See Lt. Col..
Hurlbert, Ward B.	Weybridge	Dec 24, 64	Jan 31, 65	Corp. Co. K; Reenlisted Mar 21, 64; Promoted to Sgt. Sep 1, 62; to First Lt. Co. K Jun 20, 64; Mustered out Jul 15, 65.
First Lieutenants				
Henry, William W.	Waterbury	May 20, 61	May 20, 61	Resigned Nov 5, 61.
Clark, Dayton P.	Montpelier	Jan 29, 62	Jan 29, 62	See Capt. Co. F.
Bass, John T.	Moretown	Nov 3, 63	Nov 11, 63	See Capt. Co. H.
Stone, Pratt	Readsboro	Jun 20, 64	Jul 11, 64	See Capt. Co. F.
Lesser, Alphonzo	Marshfield	Dec 24, 64	Jan 31, 65	Corp. Co. D; Reenlisted Jan 31, 64; Promoted to Sgt. Jan 8, 63; to First Sgt. Nov 1, 64; Wounded Jul 21, 61, May 5, 64 and Sep 19, 64; Mustered out Jul 15, 65.
Second Lieutenants				
Gregg, Charles C.	Waterbury	May 20, 61	May 20, 61	Dismissed from the service Jul 22, 62.
Bass, John T.	Moretown	Aug 9, 62	Aug 16, 62	See Capt. Co. H.
Tilden, Eldon A.	Barre	Nov 20, 63	Nov 24, 63	Sgt. Co. D; Promoted to First Sgt.; Mustered out Jun 29, 64.
Turner, Orlando S.	Moretown	Jun 7, 65	Jun 17, 65	Pvt. Co. D; Reenlisted Jan 31, 64; Promoted to Corp. Oct 21, 61; to Sgt. Jul 19, 64; to First Sgt. Feb 7, 65; Mustered out as First Sgt. Jul 15, 65.

Name and Rank	Residence	Date of Enlistment	Date of Muster	Remarks
Sergeants				
Canning, Charles C.	Northfield	May 7, 61	May 20, 61	See First Lt. Co. I.
Bass, John T.	Moretown	May 7, 61	May 20, 61	See Capt. Co. H.
Smith, John R.	Stowe	May 7, 61	May 20, 61	Reduced; Reenlisted Jan 31, 64; Wounded May 12, 64; Mustered out Jul 15, 65.
Tilden, Eldon A.	Barre	May 7, 61	May 20, 61	See Second Lt. Co. D.
Atkins, M. Frank	Duxbury	May 7, 61	May 20, 61	Reduced Oct 16, 61; Discharged Nov 4, 61 for disability.
Corporals				
Strong, Lemuel D.	Barre	May 7, 61	June 20, 61	Promoted to Sgt. Oct 21, 61; Wounded May 5, 64; Mustered out Jun 29, 64.
Huntley, Nathan F.	Duxbury	May 7, 61	June 20, 61	Died Aug 4, 61 of disease.
Gilman, Warren C.	Waterbury	May 7, 61	June 20, 61	Reduced; Mustered out Jun 29, 64.
Smith, Albert	Barre	May 7, 61	June 20, 61	Reduced; Discharged Nov 1, 62 for disability.

Sleeper, Tilton	Waterbury	May 7, 61	June 20, 61	Discharged Feb 5, 63 for disability.
Lesser, Alphonzo	Marshfield	May 7, 61	June 20, 61	See First Lt. Co. D.
Huntley, Frank	Waterbury	May 7, 61	June 20, 61	Reduced Oct 16, 61; Deserted Aug 28, 62.
Center, George G.	Waterbury	May 7, 61	June 20, 61	Reduced; Wounded Dec 13, 62; Transferred to V. R. C. Sep 1, 63; Discharged Apr—, 64 for disability.
Musician				
Lamont, Robert	Montpelier	Jun 15, 61	Jun 20, 61	Mustered out Jun 29, 64.
Carpenter, Franklin	Waterbury	May 7, 61	Jun 20, 61	Mustered out Jun 29, 64.
Wagoner				
Hill, Obadiah W.	Berlin	May 7, 61	Jun 20, 61	Discharged Jan 1, 63 for disability.
Privates				
Alden, Sylvester O.	Middlesex	Aug 19, 64	Aug 19, 64	Wounded Oct 19, 64; Mustered out Jun 19, 65.
Allen, Andrew H.	Montpelier	May 7, 61	Jun 20, 61	Died Jun 26, 61 of disease.
Aubry, Harvey F.	Burlington	May 7, 61	Jun 20, 61	Died Sep 27, 62 of disease.
Bean, Albert	Middlesex	Aug 15, 62	Sep 15, 62	Died Oct 3, 64 of disease.
Bean, William R.	Berlin	Aug 14, 62	Sep 22, 62	Discharged Apr 1, 63 for wounds received Dec 13, 62.
Beckley, Oren, Jr.	Barre	May 7, 61	Jun 20, 61	Promoted to Sgt.; Wounded May 5, 64; Taken prisoner May 10, 64 and died at Andersonville, Ga. Jun 6, 64.
Bickford, Riley M.	Waterbury	Sep 7, 61	Sep 20, 61	Mustered out Sep 20, 64.
Bicknell, Dennis H.	Stowe	May 7, 61	Jun 20, 61	Promoted to Corp.; Transferred to U.S. Army Jun 8, 63.
Blanchard, Origen A.	Barre	Sep 7, 61	Sep 20, 61	Promoted to Corp.; to Sgt.; Mustered out Sep 20, 64.
Braidnell, William	Duxbury	May 7, 61	Jun 20, 61	Wounded May 4, 63; Mustered out Jun 29, 64.
Brink, William F.	Waterbury	Sep 3, 61	Sep 20, 61	Reenlisted Sep 21, 63: Mustered out Jul 15, 65.
Brown, Chester	Berlin	Aug 14, 62	Sep 15, 62	Promoted to Corp. Apr 1, 65; Mustered out Jun 27, 65.
Brown Christopher P.	Waterbury	May 7, 61	Jun 20, 61	Wounded Dec 13, 62; Mustered out Jun 29, 64.
Bruce, Lucian	Duxbury	Aug 13, 62	Sep 15, 62	Wounded May 5, 64; Transferred to V. R. C. Nov 25, 64; Mustered out Jul 3, 65.
Burgin, Patrick	Montpelier	Jul 30, 62	Sep 30, 62	Died May 10, 63 of wounds received May 4, 63.
Cameron, James	Middlesex	Jul 30, 64	Jul 30, 64	Mustered out Jun 19, 65.
Camp, Iran N.	Barre	May 7, 61	Jun 20, 61	Promoted to Corp.; Wounded Dec 13, 62; Mustered out Jun 29, 65.
Churchill, Lyman	Stowe	Sep 7, 61	Sep 20, 61	Mustered out Sep 20, 64.
Clark, William	Woodstock	Feb 9, 64	Feb 9, 64	Mustered out May 12, 65.
Clough, John C.	Williamstown	Sep 7, 61	Sep 20, 61	Reenlisted Jan 31, 64; Taken prisoner May 10, 64; Escaped Jan 10, 65, Mustered out Jul 15, 65.
Coffin, Benjamin F.	Enosburgh	Jul 16, 63	Jul 16, 63	Drafted; Wounded May 5, 64; Deserted Sep 13, 64.
Colby, George W.	Stowe	May 7, 61	Jun 20, 61	Reenlisted Dec 21, 63; Wounded May 5, 64; Discharged Feb 6, 65 for disability.
Collins, Charles N.	Waterbury	May 7, 61	Jun 20, 61	Died Dec 17, 61 of disease.
Conway, Michael	Moretown	May 7, 61	Jun 20, 61	Reenlisted Jan 31, 64; Wagoner; Mustered out Jul 15, 65.
Cooley, William	Fairfield	Jul 15, 63	Jul 15, 63	Drafted; Taken prisoner May 12, 64; Died at Florence, S.C. Nov 23, 64.
Crane, Vernon F.	Moretown	Nov 20, 63	Dec 5, 63	KIA May 5, 64.
Crossman, Dexter	Middletown	Dec 30, 63	Dec 30, 63	Wounded May 5, 64; KIA Oct 19, 64.
Cummins, Jesse D.	Berlin	Aug 14, 62	Sep 15, 62	KIA May 5, 64.
Daniels, Henry F.	Eden	Sep 3, 61	Sep 20, 61	Died Mar 25, 62 of disease.
Davenport, John P.	Berlin	Aug 14, 62	Sep 22, 62	Discharged Apr 1, 63 for disability.
Davis, Leonard W.	Elmore	Jul 17, 63	Jul 17, 63	Drafted; Wounded May 5, 64; Discharged Jul 25, 65.
Deline, Albert	Waterbury	Sep 3, 61	Sep 20, 61	Mustered out Sep 20, 64.

Diamond, Henry P.	Moretown	Sep 3, 61	Sep 20, 61	Mustered out Sep 20, 64.
Diamond, James	Moretown	May 7, 61	Jun 20, 61	Wounded Jul 21, 61 and Dec 13, 62; Mustered out Jun 29, 64.
Dillingham, Martin L.	Stowe	Jul 24, 62	Sep 15, 62	Mustered out Jun 19, 65.
Dion, James	Pownal	Mar 18, 62	Apr 12, 62	Taken prisoner May 10, 64; released Dec 11, 64; Mustered out Apr 21, 65.
Dodge, Lewis H.	Barre	Sep 3, 61	Sep 3, 61	Wounded and taken prisoner Jun 29, 62; Paroled Jul 25, 62; Died Sep 1, 62 of wounds.
Dodge, Luther C.	Barre	Apr 3, 62	Apr 12, 62	Died Jun 12, 62 of disease.
Dodge, Nelson E.	Barre	Mar 8, 62	Apr 12, 62	Promoted to Corp.; to Sgt.; Taken prisoner May 10, 64; Died at Andersonville, Ga.
Dodge, Richard	Worcester	May 7, 61	Jun 20, 61	Wounded Dec 13, 62; Discharged Mar 29, 63 for disability.
Dow, Truman N.	Duxbury	May 7, 61	Jun 20, 61	Died Aug 5, 61 of disease.
Doyle, James A.	Substitute	Sep 9, 63	Sep 9, 63	Substitute for Charles Evans, Brighton; Wounded May 5, 64; Mustered out Jul 15, 65.
Dudley, Andrew J.	Barre	Sep 7, 61	Sep 20, 61	Discharged Jan 2, 63 for disability.
Dwyer, Michael	Duxbury	Aug 12, 62	Sep 15, 62	Wounded Dec 13, 62; Discharged by order of the War Dept. Jun 19, 65.
Dyer, Hiram	Elmore	Jul 17, 63	Jul 17, 63	Drafted; Died Jan 17, 64 of disease.
Edgerley, James	Middlesex	Aug 20, 64	Aug 20, 64	Died Oct 31, 64 of disease.
Fairbanks, George R.	Stowe	Aug 18, 64	Aug 18, 64	Died Mar 9, 65 of disease.
Farnham, George W.	Waterbury	May 7, 61	Jun 20, 61	Deserted Jun 22, 61 before leaving Vt..
Finnegan, Francis	Hyde Park	May 7, 61	Jun 20, 61	Wounded May 12, 64; Mustered out Jun 29, 64.
Flaherty, Patrick H.	Waterbury	May 7, 61	Jun 20, 61	Taken prisoner Jul 21, 61; Paroled Jan 3, 62; Discharged Dec 18, 62 for disability.
Fortune, John B. F.	Substitute	Aug 3, 63	Aug 3, 63	Substitute for Rodney D. Rublee, Enosburgh; Deserted Sep 14, 63.
Foster, Wilbur	Waterbury	Sep 3, 61	Sep 20, 61	Discharged Oct 20, 62 for disability.
Francis, Edgar A.	E. Montpelier	Aug 20, 64	Aug 20, 64	Mustered out Jun 19, 65.
Fuller, John H.	Chelsea	May 7, 61	Jun 20, 61	Died Apr 10, 63 of disease.
Gammash, David	Substitute	Jul 30, 63	Jul 30, 63	Substitute for Wareham Brewster, Huntington; Discharged Jul 22, 65 by order of the War Dept.
George, William S.	Berlin	Aug 14, 62	Sep 15, 62	Died Jul 9, 64 of wounds received May 5, 64.
Gilla, John	Substitute	Aug 1, 63	Aug 1, 63	Substitute for George Siples, Charlotte, Deserted Aug 30, 63.
Gilman, Charles H.	Duxbury	May 7, 61	Jun 20, 61	Discharged Sep 19, 62 for disability.
Gilman, Orin	Duxbury	May 7, 61	Jun 20, 61	Promoted to Corp. Oct 21, 61; KIA May 5, 64.
Godfrey, Timothy C.	Waterbury	Sep 2, 61	Sep 20, 61	Discharged Jun 20, 62 for disability.
Goodell, Henry	Woodbury	May 7, 61	Jun 20, 61	Reenlisted Jan 31, 64; Promoted to Corp. Apr 1, 65; Wounded Dec 13, 62, May 4, 63 and May 7, 64; Mustered out Jul 18, 65.
Goodrich, George W.	Barre	May 7, 61	Jun 20, 61	Mustered out Jun 29, 64.
Gorman, Thomas	Substitute	Jul 23, 63	Jul 23, 63	Substitute for Lafayette Wilbur, Jericho; Promoted to Corp. Feb 7, 65; Wounded May 5, 64 and Sep 19, 64; KIA Apr 2, 65.
Gowing, John	Providence	May 7, 61	Jun 20, 61	Wounded and taken prisoner Jul 21, 61; Died in Richmond, Va. Aug 21, 61.
Gravel, Alphonso	Substitute	Jul 20, 63	Jul 20, 63	Substitute for Homer M. Phelps, Burlington; Wounded May 5, 64; Mustered out Jul 15, 65.
Greenough, Frank	Monkton	Sep 12, 61	Sep 20, 61	Mustered out Sep 20, 64.
Hallock, Lucius D.	Berlin	Aug 14, 62	Sep 15, 62	Wounded Jun 21, 64; Mustered out Jun 19, 65.
Hall, Aaron P.	Woodbury	May 7, 61	Jun 20, 61	Wounded May 5, 64; Mustered out Jun 29,
Hall, James K.	Woodbury	Aug 7, 62	Sep 15, 62	KIA May 5, 64.
Hall, Marvin J.	Woodbury	Aug 11, 62	Sep 30, 62	Discharged Jan 1, 63 for disability.
Hall, William	Waterbury	Sep 2, 61	Sep 20, 61	Reenlisted Dec 21, 63; Deserted Jan 23, 63; Returned Jan 29, 63; Deserted Feb 7, 64.
Harrington, Nathan	Barre	Sep 7, 61	Sep 20, 61	Wounded May 5, 64; Mustered out Sep 20, 64.
Harron, Ira L.	Berlin	Jun 6, 61	Jun 20, 61	Deserted Sep 15, 63.
Hart, Alonzo	Waterbury	Sep 3, 61	Sep 20, 61	Discharged Feb 10, 63 for disability.

Hart, Frank	Waterbury	Feb 19, 62	Apr 12, 62	Reenlisted Apr 19, 63; Promoted to Corp. Feb 7, 65; Deserted Jul 28, 64; Returned Dec 64; Mustered out Jul 15, 65.
Hart, Frederick A.	Waterbury	Dec 14, 63	Dec 31, 63	Mustered out Jul 15, 65.
Hartwell, Charles C.	Berlin	Aug 14, 62	Sep 22, 62	Died Jan 1, 63 of wounds received Dec 13, 62.
Hatch, Zenas	Middlesex	Jul 13, 63	Jul 13, 63	Drafted; Wounded May 12, 64; Died Nov 11, 64 of wounds received Oct 19, 64.
Hill, Andrew	Cabot	May 7, 61	Jun 20, 61	Wounded Jul 21, 61; Died Jun 14, 62 of disease.
Holden, Edmund	Elmore	May 7, 61	Jun 20, 61	Discharged Dec 28, 62 for disability.
Holmes, Charles C.	Bakersfield	Nov 5, 63	Nov 5, 63	Died Jun 20, 64 of wounds received May 5, 64.
Hornbrook, Timothy	Berlin	Aug 18, 64	Aug 18, 64	Mustered out Jun 19, 65.
Houghton, Don A.	Grafton	Jul 31, 63	Jul 31, 63	Drafted; KIA May 12, 64.
Hovey, James O.	Calais	May 7, 61	Jun 20, 61	Reenlisted Dec 21, 63; Wounded Dec 13, 62 and Sep 19, 64; Discharged May 13, 65 for disability.
Hubbard, George W.	Waterbury	Sep 3, 61	Sep 20, 61	Reenlisted Jan 31, 64; Wounded Dec 13; KIA May 12, 64.
Hughes, Arthur	Substitute	Jul 24, 63	Jul 24, 63	Substitute for John Baxter, Burlington; Promoted to Corp. Apr 1, 65; Wounded Oct 19, 64; Mustered out Jul 15, 65.
Hunkins, Robert	Waterbury	May 7, 61	Jun 20, 61	KIA May 5, 64.
Hutchins, Henry D.	Substitute	Jul 29, 63	Jul 29, 63	Substitute for Americas V. Phillips, Duxbury; Discharged Apr 28, 64 for disability.
Johnson, George R.	Substitute	Aug 5, 63	Aug 5, 63	Daniel G. Spaulding, Woodstock; Deserted Sep 20, 63.
Johnson, Henry F.	Berlin	Aug 14, 62	Aug 14, 62	Promoted to Corp. Sep 1, 64; Wounded May 5, 64; Transferred to V. R. C. Nov 25, 64; Mustered out Jul 3, 65.
Jones, Henry C.	Barre	May 7, 61	Jun 20, 61	Promoted to Corp. Oct 21, 61; Wounded May 5, 64; Mustered out Jun 29, 64.
Kelley, William G.	Duxbury	May 7, 61	Jun 20, 61	Reenlisted Jan 31, 64; KIA May 5, 64.
Knapp. John	Stowe	May 7, 61	Jun 20, 61	Promoted to Corp.; Discharged Mar 8, 63 for disability.
Lawrence, George S.	Berlin	Aug 17, 64	Aug 17, 64	Wounded Oct 19, 64 and Mar 25, 65; Discharged Jul 19, 65 for disability.
Leatherland, Edwin W.	Montgomery	Jun 17, 61	Jun 20, 61	Deserted Aug 28, 62.
Leazer, Samuel	Barre	May 7, 61	Jun 20, 61	Wounded Jul 21, 61; Discharged Mar 9, 62 for disability.
Locke, Sayles	Waterbury	Sep 2, 61	Sep 20, 61	Died Apr 26, 62 of disease.
Louizell, Julius	Middlesex	Feb 8, 65	Feb 8, 65	Mustered out Jul 15, 65
Lupien, Louis	Plainfield	Feb 22, 62	Apr 11, 62	Discharged Sep 29, 62 for disability.
Marsh, Rufus H.	Moretown	May 7, 61	Jun 20, 61	Promoted to Corp.; Wounded May 12, 64; Mustered out Jun 29, 64.
Marshall, Ira A.	Waterbury	May 7, 61	Jun 20, 61	Discharged Jul 26, 62 for disability.
McCarron, Barney	Berlin	Aug 16, 64	Aug 16, 64	Mustered out Jun 19, 65.
Mee, Thomas	Ponfret	Sep 1, 64	Sep 1, 64	Mustered out Jun 19, 65.
Merriam, Luther	Waterbury	May 7, 61	Jun 20, 61	Discharged Nov 8, 61 for disability.
Moody, Hartwell	Waterbury	May 7, 61	Jun 20, 61	Taken prisoner Jun 29, 62; Paroled Sep 13, 62; Mustered out Jun 29, 64.
Morey, Samuel	Waterbury	May 7, 61	Jun 20, 61	Mustered out Jun 29, 64.
Mosier, John A.	Burlington	May 7, 61	Jun 20, 61	Mustered out Jun 29, 64.
Murphy, Edward	Moretown	May 7, 61	Jun 20, 61	Deserted Aug 28, 62.
Murray, John	Moretown	May 7, 61	Jun 20, 61	Taken prisoner Jul 21, 61; Paroled Jan 3, 62; Wounded May 3, 63; Discharged Apr 4, 64 for wounds.
Nelson, George H.	Marshfield	Dec 12, 63	Dec 31, 63	Wounded May 12, 64; Discharged May 24, 65 for wounds.
Nichols, Eugene	Middlesex	Feb 4, 65	Feb 4, 65	Mustered out Jul 15, 65.
Nichols, Henry W.	Middlesex	Aug 2, 65	Aug 2, 65	Mustered out Jun 19, 65.
Nichols, James	Moretown	May 7, 61	Jun 20, 61	Reenlisted Dec 21, 63; Wounded May 5, 64; Deserted Oct 20, 64; Returned; Discharged May 12, 65.

Nye, Cornelius	Berlin	Aug 14, 62	Sep 15, 62	KIA may 5, 64.
Parker, Henry F.	Waterbury	May 7, 61	Jun 20, 61	Discharged May 29, 62 for disability.
Perry, George W.	Hyde Park	May 7, 61	Jun 20, 61	Deserted Aug 20, 62.
Pike, George W.	Substitute	Aug 4, 63	Aug 4, 63	Substitute for Pembler Sargent, Stowe; Died Nov 2, 63 of disease.
Piper, Isiah	Braintree	Feb 3, 64	Feb 3, 64	Wounded Apr 2, 65; Mustered out Jun 24, 65.
Platt, Horatio G.	Orange	May 7, 61	Jun 20, 61	Discharged Nov 7, 62 for disability and died Nov 8, 62.
Powers, David	Marshfield	Dec 12, 63	Dec 12, 63	Discharged May 13, 65 for disability.
Pratt, Isaac S.	Stowe	May 7, 61	Jun 20, 61	Mustered out Jun 29, 64.
Prescott, Carlos	Waterbury	May 7, 61	Jun 20, 61	Discharged Jul 24, 62 for disability.
Rich, Hollis L.	Moretown	Jul 14, 63	Jul 14, 63	Drafted; Promoted to Corp.; to Sgt.; to First Sgt. Nov 1, 64; Wounded May 5, 64, May 12, 64 and Oct 19, 64; Discharged Oct 3, 65 for wounds.
Richardson, Charles L.	Barre	Sep 7, 61	Sep 20, 61	Reenlisted Jan 31, 64; Wounded May 5, 64; Transferred to V. R. C. Apr 26, 65; Mustered out Jul 20, 65.
Rickard, Henry A.	Marshfield	Dec 12, 63	Dec 31, 63	Promoted to Corp. Apr 1, 65; Mustered out Jul 15, 65.
Ripley, William C.	E. Montpelier	Jul 13, 63	Jul 13, 63	Drafted; Promoted to Corp. Oct 31, 64; to Sgt. Feb 7, 65; Wounded May 5, 64 and Sep 19, 64; Mustered out Jul 15, 65.
Roddy, John	Duxbury	Jun 9, 61	Jun 20, 61	Wounded Dec 13, 62; Mustered out Jun 29, 64.
Roddy, Terence	Hyde Park	Jun 7, 61	Jun 20, 61	Died Aug 25, 62 of wounds received Jun 29, 62.
Rollins, Winslow C.	Waterbury	Nov 3, 63	Nov 3, 63	Taken prisoner May 10, 64; Paroled Feb 23, 65; Discharged May 22, 65.
Russell, Albert W.	Stowe	May 7, 61	Jun 20, 61	Mustered out Jun 29, 64.
Russell, Charles F.	Stowe	Aug 22, 64	Aug 22, 64	Mustered out Jun 9, 65.
Russell, Joseph R.	Stowe	Sep 14, 64	Sep 14, 64	Mustered out Jun 12, 65.
Ryan, James W.	Waterville	Sep 12, 61	Sep 20, 61	Discharged Jan 22, 64 for disability.
Sanders, Asa S.	Middlesex	Aug 20, 64	Aug 20, 64	Mustered out Jun 19, 65.
Sanders, Carlisle	Berlin	Aug 14, 62	Sep 15, 62	Wounded Dec 13, 62; Died May 5, 64 of wounds received same day.
Scribner, Newell E.	Duxbury	Dec 3, 63	Dec 31, 63	Died Jul 25, 64 of wounds received May 5, 64.
Shonnio, Chancy S.	Duxbury	May 7, 61	Jun 20, 61	Sentenced Jan 18, 62 by G. C. M to serve out term of enlistment at hard labor at Dry Tortugas; Mustered out Jun 23, 64.
Slattery, Joseph	Berlin	Aug 14, 62	Sep 15, 62	Wounded May 5, 64; Mustered out May 13, 65.
Smith, Chauncey	Marshfield	May 7, 61	Jun 20, 61	Discharged Apr 28, 62 for disability.
Smith, George E.	Waterbury	May 7, 61	Jun 20, 61	Wounded May 5, 64; Mustered out Jun 29, 64.
Soper, George	Calais	May 7, 61	Jun 20, 61	Died Dec 7, 61 of disease.
Stickney, Daniel K.	Berlin	May 7, 61	Jun 20, 61	Taken prisoner Jul 21, 61; Paroled Jan 3, 62; Discharged Feb 5, 63 for disability.
Stiles, Orrin	Middlesex	Feb 4, 65	Feb 4, 65	Mustered out Jul 15, 65.
Stone, Horatio	Montpelier	Dec 9, 62	Jan 8, 63	Died May 6, 64 of wounds received same day.
Stone, Willard S.	Waterbury	Sep 7, 61	Sep 20, 61	KIA May 5, 64.
Tanner, Charles E.	Washington	May 7, 61	Jun 20, 61	Reenlisted Jan 31, 64; Promoted to Sgt. Nov 1, 64; Wounded May 3, 63, May 5, 64, Sep 19, 64 and Mar 25, 65; Mustered out Jul 17, 65.
Tanner, Howard O.	Washington	Aug 13, 64	Aug 13, 64	Mustered out Jun 19, 65.
Thurston, Quincy F.	Huntington	Jun 9, 61	Jun 20, 61	Died Aug 5, 62 of wounds received Jun 29, 62.
Travers, John	Moretown	May 7, 61	Jun 20, 61	Deserted Apr 23, 63.
Turner, Burton C.	Waterbury	Oct 30, 63	Oct 30, 63	Died Nov 4, 64 of disease.
Turner, Chauncey L.	Waterbury	Jul 14, 63	Jul 14, 63	Drafted; Wounded May 5, 64; Transferred to V. R. C. Nov 25, 64; Mustered out Jul 20, 65.
Turner, Edwin	Duxbury	May 7, 61	Jun 20, 61	Transferred to V. R. C. Sep 1, 63; Discharged Jun 19, 64.
Turner, Orlando S.	Moretown	May 7, 61	Jun 20, 61	See Second Lt. Co. D.
Warden, Alexander	Stowe	May 7, 61	Jun 20, 61	Discharged Nov 8, 61 for disability.

Watson, Josiah	Hancock	May 7, 61	Jun 20, 61	Wounded Dec 13, 62 and May 3, 63; Mustered out Jun 29, 64.
Wiley, Benjamin P.	Barre	May 7, 61	Jun 20, 61	Mustered out Jun 29, 64.
Wood, Theodore	Duxbury	Aug 12, 62	Sep 15, 62	Wounded Dec 13, 62; KIA May 5, 64.
Woodward, Lyman	Burlington	Sep 3, 61	Sep 20, 61	Reenlisted Dec 21, 63; KIA May 5, 64.
Wright, Franklin	Waterbury	Sep 3, 61	Sep 20, 61	Mustered out Sep 20, 64.
Wrisley, Jacob M.	Waterbury	Sep 3, 61	Sep 20, 61	Reenlisted Jan 31, 64; Wounded May 5, 64; Mustered out Jul 15, 65.
York, John W.	Waterbury	May 7, 61	Jun 20, 61	Reenlisted Dec 31, 63; Wounded May 3, 63; Mustered out Jul 15, 65.

Company E

Name and Rank	Residence	Date of Commission	Date of Issue	Remarks
Captains				
Smith, Richard	Tunbridge	May 21, 61	May 21, 61	Resigned Aug 1, 62.
Bixby, Orville	Royalton	Aug 4, 62	Aug 16, 62	Second Lt. Co. E; Promoted to First Lt. Jan 11, 61; KIA May 5, 64.
Morey, Charles C.	Royalton	Dec 24, 64	Jan 31, 65	Corp. Co. E; Reenlisted Jan 31, 64; Promoted to Sgt. Feb 10, 62, to First Sgt. Dec 27, 62, to First Lt. Co. C Jun 20, 64; Wounded Aug 21, 64; KIA Apr 2, 65.
Dunham, Dennis C.	Tunbridge	Jun 7, 65	Jun 17, 65	Pvt. Co. E; Reenlisted Dec 21, 63; Promoted to Corp. Feb 10, 62, to Sgt. Aug 7, 63, to QM Sgt. Sep 10, 64, to First Lt. Co. E Dec 24, 64; Mustered out Jul 15, 65.
First Lieutenants				
Whitney, Lucius C.	Tunbridge	May 21, 61	May 21, 61	Resigned Jan 8, 62.
Bixby, Orville	Royalton	Jan 11, 62	Jan 11, 62	See Capt. Co. E.
Allen, James	Tunbridge	Aug 4, 62	Aug 16, 62	Sgt. Co. E; Promoted to First Sgt. Feb 10, 62; Wounded May 5, 64; Mustered out Jun 29, 64.
Dunham, Dennis C.	Tunbridge	Dec 24, 64	Jan 31, 65	See Capt. Co. E.
Fassett, Nelson	Jericho	Jan 7, 65	Jan 17, 65	Pvt. Co. E; Reenlisted Apr 19, 64; Promoted to Sgt. Oct 18, 64, to QM Sgt. Feb 7, 65; Mustered out Jul 15, 65.
Second Lieutenants				
Bixby, Orville	Royalton	May 21, 61	May 21, 61	See Capt. Co. E.
Dewy, Harrison	Royalton	Jan 11, 62	Jan 11, 62	First Sgt.Co. E; Taken prisoner and paroled date unknown; Honorable discharge Oct 4, 62.
Hayward, Henry R.	Tunbridge	Nov 24, 62	Dec 64	Sgt. Co. E; Promoted to First Sgt. Aug 28, 62; Mustered out Jun 29, 64.
Adams, George S.	Royalton	Jun 7, 65	Jun 17, 65	Pvt. Co. E; Reenlisted Dec 21, 63; Promoted to Corp. Aug 28, 62, to Sgt. Oct 18, 64, to First Sgt. Feb 7, 65; Mustered out Jul 15, 65.

Name and Rank	Residence	Date of Enlistment	Date of Muster	Remarks
Sergeants				
Dewey, Harrison	Royalton	Apr 22, 61	Jun 20, 61	See Second Lt. Co. E.
Allen, James	Tunbridge	Apr 22, 61	Jun 20, 61	See First Lt. Co. E.
Hayward, Henry R.	Tunbridge	Apr 22, 61	Jun 20, 61	See Second Lt. Co. E.
Allen, George E.	Chelsea	May 11, 61	Jun 20, 61	Drowned Jul 9, 61.
Rowell, George W.	Tunbridge	Apr 22, 61	Jun 20, 61	Discharged Sep 10, 62 for wounds.
Corporals				
Willis, Horace S.	Tunbridge	Apr 22, 61	Jun 20, 61	Discharged Dec 1, 62 for disability.

Morey, Charles C.	Royalton	Apr 22, 61	Jun 20, 61	See Capt. Co. E.
Lunt, Cyrus W.	Tunbridge	Apr 22, 61	Jun 20, 61	Died Nov 29, 61 of disease.
Noyes, George H.	Tunbridge	Apr 22, 61	Jun 20, 61	Reduced Aug 4, 63; KIA May 12, 64.
Davis, Martin V. B.	Chelsea	May 1, 61	Jun 20, 61	Promoted to Sgt.; Reenlisted Jan 31, 64; Wounded May 3, 63, May 5, 64 and Oct 19, 64; Discharged Jun 18, 65.
Emery, Edson	Tunbridge	Apr 29, 61	Jun 20, 61	Promoted to Sgt.; Wounded May 9, 64; Mustered out Jun 29, 64.
Davis, George W.	Tunbridge	Apr 22, 61	Jun 20, 61	Promoted to Sgt.; Mustered out Jun 29, 64.
Lyman, Joel T.	Royalton	Apr 22, 61	Jun 20, 61	Discharged Nov 20, 62 for disability.
Musicians				
Bishop, Hiram J.	Burlington	Apr 22, 61	Jun 20, 61	Discharged Dec 30, 61 for disability.
Goodwin, Henry K.	Tunbridge	May 15, 61	Jun 20, 61	Taken prisoner and died at Richmond, Va., Jul 7, 62.
Wagoner				
Jones, James M.	Tunbridge	Apr 22, 61	Jun 20, 61	Discharged Sep 30, 62 for disability.
Privates				
Adams, George S.	Royalton	Apr 22, 61	Jun 20, 61	See Second Lt. Co. E.
Aldrich, Lucius C.	Vershire	Apr 25, 61	Jun 20, 61	Discharged Nov 9, 61 for disability.
Atwell, Marshall B.	Johnson	May 12, 61	Jun 20, 61	Discharged May 18, 63 for disability.
Bacon, David F.	Randolph	Sep 6, 61	Sep 27, 61	Discharged Jan 4, 64 for disability.
Baker, Henry L.	Royalton	Apr 22, 61	Jun 20, 61	Promoted to Corp.; Wounded May 5, 64; Mustered out Jun 29, 64.
Baker, Nahum C.	Royalton	Sep 9, 61	Sep 27, 61	Taken prisoner May 21, 64; Paroled; Mustered out Mar 13, 65.
Barstow, Joseph	Vershire	Aug 1, 62	Sep 15, 62	Wounded May 10, 64; Deserted Apr 4, 65; Returned May 21, 65; Mustered out Jun 19, 65.
Beckwith, Joseph D.	Royalton	Apr 21, 61	Jun 20, 61	Mustered out Jun 29, 64.
Bills, Allen	Randolph	Aug 9, 62	Sep 22, 62	Taken prisoner Jun 28, 63; Paroled same day; Died Dec 29, 64 of disease.
Bills, Franklin	Randolph	Aug 6, 62	Sep 22, 62	Mustered out Jun 26, 65.
Blake, Horatio C.	Royalton	Apr 22, 61	Jun 20, 61	Discharged Mar 8, 63 for disability.
Blakely, George	Chelsea	Apr 14, 61	Jun 20, 61	Deserted Aug 28, 62.
Blanchard, Frank F.	Royalton	Aug 4, 64	Aug 4, 64	Mustered out Jun 19, 65.
Boudreau, Stephen	E. Montpelier	Feb 25, 62	Apr 12, 62	Reenlisted Apr 19, 64; Wounded Dec 13, 62; Deserted May 29, 64.
Brooks, Joseph M.	Cornith	Aug 14, 62	Sep 22, 62	Mustered out Jun 19, 65.
Broughton, Thomas F.	Tunbridge	Apr 22, 61	Jun 20, 61	Reenlisted Dec 21, 63; Wounded Apr 6, 65; Discharged Sep 6, 65 for wounds.
Brown, Truman O.	Pittsfield	Aug 13, 62	Sep 15, 62	Died May 7, 63 of wounds received May 4, 63.
Burnham, Charles W.	Substitute	Aug 5, 63	Aug 5, 63	Substitute for Henry Stephens, Springfield; Promoted to Corp. Feb 7, 65; Wounded May 5, 64; Mustered out Jun 26, 65.
Burns, Elias	Jericho	Aug 22, 62	Sep 15, 62	Transferred to V. R. C. Jul 1, 63; Mustered out Jul 31, 65.
Buzzell, Azro	Bethel	Jul 28, 62	Sep 22, 62	Wounded Aug 21, 64 and Sep 19, 64; Taken prisoner Oct 19, 64; Died Feb 27, 65 while a prisoner.
Buzzell, Stillman C.	Chelsea	Aug 1, 62	Sep 30, 62	Promoted to Corp. Oct 18, 64; Reduced Mar 29, 65; Wounded May 5, 64; Mustered out Jun 19, 65.
Chadwick, Edwin H.	Royalton	May 2, 61	Jun 20, 61	Deserted Nov 27, 62; Returned Aug 14, 63; Deserted again; Returned Mar 21, 65; Mustered out Jul 15, 65.
Chamberlin, F. W.	Royalton	Apr 23, 61	Jun 20, 61	Wounded Dec 13, 62; KIA May 3, 63.
Cilley, John A.	Royalton	Dec 19, 63	Jan 5, 64	Wounded Sep 19, 64; Mustered out Jul 15, 65.
Clark, William	Charleston	Jul 31, 63	Jul 31, 63	Drafted; KIA May 12, 64.
Clark, William H.	Randolph	May 10, 61	Jun 20, 61	Wounded and taken prisoner Jun 29, 62; Paroled Aug 6, 62; Discharged Jan 19, 63 for wounds.

Clifford, Benjamin F.	Tunbridge	Jul 21, 62	Sep 15, 62	Wounded May 3, 63; Transferred to V. R. C. Apr 15, 64; Mustered out Jul 17, 65.
Clifford, Israel P.	Chelsea	Apr 22, 61	Jun 20, 61	Wounded and taken prisoner Jun 29, 62; Paroled Jul 22, 62; Deserted Jul 2, 63.
Colburn, Freeman L.	Tunbridge	May 6, 61	Jun 20, 61	Wounded May 5, 64; Mustered out Jun 29, 64.
Colburn, William	Chelsea	Sep 17, 61	Sep 27, 61	Discharged Dec 9, 62 for disability.
Cressey, George	Tunbridge	Dec 23, 63	Jan 2, 64	Mustered out Jul 15, 65.
Cross, Nathan	Substitute	Aug 4, 63	Aug 4, 63	Substitute for Truman Hurlburt, Richford; Mustered out Jul 15, 65.
Cushman, Daniel W.	Tunbridge	Dec 3, 63	Dec 19, 63	KIA May 12, 64.
Drake, Alonzo	Tunbridge	Dec 10, 63	Dec 19, 63	Mustered out Jul 7, 65.
Dunham, Dennis C.	Tunbridge	May 4, 61	Jun 20, 61	See Capt. Co. E.
Durrell, George W.	Tunbridge	May 1, 61	Jun 20, 61	Deserted Nov 26, 62; Returned Jan 23, 63; KIA May 5, 64.
Dustin, Azro	Bethel	Sep 5, 61	Sep 27, 61	Discharged Oct 30, 62 for disability.
Dustin, Charles H.	Tunbridge	Sep 5, 61	Sep 27, 61	Died Nov 7, 62.
Dustin, George M. D.	Bethel	Sep 17, 61	Sep 27, 61	Died Sep 24, 62 of disease.
Ellsworth, Francis P.	Royalton	Apr 22, 61	Jun 20, 61	KIA May 5, 61.
Emerson, Carlo J.	Chelsea	Apr 22, 61	Jun 20, 61	Discharged Oct 10, 61 for disability.
Emery, Philo	Tunbridge	Jun 4, 61	Jun 20, 61	Died Jun 9, 64 of wounds received May 5, 64.
Farrer, Stephen	Tunbridge	Dec 3, 63	Dec 19, 63	Discharged Apr 18, 64 for disability.
Fassett, Edwin H.	Jericho	Feb 26, 62	Apr 12, 62	Mustered out Feb 27, 65.
Fassett, Nelson	Jericho	Feb 26, 62	Apr 12, 62	See First Lt. Co. E.
Fish, John M.	Royalton	Apr 26, 61	Jun 20, 61	Died Aug 19, 61 of disease.
Fisk, Wilbur	Tunbridge	Sep 5, 61	Sep 7, 61	See QM Sgt.
Fitzgerald, Patrick	Underhill	Aug 27, 62	Sep 15, 62	Discharged Apr 6, 63 for disability.
Fitzgerald, Patrick	Underhill	Aug 29, 64	Aug 29, 64	Mustered out Jun 19, 65.
Flanders, George W.	Sharon	May 7, 61	Jun 20, 61	Dishonorable discharge for desertion Mar 10, 62; drummed out of camp.
Folsom, Francis A.	Washington	Sep 7, 61	Sep 27, 61	Died Nov 5, 62 of disease.
Foster, Benjamin F.	Tunbridge	Jan 30, 65	Jan 30, 65	Mustered out Jul 15, 65.
Foster, Jacob T.	Tunbridge	Dec 10, 63	Dec 19, 63	Transferred to V. R. C. Apr 15, 64; Discharged Jun 21, 64.
Foster, John E.	Tunbridge	May 14, 61	Jun 20, 61	KIA May 12, 64.
Foster, William S., Jr.	Royalton	Dec 10, 61	Dec 10, 61	Reenlisted Dec 21, 63; Promoted to Corp.; Wounded May 5, 64; KIA Sep 19, 64.
Frapier, Francis	Substitute	Aug 4, 63	Aug 4, 63	Substitute for Sherman Tichout, Highgate; Transferred to V. R. C. Apr 10, 64; Deserted Apr 25, 64.
French, Norman	Cornith	Aug 16, 62	Sep 22, 62	Died Dec 13, 62.
George, Lyndon A.	Chelsea	May 14, 61	Jun 20, 61	Mustered out Jun 29, 64.
Glines, Moses C.	Tunbridge	Apr 22, 61	Jun 20, 61	Wounded Jul 21, 61; Discharged Jan 4, 62 for disability.
Glover, Lucius	Substitute	Jul 22, 63	Jul 22, 63	Substitute for Fred Z. Dickenson, Brattleboro; Deserted Jan 10, 64.
Goodale, Samuel L. D.	Washington	Apr 22, 61	Jun 20, 61	Wounded May 3, 63; Mustered out Jun 29, 64.
Goodwin, Charles C.	Randolph	Jun—, 61	Jun 20, 61	Deserted Jul 27, 61; Returned Feb 5, 62; Discharged Aug 15, 62 for disability.
Goodwin, Edmund	Charleston	Jul 31, 63	Jul 31, 63	Drafted; KIA May 12, 64.
Gorton, Hosea M.	Essex	Aug 30, 62	Sep 15, 62	Died Nov 29, 62 of disease.
Gravlin, John	Montpelier	Mar 20, 62	Apr 12, 62	Reenlisted Apr 13, 64; Deserted Jan 28, 63; returned Mar 25, 63; Wounded Aug 21, 64 and Apr 2, 65; Mustered out Jul 15, 65.
Gray, John	Underhill	Aug 30, 64	Aug 30, 64	Mustered out Jun 28, 65.
Green, Mark	Randolph	May 13, 61	Jun 20, 61	Died Feb 25, 62 of disease.
Hall, George	Substitute	Aug 3, 63	Aug 3, 63	Substitute for Justin Paddleford, Hartford; Turned over to provost marshal as a deserter from 7th Mass. Inf. Apr 20, 64.
Harper, George N.	Royalton	May 6, 61	Jun 20, 61	Discharged Jul 26, 62 for disability.
Harper, George N.	Royalton	Dec 19, 63	Jan 5, 64	Wounded May 5, 64; Died Dec 28, 64 of disease.
Heath, Salmon W.	Cornith	Sep 9, 61	Sep 27, 61	Discharged Jul 14, 63 for disability.

Hendry, Thomas	Barton	Jul 31, 63	Jul 31, 63	Drafted; Promoted to Corp. May 1, 65; Wounded Jun 1, 64, Sep 19, 64 and Apr 2, 65; Mustered out Jul 15, 65.
Henry, Alfred	Braintree	May 29, 61	Jun 20, 61	Died Nov 2, 62 of disease.
Hill, Charles P.	Substitute	Aug 3, 63	Aug 3, 63	Substitute for Henry H. Taft, Woodstock; Promoted to Corp. Feb 7, 65, to Sgt.T Mar 28, 65; Mustered out Jul 15, 65.
Hill, Henry G.	Substitute	Jul 24, 63	Jul 24, 63	Substitute for John A. Butler, Jamaica, Vt.; Wounded May 12, 64; Died Oct 26, 64 of wounds received Oct 19, 64.
Holman, Frederick B.	Brattleboro	Sep 10, 62	Sep 30, 62	Wounded May 12, 64; Mustered out Jun 19, 65.
Hood, Christopher	Chelsea	Sep 16, 61	Sep 27, 61	Wounded May 3, 63 and May 5, 64; Mustered out Sep 27, 64.
Hood, Egerton	Chelsea	Sep 10, 61	Sep 27, 61	Wounded May 12, 64; Mustered out Sep 27, 64.
Hood, Marcellus F.	Chelsea	Sep 9, 61	Sep 27, 61	Discharged Sep 17, 62 for disability.
Hood, Rinaldo	Chelsea	Sep 7, 61	Sep 27, 61	Promoted to Corp.; Wounded May 12, 64; Mustered out Oct 18, 64.
Hopkins, Ebenezer	Tunbridge	Apr 23, 61	Jun 20, 61	Reenlisted Dec 21, 63; Promoted to Corp. Mar 28, 65; Wounded Apr 2, 65; Mustered out Jul 21, 65.
Hovendon, James	Royalton	Sep 7, 61	Sep 27, 61	Discharged Aug 15, 62 for disability.
Hoyt, Timothy S.	Craftsbury	Aug 20, 63	Aug 20, 63	Drafted; Discharged May 4, 64 for disability.
Hulburt, William	Substitute	Aug 4, 63	Aug 4, 63	Substitute for Henry L. Sampson, St. Albans; KIA Apr 2, 65.
Hunt, Byron	Hartford	Jul 22, 63	Jul 22, 63	Drafted; Mustered out Jul 15, 65.
Huntington, Peyton R.	Chelsea	Aug 18, 62	Sep 30, 62	Discharged Nov 27, 62 for disability.
Hurson, James S.	Jericho	Aug 30, 62	Aug 30, 62	Discharged Jan 3, 63 for disability.
Jackson, Thomas	Substitute	Aug 3, 63	Aug 3, 63	Substitute for Thomas J. Shurtleff, Hartford; Deserted Jul 16, 64.
Jerd, Alexander	Braintree	Dec 8, 63	Dec 19, 63	Transferred to V. R. C. Apr 15, 64; Discharged Jul 29, 65.
Johnson, Napoleon B.	Substitute	Aug 5, 63	Aug 5, 63	Substitute for Marcellus J. Hudson, Bridgewater; Mustered out Jul 15, 65.
Judway, Faba	Substitute	Aug 3, 63	Aug 3, 63	Substitute for John S. Kellogg, Enosburgh; Wounded May 6, 64; Deserted Jul 26, 64; Returned; Mustered out Jul 15, 65.
Kavanaugh, James	Substitute	Aug 5, 63	Aug 5, 63	Substitute for William N. Carpenter, Plymouth; Wounded Jun 1, 64 and Mar 25, 65; Mustered out Jul 15, 65.
Kent, Charles J.	Substitute	Aug 5, 63	Aug 5, 63	Substitute for Hart B. Pierce, Westminster; Discharged Jun 5, 64 for disability.
Keyes, Jacob	Substitute	Aug 3, 63	Aug 3, 63	Substitute for Henry H. Dake, West Windsor; Died Dec 28, 63 of disease.
King, Augustus	Tunbridge	Aug 1, 64	Aug 1, 64	Mustered out Jun 27, 65.
Luce, William	Braintree	May 11, 61	Jun 20, 61	Wounded May 3, 63; Mustered out Jun 29, 64.
Lucia, Oliver	Jericho	Aug 22, 62	Sep 15, 62	Wounded Sep 19, 64; Discharged Jun 2, 65 for disability.
Lunt, William B.	Tunbridge	Sep 12, 61	Sep 27, 61	Discharged Nov 8, 62 for disability.
Lyman, Horace H.	Royalton	Apr 22, 61	Jun 20, 61	Discharged Nov 10, 62 for disability.
Lyman, Horace H.	Royalton	Jul 3, 63	Jul 3, 63	Enlisted in V. R. C.; Transferred to Co. E Jan 9, 64; Taken prisoner Oct 19, 64; Died in Florence, S.C. Jan 29, 65.
Magoon, Alfred M.	Cornith	Aug 16, 62	Sep 22, 62	Wounded May 6, 64; Deserted ——, 64.
Martin, George A.	Cornith	May 10, 61	Jun 20, 61	Taken prisoner Jul 21, 61; Paroled Jan 3, 62; Discharged Sep 10, 62 for disability.
McDaniels, John B.	Underhill	Aug 30, 62	Sep 15, 62	Discharged May 16, 65 for disability.
Meader, Benjamin L.	Tunbridge	Apr 22, 61	Jun 20, 61	Reenlisted Jan 31, 64; Promoted to Corp. Oct 18, 64, to Sgt. Mar 23, 65; Wounded May 3, 63; Mustered out Jul 15, 65.
Moody, Charles H.	Tunbridge	Jul 28, 64	Jul 28, 64	Mustered out Jun 19, 65.

Moore, Orville E.	Bethel	May 10, 61	Jun 20, 61	Wagoner; Reenlisted Jan 31, 64; Wounded and taken prisoner Jun 29, 62; Paroled Aug 3, 62; Mustered out Jul 15, 65.
Morse, Henry E.	Royalton	Aug 4, 64	Aug 4, 64	Mustered out Jun 19, 65.
Murray, Edward	Burlington	Aug 21, 62	Sep 15, 62	Discharged Feb 6, 63 for disability.
Newton, Truman	Chelsea	May 13, 61	Jun 20, 61	Deserted Nov 26, 62; taken prisoner while a deserter; N. F. R.
Noyes, Calvin M.	Tunbridge	Aug 9, 64	Aug 9, 64	Died Nov 10, 64 of disease.
Noyes, Charles B.	Tunbridge	Apr 22, 61	Jun 20, 61	Died Oct 12, 62 of disease.
Noyes, William M.	Tunbridge	Apr 22, 61	Jun 20, 61	Wounded ——, 62; KIA May 5, 64.
Ordway, George B.	Chelsea	Apr 22, 61	Jun 20, 61	Reenlisted Dec 21, 63; Promoted to Sgt. Feb 7, 65; Wounded May 5, 64; Mustered out Jul 15, 65.
Orr, Richard R.	Cornith	May 14, 61	Jun 20, 61	Died Aug 14, 62 of disease.
Osgood, Henry H.	Royalton	May 22, 61	Jun 20, 61	Promoted to Corp.; Wounded May 6, 64; Mustered out Jun 29, 64.
Page, Adelbert H.	Tunbridge	May 13, 61	Jun 20, 61	Deserted Sep 18, 62.
Pearson, Arthur M.	Bethel	Sep 5, 61	Sep 27, 61	Discharged Oct 20, 62 for disability.
Pearson, Granville L.	Bethel	May 10, 61	Jun 20, 61	Mustered out Jun 29, 64.
Pember, Daniel B.	Randolph	Jun 1, 61	Jun 20, 61	Wounded Jul 21, 61; Discharged Jul 30, 62 for disability.
Pierce, George W.	Royalton	Apr 22, 61	Jun 20, 61	Discharged Aug 28, 61 for disability.
Preston, George W.	Tunbridge	Sep 1, 64	Sep 1, 64	Mustered out Jun 19, 65.
Quade, Charles	Randolph	Apr 22, 61	Jun 20, 61	Dishonorable discharge for desertion Mar 10, 62, drummed out of camp.
Reed, Charles	Tunbridge	Dec 3, 63	Dec 3, 63	Wounded May 5, 64; Mustered out Jul 15, 65.
Reed, William	Tunbridge	Dec 3, 63	Dec 3, 63	Wounded May 12, 64; Died Sep 19, 64 of wounds received the same day.
Remick, A. Wheeler	Chelsea	May 10, 61	Jun 20, 61	Died Sep 9, 62 of disease.
Richardson, Charles C.	Jericho	Aug 22, 62	Sep 15, 62	MIA May 12, 64; Supposed to have died while a POW.
Richardson, George W.	Randolph	Apr 26, 61	Jun 20, 61	Reenlisted Dec 21, 63; Promoted to Corp.; Deserted Jul 27, 64.
Richardson, William C.	Chelsea	Aug 20, 62	Sep 22, 62	Wounded May 3, 63; Mustered out Jun 19, 65.
Rogers, Owen	Substitute	Aug 7, 63	Aug 7, 63	Substitute for Ralph T. Stinehour, South Hero; Mustered out Jul 15, 65.
Rollinson, Joseph	Royalton	Sep 16, 61	Sep 27, 61	Died Sep 6, 62 of disease.
Root, Benjamin A.	Royalton	Apr 22, 61	Jun 20, 61	Mustered out Jun 29, 64.
Royce, Jason S.	Royalton	Aug 17, 64	Aug 17, 64	Mustered out Jun 19, 65.
Russin, Duff	Underhill	Sep 6, 62	Sep 15, 62	Died Nov 13, 63 of disease.
Russin, Joseph	Jericho	Aug 30, 62	Sep 15, 62	Mustered out Jun 19, 65.
Rust, Albert	Tunbridge	Apr 22, 61	Jun 20, 61	Reenlisted Dec 21, 63; Died May 18, 64 of wounds received May 5, 64.
Sanborn, Charles F.	Tunbridge	Sep 4, 61	Sep 27, 61	Reenlisted Dec 21, 63; Taken prisoner and paroled May 4, 64; Deserted May 5, 64.
Sanborn, Royal	Tunbridge	Apr 25, 61	Jun 20, 61	Reenlisted Dec 21, 63; Promoted to Corp. Mar 28, 65; Wounded May 5, 64 and May 12, 64; Mustered out Jul 15, 65.
Sanborn, William H.	Royalton	Apr 22, 61	Jun 20, 61	Promoted to Corp. Dec 27, 62; KIA May 5, 64.
Sargent, Mark J.	Tunbridge	Apr 22, 61	Jun 20, 61	Mustered out Jun 29, 64.
Scales, Carlos E.	Washington	Apr 25, 61	Jun 20, 61	Discharged Dec 30, 61 for disability.
Sleeper, Van B.	Chelsea	May 13, 61	Jun 20, 61	Transferred to Signal Corps Aug 1, 63; Mustered out Aug 16, 65.
Smith, Adam	Tunbridge	Apr 22, 61	Jun 20, 61	Promoted to Corp.; KIA Jun 29, 62.
Smith, Edward Hart	Randolph	Sep 10, 61	————	Deserted Jul 2, 62; Returned Aug 14, 63; KIA May 12, 64.
Smith, Nathan F.	Tunbridge	Dec 3, 63	Dec 19, 63	KIA May 5, 64.
Spaulding, Alonzo D.	Royalton	Apr 26, 61	Jun 20, 61	Reenlisted Dec 21, 63; Promoted to Corp. Oct 18, 64, to Sgt. Feb 7, 65; Died Mar 25, 65.
Spaulding, Reuben	Royalton	Sep 6, 61	Sep 27, 61	Discharged Feb 21, 62 for disability.

Spencer, William A.	Substitute	Jul 27, 63	Jul 27, 63	Substitute for William E. White, Panton; Deserted Sep 5, 63.
Stevens, Cornelius C.	Royalton	Sep 6, 61	Sep 27, 61	Wounded Dec 13, 62; Transferred to V. R. C. Sep 1, 63; Discharged Dec 11, 63.
Straw, James	Vershire	Apr 22, 61	Jun 20, 61	Mustered out Jun 29, 64.
Strickland, Samuel	Substitute	Aug 5, 63	Aug 5, 63	Substitute for Justus Dartt, Weathersfield; Deserted Aug 28, 63.
Terrill, Henry H.	Underhill	Aug 30, 62	Sep 15, 62	Died Dec 11, 62.
Tillison, Charles	Underhill	Aug 30, 62	Sep 15, 62	Lost overboard on voyage from City Point to Alexandria, Va., Jun 64.
Tillison, Hosea H.	Underhill	Aug 20, 64	Aug 20, 64	Wounded Apr 2, 65; Mustered out Jun 19, 65.
Tillison, Leander	Underhill	Aug 30, 62	Sep 15, 62	Discharged Feb 6, 63 for disability.
Tillison, Warren M.	Underhill	Aug 30, 62	Sep 15, 62	Wounded Apr 2, 65; deserted Apr 4, 65.
Tinkham, James G.	Bethel	Apr 26, 61	Jun 20, 61	Discharged Aug 26, 62 for disability.
Tucker, John F.	Strafford	Aug 12, 62	Sep 22, 62	Discharged Apr 17, 63 for disability.
Tullar, Elihu	Tunbridge	Sep 9, 61	Sep 27, 61	Reenlisted Dec 21, 63; Wounded May 5, 64; Mustered out Jul 15, 65.
Tullar, Myron	Royalton	Aug 25, 64	Aug 25, 64	Wounded Oct 19, 64 and Mar 14, 65; Mustered out Jun 19, 65.
Tupper, Jonathan E.	Underhill	Aug 16, 62	Sep 15, 62	Wounded May 5, 64; Died Nov 5, 64 of wounds received Oct 19, 64.
Walcott, James A.	Royalton	Apr 21, 61	Jun 20, 61	Reenlisted Dec 21, 63; Promoted Corp. Aug 7, 63; KIA Aug 21, 64.
Waldo, Albigence	Royalton	Apr 27, 61	Jun 20, 61	Died Jul 21, 61 of wounds received same day.
Waldo, Dillingham	Royalton	Sep 16, 61	Sep 27, 61	Discharged Jun 4, 62 for disability.
Wallace, Daniel	Strafford	Aug 27, 62	Sep 22, 62	Died Jan 26, 63 of disease.
Ward, Benjamin	Hancock	May 19, 61	Jun 20, 61	Mustered out Jun 29, 64.
Waterman, Elliston	Randolph	Aug 2, 62	Sep 30, 62	Wounded May 12, 64; Mustered out Jun 19, 65.
Whitney, Albert	Randolph	Aug 2, 62	Sep 30, 62	Discharged Mar 8, 63 for disability.
Wiggins, Edson	Chelsea	May 10, 61	Jun 20, 61	Discharged Dec 18, 61 for disability.
Williams, Thomas R.	Bethel	Sep 16, 61	Sep 27, 61	Promoted to Corp. Feb 10, 62; KIA May 3, 63.
Williams, Wallace E.	Bethel	Sep 16, 61	Sep 27, 61	Wounded May 3, 63; Mustered out Sep 26, 64.
Willis, Andrew J.	Tunbridge	Sep 5, 61	Sep 27, 61	Wounded May 3, 63; Mustered out Sep 26, 64.
Willis, Edward S.	Royalton	Apr 25, 61	Jun 20, 61	Discharged Dec 11, 61 for disability.
Wood, George E.	Randolph	Apr 22, 61	Jun 20, 61	Reenlisted Dec 21, 63; Wounded and taken prisoner Jun 29, 62; Paroled Jul 22, 62; Mustered out Jul 15, 65.
Woodworth, Joel P.	Underhill	Aug 16, 62	Sep 30, 62	Discharged Apr 4, 65 for disability.
York, George G.	Tunbridge	Aug 8, 64	Aug 8, 64	Mustered out Jun 19, 65.

Company F

Name and Rank	Residence	Date of Commission	Date of Issue	Remarks
Captains				
Randall, Francis V.	Montpelier	May 20, 61	May 20, 61	Resigned Sep 9, 62 to accept promotion to Col. of the 13th Vt. Inf.
Crossman, Horace F.	Montpelier	Oct 1, 62	Oct 13, 62	Second Lt. Co. F; Promoted to First Lt. Co. F Jan 24, 62; Transferred to V. R. C. Oct 30 63; Discharged for wound Aug 18, 1866.
Clark, Dayton P.	Montpelier	Nov 3, 63	Nov 11, 63	Sgt. Co. F; Promoted to First Lt. Co. D Jan 29, 62; Wounded May 3, 63; Mustered out Jun 29, 64.
Stone, Pratt	Readsboro	Dec 24, 64	Jan 31, 65	Pvt. Co. A; Reenlisted Dec 21, 63; Promoted to Sgt. Nov 1, 61, to First Sgt. Oct 17, 62, to First Lt. Co. D Jun 20, 64; Wounded May 3, 63; Resigned Jun 9, 65.

Name and Rank	Residence	Date of Enlistment	Date of Muster	Remarks
First Lieutenants				
Philips, Walter A.	Montpelier	May 20, 61	May 20, 61	Dismissed from the service Dec 31, 61 by sentence of G. M. C.
Crossman, Horace F.	Montpelier	Jan 24, 62	Jan 24, 62	See Capt. Co. F.
Worcester, Almond, Jr.	Warren	Oct 1, 62	Oct 13, 62	First Sgt. Co. F; Promoted to Second Lt. Aug. 4, 62; Wounded May 12, 64; Mustered out June 29, 64.
Ferry, Amasa W.	Roxbury	Sep 15, 64	Sep 29, 64	Corp. Co. F; Reenlisted Jan 23, 64; Promoted to Sgt. Feb 1, 62, then to First Sgt.; Wounded May 6, 64 and Oct 19, 64; Discharged Jan 4, 65 for wounds.
Flagg, George W.	Braintree	Dec 24, 64	Jan 31, 65	Pvt. Co. F.; Reenlisted Jan 31, 64; Promoted to Corp. May 20, 63, to Sgt. Dec 23, 63, to First Sgt. Oct 12, 64; Wounded May 5, 64; Mustered out Jul 15, 65.
Second Lieutenants				
Crossman, Horace F.	Montpelier	May 20, 61	May 20, 61	See Capt. Co. F.
Edgerton, Francis M.	Poultney	Jan 25, 62	Jan 25, 62	See Adjutant.
Worcester, Almond, Jr.	Warren	Aug 4, 62	Aug 16, 62	See First Lt. Co. F.
Bridgeman, George W.	Hardwick	Oct 1, 62	Oct 13, 62	Sgt. Co. F; Promoted to First Sgt.; Wounded May 5, 64; Mustered out Jun 29, 64.
George, Daniel B.	Hardwick	Jun 7, 65	Jun 17, 65	Pvt. Co. F; Reenlisted Mar 20, 64; Promoted to Corp. Jul 1, 64, to Sgt. Sep 1, 64, to First Sgt. Feb 7, 65; Wounded Apr 2, 65; Mustered out as First Sgt. Jul 15, 65.

Name and Rank	Residence	Date of Enlistment	Date of Muster	Remarks
Sergeants				
Worcester, Almond, Jr.	Warren	May 7, 61	Jun 20, 61	See First Lt. Co. F.
Camp, William H. H.	Montpelier	May 7, 61	Jun 20, 61	Wounded May 3, 63; Transferred to V. R. C. Nov 20, 63; Discharged Jun 20, 64.
Ballou, Jerome E.	Montpelier	May 7, 61	Jun 20, 61	Discharged Feb 23, 62 for disability.
Bridgeman, George W.	Hardwick	May 7, 61	Jun 20, 61	See Second Lt. Co. F.
Clark, Dayton P.	Montpelier	May 7, 61	Jun 20, 61	See Capt. Co. F.
Corporals				
Gunnison, Eri S.	Montpelier	May 7, 61	Jun 20, 61	Reduced Oct 1, 61; Wounded Jun 29, 62; Transferred to V. R. C. Oct 5, 63; Discharged Jun 20, 64 as a Pvt.
Ferry, Amasa W.	Roxbury	May 7, 61	Jun 20, 61	See First Lt. Co. F.
White, Charles A.	Williamstown	May 7, 61	Jun 20, 61	Reduced Oct 1, 61; Wounded Dec 13, 62; Mustered out Jun 29, 64.
Bacon, James T.	Barre	May 7, 61	Jun 20, 61	Reduced Oct 1, 61; Promoted to Sgt.; Wounded May 5, 64; Mustered out Jun 29, 64.
Perrin, Julius	Montpelier	May 7, 61	Jun 20, 61	Discharged Nov 7, 61 for disability.
Wright, Edwin N.	Montpelier	May 7, 61	Jun 20, 61	Discharged Jul 24, 62 for disability.
Herring, Charles J.	Montpelier	May 7, 61	Jun 20, 61	Reduced; Wounded—62; Discharged Apr 23, 63.
Burbank, Morgan A.	Warren	May 7, 61	Jun 20, 61	Discharged Dec 22, 62 for disability.
Musicians				
Field, William C.	Montpelier	May 7, 61	Jun 20, 61	Mustered out Jun 29, 64.
Taylor, Benjamin	Montpelier	May 7, 61	Jun 20, 61	Wounded and taken prisoner Jul 21, 61; Paroled Jan 3, 62; Discharged Sep 21, 63 for disability.
Wagoner				
Kelton, John A.	Montpelier	May 7, 61	Jun 20, 61	Discharged Nov 27, 62 for disability.
Privates				
Ainsworth, George J.	Warren	May 7, 61	Jun 20, 61	Wounded May 3, 63; Transferred to V. R. C. Nov 20, 63; Discharged Jun 20, 64.

Allen, Myron H.	Hardwick	May 7, 61	Jun 20, 61	Discharged Jun 16, 62 for disability.
Anderson, Stephen	Moores, N.Y.	Oct 10, 61	Oct 15, 61	Died Jun 30, 62 of wounds received Jun 29, 62.
Andrews, John S.	Moretown	May 7, 61	Jun 20, 61	Mustered out Jun 29, 64.
Ayers, George A.	Plainfield	May 7, 61	Jun 20, 61	Mustered out Jun 29, 64.
Ballou, Horace C.	Montpelier	May 7, 61	Jun 20, 61	Mustered out Jun 29, 64.
Barrett, Cephas T.	Woodbury	May 20, 61	Jun 20, 61	Discharged Mar 27, 62 for disability.
Belcher, Henry H.	Randolph	Sep 9, 61	Sep 20, 61	Deserted Sep 7, 63.
Benedict, Charles M.	Waitsfield	May 7, 61	Jun 20, 61	Deserted Aug 30, 62.
Bennett, Amos N.	Montpelier	May 11, 61	Jun 20, 61	Promoted to Corp. Oct 1, 61; KIA May 3, 63.
Bradford, Amos C.	Plainsfield	Aug 12, 62	Sep 22, 62	Wounded May 3, 63 and May 5, 64; Transferred to V. R. C; Discharged Jul 7, 65.
Bradford, John M., Jr.	Plainsfield	Aug, 14, 62	Sep 22, 62	Discharged Aug 28, 63 for wounds received May 3, 63.
Brown, Elijah S.	Woodbury	May 7, 61	Jun 20, 61	Died Feb 4, 63 of disease.
Brown, Harvey W.	Middlesex	May 7, 61	Jun 20, 61	Sentenced by G. C. M. to serve one year and 10 days after expiration of service for AWOL; Wounded May 12, 64 and Jun 4, 64; Transferred to V. R. C. Mar 23, 65; Mustered out Jun 30, 65.
Brown, William H.	Moretown	Sep 9, 61	Sep 20, 61	Mustered out Sep 19, 64.
Buxton, Anson	Dummserston	Aug 21, 62	Sep 30, 62	Discharged Feb 12, 63 for disability.
Caffrey, John	Middlebury	Oct 3, 61	Oct 17, 61	Died Dec 21, 61 of disease.
Carpenter, Ira M.	Substitute	Jul 25, 63	Jul 25, 63	Substitute for Daniel McAllister, Jr., Warren; Promoted to Corp. Sep 1, 64; Wounded May 5, 64; Mustered out Jul 15, 65.
Cass, Elisha	Warren	May 7, 61	Jun 20, 61	Discharged Nov 12, 61 for disability.
Clark, William	————	Jul 1, 61	Jul 1, 61	Wounded Jun 29, 62; Discharged Jan 16, 63 for disability.
Clough, Ephraim	Granville	May 7, 61	Jun 20, 61	Reenlisted Jan 31, 64; Wounded Mar 25, 64; Mustered out Jul 17, 65.
Clury, Thomas	Williamstown	May 7, 61	Jun 20, 61	Promoted to Sgt.; Wounded Jul 21, 61; Mustered out Jun 29, 64.
Cochran, Thomas	Vergennes	Sep 27, 61	Oct 18, 61	Wounded May 5, 64; Mustered out Oct 18, 64.
Cole, William T.	Weybridge	Sep 20, 61	Oct 17, 61	Died Nov 27, 61 of disease.
Constant, Augustus	Montpelier	Jun 9, 61	Jun 20, 61	Discharged Feb 12, 63 for disability.
Constant, Augustus	Substitute	Jul 11, 63	Jul 11, 63	Substitute for Alonzo G. Bradish, Montpelier; Mustered out Jul 15, 65.
Cross, John	Hardwick	Aug 11, 62	Sep 30, 62	Wounded May 3, 63, Sep 19, 64 and Apr 2, 65; Discharged Jun 28, 65 for disability.
Cross, Oliver W.	Hardwick	Aug 4, 62	Sep 30, 62	Mustered out Jul 15, 65.
Darling, Albert	Berlin	Dec 19, 63	Jan 2, 64	Wounded May 5, 64; Mustered out Jul 15, 65.
Devine, Robert	Granville	May 20, 61	Jun 20, 61	Mustered out Jun 29, 64.
Ditty, John Q. A.	Roxbury	May 7, 61	Jun 20, 61	Wounded Dec 13, 62; Transferred to V. R. C. Sep 1, 63; Discharged Jun 26, 64.
Ditty, Ralph	Roxbury	May 7, 61	Jun 20, 61	Wounded May 3, 63; Mustered out Jun 29, 64.
Dodge, Charles C.	Troy	May 7, 61	Jun 20, 61	Wounded and taken prisoner Jun 29, 62; Paroled Sep 13, 62; Transferred to V. R. C. Jan 15, 64; Discharged Jun 20, 64.
Donnelly, Patrick	Middlebury	Oct 3, 61	Oct 18, 61	Reenlisted Dec 21, 63; Promoted to Corp. Apr 1, 65; Wounded May 5, 64; Mustered out Jul 15, 65.
Donnelly, Peter	Substitute	Aug 1, 63	Aug 1, 63	Substitute for F. J. Haven, North Hero; Wounded May 12, 64; Mustered out Jul 15, 65.
Doty, George W	Morristown	May 7, 61	Jun 20, 61	Promoted to Corp. Oct 1, 61; Wounded Dec 13, 62; Transferred to V. R. C. Sep 1, 63; Discharged Jun 29, 64.
Eaton, Charles H.	Calais	Jul 11, 63	Jul 11, 63	Drafted; Promoted to Corp. Jul 1, 64; Wounded May 5, 64; Mustered out May 13, 65.
Field, William C.	Poultney	Sep 9, 64	Sep 9, 64	Drummer; Mustered out Jun 19, 65.
Flagg, George W.	Braintree	May 7, 61	May 20, 61	See First Lt. Co. F.
Flanders, Luke A.	Orange	Aug 19, 62	Sep 22, 62	Died Feb 28, 63 of disease.
Flanders, Royal C.	Orange	May 7, 61	Jun 20, 61	Discharged Apr 21, 63 for disability.

Fortin, Benjamin L.	Vergennes	Sep 6, 61	Sep 26, 61	KIA May 5, 64.
Fuller, Ellick	Addison	Sep 3, 61	Sep 20, 61	Died May 18, 62 of disease.
Fuller, Joseph	Waltham	Sep 3, 61	Sep 20, 61	Discharged Jun 15, 63 for wounds received May 4, 63.
Fuller, William	Addison	Sep 3, 61	Sep 20. 61	KIA Apr 16, 62.
George, Daniel R.	Hardwick	May 7, 61	Jun 20, 61	See Second Lt. Co. F.
George, Leonard	Williamstown	Aug 25, 62	Oct 2, 62	No record since muster.
George, Orlenzo M.	Lowell	Jul 24, 62	Sep 30, 62	Wounded May 3, 63; Transferred to V. R. C. Feb 15, 64; Mustered out Jul 4, 65.
Goodrich, Victor	Roxbury	May 7, 61	Jun 20, 61	KIA Jul 21, 61.
Goron, Joseph N.	E. Montpelier	Aug 16, 62	Sep 22, 62	Promoted to Corp. Sep 1, 64, to Sgt. Jan 1, 65; Wounded May 12, 64; Mustered out Jul 10, 65.
Guinan, Edward	Montpelier	May 7, 61	Jun 20, 61	Discharged Jul 25, 63 for disability.
Guyett, Cerel G.	Montpelier	May 7, 61	Jun 20, 61	See Commissary Sgt.
Hall, Harry	Washington	May 7, 61	Jun 20, 61	KIA May 3, 63.
Hargin, Ira J.	E. Montpelier	Aug 14, 62	Sep 22, 62	KIA May 10, 64.
Harran, Charles	Berlin	May 7, 61	Jun 20, 61	Wounded Jul 21, 61 and Jun 1, 64; Mustered out Jun 29, 64.
Harran, Selden B.	Montpelier	May 7, 61	Jun 20, 61	Died Nov 14, 61 of disease.
Harris, Henry L.	Orange	May 18, 61	Jun 20, 61	Wounded and taken prisoner Jun 29, 62; Paroled Jul 22, 62; Discharged Aug 26, 62 for wounds.
Harris, Lester K.	Fayston	Aug 18, 62	Sep 22, 62	Died May 18, 63 of wounds received May 3, 63.
Hastings, Frank J.	Elmore	May 7, 61	Jun 20, 61	Discharged Nov 8, 63 for disability.
Hayward, Frederick E.	Westminster	Jul 25, 63	Jul 25, 63	Drafted; Wounded Sep 22, 64; Mustered out Jul 15, 65.
Houghton, John P.	Substitute	Jul 23, 63	Jul 23, 63	Substitute for John A. Bedard, St. Albans; Wounded May 12, 64; Mustered out Jul 15, 65.
Hutchinson, Stearns S.	Roxbury	May 7, 61	Jun 20, 61	Promoted to Corp.; Wounded May 5, 64; Mustered out Jun 29, 64.
Jacko, Cornelius V.	Substitute	Jul 28, 63	Jul 28, 63	Substitute for Allen P. Foster, Waterbury; Died May 16, 64 of wounds received May 5, 64.
January, George	Burlington	Aug 29, 62	Sep 28, 62	Deserted Nov 19, 62.
Jenne, Samuel F.	Substitute	Aug 26, 63	Aug 26, 63	Substitute for Martin V. Spiller, Morristown; Transferred to V. R. C. Dec 7, 64; Discharged Aug 22, 65.
Johnson, Merritt	Pownal	Aug 18, 63	Aug 18, 63	Drafted; Died May 12, 64 of wounds received May 5, 64.
Johnson, Norman W.	Marshfield	Dec 11, 63	Jan 5, 64	Wounded May 12, 64; Transferred to V. R. C. Dec 4, 64; Discharged May 10, 65.
Kelton, Kneeland	Worcester	Oct 10, 61	Oct 24, 61	Taken prisoner Jun 29, 62; Paroled Aug 5, 62; Mustered out Oct 23, 64.
Kelton, William A.	Worcester	Oct 10, 61	Oct 24, 61	KIA May 5, 64.
Kent, George A.	Northfield	Jul 13, 63	Jul 13, 63	Drafted; Discharged Dec 12, 63 for disability.
Labounty, Edward	Substitute	Jul 28, 63	Jul 28, 63	Substitute for Ira J. Flanigan, Burlington; Mustered out Jul 15, 65.
Labounty, William	Substitute	Aug 7, 63	Aug 7, 63	Substitute for James L. Neal, Norwich; Wounded May—, 64; Transferred to V. R. C. Feb 21, 65; Mustered out Jul 20, 65.
Laport, Daniel Marcus	Braintree	May 7, 61	Jun 20, 61	Mustered out Jun 29, 64.
Laport, Julius D.	Braintree	Sep 16, 61	Oct 1, 61	Deserted Sep 7, 63; Returned under presidential proclamation Apr 12, 65; Mustered out Jul 15, 65.
Late, John B.	Bakersfield	Jul 15, 63	Jul 15, 63	Drafted; Wounded May 5, 64; Died Oct 19, 64 of wounds received same day.
Laurie, Clavius	Substitute	Aug 7, 63	Aug 7, 63	Substitute for Edward Gordon, Grand Isle; Wounded Jun 1, 64; Deserted Jul 24, 64.
Lawrence, George	Berlin	Aug 14, 62	Sep 22, 62	Promoted to Corp.; Died May 21, 64 of wounds received May 5, 64.
Lawrence, Leonard P.	Berlin	Mar 25, 62	Apr 12, 62	Mustered out Apr 14, 65.

Loomis, Elverton W.	Montpelier	May 7, 61	Jun 20, 61	Wounded and taken prisoner Jun 29, 62; Paroled Aug 3, 62; Discharged Sep 13, 62 for wounds.
Lucas, Alfred E.	Barnard	Jul 22, 63	Jul 22, 63	Drafted; Mustered out Jun 13, 65.
Lucas, Thomas	Substitute	Jul 20, 63	Jul 20, 63	Substitute for Stephen Totman, Burlington; Wounded May 5, 64; Discharged Feb 22, 65 for wounds.
Luce, Frank R.	Braintree	May 7, 61	Jun 20, 61	Transferred to V. R. C. Sep 1, 63; Discharged Jun 21, 64.
Lupien, Cyprien	East Montpelier	Feb 24, 62	Apr 12, 62	Reenlisted Apr 13, 64; Wounded Sep 19, 64; Transferred to V. R. C. Apr 20, 65; Mustered out Jul 20, 65.
Lupien, Joseph	East Montpelier	Feb 25, 62	Apr 12, 62	Discharged Feb 13, 62 for disability.
Lupien, Nelson	Montpelier	Mar 1, 62	Apr 12, 62	Discharged Mar 8, 63 for disability.
Lynde, John M.	Substitute	Aug 5, 63	Aug 5, 63	Substitute for Joel B. Slack, Plymouth; Wounded May 5, 64; Mustered out Jul 15, 65.
Mahar, Patrick	Marshfield	May 7, 61	Jun 20, 61	Discharged Oct 31, 62 for wounds.
Mahoney, Sylvester D.	Substitute	Jul 27, 63	Jul 27, 63	Substitute for James Bixby, Essex; KIA May 12, 64.
Manahan, Thomas	Substitute	Jul 23, 63	Jul 23, 63	Substitute for Kimball Blanchard, Barre; Mustered out Jul 15, 65.
Marcou, Alfred	Montpelier	May 20, 61	Jun 20, 61	Wounded Dec 13, 62; Mustered out Jun 29, 64.
Marshall, George A.	Substitute	Aug 1, 63	Aug 1, 63	Substitute for George H. Fay, Richmond; Wounded May 10, 64; Discharged Jan 12, 65 for wounds.
Martin, Francis S.	Substitute	Sep 17, 63	Sep 17, 63	Substitute for George W. Chandler, Randolph; Wounded May 5, 64 and Oct 19, 64; Discharged Aug 25, 65.
Martin, Joseph	Substitute	Jul 29, 63	Jul 29, 63	Substitute for Jason C. Knight, Dummerston; Taken prisoner May 27, 64; Paroled Nov 26, 64; Deserted Jan 17, 65.
Matott, Nelson	Substitute	Aug 3, 63	Aug 3, 63	Substitute for George D. Marsh, Burlington; Wounded May 5, 64 and Apr 2, 65; Mustered out Jul 15, 65.
Maxwell, Thomas S.	Fayston	May 7, 61	Jun 20, 61	Discharged Feb 21, 63 for disability.
McCauley, Thomas H.	Montpelier	May 7, 61	Jun 20, 61	Reenlisted Jan 26, 64; Promoted to Sgt. Sep 1, 64; Wounded Oct 19, 64; Mustered out Jul 15, 65.
McIntyre, Burnham	Substitute	Aug 7, 63	Aug 7, 63	Substitute for Miles E. Baker, Enosburgh; Wounded May 12, 64; Mustered out Jul 15, 65.
McNellis, Edward	Substitute	Aug 1, 63	Aug 1, 63	Substitute for Calvin S. Root, Charlotte; Deserted Dec 9, 64; Returned Jan 12, 65; Mustered out Jul 15, 65.
Miles, Alvah H.	Marshfield	May 7, 61	Jun 20, 61	Deserted Oct 17, 62; Returned Nov 16, 63; Deserted—, 64.
Miller, John	Substitute	Jul 24, 63	Jul 24, 63	Substitute for Solon N. Alexander, Athens; Wounded May 12, 64; Discharged May 27, 65 for wounds.
Miller, John 2nd	Substitute	Aug 7, 63	Aug 7, 63	Substitute for unknown person; Deserted Oct 10, 63.
Miller, John B.	Substitute	Jul 30, 63	Jul 30, 63	Substitute for James S. Cole, Weybridge; Taken prisoner Oct, 14, 63 and died at Richmond, Va., Feb 27, 64.
Mills, Hiram F.	Warren	May 7, 61	Jun 20, 61	Died Jun 16, 62 of disease.
Minard, Franklin E.	Orange	Aug 16, 62	Sep 22, 62	KIA May 3, 63.
Miner, Charles	Panton	Sep 3, 61	Sep 20, 61	Discharged Dec 22, 62 for disability.
Mitchell, Jacob	Burlington	Dec 7, 63	Dec 9, 63	Mustered out Jul 15, 65.
Mitchell, Joseph	Substitute	Jul 20, 63	Jul 20, 63	Substitute for George W. Hopkins, Burlington; KIA May 5, 64.
Mitchell, Prosper	Substitute	Jul 28, 63	Jul 28, 63	Substitute for Andrew C. McBride, Burlington; Wounded May 5, 64; Transferred to V. R. C. Nov 25, 64; Discharged May 16, 65.
Moore, Heman A.	Fayston	Aug 2, 62	Sep 30, 62	Mustered out Jun 19, 65.
Moore, LaFayette	Fayston	Jul 30, 62	Sep 30, 62	Wounded May 3, 63; Died Feb 29, 64 of disease.

Morse, Henry A.	Northfield	May 20, 61	Jun 20, 61	Reenlisted Jan 23, 64; Promoted to Sgt. Feb 7, 65; Wounded May 12, 64; Transferred to V. R. C. Apr 26, 65; Mustered out Jul 20, 65.
Nelson, George E.	Substitute	Jul 11, 63	Jul 11, 63	Substitute for Edward S. Fay, Reading; Deserted Sep 25, 63.
Norris, William C.	Hardwick	May 20, 61	Jun 20, 61	Wagoner; Reenlisted Jan 31, 64; Taken prisoner Jul 21, 64; Paroled Feb 22, 65; Mustered out Jul 15, 65.
Noyes, Wallace W.	Substitute	Jul 21, 63	Jul 21, 63	Substitute for Joseph Sterling, Montpelier; Wounded Apr 2, 65; Mustered out Oct 21, 65.
O'Leary, Jeremiah	Substitute	Jul 28, 63	Jul 28, 63	Substitute for Henry W. Hammond, Middlebury; Mustered out Jul 15, 65.
Ormsbee, Mansur O.	East Montpelier	May 6, 61	Jun 20, 61	Discharged Jan 14, 63 for disability.
Ovitt, David H.	Substitute	Jul 31, 63	Jul 31, 63	Substitute for John A. Perkins, Bakersfield; Wounded Aug 21, 64; Mustered out Jul 15, 65.
Parker, Jared	Montpelier	May 7, 61	Jun 20, 61	Transferred to V. R. C. Sep 1, 63; Discharged Nov 15, 65.
Parker, Samuel B.	Lowell	Jul 30, 63	Jul 30, 63	Drafted; Discharged Mar 26, 64 for disability.
Pierce, Ira	Substitute	Aug 17, 63	Aug 17, 63	Substitute for Horace S. Ashley, Barnard; Mustered out Jun 9, 65.
Pierce, Isaac	Substitute	Aug 7, 63	Aug 7, 63	Substitute for Phillip Royce, Jr., Bridgewater; Discharged May 3, 64 for disability.
Platt, Charles H.	Vergennes	Sep 30, 61	Oct 19, 61	Taken prisoner Jul 2, 62; Paroled Aug 6, 62; Deserted Aug 25, 62.
Price, Charles	Vergennes	Sep 25, 61	Oct 18, 61	Reenlisted Dec 21, 63; Promoted to Corp. Jan 1, 65; Wounded Jun 23, 64; Mustered out Jul 15, 65.
Quimby, William H. E.	Warren	May 7, 61	Jun 20, 61	Wounded—, 62; Transferred to V. R. C Jul 1, 63; Discharged Nov 16, 65.
Rollins, Elisha E.	Greensboro	May 7, 61	Jun 20, 61	Promoted to Corp.; Mustered out Jun 29, 64.
Rose, William	Montpelier	Feb 18, 62	Apr 12, 62	Reenlisted Apr 13, 64; Promoted to Corp. Jan 1, 65 to Sgt. Feb 28, 65; Mustered out Jul 15, 65.
Saunders, Joseph A.	Montpelier	May 7, 61	Jun 20, 61	Reenlisted Dec 21, 63; Mustered out Jul 15, 65.
Savage, Lucius D.	Waitsfield	May 7, 61	Jun 20, 61	Wounded and taken prisoner Jun 29, 62; Paroled Jul 25, 62; Discharged Nov 29, 62 for wounds.
Seger, George	Stamford	Aug 19, 62	Sep 15, 62	Wounded May 12, 64; Mustered out Jun 19, 65.
Selleck, Albert H.	Waitsfield	May 20, 61	Jun 20, 61	Wounded Jul 21, 61; Discharged Mar 21, 63 for disability.
Shorey, Alcine	Montpelier	May 7, 61	Jun 20, 61	Reenlisted Dec 21, 63; Promoted to Corp.; KIA May 12, 64.
Shorey, Joseph	Plainfield	Aug 12, 62	Sep 22, 62	Wounded May 10, 64; Transferred to V. R. C. Nov 27, 64; Mustered out Jul 3, 65.
Shorey, Theodore	East Montpelier	May 7, 61	Jun 20, 61	Reenlisted Dec 21, 63; Promoted to Corp. Sep 1, 62; to Sgt. Apr 1, 65; Wounded Oct 19, 64; Mustered out Jul 15, 65.
Smith, Daniel	Addison	Sep 3, 61	Oct 19, 61	Died Apr 30, 62.
Smith, Edward H.	Substitute	Aug 7, 63	Aug 7, 63	Substitute for Chauncey M. Kimball, Weathersfield; Deserted Sep 29, 63.
Smith, William S.	Middlesex	May 7, 61	Jun 20, 61	Died Sep 25, 61 of disease.
Somers, Seth P.	Greensboro	May 7, 61	Jun 20, 61	Wounded and taken prisoner Jun 29, 62; Paroled Jul 18, 62; Discharged Nov 6, 62 for disability.
Stearns, Henry	Montpelier	May 7, 61	Jun 20, 61	Promoted to Corp. Oct 1, 61; reduced; Taken prisoner Jun 29, 62; Paroled Aug 5, 62; Mustered out Jun 29, 64.
Stearns, Parrish L.	Montpelier	Oct 10, 61	Oct 24, 61	Mustered out Oct 12, 64.
Stoddard, Harlen P.	Waitsfield	May 7, 61	Jun 20, 61	Wounded and taken prisoner Jun 29, 62; Paroled Jul 25, 62; Discharged Jul 30, 63 for disability.
Stoddard, Horace B.	Waitsfield	Sep 9, 61	Oct 10, 61	KIA May 5, 64.
Storrs, Charles W.	Montpelier	May 7, 61	Jun 20, 61	Discharged Oct 25, 61 for disability.

Stowe, William	Calais	May 7, 61	Jun 20, 61	Promoted to Corp.; KIA May 5, 64.
Sullivan, Charles	Substitute	Aug 5, 63	Aug 5, 63	Substitute for Charles W. Perkins, Weathersfield; Deserted Sep 29, 63.
Taft, Sanborn B.	Substitute	Jul 29, 63	Jul 29, 63	Substitute for John H. Orvis, Starksboro; Discharged Jan 9, 64 for disability.
Taylor, Stephen	Plainfield	May 7, 61	Jun 20, 61	Fifer; Reenlisted Jan 31, 64; Taken prisoner Jun 29, 62; Paroled—, 62; Wounded Dec 13, 62; Mustered out Jul 15, 65.
Thibo, Antoine	East Montpelier	Aug 28, 62	Sep 22, 62	Died Dec 24, 62 of disease.
Tourvill, Louis	Vergennes	Sep 6, 61	Sep 20, 61	Reenlisted Dec 21, 63; Promoted to Corp. Jan 1, 65; Wounded May 5, 64 and Sep 19, 64; Mustered out Jul 15, 65.
Town, Josiah	Montpelier	May 7, 61	Jun 20, 61	Mustered out Jun 29, 64.
Voodry, George B.	Woodbury	May 20, 61	Jun 20, 61	Promoter to Corp.; Mustered out Jun 29, 64.
Wade, Charles, Jr.	Montpelier	May 7, 61	Jun 20, 61	Discharged Dec 4, 62 for disability.
Williams, Frederick	Vergennes	Sep 3, 61	Sep 20, 61	Mustered out Sep 19, 64.
Williams, Ira	Brookfield	May 7, 61	Jun 20, 61	Discharged Nov 16, 62 for disability.
Withers, George	Greensboro	May 7, 61	Jun 20, 61	Wounded and taken prisoner Jun 29, 62; Paroled Jul 22, 62; Died Jul 28, 62 of wounds.
Woodcock, Carlton A.	Plainfield	Aug 12, 62	Sep 22, 62	Wounded Sep 19, 64; Discharged Jun 12, 65.
Worcester, Earl C.	Warren	May 20, 61	Jun 20, 61	Mustered out Jun 29, 64.

Company G

Name and Rank	Residence	Date of Commission	Date of Issue	Remarks
Captains				
Drew, John T.	Burlington	May 20, 61	May 20, 61	Taken prisoner Jul 21, 61; Paroled Aug 17, 62; Resigned Oct 8, 62.
Chase, Phillips E.	Mt. Holly	Oct 17, 62	Nov 5, 62	Sgt. Co. I; Promoted to First Sgt. Oct 15, 61; to Second Lt. Co. A Jan 24, 62; to First Lt. Co. A May 21, 62; Wounded May 5, 64; Mustered out Jun 29, 64.
Harrington, Ephriam W.		Kirby	Dec 24, 64	Jan 31, 65 Sgt. Co. G; Reenlisted Dec 21, 63; Promoted to Second Lt. Co. B Jun 20, 64; to First Lt. Co. G Aug 8, 64; Bvt Maj. Apr 2, 65 for gallantry at Petersburg; Wounded May 3, 63; Mustered out Jul 15, 65.
First Lieutenants				
Sharpley, David L.	Burlington	May 20, 61	May 20, 61	Resigned Jun 24, 62.
Weed, Anson H.	Hinesburgh	Jul 5, 62	Jul 5, 62	Second Lt. Co. G; Resigned Mar 5, 63.
Bain, John J., Jr.	Burlington	Mar 10, 63	Mar 17, 63	First Sgt. Co. G; Promoted to Second Lt. Co. G Jul 5, 62; Wounded May 5, 64; Mustered out Jun 29, 64.
Harrington, Ephriam W.	Kirby	Aug 8, 64	Aug 23, 64	See Capt. Co. G.
Ward, Byron C.	Underhill	Dec 24, 64	Jan 31, 65	Pvt. Co. G; Promoted to Sgt. Sep 1, 64; to First Sgt. Dec 24, 64; Wounded May 5, 64; Mustered out Jun 19, 65.
Second Lieutenants				
Weed, Anson H.	Hinesburgh	May 20, 61	May 20, 61	See First Lt. Co. G.
Bain, John J., Jr.	Burlington	Jul 5, 62	Jul 5, 62	See First Lt. Co. G.
Worcester, George B.	Ferrisburgh	Mar 10, 63	Mar 17, 63	Sgt. Co. G.; Dismissed from the service Apr 5, 64.
Ward, Edwin R.	Underhill	Jun 7, 65	Jun 17, 65	Pvt. Co. G; Promoted to Sgt. Sep 1, 64; to First Sgt. Feb 8, 65; Wounded May 5, 64 and May 18, 64; Mustered out as First Sgt. Jun 19, 65.

Name and Rank	Residence	Date of Enlistment	Date of Muster	Remarks
Sergeants				
Bain, John J., Jr.	Burlington	May 7, 61	Jun 20, 61	See First Lt. Co. G.
Harrington, Ephriam W.	Kirby	May 7, 61	Jun 20, 61	See Capt. Co. G.
Worcester, George B.	Ferrisburgh	May 7, 61	Jun 20, 61	See Second Lt. Co. G.
Woodward, George W.	Westford	May 7, 61	Jun 20, 61	Discharged Aug 9, 62 for disability.
Stuart, Benjamin F.	Hardwick	May 7, 61	Jun 20, 61	Discharged Dec 26, 62 for disability.
Corporals				
Aldrich, Morey S.	Burlington	May 18, 61	Jun 20, 61	Promoted to Sgt. Sep 23, 61; to First Sgt. Mar, 63; Mustered out Jun 29, 64.
Fletcher, Winfield S.	South Hero	May 7, 61	Jun 20, 61	Wounded Jun 29, 62; Discharged Apr 5, 63.
Naramore, Rollin C.	Underhill	May 7, 61	Jun 20, 61	Reduced; Discharged Oct 10, 62 for disability.
Nichols, Leroy B.	Williston	May 7, 61	Jun 20, 61	Promoted to Sgt.; Wounded May 12, 64; Mustered out Jun 29, 64.
Hilton, J. Walter	Bristol	May 7, 61	Jun 20, 61	Reenlisted Jan 20, 64; Promoted to Sgt.; Wounded May 3, 63; Reduced Mar 20, 64; Taken prisoner May 21, 64; Paroled Nov 19, 64; Mustered out Jul 26, 65.
Wilcox, Henry	Hinesburgh	May 7, 61	Jun 20, 61	Discharged Dec 18, 61 for disability.
Russell, Edward S.	Burlington	May 7, 61	Jun 20, 61	Discharged Jan 2, 62 for disability.
Henry, Alvin H.	Westford	May 7, 61	Jun 20, 61	Discharged Jan 2, 62 for disability.
Musicians				
Hickock, Helmas W.	Westford	May 7, 61	Jun 20, 61	Died Sep 1, 62 of disease.
Sharpley, David T.	Burlington	May 7, 61	Jun 20, 61	See Principal Musicians.
Wagoner				
McCarty, John L.	Burlington	May 7, 61	Jun 20, 61	Mustered out Jun 29, 64.
Privates				
Amblow, Henry	Burlington	May 7, 61	Jun 20, 61	Reenlisted Jan 20, 64; Died Jun 9, 64 of wounds received May 18, 64.
Archer, Foster E.	Plymouth	Mar 6, 62	Mar 22, 62	Reenlisted Apr 18, 64; Mustered out Jul 15, 65.
Arnold, George	Essex	May 7, 61	Jun 20, 61	Reenlisted Jan 31, 64; Wounded May 5, 64; Mustered out Jul 15, 65.
Aubrey, Cornelius E.	Burlington	May 7, 61	Jun 20, 61	Mustered out Jun 29, 64.
Ayers, Sanford	Vergennes	Sep 9, 61	Oct 18, 61	Died Jan 25, 62 of disease.
Barber, Edgar	Richmond	May 7, 61	Jun 20, 61	Reenlisted Jan 21, 64; Promoted to Corp. Feb 8, 65; to Sgt. Mar 22, 65; Mustered out Jul 15, 65.
Barton, Rollin W.	Charlotte	May 7, 61	Jun 20, 61	Promoted to Corp.; Wounded Dec 13, 62 and May 18, 64; Mustered out Jun 29, 64.
Bass, Henry J.	Underhill	Jun 14, 61	Jun 20, 61	Promoted to Corp.; KIA May 12, 64.
Bates, Martin, Jr.	Westford	May 7, 61	Jun 20, 61	Died Aug 4, 61 of disease.
Benedict, Wait M.	Underhill	Mar 13, 65	Mar 13, 65	Mustered out Jul 15, 65.
Bennett, Alexander	Hinesburgh	May 7, 61	Jun 20, 61	Deserted Sep 12, 63.
Bell, John H.	Essex	May 7, 61	Jun 20, 61	Wounded Jul 21, 61; Mustered out Jun 29, 64.
Bellows, Eugene C.	Westford	May 7, 61	Jun 20, 61	Wounded May 5, 64; Mustered out Jun 29, 64.
Blood, Robert R.	Westford	May 7, 61	Jun 20, 61	Discharged Dec 18, 61 for disability.
Bowen, Isaac	Hardwick	May 7, 61	Jun 20, 61	Discharged Dec 1, 62 for disability.
Bragg, Edmund C.	Waterbury	Sep 3, 61	Sep 25, 61	KIA Jun 3, 64.
Bragg, James	Waterbury	Sep 3, 61	Sep 25, 61	Deserted Oct 22, 62.
Brewster, Elihu B.	Underhill	Aug 30, 62	Sep 15, 62	Mustered out Jun 19, 65.
Brown, Daniel R.	Saratoga, NY	May 7, 61	Jun 20, 61	Reenlisted Jan 31, 64; Wounded May 5, 64; Transferred to V. R. C. Feb 21, 65; Mustered out Jul 20, 65.
Buley, John	Burlington	May 7, 61	Jun 20, 61	Wounded May 5, 64; Mustered out Aug 23, 64.
Chelsea, William	Burlington	May 7, 61	Jun 20, 61	Discharged Nov 7, 62 for disability.
Cherbino, George	Weybridge	Oct 17, 61	Oct 18, 61	Wounded May 4, 63; Discharged Mar 16, 64.

Church, Chancey L.	Jericho	Aug 20, 62	Sep 15, 62	KIA May 4, 63.
Clark, Abel N.	Underhill	Aug 29, 62	Sep 15, 62	Mustered out Jun 19, 65.
Coagle, Edward	Substitute	Aug 3, 63	Aug 3, 63	Substitute for George W. Brown, Starksboro; Deserted Sep 25, 63.
Collins, Augustus H.	Stowe	Sep 14, 61	Sep 25, 61	Reenlisted Jan 31, 64; Died Apr 19, 64 of disease.
Colt, Frank	Hinesburgh	May 15, 61	Jun 20, 61	Wounded May 3, 63; Transferred to V. R. C. Nov 20, 63; Discharged Apr 29, 64.
Condon, James	Hinesburgh	Aug 22, 62	Sep 15, 62	Mustered out Jun 19, 65.
Conro, Henry W.	South Hero	May 7, 61	Jun 20, 61	Promoted to Corp.; Taken prisoner Jul 21, 61; paroled Jun 2, 62; Wounded May 5, 64; Mustered out Jun 29, 64.
Cook, Franklin M.	Shelburne	Aug 18, 62	Sep 15, 62	Wounded May 4, 63; Died Jun 2, 64 of wounds received May 12, 64.
Cook, William W.	Shelburne	Aug 29, 62	Sep 15, 62	Wounded May 3, 63; Discharged Apr 12, 64 for wounds.
Corse, Henry P.	Cambridge	May 7, 61	Jun 20, 61	Promoted to Corp.; Discharged Mar 8, 63 for disability.
Crowley, John	Substitute	Jul 23, 63	Jul 23, 63	Substitute for Dennis Quinn, Northfield; No record since muster.
Daniel, John	Charlotte	May 7, 61	Jun 20, 61	Taken prisoner May 4, 63; Paroled May 13, 63; Discharged Jan 2, 64 for disability.
Davis, Philo	Bakersfield	May 7, 61	Jun 20, 61	Transferred to V. R. C. Sep 1, 63; Discharged Jun 20, 64.
Day, Converse E.	Underhill	Aug 28, 62	Sep 15, 62	KIA May 5, 64.
Dickinson, Harvey	Underhill	Dec 8, 63	Dec 18, 63	Wounded May 18, 64; Died Jul—, 64 of wounds.
Drake, William	Substitute	Aug 4, 63	Aug 4, 63	Substitute for Calvin McBride, South Hero; Deserted Sep 25, 63.
Edgell, Albert B.	Burlington	Jun 10, 61	Jun 20, 61	Discharged Nov 26, 61 for disability.
Fargo, Ransom B.	Shelburne	Aug 16, 62	Sep 15, 62	Wounded May 5, 64; Mustered out May 13, 65.
Farrell, John	Shelburne	Aug 19, 62	Sep 15, 62	Mustered out Jun 19, 65.
Ford, Hadley P.	Brandon	Oct 17, 61	Oct 23, 61	Reenlisted Dec 21, 63; Died May 18, 64 of wounds received same day.
Foy, Abial	Hardwick	May 7, 61	Jun 20, 61	Mustered out Jun 29, 64.
Garrow, Oliver	Burlington	May 7, 61	Jun 20, 61	Wounded and taken prisoner May 4, 63; Paroled May 16, 63; Mustered out Jun 29, 64.
Gibbs, E. Payson	Westford	May 7, 61	Jun 20, 61	Reenlisted Dec 21, 63; Promoted to Corp. Mar 10, 64; Died May 6, 64 of wounds received May 5, 64.
Goodness, Jeremiah	Waterville	Mar 25, 62	Apr 12, 62	Deserted Aug 23, 62.
Gorman, Joseph	Substitute	Aug 26, 64	Aug 26, 64	Substitute for David J. Lamson, Newfane; Mustered out Jul 15, 65.
Green, John C.	Richmond	May 7, 61	Jun 20, 61	Deserted Apr 14, 62.
Green, Orlando R.	St. Albans	May 7, 61	Jun 20, 61	Discharged Dec 15, 62 for disability.
Greenough, John	Substitute	Jul 30, 63	Jul 30, 63	Substitute for Henry Bixby, Essex; Deserted Jun 4, 64.
Guyette, Joseph	Burlington	May 7, 61	Jun 20, 61	Mustered out Jun 29, 64.
Hammer, Philip	Burlington	May 7, 61	Jun 20, 61	Mustered out Jun 29, 64.
Hanley, Daniel	Burlington	Mar 10, 62	Apr 12, 62	Died May 15, 64 of wounds received May 13, 64.
Harrington, Garrison	Ferrisburgh	Sep 1, 61	———	Discharged Oct 21, 62 for disability.
Haselton, David	Westford	May 7, 61	Jun 20, 61	KIA May 4, 63.
Hennessey, Matthew	Poultney	Sep 13, 61	Sep 25, 61	Discharged Jan 20, 63 for disability.
Higby, William	Monkton	Sep 17, 61	Sep 29, 61	Died Oct 6, 62 of disease.
Hodgeman, George W.	Underhill	Aug 30, 62	Sep 15, 62	Died Jul 26, 63 of disease.
Howard, George	Westford	May 7, 61	Jun 20, 61	Mustered out Jun 29, 64.
Humphrey, Amos C.	Underhill	Jun 14, 61	Jun 20, 61	Promoted to Corp.; Wounded Dec 13, 62 and May 5, 64; Mustered out Jun 29, 64.
Irish, Rufus C.	Hinesburgh	Aug 22, 62	Sep 15, 62	Promoted to Corp. Feb 8, 65; Mustered out Jun 19, 65.
Isham, Myron	Essex	Aug 15, 62	Sep 15, 62	Mustered out Jun 19, 65.
Jackson, John	Burlington	Aug 23, 62	Sep 15, 62	Wounded May 4, 63; Mustered out Jun 19, 65.

Jennings, Stephen E.	Whiting	Dec 9, 63	Dec 11, 63	Wounded May 5, 64 and Mar 25, 64; Mustered out Jul 15, 65.
Jerough, Benjamin	Hinesburgh	Aug 23, 62	Sep 15, 62	Wounded May 12, 64; Mustered out Jun 19, 65.
Jones, William L	Burlington	May 7, 61	Jun 20, 61	Wounded Jul 21, 61; Dishonorably discharged Sep 1, 61 by sentence of G. C. M.
Kehoe, Joseph	Charlotte	Sep 8, 61	Oct 18, 61	Reenlisted Dec 21, 63; Deserted; Returned Jan 25, 63; KIA May 18, 64.
Knapp, Horace M.	Burlington	Jun 11, 61	Jun 20, 61	Died Aug 1, 62 of disease.
Labounty, William	Burlington	Mar 19, 62	Apr 12, 62	Discharged Jul 30, 62 for disability.
Landon, Charles C.	South Hero	May 7, 61	Jun 20, 61	Promoted to Corp.; Wounded May 18, 64; Mustered out Jun 29, 64
LaPlant, Charles	Substitute	Jul 30, 63	Jul 30, 63	Substitute for John S. Palmer, Charlotte; Deserted Oct 19, 63.
Larose, Joseph A.	Hinesburgh	May 7, 61	Jun 20, 61	Reenlisted Dec 21, 63; Promoted to Corp. Oct 18, 61; to Sgt. Jan 18, 65; Reduced Mar 11, 65; Promoted to Corp. Apr 10, 65; Mustered out Jul 15, 65.
Leo, Michael	Burlington	Sep 16, 61	Oct 18, 61	Wounded May 5, 64; Mustered out Sep 24, 64.
Lessor, Baptisie	Pawlet	Sep 1, 64	Sep 1, 64	Wounded Apr 2, 65; Mustered out Jun 2, 65.
Loggins, Harrison B.	St. George	Aug 20, 61	Sep 13, 61	Mustered out Sep 12, 64.
Marks, Lorenzo J.	Shelburne	May 7, 61	Jun 20, 61	Wounded Sep 17, 62 and May 18, 64; Mustered out Jun 29, 64.
Martin, Benjamin	South Hero	May 7, 61	Jun 20, 61	Taken prisoner Jul 21, 61; Paroled Jun 2, 62; Taken prisoner May 4, 63; Paroled May 15, 63; Mustered out Jun 29, 64.
Martin, Thomas	South Hero	May 7, 61	Jun 20, 61	Taken prisoner Jun 29, 62; Paroled Aug 5, 62; Discharged Dec 21, 63 for enlistment in 1st N.Y. Independent Battery.
Massey, Walter	Substitute	Sep 5, 63	Sep 5, 63	Substitute for James L. Davis, Brighton; Dishonorable discharge Apr 10, 64 by sentence of G. C. M.
McDermott, James	Burlington	Aug 23, 63	Sep 5, 63	Wounded May 5, 64; Mustered out Jun 19, 65.
McDonald, James	Substitute	Sep 5, 63	Sep 5, 63	Substitute for Stephen Flynn, Milton; Mustered out Jul 15, 65.
McGuire, James	Shelburne	Aug 14, 62	Apr 15, 62	Taken prisoner May 21, 64 and died at Andersonville, Ga. Sep 20, 64.
Merriam, Dudley C.	Westford	May 7, 61	Jun 20, 61	See Hospital Steward.
Moore, Curtis B.	Elmore	Sep 16, 61	Sep 25, 61	Wounded and taken prisoner Jun 29, 62 and died Jul 9, 62 while a POW.
Moore, John	Substitute	Sep 5, 63	Sep 5, 63	Substitute for Anthony Flaherty, Brighton; Wounded May 5, 64; Deserted May 2, 65.
Morrill, George W.	Substitute	Aug 11, 63	Aug 11, 63	Substitute for George O. Rogers, Guildhall; Mustered out Jul 15, 65.
Morrissey, Michael	Waterbury	Sep 8, 61	Sep 25, 61	Discharged Dec 21, 63 for enlistment in 1st N.Y. Independent Battery.
Mulligan, Peter	Burlington	May 7, 61	Jun 20, 61	Mustered out Jun 29, 64.
Mumford, Thomas	Rutland	Jul 22, 63	Jul 22, 63	Drafted; Wounded May 5, 64; Deserted Dec —, 64.
Munson, Russell C.	Burlington	Aug 21, 62	Sep 15, 62	Transferred to V. R. C. Mar 8, 64; Discharged Jul 14, 65.
Nash, Horace C.	Jericho	Mar 7, 62	Apr 12, 62	Transferred to the Regular Army Jul 30, 63.
Nelson, Ferguson	Burlington	May 7, 61	Jun 20, 61	Discharged Dec 16, 61 for wounds received Jul 21, 61.
Nichols, Norman J.	Essex	Aug 28, 62	Sep 15, 62	Wounded May 5, 64; Discharged May 27, 65.
O'Neil, Edmund	Burlington	Aug 30, 62	Sep 15, 62	Promoted to Sgt. Mar 22, 65; Wounded Jul 3, 63, May 5, 64 and Mar 25, 65; Mustered out Jun 30, 65.
Page, Albert	Monkton	Oct 7, 61	Oct 18, 61	Discharged Mar 23, 62 for disability.
Page, Henry C.	Substitute	Aug 4, 63	Aug 4, 63	Substitute for Leonard M. Knight, Johnson; Wounded May 5, 64 and Jun 1, 64; Mustered out Jun 24, 65.

Palmer, Myron C.	Hinesburgh	Aug 27, 62	Sep 15, 62	Wounded Dec 13, 62, May 5, 64 and May 18, 64; Taken prisoner May 21, 64 and died at Savannah, Ga. Nov 1, 64.
Palmer, Oscar	Hinesburgh	May 7, 61	Jun 20, 61	Wounded May 3, 63; Transferred to V. R. C. Sep 1, 63; Discharged Jun 28, 64.
Peck, Levi B.	Substitute	Jul 31, 63	Jul 31, 63	Substitute for Moses F. Gove, Lincoln; Discharged May 22, 65 for disability.
Perry, Charles B.	Burlington	Jul 13, 63	Jul 13, 63	Drafted; Wounded May 5, 64; Deserted Jun —, 64; Returned under presidential proclamation Apr 22, 65; Dishonorable discharge May 12, 65.
Phelps, Buel	Morristown	Sep 14, 61	Sep 25, 61	Discharged Dec 20, 62 for disability.
Phenesy, Philip	Shelburne	Aug 18, 62	Sep 15, 62	Taken prisoner May 4, 63; Paroled May 15, 63; Wounded May 5, 64; Mustered out May 13, 65.
Ploof, Abraham	Ferrisburgh	Oct 4, 61	Oct 18, 61	Wounded on gunboat, date unknown; Discharged Nov 25, 62.
Pollard, Sherman C.	Colchester	Jan 13, 65	Jan 13, 65	Mustered out Jun 26, 65.
Porter, Elijah	Underhill	Dec 7, 63	Dec 18, 63	Wounded May 5, 64 and Jun 1, 64; Discharged Jun 18, 65 for wounds.
Powell, Orrin	Hinesburgh	Aug 21, 62	Sep 15, 62	Discharged Apr 28, 65 for wounds received Oct 19, 64.
Preston, Charles	Underhill	Aug 25, 64	Aug 25, 64	Mustered out Jun 19, 65.
Prior, Cyrus	Underhill	Dec 7, 63	Dec 18, 63	Promoted to Corp. Sep 1, 64; to Sgt. Feb 8, 65; Wounded Apr 2, 65; Mustered out Jul 15, 65.
Prior, Sidney	Underhill	Aug 19, 64	Aug 19, 64	Wounded Mar 27, 65; Mustered out Jun 30, 65.
Ravey, John	Underhill	Mar 13, 65	Mar 13, 65	Mustered out Jul 15, 65.
Ray, Orman P.	Essex	Aug 30, 62	Sep 15, 62	See Adjutant.
Redmond, John	Carterville, NY	May 7, 61	Jun 20, 61	Reenlisted Dec 21, 63; Promoted to Corp. Mar 20, 64; to Sgt. Sep 1, 64; Taken prisoner Jul 21, 61; Paroled Jun 2, 62; Wounded May 3, 63 and May 5, 64; Discharged Jun 14, 65.
Reed, Charles A.	Ludlow	Mar 6, 62	Apr 12, 62	Promoted to Corp. Sep 1, 64; to Sgt. Feb 8, 65; Mustered out Mar 22, 65.
Reed, Henry	Burlington	May 7, 61	Jun 20, 61	Reenlisted Dec 21, 63; Promoted to Corp. Oct 18, 61; to Sgt.; Died May 26, 64 of wounds received May 12, 64.
Reed, Philander W.	Fletcher	May 7, 61	Jun 20, 61	Reenlisted Jan 20, 64; Died Jun 19, 64 of wounds received May 5, 64.
Reed, Thomas	Burlington	May 7, 61	Jun 20, 61	Mustered out Jun 29, 64.
Remington, Loyal	Essex	Aug 28, 62	Sep 15, 62	Discharged Mar 10, 63 for disability.
Ross, Thomas C.	Sheldon	Dec 31, 63	Dec 31, 63	Transferred to V. R. C. Apr 15, 64; Mustered out Jul 29, 65.
Royce, Daniel	Burlington	May 7, 61	Jun 20, 61	Discharged Oct 31, 62 for disability.
Ryan, James	St. Albans	May 7, 61	Jun 20, 61	Died May 12, 63 of wounds received May 4, 63.
Ryan, John	Essex	May 7, 61	Jun 20, 61	Reenlisted Jan 31, 64; Wounded May 5, 64; discharged Jun 13, 65 for disability.
Saltus, Frank	Burlington	May 7, 61	Jun 20, 61	Reenlisted Dec 21, 63; Died May 6, 64 of wounds received same day.
Sharpley, George W.	Colchester	Jan 13, 65	Jan 13, 65	KIA Apr 2, 65.
Sharpley, John F.	Colchester	Jan 13, 65	Jan 13, 65	Mustered out Jul 15, 65.
Sherman, Alonzo H.	Underhill	Mar 13, 65	Mar 13, 65	Enlisted for one year; Mustered out Jul 15, 65.
Sibley, Eben K.	Westford	May 13, 61	Jun 20, 61	Discharged Dec 22, 61 for disability.
Smith, Warren S.	Burlington	Jun 14, 61	Jun 20, 61	Reenlisted Jan 31, 64; Died May 13, 64 of wounds received May 12, 64.
Somerville, Samuel	Burlington	Aug 21, 62	Sep 15, 62	Wounded May 18, 64; Discharged May 13, 65.
Spaulding, Andrew	Burlington	May 7, 61	Jun 20, 61	Deserted Apr 14, 62.
Spaulding, J. Seely	Burlington	Jun 10, 61	Jun 20, 61	Promoted to Corp.; to Sgt. Mar 20, 64; Wounded May 4, 63 and May 5, 64; Mustered out Jun 29, 64.
Spear, Alonzo	Burlington	May 7, 61	Jun 20, 61	Reenlisted Jan 31, 64; Promoted to Corp. Feb 8, 65; Wounded Jun 1, 64; Mustered out Jul 15, 65.

Sterling, Lyman, Jr.	Burlington	May 9, 61	Jun 20, 61	Mustered out Jun 29, 64.
Stewart, Benjamin F.	Hardwick	Nov 11, 61	————	Discharged Dec 26, 62 for disability.
Stowe, Horiato	Waterbury	Sep 14, 61	————	Discharged May 12, 62 for disability.
Terrill, Alexander W.	Burlington	May 7, 61	Jun 20, 61	Discharged Jan 31, 63 for disability.
Tilley, Hiram H.	St. George	Aug 20, 61	Sep 13, 61	Wounded May 4, 63; Transferred to V. R. C. Jul 1, 63; Discharged Sep 13, 64.
Tilley, Silas H.	St. George	Aug 20, 61	Sep 13, 61	Mustered out Sep 13, 64.
Tilley, Sydney N.	St. George	May 7, 61	Jun 20, 61	Transferred to V. R. C. Dec 1, 63; Discharged Feb 22, 64.
Train, Thaddeus	Moriah, NY	Sep 3, 61	Oct 18, 61	Reenlisted Dec 21, 63; Wounded May 3, 63; KIA May 10, 64.
Tryon, Hollis	Burlington	Jul 20, 64	Jul 20, 64	Mustered out Jul 15, 65.
Tupper, Charles E.	Bakersfield	May 13, 61	Jun 20, 61	Died Dec 11, 61 of disease.
Vancor, Henry	Morristown	Feb 1, 65	Feb 1, 65	Mustered out Jul 15, 65.
Wait, Roswell C.	Westford	May 7, 61	Jun 20, 61	Mustered out Jun 29, 64.
Ward, Byron C.	Underhill	Aug 26, 62	Sep 15, 62	See First Lt. Co. G.
Ward, Edwin, R.	Underhill	Aug 28, 62	Sep 15, 62	See Second Lt. Co. G.
Wells, John C.	Underhill	Dec 8, 63	Dec 18, 63	Wounded May 12, 64 and Sep 19, 64; Deserted May 9, 65.
Weston, David W.	Cambridge	Mar 24, 65	Mar 24, 65	Mustered out Jul 15, 65.
White, Roderick S.	Huntington	May 7, 61	Jun 20, 61	Mustered out Jun 29, 64.
Wilder, George H.	Underhill	Aug 21, 62	Sep 15, 62	Died May 10, 64 of wounds received May 5, 64.
Wilkins, George F.	Ferrisburgh	Sep 12, 61	Oct 18, 61	Wounded May 4, 63; Transferred to V. R. C. Sep 1, 63; Discharged Oct 17, 64.
Wills, Hiram	Burlington	May 7, 61	Jun 20, 61	Wounded May 5, 64; Mustered out Jun 29, 64.
Wilson, Lewis M.	Bakersfield	May 13, 61	Jun 20, 61	Wounded and taken prisoner May 4, 63; Paroled May 16, 63; Mustered out Jun 29, 64.
Winchell, Martin H.	Cambridge	Mar 27, 65	Mar 27, 65	Mustered out Jul 15, 65.
Wright, John E. P.	Burlington	Aug 21, 62	Sep 15, 62	Discharged Jul 28, 64 for wounds received May 12, 64.
Youatt, Martin	Burlington	May 7, 61	Jun 20, 61	Deserted Aug 23, 62.

Company H

Name and Rank	Residence	Date of Commission	Date of Issue	Remarks
Captains				
Burnham, William T.	Montpelier	May 23, 61	May 23, 61	Resigned Oct 25, 61.
Tracy, Amasa S.	Middlebury	Jan 24, 62	Jan 24, 62	See Col.
Bass, John T.	Moretown	Jun 20, 64	Jul 11, 64	Sgt. Co. D; Promoted to First Sgt. Jan 28, 62; to Second Lt. Co. D Aug 9, 62; to First Lt. Co. D Nov 3, 63; Mustered out Dec —, 69.
First Lieutenants				
Case, Jerome B.	Fletcher	May 23, 61	May 23, 61	Discharged Sep 14, 61 for disability.
Leach, Chester K.	Fletcher	Sep 14, 61	Sep 14, 61	Second Lt. Co. H; Mustered out Jun 29, 64.
Prouty, Henry H.	Brattleboro	Apr 24, 64	May 5, 64	See Capt. Co. B.
Buck, George, Jr.	Fairfax	Dec 24, 64	Jan 31, 65	Corp. Co. H; Reenlisted Jan 31, 64; Promoted to Sgt. Aug 1, 63; to First Sgt. Sep 1, 64; Wounded May 5, 64; Mustered out Jul 15, 65.
Second Lieutenants				
Leach, Chester K.	Fletcher	May 23, 61	May 23, 61	See First Lt. Co. H.
Appleton, Edward W.	Bennington	Sep 14, 61	Sep 14, 61	See First Lt. Co. B.
Sawyer, Joshua P.	St. Albans	Jan 25, 62	Jan 25, 62	See First Lt. Co. C.
Prouty, Henry H.	Brattleboro	Nov 2, 63	Nov 11, 63	See Capt. Co. B.
Westman, Orson C.	Cambridge	Jun 7, 65	Jun 28, 65	Pvt. Co. H; Reenlisted Jan 31, 64; Promoted to Corp. Sep 1, 62; to Sgt. Sep 1, 64; to First Sgt. Feb 8, 65; Mustered out as First Sgt. Jul 15, 65.

Name and Rank	Residence	Date of Enlistment	Date of Muster	Remarks
Sergeants				
Woodbury, Urban A.	Elmore	May 25, 61	Jun 20, 61	Wounded and taken prisoner Jul 21, 61; Paroled Oct 5, 61; Discharged Oct 18, 61 for wounds received Jul 21, 61.
Sawyer, Joshua P.	St Albans	May 7, 61	Jun 20, 61	See First Lt. Co. C.
Ford, Abram	Montpelier	Jun 17, 61	Jun 20, 61	Discharged Nov 20, 62 for disability.
Ellenwood, Eli	Cambridge	May 25, 61	Jun 20, 61	Died Aug 5, 62 of disease.
Smith, Edwin R.	Cambridge	May 23, 61	Jun 20, 61	Reduced; Mustered out Jun 29, 61.
Corporals				
Ballard, Henry L.	Georgia	May 18, 61	Jun 20, 61	Promoted to Sgt.; Wounded May 3, 63 and May 5, 64; Transferred to V. R. C. Nov 20, 63; Discharged Oct 2, 64.
Royce, Samuel W.	Fletcher	May 7, 61	Jun 20, 61	Discharged Jan 14, 63 for disability.
Wells, William L.	Fairfax	May 14, 61	Jun 20, 61	Died Oct 22, 63 of disease.
Hulburd, Loyal P.	Waterville	May 7, 61	Jun 20, 61	Promoted to Sgt. Sep 1, 62; Wounded May 12, 64; Mustered out Jun 29, 64.
Buck, George, Jr.	Fairfax	May 14, 61	Jun 20, 61	See First Lt. Co. H.
Meeker, Henry V.	Cambridge	May 7, 61	Jun 20, 61	Reduced; Mustered out Jun 29, 64.
Graves, Thaddeus O.	Wolcott	May 25, 61	Jun 20, 61	Reduced Oct 1, 61; Transferred to V. R. C. Sep 1, 63; Discharged May 25, 64.
Ufford, Zadock	Fairfax	May 18, 61	Jun 20, 61	See Sgt. Maj.
Musicians				
Kinsley, Chellis	Georgia	May 18, 61	Jun 20, 61	Transferred to V. R. C. Dec 1, 63; Discharged Jun 27, 64.
Montague, Hollis R.	Fletcher	May 7, 61	Jun 20, 61	Mustered out Jun 29, 64.
Wagoner				
Fletcher, William H.	Waterville	May 10, 61	Jun 20, 61	Mustered out Jun 29, 64.
Privates				
Akey, Peter	South Hero	Aug 23, 62	Sep 30, 62	Discharged Feb 7, 63 for disability.
Aldrich, Caleb A.	Fletcher	Dec 8, 63	Dec 30, 63	Mustered out Jul 15, 65.
Allen, Henry	Weathersfield	Apr 3, 62	Apr 3, 62	Discharged Jan 17, 63 for disability.
Austin, James	Cambridge	May 7, 61	Jun 20, 61	Died Oct 4, 63 of disease.
Ayres, John	Bakersfield	May 17, 61	Jun 20, 61	Reenlisted Jan 31, 64; Promoted Corp.; Wounded May 5, 64; Transferred to V. R. C Aug 2, 64; Mustered out Aug 23, 65.
Bailey, Jehial S., Jr.	Waterville	May 24, 61	Jun 20, 61	Promoted to Corp.; Wounded May 12, 64; Discharged Jul 29, 64.
Barnes, Sanford R.	Bakersfield	May 15, 61	Jun 20, 61	Promoted to Corp.; Discharged Oct 21, 62 for disability.
Beales, Charles	Shaftsbury	Aug 18, 63	Aug 18, 63	Drafted; Wounded May 5, 64; Transferred to V. R. C. Feb 21, 65; Mustered out Jul 20, 65.
Billings, Stephen, Jr.	Cambridge	May 20, 61	Jun 20, 61	Reenlisted Dec 21, 63; Mustered out Jul 15, 65.
Bingham, Charles W.	Fletcher	May 7, 61	Jun 20, 61	Discharged Dec 31, 62 for disability.
Bingham, Leroy M.	Fletcher	May 7, 61	Jun 20, 61	Promoted to Corp.; Wounded May 3, 63 and May 5, 64; Mustered out Jun 29, 64.
Blair, Charles R.	Fletcher	May 7, 61	Jun 20, 61	Mustered out Jun 29, 64.
Blake, Sarvarnard J.	Fairfax	May 15, 61	Jun 20, 61	Deserted Sep 30, 62.
Blakesley, James	Substitute	Jul 30, 63	Jul 30, 63	Substitute for Prosper Bacon, Shelburne; Deserted Sep 24, 63.
Boughton, William	Monkton	May 15, 61	Jun 20, 61	Reenlisted Dec 21, 63; Feb 11, 61.
Bradley, Albert G.	Jericho	Aug 23, 62	Sep 15, 62	Wounded Oct 19, 64; Promoted to Corp.; Discharged Jul 1, 65.
Brooks, Lewis	Ferrisburgh	Oct 4, 61	Oct 28, 61	Reenlisted Dec 21, 63; KIA May 5, 64.
Brush, Edwin R.	Cambridge	Jul 17, 63	Jul 17, 63	See Asst. Surgeon.
Burnham, Andrew J.	Montpelier	Aug 20, 61	Sep 13, 61	Discharged Dec 17, 61 for disability.

Butler, Jed C.	Fairfax	Mar 22, 62	Apr 12, 62	Reenlisted Apr 18, 64; Mustered out Jul 15, 65.
Casavaint, Thomas L.	Moretown	Aug 20, 61	Sep 12, 61	Reenlisted Jan 31, 64; Promoted to Corp. Sep 1, 62; to Sgt. Sep 1, 64; Mustered out Jul 15, 65.
Celley, Charles M.	Berlin	Aug 20, 61	Sep 13, 61	Discharged Sep 1, 62 for disability.
Champaigny, Joseph	Vergennes	Oct 4, 61	Oct 28, 61	Discharged Jun 27, 64 for disability.
Chase, Bingham K.	Fletcher	May 15, 61	Jun 20, 61	Mustered out Jun 29, 64.
Chase, Jonathan E.	Jay	May 7, 61	Jun 20, 61	Discharged Sep 1, 63 for disability.
Chase, Walter	Fairfield	May 20, 61	Jun 20, 61	Discharged Mar 25, 63 for disability.
Clark, Charles	Montpelier	Jun 17, 61	Jun 20, 61	Discharged Mar 6, 62 for disability.
Coveney, John W.	Substitute	Aug 26, 64	Aug 26, 64	Substitute for Thomas S. Ladd, Corinth; Promoted to Corp. Feb 8, 65; Mustered out Jul 15, 65.
Crown, George	Grand Isle	Aug 16, 62	Sep 30, 62	Wounded May 10, 64 and Sep 19, 64; Discharged Jun 6, 65 for wounds.
Crown, Samuel	Fletcher	Jun 3, 61	Jun 20, 61	Reenlisted Dec 21, 63; Wounded May 5, 64; Promoted to Corp. Nov 1, 61; Mustered out Jul 15, 65.
Cutler, Jerome	Waterville	May 16, 61	Jun 20, 61	Wounded May 3, 63; Mustered out Jun 29, 64.
Davis, David H.	Belvidere	May 7, 61	Jun 20, 61	Killed on western gunboat *Mound City* Jun 30, 62.
Davis, Timothy C.	Johnson	May 7, 61	Jun 20, 61	Died Oct 27, 62 of disease.
Doane, Oramillo W.	Bakersfield	May 17, 61	Jun 20, 61	Died Dec 25, 62 of disease.
Doran, James H.	Cambridge	Aug 16, 62	Sep 30, 62	Wounded Dec 13, 62; Promoted to Corp. Jan 1, 65; Reduced Mar 1, 65; Mustered out Jun 19, 65.
Dubois, Ansel	Substitute	Jul 31, 63	Jul 31, 63	Substitute for Charles C. Marcy, West Windsor; Deserted Sep 24, 63.
Dunbar, Norman	Fairfax	May 21, 61	Jun 20, 61	Discharged Sep 14, 61 for disability.
Ellis, Edgar D.	Fletcher	Feb 20, 62	Apr 12, 62	Discharged Mar 30, 63 for disability.
Ellis, Frederick D.	Fletcher	Dec 14, 63	Dec 30, 63	Discharged Jun 12, 65 for disability.
Estes, Lewis H.	Elmore	Jun 3, 61	Jun 20, 61	Discharged Dec 25, 61 for disability.
Estes, Lewis H.	Cambridge	Aug 16, 62	Sep 22, 62	Wounded May 4, 63; Discharged Jul 2, 65.
Felton, Joseph C.	Fairfax	Mar 5, 62	Apr 12, 62	Reenlisted Apr 18, 64; KIA Jun 8, 64.
Fitzgerald, Timothy	Montpelier	Aug 20, 61	Sep 12, 61	Reenlisted Dec 21, 63; Deserted Aug 17, 63; Returned Sep 2, 63; Deserted Feb 11, 64.
Fletcher, Enos	Waterville	May 7, 61	Jun 20, 61	Discharged Oct 18, 61 for disability.
French, Alfred E.	Fairfax	May 20, 61	Jun 20, 61	Discharged Aug —, 61 for disability.
Fulton, Robert M.	Fletcher	Dec 11, 63	Dec 30, 63	Wounded May 10, 64 and Sep 19, 64; Mustered out Jul 15, 65.
Glougie, John R.	Cambridge	Aug 16, 62	Sep 22, 62	Wounded May 5, 64; Discharged Feb 22, 65.
Goodness, Joseph	Fairfield	Mar 25, 62	Apr 12, 62	Deserted Aug 23, 62; Returned; Deserted Jul 1, 63.
Greenleaf, William H.	Bethel	Mar 22, 62	Apr 12, 62	Reenlisted Apr 18, 64; Promoted to Corp. Sep 1, 64; Mustered out Jul 15, 65.
Griffin, Sherman	Fletcher	May 7, 61	Jun 20, 61	Discharged May 28, 62 for disability.
Hale, Martin	Substitute	Aug 26, 64	Aug 29, 64	Substitute for William M. Wilson, Corinth; Wounded Sep 19, 64 and Apr 2, 65; Deserted Jul 31, 65
Hebb, Louis S.	Cambridge	Jun 17, 61	Jun 20, 61	Taken prisoner Jun 29, 62; Paroled Sep 13, 62; Transferred to V. R. C. Jan 15, 64; Discharged Jun 20, 64.
Hewitt, Orrin D.	Warren	Aug 20, 61	Sep 13, 61	Died Jan 9, 62 of disease.
Hogaboom, Jay	Fairfield	Dec 18, 63	Dec 31, 63	Discharged Apr 22, 64 for disability.
Hogan, Dennis	Montpelier	Aug 20, 61	Sep 12, 61	Discharged Sep 9, 63 for disability.
Holmes, Horace B.	Woodbury	Aug 20, 61	Sep 12, 61	Transferred to V. R. C. Nov 20, 63; Discharged Sep 12, 64.
Howard, Ansel H.	Burlington	Aug 20, 61	Sep 12, 61	Reenlisted Dec 21, 63; Promoted to Corp. Apr 1, 63; to Sgt. Sep 1, 64; Wounded Sep 19, 64; Mustered out Jul 15, 65.
Howard, Isaac	Burlington	Aug 20, 61	Sep 12, 61	Wounded May 5, 64 and May 12, 64; Mustered out Sep 13, 64.

Howard, Wells	Jamaica	Jul 13, 63	Jul 13, 63	Drafted; Wounded May 5, 64 and May 12, 64; Died Nov 1, 64 of wounds received Oct 19, 64.
Howe, Henry	Jamaica	Jul 31, 63	Jul 31, 63	Drafted; KIA May 5, 64.
Hubbard, George W.	Cambridge	Aug 16, 62	Sep 22, 62	Wounded May 5, 64 and May 12, 64; Discharged Feb 6, 65 for wounds.
Hulburd, Benjamin F.	Stowe	Dec 5, 63	Dec 18, 63	KIA Oct 19, 64.
Hulburd, Daniel C.	Waterville	May 7, 61	Jun 20, 61	Discharged Oct 14, 62 for disability.
Hutchinson, James C.	Roxbury	Aug 20, 61	Sep 12, 61	Reenlisted Jan 31, 64; Promoted to Corp.; to Sgt.; KIA Aug 21, 64.
Kinsley, Alonzo	Fletcher	May 7, 61	Jun 20, 61	Wounded Jul 21, 61; Transferred to V. R. C. Mar 15, 64; Discharged Jun 21, 64.
Kinsley, William L.	Fletcher	Aug 22, 64	Aug 22, 64	Wounded Oct 19, 64 and Apr 2, 65; Promoted to Corp. Jan 1, 65; Mustered out Jun 19, 65.
Kneeland, George A.	Substitute	Jul 28, 63	Jul 28, 63	Substitute for L. C. Kendall, Enosburgh; KIA May 6, 64.
Kneeland, James	St. Albans	Dec 31, 63	Dec 31, 63	Wounded May 5, 64 and May 12, 64; Deserted Aug 3, 64.
Laird, John	Braintree	Aug 20, 61	Sep 12, 61	Died May 18, 64 of wounds received May 5, 64.
Larrabee, Lyman H.	Underhill	May 7, 61	Jun 20, 61	Discharged Sep 17, 62 for disability.
Lathrop, Napoleon B.	Cambridge	Jun 10, 61	Jun 20, 61	Discharged Nov 11, 61 for disability.
Lawson, Norman C.	Woodbury	Aug 20, 61	Sep 12, 61	Wounded and taken prisoner Jun 29, 62; Paroled Aug 3, 62; Wounded May 3, 63; Transferred to V. R. C. Apr 15, 64; Discharged Sep 20, 64.
Layth, Isaac C.	Fairfax	Mar 13, 62	Apr 12, 62	Deserted Aug 5, 62.
Leach, Albert G.	Fletcher	Dec 19, 63	Dec 30, 63	Wounded Oct 19, 64; Discharged May 12, 65 for wounds.
Leach, George W.	Waterville	Dec 19, 61	Dec 30, 61	Discharged Feb 21, 62 for disability.
Leach William H.	Fletcher	Dec 19, 63	Dec 30, 63	Discharged Mar 24, 64 for disability.
Loomis, Alden C.	Roxbury	Aug 20, 61	Sep 12, 61	Wounded Sep 14 and Dec 13, 62; Transferred to V. R. C. Sep 1, 63; Discharged Nov 15, 65.
Loomis, Osmond E.	Braintree	Aug 20, 61	Sep 12, 61	Died Jan 23, 62 of disease.
Loveland, Lucius V.	Fairfax	May 15, 61	Jun 20, 61	Reenlisted Dec 21, 63; Wounded May 12, 64 and Aug 21, 64; Deserted Dec 22, 64; Returned Feb 1, 65; Discharged Feb 27, 65.
Maloney, Thomas	Montpelier	Aug 20, 61	Sep 12, 61	Wounded May 5, 64; Mustered out Sep 12, 64.
Marshall, Frederick	Waterville	May 7, 61	Jun 20, 61	Reenlisted Dec 21, 63; Wounded Jul 21, 61; KIA May 12, 64.
Martin, John, Jr.	Westfield	May 20, 61	Jun 20, 61	Taken prisoner Jun 29, 62; Paroled Sep 13, 62; Wounded May 5, 64; Mustered out Jun 29, 64.
Maxfield, Hampton L.	Fairfax	May 7, 61	Jun 20, 61	Reenlisted Dec 21, 63; Promoted to Corp. Jun 1, 63; to Sgt. Sep 1, 64; Wounded May 3, 63 and May 5, 64; Mustered out Jul 15, 65.
McCarty, James	Fairfax	Jun 1, 61	Jun 20, 61	Discharged Sep 14, 61 for wounds received Jul 21, 61.
McLoud, D. Brooks	Woodbury	Aug 20, 61	Sep 12, 61	Wounded Dec 13, 62; KIA May 5, 64.
McNamara, John	Montpelier	Aug 20, 61	Sep 12, 61	Deserted Jul 11, 62.
Mears, Joseph	Poultney	Aug 12, 62	Sep 15, 62	Drummer; Mustered out Jun 19, 65.
Merrill, Adrain J.	Fairfax	May 20, 61	Jun 20, 61	Promoted to Corp.; to Sgt.; Wounded Jul 21, 61, May 3, 63 and May 5, 64; Discharged Jun 29, 64.
Merrill, Theodore	Springfield	Apr 3, 62	Apr 12, 62	Wounded May 3, 63 and Jun 1, 64; Mustered out Apr 14, 65.
Meslo, Julius	Substitute	Jul 31, 63	Jul 31, 63	Substitute for Isaac Farnsworth, St. Albans; Deserted Sep 24, 63.
Metras, Edward	Fletcher	Dec 12, 63	Dec 30, 63	Wounded May 5, 64; Mustered out Jul 15, 65.
Miller, Robert H.	Substitute	Sep 9, 63	Sep 9, 63	Substitute for Jesse B. Sanborn, Brighton; Wounded May 12, 64; Discharged Aug 25, 64.
Minogue, William	Rutland	Aug 20, 61	Sep 12, 61	KIA May 5, 64.
Montague, Edgar K.	Fletcher	Dec 14, 63	Dec 30, 63	Mustered out Jul 15, 65.
Morgan, Harrison A.	Cambridge	Aug 17, 62	Sep 22, 62	Promoted to Corp.; Wounded Aug 14, 64; Promoted to Sgt. Feb 8, 65; Transferred to V. R. C. Feb 21, 65; Mustered out Jul 8, 65.

Morse, Andrew G.	Elmore	Aug 20, 61	Sep 12, 61	Discharged Dec 25, 61 for disability.
Morse, Charles W.	Elmore	Aug 20, 61	Sep 12, 61	Died Aug 27, 62 of disease.
Morse, Joseph, Jr.	East Montpelier	Aug 20, 61	Sep 12, 61	Mustered out Sep 13, 64.
Morton, Joseph W.	Cambridge	May 7, 61	Jun 20, 61	Died Aug 14, 62 of disease.
Naylor, Francis, Jr.	Fairfax	————	Jun 20, 61	Deserted Jun 20, 61.
Ormsbee, Charles E.	Calais	Jun 17, 61	Jun 20, 61	Reenlisted Dec 21, 63; Promoted to Corp. Mar 1, 65; Wounded Jul 21, 61; Mustered out Jul 15, 65.
Osgood, Isaac C.	Milton	Aug 12, 63	Aug 12, 63	Drafted; Wounded May 5, 64; Mustered out Jul 15, 65.
Page, Charles	Substitute	Aug 26, 64	Aug 28, 64	Substitute for Charles Spaulding, Cavendish; Deserted from U.S. Hospital —, 64.
Parker, Sumner E.	Fletcher	May 15, 61	Jun 20, 61	KIA May 3, 63.
Parris, Alonzo W.	Fairfax	May 20, 61	Jun 20, 61	Wounded and taken prisoner Jul 21, 61; Paroled Feb 20, 62; Died Aug 26, 62 of disease.
Peckham, John G.	Burlington	Aug 20, 61	Sep 12, 61	Discharged Jan 4, 62 for disability.
Pelkey, Moses	Substitute	Jul 29, 63	Jul 29, 63	Substitute for Horace M. Burritt, Chester; KIA May 5, 64.
Perkins, Lafavor C.	Essex	May 25, 61	Jun 20, 61	Reenlisted Dec 21, 63; Died Feb 6, 64 of injuries received on railroad.
Perry, Martin	Milton	Aug 12, 63	Aug 12, 63	Drafted; Mustered out Jul 15, 65.
Picknell, Walter S.	Fairfax	Jun 1, 61	Jun 20, 61	Deserted Jun 20, 61.
Powers, Charles F.	Milton	Aug 12, 63	Aug 12, 63	Drafted; Wounded Sep 19, 64; Transferred to V. R. C. Feb 21, 65; Mustered out Jul 20, 65.
Powers, Chester	Moretown	May 25, 61	Jun 20, 61	Taken prisoner Jul 1, 63; Paroled—; Taken prisoner Oct 23, 63; Paroled Dec 2, 63; Mustered out Jun 29, 64.
Quinn, John C.	Montpelier	May 25, 61	Jun 20, 61	Mustered out Jun 29, 64.
Ranneau, Francis	Substitute	Aug 21, 63	Aug 21, 63	Substitute for Henry C. Wells, Marshfield; Wounded May 5, 64; Mustered out Jul 15, 65.
Rappallo, John	Substitute	Aug 5, 63	Aug 5, 63	Substitute for Davis G, Moore, Rutland; Deserted Oct 25, 63; Returned; Wounded Oct 19, 64; Deserted Mar 22, 65.
Reed, Levant M.	Jamaica	Jul 13, 63	Jul 13, 63	Drafted; Wounded May 5, 64; Transferred to V. R. C. Feb 21, 65; Mustered out Jul 19, 65.
Reynolds, Philo	Belvidere	May 20, 61	Jun 20, 61	Died Nov 22, 61 of disease.
Riggs, Alfred	Fletcher	Dec 26, 63	Dec 26, 63	Mustered out May 13, 65.
Riley, Patrick	Substitute	Jul 30, 63	Jul 30, 63	Substitute for Joseph A. Lovett, Shelburne; Wounded May 5, 64; Discharged Feb 22, 65 for disability.
Robinson, George E.	Fletcher	Dec 19, 63	Dec 30, 63	Transferred to V. R. C. Jul 26, 64; Mustered out Jul 20, 65.
Robinson, Joseph	Substitute	Jul 23, 63	Jul 23, 63	Substitute for Edward Laduke, Burlington; Wounded May 5, 64 and Apr 2, 65; Discharged May 3, 65 for wounds.
Robinson, Thomas	Substitute	Jul 27, 63	Jul 27, 63	Substitute for David R. Bigelow, Jericho; Wounded May 6, 64; Mustered out Jul 15, 65.
Rood, Vernon D.	Fletcher	May 16, 61	Jun 20, 61	Wounded Jul 21, 61; Wounded and taken prisoner Jun 29, 62; Paroled Jul 25, 62; Transferred to V. R. C. Sep 1, 63; Discharged Jun 27, 64.
Rose, Peter	Montpelier	May 25, 61	Jun 20, 61	Discharged Feb 16, 63 for disability.
Russell, Archelaus	Substitute	Jul 20, 63	Jul 20, 63	Substitute for W. S. Blaisdell, Richford; Wounded May 5, 64; Died of wounds date unknown.
Ryan, William	Substitute	Jul 31, 63	Jul 31, 63	Substitute for George W. Brown, St. Albans; Taken prisoner May 21, 64; Paroled Apr 28, 65; Mustered out May 23, 65.
Ryder, Henry R.	Jamaica	Jul 13, 63	Jul 13, 63	Mustered out Jul 15, 65.
Scott, Orange	Plainfield	Jun 3, 61	Jun 20, 61	Died Nov 4, 61 of disease.
Scott, Wait	Fletcher	Dec 19, 63	Dec 30, 63	Wounded May 5, 64; Promoted to Corp. Sep 1, 64; Mustered out Jul 15, 65.

Seymour, Charles H.	Substitute	Aug 7, 63	Aug 7, 63	Substitute for Merritt Quincy, Underhill; Deserted Oct 19, 63.
Shattuck, Henry B.	————	————	————	Discharged Nov 11, 61 (no descriptive list)
Sherry, John W.	Lowell	Jun 1, 61	Jun 16, 61	See Hospital Steward.
Shonion, Henry	Substitute	Aug 7, 63	Aug 7, 63	Substitute for Henry C. Mooney, North Hero; Discharged May 17, 65 for wounds received Jun 9, 64.
Sleeper, Eugene C.	Strafford	Jun 17, 61	Jun 20, 61	Taken prisoner Oct 26, 63; Paroled Nov 26, 64; Mustered out Feb 4, 65.
Smith, Isaac L.	Burlington	Aug 30, 62	Sep 15, 62	Mustered out Jun 19, 65.
Snow, Edward, E.	Milton	Jun 17, 61	Jun 20, 61	Reenlisted Mar 20, 64; Mustered out Jul 15, 65.
Snow, William E.	Milton	Jun 17, 61	Jun 20, 61	Wounded and taken prisoner Sep 30, 61 and died same day.
Soule, Hiram E.	Fairfax	May 7, 61	Jun 20, 61	Died Jul 7, 63 of wounds received May 3, 63.
Spaulding, Charles	Fletcher	Dec 14, 63	Dec 30, 63	Wounded May 5, 64; Transferred to V. R. C.; Mustered out Jul 20, 65.
Squires, Ezra W.	Fletcher	Dec 19, 63	Dec 30, 63	KIA May 5, 64.
Start, Storrs W.	Bakersfield	May 15, 61	Jun 20, 61	Wounded May 6, 64; Mustered out Jun 29, 64.
Stowe, Charles H.	Fletcher	Aug 23. 64	Aug 23, 64	Died Nov 14, 64 of wounds received Oct 19, 64.
Streeter, Andrew	————	————	————	Discharged Dec 17, 61 (no descriptive list).
Streeter, George	Colchester	May 25, 61	Jun 20, 61	Wounded and taken prisoner Jul 21, 61; Paroled Oct 5, 61; Discharged Dec 16, 61.
Sullivan, Daniel	Substitute	Aug 4, 63	Aug 4, 63	Substitute for Samuel F. Corliss, Sheldon; Deserted Sep 18, 64.
Trefren, John P.	Substitute	Aug 21, 63	Aug 21, 63	Substitute for Joseph Bullard, Georgia; Deserted Feb 5, 64; Returned May 10, 65 under presidential proclamation; Dishonorably discharged Jun 12, 65.
Trow, George E.	East Montpelier	Aug 20, 61	Sep 12, 61	Mustered out Sep 12, 64.
Turner, Sylvester	Enosburgh	May 23, 61	Jun 20, 61	Mustered out Jun 29, 64.
Ward, Frank	Williston	May 25, 61	Jun 20, 61	Reenlisted Jan 31, 64; Promoted to Corp. Sep 1, 64; Mustered out Jul 15, 65.
Ward, Philip	Burlington	May 25, 61	Jun 20, 61	Wounded and taken prisoner Jun 29, 62; Paroled Aug 3, 62; Discharged Jan 5, 63.
Westman, Orson C.	Cambridge	May 25, 61	Jun 20, 61	See Second Lt. Co. H.
Whicher, Edwin P.	Burlington	May 25, 61	Jun 20, 61	Mustered out Jun 29, 64.
White, George A.	Wooodbury	Aug 20, 61	Sep 12, 61	Reenlisted Dec 21, 63; Wounded May 3, 63; Died May 25, 64 of wounds received May 12, 64.
Wilcox, Samuel J.	Cambridge	May 25, 61	Jun 20, 61	Died Jan 7, 62 of disease.
Witherell, Philander	Waterville	May 15, 61	Jun 20, 61	Reenlisted Dec 12, 63; Wounded May 5, 64; Mustered out Jul 15, 65.
Worthing, James M.	Bakersfield	Aug 7, 62	Aug 30, 62	Promoted to Corp.; Wounded May 10, 64; Transferred to V. R. C. Dec 10, 64; Reduced Jan 1, 65; Mustered out Jun 29, 65.
Worthing, Robert N.	Bakersfield	May 15, 61	Jun 20, 61	Died Jun 7, 63 of wounds received May 3, 63.

Company I

Name and Rank	Residence	Date of	Date of	Remarks
Commission	Issue			
Captains				
Fullam, Volney S.	Ludlow	May 22, 61	May 22, 61	Promoted to Lt. Col. 7th Vt. Jan 18, 62.
Stone, Newton	Bennington	Jan 22, 62	Jan 22, 62	See Col.
White, Daniel S.	Cavendish	Jan 26, 63	Feb 23, 63	Sgt. Co. I; Promoted to First Sgt. Feb 9, 62; to Second Lt. Co. I, Jan 8, 63; Discharged Oct 24, 64 for wounds received May 5, 64.
Taylor, Horatio F.	Jamaica	Dec 24, 64	Jan 31, 65	Pvt. Co. I; Reenlisted Dec 21, 63; Promoted to Corp. Nov 1, 61; to Sgt. Jan 20, 63; to First Sgt. Feb 26, 63; to First Lt. Co. I, Jun 20, 64; Mustered out Jul 15, 65.

First Lieutenants				
Parkhurst, Sherman W.	Cavendish	May 22, 61	May 22, 61	Resigned Nov 9, 61.
Canning, Charles C.	Northfield	Jun 28, 62	Jun 28, 62	First Sgt. Co. D; Resigned Feb 8, 63.
Priest, Ethan A.	Mt. Holly	Feb 10, 63	Feb 23, 63	Sgt. Co. I; Promoted to First Sgt. Jan 20, 63; Wounded Jul 21, 61, Jun 27, 62 and May 12, 64; Mustered out Jun 29, 64.
Taylor, Horatio F.	Jamaica	Jun 20, 64	Jul 11, 64	See Capt. Co. I.
Beckwith, Albert D.	Weston	Dec 24, 64	Jan 31, 65	Sgt. Co. I; Reenlisted Dec 21, 63; Promoted to First Sgt. Oct 18, 64; Wounded Dec 13, 62 and May 5, 64; Mustered out Jul 15, 65.
Second Lieutenants				
Wadleigh, Isaac N.	Ludlow	May 22, 61	May 22, 61	Resigned Dec 14, 61.
Stone, James E.	Northfield	Dec 14, 61	Dec 14, 61	Principal Musician; Resigned Jan 6, 63.
White, Daniel S.	Cavendish	Jan 8, 63	Jan 19, 63	See Capt. Co. I.
Howe, Oramel G.	Ludlow	Feb 10, 63	Feb 23, 63	Corp. Co. I; Promoted to Sgt. Oct 17, 62; Mustered out Jun 29, 64.
May, Albert A.	Ludlow	Jun 7, 65	Jun 17, 65	Pvt. Co. I; Reenlisted Dec 21, 63; Promoted to Corp. Aug 19, 62; to Sgt. Jan 20, 65; to First Sgt. Feb 15, 65; Wounded May 5, 64; Mustered out as First Sgt. Jul 15, 65.

Name and Rank	Residence	Date of Enlistment	Date of Muster	Remarks
Sergeants				
Ballou, Erastus G.	Boston, Mass.	May 7, 61	Jun 20, 61	See Maj.
Chase, Phillips E.	Mt. Holly	May 7, 61	Jun 20, 61	See Capt. Co. G.
White, Daniel S.	Cavendish	May 7, 61	Jun 20, 61	See Capt. Co. I.
Priest, Ethan A.	Mt. Holly	May 7, 61	Jun 20, 61	See First Lt. Co. I
Beckwith, Albert D.	Weston	May 7, 61	Jun 20, 61	See First Lt. Co. I.
Corporals				
Parmenter, Benjamin F.	Mt. Holly	May 7, 61	Jun 20, 61	Deserted Sep—, 62; Returned; reduced; Discharged Jan—, 63 for disability.
Peabody, Harland O.	Andover	May 11, 61	Jun 20, 61	Promoted to Sgt. Nov 1, 61; Discharged May 1, 62 for disability.
Hall, Artemas W.	Ludlow	May 7, 61	Jun 20, 61	Promoted to Sgt. Jan 24, 62; Deserted Oct 26, 62.
Mandigo, Henry H.	Ludlow	May 7, 61	Jun 20, 61	Promoted to Sgt.; Died Oct 14, 62 of disease.
Austin, Harvey K.	Weston	May 7, 61	Jun 20, 61	Discharged Nov 23, 61 for wounds received Jul 21, 61.
Howe, Oramel G.	Ludlow	May 7, 61	Jun 20, 61	See Second Lt. Co. I.
Gleason, Seneca B.	Jamaica	May 15, 61	Jun 20, 61	Reenlisted Dec 21, 63; KIA May 5, 64.
Black, Edward E.	Ludlow	May 7, 61	Jun 20, 61	Reduced Dec 1, 61; Taken prisoner May 4, 63; Paroled May 14, 63; Mustered out Jun 29, 64.
Musicians				
Carr, Isaac B.	Moretown	May 7, 61	Jun 20, 61	Mustered out Jun 29, 64.
Lewis, George H.	Shrewsbury	May 7, 61	Jun 20, 61	Taken prisoner Jul 21, 61; Paroled Jan 3, 62; Mustered out Jun 29, 64.
Wagoner				
Moore, Armin E.	Ludlow	May 7, 61	Jun 20, 61	Discharged Sep 25, 62 for disability.
Privates				
Adams, John W.	Ludlow	May 7, 61	Jun 20, 61	Died Jun 10, 64 of wounds received Jun 1, 64.
Allen, Hiram	Landgrove	Dec 1, 63	Dec 24, 63	Mustered out Jul 15, 65.
Allen, Joseph	Londonderry	Mar 8, 65	Mar 8, 65	Mustered out Jul 15, 65.
Bailey, Samuel W.	Brandon	May 15, 61	Jun 20, 61	Reenlisted Dec 21, 63; Promoted to Corp. Oct 10, 62; to Sgt. Feb 26, 63; Died Oct 21, 64 of wounds received Sep 19, 64.
Barrett, Henry	Mt. Holly	Aug 24, 64	Aug 24, 64	Mustered out Jun 19, 65.

Barrett, John	Ludlow	Feb 20, 62	Apr 12, 62	Transferred to V. R. C. Sep 1, 63; Discharged Mar 25, 65.
Barrett, William	Ludlow	Feb 20, 62	Mar 25, 62	Wounded May 5, 64 and Sep 22, 64; Mustered out Mar 25, 65.
Beckwith, Milan N.	Weston	Sep 6, 64	Sep 6, 64	Mustered out May 24, 65.
Benson, Austin L.	Mt. Holly	Aug 16, 64	Aug 16, 64	Died Apr 13, 65 of wounds received Apr 2, 65.
Bixby, Hiram P.	Ludlow	Oct 7, 61	Oct 18, 61	Wounded Dec 13, 62 and May 3, 63; Discharged Jan 11, 64 for wounds.
Bolster, David	Landgrove	May 7, 61	Jun 20, 61	Discharged Mar 5, 62 for disability.
Brush, Henry B.	Rutland	Jul 16, 61	Jul 16, 61	Wounded May 5, 64; Mustered out Jul 16, 64.
Burbank, George B.	Ludlow	May 15, 61	Jun 20, 61	Promoted to Corp. Jan 8, 63; to Sgt. Feb 26, 63; Wounded May 5, 64; Mustered out Jun 29, 64.
Butterfield, Byron H.	Andover	Feb 24, 62	Apr 12, 62	Discharged Mar 12, 63 for wounds received Dec 13, 62.
Butterfield, Joseph E.	Winhall	May 27, 61	Jun 20, 61	Wounded Dec 13, 62; KIA May 5, 64.
Buxton, Willard	Londonderry	Mar 7, 65	Mar 7, 65	Mustered out Jul 24, 65.
Cannon, Daniel	Mt. Holly	May 7, 61	Jun 20, 61	Wounded Dec 13, 62, May 3, 63 and May 5, 64; Mustered out Jun 29, 64.
Chase, Edwin B.	Mt. Holly	Aug 19, 64	Aug 19, 64	Died Nov 27, 64 of disease.
Chase, Peter S.	Weston	Aug 14, 62	Sep 30, 62	Wounded Dec 13, 62 and May 5, 64; Discharged May 16, 65 for wounds.
Clark, Ira D.	Duxbury	Aug 12, 62	Sep 15, 62	Wounded May 3, 63; KIA May 12, 64.
Clark, Jasper N.	Ludlow	Sep 10, 61	Oct 18, 61	Discharged Oct 31, 62 for disability.
Colby, Henry W.	Ludlow	May 26, 61	Jun 20, 61	Discharged Jun 3, 62 for disability.
Colby, John H.	Weston	May 15, 61	Jun 20, 61	Discharged Mar 19, 63 for disability.
Colby, Joseph	Mt. Holly	Aug 19, 64	Aug 19, 64	Mustered out Jun 19, 65.
Comstock, Henry A.	Andover	May 7, 61	Jun 20, 61	Reenlisted Dec 21, 63; Wounded Jun 8, 64; promoted to Corp. Feb 15, 65; Mustered out Jul 15, 65.
Crosby, John	Reading	Aug 12, 62	Sep 30, 62	Wounded Jul 10, 63 and May 19, 64; Discharged Dec 20, 64 for wounds.
Crosby, Philip W.	Plymouth	Sep 23, 61	Oct 18, 61	KIA May 3, 63.
Derby, Webster D.	Townshend	May 23, 61	Jun 20, 61	Wounded May 3, 63; Transferred to V. R. C. Nov 20, 63; Discharged Jun 20, 64.
Dodge, Lorenzo A.	Ludlow	Sep 9. 61	Oct 18, 61	Reenlisted Dec 21, 63; Wounded Jun 20, 64; Promoted to Corp. Oct 18, 64; Mustered out Aug 10, 65.
Dorset, David G.	Mt. Holly	Aug 22, 64	Aug 22, 64	Died Dec 2, 64 of disease.
Downing, Ezekiel K.	Landgrove	May 7, 61	Jun 20, 61	Died Jul 18, 61 of disease.
Emery, Elmer A.	Reading	Aug 14, 62	Sep 30, 62	Promoted to Corp. Aug 4, 64; to Sgt. Oct 18, 64; Mustered out Jun 19, 65.
Fish, Fredrick A.	Jamaica	May 15, 61	Jun 20, 61	Promoted to Corp. Dec 1, 61; to Sgt. Oct 14, 62; Mustered out Jun 29, 64.
French, George A.	Springfield	Dec 24, 63	Jan 2, 64	KIA May 12, 64.
Frost, Daniel	Mt. Holly	May 7, 61	Jun 20, 61	Discharged Jan 4, 63 for disability.
Frost, Stephen	Mt. Holly	May 7, 61	Jun 20, 61	Wounded May 5, 64; Mustered out Jun 29, 64.
Gilligan, Michael	Ludlow	Sep 11, 61	Oct 15, 61	Reenlisted Mar 20, 64; Wounded Dec 13, 62, May 3, 63 and Jul 3, 63; Deserted May 11, 64.
Gilson, Forest D.	Reading	May 7, 61	Jun 20, 61	Wounded May 3, 63; Mustered out Jun 29, 64.
Gleason, David W.	Londonderry	Jul 31, 63	Jul 31, 63	Drafted; Discharged Jan 23, 64 for disability.
Grant, Charles C.	Reading	Sep 14, 61	Oct 18, 61	Reenlisted Dec 21, 63; Died May 7, 64 of wounds received May 5, 64.
Grover, Martin E.	Ludlow	Sep 23, 61	Oct 18, 61	Reenlisted Dec 21, 63; Died Jun 19, 64 of wounds received May 5, 64.
Hall, Eleazer A.	Plymouth	May 7, 61	Jun 20, 61	Discharged May 27, 63 for wounds received May 3, 63.
Hall, George H.	Tinmouth	Aug 25, 64	Aug 25, 64	Mustered out 19 Jun 65.
Halpin, Philip	Reading	Aug 15, 62	Sep 30, 62	Wounded Dec 13, 62; Died Jul 12, 64 of wounds received May 10, 64.
Hastings, Joseph S.	Ludlow	May 28, 61	Jun 20, 61	KIA Dec 13, 62.

Hathorn, Albert	Rutland	May 20, 61	Jun 20, 61	Reenlisted Dec 21, 63; Wounded Dec 13, 62 and May 5, 64; Promoted to Corp. Feb 15, 65; KIA Mar 25, 65.
Haven, Lowell W.	Ludlow	Sep 9, 61	Oct 18, 61	Reenlisted Dec 21, 63; Wounded May 5, 64; Mustered out Jul 15, 65.
Hayward, George	Vershire	Jan 25, 64	Jan 25, 64	Transferred to V. R. C. Apr 15, 64; Discharged Jun 8, 64.
Headle, Elwin	Plymouth	May 7, 61	Jun 20, 61	Mustered Jun 29, 64.
Hemenway, Daniel D.	Ludlow	May 7, 61	Jun 20, 61	Wounded May 5, 64; Mustered out Jun 29, 64.
Hemenway, Henry G.	Ludlow	May 7, 61	Jun 20, 61	Wounded Dec 13, 62; Mustered out Jun 29, 64.
Henry, Haskell A.	Westford	Jun 20, 61	Jun 20, 61	Discharged Jan 12, 63 for disability.
Heselton, Moses P.	Ludlow	Sep 14, 61	Oct 18, 61	Discharged Jan 5, 63 for disability.
Heselton, William W.	Weston	May 7, 61	Jun 20, 61	Mustered out Jun 29, 64.
Holden, Philemon	Reading	Aug 15, 62	Sep 30, 62	Wounded Dec 13, 62; Died Feb 27, 63 of disease.
Holmes, Elmer G.	Reading	Aug 14, 62	Oct 16, 62	KIA May 12, 64.
Holmes, James T	Mt. Holly	Sep 19, 61	Oct 19, 61	Wounded May 3, 63; Mustered out Oct 18, 64.
Houghton, Levi	Londonderry	May 7, 61	Jun 20, 61	Died Nov 27, 62 of disease.
Houghton, Stephen	Londonderry	Aug 9, 62	Sep 30, 62	Mustered out Jun 19, 65.
Hubbard, Myron E.	Reading	Sep 10, 61	Oct 18, 61	Reenlisted Dec 21, 63; Promoted to Corp. Jan 26, 63; Wounded May 3, 63 and May 5, 64; Reduced Oct 18, 64; Mustered out Jul 15, 65.
Jaquith, Thomas J.	Londonderry	May 20, 61	Jun 20, 61	Wounded Dec 13, 62 and May 10, 64; Mustered out Jun 29, 64.
Jenkins, Amos H.	Landgrove	Dec 1, 63	Dec 24, 63	Discharged Jan 23, 64 for disability.
Johnson, W. R. F.	Weston	May 7, 61	Jun 20, 61	Wounded May 3, 63 and May 5, 64; Mustered out Jun 29, 64.
Kelley, Francis	Ludlow	Oct 7, 61	Oct 18, 61	Deserted Aug 30, 63.
Kidder, Charles E.	Substitute	Aug 3, 63	Aug 3, 63	Substitute for John S. Eaton, Woodstock; Transferred to U.S. Navy Apr 14, 64; Discharged Jul 29, 65.
Kilburn, Joseph W.	Jamaica	May 15, 61	Jun 20, 61	Promoted to Corp. Oct 11, 63; Wounded May 12, 64; Mustered out Jun 29, 64.
King, Wallace D.	Londonderry	May 16, 61	Jun 20, 61	Discharged Jul 23, 62 for disability.
Lawrence, Henry E.	Ludlow	Sep 12, 61	Oct 18, 61	Promoted to Corp. Jun 10, 62; Discharged Jan 8, 63 for disability; Died at N.Y. Jan 18, 63.
Lawrence, Henry H.	Substitute	Jul 20, 63	Jul 20, 63	Substitute for Philip Pryor, Jericho; Deserted Jan 4, 64.
Leonard, John	Shrewsbury	May 7, 61	Jun 20, 61	Wounded and taken prisoner Jul 21, 61; Died at Richmond, Va. Sep 7, 61 of wounds.
Leslie, Warren S.	Plymouth	May 18, 61	Jun 20, 61	Discharged Feb 12, 63 for disability.
Lovejoy, Henry A.	Andover	Oct 1, 61	Oct 18, 61	Died Dec 4, 61 of disease.
Mandigo, William S.	Mt. Holly	May 7, 61	Jun 20, 61	Discharged Sep 7, 63 for disability.
Marsh, Vernon A.	Andover	Jun 17, 61	Jun 20, 61	Discharged Oct 4, 61 for wounds received Jul 21, 61.
Marsh, Vernon A.	Weston	Mar 20, 65	Mar 20, 65	Mustered out Jul 15, 65.
Marshall, Myron E.	Chester	May 16, 61	Jun 20, 61	Discharged Mar 9, 63 for disability.
Martin, Edwin	Corinth	Aug 27, 62	Sep 22, 62	Died Jan 18, 63 of wounds received Dec 13, 62.
May, Albert A.	Ludlow	May 7, 61	Jun 20, 61	See Second Lt. Co. I.
McDonald, Charles	Substitute	Jul 27, 63	Jul 27, 63	Substitute for Hopkins F. Gaines, Panton; Taken prisoner Sep 17, 63; Paroled May 8, 64; Deserted from Camp Parole, Md., Oct —, 64.
Moore, Alonzo E.	Ludlow	May 7, 61	Jun 20, 61	KIA Dec 13, 62.
Newton, Oscar S.	Shelburne	Aug 15, 64	Aug 15, 64	Wounded Apr 2, 65; Mustered out May 25, 65.
Nichols, Amos E.	Reading	Feb 13, 65	Feb 13, 65	Mustered out Jul 15, 65.
Nichols, Henry J.	Underhill	May 22, 61	Jun 20, 61	Mustered out Jun 29, 64.
Nolet, Henry	Mt. Holly	May 7, 61	Jun 20, 61	Deserted Sep 20, 62.
O'Reilly, James	Substitute	Aug 26, 64	Aug 26, 64	Substitute for Edgar F. Watkins, Sharon; Promoted to Corp. Mar 1, 65; Mustered out Jul 15, 65.
Osier, Joseph	Jamaica	May 15, 61	Jun 20, 61	Wounded Jul 21, 61; Deserted Sep 25, 62.
Parker, George W.	Plymouth	May 13, 61	Jun 20, 61	Died May 14, 64 of wounds received May 5, 64.

Parker, Henry M.	Plymouth	Aug 13, 62	Sep 30, 62	Wounded May 3, 63, May 5, 64 and Sep 19, 64; Mustered out Jun 19, 65.
Parkhurst, Simeon L.	Ludlow	May 7, 61	Jun 20, 61	Reenlisted Dec 21, 63; Promoted to Corp. Oct 18, 64; Mustered out Jul 15, 65.
Patterson, Samuel	Londonderry	Mar 17, 65	Mar 17, 65	Mustered out Jul 15, 65.
Pease, Silas H.	Weston	Aug 9, 62	Sep 30, 62	Transferred to V. R. C. Sep 1, 63; Discharged Nov 10, 64.
Peck, Henry H.	Weston	Aug 15, 62	Sep 30, 62	Wounded May 5, 64; Discharged May 13, 65 for disability.
Peck, Hiram H.	Landgrove	Dec 2, 63	Dec 24, 63	Mustered out Jul 15, 65.
Perkins, Daniel P.	Andover	Sep 12, 61	Oct 18, 61	Wounded May 5, 64; Mustered out Oct 18, 64.
Pierce, Rufus F.	Reading	Feb 13, 65	Feb 13, 65	Died Apr 2, 65 of disease.
Pike, Daniel R.	Rutland	Jul 15, 61	Jul 16, 61	Deserted Jul 3, 63; Dishonorably discharged to date Jul 3, 63 by special order Dept. of the East Dec 5, 67.
Pollard, John B.	Ludlow	Sep 12, 61	Oct 18, 61	Promoted to Corp. Jan 26, 63; to Sgt. Aug 4, 64; Wounded May 3, 63; Mustered out Oct 18, 64.
Pratt, Augustus H.	Ludlow	May 7, 61	Jun 20, 61	Promoted to Corp. Oct 17, 62; Wounded May 3, 63; Transferred to V. R. C. Sep 1, 63; Discharged Apr 1, 64.
Prentice, Benjamin B.	Substitute	Jul 24, 63	Jul 24, 63	Substitute for Henry W. Dana, Burlington; Wounded May 5, 64; Mustered out May 13, 65.
Priest, Charles W.	Mt. Holly	Aug 16, 64	Aug 16, 64	Wounded Oct 19, 64; Mustered out Jun 19, 65.
Priest, Darius D.	Mt. Holly	May 7, 61	Jun 20, 61	Wounded May 12, 64; Mustered out Jun 29, 64.
Prior, Elbridge W.	Plymouth	May 11, 61	Jun 20, 61	Wounded may 3, 63 and May 5, 64; Promoted to Corp. Jan 8, 63; Mustered out Jun 29, 64.
Ray, Abel, Jr.	Cavendish	Sep 2, 64	Sep 2, 64	Mustered out Jul 15, 65.
Ray, Charles H.	Mt. Holly	Aug 16, 64	Aug 16, 64	Mustered out Jun 19, 65.
Reed, Sullivan E.	Ludlow	May 7, 61	Jun 20, 61	Wounded Dec 13, 62; Transferred to V. R. C. Jul 1, 63; Discharged May 7, 64.
Richardson, John C.	Londonderry	May 16, 61	Jun 20, 61	Wounded May 5, 64; Mustered out Jun 29, 64.
Riggs, Henry H.	Ludlow	Mar 24, 62	Apr 12, 62	Promoted to Corp. Oct 7, 62; Wounded May 3, 63; Mustered out Mar 25, 65.
Roberts, Burton N.	Weston	May 7, 61	Jun 20, 61	Wounded May 5, 64; Mustered out Jun 29, 64.
Rogers, Hoxxey C.	Mt. Holly	May 7, 61	Jun 20, 61	Reenlisted Dec 21, 63; Promoted to Corp. Aug 4, 64; to Sgt. Nov —, 64; Mustered out Jul 15, 65.
Ross, Duane O.	Ludlow	May 7, 61	Jun 20, 61	Wounded May 3, 63; Transferred to V. R. C. Sep 1, 63; Discharged Jun 20, 64.
Royce, Alba	Substitute	Aug 5, 63	Aug 5, 63	Substitute for Addison R. Royce, Ludlow; Wounded Aug 21, 64; Mustered out Jul 15, 65.
Sanders, Thomas	Substitute	Sep 7, 63	Sep 7, 63	Substitute for Ebenezer M. Wilson, Barnard; Wounded May 10, 64; Mustered out Jul 15, 65.
Sawyer, Leroy W.	Plymouth	Mar 23, 65	Mar 23, 65	Mustered out Jun 13, 65.
Scofield, Daniel A.	Hinesburgh	Aug 7, 62	Sep 30, 62	Died May 7, 64 of wounds received May 5, 64.
Severy, Jehial	Salisbury	Oct 23, 61	Oct 23, 61	Discharged May 18, 63 for disability.
Shatner, Joseph	Substitute	Jul 22, 63	Jul 22, 63	Substitute for Charles L. Mead, Brattleboro; Deserted Oct 25, 63; Returned Nov 15, 63; Discharged Jan 21, 64.
Shatner, Moses	Substitute	Jul 31, 63	Jul 31, 63	Substitute for Ebenezer M. Wilson, Barnard; Wounded May 10, 64; Mustered out Jul 15, 65.
Shattuck, Samuel A.	Londonderry	May 27, 61	Jun 20, 61	Wounded Jun 27, 62; Discharged Dec 30, 63 for disability.
Shaw, George B.	Landgrove	Dec 4, 63	Dec 24, 63	Wounded May 5, 64; Mustered out Jul 12, 65.
Shippy, Loring	Weston	Sep 2, 64	Sep 2, 64	Mustered out Jun 19, 65.
Shufelt, Jared	Substitute	Jul 31, 63	Jul 31, 63	Substitute for Harlow Button, Sheldon; Deserted Feb 17, 64.
Simonds, Erastus M.	Ludlow	Jun 10, 61	Jun 20, 61	Died Jul 29, 62 of disease.
Simonds, Hiram	Mt. Holly	Aug 16, 64	Aug 16, 64	Discharged Jun 19, 65.
Sinnott, William	East Montpelier	Aug 27, 62	Sep 22, 62	Discharged May 18, 63 for wounds received 13, Dec 62.

Slater, William	Substitute	Jul 31, 63	Jul 31, 63	Substitute for Andrew Lamb, Fletcher; Wounded May 12, 64 and Apr 2, 65; Promoted to Corp. Aug 4, 64; to Sgt. Feb 16, 65; Mustered out Jul 15, 65.
Smalley, John	Shrewsbury	May 7, 61	Jun 20, 61	Mustered out Jun 29, 64.
Smith, John	Substitute	Sep 7, 63	Sep 7, 63	Substitute for Dewitt C. Stowell, Weathersfield; Deserted Feb 17, 64.
Smith, Joseph	Substitute	Jul 29, 63	Jul 29, 63	Substitute for Wallace W. Cook, Brattleboro; Deserted Sep 22, 63.
Snell, Hiland	Ludlow	Jun 11, 61	Jun 20, 61	Wounded May 3, 63; Transferred to V. R. C. Nov 1, 63; Discharged Jun 20, 64.
Sprague, Wooster C.	Rutland	May 20, 61	Jun 20, 61	Died Apr 22, 62 of disease.
Stebbins, John	————	Jul 25, 61	Jul 25, 61	Discharged Oct 5, 62 for disability.
Stevens Henry A.	Weston	May 27, 61	Jun 20, 61	Taken prisoner Jul 21, 61; Paroled; Discharged Jul 11, 62 for disability.
Stevens, James M.	Weston	Aug 11, 62	Sep 30, 62	Wounded Dec 13, 62; Discharged Apr 29, 64 for disability.
Stickney, Frederic B.	Ludlow	Sep 12, 61	Oct 18, 61	Taken prisoner Jun 29, 62; Paroled Sep 3, 62; Died Oct 16, 62 of disease.
Story, Joseph	Substitute	Jul 29, 63	Jul 29, 63	Substitute for James Peck, Burlington; Died May 14, 64 of wounds received May 5, 64.
Sullivan, John	Substitute	Jul 29, 63	Jul 29, 63	Substitute for John A. Stanley, Washington; Deserted Sep 22, 63.
Swasey, Parker	Cabot	Jul 11, 63	Jul 11, 63	Drafted; MIA May 5, 64 (supposed killed).
Sweeney, John	Substitute	Sep 4, 63	Sep 4, 63	Substitute for Norman Learned, Milton; KIA May 5, 64.
Sweeney, Theophilus	Substitute	Sep 4, 63	Sep 4, 63	Substitute for A. B. Ashley, Milton; Mustered out Jul 15, 65.
Sweetland, Artemas	Substitute	Jul 23, 63	Jul 23, 63	Substitute for Willard V. B. Stanclift, Marlboro; Died May 30, 64 of wounds received May 5, 64.
Taylor, Horatio F.	Jamaica	May 15, 61	Jun 20, 61	See Capt. Co. I.
Tenney, Whitney	Londonderry	Jul 31, 63	Jul 31, 63	Drafted; Wounded May 5 and Aug 24, 54, 64; Mustered out Jul 15, 65.
Tole, Henry	Mt. Holly	May 7, 61	Jun 20, 61	Wounded Jul 21, 61; Mustered out Jun 29, 64.
Turner, Bradbury H.	Substitute	Jul 31, 63	Jul 31, 63	Substitute for C. R. Churchill, Stowe; Deserted Sep 21, 64.
Twiss, Samuel B.	Reading	Aug 14, 62	Sep 30, 62	Wounded May 5, 64; Mustered out Jun 19, 65.
Ward, Oric R.	Plymouth	May 7, 61	Jun 20, 61	Promoted to Corp. Oct 11, 63; KIA May 5, 64.
Warner, Hiram L.	Mt. Holly	Aug 19, 64	Aug 19, 64	Mustered out Jun 19, 65.
Way, Sidney D.	Weston	May 7, 61	Jun 20, 61	Discharged Mar 5, 62 for disability.
Webster, Addison	Mendon	Aug 12, 62	Sep 15, 62	Wounded Dec 13, 62; Deserted Jan 20, 63; Returned Aug —, 63; Deserted Jan 1, 64.
Wells, Perry G.	Mt. Holly	May 7, 61	Jun 20, 61	Reenlisted Mar 20, 64; Wagoner; Mustered out Jul 15, 65.
Wheeler, Cyril	East Montpelier	Aug 20, 62	Sep 22, 62	Discharged May 11, 63 for wounds received Dec 13, 62.
Whitcomb, Asahel S.	Ludlow	May 7, 61	Jun 20, 61	Mustered out Jun 29, 64.
Whitcomb, Orrin L.	Londonderry	May 21, 61	Jun 20, 61	Discharged Jun 17, 62 for promotion as Hospital Steward in U. S. Army.
Whitman, Edwin H.	Londonderry	May 21, 61	Jun 20, 61	Wounded —, 62; Transferred to V. R. C. Sep 1, 63; Died Apr 28, 64.
Whitney, Alonzo	Plymouth	Aug 20, 62	Sep 22, 62	Discharged Mar 10, 65 for wounds received Oct 19, 64.
Whitney, Eben E.	Plymouth	Sep 14, 61	Oct 18, 61	KIA Dec 13, 62.
Wiley, John, Jr.	Mt. Holly	Aug 16, 64	Aug 16, 64	Mustered out Jun 19, 65.
Wilkins, Wallace W.	Reading	Aug 15, 62	Sep 30, 62	Wounded May 5, 64; Mustered out Jun 29, 64.
Woodcock, Hiram	Londonderry	May 11, 61	Jun 20, 61	Died Oct 16, 62 of disease.
Woodward, Charles L.	Manchester	May 14, 61	Jun 20, 61	Wounded May 3, 63; Discharged Mar 21, 64 for disability.

Company K

Name and Rank	Residence	Date of Commission	Date of Issue	Remarks
Captains				
Eaton, Solon	Addison	May 28, 61	May 28, 61	Resigned Aug 4, 62.
Ballou, Erastus G.	Boston, Mass.	Aug 4, 62	Aug 16, 62	See Maj.
Decelle, Augustus A.	Shoreham	Jun 7, 65	Jun 17, 65	Pvt. Co. K; Reenlisted Jan 31, 64; Promoted to Corp. Dec 31, 62; to Sgt. Aug 4, 64; to First Sgt. Dec 24, 64; to First Lt. Co. K Dec 24, 64; Mustered out First Lt. Jul 15, 65.
First Lieutenants				
Tracy, Amasa S.	Middlebury	May 28, 61	May 28, 61	See Col.
Ballou, Erastus G.	Boston, Mass.	Jun 27, 62	Jun 27, 62	See Maj.
Drury, Eben N.	Vergennes	Aug 9, 62	Aug 16, 62	Sgt. Co. K; Promoted to First Sgt.; Wounded Jul 10, 63 and May 5, 64; Mustered out Jun 29, 64.
Hurlburt, Ward B.	Weybridge	Jun 20, 64	Jul 11, 64	See Capt. Co. D.
Decelle, Augustus A.	Shoreham	Dec 24, 64	Jan 31, 65	See Capt. Co. K.
Greenleaf, Charles F.	Salisbury	Jun 7, 65	Jun 17, 65	Pvt. Co. K; Reenlisted Jan 31, 64; Promoted to Corp. Apr 1, 64; to Sgt. Oct 18, 64; to First Sgt. Feb 6, 65; Wounded May 12, 64 and Sep 19, 64; Mustered out as First Sgt. Jul 15, 65.
Second Lieutenants				
Hoyt, Jonathan M.	New Haven	May 28, 61	May 28, 61	Resigned Jul 17, 62.
Carroll, Henry	New Haven	Jul 23, 62	Jul 31, 62	First Sgt. G Co. K; Wounded Jul 10, 63; Taken prisoner May 6, 64; Escaped Nov 1, 64; Mustered out Jan 6, 65.
Fisk, Russell	Bennington	Jun 7, 65	Jun 17, 65	Pvt. Co. A.; Promoted to Sgt. Maj. Feb 7, 65; Mustered out as Sgt. Maj. Jul 15, 65.

Name and Rank	Residence	Date of Enlistment	Date of Muster	Remarks
Sergeants				
Carroll, Henry	New Haven	May 15, 61	Jun 20, 61	See Second Lt. Co. K.
Beach, John T.	Salisbury	May 18, 61	Jun 20, 61	Promoted to First Sgt. Jun 24, 62; Mustered out Jun 29, 64.
Ward, George W.	New Haven	May 7, 61	Jun 20, 61	Discharged Aug 15, 62 for disability.
Drury, Eben N.	Vergennes	May 15, 61	Jun 20, 61	See First Lt. Co. K.
Sullivan, James	New Haven	May 20, 61	Jun 20, 61	Reduced to Corp.; Mustered out Jun 29, 64.
Corporals				
White, George A.	Panton	May 7, 61	Jun 20, 61	Died Aug 23, 62 of disease.
Adams, George W.	Vergennes	May 20, 61	Jun 20, 61	Discharged May 10, 62 for disability.
Matthews, Charles H.	Panton	May 7, 61	Jun 20, 61	Mustered out Jun 29, 64.
Hight, Bradbury W.	Burlington	May 20, 61	Jun 20, 61	See Second Lt. Co. C.
Shadwick, James	New Haven	May 20, 61	Jun 20, 61	Discharged Oct 4, 61 for disability.
Hurlburt, Ward B.	Weybridge	May 20, 61	Jun 20, 61	See Capt. Co. D.
Sloan, Casper B.	Shoreham	May 19, 61	Jun 20, 61	Reduced; Mustered out Jun 29, 64.
Lyman, Henry C.	Hinesburg	May 24, 61	Jun 20, 61	Died Aug 11, 61 of disease.
Musicians				
Baldwin, Josiah	Ferrisburgh	May 13, 61	Jun 20, 61	Mustered out Jun 29, 64.
Hoadley, Lucius J.	Lincoln	May 11, 61	Jun 20, 61	Died Dec 14, 61 of disease.
Wagoner				
McLaughlin, Robert E.	Vergennes	May 7, 61	Jun 20, 61	Mustered out Jun 29, 64.

Privates

Adams, Franklin	Vergennes	Aug 9, 61	Aug 30, 61	Taken prisoner Jun 29, 62; Paroled Aug 5, 62; Discharged Nov 13, 63.
Atwood, George H.	Lincoln	May 10, 61	Jun 20, 61	Wounded Jun 1, 64; Mustered out Jun 29, 64.
Austin, Alonzo	Weybridge	May 9, 61	Jun 20, 61	Discharged Nov 12, 61 for disability.
Backman, Samuel	Addison	May 29, 61	Jun 20, 61	Discharged Mar 8, 63 for disability.
Bartley, Jeremiah J.	Vergennes	Oct 1, 61	Oct 3, 61	Discharged May 2, 63 for disability.
Bartley, John	Vergennes	May 17, 61	Jun 20, 61	Discharged Oct 31, 62 for disability.
Beals, William	Pownal	Mar 11, 62	Apr 12, 62	Mustered out —, 65.
Bombard, Franklin	Panton	Aug 8, 61	Aug 30, 61	Discharged Jan 19, 63 for disability.
Bovia, Joseph	Salisbury	May 20, 61	Jun 20, 61	Reenlisted Jan 31, 64; Promoted to Corp. Sep 1, 62; to Sgt. Aug 27, 63; Died May 8, 64 of wounds received May 5, 64.
Bowers, Cyrus	Addison	May 9, 61	Jun 20, 61	Promoted to Corp. Sep 12, 62; Discharged Mar 4, 64 for wounds received May 3, 63.
Briggs, Alfred S.	Salisbury	May 16, 61	Jun 20, 61	Deserted Sep 10, 62.
Bristol, Aaron	Bridport	Aug 5, 61	Aug 30, 61	Deserted Dec 1, 62.
Brooks, Elbridge	Windham	Feb 21, 62	Apr 12, 62	KIA May 5, 64.
Brown, Luther T.	Substitute	Sep 7, 63	Sep 7, 63	Substitute for Martin P. Blanchard, Orange; Transferred to V. R. C. Apr 15, 64; Deserted —, 64.
Bryant, Eliphalet	Montpelier	May 16, 61	Jun 20, 61	Discharged Nov 23, 61 for disability.
Bull, Asahel J.	Monkton	Aug 17, 61	Aug 30, 61	Discharged Mar 4, 62 for disability.
Bushey, Henry H.	Salisbury	May 23, 61	Jun 20, 61	Discharged May 16, 62 for disability.
Button, Jonathan	Underhill	Dec 5, 63	Dec 18, 63	Transferred to U.S. Navy Apr 18, 64; Discharged Aug 19, 65.
Casey, Edward	Addison	May 15, 61	Jun 20, 61	Mustered out Jun 29, 64.
Center, Franklin T.	Shoreham	May 20, 61	Jun 20, 61	Discharged Dec 25, 61 for disability.
Cilley, Edwin H.	Woodbury	Jul 25, 63	Jul 25, 63	Drafted; Wounded May 5, 64; Mustered out Jul 15, 65.
Clair, Calvin	Cornwall	Aug 9, 61	Aug 30, 61	KIA Jun 29, 62.
Clair, Oliver	Cornwall	May 18, 61	Jun 20, 61	Reenlisted Dec 21, 63; Wounded Sep 19, 64; Mustered out Jul 15, 65.
Cloyes, Gideon H.	Salisbury	May 18, 61	Jun 20, 61	Discharged Aug 17, 61 for disability.
Comstock, John	Salisbury	May 13, 61	Jun 20, 61	Wounded Jul 10, 63; Mustered out Jun 29, 64.
Comstock, Lewis	Middlebury	Dec 12, 62	Jan 8, 63	Transferred to V. R. C. Aug 26, 64; Mustered out Jul 1, 64.
Conant, William J.	Ferrisburgh	May 17, 61	Jun 20, 61	Discharged Jun 8, 62 for disability.
Converse, George W.	Addison	May 9, 61	Jun 20, 61	Promoted to Corp. Sep 1, 62; to Sgt. Dec 12, 62; Mustered out Jun 29, 64.
Converse, Jesse G.	Panton	Aug 18, 62	Sep 15, 62	Discharged Oct 5, 63 for disability.
Cross, William	Panton	Aug 16, 62	Sep 15, 62	Deserted Jul 3, 63.
Daggett, Hiram S.	Salisbury	May 17, 61	Jun 20, 61	Promoted to Corp. Dec —, 61; Died Dec 25, 61 of disease.
Dake, Orrin L.	Shoreham	May 18, 61	Jun 20, 61	Discharged Mar 19, 63 for disability.
Dana, Lewis	Burlington	Jun 20, 61	Jun 20, 61	Reenlisted Dec 21, 63; Mustered out Jul 15, 65.
Daniels, Joseph	Panton	May 4, 61	Jun 20, 61	Reenlisted Dec 21, 63; Promoted to Corp. Aug 4, 64; to Sgt. Jan 1, 65; Mustered out Jul 15, 65.
Daniels, Mitchell	Panton	Mar 10, 62	————	Discharged Feb 11, 63 for disability.
Decelle, Augustus A.	Shoreham	May 20, 61	Jun 20, 61	See Capt. Co. K.
Dickinson, Clay N.	Weybridge	May 27, 61	Jun 20, 61	Discharged Oct 4, 61 for disability.
Dompier, Theophilus	Vergennes	Aug 8, 61	Aug 30, 61	Discharged Mar 6, 62 for disability.
Drake, Oliver B.	Bristol	May 22, 61	Jun 20, 61	Discharged Apr 19, 63 for wounds received Sep 17, 62.
Elmer, Henry	Addison	Aug 11, 61	Aug 11, 61	Discharged Aug 1, 62 for disability.
Elmer, William F.	Addison	Aug 1, 61	Aug 30, 61	Promoted to Corp. Sep 21, 62; Wounded Jul 10, 63; Mustered out Aug 30, 64.
Farrington, William R.	Rutland	Aug 10, 61	Aug 30, 61	Reenlisted Jan 31, 64; Promoted to Corp. Apr 18, 64; to Sgt. Aug 4, 64; Wounded May 5, 64; Taken prisoner Oct 19, 64; Paroled Feb 15, 65; Mustered out Jun 9, 65.

Felch, Harlan E.	Bradford	Dec 27, 62	Jan 8, 63	Wounded Mar 27, 65; Mustered out Jul 15, 65.
Field, Alonzo H.	New Haven	Aug 13, 62	Sep 15, 62	KIA Sep 19, 64.
Fish, Thomas	Substitute	Jul 23, 63	Jul 23, 63	Substitute for Edgar W. Burrett, Burlington; Deserted Nov 30, 63.
Fitzsimmons, John	Vergennes	Mar 27, 62	Apr 12, 62	Wounded May 5, 64; Promoted to Corp. Feb 6, 65; to Sgt. Mar —, 65; to First Sgt. —, 65; Mustered out Apr 14, 65.
Flint, Almon Warner	Leicester	Sep 10, 62	Sep 15, 62	Promoted to Corp. Aug 4, 64; Mustered out Jun 19, 65.
Flynn, Francis	Underhill	May 17, 61	Jun 20, 61	G. C. M. Feb 6, 62 for being drunk and disorderly; Transferred to 1st N.Y. Independent Artillery Battery Jan 10, 64.
Foley, Michael	Clermont, Va.	Jul 16, 61	Aug 30, 61	Reenlisted Dec 21, 63; Wounded Dec 13, 62 and May 6, 64; Promoted to Corp. Mar 1, 65; Mustered out Jul 15, 65.
Forrest, Edwin	Salisbury	Oct 21, 61	Oct 23, 61	Died Dec 27, 61 of disease.
Freeman, John A.	Middlebury	May 22, 61	Jun 20, 61	Deserted Dec 17, 62.
Gaffney, James	Colchester	Mar 1, 62	Apr 20, 62	Discharged Feb 19, 63 for disability.
Gale, Albert	Substitute	Aug 1, 63	Aug 1, 63	Substitute for Henry J. Harris, Stowe; Wounded May 12, 64; Mustered out Jul 15, 65.
Gambell, Samuel J.	Salisbury	May 17, 61	Jun 20, 61	Reenlisted Jan 31, 64; Taken prisoner May 21, 64; Paroled Dec 11, 64; Mustered out Jun 9, 65.
Gardner, Truman G.	Panton	Apr 18, 62	Sep 15, 62	KIA May 12, 64.
Grant, Frederick	Salisbury	May 25, 61	Jun 20, 61	Discharged Oct 16, 61 by Special Order of the War Dept.
Grant, John W.	Middlebury	May 13, 61	Jun 20, 61	Reenlisted Dec 21, 63; Deserted Jul 3, 63; Returned Sep 23, 63; KIA May 12, 64.
Graves, Hiram	Marshfield	Dec 14, 63	Jan 2, 64	Discharged Aug 25, 64 for disability.
Greenleaf, Charles F.	Salisbury	May 13, 61	Jun 20, 61	See First Lt. Co. K.
Grinnell, Edgar E.	Weybridge	May 21, 61	Jun 20, 61	Reenlisted Jan 31, 64; Taken prisoner Jul 21, 61; Paroled Jan 3, 62; Deserted Mar —, 64.
Grover, Luther	Sudbury	Dec 8, 63	Dec 17, 63	Discharged Apr 18, 64 by reason of old age.
Guyett, Edward	Shoreham	May 17, 61	Jun 20, 61	Deserted Feb 27, 63.
Hamlin, Moses J.	Fairfax	May 10, 61	Jun 20, 61	Discharged Dec 29, 61 for disability.
Harris, Fayett A.	Addison	May 9, 61	Jun 20, 61	Promoted to Corp. Aug 27, 63; Wounded May 4, 63; Mustered out Jun 29, 64.
Hatch, Isaac	Panton	Aug 3, 61	Aug 30, 61	Wounded May 5, 64; Mustered out Aug 29, 64.
Higgins, William	Shoreham	May 17, 61	Jun 20, 61	Taken prisoner Jun 29, 62; Paroled Aug 5, 62; Promoted to Corp. Dec 31, 62; KIA May 4, 63.
Hunter, Truman M.	Weybridge	May 17, 61	Jun 20, 61	KIA Jun 29, 62.
Huntley, Henry	Salisbury	May 10, 61	Jun 20, 61	Discharged May 19, 62 for disability.
Huntley, Loomis D.	Salisbury	May 10, 61	Jun 20, 61	Discharged May 21, 62 for disability.
Hurd, Walter J.	Addison	Aug 1, 61	Aug 30, 61	Promoted to Corp. Sep 1, 62; KIA Jul 10, 63.
Hurlburt, Louis	Ferrisburgh	Aug 17, 61	Aug 30, 61	Discharged Dec 25, 61 for disability.
Jabonzie, Charles	Montpelier	Dec 29, 62	Jan 8, 63	Wounded May 3, 63; Deserted Jul 18, 63.
Jacobs, Alfred	Bradford	Dec 10, 62	Jan 8, 63	Drummer; Mustered out Jul 15, 65.
Kelley, John	Shoreham	May 17, 61	Jun 20, 61	Reenlisted Jan 31, 64; Promoted to Corp. Sep 1, 62; to Sgt. Aug 27, 63; Wounded —, 62 and May 3, 63; KIA May 12, 64.
Kennedy, John	Rutland	May 8, 61	Jun 20, 61	Discharged Jun 8, 62 for disability.
King, Edmund W.	Vergennes	Aug 14, 61	Aug 30, 61	Died Jan 29, 63 of disease.
Larock, William	Berlin	Mar 25, 62	Apr 12, 62	Died May 15, 62 of disease.
Lavake, Joseph S.	Burlington	Aug 23, 62	Sep 15, 62	Taken prisoner Aug 1, 63; Paroled Nov 20, 64; Wounded Apr 2, 65; Mustered out Jun 8, 65.
Lawrence, Anthony	New Haven	May 23, 61	Jun 20, 61	Died Sep 16, 61 of disease.
Lawson, George H.	Vergennes	Aug 1, 61	Aug 30, 61	Deserted Nov 5, 62; Returned Mar 18, 63; Mustered out Aug 29, 64.
Maloney, John	Burlington	May 20, 61	Jun 20, 61	Taken prisoner Jul 2, 62; paroled Aug 5, 62; Deserted Aug 24, 62.
Marlow, Patrick,	Underhill	Dec 7, 63	Dec 18, 63	Taken prisoner May 4, 63; and died in a Confederate prisoner of war camp date unknown.

Martin, James	Vergennes	Aug 3, 61	Aug 30, 61	Deserted Aug 24, 63.
Matthews, Hiram P.	Panton	May 20, 61	Jun 20, 61	Promoted to Sgt.; Wounded May 4, 63; Transferred to V. R. C. Sep 1, 63.
Matthews, Levi P.	Panton	Aug 18, 62	Sep 15, 62	Died Jan 8, 63 of disease.
Mayo, Sylvester W.	Lincoln	May 22, 61	Jun 20, 61	Reenlisted Dec 21, 63; Wounded May 6, 64; Transferred to V. R. C. Oct 11, 64; Mustered out Jul 19, 65.
McCue, George	Weybridge	May 23, 61	Jun 20, 61	Discharged Oct 4, 61 for disability.
McGelley, Thomas	Underhill	Dec 8, 63	Dec 18, 63	KIA Sep 9, 64.
McKenzie, Edwin	Addison	May 26, 61	Jun 20, 61	Discharged Oct 1, 63 for disability.
McKinn, Daniel	Vergennes	May 7, 61	Jun 20, 61	Promoted to Corp. Feb 22, 62; to Sgt. Sep 1, 62; Wounded Dec 13, 62; KIA May 3, 63.
McLeod, Angus	Underhill	Dec 8, 63	Dec 18, 63	Died Feb 29, 64 of disease.
Meigs, George W.	Vergennes	Aug 10, 61	Aug 30, 61	Died Apr 16, 62 of disease.
Montgomery, Charles	Pownal	Mar 16, 62	Apr 12, 62	Died Jan 27, 63 of disease.
Morgan, James	Addison	Aug 14, 61	Aug 30, 61	Reenlisted Jan 31, 64; Taken prisoner Dec 8, 64; Paroled Jun 2, 65; Mustered out Jul 15, 65.
Morgan, Julius S.	Sudbury	Oct 23, 61	Oct 23, 61	Discharged Dec 27, 62 for disability; Enlisted again Dec 8, 63; Discharged Jan 25, 65 for wounds received May 5, 64.
Munson, Reuben L.	Corinth	Aug 21, 62	Sep 22, 62	Discharged Feb 2, 64 for disability.
Neveux, Seraphin	Montpelier	Mar 11, 62	Apr 12, 62	Reenlisted Apr 18, 64; Promoted to Corp. Oct 18, 64; Mustered out Jul 15, 65.
Norton, Covel L.	Addison	Aug 1, 61	Aug 30, 61	KIA May 6, 64.
O'Brien, Patrick	Vergennes	Aug 10, 61	Aug 30, 61	Wounded May 3, 63; Deserted Jul 3, 63.
Packman, Samuel	Vergennes	May 23, 61	Jun 20, 61	Discharged Mar 8, 63 for disability.
Palmer, William H.	Ferrisburgh	May 22, 61	Jun 20, 61	Discharged Jan 21, 63 for disability.
Papin, Joseph	Georgia	Aug 6, 61	Aug 30, 61	Deserted Jan 27, 64.
Pecu, Frank	Ferrisburgh	Aug 5, 61	Aug 30, 61	Died Jan 3, 62 of disease.
Pecu, John	Ferrisburgh	May 18, 61	Jun 20, 61	Wounded Jul 21, 61; Discharged Jul 26, 62 for disability.
Pelkey, Leander	Rutland	Aug 16, 62	Sep 15, 62	Deserted Jun 5, 63.
Perry, Albert	Panton	Aug 16, 62	Sep 15, 62	Deserted Jul 21, 63; Returned Aug 24, 63; wounded May 10, 64; Mustered out Jun 19, 65.
Perry, Henry	Panton	Aug 16, 62	Sep 15, 62	Mustered out Jun 19, 65.
Perry, John P.	Panton	Aug 11, 62	Sep 15, 62	KIA May 4, 63.
Phillips, Rollin	Pittsford	May 18, 61	Jun 20, 61	Deserted Jul 16, 61; Returned; Mustered out Jun 29, 64.
Pratt, Oliver E.	Shoreham	May 19, 61	Jun 20, 61	Discharged Mar 7, 62 for disability.
Raymond, Louis	Panton	Aug 19, 61	Aug 30, 61	Died Feb 28, 62 of disease.
Sands, Alexander	Vergennes	Sep 2, 61	Oct 15, 61	Mustered out Oct 14, 64.
Sardini, Eugene	Substitute	Aug 4, 63	Aug 4, 63	Substitute for Rollin C. Wilcox, Orwell; Wounded May 10, 64; Deserted Sep 13, 64.
Schmidt, John	Substitute	Aug 5, 63	Aug 5, 63	Substitute for Hosea Paddleford, Hartland; Taken prisoner Nov 2, 63; Paroled Nov 24, 64; Mustered out Jul 15, 65.
Segaun, Joseph	Substitute	Sep 9, 63	Sep 9, 63	Substitute for Rodney B. Mears, Milton; Died Jul 15, 64 of disease.
Severy, Walter J.	Salisbury	May 9, 61	Jun 20, 61	Discharged Oct 10, 62 for disability.
Shaffer, John	Substitute	Aug 7, 63	Aug 7, 63	Substitute for George A. Gardner, West Windsor; Deserted Nov 30, 63.
Simpson, Thomas	Substitute	Sep 5, 63	Sep 5, 63	Substitute for George Wetmore, Milton; Taken prisoner May 5, 64 and died at Florence, S.C., date unknown.
Skiddy, John	Rutland	Aug 12, 62	Sep 15, 62	Taken prisoner May 5, 64 and died at Andersonville, Ga. Aug 19, 64.
Smith, Charles W.	Substitute	Sep 9, 63	Sep 9, 63	Substitute for Monroe S. Preble, Newport; Died Apr 15, 64 of disease.
Smith, George	Substitute	Jul 30, 63	Jul 30, 63	Substitute for Florentine D. Moody, Chelsea; Deserted Aug 29, 63.
Smith, Henry	Vergennes	May 28, 61	Jun 20, 61	Discharged Jan 8, 63 for disability.

Solei, Joseph	Substitute	Jul 29, 63	Jul 29, 63	Substitute for Charles E. Chase, Jr., Rockingham; Deserted Sep 22, 63; Returned Dec 10, 63; Wounded May 12, 64; Deserted Oct 5, 64.
Stevens, Francis	Lincoln	May 28, 61	Jun 20, 61	Deserted Sep 26, 61.
Stokes, Alvin R.	Charleston	Jul 31, 63	Jul 31, 63	Drafted; Mustered out Sep 2, 65.
Stow, Lewis A.	Calais	Feb 20, 62	Apr 12, 62	Discharged Oct 2, 62 for disability.
Sturdevant, Freeman D.	Weybridge	May 15, 61	Jun 20, 61	Wounded May 3, 63; Mustered out Jun 29, 64.
Sturdevant, William H.	Weybridge	May 26, 61	Jun 20, 61	Discharged Jul 14, 61 for disability.
Sturgis, Joseph	Substitute	Jul 22, 63	Jul 22, 63	Substitute for Samuel Swan, Brattleboro; Wounded May 5, 64; Discharged Jun 24, 64 by Special Order of the War Dept.
Swetser, James C.	Charleston	Aug 31, 63	Aug 31, 63	Drafted; Died Nov 3, 64 of wounds received Oct 19, 64.
Tatro, Abraham	Substitute	Jul 31, 63	Jul 31, 63	Substitute for Francis N. Nason, Middlebury; Wounded May 6, 64; Mustered out Jul 15, 65.
Tatro, Joseph	Substitute	Aug 4, 63	Aug 4, 63	Substitute for Charles Baker, Montgomery; Wounded May 6, 64; Discharged May 22, 65 for wounds.
Taylor, William	Middlebury	May 23, 61	Jun 20, 61	Deserted Jun 20, 62.
Thomas, Nathan C.	Rutland	Dec 9, 63	Dec 15, 63	Wounded Aug 21, 64; Mustered out Jul 15, 65.
Thomas, William W.	Salisbury	May 18, 61	Jun 20, 61	Discharged May 18, 64 for disability.
Tremble, Frank	Bridport	May 17, 61	Jun 20, 61	Promoted to Corp.; Discharged Dec 14, 62 for disability.
Tremble, Josephus	Bridport	Aug 18, 61	Aug 30, 61	Deserted Sep 10, 62.
Ubar, Lewis, Jr.	Substitute	Jul 25, 63	Jul 25, 63	Substitute for Charles W. Bragg, Warren; Mustered out Jul 15, 65 by Special Order of the War Dept.
Vanderhoof, John L.	Addison	May 9, 61	Jun 20, 61	Died May 13, 62 of disease.
Vanderhoof, Oliver S.	Addison	Mar 25, 62	Apr 12, 62	Deserted Dec 1, 62; Returned May 26, 63; Wounded and taken prisoner May 5, 64; Paroled Mar 3, 65; Mustered out May 9, 65.
Vassar, Charles	Substitute	Jul 20, 63	Jul 20, 63	Substitute for Charles Nash, Burlington; Died Jan 8, 64 of disease.
Vaundell, Lewis	Woodstock	May 11, 61	Jun 20, 61	Reenlisted Jan 31, 64; Dishonorable discharge Apr 21, 64 for desertion and sent to Dry Tortugas, Fla. for one year by sentence of G. C. M.
Vose, William	Substitute	Jul 23, 63	Jul 23, 63	Substitute for Tyler I. Whipple, Dover; Wounded May 5, 64 and Apr 2, 65; Mustered out May 13, 65.
Walker, Foster	Lincoln	May 26, 61	Jun 20, 61	Died Dec 20, 61 of disease.
Walker, James	Lincoln	May 23, 61	Jun 20, 61	Reenlisted Dec 21, 63; Taken prisoner Jun 29, 62; Paroled Aug 5, 62; Wounded Jul 21, 61, May 3, 63, and Apr 2, 65; Promoted to Corp. Apr —, 64; Reduced Feb 20, 65; Promoted to Sgt. Jun 16, 65; Mustered out Jul 15, 65.
Walker, William	Substitute	Aug 4, 63	Aug 4, 63	Substitute for Uri Fletcher, Richford; Deserted Mar 1, 64.
Ward, Arthur	Substitute	Jul 20, 63	Jul 20, 63	Substitute for H. W. Field, Essex; Died Oct 15, 64 of wounds received Oct 19, 64.
Washburn, Calvin	Substitute	Aug 5, 63	Aug 5, 63	Substitute for James C. Platt, Colchester; Died Apr 1, 64 of disease.
Washburn, Erastus T.	Substitute	Jul 23, 63	Jul 23, 63	Substitute for John Rolfe, Colchester; Died Dec 5, 63 of disease.
Welcome, Lewis	Substitute	Jul 27, 63	Jul 27, 63	Substitute for Benjamin Harrington, Shelburne; Died Oct 12, 64 of wounds received Sep 19, 64.
Welsh, John W.	Substitute	Aug 7, 63	Aug 7, 63	Substitute for Gilbert W. Atwood, Hartland; Deserted Oct 20, 63.
Wheeler, Charles S.	Substitute	Aug 1, 63	Aug 1, 63	Substitute for Loomis D. Sessions, Middlebury; Wounded May 12, 64; Deserted Sep 23, 64.
Wheeler, Fordyce N.	Substitute	Jul 31, 63	Jul 31, 63	Substitute for Abel Barber, Charlotte; Died Feb 2, 64 of disease.

White, Ronello C.	Substitute	Aug 3, 63	Aug 3, 63	Substitute for William Davenport, Wallingford; Mustered out Jul 15, 65.
Williams, Robert F.	Substitute	Aug 1, 63	Aug 1, 63	Substitute for Eber B. Tracy, Lincoln; Wounded May 5, 64; Mustered out Jul 15, 65.
Williamson, Arthur	New Haven	Sep 6, 61	Oct 15, 61	Reenlisted Jan 31, 64; Deserted Mar 21, 64.
Williamson, John	New Haven	May 18, 61	Jun 20, 61	Reenlisted Jan 31, 64; Taken prisoner Aug 18, 62; Paroled Sep 13, 62; Promoted to Corp. Aug 27, 63; Deserted Mar 21, 64.
Witham, Thomas	Marshfield	Dec 19, 63	Jan 2, 64	Taken prisoner May 5, 64 and died at Florence, S.C. Sep 29, 64.
Wood, James	Substitute	Jul 27, 63	Jul 27, 63	Substitute for Clark Whitney, Westminster; Deserted Oct 8, 63.
Woods, Stephen	Pawlet	Aug 30, 62	Sep 15, 62	Discharged May 13, 65 for disability.
Woods, Willard	Wells	Aug 26, 62	Sep 15, 62	Discharged to date Jul 15, 63 by Special Order of the Dept. of the Lakes.
Woodward, Harrison	Middlesex	Jul 11, 63	Jul 11, 63	Drafted; Discharged Jan 23, 64 for disability.
Woodward, John S.	Holland	Jul 31, 63	Jul 31, 63	Drafted; Promoted to Corp. Dec 24, 64; Wounded Apr 2, 65; Mustered out Jul 15, 65.
Wright, Eugene F.	Shoreham	May 17, 61	Jun 20, 61	Mustered out Jun 29, 64.
Wright, Sidney S.	Substitute	Aug 5, 63	Aug 5, 63	Substitute for Francis A. Newell, Weathersfield; Died Apr 11, 64 of disease.
York, George W.	Waterbury	Jul 14, 63	Jul 14, 63	Drafted; Died May 31, 64 of wounds received May 5, 64.

NOTES

1. Off to Save the Union

1. Kenneth Nebenzahl, ed., *Atlas of the American Revolution* (Chicago: Rand McNally Company, 1977), pp. 43, 99, 101; Walter Hill Crockett, *Vermont: The Green Mountain State* (New York: The Century History Company, 1921), pp. 101–164, 430–445, hereinafter cited as Crockett; George G. Benedict, *Vermont in the Civil War*, 2 vols. (Burlington, Vt.: The Free Press Association, 1886), pp. 8–9, hereinafter cited as Benedict; unless otherwise noted all references are to vol. 1.

2. Benedict, pp. 8–9.

3. Ibid., pp. 9–10.

4. Ibid., pp. 10–11.

5. Ibid., p. 11.

6. William C. Davis, *Battle at Bull Run* (Garden City, N.Y.: Doubleday, 1977), p. 3, hereinafter cited as Davis.

7. Benedict, p. 12; Davis, p. 4; Charles E. Heller and William A. Stofft, *America's First Battles, 1776–1965* (Lawrence, Kans.: University Press of Kansas, 1986), p.82, hereinafter cited as *America's First Battles.*

8. Benedict, pp. 18, 24.

9. Ibid., pp. 19–20.

10. Ibid., pp. 20–27.

11. Ibid., pp. 28–61.

12. Benedict, pp. 42–54; Mark M. Boatner, *The Civil War Dictionary*, rev. ed. (New York: Vintage Books, 1991), p. 63, hereinafter cited as *The Civil War Dictionary*; George Grenville Benedict, *The Service of the Vermont Troops: An Oration before the Re-Union Society of Vermont Officers, in the Representatives' Hall, Montpelier, Vt., November 2, 1882.* Montpelier: Watchman and Journal Press, 1882, p.5.

13. Benedict, pp. 60–61.

14. Benedict, pp. 27, 62–63; *America's First Battles*, p. 84; *Daily Free Press*, 6 June 1861.

15. *Daily Free Press*, 6 June 1861.

16. *Daily Free Press*, 6 June 1861.

17. Mark M. Boatner, *Military Customs and Traditions* (Westport, Conn.: Greenwood Press, 1956; repr., New York: D. McKay, 1976), p. 88; U.S. War Department, *Revised Regulations for the Army of the United States, 1861* (1861; reprint, Harrisburg: National Historical Society, 1980), p. 519, hereinafter cited as *Revised Regulations for the Army, 1861.*

18. *Revised Regulations for the Army of the United States, 1861*, pp. 36, 519.

19. Peter S. Chase, *Reunion Greeting, Together with an Historical Sketch, and a Complete Descriptive List of the Members of Co. I, 2d Regt., Vt. Vols* (Brattleboro, Vt.: Phoenix Job Printing Office, 1891), p. 4–16, hereinafter cited as *Historical Sketch of Co. I.*

20. Benedict, p. 63.

21. Benedict, p. 63–64; Henry Whiting's military service record, Records of the Adjutant General's Office, 1780–1917. Record Group 94, National Archives Building, Washington, DC., hereinafter cited as the individuals name and military service record.

22. Benedict, p. 64; George J. Stannard's military service record; Hiram Carlton, *Genealogical and Family History* of the *State of Vermont.* 2 vols. (New York: Lewis Publishing Co., 1903), Vol. 1 pp. 150–151, hereinafter cited as Carlton; Otis F. R. Waite, *Vermont in the Great Rebellion* (Claremont, N.H.: Tracy, Chase and Co., 1869), pp. 251–252, hereinafter cited as Waite.

23. Benedict, p. 64; Charles H. Joyce's military service record; Crockett, p. 370–371; John Gregory, *1776–1876 Centennial Proceedings and Historical Incidents of the Early Settlers of Northfield, Vermont, With Biographical Sketches of Prominent Business Men Who have been and are now Residents of the Town* (Montpelier: Argus and Patriot Book and Job Printing House, 1878), p. 164–167; Carlton, vol. 1, pp. 64–67.

24. Benedict, pp. 64–65.

25. Benedict, p. 65; *Daily Free Press*, 11, 14, 18 June 1861;

Chester K. Leach, Civil War letters, Special Collections, Bailey/ Howe Library, University of Vermont, Burlington, Vermont, hereinafter cited as Chester K. Leach letters; *Revised Regulations for the Army, 1861*, p. 76; *The Burlington Times*, 8 June 1861; *Green Mountain Freeman*, 6 June 1861.

26. *Daily Free Press*, 6 June 1861.

27. *Daily Free Press*, 6 June 1861; Bell Ivrin Wiley, *The Life of Billy Yank* (Baton Rouge: Louisiana State University Press, 1986), pp. 45–46, hereinafter cited as *The Life of Billy Yank*; Edson Emery, Civil War diary, 1861, Special Collections, Bailey/ Howe Library, University of Vermont, Burlington, Vermont, hereinafter cited as Edson Emery diary; Chester K. Leach letters.

28. *The Life of Billy Yank*, pp. 49–50.

29. *The Life of Billy Yank*, pp. 446–47.

30. Chester K. Leach letters; *Daily Free Press*, 14 June 1861; *Green Mountain Freeman*, 11 Jun 1861.

31. *Daily Free Press*, 8 July 1861; Chester K. Leach letters; *The Life of Billy Yank*, p. 50.

32. Chester K. Leach letters; Edson Emery diary; *Daily Free Press*, 11, 23, 24 June 1861; Herbert Klynstra and John Stutsman, eds., *Letters of Jerome Cutler Waterville, Vermont during his enlistment in the Union Army 2nd Vermont Volunteers 1861–1864* (n.p., n.d.), p. 1, hereinafter cited as Jerome Cutler.

33. *Rutland Daily Herald*, 24 June 1861; *The Burlington Times*, 15 June 1861.

34. Edson Emery diary; *The Life of Billy Yank*, pp. 47–48.

35. Edson Emery diary; *The Life of Billy Yank*, p. 45.

36. *Daily Free Press*, 7–8 June 1861; *The Burlington Times*, 15 June 1861; *Green Mountain Freeman*, 11 June 1861.

37. *Daily Free Press*, 8, 11–13 June 1861; *Rutland Daily Herald*, 19 June 1861; *The Burlington Times*, 15 June 1861; *The Vermont Phoenix*, 20 June 1861; *The Life of Billy Yank*, p. 24.

38. Benedict, pp. 31–32, 66; *The Civil War Dictionary*, p. 676; Peggy Robbins, "Bomb Brothers," *Civil War Times Illustrated 36*, no. 4 (August, 1997), pp. 40–46.

39. *Daily Free Press*, 10 June 1861.

40. *Daily Free Press*, 10 June 1861.

41. Benedict, p. 64–65; *Daily Free Press*, 13–14 June 1861; *The Burlington Times*, 15 June 1861; *The Vermont Historical Gazetteer*, vol. 4, p. 341.

42. Benedict, p. 32, 65; *Daily Free Press*, 12–13 June 1861; *The Burlington Times*, 15 June 1861; *Rutland Daily Herald*, 19 June 1861; Howard C. Coffin, *Nine Months to Gettysburg* (Woodstock, Vt.: Country Press, 1997), p. 21, hereinafter cited as *Nine Months to Gettysburg*.

43. *Daily Free Press*, 12, 13, 18 June 1861; *Rutland Daily Herald*, 19 June 1861; *Nine Months to Gettysburg*, p. 21.

44. Benedict, p. 65; Edson Emery diary; Chester K. Leach letters; *Daily Free Press*, 13, 14, 17 June 1861; *Rutland Daily Herald*, 19 June 1861; *The Life of Billy Yank*, p. 22.

45. *Daily Free Press*, 17 June 1861; Edson Emery letters; Francis A. Lord, *Civil War Collector's Encyclopedia* (New York: Castle Books, 1965), p. 119, hereinafter cited as Lord.

46. Benedict, p. 66; Lord, p. 119.

47. *Daily Free Press*, 17 June 1861; *Rutland Daily Herald*, 19 June 1861; Lord, pp. 119–121.

48. Chester K. Leach letters; *Daily Free Press*, 20–21 June 1861; *Revised Regulations for the Army, 1861*, pp. 112, 284, 489, 525.

49. Benedict, p. 65; Edson Emery diary; *Daily Free Press*, 17 June 1861; *Rutland Daily Herald*, 19 June 1861; Theodore S. Peck, *Revised Roster of Vermont Volunteers and Lists of Vermonters who Served in the Army and Navy of the United States During the War of the Rebellion* (Montpelier, Vt.: Watchman Co., 1892), p. 32, hereinafter cited as Peck.

50. *Daily Free Press*, 17 June 1861; *Rutland Daily Herald*, 19 June 1861; Edson Emery diary.

51. *Daily Free Press*, 19 June 1861; *Rutland Daily Herald*, 17 June 1861.

52. Benedict, pp. 65–66.

53. Lord, pp. 16, 243.

54. Lord, p. 17; William B. Edwards, *Civil War Guns* (Harrisburg: Stackpole, 1962), pp. 13, 17–19; Harold L. Peterson, ed., *Encyclopedia of Firearms* (New York: E. P. Dutton, 1964), pp. 72, 219; Irwin Bell Wiley, *They Who Fought Here* (New York: Bonanza Books, 1959), p. 114; William M. Wallace, *Soul of the Lion* (Gettysburg: Stan Clark Military books, 1960; reprint, 1995), p. 133.

55. *America's First Battles*, p. 86; *Soul of the Lion*, p. 133; Grady McWhitney and Perry D. Jamieson, *Attack and Die* (University, Ala.: University of Alabama Press, 1982), pp. 50, 82, hereinafter cited as *Attack and Die*; *The Life of Billy Yank*, pp. 187–189.

56. Bruce Catton, *The Army of the Potomac: Mr. Lincoln's Army* (Garden City, N.Y.: Doubleday, 1951), pp. 187–188, hereinafter cited as *Mr. Lincoln's Army*.

57. William J. Hardee, *Hardee's Rifle and Light Infantry Tactics*, (Memphis: E. C. Kirk & Co., 1861), p. 6

58. George A. Merrill to Lucius E. Chittenden, 28 May 1861, Ed Italo collection; *Rutland Daily Herald*, 21–22 June 1861; *Burlington Weekly Sentinel*, 21 June 1861.

59. Benedict, p. 66; *Rutland Daily Herald*, 22 June 1861; Ephriam W. Harrington's military service record; *Green Mountain Freeman*, 25 June 1861.

60. Benedict, p. 66; Edson Emery diary: *Daily Free Press*, 24 June 1861; *Burlington Weekly Sentinel*, 21 June 1861: *Rutland Daily Herald*, 24 June 1861.

61. Benedict, p. 66; *Daily Free Press*, 24 June 1861; *Burlington Weekly Sentinel*, 28 June 1861.

62. Benedict, p. 67; *Daily Free Press*, 10–11 June 1861; *Rutland Daily Herald*, 8 July 1861; Walter A. Philips's military service record; *The Burlington Times*, 15 June 1861; Robert G. Poirier, *By the Blood of our Alumni* (Mason City, Iowa: Savas Publishing Company. 1999), p. 24.

63. Benedict, pp. 66–67; *Daily Free Press*, 24 June 1861; *Burlington Weekly Sentinel*, 28 June 1861

64. *Daily Free Press*, 24 June, 1861; *Burlington Weekly Sentinel*, 28 June 1861.

65. Benedict, p. 67; *Daily Free Press*, 24 June 1861; *Burlington Weekly Sentinel*, 28 June 1861; Janet B. Hewett, Bryce A. Suderow, and Noah Andre Trudeau, eds. *Supplement to the Official Records of the Union and Confederate Armies* (Wilmington, N.C.: Broadfoot Publishing Company, 1998), Part II-Record of Events, Vol. 69, Serial No. 81, p. 239, hereinafter cited as *Supplement to the Official Records*.

66. Moses C. Glines, Civil War letters, letters in the pos-

session of Kenneth E. Prohel; *The Vermont Historical Gazetteer*, vol. 2, p. 1126.

67. Benedict, 67; *Daily Free Press*, 25 June, 1 July 1861; Edson Emery diary.

68. Benedict, p. 67; *Daily Free Press*, 1 July 1861; *Green Mountain Freeman*, 3 July 1861; Edson Emery letters.

69. *Daily Free Press*, 1 July 1861.

70. Benedict, p. 68; Chester K. Leach letters; Edson Emery diary; *Daily Free Press*, 1 July 1861; C. Wilson Wright, *Our Harford Heritage; A History of Harford County, Maryland*, 3d ed. (Glen Burnie, Md.: French-Bray Printing Company, 1980), pp. 128, hereinafter cited as Wright.

71. Benedict, p. 68; Chester K. Leach letters; Edson Emery diary; *Daily Free Press*, 1 July 1861; Wright, pp. 116, 128; United States War Department. *War of the Rebellion: A Compilation of the Official Records of the Union and Confederate Armies* (Washington: Government Printing Office, 70 vols., in 128 parts,1881–1902), series 1, vol. 5, p. 570, hereinafter cited as OR. All references will be to series 1, part 1 unless otherwise stated; Jeffery K. Smart, "Burning Bridges: The Events leading Up to the Military Occupation of Harford County in 1861," *Harford Historical Bulletin 72* (Spring 1997), pp. 8, 11, 27–29, 50–52, hereinafter cited as Burning Bridges.

72. Lucius D. Savage, Civil War diary, Vermont Historical Society, Montpelier, Vermont, hereinafter cited as Lucius Savage diary; *The Vermont Historical Gazetteer*, vol. 4, p. 773.

73. Benedict, p. 68; Alfred H. Guernsey and Henry M. Alden, *Harper's Pictorial History of the Civil War*, 2 vols., (New York: Fairfax Press, 1866), vol. 1, p.86, hereinafter cited as *Harper's Pictorial History of the Civil War*; *Daily Free Press*, 1 July 1861; Chester K. Leach letters; Edson Emery diary; Margaret Leech, *Reveille in Washington 1860–1865* (New York: Harper & Brothers Publishers, 1941), pp.60–61, hereinafter cited as *Reveille in Washington*; Sherry H. Olson, *Baltimore* (Baltimore: Johns Hopkins University Press, 1980), pp. 107, 226; Burning Bridges, pp. 21–24.

74. Benedict, p. 68; *Reveille in Washington*, p. 76; *Harper's Pictorial History of the Civil War*, p. 86; *Supplement to the Official Records*, Part II-Record of Events, Vol. 69, Serial No. 81, p. 239; Lucius Savage diary.

75. Benedict, p. 68; *Supplement to the Official Records*, Part II—Record of Events, Vol. 69, Serial No. 81, p. 239; Henry Whiting's military service record; *Reveille in Washington*, pp. 76, 86

76. Chester K. Leach letters; *Reveille in Washington*, p. 78; *Daily Free Press*, 8 July 1861; *The Vermont Phoenix*, 18 July 1861; *Green Mountain Freeman*, 3 July 1861.

77. Chester K. Leach letters.

78. *The Vermont Phoenix*, 18 July 1861.

79. *Daily Free Press*, 8 July 1861; Chester K. Leach letters; Edson Emery diary.

80. Chester K. Leach letters; *Reveille in Washington*, pp. 56; Davis, p. 41.

81. Chester K. Leach letters; Edson Emery diary; *The Vermont Historical Gazetteer*, vol. 2, p. 1126.

82. Sanford R. Barnes, Civil War letters, Special Collections, Bailey/Howe Library, University of Vermont, Burlington, Vermont, hereinafter cited as Sanford R. Barnes letters; Sanford R. Barnes's military service record.

83. Chester K. Leach letters; *Reveille in Washington*, pp. 260–261.

84. Geraldine F. Chittick, ed., In the Field: Doctor Melvin John Hyde, Surgeon, 2nd Vermont Volunteers (Newport, Vt.: Vermont Civil War Enterprises, 1999), p. 177, hereinafter cited as In the Field.

85. Descriptive Rolls of Company B, 2nd Vermont Volunteer Infantry Regiment, Vermont Historical Society, Montpelier, Vermont; Peck, p. 38.

86. Jerome Cutler, p. 3.

87. Chester K. Leach letters.

88. *Rutland Daily Herald*, July 15, 1861; Henry R. Hayward, History of Co. E, 2nd Regt. Vt. Vols., Tunbridge Historical Society, Tunbridge, Vermont, p. 3, hereinafter cited as *History of Co. E.*

89. Chester K. Leach letters; *Daily Free Press*, 8, 17 July 1861; Mary R. Cabot, *Annals of Brattleboro Vermont*, vol. 2 (Brattleboro, Vt.: Press of E. L. Hildreth & Co., 1922), p. 765, hereinafter cited as *Annals of Brattleboro Vermont*; *The Vermont Phoenix*, 15, July, 1861.

90. Davis, p. 8.

91. Davis, p. 9; James G. Barber, *Alexandria in the Civil War* (Lynchburg, Va.: H. E. Howard, 1988), pp. 14–15, hereinafter cited as Barber; *Reveille in Washington*, p. 81.

92. Davis, p. 8; *America's First Battles*, p. 88

93. Davis, pp. 9–10; *America's First Battles*, p. 88.

94. Davis, pp. 11–12; *America's First Battles*, p. 88.

95. Davis, pp. 12, 14.

96. Oliver O. Howard, *Autobiography of Oliver Otis Howard*, vol. 1 (Freeport, NY: Books For Libraries, 1971), p. 143. hereinafter cited as Howard.

97. Chester K. Leach letters; Edson Emery diary; *Daily Free Press*, 17, 20 July 1861.

98. Chester K. Leach letters; Edson Emery diary; *Daily Free Press*, 17, 20 July 1861; Elijah S. Brown, Civil War letters, Vermont Historical Society, Montpelier, Vermont, hereinafter cited as Elijah S. Brown letters.

99. Chester K. Leach letters; Edson Emery diary; *Daily Free Press*, 17, 20 July 1861; *The Burlington Times*, 20 July 1861; *Green Mountain Freeman*, 17 July 1861.

100. Chester K. Leach letters; Edson Emery diary; *Daily Free Press*, 17 July 1861; Dallas M. Lancaster and Mary H. Lancaster, eds., *The Civil War Diary of Anne S. Frobel* (McLean, Va.: EPM Publications, 1992), pp. 40–41, hereinafter cited as Lancaster.

101. *Daily Free Press*, 17 July 1861: Barber, p. 95.

102. Benedict, pp. 68–69; George W. Bicknell, *History of the Fifth Regiment Maine Volunteers* (Portland, Me.: Hall L. Davis, 1871), p. 40, hereinafter cited as Bicknell; William E. S. Whitman and Charles H. True, *Maine in the War for the Union* (Lewiston, Maine: Nelson Dingley Jr. & Co., 1865), pp. 84, 113, hereinafter cited as *Maine in the War for the Union*.

103. Benedict, p. 69; *Rutland Daily Herald*, 20 July 1861.

104. *Rutland Daily Herald*, 20 July 1861; *The Burlington Times*, 20 July 1861.

105. Howard, pp. 143–144.

106. Benedict, p. 83; Jerome Cutler, p. 6

107. James W. Bromley's military service record; James W.

Bromley Civil War letters, Vermont Historical Society, Montpelier, Vermont, hereinafter cited as James W. Bromley letters; J. C. Williams, *The History and Map of Danby, Vermont* (Rutland, Vt.: Printed by McLean & Robbins, 1869), pp. 311–312.

108. Benedict, p. 83.

2. The Disgraceful Affair at Bull Run

1. OR, vol. 2, pp. 303–305.

2. Benedict, p. 69; Davis, pp. 90–91; *The Burlington Times*, 10 August 1861; *Vermont Phoenix*, 15 August 61.

3. Davis, p. 93; Howard, pp. 147–148.

4. Benedict, p. 70; Lucius D. Savage diary.

5. Benedict, p. 70; Davis, p. 95; Bicknell, p. 23; Howard, p. 148; Chester K. Leach letters.

6. Benedict, p. 70; Chester K. Leach letters; Sanford R. Barnes letters; Lucius D. Savage diary.

7. *Mr. Lincoln's Army*, p. 181; *The Life of Billy Yank*, p. 237.

8. *Mr. Lincoln's Army*, pp. 181–182; *The Life of Billy Yank*, p. 239.

9. *Mr. Lincoln's Army*, p. 182; *The Life of Billy Yank*, pp. 240–241.

10. Benedict, p. 70; Howard, pp. 149–150.

11. Benedict, p. 70.

12. Benedict, p. 70; Howard, pp. 149–150; *America's First Battles*, p. 95; Elijah S. Brown letters.

13. *Daily Free Press*, 25 July 1861; *The Burlington Times*, 10 August 1861.

14. Lucius D. Savage diary.

15. Elijah S. Brown letters.

16. *America's First Battles*, p. 95; Davis, p. 155.

17. *America's First Battles*, pp. 95–96; Davis, pp. 113, 136.

18. Benedict, pp. 71–72; Howard, p. 152; *The Burlington Times*, 10 August 1861.

19. Benedict, p. 72; Bicknell, p. 27; Sanford R. Barnes letters; *Rutland Daily Herald*, 2 August 1861.

20. *America's First Battles*, p. 97; Lloyd Lewis, *Sherman, Fighting Prophet* (New York: Harcourt, Brace, 1932), p. 173, hereinafter cited as *Sherman*; OR, vol. 2, p. 417; Davis, pp. 156–166.

21. Benedict, p. 72; Howard, pp. 153–154; *America's First Battles*, p. 97; OR, vol. 2, p. 418; Davis, p. 168.

22. *America's First Battles*, p. 97–99; Howard, pp. 153–154; Davis, p. 171.

23. *America's First Battles*, p. 99; Davis, p. 175.

24. *America's First Battles*, p. 99; Davis, pp. 176–188.

25. Benedict, p. 75; Howard, p. 157; Sanford R. Barnes letters; Chester K. Leach letters; *Rutland Daily Herald*, 2 August 1861; *The Burlington Times*, 10 August 1861; *Supplement to the Official Records*, Part II-Record of Events, Vol. 69, Serial No. 81, p. 239; OR, vol. 2, p. 418; Jerome Cutler, p. 7.

26. *America's First Battles*, pp. 99–100; Davis, pp. 187–188.

27. *America's First Battles*, p. 100; Davis, pp. 192–198.

28. *America's First Battles*, pp. 100–101; Davis, pp. 200–204.

29. *America's First Battles*, p. 101; Davis, pp. 203–213; *Sherman*, p. 175.

30. Benedict, p. 75; *Rutland Daily Herald*, 3 August 1861; *Supplement to the Official Records*, Part II-Record of Events, Vol. 69, Serial No. 81, p. 239; OR, Vol. 2, p. 422.

31. Howard, pp. 157–158.

32. *The Burlington Times*, 10 August 1861.

33. Howard, p. 158.

34. Benedict, pp. 76–77; OR, vol. 2, p. 422.

35. Benedict, p. 77; *The Vermont Phoenix*, 1 August 1861.

36. Benedict, p. 77; Urban A. Woodbury's military service record; Carlton, pp. 151–152.

37. Benedict, pp. 76–77; Sanford R. Barnes letters; Chester K. Leach letters; *Daily Free Press*, 31 July, 1861; *The Burlington Times*, 10 August 1861; *The Vermont Phoenix*, 1 August 1861.

38. Benedict, p. 77; Howard, p. 158; OR, vol. 2, p. 418.

39. Jerome Cutler, pp. 7–8.

40. Benedict, pp. 77–78; Howard, pp. 158–159; *Daily Free Press*, 30 July 1861; *Rutland Daily Herald*, 2 August 1861; *Supplement to the Official Records*, Part II-Record of Events, Vol. 69, Serial No. 81, p. 239; OR, vol. 2, pp. 418, 422; Edward K. Gould, *Major-General Hiram G. Berry* (Rockland, Maine: Press of the Courier-Gazette, 1899), pp. 62–63, hereinafter cited as *Major-General Hiram G. Berry*.

41. Davis, p. 220; *Daily Free Press*, 29 July 1861; *Major-General Hiram G. Berry*, p. 64.

42. Benedict, p. 81, 83; *The Vermont Phoenix*, 1 August 1861; Dorothy Sutherland Melville, *Tyler-Browns of Brattleboro* (New York: Exposition Press, 1973) p. 49, hereinafter cited as *Tyler-Browns of Brattleboro*.

43. Benedict, p. 23; *The Vermont Historical Gazetteer*, vol. 4, p. 342; Peck, 40.

44. Abby Maria Hemenway, *The History of the Town of Montpelier, Including that of the Town of East Montpelier, for the First One Hundred and Two Years*. Montpelier: Published by Miss A. M. Hemenway, 1882; William Guinan's military service record; Peck, p. 31.

45. Benedict, p. 83; *Daily Free Press*, 24, 29 July 1861; Andrew J. Noyes's pension record, Records of the Office of the Secretary of the Interior, Record Group 48, National Archives Building, Washington, D.C., hereinafter cited as the individual's name and military pension record.

46. Eli Ellenwood, Civil War letter. U.S. Army Military History Institute, Carlisle Barracks, Pennsylvania.

47. Peck, p. 40, 42; Charles B. Rice's pension record; *The Vermont Phoenix*, 8 August and 17 October 1861.

48. The Burlington Times, 10 August 1861; *Daily Free Press*, 30 July 1861.

49. *The Black River Tribune*, 1 November 1995; Ethan Allen Priest's military service record.

50. *Major-General Hiram G. Berry*, pp. 64–65.

51. *First Manassas Battlefield Map Study*, p. 72; Howard, p. 159; *Maine in the War for the Union*, p. 113; OR, vol. 2, p. 418.

52. *First Manassas Battlefield Map Study*, pp. 64–66; OR, vol. 2, p. 483.

53. Benedict, pp. 78–79; Howard, p. 159.

54. Benedict, p. 79.

55. Benedict, p. 79; Howard, p. 159; English Combatant, *Battle-Fields of the South, from Bull Run to Fredericksburg; with Sketches of Confederate Commanders, and Gossip of the Camps*

(Time-Life Books, reprint, 1984), p. 55, hereinafter cited as English Combatant.

56. Howard, pp. 156–160; OR, vol. 2, p. 418.

57. Elijah S. Brown letters.

58. Oramel G. Howe, Three Years in the Civil War, 1861–1864 (n. p., 1912), Vermont Historical Society, Montpelier, Vermont, hereinafter cited as Oramel Howe; *Historical Sketch of Co. I*, p. 5–6

59. *The Burlington Times*, 10 August 1861; Orlando S. Turner, Civil War letters, Vermont Historical Society, Montpelier, Vermont.

60. *Daily Free Press*, 29 July 1861; Peck, p. 51; *Rutland Daily Herald*, 29 July 1861.

61. Benedict, p. 79; OR vol. 2, p. 390.

62. Jubal A. Early, *War Memoirs* (Bloomington: Indiana University Press, 1960) , p. 23, hereinafter cited as Early.

63. Early, pp. 23–25.

64. Benedict, pp. 79–80.

65. Early, pp. 25–26.

66. Davis, pp. 237–238.

67. Benedict, pp. 80–81; Howard, p. 162.

68. *Daily Free Press*, 30 July 1861.

69. Peck, P. 38; Warren Gifford's military service record.

70. *Daily Free Press*, 31 July 1861; *Supplement to the Official Records*, Part II-Record of Events, Vol. 69, Serial No. 81, p. 239.

71. Benedict, p. 85.

72. Benedict, p. 85; *Daily Free Press*, 30 July 1861; *Rutland Daily Herald*, 3 August 1861.

73. Benedict, pp. 85–86; *Daily Free Press*, 30 July 1861; *Rutland Daily Herald*, 1 August 1861.

74. Benedict, p. 86.

75. Benedict, p. 84; *The Burlington Times*, 28 September 1861; Peck, pp. 40–41, 45, 61; *The Civil War Dictionary*, p. 101; Elisha Keables's military service record.

76. Benedict, p. 83; Peck, p. 53; *Daily Free Press*, 9, 10, 26 August 1861.

77. Patrick F. Flaherty's military service and pension record; Peck, p. 44.

78. Davis, p. 238.

79. Benedict, pp. 80–81; Chester K. Leach letters; Edson Emery diary; *Supplement to the Official Records*, Part II-Record of Events, Vol. 69, Serial No. 81, p. 239.

80. Benedict, p. 87; Chester K. Leach letters.

81. *Daily Free Press*, 30 July 1861; Lucius D. Savage diary.

82. Benedict, p. 88.

83. Benedict, p. 88; Howard, p.163; Lucius D. Savage diary.

84. OR, vol. 2, p. 371.

85. George W. Flanders's court-martial record, Records of the Office of the Judge Advocate General (Army), Record Group 153, National Archives Building, Washington, D.C, hereinafter cited as the individual's name and court-martial record.

86. Charles W. Goodwin's court-martial record.

87. Charles Quade's court-martial record.

88. George W. Flander's court-martial record; Charles W. Goodwin's court-martial record; Charles Quade's court martial record.

89. Sanford R. Barnes letters.

90. William H. Bond, Civil War Letters in the possession of Thomas R. Baine, hereinafter cited as William H. Bond letters.

91. *Burlington Weekly Sentinel*, 2 August 1861.

92. *Rutland Daily Herald*, 26 July 1861.

93. *Daily Free Press*, 29 July 1861; Curtis A. Coburn, Civil War letter, Special Collections, Bailey/Howe Library, University of Vermont, Burlington, Vermont.

94. *The Burlington Times*, 24 August 1861.

95. Benedict, p. 89; *Revised Regulations for the Army*, p. 38; *The Weekly Times*, 24 August 1861; *The Burlington Times*, 24 August 1861.

96. Benedict, pp. 89–90; OR, vol. 2, p. 419; *Daily Free Press*, 26 August 1861; *Rutland Daily Herald*, 3 August 1861.

97. Chester K. Leach letters.

3. He Died a Hero

1. Howard, pp. 166, 168–169; *Mr. Lincoln's Army*, pp. 61–64.

2. Chester K. Leach letters; Edson Emery diary.

3. Chester K. Leach letters; Edson Emery diary.

4. Barber, pp. 19, 109; *Green Mountain Freeman*, 7 August 1861; William H. Bond letters; William F. Murray's court-martial record.

5. Volney Fullam letters, Vermont Historical Society, Montpelier, Vermont; *Historical Sketch of Co. I*, p. 4.

6. Oramel Howe.

7. Benedict, pp. 90–91, 130–131; *The Civil War Dictionary*, pp. 932–935; James Hagemann, *The Heritage of Virginia* (West Chester, Pa.: Whitford Press, 1988), p. 42, hereinafter cited as *The Heritage of Virginia*; Noel G. Harrison, "Atop an Anvil," *The Virginia Magazine of History and Biography*, Spring 1998, p. 136. The name Chain Bridge is a misnomer. This bridge was actually a wooden truss structure resting on seven concrete piers. The name came from the previous bridge, built in 1810, which was a chain suspension bridge. It had been replaced with the wooden structure in 1852, but retained the name Chain Bridge, as it does today.

8. Benedict, pp. 130–131; William F. Smith, *Autobiography of Major General William F. Smith 1861–1864*, ed. Herbert M. Schiller (Dayton, Ohio: Morningside House, 1990), pp. 29–30, hereinafter cited as W. F. Smith.

9. *The Civil War Dictionary*, pp. 775–776.

10. Benedict, pp.235–236; W. F. Smith, p. 30.

11. Chester K. Leach letters; *Supplement to the Official Records*, Part II-Record of Events, Vol. 69, Serial No. 81, p. 240.

12. Barber, p. 114; Frobel, p. 176.

13. Chester K. Leach letters.

14. Benedict, p. 132.

15. *Tyler-Browns of Brattleboro*, p. 55.

16. Jerome Cutler, pp. 12–13.

17. Chester K. Leach letters; Edson Emery diary; Benedict, pp. 90–91, 129–130; *Supplement to the Official Records*, Part II-Record of Events, Vol. 69, Serial No. 81, p. 240; Charles C. Morey, Civil War diaries, U.S. Army Military History Institute, Carlisle Barracks, Pennsylvania, hereinafter cited as Charles C. Morey diaries.

18. Chester K. Leach letters; Edson Emery diary; *Supplement to the Official Records*, Part II-Record of Events, Vol. 69, Serial No. 81, p. 240.

19. *The Vermont Gazetteer*, pp. 706–708; Francis V. Randall's pension record.

20. William H. Jeffery, *Successful Vermonters (Lamoille, Franklin and Grand Isle Cities)* (East Burke, Vt.: Historical Publishing Co., 1907), pp. 57–58; Biographical Sketch Book, James M. Warner Post No. 4, Grand Army of the Republic, Noyes House Museum, Morristown Historical Society, Morrisville, Vermont.

21. Chester K. Leach letters; Edson Emery diary; *Supplement to the Official Records*, Part II-Record of Events, Vol. 69, Serial No. 81, p. 240; Lucius D. Savage diary; *Green Mountain Freeman*, 2 September 1861.

22. Chester K. Leach letters; Edson Emery diary.

23. Chester K. Leach letters; Edson Emery diary; Edwin N. Turner, Civil War letters, Vermont Historical Society, Montpelier, Vermont, hereinafter cited as Edwin N. Turner Letters; Charles C. Morey diaries.

24. Benedict, pp. 91–92; Edson Emery diary; *Daily Free Press*, 20 September 1861; *Supplement to the Official Records*, Part II-Record of Events, Vol. 69, Serial No. 81, p. 240.

25. George W. Megis, Civil War letters, Special Collections, Bailey/Howe Library, University of Vermont, Burlington, Vermont.

26. Benedict, p. 92; Edson Emery diary; *Daily Free Press*, 20 September 1861; Lucius D. Savage diary.

27. Benedict, pp. 92–93, 134–135; OR, vol. 3, pp. 167–185; Lucius D. Savage diary.

28. Benedict, p. 88.

29. Jerome Cutler, p. 38.

30. Benedict, p. 92; William E. Snow's military service record; *Daily Free Press*, 1 October 1861.

31. Benedict, p. 93.

32. *Daily Free Press*, 28 September 1861; *Green Mountain Freeman*, 27 September 1861.

33. Benedict, p. 90; *Green Mountain Freeman*, 27 September 1861.

34. Benedict, p. 93; OR, vol. 3, p. 611.

35. Walter A. Philips's military service record; *Green Mountain Freeman*, October 28 1861.

36. *Green Mountain Freeman*, October 28 1861; Walter A, Philips's military service record; Benedict, p. 94; Edwin N. Turner letters; Lucius D. Savage diary.

37. Benedict, p. 95; Walter A. Philips's military service record; *Green Mountain Freeman*, October 28 1861.

38. *Green Mountain Freeman*, October 28 1861; Edwin N. Turner letters; Benedict, pp. 93–94; Lucius D. Savage diary.

39. Edwin N. Turner letters.

40. Benedict, pp. 93–95; OR, vol. 5, pp. 217–220; *Green Mountain Freeman*, October 28 1861; Lucius D. Savage diary; *Green Mountain Freeman*, October 28 1861; Samuel P. Bates, *History of Pennsylvania Volunteers 1861–5*, vol. 2 (Harrisburg, Pa.: B. Singerly, State Printer, 1869), pp. 697, 788–789, hereinafter cited as Bates.

41. Bates, pp. 697, 788–789; Benedict, pp. 94–95; *Green Mountain Freeman*, 28 October 1861; Lucius D. Savage diary; Elisha S. Brown letters; Hiram H. Tilly, Civil War letter book, 1861–1864, *The Pearce Civil War Documents Collection*, Navarro College, Corsicana, Texas, pp. 13, 22, hereinafter cited as Hiram H. Tilly letter book.

42. Benedict, p. 94; *Green Mountain Freeman*, 28 October 1861; Walter A. Philips's military service record.

43. Benedict, p. 95; Edwin N. Turner letters; *Green Mountain Freeman*, 28 October 1861.

44. Benedict, p. 95, vol. 2, pp. 405–406; Chester K. Leach letters; *The Vermont Phoenix*, 6 February 1862; *Green Mountain Freeman*, 28 October 1861; *The Burlington Times*, 12 October 1861

45. Benedict, p. 95, vol.2, 720–730; Walter A. Philips's military service record; Abby Maria Hemenway, *The History of the Town of Montpelier, Including that of the Town of East Montpelier, for the First One Hundred and Two Years* (Montpelier, Vt.: Published by Miss A. M. Hemenway, 1882), pp. 521–522, hereinafter cited as History of Montpelier; *Pictorial History, Thirteenth Regiment, Vermont Volunteers*, p. 655; William Arba Ellis, ed., *Norwich University, 1819–1911: Her History, Her Graduates; Her Honor Roll* (Montpelier, Vt.: Capital City Press, 1911), p. 665.

46. Benedict, pp. 95–96; Henry L. Franklin, Civil War letters, Rare Book, Manuscript, and Special Collections Library, Duke University, Durham, North Carolina, hereinafter cited as Henry L. Franklin letters.

47. Benedict, p. 97; *The Civil War Dictionary*, p. 89.

48. W. F. Smith, p. 30.

49. Benedict, p. 96; *Supplement to the Official Records*, Part II-Record of Events, Vol. 69, Serial No. 81, p. 240.

50. Benedict, p. 96; Chester K. Leach letters; Edson Emery diary.

51. Benedict, pp. 96–97; *Rutland Daily Herald*, 13 November 1861, 11 February 1862.

52. Peck, p. 41; George P. Butterfield's court-martial record.

53. Peck, p. 41; Joel P. Butterfield's court-martial record.

54. *Green Mountain Freeman*, 17 December 1861.

55. Benedict, p. 210.

56. Emil and Ruth Rosenblatt, eds., *Hard Marching Every Day: The Civil Letters of Private Wilbur Fisk, 1861–1865* (Lawrence, Kans.: University Press of Kansas, 1992), p. xiv, hereinafter cited as Rosenblatt; *Green Mountain Freeman*, 17 December 1861.

57. Benedict, p. 100; Chester K. Leach letters.

58. *Lamoille Newsdealer*, 13 December, 1861.

59. Jerome Cutler, pp. 36.

60. Chester K. Leach letters; *Tyler-Browns of Brattleboro*, p. 62.

61. Benedict, pp. 98–100.

62. Benedict, p. 100; Henry Whiting's military service record.

63. Peck, pp. 33–63; *The Burlington Times*, 8 February 1862.

64. Benedict, p. 100; Peck, p. 32; *The Burlington Times*, 28 December 1861.

65. Benedict, pp. 237–238.

66. Benedict, pp. 237–240; OR, vol. 5, p. 92; *Green Mountain Freeman*, 6 December 1861.

67. Jerome Cutler, p. 29; Peck, p. 58.

68. Benedict, pp. 236–240; OR, vol. 5, pp. 108, 713; Peck, pp. 30–66; Chester K. Leach letters.

69. Hiram H. Tilly letter book, p. 37.

70. *Daily Free Press*, 8 March, 1862.

71. Benedict, p. 240; Chester K. Leach letters; *The Burlington Times*, 1 February 1862.

72. Chester K. Leach letters; Henry L. Franklin letters.

73. Wiley, p. 250; Ted Tunnell, "With Banner, Gun, and Sword: Marshall Harvey Twitchell and the 4th Vermont Regiment Go to War," *Vermont History 59*, no. 2, p. 80, hereinafter cited as With Banner, Gun and Sword.

74. Francis Flynn's court-martial and military service record; Charles C. Morey diaries.

75. Henry L. Franklin letters.

76. Jerome Cutler, pp. 25–26, 47.

77. Lucius D. Savage diary; Joseph E. Butterfield, Civil War diary, in the possession of Kenneth E. Proehl, hereinafter cited as Joseph E. Butterfield diary; Charles C. Morey diaries.

78. *Green Mountain Freeman*, 4 March 1862; Chester K. Leach letters; Charles M. Hapgood diary; Lucius D. Savage diary.

79. Benedict, pp. 100–101; Chester K. Leach letters; Charles M. Hapgood diary; *Daily Free Press*, 14 March 1862; *Rutland Daily Herald*, 13 March 1862; *The Burlington Times*, 1 February, 22 March 1862; James Morwood, *A Dictionary of Latin Words and Phrases* (Oxford: Oxford University Press, 1998), p. 65; *The Vermont Historical Gazetteer*, vol. 2, p. 204.

80. *Daily Free Press*, 14 March 1862; *Rutland Daily Herald*, 13 March 1862.

81. *Rutland Daily Herald*, 13 March 1862.

82. *Rutland Daily Herald*, 27 February 1862.

83. Hiram H. Tilly letter book, pp. 55, 67.

84. Frank J. Welcher, *The Union Army, 1861–1865, Organization and Operations*, vol. 1 (Bloomington: Indiana University Press, 1989), pp. 795–796, hereinafter cited as Welcher. Alexander S. Webb, *The Peninsula* (New York: Scribner's, 1881), pp. 22, 26, hereinafter cited as Webb.

85. Welcher, p. 796; Webb, pp. 18–24.

86. Welcher, p.796; Webb. pp. 24–28, 32.

4. "A Dam Failure"

1. Benedict, p. 241; *Green Mountain Freeman*, 1 April 1862; Charles M. Hapgood diary; *Supplement to the Official Records*, Part II-Record of Events, Vol. 69, Serial No. 81, p. 241.

2. Benedict, p. 241; *Green Mountain Freeman*, 1 April 1862; Chester K. Leach letters; *With Banner, Gun and Sword*, p. 83; *Supplement to the Official Records*, Part II-Record of Events, Vol. 69, Serial No. 81, p. 241; Henry L. Franklin letters.

3. Benedict, p. 242; *Green Mountain Freeman*, 1 Apr 1862; Lord, p. 279; Chester K. Leach letters.

4. *Green Mountain Freeman*, 1 April 1862; Charles M. Hapgood diary.

5. Benedict, p. 242; Charles M. Hapgood diary.

6. *Green Mountain Freeman*, 1 April 1862.

7. Benedict, p. 242; *Green Mountain Freeman*, 1 April 1862.

8. Welcher, p. 796; Webb, pp. 27–32.

9. Welcher, p. 796; Webb, p. 32.

10. *Green Mountain Freeman*, 1 April 1862.

11. *Green Mountain Freeman*, 1 Apr 1862; Chester K. Leach letters; Lucius Savage diary; Jerome Cutler, p. 48.

12. Benedict, p. 243; *Green Mountain Freeman*, 1 April 1862; Chester K. Leach letters; Charles M. Hapgood diary; *Supplement to the Official Records*, Part II-Record of Events, Vol. 69, Serial No. 81, p. 241; Elijah S. Brown letters.

13. Chester K. Leach letters.

14. Benedict, pp. 101, 243–244; *Green Mountain Freeman*, 29 April 1862; Chester K. Leach letters; *Supplement to the Official Records*, Part II-Record of Events, Vol. 69, Serial No. 81, p. 241; Joseph E. Butterfield diary.

15. Chester K. Leach letters; Charles M. Hapgood diary; *Supplement to the Official Records*, Part II-Record of Events, Vol. 69, Serial No. 81, p. 241; Lucius Savage diary.

16. Stephen W. Sears, *To the Gates of Richmond* (New York: Ticknor & Fields, 1992), p. 27, hereinafter cited as *To the Gates of Richmond*; Chester K. Leach letters; Charles M. Hapgood diary.

17. *To the Gates of Richmond*, p. 27; Chester K. Leach letters; Charles M. Hapgood diary.

18. Benedict, pp. 101, 243–244; *Green Mountain Freeman*, 29 April 1862; George T. Stevens, *Three Years in the Sixth Corps* (Albany: S. R. Gray, 1866; repr., Time-Life 1984), pp. 26–28. hereinafter cited as Stevens; Chester K. Leach letters; Charles M. Hapgood diary.

19. Benedict, pp. 101, 243–244; *Green Mountain Freeman*, 29 April 1862; Stevens, pp. 26–28; Chester K. Leach letters; *The Heritage of Virginia*, pp. 219; David W. Blight, ed., *When This Cruel War is Over: The Civil War Letters of Charles Harvey Brewester* (Amherst, Mass.: University of Massachusetts Press, 1992), p. 106, hereinafter cited as Blight; *Tyler-Browns of Brattleboro*, p. 72.

20. Benedict, p. 244; *Green Mountain Freeman*, 29 April 1862; Stevens, p. 29; Chester K. Leach letters; Charles M. Hapgood diary; *Daily Free Press*, 7 April 1862.

21. Benedict, pp. 244–245; Chester K. Leach letters; *Daily Free Press*, 7 April 1862.

22. Benedict, pp. 244–245; Chester K. Leach letters; *Daily Free Press*, 7 April 1862; *Supplement to the Official Records*, Part II-Record of Events, Vol. 69, Serial No. 81, p. 241.

23. *Daily Free Press*, 7 April 1862.

24. Benedict, pp. 244–245; *Green Mountain Freeman*, 29 April 1862; Stevens, pp. 29–30; Chester K. Leach letters; Charles M. Hapgood diary; *Supplement to the Official Records*, Part II-Record of Events, Vol. 69, Serial No. 81, p. 241.

25. Benedict, p. 245; Stevens, pp. 31–32, Chester K. Leach letters; Charles M. Hapgood diary; *Daily Free Press*, 7 April 1862; Lucius Savage diary; Jerome Cutler, p. 51.

26. Welcher, p. 797; OR, vol. 11, pp. 5–6.

27. Welcher, p. 797; OR, vol. 11, pp. 6–8.

28. OR, vol. 11, p. 9

29. OR, vol. 11, p. 9.

30. *Green Mountain Freeman*, 29 April 1862; Charles M. Hapgood diary.

31. Benedict, p. 245; *Green Mountain Freeman*, 29 April 1862; OR, vol. 11, pp. 300, 358; *Supplement to the Official Records*, Part II-Record of Events, Vol. 69, Serial No. 81, p. 242.

32. Benedict, p. 246; OR, vol. 11, pp. 300, 358; Blight, p. 109; Joseph K. Newell, *"Ours," Annals of the Tenth Regiment:*

Massachusetts Volunteers in the Rebellion (Springfield, Mass.: C.A. Nichols & Co., 1875), p. 80, hereinafter cited as Newell; Robert H. Rhodes, *All for the Union: A History of the 2nd Rhode Island Volunteer Infantry in the War of the Great Rebellion as told by the Diary of Elisha Hunt Rhodes* (New York: Orion, 1991), p. 62, hereinafter cited as Rhodes; Civil War letters of Orin Rugg (Internet *www.gunsites.com/77th/letters.html*), hereinafter cited as Rugg.

33. Benedict, p. 246; OR, vol. 11, pp. 300, 358; *Supplement to the Official Records*, Part II-Record of Events, Vol. 69, Serial No. 81, p. 242.

34. Webb, pp. 47–48.

35. Benedict, p. 245; *Green Mountain Freeman*, 29 April 1862; OR, vol. 11, pp. 300, 358; Rhodes, p. 62; *Supplement to the Official Records*, Part II-Record of Events, Vol. 69, Serial No. 81, p. 242.

36. Benedict, p. 246–247; OR, vol. 11, p. 258; *Supplement to the Official Records*, Part II-Record of Events, Vol. 69, Serial No. 81, p. 242; Stevens, p. 34.

37. Benedict, p. 247; *Green Mountain Freeman*, 29 April 1862; OR, vol. 11, pp. 358–359; William T. H. Brooks, Civil War letters, U.S. Army Military History Institute, Carlisle Barracks, Pennsylvania, herein after cited as W. T. H. Brooks letters.

38. OR, vol. 11, p. 358; Stevens, pp. 34, 36; W. T. H. Brooks letters.

39. Stevens, p. 34; *Green Mountain Freeman*, 29 April 1862.

40. OR, vol. 11, p. 359.

41. Benedict, pp. 247–248; Webb, pp. 48–50; OR, vol. 11, pp. 317–318, 359; English, p. 167; *To the Gates of Richmond*, pp. 37–38.

42. Welcher, pp. 797–798; *To the Gates of Richmond*, p. 46.

43. Benedict, p. 248; *Green Mountain Freeman*, 29 April 1862; Stevens, p. 37; Charles M. Hapgood diary.

44. OR, vol. 11, part 2, p. 10; *To the Gates of Richmond*, p. 39; Webb, p. 58.

45. Benedict, p. 248; Stevens, p. 38.

46. Benedict, pp. 248–249; Charles M. Hapgood diary; Lucius Savage diary.

47. Smith, p. 34.

48. Benedict, pp. 248–249; Stevens, p. 38; Charles M. Hapgood diary; Chester K. Leach letters; *Supplement to the Official Records*, Part II-Record of Events, Vol. 69, Serial No. 81, p. 242.

49. *Tyler-Browns of Brattleboro*, p. 72.

50. Welcher pp. 198–199.

51. Newell, p. 83; English, p. 173; Charles M. Hapgood diary; Blight, p. 111.

52. Richard Wheeler, *Sword Over Richmond* (New York: Harper & Row, 1986), pp. 137–138.

53. Chester K. Leach letters; Charles M. Hapgood diary.

54. Webb, p. 63; Benedict, p. 250; OR, vol. 11, pp. 416–418.

55. Webb, p. 64; Benedict, pp. 249–250; OR, vol. 11, p. 418.

56. OR, vol. 11, p. 372; Benedict, p. 251; *Daily Free Press*, 28 April 1862; Lucius Savage diary.

57. OR, vol. 11, p. 364; Benedict, p. 253.

58. OR, vol. 11, pp. 319, 372, 417; Benedict, pp. 251–252.

59. OR, vol. 11, p. 372; Benedict, p. 253.

60. OR, vol. 11, pp. 419, 421.

61. Benedict, p. 252; Chester K. Leach letters.

62. OR, vol. 11, p. 372; Benedict, p. 253.

63. Chester K. Leach letters; *Green Mountain Freeman*, 6 May 1862; Peck, p. 51; Erastus Worthen, Civil War letter, special collections, Bailey/Howe Library, University of Vermont, Burlington, Vermont; *Daily Free Press*, 7 May 1862; *Supplement to the Official Records*, Part II-Record of Events, Vol. 69, Serial No. 81, p. 242; Lucius Savage diary.

64. OR, vol. 11, pp. 372, 375; Benedict, pp. 254–256; Chester K. Leach letters; John E. Balzel, *Buck's Book; A View of the Third Vermont Infantry Regiment* (Burlington, Ill.: Balzer & Associates, 1993), pp. 27–28, hereinafter cited as *Buck's Book*.

65. OR, vol. 11, pp. 415, 417, 419–422; Benedict, p. 256.

66. OR, vol. 11, pp. 375; Benedict, pp. 256–258; *Buck's Book*, p. 30.

67. OR, vol. 11, pp. 364, 373, 376, 378; Benedict, pp. 259–264; *Green Mountain Freeman*, 6 May 1862.

68. Benedict, p. 264.

69. Benedict, pp. 264–265.

70. Benedict, pp. 264–266; Smith, p. 35; Albert C. Eisenberg, ed., "'The Third Vermont has won a name': Corporal Albert C. French's Account of the Battle of Lee's Mill," *Vermont History 49*, no. 4 (Fall 1981), p. 227; *Rutland Daily Herald*, 9 May 1862.

71. *Green Mountain Freeman*, 6 May 1862; *Tyler-Browns of Brattleboro*, p. 74.

72. OR, series I, vol. 11, part III, p. 450; Chester K. Leach letters; Rhodes, p. 63; *Daily Free Press*, 28 April 1862.

73. John S. Tyler letters.

74. Edwin N. Turner letters.

75. Chester K. Leach letters; *Green Mountain Freeman*, 6 May 1862; Charles M. Hapgood diary; *Daily Free Press*, 7 May 1862; John H. Savory's military pension record; Horace G. Ross's military pension record.

76. Benedict, pp. 267–268; Charles M. Hapgood diary; Chester K. Leach letters; Blight, p. 115.

77. *Buck's Book*, p. 32; Chester K. Leach letters; *Green Mountain Freeman*, 6 May 1862; Blight, p. 116.

78. *Buck's Book*, p. 32.

79. Peck, pp. 33–66; Chester K. Leach letters; Lucius Savage diary.

80. Peck, pp. 30–36; Benedict, p. 101; Chester K. Leach letters; Charles M. Hapgood diary; *Daily Free Press*, 7 May 1862; *Supplement to the Official Records*, Part II-Record of Events, Vol. 69, Serial No. 81, p. 242; *The Vermont Phoenix*, 12, 15 May 1862; Lucius Savage diary; Horace G. Ross's military pension record.

81. Benedict, p. 101; Chester K. Leach letters; Charles M. Hapgood diary; Horace G. Ross's military pension record.

82. Charles M. Hapgood diary; Benedict, p. 101; Lucius Savage diary.

83. Benedict, p. 268; *To the Gates of Richmond*, p. 61; Jeffery D. Wert, *General James Longstreet: The Confederacy's Most Controversial Soldier: A Biography* (New York: Simon & Shuster, 1994), p. 103, hereinafter cited as *General James Longstreet*.

84. *Green Mountain Freeman*, 27 May 1862.

85. Stevens, p. 47; Welcher, p. 801; OR, vol. 11, part 3, p.

140; *Supplement to the Official Records*, Part II-Record of Events, Vol. 69, Serial No. 81, p. 242.

86. *The Civil War Dictionary*, pp. 470, 676; Robins, pp. 42–43; *General James Longstreet*, p. 104.

87. Benedict, pp. 268–269; *Supplement to the Official Records*, Part II-Record of Events, Vol. 69, Serial No. 81, p. 242.

88. Benedict, pp. 268–269; Welcher, p. 801, Webb, p. 72.

89. Benedict, p. 269; Welcher, p. 801.

90. *To the Gates of Richmond*, p. 68, 70; Benedict, p. 269; Earl C. Hastings, Jr. and David Hastings. *A Pitiless Rain: The Battle of Williamsburg, 1862* (Shippensburg, Pa: White Mane, 1997), pp. 55–56, hereinafter cited as *A Pitiless Rain.*

91. Benedict, p. 270; *Green Mountain Freeman*, 27 May 1862; Charles M. Hapgood diary; Webb, p. 73.

92. Benedict, p. 271; *To the Gates of Richmond*, pp. 73–74; *Green Mountain Freeman*, 27 May 1862.

93. Benedict, p. 270; *The Civil War Dictionary*, p. 929; *To the Gates of Richmond*, p. 73; Welcher, p. 801; Webb, pp. 73–74; *A Pitiless Rain*, pp. 63–66, 71.

94. Benedict, p. 271; *To the Gates of Richmond*, pp. 73–74; Webb, p. 77.

95. Benedict, p. 272; *To the Gates of Richmond*, p. 74; Webb, p. 78.

96. Benedict, p. 272.

97. Benedict, p. 272.

98. Benedict, p. 273; Smith, p. 37.

99. Benedict, p. 273; *To the Gates of Richmond*, p. 81; Welcher, p. 802; *A Pitiless Rain*, p. 105.

100. Benedict, p. 274; *To the Gates of Richmond*, pp. 76–77.

101. *Green Mountain Freeman*, 27 May 1862; *To the Gates of Richmond*, p. 83; Kirk Rand, Civil War letters, Sallie Joy White Collection, Schlesinger Library, Radcliffe College, Cambridge, Massachusetts, hereinafter cited as Kirk Rand letters.

102. *To the Gates of Richmond*, p. 82; Webb, p. 81.

103. *To the Gates of Richmond*, p. 82; Benedict, p. 274; Webb, p. 81; Lucius Savage diary.

104. *Green Mountain Freeman*, 27 May 1862.

105. Chester K. Leach letters.

106. Lucius Savage diary.

5. "The Awfullist Thing That Ever Was"

1. Benedict, p. 275; Chester K. Leach letters; Charles M. Hapgood diary; Stevens, p. 58; *Daily Free Press*, 20 May 1862; Webb, p. 83.

2. *To the Gates of Richmond*, pp. 107–108; OR, vol. 11, part 2, p. 23, *Green Mountain Freeman*, 3 June 1862; Chester K. Leach letters; *Daily Free Press*, 20 May 1862.

3. Benedict, p. 275; Chester K. Leach letters; Charles M. Hapgood diary; *Green Mountain Freeman*, 3 June 1862; Stevens, p. 58.

4. Stevens, p. 60; Chester K. Leach letters; Lucius Savage diary; Kirk Rand letters.

5. OR, vol. 11, part 3, p. 24; Stevens, p. 60; Chester K. Leach letters.

6. Stevens, p. 60; Chester K. Leach letters; Charles M. Hapgood diary; *Green Mountain Freeman*, 3 June 1862; Lucius Savage diary; Kirk Rand letters.

7. *To the Gates of Richmond*, p. 104.

8. *To the Gates of Richmond*, p. 104.

9. Welcher, pp. 804–806; Webb, p. 84.

10. *Green Mountain Freeman*, 3 June 1862.

11. Benedict, pp. 276–278; Chester K. Leach letters; Charles M. Hapgood diary; Stevens, pp. 65–66; Smith, p. 39; Lucius Savage diary; *To the Gates of Richmond*, p. 110.

12. Welcher, p. 807.

13. Stevens, pp. 65–66; Benedict, p. 277.

14. Chester K. Leach letters; Charles M. Hapgood diary; Stevens, p. 67; Benedict, p. 279; *To the Gates of Richmond*, pp. 138; *The Civil War Dictionary*, p. 273.

15. Benedict, p. 102; Peck, pp. 30, 33; Chester K. Leach letters; George J. Stannard's military service record; Lucius Savage diary; Kirk Rand letters.

16. Benedict, p. 102; Peck, p. 31; *The Vermont Historical Gazetteer*, vol. 4, p. 632.

17. Benedict, p. 280; Chester K. Leach letters. Charles M. Hapgood diary; Lucius Savage diary.

18. Kirk Rand letters.

19. Benedict, pp. 280–281; Chester K. Leach letters; Charles M. Hapgood diary; Smith. P. 40.

20. Benedict, p. 281; Smith, p. 40; *Green Mountain Freeman*, 1 July 1862; Chester K. Leach letters; Lucius Savage diary.

21. William Clark's military pension record; Peck, p. 51.

22. Lucius Savage diary; John S. Tyler letters.

23. Chester K. Leach letters; Lucius Savage diary.

24. Peck, p. 53; David L. Sharpley's military pension record; *The Burlington Times*, 5 July 1862.

25. Chester K. Leach letters; *History of Montpelier*, p. 521; *The Vermont Phoenix*, 19 June 1862; Cause of death ledger in the town clerk's office, Montpelier, Vermont.

26. *The Civil War Dictionary*, pp. 540–541.

27. *The Civil War Dictionary*, p. 321.

28. *To the Gates of Richmond*, pp. 216–217; Benedict, p. 284.

29. Benedict, pp. 284–285; *Green Mountain Freeman*, 29 July 1862; *Battles and Leaders*, p. 367; Charles M. Hapgood diary; Smith, p. 41;Welcher, p. 821.

30. Benedict, pp. 284–285; *The Civil War Dictionary*, p. 325; *Green Mountain Freeman*, 29 July 1862; Charles M. Hapgood diary.

31. Benedict, pp. 287–288; Smith, p. 42; Chester K. Leach letters; Charles M. Hapgood diary; Lucius Savage diary; *Tyler-Browns of Brattleboro*, p. 81.

32. Peck, p. 42.

33. Benedict, p. 289; OR, vol. 11, part 2, pp. 463–464; Lucius Savage diary.

34. Stevens, p. 95; *Green Mountain Freeman*, 29 July 1862; Lucius Savage diary; Kirk Rand letters.

35. Benedict, p. 289; OR, vol. 11, part 2, p. 464; Kirk Rand letters.

36. Stevens, pp. 100–101; Smith, p. 43; OR, vol. 11, part 2, p. 464; *Battles and Leaders*, vol. 2, p. 272.

37. Benedict, pp. 291–292; Stevens, p. 101; *To the Gates of Richmond*, pp. 269–272; OR, vol. 11, part 2, p. 464.

38. Benedict, p. 292; *To the Gates of Richmond*, pp. 270–272.

39. Benedict, p. 293; OR, vol. 11, part 2, pp. 477–478.

40. Benedict, p. 293; OR, vol. 11, part 2, pp. 477–478, 732; Charles M. Hapgood diary.

41. Benedict, p. 295; OR, vol. 11, part 2, pp. 477–478.

42. Daniel M. Priest's military pension record; Peck, p. 35.

43. James H. Shippee's military pension record; Peck, pp. 36, 454.

44. Benedict, p. 295; OR, vol. 11, part 2, pp. 477–478; Charles M. Hapgood diary; Lucius Savage diary.

45. Benedict, pp. 296–298; OR, vol. 11, part 2, pp. 477–478; *Green Mountain Freeman*, 29 July 1862.

46. Benedict, p. 298.

47. Benedict, pp. 298–299.

48. Charles C. Dodge's military pension record; Peck, p. 51; Elijah S. Brown letters; Biographical Sketch Book, James M. Warner Post No. 4, Grand Army of the Republic, Morristown Historical Society, Morristown, Vermont.

49. Henry L. Harris's military pension record, Peck, p. 51.

50. Harlan P. Stoddard's military pension record; Peck, p. 52.

51. OR, Vol. 11, part 2, p. 721; William H. Clark's military pension record.

52. Vernon D. Rood's military pension record; Peck, p. 59; *The Vermont Historical Gazetteer*, vol. 2, p. 204.

53. Lucius Savage diary.

54. Benedict, p. 299.

55. Benedict, pp. 299, 301; OR, vol. 11, part 2, p. 721.

56. Benedict, pp. 299–300; Elijah S. Brown letters; W. T. H. Brooks letters.

57. Stevens, p. 103.

58. Benedict, pp. 181, 303; OR, vol. 11, part 2, p. 477.

59. Lucius Savage diary.

60. Lucius Savage diary; Peck, p. 52.

61. Benedict, p. 300.

62. Oric R. Ward, civil war letter, from the private collection of Ed Italo; *Historical Sketch of Co. I.*, p. 16.

63. Benedict, p. 303; OR, vol. 11, part 2, p. 464; Charles M. Hapgood diary.

64. Benedict, p. ; Stevens, pp. 102–103; *Tyler-Browns of Brattleboro*, p. 82.

65. Smith, p. 45.

66. Benedict, pp. 304; Welcher, p. 824.

67. Benedict, pp. 304–305; Stevens, p. 104–105; Smith, pp. 45–46; *To the Gates of Richmond*, pp. 285–286; Charles M. Hapgood diary; Chester K. Leach letters.

68. *Tyler-Browns of Brattleboro*, p. 82.

69. Benedict, pp. 305–306; *Daily Free Press*, 2 August 1862; Oramel Howe; *Tyler-Browns of Brattleboro*, p. 82.

70. Benedict, p. 307; Smith, p. 46; Charles M. Hapgood diary.

71. Benedict, p. 308; *Green Mountain Freeman*, 29 July 1862; Smith, p. 47; OR, vol. 11, part 2, p. 464.

72. Benedict, 308; *Green Mountain Freeman*, 29 July 1862; Charles M. Hapgood diary; OR, vol. 11, part 2, p. 464; Welcher, p. 829; Oramel Howe; *The Civil War Dictionary*, p. 507.

73. Benedict, pp. 309–310; *Green Mountain Freeman*, 29 July 1862; OR, vol. 11, partl2, pp. 72, 464; Kirk Rand letters.

74. Benedict, pp. 309–310; *Green Mountain Freeman*, 29 July 1862; Smith, p. 49; *To the Gates of Richmond*, p. 338; OR, vol. 11, part 2, pp. 72, 464; Gunnison's military pension record.

75. *To the Gates of Richmond*, pp. 338–339; Heritage, pp. 114–115; Paul Wilstach, *Tidewater Virginia* (New York: Tudor, 1945), p. 141, hereinafter cited as Wilstach; D. Gardiner Tyler, *A History Pictorial Review of Charles City County, Virginia* (Expert Graphics, 1990), p. 58, hereinafter cited as Gardiner Tyler.

76. *Battles and Leaders*, p. 427; Kirk Rand letters.

77. Benedict, p. 311; Chester K. Leach letters; *To the Gates of Richmond*, p. 340; *Battles and Leaders*, pp. 427–428; OR, vol. 11, part 2, p. 464.

78. Benedict, p. 311; *Battles and Leaders*, p. 428; Chester K. Leach letters.

79. *Heritage of Virginia*, p. 264; Chester K. Leach letters; Hollis Montegue letters.

80. Jerome Cutler, p. 62.

81. Benedict, p. 102; Peck, p. 30,31; *Daily Free Press*, 2 August 1862.

82. Benedict, p. 311; Chester K. Leach; Hollis Montegue letters; *Mr. Lincoln's Army*, p. 147.

83. Chester K. Leach letters; Charles C. Morey Diaries; Peck, pp. 47; George E. Allen's military service record.

84. Charles C. Morey diaries.

85. Ibid.

86. Chester K. Leach letters; Hollis Montegue letters.

87. Charles C. Morey diaries.

88. *To the Gates of Richmond*, p. 348.; Chester K. Leach letters.

89. Oric R. Ward.

90. Warren Leslie; *Historical Sketch of Co.* I, p. 16; Peck, p. 61.

91. *To the Gates of Richmond*, p. 348.

92. Warren S. Leslie.

93. Oric R. Ward.

94. Benedict, p. 311.

95. *Daily Free Press*, 30 July 1862; Peck, pp. 34, 38; Jerome Draper's military service record.

96. Charles H. Joyce's military service record.

97. Charles H. Joyce's military service record.

98. *Harper's Pictorial History of the Civil War*, p. 380; *To the Gates of Richmond*, p. 351–354; *Mr. Lincoln's Army*, pp. 155–156.

99. Kirk Rand letters.

100. *Harper's Pictorial History of the Civil War*, p. 380; OR, vol. 11, p. 74

101. Chester K. Leach letters; Peck, pp. 46, 63.

102. *To the Gates of Richmond*, pp. 354–355; OR, vol. 11, pp. 77–78; Harper's, p. 380; *Mr. Lincoln's Army*, p. 156.

103. Chester K. Leach letters.

104. Chester K. Leach letters; Charles M. Hapgood diary; Benedict, p. 312.

105. Chester K. Leach letters; Benedict, p. 312.

106. Chester K. Leach letters; Benedict, p. 312.

107. Kirk Rand letters.

108. Chester K. Leach letters; Charles M. Hapgood diary; Benedict, p. 313; Kirk Rand letters.

6. "The Greatest Battle Yet Fought"

1. *Mr. Lincoln's Army*, p. 28, *To the Gates of Richmond*, pp. 349–350; *The Civil War Dictionary*, p. 101, *Battles and Leaders*, vol. 1, p. 458.

2. *Battles and Leaders*, vol.1, p. 449; *The War Dictionary*, pp. 101, 659.

3. *To the Gates of Richmond*, pp. 349–350; *The Civil War Dictionary*, p. 108; Douglas S. Freeman, *R. E. Lee: A Biography* (New York: Charles Scribner's Sons, 1936), vol. 2, pp. 257–258, hereinafter cited as *R. E. Lee*.

4. *The Civil War Dictionary*, p. 102; *Battles and Leaders*, vol.1, p. 459; *R. E. Lee*, vol. 2, pp. 261–266, 271–272; *To the Gates of Richmond*, p. 350.

5. *The Civil War Dictionary*, p. 102; *R. E. Lee*, vol. 2, pp. 277–288.

6. *The Civil War Dictionary*, pp. 102–103; *R. E. Lee*, vol. 2, pp. 292–310.

7. *The Civil War Dictionary*, p. 103; *R. E. Lee*, vol. 2, pp. 304–310.

8. *The Civil War Dictionary*, p. 103.

9. *The Civil War Dictionary*, pp. 103–104; *R. E. Lee*, vol. 2, pp. 312–316.

10. *The Civil War Dictionary*, pp. 104–105; *R. E. Lee*, vol. 2, pp. 317–328.

11. Benedict, p. 131; Chester K. Leach letters; Charles M. Hapgood diary; *Battles and Leaders*, vol. 1, p. 539.

12. Benedict, p. 131; Chester K. Leach letters; Charles M. Hapgood diary.

13. Benedict, p. 316; Peck, pp. 30–66; Warren S. Leslie, Civil War letters, Special Collections, Bailey/Howe Library, University of Vermont, Burlington, Vermont.

14. Benedict, p. 316; *Battles and Leaders*, vol. 1, p. 540; Chester K. Leach letters; Charles M. Hapgood diary.

15. Benedict, p. 316; *Battles and Leaders*, vol. 1, p. 540; Charles M. Hapgood diary.

16. *Green Mountain Freeman*, 19 September 1862.

17. Stevens, p. 130.

18. Benedict, p. 316; Stevens, pp. 130–131; *Battles and Leaders*, vol. 1, p. 540.

19. Benedict, pp. 316–317; *Battles and Leaders*, vol. 1, p. 540.

20. OR, vol. 11, p. 98.

21. *Tyler-Browns of Brattleboro*, p. 92.

22. Benedict, p. 317.

23. Benedict, p. 317; *R. E. Lee*, vol. 2, pp. 350–354; Timothy J. Reese, *Sealed With Their Lives: The Battle for Crampton's Gap, Burkittsville, Maryland, September 14, 1862* (Baltimore: Butternut and Blue, 1998), pp. 2–7, hereinafter cited as Reese.

24. Benedict, p. 317; Chester K. Leach letters; Charles M. Hapgood diary.

25. Benedict, pp. 317–318; Chester K. Leach letters.

26. *R. E. Lee*, vol. 2, pp. 359–364; *Mr. Lincoln's Army*, pp. 211–215; William D. Henderson, *12th Virginia Infantry* (Lynchburg, Va.: H. E. Howard, Inc., 1984), p. 33, hereinafter cited as *12th Virginia Infantry*.

27. Benedict, p. 318; Chester K. Leach letters.

28. Henry Whiting's military service record; Charles H. Joyce's military service record; OR, vol. 19, part 2, p. 408; Chester K. Leach letters.

29. Auburn T. Patch's court-martial file; Peck, p. 39.

30. *Mr. Lincoln's Army*, p. 221; Benedict, p. 319; OR, vol. 19, p. 45.

31. OR, vol. 19, pp. 45–46.

32. OR, vol. 19, pp. 370, 374, 380; Stephen W. Sears, *Landscape Turned Red: The Battle of Antietam* (Boston: Houghton Mifflin, 1983), pp. 145–146, hereinafter cited as *Landscape Turned Red*; Reese, pp. 42–44.

33. Benedict, p. 320; *Landscape Turned Red*, p. 145; *Sealed With Their Lives*, p. 148.

34. D. Archie Ridout, "War at my Front Door," *Civil War Times Illustrated 37*, no. 3 (June 1998), pp.18–22; *12th Virginia Infantry*, p. 35; OR, vol. 19, pp. 826, 853; Reese, pp. 45–51, 73.

35. Reese, p. 54; OR, vol. 19, p. 853, 881.

36. Benedict, p. 320; OR, vol. 19, pp. 875–876; Reese, pp. 54, 58, 69–72, 95.

37. *Landscape Turned Red*, p. 146; OR, vol. 19, pp. 826, 873, 876, 881; Reese, pp. 72–85.

38. Benedict, pp. 320–321; OR, vol. 19, p. 380; Reese, pp. 81–128.

39. Benedict, p. 321; Oramel Howe; OR, vol. 19, part 2, pp. 375, 401, 407–408; Chester K. Leach letters; Reese, p. 95.

40. Benedict, p. 322; Chester K. Leach letters.

41. Benedict, pp. 321–322; *Landscape Turned Red*, p. 147; OR, vol. 19, pp. 375–376, 401, 408; Reese, pp. 95, 102–103.

42. John Conline, "Recollections of the Battle of Antietam and the Maryland Campaign," in *War Papers Read Before The Michigan Commandery of the Military Order of the Loyal Legion of the United States*, vol.2. (Detroit: James H. Stone & Co., 1898), p. 114–115, hereinafter cited as Conline; Reese, p. 102–103.

43. Conline, pp. 114–115; Reese, p. 102–103.

44. Benedict, p. 322; *Landscape Turned Red*, p. 147; Reese, pp. 128–132, 150; Conline, p. 115.

45. Benedict, p. 322; OR, vol. 19, p. 408; *Landscape Turned Red*, p. 148; Conline, p. 115; Reese, p. 150.

46. Benedict, p. 322; OR, vol. 19, pp. 401, 408; Conline, p. 115; Reese; p. 150.

47. OR, vol. 19, p. 870; Reese, pp. 115–116, 126–128.

48. Benedict, p. 322; OR, vol. 19, p. 408; Reese, p. 151–152.

49. Benedict, p. 322; *Landscape Turned Red*, p. 148; OR, vol. 19, pp. 827, 870, 873; Reese, pp. 159–166.

50. Reese, pp. 117, 162–163, 165.

51. Benedict, pp. 322–323, Chester K. Leach letters, *Vermont Phoenix*, 2 October 1862; OR, vol. 19, pp. 401, 408; Chester K. Leach letters; Hiram H. Tilly letter book, p. 104; Kirk Rand letters; Conline, p. 115; Reese, p. 166; Jerome Cutler, p. 72.

52. Benedict, p. 323; *Landscape Turned Red*, p. 149; OR, vol. 19, p. 408; Reese, p. 173.

53. Benedict, p. 323; *Landscape Turned Red*, p, 149; OR, vol. 19, p. 376; Reese, pp. 269, 302–303.

54. *Landscape Turned Red*, p, 142.

55. Benedict, p. 324; Reese, p. 174.

56. Benedict, p. 325.

57. Ibid.

58. Benedict, p. 326; OR, vol. 19, p. 376.

59. *Mr. Lincoln's Army*, p. 266; *Landscape Turned Red*, p. 180.

60. Benedict, p. 326; *Landscape Turned Red*, pp. 202–215.

61. Benedict, p. 326.

62. *Mr. Lincoln's Army*, pp. 291–292; *Landscape Turned Red*, p. 236.

63. *Mr. Lincoln's Army*, pp. 291–294; *Landscape Turned Red*, pp. 235–242.

64. *Mr. Lincoln's Army*, pp. 294–297; *Landscape Turned Red*, pp. 244–247.

65. *Mr. Lincoln's Army*, pp. 290–298.

66. Benedict, p. 326; OR, vol. 19, pp. 376, 402, 408; *Landscape Turned Red*, p. 256.

67. Benedict, pp. 326–327; *Mr. Lincoln's Army*, p. 299; OR, vol. 19, pp. 376–377, 402, 408; Conline, p. 117. Conline estimated the distance to the sunken road as 150 yards, but the Antietam National Battlefield historical marker for the Vermont Brigade put the distance as 170. I chose to use the latter.

68. Benedict, pp. 326–327; *Mr. Lincoln's Army*, p. 299; OR, vol. 19, pp. 376–377, 402, 408; *Vermont Phoenix*, 2 October 1862; Conline, p. 117.

69. Chester K. Leach letters.

70. George Pierce's military pension record; Oliver Drake's military service and pension record; Peck, pp. 41, 64; Grand Army of the Republic records, Putney Historical Society, Putney, Vermont; Lorenzo J. Marks's military pension record; Dorr Blood's military service record.

71. Benedict, pp. 328–329.

72. *Mr. Lincoln's Army*, p. 299.

73. Frances H. Kennedy, ed. *The Civil War Battlefield Guide* (Boston: Houghton Mifflin, 1990), pp. 82–85, hereinafter cited as *The Civil War Battlefield Guide.*

74. Benedict, pp. 329–330; Oramel Howe.

75. Benedict, p. 330; Oramel Howe.

76. *Vermont Phoenix*, 2 October 1862.

77. Hiram H. Tilly letter book, p. 106.

78. Benedict, p. 330; *Battles and Leaders*, vol. 2, pp. 600, 603.

79. Benedict, p. 330; Hiram H. Tilly letter book, p. 107.

80. Benedict, pp. 330–331; Oramel Howe; *Vermont Phoenix*, 2 October 1862.

81. Jerome Cutler, p. 70.

82. Benedict, p. 331; Charles M. Hapgood diary.

83. Kelly A. Nolin, ed., *S. E. and S. M. Pingree Civil War Letters, 1861-1864*, Vermont Historical Society, Montpelier, Vermont, hereinafter cited as either Stephen E. Pingree or Samuel M. Pingree letters.

84. Benedict, p. 331.

85. Chester K. Leach letters.

86. Chester K. Leach letters.

87. Charles Tillison, Civil War letters. Vermont Historical Society, Montpelier, Vermont.

88. Benedict, p. 331; *Landscape Turned Red*, p. 327; OR, vol. 19, p. 52.

89. *Landscape Turned Red*, p. 328; OR, vol. 19, pp. 52–53.

90. Benedict, pp. 331–332; Stephen M. Pingree letters.

91. Benedict, p. 332; Charles M. Hapgood diary.

92. Benedict, p. 332; Irs S. Dodd, *The Song of the Rappahannock* (New York: Dodd, Mead, 1898), p. 34, hereinafter cited as *The Song of the Rappahannock.*

93. *Tyler-Browns of Brattleboro*, p. 99; Peck, p. 674.

94. *Tyler-Browns of Brattleboro*, pp. 120, 200.

95. Benedict, p. 332; Chester K. Leach letters; Charles M. Hapgood diary.

96. Charles C. Morey letters.

97. Chester K. Leach letters.

98. Benedict, p. 334; Chester K. Leach letters; Charles M. Hapgood diary, Peck, p. 36; Edward J. Stackpole, *Drama on the Rappahannock: The Fredericksburg Campaign* (Harrisburg: Military Service Publishing Co., 1957), p. 28, hereinafter cited as *The Fredericksburg Campaign*; *Mr. Lincoln's Army*, p. 327.

99. Benedict, p. 334; Chester K. Leach letters; Charles M. Hapgood diary.

100. *For the Glory of the Union*, p. 91.

101. Benedict, p. 334; Kirk Rand Letters.

102. Benedict, p. 334; Chester K. Leach letters; Charles M. Hapgood diary.

103. *For the Glory of the Union*, p. 92.

104. Ibid. p. 93.

105. Ralph Ditty's court-martial record; *The Revised Regulations for the Army, 1861.*

106. Benedict, p. 334; *Landscape Turned Red*, pp. 323–324, 340–342; *Mr. Lincoln's Army*, pp. 325–328; T. Harry Williams, *Lincoln and his Generals* (New York: Alfred A. Knopf, 1952), p. 179; hereinafter cited as *Lincoln and his Generals.*

107. Benedict, p. 336; Stevens, pp. 163–164; Chester K. Leach letters; *Mr. Lincoln's Army*, p. 329.

108. *Landscape Turned Red*, pp. 323–324

7. "Another Good Defeat"

1. Benedict, pp. 334–335; Stevens, p. 165.

2. Benedict, p. 335.

3. Ibid., pp. 335–336.

4. Benedict, p. 336; *The Fredericksburg Campaign*, pp. 65–66.

5. Benedict, p. 336; Chester K. Leach letters; Charles M. Hapgood diary.

6. Chester K. Leach letters.

7. Carroll R. Tarbell, *The History of Mount Holly* (Publisher unknown, 1987), p. 266–267; Hiram H. Tilly letter book, pp. 111, 114, 138; Peck, p. 53.

8. Hiram H. Tilly letter book, pp. 115–116.

9. Kirk Rand letters.

10. *Battles and Leaders*, vol. 2, pp. 70–72, 107.

11. Benedict, pp. 337–338; Chester K. Leach letters; Charles M. Hapgood diary.

12. Lauriston L. Stone, Civil War letters. Special Collections, Bailey/Howe Library, University of Vermont, Burlington, Vermont, hereinafter cited as Lauriston L. Stone letters.

13. *The Fredericksburg Campaign*, pp. 123–124, 129–132; Bruce Catton, *Army of the Potomac: Glory Road* (Garden City, N.Y.: Doubleday, 1952), pp. 34, 40–41, hereinafter cited as *Glory Road.*

14. Benedict, pp. 338–339; *The Fredericksburg Campaign*, pp. 151–152.

15. Benedict, pp. 341–342; OR, vol. 21, pp. 148–149; Stevens, pp. 166–167; *The Civil War Battlefield Guide*, p. 97.

16. Benedict, pp. 341–342; *The Fredericksburg Campaign*, pp. 133–138; *Glory Road*, pp. 35–38; *The Civil War Battlefield Guide*, pp. 97–100.

17. Benedict, p. 342; *The Fredericksburg Campaign*, pp. 133–138; *The Civil War Battlefield Guide*, p. 100.

18. Benedict, p. 342; Stevens, p. 169.

19. Benedict, p. 342; Stevens, p. 169.

20. OR, vol. 21, p. 449.

21. Ibid., p. 523.

22. Benedict, p. 342; OR, vol. 21, pp. 532–533.

23. OR, vol. 21, pp. 449–450; *The Fredericksburg Campaign*, p. 280; *The Civil War Battlefield Guide*, pp. 100–102.

24. OR, vol. 21, p. 530.

25. Benedict, p. 343; OR, vol. 21, p. 533; Oramel Howe.

26. Henry P. Diamond's and Chauncy S. Shonio's court-martial record.

27. Henry Holden's military pension record; Peck, p. 35.

28. George G. Center's military pension record; Peck, p. 43.

29. OR, vol. 21, p. 530.

30. Edwin N. Turner letters letters.

31. Henry C. Smith's military pension record; Peck, p. 39.

32. Henry G. Hemenway's military pension record; Peck, p. 61; *Historical Sketch of Co. I*, p. 10.

33. William Sinnott's military service record and military pension record. Sinnott family history provided by Robert Norris; *Historical Sketch of Co. I*, p.22.

34. Cyrill Wheeler's military pension record; *History of Montpelier*, p. 523; Peck, p. 62; *Historical Sketch of Co. I*, p. 22.

35. Alden C. Loomis's military pension record; Peck, p. 58.

36. Richard Dodge's military pension record; Peck, p. 44, 596; *The Vermont Historical Gazetteer*, vol. 4, p. 341.

37. John Q. A. Ditty's military pension record; Peck, p. 51, 668.

38. Stevens, p. 171; *The Civil War Dictionary*, p. 879.

39. George W. Doty's military pension record; Peck, p. 51; Biographical Sketch Book, James M. Warner Post No. 4, Grand Army of the Republic, Noyes House Museum, Morristown Historical Society, Morrisville, Vermont.

40. Thomas J. Jaquith's military pension record; Peck, p. 61; *Historical Sketch of Co. I*, p.10.

41. Warren S. Leslie's military service record.

42. Cornelius Nye, Civil War letters, Vermont Historical Society, Montpelier, Vermont, hereinafter cited as Cornelius Nye letters.

43. Charles C. Hartwell's military pension records; Peck, p. 45.

44. Storrs W. Start, Civil War letters, Fredericksburg and Spottsylvania National Military Park, Fredericksburg, Va., hereinafter cited as Storrs W. Start letters.

45. Joseph E. Butterfield diary.

46. Benedict, p. 345.

47. Hiram H. Tilly letter book, p. 125.

48. *The Fredericksburg Campaign*, pp. 108–110; *The Civil War Battlefield Guide*, p. 103.

49. *The Fredericksburg Campaign*, pp. 199–218; *The Civil War Battlefield Guide*, p. 103.

50. Benedict, p. 346; OR, vol. 21, p. 530.

51. Joseph E. Butterfield diary.

52. Benedict, p. 346; OR, vol. 21, p. 523; *The Civil War Battlefield Guide*, p. 103; Orin T. Leach, Personal Reminiscences of the Civil War, (n. p., n. d.), p. 14, Special Collections, Bailey/Howe Library, University of Vermont, Burlington, Vermont, hereinafter cited as *Personal Reminiscences of the Civil War*.

53. Benedict, p. 346; Chester K. Leach letters, Charles M. Hapgood diary.

54. Chester K. Leach letters, Charles M. Hapgood diary.

55. Henry P. Diamond's and Chauncy S. Shonio's court-martial record.

56. John Gregory, *1776–1876 Centennial Proceedings and Historical Incidents of the Early Settlers of Northfield, Vermont, With Biographical Sketches of Prominent Business Men Who have been and are now Residents of the Town* (Montpelier, Vt.: Argus and Patriot Book and Job Printing House, 1878), pp. 164–167; Walter Hill Crockett, *Vermont the Green Mountain State* (New York: Century History Company, Inc., 1923), pp. 370–371.

57. *Tyler-Browns of Brattleboro*, p. 106.

58. Benedict, p. 347; *Glory Road*, pp. 84–85.

59. Benedict, p. 347; *Glory Road*, p. 86; Stevens, p. 175.

60. Chester K. Leach letters.

61. Hiram H. Tilly letter book, p. 129.

62. Benedict, pp. 347–348; Stevens, p. 176; William H. Bond letters.

63. Chester K. Leach letters.

64. Benedict, p. 348; Stevens, p. 178.

65. William H. Bond's military service record; William H. Bond letters; Philip Halpin, Civil War diary (1863) (typescript). Pittsford Historical Society, Pittsford, Vermont, hereinafter cited as Philip Halpin diary; Philip Halpin's military service record; Peck, p. 61; *Historical Sketch of Co. I*, p. 20.

66. Benedict, pp. 104, 348; Chester K. Leach letters; William H. Bond letters; Jerome Cutler, p. 83.

67. Joseph C. Felton, Civil War letters, Felton Collection, The Lincoln Memorial Shrine, Redlands, Calif., hereinafter cited as Joseph C. Felton letters; Joseph C. Felton's military service record.

68. Benedict, pp. 348–349.

69. *The Civil War Dictionary*, p. 409; *Lincoln and his Generals*, p. 213.

70. Jerome Cutler, p. 88.

71. Joseph E. Butterfield diary.

72. James W. Bromley letters.

73. William H. Bond letters.

74. *Glory Road*, p. 98; *Reveille in Washington*, p. 226; William H. Bond letters.

75. *Glory Road*, p. 98; OR, vol. 25, part 2, p. 73.

76 . Bruce Catton, *Reflections on the Civil War* (New York: Promontory Press, 1998), pp. 64–65, hereinafter cited as *Reflections on the Civil War*.

77. Rosenblatt, pp. viii-ix; Wilbur Fisk, Civil War diaries, 1863 and 1864 (typescript), Library of Congress, Washington, D.C., hereinafter cited as Wilbur Fisk diaries.

78. William H. Bond letters; Chester K. Leach letters.

79. *Glory Road*, p. 102.
80. Chester K. Leach letters.
81. *The Civil War Dictionary*, pp. 74–75, 172; *Reflections on the Civil War*, pp. 56–58.
82. William H. Bond letters.
83. *Glory Road*, pp. 142–143; OR, vol. 25, part 2, pp. 57, 491–492.
84. Jerome Cutler, p. 87.
85. Joseph C. Felton letters.
86. Chester K. Leach letters.
87. Wilbur Fisk diaries.
88. William H. Bond letters.
89. Chester K. Leach letters.
90. Benedict, p. 332; Chester K. Leach letters; *Green Mountain Freeman*, 9 May 1863; Alan A. Siegel, *For the Glory of the Union: Myth, Reality, and the Media in Civil War New Jersey* (Rutherford, N.J.: Fairleigh Dickinson University Press, 1984), p. 128, hereinafter cited as *For the Glory of the Union*.
91. Chester K. Leach letters.
92. Wilbur Fisk diary.
93. *Green Mountain Freeman*, 9 May 1863.
94. Chester K. Leach letters.
95. Lawson M. Perkins's court-martial record, Peck, p. 156–157.
96. *The Civil War Dictionary*, pp. 775–776; Stevens, pp. 186–187; Smith, pp. 66–67.
97. *The Civil War Dictionary*, p. 730; Stevens, pp. 186–187; Benedict, pp. 351–352.
98. Benedict, pp. 105–106; Henry Whiting's military service record.
99. Benedict, p. 106; F. B. Heitman, *Historical Register of the United States Army from its Organization: September 29, 1789, to September 29, 1889* (Washington, D.C.: The National Tribune, 1890), p. 691.
100. Stephen E. Pingree letters.
101. Chester K. Leach letters.
102. Benedict, pp. 106–107; *Sherman* pp. 92–93; Hiram Carelton, *Genealogical and Family History of the State of Vermont* (New York: Lewis Publishing Co., 1903), pp. 217–218; William Gedney, compiler, *Descendants of Henry Walbridge who Married Anna Amos, Dec. 25, 1688 at Preston, Connecticut* (Litchfield, Conn.: Press of Franklin Company, Phila., 1898), pp. 230–231.
103. Benedict, pp. 107, 112; *Historical Sketch of Co. I*, p. 4.
104. Benedict, p. 107; Wilbur Fisk diary; *The Vermont Gazetteer*, vol. 3, pp. 153–154.
105. Peck, pp. 40, 53, 59–60; *The Green Mountain Freeman*, 31 May 1863.
106. Benedict, p. 352; Chester K. Leach letters.
107. Lewis A. Grant's military pension record.
108. *Green Mountain Freeman*, 21 April 1863.
109. Joseph C. Felton letters.
110. Wilbur Fisk diaries.
111. Ibid.
112. OR, vol. 25, part 2, pp. 152, 471; *The Civil War Dictionary*, pp. 37–38.
113. William H. Bond letters.
114. Daniel K. Stickney's military pension record.
115. Chester K. Leach letters.
116. Benedict, p. 355

8. Covered with Glory

1. Benedict, p. 355; *The Civil War Dictionary*, p. 136; Stephen W. Sears, *Chancellorsville* (Boston: Houghton Mifflin, 1996), p. 140, hereinafter cited as *Chancellorsville*; Ernest B. Furgurson, *Chancellorsville 1863; The Souls of the Brave* (New York: Knopf, 1992), p. 67, hereinafter cited as Furgurson.
2. Benedict, p. 358; Wilbur Fisk diary; *Green Mountain Freeman*, 14 May 1863; Chester K. Leach letters; OR, vol. 25, p. 557.
3. Wilbur Fisk diary; *Green Mountain Freeman*, 14 May 1863; OR, vol. 25, p. 557.
4. Stevens, pp. 188–189; *Chancellorsville*, p. 140; OR, vol. 25, p. 557
5. Stevens, pp.190; OR, vol. 25, p. 558.
6. Stevens, pp. 189–190; *Green Mountain Freeman*, 14 May 1863; *The Civil War Battlefield Guide*, p. 108; OR, vol. 25, p. 171.
7. Stevens, p. 190; *The Civil War Battlefield Guide*, p. 108–110; *Glory Road*, p. 167; OR, vol. 25, p. 558.
8. *The Civil War Battlefield Guide*, p. 110; *The Civil War Dictionary*, p. 137; Abner Doubleday, *Chancellorsville and Gettysburg* (New York: Charles Scribner's Sons, 1886), pp. 13–19, hereinafter cited as Doubleday.
9. OR, vol. 25, pp. 558–559; *Green Mountain Freeman*, 19 May 1863; Doubleday, p. 21.
10. *The Civil War Battlefield Guide*, p. 110; *The Civil War Dictionary*, p. 137.
11. Benedict, pp. 359–360; *Chancellorsville*, pp. 303–304.
12. Benedict, p. 361; Stevens, pp. 192–193; *Chancellorsville*, pp. 303–306; *Green Mountain Freeman*, 19 May 1863.
13. Benedict, p. 361; *Chancellorsville*, pp. 350–352; OR, vol. 25, p.559.
14. *Chancellorsville*, pp. 309–310.
15. Benedict, pp. 361–362; Noel G. Harrison, *Fredericksburg Civil War Sites, December 1862-April 1865* (Lynchburg: H. E. Howard, 1995), p. 153.
16. *Chancellorsville*, p. 348; Welcher, p. 680; OR, vol. 25, pp. 815, 847.
17. Benedict, pp. 362–363; *Report of the Adjutant & Inspector General of the State of Vermont, from November 1, 1862 to October 1, 1863* (Montpelier, Vt.: Walton's Steam Printing Establishment, 1863), p. 78, hereinafter cited as *Vermont A&IG Report, 1863*; Jed Hotchkiss and William Allan, *Chancellorsville: Embarking the Operations of the Army of Northern Virginia, from the First Battle of Fredericksburg to the Death of Lieutenant General Jackson* (New York: D. Van Nostrand, 192 Broadway, 1867), p. 81, hereinafter cited as Hotchkiss and Allan.
18. Benedict, p. 362; OR, vol. 25, pp. 599, 602, 609; *Vermont A&IG Report, 1863*, p. 78.
19. *For the Glory of the Union*, p. 164; *The Song of the Rappahannock*, p. 76–78.
20. William Stowe letters; OR, vol. 25, p. 602; *Vermont A&IG Report, 1863*, p. 78.

21. *Green Mountain Freeman*, 19 May 1863; William Stowe letters; Stevens, p. 195; *Vermont A&IG Report, 1863*, p. 78; OR, vol. 25, pp. 599, 602, 609.

22. Chester K. Leach letters; Hampton L. Maxfield's military pension record; Joseph C. Felton letters.

23. LeRoy M. Bingham's military pension record; Levi L. Munson's military pension record.

24. Henry M. Parker's military pension record; *Historical Sketch of Co. I*, p. 20.

25. Albert Parkhurst's military pension record.

26. Biographical Sketch Book, James M. Warner Post No. 4, Grand Army of the Republic, Morristown Historical Society, Morristown, Vermont; Peck, p. 51.

27. *For the Glory of the Union*, p. 165.

28. OR, vol. 25, p. 602.

29. Stevens, pp. 196–197; OR, vol. 25, pp. 608–609, 815–816, 1000; *Vermont A&IG Report, 1863*, pp. 78–79; Edward J. Stackpole, *Chancellorsville: Lee's Greatest Battle* (Harrisburg: Stackpole, 1958), p. 324; Early, pp. 207–208.

30. Benedict, p. 364–365; Oramel Howe, p. 10; William Stowe letters; *Vermont A&IG Report, 1863*, p. 78; *Green Mountain Freeman*, 19 May 1863; William Miller Owens, *In Camp and battle with the Washington Artillery of New Orleans* (Boston: Ticknor and Co., 1885), p. 213; Early, p. 208.

31. OR, vol. 25, pp. 815, 840, 847.

32. Benedict, pp. 363–365; OR, vol. 25, p. 602; Furgurson, p. 259; Jerome Cutler letters, p. 95; *Vermont Watchman and State Journal*, 15 May 1863; Fredericksburg and Spottsylvania National Military Park, Fredericksburg, Va.

33. *Green Mountain Freeman*, 19 May 1863.

34. Benedict, pp. 363–365; OR, vol. 25, pp. 602, 847; Furgurson, p. 259.

35. *Green Mountain Freeman*, 19 May 1863.

36. *Green Mountain Freeman*, 19 May 1863; Hamilton Child, *Gazetteer of Orange County, 1762–1888* (Syracuse: Syracuse Journal Company, 1888), p. 239, hereinafter cited as *Gazetteer of Orange County*; Martin V. B. Davis's military pension record.

37. Benedict, p. 365; OR, vol. 25, pp. 608, 840.

38. *Green Mountain Freeman*, 19 May 1863; William Stowe letters; Jerome Cutler letters, p. 95.

39. Benedict, p. 365; William Stowe letters; *Vermont A&IG Report, 1863*, p. 78.

40. *Vermont Watchman and State Journal*, 15 May 1863.

41. William H. H. Camp's military pension record; *Vermont Watchman and State Journal*, 15 May 1863; Peck, p. 50.

42. *Green Mountain Freeman*, 19 May 1863; Charles C. Morey letters.

43. Charles C. Morey letters; Peck, p. 49.

44. Hiland Snell's military pension record; *History of Ludlow Vermont*, p. 156; *Historical Sketch of Co. I*, p. 14.

45. Norman C. Lawson's military pension record; Peck, p. 58.

46. Joseph N. Harris, *History of Ludlow Vermont* (Charlestown, N.H.: Mrs. Ina Harris Harding and Mr. Archie Frank Harding Publishers, 1949, p. 25, hereinafter cited as *History of Ludlow Vermont*; *Historical Sketch of Co. I*, p. 13, 60; Hiram P. Bixby's military pension and military service record; *History of Co. I*, pp. 16–17.

47. Lewis A. Grant's military pension record.

48. Amasa S. Tracy's military pension record; Chester K. Leach letters; *Green Mountain Freeman*, 19 May 1863.

49. Horace F. Crossman's military pension record.

50. Ambrose Pratt Stone's military pension record.

51. Chester K. Leach letters.

52. William H. Foster's military pension record; *Annals of Brattleboro Vermont*, p. 764.

53. Jerome Cutler's military pension record; Jerome Cutler letters, p. 95.

54. Dr. Henry L. Janes, medical journal, Special Collections, Bailey/Howe Library, University of Vermont, Burlington, Vermont, p. 369, hereinafter cited as Dr. Janes's journal.

55. Orlenzo M. George's military pension record.

56. William Coagle's military pension record.

57. *Green Mountain Freeman*, 19 May 1863.

58. Benedict, p. 365; OR, vol. 25, pp. 602–603, 614, 847, 856, 1001; *Vermont A&IG Report, 1863*, p. 78.

59. *Vermont A&IG Report, 1863*, p. 79.

60. *Vermont A&IG Report, 1863*, p. 79; Sears, p. 374; Early, p. 210.

61. Jerome Cutler letters, p. 95; Chester K. Leach letters; *For the Glory of the Union*, p. 167.

62. William Stowe letters.

63. Benedict, p. 366; OR, vol. 25, p. 603.

64. Benedict, p. 365–366; Hotchkiss and Allan, p. 82; OR, vol. 25, p. 820.

65. Benedict, pp. 366, 377; Sears, p. 357; Joseph C. Felton letters.

66. W. F. Beyer and O. F. Keydel, *Deeds of Valor*, (Stamford, Conn.: Republished, Longmeadow Press, 1993), pp. 145–147, hereinafter cited as *Deeds of Valor*; Lewis A. Grant's military pension record.

67. Benedict, p. 367; William Stowe letters.

68. *R. E. Lee*, vol. 2, pp. 537–544; Doubleday, pp. 45–51; *Chancellorsville*, p. 339.

69. *R. E. Lee*, vol. 2, p. 545.

70. Doubleday, p. 59; Hotchkiss and Allan, pp. 82–84.

71. Doubleday, pp. 60–61; Hotchkiss and Allan, pp. 85–88.

72. Doubleday, pp. 61–62.

73. Doubleday, p. 62; Hotchkiss and Allan, p. 92.

74. Historian's record, Col. W. H. Greenwood Post No. 90, Grand Army of the Republic; *Historical Sketch of Company I*, pp. 10–11.

75. Hotchkiss and Allan, pp. 89–91.

76. *Chancellorsville*, p. 394.

77. Hotchkiss and Allan, p. 91.

78. Ibid., p. 93.

79. Doubleday, p. 64; OR, vol. 25, p. 560.

80. *Green Mountain Freeman*, 20 May 1863.

81. *For the Glory of the Union*, pp. 179–183.

82. Benedict, p. 368; Doubleday, p. 64; Early, 226; Stevens, p. 203.

83. Benedict, p. 368.

84. Benedict, pp. 368–369; OR, vol. 25, p. 604; *Vermont A&IG Report, 1863*, p. 75.

85. Benedict, p. 368–369.

86. Early, p. 229; *Chancellorsville*, p. 415.
87. Benedict, pp. 368–369; OR, vol. 25, p. 604.
88. Benedict, p. 369.
89. Ibid., p. 370.
90. Benedict, p. 370; *Green Mountain Freeman*, 20 May 1863; OR, vol. 25, p. 605; *Vermont A&IG Report, 1863*, p. 75.
91. Benedict, pp. 370–371; William Stowe letters; OR, vol. 25, p. 605; *Vermont A&IG Report, 1863*, p. 75; *For the Glory of the Union*, p. 169.
92. Peck, p. 54; E. H. Lane, *The Soldier's Record of Jericho, Vermont* (Burlington: R. S. Styles, 1868), p. 20, hereinafter cited as *The Soldier's Record of Jericho, Vermont*; Charles Tillison letters.
93. Lewis M. Wilson's military pension record.
94. Hiram H. Tilly letter book, p. 150.
95. Hiram H. Tilly letter book, p. 150; Hiram H. Tilly's military pension record.
96. Henry Prouty's military pension record.
97. William Wiggins's military pension record; Hiram P. Matthews's military pension record; Fayette A. Harris's military pension record.
98. *Green Mountain Freeman*, 19 May 1863; Patrick Burgin's military service record; Peck, p. 44.
99. Truman O. Brown's military pension record and military service record.
100. Benedict, pp. 370–371; OR, vol. 25, p. 605; *Vermont A&IG Report, 1863*, pp. 75–76.
101. Benedict, p. 371; OR, vol. 25, p. 605.
102. Benedict, p. 371; OR, vol. 25, p. 605; *For the Glory of the Union*, p. 170; *The Song of the Rappahannock*, p. 34.
103. Benedict, p. 371; OR, vol. 25, p. 605; *For the Glory of the Union*, p. 170; *The Song of the Rappahannock*, pp. 34–35.
104. Benedict, p. 372; Samuel E. Pingree letters; William Stowe letters; *Green Mountain Freeman*, 20 May 1863.
105. OR, vol. 25, p. 601.
106. Benedict, p. 372.
107. Benedict, p. 373; Furgurson, pp. 299–304; *Chancellorsville*, pp. 410–417.
108. *Vermont A&IG Report, 1863*, p. 76; *For the Glory of the Union*, p. 170; *Chancellorsville*, p. 417.
109. Benedict, pp. 373, 377; OR, vol. 25, pp. 561, 601.
110. Benedict, p. 373; *Vermont A&IG Report, 1863*, p. 76; OR, vol. 25, p. 606.
111. Benedict, pp. 373–374; Chester K. Leach letters; Stevens, p. 220.
112. Chester K. Leach letters.
113. *Green Mountain Freeman*, 20 May 1863; OR, vol. 25, p. 561.
114. *Chancellorsville*, pp. 426–429; *Glory Road*, p. 208; OR, vol. 25, p. 215.
115. *Glory Road*, p. 211.
116. Wilbur Fisk diary.
117. Benedict, p. 378; Chester K. Leach letters.
118. *Green Mountain Freeman*, 13 June 1863.
119. Chester K. Leach letters.
120. George W. Durrell's military service record.
121. *Historical Sketch of Company I*, p. 63.
122. Chester K. Leach letters.
123. Ibid.
124. Ibid.
125. *Green Mountain Freeman*, 13 June 1863.
126. Benedict, p. 378; Stevens, p. 216; *Green Mountain Freeman*, 13 June 1863.
127. William C. Jackson, Civil War letters, Vermont Historical Society, Montpelier, Vermont, hereinafter cited as William C. Jackson letters.
128. Charles C. Morey letters.
129. *R. E. Lee*, vol. 3, pp. 8–14.
130. Ibid., pp. 18–25.
131. Benedict, pp. 378–379; *Vermont A&IG Report, 1863*, p. 80.
132. *Vermont A&IG Report, 1863*, pp. 80–81.
133. Benedict, p. 380.
134. *For the Glory of the Union*, p. 187; *The song of the Rappahannock*, p. 153.
135. *The song of the Rappahannock*, pp. 162–163.
136. Benedict, pp. 379–381; *Vermont A&IG Report, 1863*, pp. 81–82; Stevens, p. 219.
137. Benedict, p. 381.
138. Ibid.
139. Ibid., p. 382.
140. Benedict, p. 382; *Green Mountain Freeman*, 20 June 1863.
141. Chester K. Leach letters.
142. William Stowe letters.
143. *Green Mountain Freeman*, 20 June 1863

9. A Reprieve at Gettysburg

1. Benedict, p. 382; *Glory Road*. pp. 242–247; *The Civil War Dictionary*, pp. 80–81,655–656
2. Benedict, p. 383; *Green Mountain Freeman*, 27 June 1863.
3. *Green Mountain Freeman*, 27 June 1863.
4. Benedict, p. 383, Jerome Cutler letters, p. 101; Stevens, p. 227; *Green Mountain Freeman*, 27 June 1863.
5. Benedict, p. 383; Stevens, p. 227.
6. Benedict, pp. 383–384; Stevens, p. 228.
7. Benedict, p. 384; Chester K. Leach letters.
8. Benedict, pp. 384–385; Chester K. Leach letters.
9. Benedict, p. 385.
10. Benedict, p. 385; *The Civil War Dictionary*, pp. 334–335.
11. Benedict, p. 385.
12. Benedict, vol. 2, p. 448; *The Civil War Dictionary*, pp. 335–336; *Glory Road*, pp. 285–286.
13. Benedict, vol. 2, pp. 448–456; *The Civil War Dictionary*, pp. 336–337; *R. E. Lee*, vol. 3, pp. 98–100.
14. Benedict, vol. 2, pp. 448–456; *The Civil War Dictionary*, pp. 336–337; *R. E. Lee*, vol. 3, pp. 98–100.
15. Benedict, pp. 385–386; Stevens, 240.
16. Benedict, p. 386.
17. Ibid., p. 387.
18. Benedict, pp. 387–388; *Green Mountain Freeman*, 22 July 1863; OR, vol. 27, pp. 675–676, 678.

19. Benedict, pp. 460–461; *The Civil War Dictionary*, pp. 337–338.

20. Benedict, pp. 462–476; *The Civil War Dictionary*, pp. 338–339.

21. Benedict, p. 388; OR, vol. 27, p. 678.

22. Benedict, p. 388; OR, vol. 27, p. 678.

23. Benedict, p. 388; *Green Mountain Freeman*, 25 July 1863; OR, vol. 27, p. 145.

24. Benedict, p. 388; Chester K. Leach letters.

25. Benedict, pp. 388–389.

26. Benedict, pp. 388–389; Jerome Cutler letters, pp. 105–106.

27. Benedict, p. 389; OR, vol. 27, p. 146.

28. Benedict, pp. 389–390; *Vermont A&IG Report, 1863*, p. 83; Ted Alexander, "Ten Days in July: The Pursuit to the Potomac," *North & South 2*, no. 6 (August 1999), pp. 27–28, hereinafter cited as Ted Alexander; OR, vol. 27, part 2, p. 704.

29. Benedict, pp. 390–391; *Vermont A&IG Report, 1863*, p. 83;.Ted Alexander, p. 28; Roger S. Keller, *Events of the Civil War in Washington County, Maryland* (Shippenburg, Pa.: Burd Street Press, 1995), p. 249, hereinafter cited as Keller; OR, vol. 27, p. 929.

30. Benedict, pp. 390–391; *Vermont A&IG Report, 1863*, p. 83; Ted Alexander, p. 28; Keller, p. 251; OR, vol. 27, p. 692.

31. Benedict, p. 391.

32. Benedict, p. 391; *Vermont A&IG Report, 1863*, p. 83; Ted Alexander, p. 28.

33. Benedict, p. 391; *Vermont A&IG Report, 1863*, p. 84.

34. Benedict, p. 392; *Vermont A&IG Report, 1863*, p. 84; Keller, p. 251.

35. John Comstock's military pension record.

36. George M. Colt's military pension record.

37. Benedict, p. 392; *Vermont A&IG Report, 1863*, p. 84; Jerome Cutler letters, p. 105; *Green Mountain Freeman*, 4 Aug 1863; Keller, p. 251.

38. *Vermont A&IG Report, 1863*, p. 84.

39. Benedict, pp. 392–393; *Vermont A&IG Report, 1863*, p. 84; Jerome Cutler letters, p. 105.

40. Benedict, p. 394; *Vermont A&IG Report, 1863*, p. 84.

41. Benedict, p. 394; Ted Alexander, p. 28; Kent M. Brown, "A Golden Bridge: Lee's Williamsport Defense Lines and His Escape Across the Potomac," *North & South Magazine 2*, no. 6 (August 1999), p. 60.

42. Chester K. Leach letters.

43. Benedict, pp. 394–395.

44. Benedict, p. 395; Wilbur Fisk diary; Jerome Cutler letters, p. 108.

45. Benedict, p. 395.

46. *Green Mountain Freeman*, 22 Aug 1863.

47. Benedict, pp. 396–397; *The Civil War Dictionary*, pp. 245–246.

48. Benedict, pp. 396–397; Wilbur Fisk diary; *Green Mountain Freeman*, 5 Sep 1863; Chester K. Leach letters.

49. Wilbur Fisk diary.

50. Wilbur Fisk diary; Jerome Cutler letters, p. 110; Philip Halpin diary.

51. Jerome Cutler letter, p. 110.

52. Benedict, p. 397; Wilbur Fisk diary; Charles Tillison letters.

53. Benedict, pp. 396–397; *Green Mountain Freeman*, 5 September 1863; Chester K. Leach letters; Philip Halpin diary; *Burlington Free Press*, 10 Sep, 1863; Joseph C. Felton letters.

54. Jerome Cutler letters, p. 110.

55. *Green Mountain Freeman*, 12 September 1863.

56. Benedict, p. 398; Philip Halpin diary; *Green Mountain Freeman*, 19 Sep 1863; Wilbur Fisk diary; *Poughkeepsie Daily Eagle*, 7 Sep 1863.

57. Benedict, p. 398; Philip Halpin diary; *Green Mountain Freeman*, 19 Sep 1863; Wilbur Fisk diary; *Poughkeepsie Daily Eagle*, 7 Sep 1863.

58. Benedict, p. 398; Philip Halpin diary; *Green Mountain Freeman*, 19 Sep 1863; Wilbur Fisk diary; *Poughkeepsie Daily Eagle*, 10 Sep 1863.

59. Peck, p. 53; Family information from Steve Taylor, Pvt. Stephen M. Taylor's great-great-grandson.

60. Benedict, p. 398; Philip Halpin diary; *Green Mountain Freeman*, 30 Oct 1863; Chester K. Leach letters; *Poughkeepsie Daily Eagle*, 14 Sep 1863.

61. Benedict, p. 398; Philip Halpin diary; *Green Mountain Freeman*, 30 Oct 1863.

62. Benedict, p. 398; Philip Halpin diary; Chester K. Leach letters.

63. Benedict, pp. 398–399; Chester K. Leach letters; Wilbur Fisk diary.

64. Benedict, p. 399; Chester K. Leach letters; Wilbur Fisk diary.

65. Benedict, pp. 111, 399–400; Wilbur Fisk diary; Samuel M. Pingree letters.

66. Chester K. Leach letters.

67. Chester K. Leach letters; Edwin R. Brush's military service record; Peck, pp. 31, 57.

68. Chester K. Leach letters.

69. Ibid.

70. Benedict, p. 400; Wilbur Fisk diary; Chester K. Leach letters.

71. *R. E. Lee*, vol. 3, pp., 163, 166, 168; Martin F. Graham and George F. Skoch, *Mine Run: A Campaign of Lost Opportunities, October 21, 1863-May 1, 1864* (Lynchburg, Va.: H. E. Howard, 1987), p. 1, hereinafter cited as *Mine Run*.

72. *R. E. Lee*, vol. 3, pp. 169–170.

73. Benedict, pp. 400–401; *R. E. Lee*, vol. 3, p. 171.

74. Benedict, pp. 400–401; Chester K. Leach letters.

75. Benedict, pp. 400–401; *The Civil War Dictionary*, p. 87; *R. E. Lee*, vol. 3, pp. 181–183; *Mine Run*, pp. 1–2.

76. Benedict, pp. 401–402; Chester K. Leach letters; *Mine Run*, p. 2.

77. Benedict, p. 402; Chester K. Leach letters; Peck, pp. 33, 52, 144, 735.

78. Benedict, pp. 402–403.

79. Ibid.

80. Benedict, p. 110; Peck, pp. 30, 59; Lauriston L. Stone letters; Bruce Catton, *The Army of the Potomac: A Stillness at Appomattox* (Garden City, N.Y.: Doubleday, 1953), p. 57, hereinafter cited as *A Stillness at Appomattox*.

81. *The Vermont Gazetteer*, pp. 764–765.

82. Peck, pp. 30, 59; Lauriston L. Stone letters.

83. *Green Mountain Freeman*, 21 Nov 1863; Peck, p. 42, 65; Charles S. Wheeler's court-martial record.

84. Benedict, p. 403; Wilbur Fisk diary; Chester K. Leach letters; *Mine Run*, pp. 8–9.

85. Benedict, pp. 403–404; *Mine Run*, pp. 9–10.

86. Wilbur Fisk diary; *Green Mountain Freeman*, 5 Nov 1863.

87. Benedict, pp. 403–404; *Mine Run*, pp. 10–19.

88. Benedict, pp. 403–404; *Green Mountain Freeman*, 5 Nov 1863; *Mine Run*, p. 16.

89. Joseph C. Felton letters.

90. Benedict, pp. 404–405; *Mine Run*, pp. 18–28.

91. Benedict, p. 405; *R. E. Lee*, vol. 3, p. 192; *Mine Run*, pp. 24, 30–34.

92. Benedict, p. 405–406; *The Wilderness Campaign*, p. 112; *Mine Run*, pp. 34–35; Jeffrey D. Marshall, ed., *A War of the People: Vermont Civil War Letters* (Hanover, N.H.: University Press of New England, 1999), p. 226.

93. Chester K. Leach letters; Peck, pp. 31, 40, 43, 50, 56, 57.

94. Chester K. Leach letters; Wilbur Fisk diary; Albert J. Reid, Civil War diary, 1863, in the possession of Barbara F. Earle, hereinafter cited as Albert J. Reid diary; Charles C. Morey Diaries.

95. Benedict, p. 406; Stevens, p. 290.

96. Benedict, p. 406; Stevens, p. 291.

97. Stevens, p. 291.

98. Benedict, pp. 406–407; Stevens, p. 291.

99. Benedict, p. 407, vol. 2, p. 291.

100. Stevens, p. 294.

101. Ibid., pp. 294–295.

102. Benedict, p. 408; *Green Mountain Freeman*, 22 Dec 1863; Stevens, pp. 295–297.

103. Benedict, pp. 408–409.

104. Benedict, p. 409; Stevens, pp. 297–298; *R. E. Lee*, vol. 3, pp. 201–202.

105. Benedict, p. 409; Stevens, p. 298.

106. Benedict, pp. 112, 410; *Green Mountain Freeman*, 5 Jan 1864.

107. *Green Mountain Freeman*, 12 Jan 1864.

108. Eben N., Drury, Civil War letter, U.S. Army Military History Institute, Carlisle Barracks, Pennsylvania.

109. *Burlington Free Press*, 11 Feb 1864; *Green Mountain Freeman*, 12 Jan 1864; Peck, pp. 30–66.

110. Benedict, p. 111; George E. Blowers's military service record and court-martial record; William Blowers's military service record.

111. George E. Blowers's military service record and court-martial record; William Blowers's military service record.

112. George E. Blowers's military service record and court-martial record.

113. Ibid.

114. William Blowers's military service record.

115. Benedict 111; Albert J. Reid diary; *Green Mountain Freeman*, 5 Jan 1864; Joseph C. Felton letters.

116. *Green Mountain Freeman*, 5 Jan 1864.

117. Joseph Solie's, John Rapalle's, and Giovanni Arbatraca's court-martial records; John Rapalle's personnel service record.

118. Joseph Solie's, John Rapalle's, and Giovanni Arbatraca's court-martial records; John Rapalle's military personnel record; Peck, pp. 37, 58, 65

10. "A Wilderness of Woe"

1. Chester K. Leach Letters.

2. *Tyler-Browns of Brattleboro*, p. 128.

3. Charles H. Richardson, Civil War diary, Library of Congress, Washington, D.C., hereinafter cited as the Charles H. Richardson diary.

4. John Casey's, Charles Coe's, Arthur Devine's, James Fitzgerald's, Samuel Glover's, Alvah H. Miles's, and Walter Massey's courts-martial record; *Green Mountain Freeman*, 26 April 1864.

5. John Casey's, Charles Coe's, Arthur Devine's, James Fitzgerald's, Samuel Glover's, Alvah H. Miles's, and Walter Massey's courts-martial record.

6. John Casey's, Charles Coe's, James Fitzgerald's, Samuel Glover's, Walter Massey's, and Arthur Devine's courts-martial records.

7. General Order No. 14, April 28th, 1864. National Archives, Washington, DC.

8. Timothy S. Hoyt to Cate Hoyt, 17 Dec, 1863. In the possession of Douglas Williams.

9. Stevens, p. 300.

10. Wilbur Fisk diary.

11. Chester K. Leach letters.

12. *A Stillness at Appomattox*, p. 4; *The Civil War Dictionary*, pp. 450–460.

13. *A Stillness at Appomattox*, p. 9; *The Civil War Dictionary*, p. 460.

14. *Green Mountain Freeman*, 15 March 1864; Wilbur Fisk diary.

15. *Green Mountain Freeman*, 15 March 1864.

16. Norman W. Johnson, Civil War diary, Vermont Historical Society, Montpelier, Vermont, hereinafter cited as the Norman W. Johnson diary.

17. *Green Mountain Freeman*, 15 March 1864; Chester K. Leach letters.

18. *Green Mountain Freeman*, 15 March 1864; Norman W. Johnson diary.

19. Wilbur Fisk diary; Chester K. Leach letters.

20. *A Stillness at Appomattox*, pp. 16–18; *The Civil War Dictionary*, pp. 460–461; *Green Mountain Freeman*, 15 March 1864.

21. Charles H. Richardson diary; Wilbur Fisk diary; *Personal Reminiscences of the Civil War*, p. 32; "The 1864 Diary of Private John T. Kelly, Second Vermont Regiment," ed. Don Wickman, *Rutland Historical Society Quarterly 24*, no. 2, (1994), p. 24, hereinafter cited as the John T. Kelly diary; *Green Mountain Freeman*, 5 April 1864.

22. *Green Mountain Freeman*, 5 April 1864; Wilbur Fisk diary; *Personal Reminiscences of the Civil War*, p. 32.

23. *Personal Reminiscences of the Civil War*, p. 32.

24. *Green Mountain Freeman*, 5 April 1864.

25. Benedict, pp. 412–413; *A Stillness at Appomattox*, pp. 48–53.

26. *In the Field*, pp. 78–79.

27. Peck, p. 30; Chester K. Leach letters.

28. Amasa S. Tracy's military pension record; Peck, p. 30; Chester K. Leach letters; *The State of Vermont*, vol. 2, pp. 513–514.

29. Peck, pp. 144, 747–748.

30. Chester K. Leach letters.

31. Gordon C. Rhea, *The Battle of the Wilderness* (Baton Rouge: Louisiana State University Press, 1994), pp. 42–46, hereinafter cited as *The Battle of the Wilderness.*

32. *A Stillness at Appomattox*, pp. 57–58; Gary W. Gallagher, ed., *The Wilderness Campaign, May 5–6, 1864*, *"Great Expections"* by Brooks D. Simpson (Chapel Hill, N.C.: The University of North Carolina Press, 1997), pp. 6–7, hereinafter cited as *The Wilderness Campaign*; *The Battle of the Wilderness*, p. 47.

33. *The Wilderness Campaign*, *"Union Cavalry in the Wilderness"* by Gordon C. Rhea, p. 113; *A Stillness at Appomattox*, p. 57; *The Battle of the Wilderness, The Army of Northern Virginia*, by Gary W. Gallagher, pp. 51–53.

34. *Place Names of Virginia*, pp. 268; *A Stillness at Appomattox*, p. 56; Donald C. Pfanz, *Richard S. Ewell: A Soldier's Life* (Chapel Hill, N.C.: The University of North Carolina Press, 1998), p. 362, hereinafter cited as *Richard S. Ewell.*

35. *A Stillness at Appomattox*, pp. 56–57; *Richard S. Ewell*, p. 361.

36. *A Stillness at Appomattox*, p. 60; *The Battle of the Wilderness*, p. 54.

37. *The Wilderness Campaign*, *"Union Cavalry in the Wilderness"* by Gordon C. Rhea, p. 113; *The Battle of the Wilderness*, pp. 54–55, 60.

38. Chester K. Leach letters.

39. Orville Bixby, Civil War letter, in the possession of Ed Italo.

40. Charles C. Morey letters.

41. Benedict, p. 112; *The Battle of the Wilderness*, p. 64; Wilbur Fisk diary; *Report of the Adjutant & Inspector General of the State of Vermont, from October 1, 1863 to October 1, 1864*, Montpelier, Vt.: Walton's Steam Press, 1864, p. 60.

42. *The Wilderness Campaign*, *"Union Cavalry in the Wilderness"* by Gordon C. Rhea, pp. 113–115; *The Battle of the Wilderness*, pp. 60–65.

43. *The Battle of the Wilderness*, pp. 70–71.

44. *The Wilderness Campaign*, *"Lewis A. Grant and the Vermont Brigade"* by Carol Reardon, p. 205; *The Battle of the Wilderness*, pp. 74–75; OR, vol. 36, p. 676.

45. Wilbur Fisk diary.

46. *The Wilderness Campaign*, *"Ewell and Hill at the Wilderness"* by Peter S. Carmichael, p. 145; *The Battle of the Wilderness*, pp. 81–82; *Richard S. Ewell*, p. 362.

47. *The Battle of the Wilderness*, p. 94.

48. Benedict, p. 419; *The Wilderness Campaign*, *"Lewis A. Grant and the Vermont Brigade"* by Carol Reardon, p. 205; *Green Mountain Freeman*, 31 May 1864.

49. *The Battle of the Wilderness*, pp., 104–106; *Richard S. Ewell*, pp. 363–364.

50. *The Civil War Dictionary*, p. 922; OR, vol. 36, p. 676; *Richard S. Ewell*, p. 364.

51. *The Battle of the Wilderness*, p. 108.

52. *The Battle of the Wilderness*, pp. 133, 188; OR, vol. 36, p. 676; *National Tribune*, 28 Jan 1897.

53. Benedict, p. 422; *The Battle of the Wilderness*, pp. 134–135; OR, vol. 36, p. 676.

54. *The Battle of the Wilderness*, p. 135; OR, vol. 36, p. 676.

55. *The Battle of the Wilderness*, pp. 135, 189; OR, vol. 36, p. 676.

56. Benedict, p. 423; OR, vol. 36, p. 696.

57. Benedict, p. 423; OR, vol. 36, p. 696; *The Wilderness Campaign*, *"Lewis A. Grant and the Vermont Brigade"* by Carol Reardon, p. 207; *The Battle of the Wilderness*, p. 191; *National Tribune*, 28 Jan 1897.

58. OR, vol. 36, pp. 696–697, 709; *The Wilderness Campaign*, *"Lewis A. Grant and the Vermont Brigade"* by Carol Reardon, p. 207; *The Battle of the Wilderness*, pp. 195–196; *National Tribune*, 28 Jan 1897.

59. *The Battle of the Wilderness*, pp. 193–194; OR, vol. 36, p. 697.

60. Benedict, p. 424; OR, vol. 36, p. 697.

61. OR, vol. 36, p. 697.

62. George W. Colby's military pension record; Peck, p. 44.

63. Henry M. Parker's military pension record; Peck, p. 61; *Historical Sketch of Co. I*, p. 20.

64. Daniel D. Hemenway's military pension record, in the possession of Alan Poore; *Historical Sketch of Co. I*, p. 10.

65. Dr. Henry L. Janes, medical journal, Special Collections, Bailey/Howe Library, University of Vermont, Burlington, Vermont, p. 372, hereinafter cited as Dr. Henry L. Janes medical journal; Peck, p. 34.

66. Theodore Wood's military pension record; Theodore Wood's Army discharge paper, in the possession of Susan Hunziker; Peck. P. 46.

67. Eben N. Drury's military service and military pension records.

68. Francis P. Ellsworth's military service record.

69. Benedict, pp. 424–425; *The Army of the Potomac: A Stillness at Appomattox*, p. 73.

70. Benedict, pp. 424–425; *Green Mountain Freeman*, 31 May 1864.

71. Benedict, pp. 424–425; Wilbur Fisk diary.

72. *Green Mountain Freeman*, 31 May 1864; Wilbur Fisk diary.

73. Wilbur Fisk diary; Peck, pp. 46–49; James Allen's military pension record.

74. Phillips E. Chase's military pension record; Peck, pp. 53, 60.

75. George M. Colt's military pension record; Peck, p. 41.

76. Kirk Rand's military pension record; Dr. Henry L. Janes medical journal, p. 298; Peck. 42; Nelson S. Cole.

77. Alfred Guyett's military service record; Peck, pp. 42, 755.

78. Dr. Henry L. Janes medical journal, p. 188; Peck. 35.

79. Bradley P. Bengtson, M.D., and Julian E. Kuz, M.D., eds. *Photographic Atlas of Civil War Injuries: Surgical Cases and Specimens, Otis Historical Archives* (Grand Rapids, Mich.: Medical Staff Press in association with Kennesaw Mountain Press, 1996), p. 117.

80. Elijah Wales's military pension record; Waite, pp. 267–269; Nelson S. Cole, Civil War Recollections, in the possession of Douglas W. Ronaldson, hereinafter cited as Nelson S. Cole; Peck, p. 40.

81. Joshua P. Sawyer's military pension record; Peck, pp. 40, 56.

82. Howard Coffin, *Full Duty: Vermonters in the Civil War* (Woodstock, Vt.: Countryman Press, 1993), p. 236; *The State of Vermont*, pp. 736–737; George W. Flagg's military pension and military service record; Peck, pp. 50–51.

83. L. Fay Bowker's military pension and personnel service records; Peck, p. 41

84. Warren Clough's military pension record; Joseph Slattery's military pension record; Amos C. Humphrey's military pension record; Hampton L. Maxfield's military pension record; Elbridge W. Prior's military pension record; Henry H. Bushy's military service record; Peck, pp. 34, 46, 54, 58, 61; *Historical Sketch of Co. I*, p. 14.

85. Joseph E. Butterfield's military pension record, *Historical Sketch of Co. I*; p. 8–9; Peck, p. 60.

86. *Vermont Gazetteer*, vol. 4, p. 167.

87. Ira M. Carpenter's military service record and military pension record; Peck, p. 51. Carpenter moved to California in 1874 where he died at Lakefork, September 6, 1907, of what the coroner described as 40 years of hard drinking

88. Isaac Howard's military pension record; Peck, pp. 57–58. In 1882 Howard applied for a pension because of his deteriorating mental capacity that was assumed to have been caused by his head wound. In his pension application his doctor stated, "At the time of seeing him first he appeared so strange that I thought him either deranged or idiotic." In 1883 another doctor stated, "There was loss of memory and irritable temper, unsteady gait." A year later, however, a doctor in the Bureau of Pensions stated that, "From a medical standpoint the wound of the head has not produced any special disability aside from cicatrix, and neuralgic pains due to involvement of superficial nerves in the scar, and the impairment of mind, somnolency, dizziness, etc., are due to causes unconnected with the pensioned wound." His application for a pension was denied.

89. James G. Howard's military pension record; Peck, pp. 33, 35.

90. Norman J. Nichols's military pension record; Peck, p. 55.

91. LeRoy B. Nichols's military pension record; Peck, p. 53.

92. George B. Ordway's military pension record; Peck, p. 49.

93. OR, vol. 36, p. 697; *The Wilderness Campaign*, "*Lewis A. Grant and the Vermont Brigade*" by Carol Reardon, pp. 214–215.

94. Benedict, pp. 425–426; OR, vol. 36, pp. 697, 714.

95. *The Battle of the Wilderness*, p. 469; OR, vol. 36, p. 469.

96. OR, vol. 36, p. 677; *Historical Sketch of Company I*, p. 51; H. Martyn Harwood military pension record; Peck, p. 34.

97. Albert A. May's military pension record; Peck, pp. 60–61; *Historical Sketch of Co. I*, p. 12.

98. Daniel S. White's military pension record; Peck, pp. 59–60.

99. Benedict, pp. 113, 425; *Historical Sketch of Company I*, p. 51; OR, vol. 36, p. 700.

100. Benedict, pp. 113, 425; *Historical Sketch of Company I*, p. 51; OR, vol. 36, p. 700; *Tyler-Browns of Brattleboro*, p.138.

101. *Tyler-Browns of Brattleboro*, p. 141–143; Mary R. Cabot, *Annals of Brattleboro Vermont* (Brattleboro, Vt.: Press of E. L. Hildreth & Co., 1922), vol. 2, pp. 780–781, hereinafter cited as *Annals of Brattleboro.*

102. Benedict, p. 425; OR, vol. 36, pp. 700–701.

103. OR, vol. 36, p. 697.

104. *The Battle of the Wilderness*, pp. 197–198.

105. Charles H. Richardson's military pension; Charles H. Richardson diary; Peck, p. 45.

106. *Historical Sketch of Company I*, pp. 20–21, 51; *The Vermont Phoenix*, 30 January 1891.

107. Nelson S. Cole; Elijah Wales's military pension record.

108. OR, vol. 36, p. 697; *Green Mountain Freeman*, 31 May 1864.

109. Isaac C. Osgood's military pension record; Peck, p. 58.

110. *The Vermont Phoenix*, 30 Jan 1891.

111. Edward Payson Gibbs's military pension record; Peck, p. 54.

112. OR, vol. 36, p. 700; John T. Kelly diary, p. 26.

113. Nelson S. Cole.

114. Kirk Rand's military pension record; Dr. Henry L. Janes medical journal, p. 298.

115. OR, vol. 36, p. 698.

116. *The Battle of the Wilderness*, pp. 245–247; *Richard S. Ewell*, pp. 365–369.

117. *The Battle of the Wilderness*, pp. 273–280; Benedict, pp. 428–429.

118. Benedict, p. 429.

119. *National Tribune*, 4 Feb 1897.

120. Wilbur Fisk diary.

121. *Green Mountain Freeman*, 31 May 1864.

122. Samuel E. Pingree letters.

123. Samuel E. Pingree letters; *Genealogical and Family History of the State of Vermont*, pp. 16–18.

124. Benedict, p. 429; *Richard S. Ewell*, p. 370.

125. Benedict, p. 429.

126. *Green Mountain Freeman*, 31 May 1864.

127. *National Tribune*, 4 Feb 1897.

128. Benedict, p. 429; Craig S. Chapman, *More Terrible than Victory: North Carolina's Bloody Bethel Regiment, 1861–1865* (Washington: Brassey's, 1998), pp. 159–160, hereinafter cited as *More Terrible than Victory.*

129. Benedict, p. 429.

130. Benedict, p. 429; *The Battle of the Wilderness*, pp. 299–309.

131. Benedict, p. 429; Robert Garth Scott, *Into the Wilderness with the Army of the Potomac* (Bloomington: Indiana University Press, 1957), p. 214, hereinafter cited as *Into the Wilderness.*

132. *The Battle of the Wilderness*, pp. 309, 310; *Into the Wilderness*, p. 214; *National Tribune*, 4 Feb 1897.

133. OR, vol. 36, p. 699.

134. OR, vol. 36, p. 699; *National Tribune*, 4 Feb 1897.

135. OR, vol. 36, p. 699.

136. OR, vol. 36, p. 699; *National Tribune*, 4 Feb 1897.

137. Wilbur Fisk diary; Charles C. Morey letters.

138. Joseph Tatro and Abraham Tatro's military pension record; Peck, p. 65. After the war Abraham Tatro married and moved to Rhode Island, where he died April 15, 1900. Upon filing for a widow's pension after his death, his wife Lucy found that Abraham had conveniently forgotten to tell her he was already married. His first wife Sophia had divorced him 1871, after he had deserted her and married Lucy; however, Sophia had filed for a widow's pension before Lucy. The Pension Bureau ruled in favor of his first wife.

139. William H. Foster's military pension record; Peck, p. 41.

140. OR, vol. 36, p. 699.

141. Ibid.

142. Wilbur Fisk diary.

143. Ibid.

144. Benedict, p. 115.

145. *The Battle of the Wilderness*, pp. 366–374; *The Wilderness Campaign, Longstreet's Flank Attack* by Robert E. L. Krick, p. 257.

146. OR, vol. 36, p. 699.

147. Samuel E. Pingree letters.

148. *The Vermont Phoenix*, 30 Jan 1891.

149. Benedict, p. 435.

150. *The Battle of the Wilderness*, pp. 435, 440

11. "The Slaughter Pen"

1. Benedict, 437; OR, vol. 36, part 1, pp. 700, 768; Gordon C. Rhea, *The Battles for Spotsylvania Court House and the Road to Yellow Tavern, May 7–12, 1864* (Baton Rouge: Louisiana State University Press, 1997), p. 29, hereinafter cited as *The Battles for Spotsylvania Court House*; Wilbur Fisk diary; *National Tribune*, 4 Feb 1897.

2. Benedict, 437; OR, vol. 36, part 1, p. 700; *National Tribune*, 4 Feb 1897.

3. *The Battles for Spotsylvania Court House*, pp. 13–14.

4. Ibid., pp. 14–15.

5. Benedict, p. 437; OR, vol. 36, partl, p. 715; *In the Field*, pp. 83–84.

6. Peter Chase, "The Wilderness," *The Vermont Phoenix*, 30 Jan 1891.

7. *The Battles for Spotsylvania Court House*, pp. 27–30, 43; *Richard S. Ewell*, pp. 375–376.

8. Benedict, p. 438; John T. Kelly diary, p. 26; OR, vol. 36, part 1, pp. 700–702.

9. Benedict, p. 438; *The Battles for Spotsylvania Court House*, pp. 44, 59, 73.

10. Benedict, pp. 438–439; OR, vol. 36, part 1, p. 702.

11. Benedict, p. 440 ; *The Battles for Spotsylvania Court House*, pp. 89–90; *The Civil War Dictionary*, p. 1.

12. *The Battles for Spotsylvania Court House*, p. 91.

13. Benedict, pp. 440–441.

14. Benedict, pp. 440–441; Wilbur Fisk diary; John T. Kelly diary, p. 27; Fisk, p. 219.

15. Benedict, p. 442; *The Civil War Dictionary*, p. 949; *Full Duty*, pp. 245–246.

16. Benedict, pp. 442–443; *The Battles for Spotsylvania Court House*, pp. 161–168; OR, vol. 36, part 1, pp. 667, 679, 703.

17. Albert Perry's military pension record; Peck, p. 65.

18. Benedict, pp. 442–443; *The Battles for Spotsylvania Court House*, p. 164; Rosenblatt, p. 220; *Ewell*, p. 379; *A Stillness at Appomattox*, p. 113.

19. Benedict, p. 444; *The Battles for Spotsylvania Court House*, p. 169; Rosenblatt, p. 221; *A Stillness at Appomattox*, p. 114; *Ewell*, p. 379; OR, vol. 36, part 1, pp. 667–668, 703; Stevens, pp. 331–332.

20. Rosenblatt, pp. 296–297.

21. Benjamin Jerough's military pension record; Peck, p. 55.

22. Ethan Allen Priest's military pension and service records; Peck, p. 59; Historical Sketch of Co. I, p. 5; Ethan Allen Priest's eulogy in the possession of Dennis Devereux.

23. Benedict, p. 444; *The Battles for Spotsylvania Court House*, p. 174; *A Stillness at Appomattox*, pp. 114–115.

24. Rollin C. Ward's military pension record; Peck, pp. 36–37. After the war Ward, with his second wife, settled in Franklin, Mass. Because of the pain caused by his leg wound, Ward was on a painkiller, probably opium. The drug, unfortunately, caused him mood swings and he would sometimes abuse his wife. Their family pastor stated, after visiting their house in the spring of 1901, "She came out with finger marks upon her throat and then she was excited and told me that her husband choked her and roughly assaulted her. I am sure that these marks were made by the hand of a man. She frequently complained to me that he assaulted her and that the cause therefore was the use of a drug by him." They legally separated that summer and Ward moved in with his niece, Ella Dunnett, in St. Johnsbury, where he died December 8, 1913, without ever reconciling with his wife.

25. Egerton Hood's military pension record; Peck, p. 48. Hood returned to Chelsea after his discharge from the service, the following September. He married a widow in 1877and adopted her child from her first marriage, but after several years she left him for someone else. He never remarried.

26. Benedict, p. 444; *Ewell*, pp. 379–380; OR, vol. 36, part 1, p. 668.

27. John Miller's military pension record; Peck, p. 52.

28. Joseph N. Goron's military pension file; James M. Worthing's military pension file; Peck, pp. 51, 59.

29. Benedict, pp. 444–445; Rosenblatt, p. 297; OR, vol. 36, part 1, pp. 679, 703.

30. David P. Bateman's military pension record; Peck, pp. 37, 44.

31. John P. Abbott's military pension record; Peck, p. 33.

32. John A. Freelove's military pension record; Peck, p. 37; Charles C. Morey letters.

33. John C. Clough's military pension record; Peck, p. 44.

34. James Dion's military pension record; Peck, p. 44.

35. Winslow C. Rollins's military pension record; Peck, p. 45.

36. Samuel E. Pingree letters.

37. Benedict, p. 445.

38. *The Battles for Spotsylvania Court House*, pp. 206–209, 321; *Ewell*, pp. 381–382.

39. Benedict, p. 446; John T. Kelly diary, p. 27.

40. Benedict, pp. 445–446; *Ewell*, p. 382; *The Battles for Spotsylvania Court House*, pp. 214–215.
41. *Ewell*, p. 382; *The Battles for Spotsylvania Court House*, pp. 225–226.
42. Benedict, pp. 445–446; *Ewell*, pp. 385–386; *The Battles for Spotsylvania Court House*, pp. 230–242; *A Stillness at Appomattox*, p. 121; *The Civil War Battlefield Guide*, p. 209.
43. *The Battles for Spotsylvania Court House*, p. 259
44. Benedict, p. 446; OR, vol. 36, p. 703; *The Battles for Spotsylvania Court House*, p. 264.
45. Charles F. Greenleaf's military pension record; Peck, pp. 63–64.
46. Benedict, p. 446; OR, vol. 36, part 1, p. 703; *The Battles for Spotsylvania Court House*, p. 272.
47. Benedict, pp. 116, 446–447.
48. OR, vol. 36, part 1, p. 704.
49. Charles M. Hapgood's military pension record; Peck, p. 34.
50. LeRoy B. Nichols's military pension record; Peck, p. 53.
51. Rufus H. Marsh's military pension record; Peck, p. 45.
52. Franklin M. Cook's military pension record; Peck, p. 54.
53. Giles J. Burgess's military pension record; Peck, p. 33.
54. Jeheil S. Bailey's military pension and personnel service records; Peck, p. 57.
55. Augustus J. Robbins's military pension record; Peck, 36.
56. W. F. Beyer and O. F. Keydel, *Deeds of Valor* (Stamford, Conn.: Reprint, Longmeadow Press, 1993), p. 334, hereinafter cited as *Deeds of Honor*.
57. *Deeds of Honor*, p. 334; *Rutland Herald* 21 May 2000.
58. Charles C. Morey letters.
59. Francis A. Bush's military pension and military service records; Peck, p. 37. Bush returned home after being discharged and married a 22-year-old war widow named Matilda on March 22, 1865. She left him seven years later and moved in with a man named Thomas Hughes. Thomas and Matilda had several children, but were never married. When Francis died in West Chazy, N.Y., December 16, 1892, Matilda moved out of Thomas Hughes's house and tried to claim Francis's pension as his widow. A Mr. W. H. Stratton, of West Chazy, wrote the pension commissioner and reported her "adulterous cohabitation" and she was denied the pension.
60. Charles S. Wheeler's military pension record, Peck, 66.
61. *Historical Sketch of Co. I*, pp. 14–15, Peck, p. 61; Darius D. Priest's Civil War letters, in the possession of Nancy D. Wilson.
62. Benedict, p. 449; *Ewell*, p. 387.
63. Benedict, p. 449.
64. Benedict, pp. 449–450; Rosenblatt, p. 297; *Ewell*, p. 389; *The Civil War Battlefield Guide*, p. 209.
65. Benedict, p. 450; *The Battles for Spotsylvania Court House*, pp. 311–312.
66. Benedict, p. 451; John T. Kelly diary, p. 27; Wilbur Fisk diary; Rosenblatt, p. 221.
67. OR, vol. 36, part 1, p. 704.
68. Jerome Cutler, p. 134
69. Samuel E. Pingree letters.
70. Chester K. Leach letters; Charles C. Morey letters.
71. Benedict, p. 451; *The Civil War Battlefield Guide*, p. 209.
72. Benedict, p. 451, vol. 2, pp. 345–347; Peck, p. 409; OR, vol. 36, part 1, p. 704.
73. Benedict, p. 452.
74. Benedict, p. 452; OR, vol. 36, part 1, p. 705.
75. Benedict, p. 453.
76. Benedict, p. 116; Peck, pp. 41–42, 55; Wilbur Fisk diary; George Dow's military pension record; Joseph Kehoe's military record.
77. Benedict, pp. 453–455; Chester K. Leach letters; Peck, p. 55, 59; Myron Palmer's military pension record; *The Civil War Dictionary*, p. 15.
78. Rosenblatt, p. 223–225.
79. Benedict, pp. 455–456; *The Civil War Battlefield Guide*, p. 213; Chester K. Leach letters.
80. Benedict, p. 457–458; *The Civil War Battlefield Guide*, p. 213; OR, vol. 36, part 1, p. 706.
81. Benedict, p. 458; OR, vol. 36, part 1, pp. 706–707.
82. Benedict, p. 459; *The Civil War Battlefield Guide*, p. 215.
83. Benedict, pp. 459–460; *The Civil War Battlefield Guide*, p. 217.
84. Benedict, 461–462.
85. Benedict, p. 459; *The Civil War Battlefield Guide*, p. 217; Andrew A. Humphreys, *The Virginia Campaign of '64 and '65: The Army of the Potomac and the Army of the James* (New York: Charles Scribner's Sons, 1907), p. 17, hereinafter cited as Humphreys.
86. Benedict, pp. 461–462; OR, vol. 36, part 1, p. 707; Harrison A. Morgan's Military pension record; Peck, 57.
87. Benedict, pp. 461–462; OR, vol. 36, part 1, p. 707.
88. Wilbur Fisk diary.
89. History of Co. E, 2nd Regt. Vt. Vols., pp. 15–16.
90. Leander E. Shippee's military pension record; Peck, p. 36.
91. Benedict, pp. 461–462; OR, vol. 36, part 1, p. 707.
92. Benedict, pp. 462–463.
93. Wilbur Fisk diary.
94. Henry C. Page's military pension record; Peck, p. 55.
95. Nahum C. Baker's military service record; Peck, p. 47.
96. Benedict, pp. 462–463.
97. Benedict, p. 463; *The Civil War Battlefield Guide*, p. 217.
98. Benedict, p. 463.
99. Wilbur Fisk diary.
100. OR, vol. 36, part 1, p. 708.
101. Benedict, p. 464.
102. Benedict, p. 464; *A Stillness at Appomattox*, p. 159; Humphreys, pp. 175, 182.
103. Benedict, p. 464.
104. Wilbur Fisk diary; Peck, p. 36–37; Hiram Bailey's personnel service record; John T. Kelley diary, p. 29.
105. Benedict, p. 465.
106. Benedict, pp. 465–466; *The Civil War Battlefield Guide*, p. 220; *A Stillness at Appomattox*, p. 162.
107. Benedict, p. 466.

108. Wilbur Fisk diary.

109. Benedict, p. 467.

110. Benedict, p. 467; *A Stillness at Appomattox*, pp. 177–178; Humphreys, pp. 194–195.

111. Benedict, pp. 468–469, 484; Humphreys, pp. 190–192; OR, vol. 36, part 1, p. 708.

112. Chester K. Leach letters.

113. Hiland A Fuller's military pension record; Peck, p. 34.

114. Rosenblatt, p. 228.

115. Jerome Cutler letters, p. 135.

116. *The Daily Free Press*, 22 June 1864.

117. Chester K. Leach letters.

118. Charles C. Morey diary.

119. Chester K. Leach letters.

120. Joseph C. Felton letters.

121. Rosenblatt, p. 227.

122. Charles H. Reed, Civil War letters, in the possession of Brad Limoge.

123. Humphreys, p. 427.

124. Humphreys, p. 427.

125. Benedict, pp. 470–471; Wilbur Fisk diary; Rosenblatt, p. 229.

126. Benedict, p. 471; Wilbur Fisk diary; Rosenblatt, p. 230; Charles C. Morey diaries.

127. Benedict, p. 471; John Horn, *The Petersburg Campaign: June 1864-April 1865* (Conshohocken, Penn.: Combined Publishing, 1993), p. 53, hereinafter cited as Horn.

128. Horn, pp. 47–49; Humphreys, pp. 194–195.

129. Benedict, p. 471; Horn, pp. 56–59.

130. Benedict, pp. 471–472; Horn, pp. 53–59.

131. Benedict, p. 472.

132. Ibid.

133. Ibid., pp. 472–473.

134. Charles C. Morey diaries.

135. Rosenblatt, pp. 230–231.

136. Benedict, pp. 118–119; Rosenblatt, p. 235; Charles C. Morey diaries; John T. Kelly diary, p. 32.

137. Benedict, p. 118.

138. Wilbur Fisk diary.

139. Charles C. Morey diaries.

140. Benjamin P. Wheeler's military pension record; Peck, 39.

141. Lorenzo A. Dodge's military pension record; Peck, p. 60.

142. Benedict, p. 473; Horn, pp. 77–78.

143. Benedict, pp. 473–474; Charles C. Morey diaries; Horn, pp. 79–81; John T. Kelly diary, p. 33.

144. Benedict, p. 475.

145. Ibid., pp. 475–476.

146. Ibid., p. 476.

147. Ibid., pp. 476–477.

148. Benedict, pp. 478–481; Horn, p. 85.

149. Benedict, pp. 481–482; Wilbur Fisk diary.

150. Benedict, pp. 482–483; Charles C. Morey letters; Horn, pp. 91–95; John T. Kelly diary, p. 33

12. Duty in the Shenandoah Valley

1. Benedict, p, 484; Humphreys, p. 243; George E. Pond, *The Shenandoah Valley in 1864* (1883. Wilmington, N.C.: Broadfoot, 1989), p. 46, 54, hereinafter cited as Pond; *Reveille in Washington*, p. 334; Gloria Baker Swift and Gail Stephens, "Honor Redeemed: Lew Wallace's Military Career and the Battle of Monocacy," *North & South 4*, no. 2 (January 2001), p. 41–42, hereinafter cited as Swift and Stephens.

2. Benedict, pp. 484; Humphreys, p. 244; Swift and Stephens, p. 44; John T. Kelly diary, p. 33.

3. Benedict, p. 485, vol. 2, p. 352; *In the Field*, p. 91.

4. Benedict, p. 486; Pond, p. 66.

5. Benedict, p. 486; *A Stillness at Appomattox*, p. 263; Stevens, p. 372.

6. Benedict, pp. 486–487; *A Stillness at Appomattox*, p. 263; Aldace F. Walker, *The Vermont Brigade in the Shenandoah Valley, 1864* (Burlington, Vt.: Free Press Association, 1896), pp. 27–28 , hereinafter cited as Walker; *Reveille in Washington*, pp. 336–339; John T. Kelly diary, p. 34.

7. Benedict, p. 487.

8. Benedict, p. 488; Benjamin F. Hulburd letters; Walker, p. 29.

9. Benedict, pp. 488–489; Walker, p. 31.

10. Benedict, p. 490.

11. Benedict, p. 490; Walker, p. 37; John T. Kelly diary. P. 34.

12. Benedict, p. 491; Wilbur Fisk diary; John T. Kelly, p. 34.

13. Benedict, p. 491; Walker, pp. 39–40; John T. Kelly diary, p. 34.

14. Benedict, pp. 491–492; Walker, p. 41; John T. Kelly diary, p. 34.

15. Benedict, p. 492; Walker, pp. 41–42; John T. Kelly diary, p. 34.

16. Benedict, p. 493; Benjamin F. Hulburd letters; John T. Kelly diary, p. 34.

17. Benedict, p. 493; John T. Kelly diary, p. 35.

18. Benedict, pp. 493–494.

19. Ibid., pp. 494–495.

20. *In the Field*, p. 92.

21. William W. Noyes Civil War letter in the possession of Ed Italo.

22. Benedict, p. 495.

23. Benedict, pp. 495–496; *The Civil War Dictionary*, p. 136.

24. Pond, pp. 2–8; Richard O'Connor, *Sheridan the Inevitable* (Indianapolis: Bobbs-Merrill, 1953), p. 193, hereinafter cited as O'Connor; *A Stillness at Appomattox*, p. 275.

25. O'Connor, p. 192.

26. Benedict, pp. 496–498; Walker, p. 49; O'Connor, pp. 192–193; *A Stillness at Appomattox*, p. 275.

27. Benedict, p. 500; Walker, pp. 51–52; *From Winchester to Cedar Creek*, p. 22.

28. Benedict, p. 499; John T. Kelly diary, p. 35.

29. Benedict, p. 501; Walker, p. 52; Pond, p. 126; *From Winchester to Cedar Creek*, p. 26.

30. Benedict, p. 501.

31. Benedict, pp. 501–502; Walker, p. 57.

32. *In the Field*, p. 102.

33. Benedict, p. 502; Charles C. Morey diaries; *In the Field*, p. 104; John T. Kelly diary, p. 36.

34. Elijah Wales military pension record; Harrison A. Morgan's military pension record; Peck, p. 58.

35. Benedict, pp. 502–503; Walker, pp. 57–58.

36. Benedict, p. 503; Walker, p. 59; John T. Kelly diary, p. 36.

37. Benedict, p. 503; Walker, p. 59.

38. Benedict, pp. 504–505; Walker, pp. 60–61; Pond, p. 135; *Battles and Leaders*, vol. 4, p., 504; *In the Field*, p. 105; John T. Kelly diary, p. 36.

39. Benedict, p. 505; Walker, pp. 61–62; Stevens, p. 394; OR, vol. 43, p. 211; Jonathan Camp's military pension record; Peck, p. 34.

40. James C. Hutchinson's military pension record; Peck, 58.

41. Hamilton Ovitt's military pension record; Peck, 52.

42. Benedict, p. 505; Walker, pp. 61–62; OR, vol. 43, p. 211.

43. Abraham Sherman's military pension record; Peck, p. 36.

44. Charles C. Morey letters.

45. *Bennington Banner*, July 21, 1881. After the war O'Brian returned to farming in Vermont. On July 19, 1881, after spending several hours in a saloon, he got into a wagon race in North Bennington with a young tough named Keefe, whom the *Bennington Banner* described as "a thoroughly bad offshoot of a respectable family." During the race the hat of a man riding with O'Brian blew off and O'Brian stopped to let him retrieve it. As the other man was picking up his hat, Keefe passed O'Brian's wagon and hit one of O'Brian's horses with his whip. When O'Brian finally caught up with Keefe he hit one of Keefe's horses with a whip and a fight ensued. During the fight, Keefe got O'Brian down on the ground and started kicking him. One of Keefe's kicks broke one of O'Brian's ribs, which then punctured his left lung. He lived only a few hours afterward.

46. Charles Hammond's military service record; Peck, p. 38.

47. Alba Royce's military pension record; Peck, p. 62; *Historical Sketch of Co. I*, p. 24.

48. *In the Field*, pp. 105–106.

49. Benedict, pp. 505–506; Walker, pp. 62–66; *From Winchester to Cedar Creek*, p. 35.

50. Benedict, pp. 508–509; Walker, p. 69; John T. Kelly diary, p. 36.

51. Benedict, p. 509.

52. Ibid.

53. Benedict, p. 510; Walker, p. 71.

54. Walker, pp. 73–74; Benjamin F. Hulburd letters.

55. Walker, pp. 73–74; *In the Field*, pp. 113–114.

56. Walker, pp. 73–74; *In the Field*, pp. 113–114.

57. Benedict, p. 511.

58. Ibid.

59. Benedict, p. 513; Walker, p. 91; OR, vol. 43, p. 191.

60. Benedict, p. 513; Pond, p. 155.

61. O'Connor, pp. 200–201.

62. Benedict, p. 514; Walker, p. 91; OR, vol. 43, p. 191; Pond, p. 157; *From Winchester to Cedar Creek*, pp. 47–49.

63. Walker, pp. 92–93; Stevens, p. 398.

64. O'Connor, p. 202; Pond, p. 159.

65. Benedict, p. 514; OR, vol. 43, part 1, p. 207; Benjamin F. Hulburd letters; Horatio C. Blake, Civil War letter, Tunbridge Historical Society, Tunbridge, Vermont.

66. Walker, p. 96.

67. Walker, p. 96; OR, vol. 43, part 1, p. 207; *From Winchester to Cedar Creek*, p. 64.

68. Laroy Wyman's military service record; Peck, p. 36.

69. William Reed's military pension record; Peck, p. 49.

70. Charles F. Powers's military pension record; Peck, p. 58.

71. Walker, p. 96.

72. Ibid.

73. Benedict, p. 516; *A Stillness at Appomattox*, p. 297; O'-Connor, pp. 202–203; Pond, p. 162; *From Winchester to Cedar Creek*, p. 66.

74. Benedict, p. 516; *A Stillness at Appomattox*, p. 297; O'-Connor, pp. 202–203; Pond, p. 162; *From Winchester to Cedar Creek*, p. 67.

75. Benedict, pp. 515–516; Pond, pp. 163–166.

76. Oliver Lucia's military pension record; Peck, 48; *The Soldier's Record of Jericho, Vermont*, p. 21.

77. John Cilly's military pension record; Peck, p. 47.

78. George Seger's military pension record. After the war Seger received a pension for the disability caused by his wounds and was described as a "a wicked drinking man, he was considered partly insane from drink." Sometime before the turn of the century Seger left his wife and returned to Germany where he died October 22, 1904. His wife learned of his death and the members of the C. D. Sanford Post, No. 79, of the Grand Army of the Republic in North Adams, Mass., helped her apply for a pension. She was described as "very old about as feeble in mind as body, memory gone." She "had absolutely nothing" and lived with her only son who was almost as poor as she was. She received her widow's pension.

79. Walker, p. 104.

80. Ibid., p. 117.

81. Charles F. Powers's military pension record.

82. George Crown's military pension record; Peck, p. 57.

83. Oliver Clair's military pension record; Peck, p. 64.

84. Benedict, p. 517; O'Connor, p. 203.

85. Walker, p. 107; Pond, pp. 168–169; *From Winchester to Cedar Creek*, p. 103.

86. Wilbur Fisk diary.

87. Oliver Lucia's military pension record; *The Soldier's Record of Jericho, Vermont*, p. 21.

88. *In the Field*, pp. 118–119.

89. Benedict, p. 527; Walker, p. 110.

90. Benedict, pp. 526–527, O'Connor, p. 206; Pond, p. 174.

91. Benedict, p. 527; Pond, 174.

92. Benedict, 528; Walker, p. 114; Rosenblatt, p. 258.

93. *In the Field*, p. 119.

94. Benedict, p. 528; Walker, p. 115; *From Winchester to Cedar Creek*, p. 117.

95. Benedict, p. 529; Walker, p. 116

96. Benedict, pp. 529–530; Walker, p. 117; Benjamin F. Hulburd letters.

97. Benedict, p. 530; Wilbur Fisk diary; *From Winchester to Cedar Creek*, p. 121.

98. Benedict, pp. 530–532; Walker, pp. 119–120; O'Connor, p. 209.

99. Benedict, p. 532–533; *From Winchester to Cedar Creek*, pp. 128–129.

100. Benjamin F. Hulburd letters.

101. Benedict, p. 534.

102. Benedict, pp. 534–536; *From Winchester to Cedar Creek*, pp. 133–135

103. Benedict, p. 536; Walker, p. 126.

104. Benedict, p. 536; Wilbur Fisk diary.

105. Benedict, pp. 536–537; Walker, p. 128; *From Winchester to Cedar Creek*, p. 159; Benjamin F. Hulburd letters.

106. *In the Field*, p. 124.

107. Benedict, p. 537.

108. Ibid., pp. 535–537.

109. Benedict, p. 538; *From Winchester to Cedar Creek*, pp. 165–169.

110. Benedict, pp. 538–539.

111. Benedict, p. 539; *From Winchester to Cedar Creek*, p. 169.

112. Benedict, pp. 540–542; Walker, pp. 131–132; *From Winchester to Cedar Creek*, pp. 170–171; *The Civil War Battlefield Guide*, p. 246.

113. Benedict, pp. 542–544; *Battles and Leaders*, p. 526; *The Civil War Battlefield Guide*, p. 246.

114. Benedict, p. 544.

115. Benedict, pp. 544–545; Thomas A. Lewis, *The Guns of Cedar Creek* (Strasburg, Va.: Heritage Associates, 1988), p. 167, hereinafter cited as *The Guns of Cedar Creek*.

116. Benedict, pp. 545–546; *The Guns of Cedar Creek*, p. 172.

117. Benedict, pp. 546–547; Walker, pp. 137–138; *The Guns of Cedar Creek*, pp. 175–182.

118. Amasa S. Tracy, "My recollections of the Battle of Cedar Creek," Harrisburg Civil War Round Table Collection, U.S. Army Military History Institute, Carlisle Barracks, Pennsylvania, hereinafter cited as "My recollections of the Battle of Cedar Creek."

119. Benedict, p. 548; *The Guns of Cedar Creek*, pp. 184–186.

120. Walker, pp. 139–140.

121. Benedict, p. 548; *The Guns of Cedar Creek*, p. 186.

122. Benedict, pp. 550–551; Walker, pp. 140–141; Stevens, p. 418; *The Guns of Cedar Creek*, p. 188; *Battles and Leaders*, p. 527; *From Winchester to Cedar Creek*, p. 198.

123. Benedict, p. 551; Walker, p. 141; *The Guns of Cedar Creek*, pp. 189–190.

124. Benedict, p. 551; Walker, p. 141; *The Guns of Cedar Creek*, pp. 189–190; Lewis A. Grant, "The Second Division of the Sixth Corps at Cedar Creek," in *Glimpses Of the Nation's Struggle, Sixth Series, Papers Read Before the Minnesota Commandery the Loyal Legion of the United States, January, 1903–1908* (Minneapolis: Aug. Davis, Publisher, 1909), p. 17, hereinafter cited as Lewis A. Grant.

125. *Battles and Leaders*, p. 527; Lewis A. Grant, p. 18.

126. "My recollections of the Battle of Cedar Creek."

127. Albert G. Leach's military pension record; Peck, p. 58. After Leach returned home to Fletcher, he developed what his daughter described as "a roving, discontented mind or disposition" with "a marked uneasiness" which she attributed to the effects of his wound and boredom from not being able to work. For nearly 20 years he moved his family throughout most of the Central and Western states. Sometime in 1885, he got the urge to move to Nebraska with the idea of claiming a plot of government land, telling his family, "that they could live in a dug-out or a mud hut as well as anywhere." His wife put her foot down and refused to go. For the next five years he would from time to time go into fits of rage and beat and choke her until she finally left him and, with her children, moved back to Vermont from Nebraska. Albert eventually moved back to his hometown of Fletcher, Vt., where he died of bronchitis the day after Christmas 1912.

128. Wells Howard's military pension record; Peck, p. 58.

129. Hollis L. Rich's military pension record; Peck, p. 45.

130. Benedict, pp. 551–552; Walker, p. 142; *Battles and Leaders*, p. 527; Lewis A. Grant, p. 18.

131. "My recollections of the Battle of Cedar Creek"; George L. Crozier's military pension record, Peck, p. 34.

132. Benedict, p. 551–552; Walker, pp. 143–144; *Battles and Leaders*, p. 527.

133. William L. Kinsley's military pension record; Peck, p. 58.

134. William B. Nichols's military pension record; Peck, p. 35.

135. Alonzo Goodenough's military pension record; Peck, p. 34.

136. Benedict, pp. 552; Walker, pp. 142–143; *Battles and Leaders*, p. 527.

137. John Rappallo's military pension record; Peck, p. 58.

138. Michael Lynch's military pension record; Peck, p. 42.

139. Walker, p. 144; *The Guns of Cedar Creek*, p. 200; "My recollections of the Battle of Cedar Creek."

140. Walker, pp. 144–145; *The Guns of Cedar Creek*, pp. 200–201.

141. William R. Farrington's personnel service record.

142. Walker, p. 146; *The Guns of Cedar Creek*, pp. 201–202.

143. Walker, p. 147.

144. Walker, p. 147; *The Guns of Cedar Creek*, pp. 207–210.

145. Walker, pp. 147–148; "My recollections of the Battle of Cedar Creek."

146. "My recollections of the Battle of Cedar Creek."

147. Walker, p. 149; *The Guns of Cedar Creek*, p. 222; Stevens, p. 424.

148. "My recollections of the Battle of Cedar Creek"; Amasa S. Tracy's military pension record.

149. Walker, p. 149.

150. Walker, p. 149–150; *The Guns of Cedar Creek*, p. 228; *From Winchester to Cedar Creek*, pp. 232–233.

151. Walker, p. 150.

152. Walker, p. 151; *The Guns of Cedar Creek*, p. 230.

153. Walker, pp. 151–153; *The Guns of Cedar Creek*, p. 238.

154. Dr. Henry L. Janes medical journal, p. 369; Peck, p. 52

155. Walker, pp. 151–155; John T. Kelly diary, p. 39.

156. Benedict, p. 564; *The Guns of Cedar Creek*, p. 254.

13. The End in Sight

1. Benedict, p. 566; Walker, p 162.
2. Benedict, pp. 566–567 John T. Kelly diary, p. 40.
3. Benedict, p. 567.
4. Benedict, p. 567; John T. Kelly diary, p. 40.
5. Benedict, pp. 567–568.
6. Benedict, p. 568; Rosenblatt, pp. 288–289; John T. Kelly diary, p. 41.
7. Benedict, pp. 569–570; Rosenblatt, pp. 290–291; Charles C. Morey diary; John T. Kelly diary, p. 41.
8. Benedict, p. 570; *A Stillness at Appomattox*, pp. 319–320.
9. Benedict, p. 571.
10. Ibid.
11. Benedict, pp. 571–572; John T. Kelly diary, p. 43.
12. Benedict, p. 573.
13. Henry L. Franklin's court-martial record.
14. Ibid.
15. Ibid.
16. Charles C. Morey letters.
17. Benedict, pp. 573–574.
18. Ibid, p. 574.
19. Horn, pp. 212–213.
20. Benedict, p. 574; Horn, pp. 214–216; Hazard Stevens, "The Storming of the Lines of Petersburg by the Sixth Corps." *Personal Narratives of the Events in the War of the Rebellion being Papers Read Before the Rhode Island Soldiers and Sailors Historical Society*, vol. 9. (Providence, R.I.: The Society, 1903–1905), p. 391, hereinafter cited as Hazard Stevens.
21. Benedict, p. 576–577; Hazard Stevens, pp. 391–392.
22. Benedict, p. 577; Burr T. Cole's military pension record; Hazard Stevens, p. 392.
23. Antoine Gravlin's military pension record.
24. James Kavanaugh's military pension record.
25. George L. Lawrence's military service record; Peck, p. 45.
26. Benedict, p. 577.
27. Ibid.; A. Wilson Greene, *Breaking the Backbone of the Rebellion: The Final Battles of the Petersburg Campaign* (Mason City, Iowa: Savas, 2000), pp. 168, 180, hereinafter cited as Greene; The Jones House on Church Road belonged to Robert H. Jones and should not be confused with the Jones House near the Jerusalem Plank Road, Greene, p. 191.
28. Benedict, p. 577.
29. Ibid., p. 578.
30. Ibid., p. 579; Greene, pp. 158, 182–183.
31. Lewis A. Grant, "The Old Vermont Brigade at Petersburg," in *Glimpses Of the Nation's Struggle, A Series of Papers Read Before the Minnesota Commandery* (St. Paul, Minn.: St. Paul Book & Stationary Co., 1887), p. 18, hereinafter cited as "The Old Vermont Brigade at Petersburg"; Hazard Stevens, pp. 396–397. Greene, p. 261.
32. "The Old Vermont Brigade at Petersburg," pp. 18–19; Hazard Stevens, pp. 398–399.
33. Benedict, p. 579; Greene, p. 200.
34. Benedict, p. 579; Greene, pp. 201–205.
35. Benedict, pp. 580; *The Civil War Battlefield Guide*, p. 273.
36. Benedict, pp. 580–581; *The Civil War Battlefield Guide*, pp. 274–276.
37. Benedict, p. 581; Chris M. Calkins, *The Appomattox Campaign: March 29–April 9, 1865* (Conshohocken, Pa.: Combined Books, 1997), p. 45, hereinafter cited as *The Appomattox Campaign*; OR, vol. 46, pp. 902.
38. Benedict, p. 581; OR, vol. 46, p. 902.
39. Benedict, p. 582; *The Appomattox Campaign*, p. 45; Greene, pp. 260, 265.
40. "The Old Vermont Brigade at Petersburg," p. 19; Greene, p. 265.
41. "The Old Vermont Brigade at Petersburg," p. 21.
42. Benedict, pp. 582–583; "The Old Vermont Brigade at Petersburg," p. 22; OR, vol. 46, pp. 954, 968; Greene, p. 272; Hazard Stevens, p. 401.
43. Benedict, pp. 583–584; OR, vol. 46, p. 902; Greene, p. 275; Hazard Stevens, pp. 401–402.
44. Benedict, p. 584; Lewis A. Grant's military pension record; Baptise Lessor's military pension record; Peck, p. 55 ; OR, vol. 46, pp. 903, 954, 968; Hazard Stevens, pp. 403–404.
45. Benedict, p. 584; Greene, p. 274.
46. Benedict, pp. 585–586; "The Old Vermont Brigade at Petersburg," p. 23; OR, vol. 46, pp., 902, 954, 968–969; Hazard Stevens, p. 404; Hazard Stevens, pp. 405–406; Greene, p. 297.
47. William W. Noyes's military pension record; Peck, p. 52; Greene, p. 297.
48. Norman H. Ryan's military pension record; Peck, p. 36; Manchester town clerk's book of deaths; William W. Beals's military pension record; William W. Beals's Vermont Veteran's Home records; Peck, p. 34; Henry G. Seger's military pension record; Peck, p. 36.
49. Horace G. Ross's military pension record; Peck, p. 39.
50. Martin Hale's military pension record, Peck, p. 57.
51. William W. Vose's military pension record; Peck, p. 65.
52. Joseph S. Lavake's military pension record; Peck, p. 64.
53. OR, vol. 46, p. 973.
54. Benedict, pp. 584–587; OR, vol. 46, pp. 968–970; "The Old Vermont Brigade at Petersburg," p. 23; Greene, pp. 200–301; Hazard Stevens, p. 407; Greene, pp. 353, 358, 363.
55. Benedict, p. 588; *The Appomattox Campaign*, p. 46; OR, vol. 46, pp. 903, 955, 969–970.
56. William L. Kinsley's military pension record; Peck, p. 58.
57. Merritt P. Maranville's military pension and service records, Peck, p. 38.
58. Benedict, pp. 590–591; *The Appomattox Campaign*, p. 52; OR, vol. 46, pp. 904, 955, 970; Hazard Stevens, p. 415.
59. Greene, pp. 363–365.
60. Benedict, pp. 590–591; *The Appomattox Campaign*, p. 52; OR, vol. 46, pp. 904, 955, 970; Hazard Stevens, pp. 417–418; Greene, pp. 387–388.
61. Hazard Stevens, pp. 418–419; Greene, p. 421.
62. Benedict, pp. 590–591; *The Appomattox Campaign*, p. 52; OR, vol. 46, pp. 904, 955, 970.

63. Ephraim Harrington, Civil War letter, S. Goldman Collection, U.S. Army Military History Institute, Carlisle Barracks, Pennsylvania.
64. Isaiah Piper's military pension record; Peck, p. 45.
65. John S. Woodward's military pension record; Peck, p. 66.
66. Daniel B. George's military pension record; Peck, pp. 50–51.
67. Benedict, pp. 591–592, 955.
68. OR, vol. 46, p. 973.
69. Benedict, p. 592.
70. Ibid., p. 592.
71. Ibid., pp. 603–604.
72. *The Appomattox Campaign*, pp. 47–48.
73. Ibid., p. 58.
74. Ibid., pp. 58–59.
75. Benedict, pp. 605–606; *The Appomattox Campaign*, p. 67.
76. Benedict, p. 606; *The Appomattox Campaign*, p. 74.
77. Benedict, p. 606; *The Appomattox Campaign*, p. 74.
78. Benedict, p. 606; *The Appomattox Campaign*, pp. 74, 78.
79. *The Appomattox Campaign*, pp. 75–76, 85.
80. Benedict, p. 606; *The Appomattox Campaign*, p. 89.
81. Benedict, p. 606; *The Appomattox Campaign*, p. 93.
82. Benedict, pp. 606–607; *The Appomattox Campaign*, p. 91.
83. *A Stillness at Appomattox*, pp. 369–370; *In the Field*, p. 169.
84. Benedict, p. 607; *The Civil War Battlefield Guide*, pp. 278–280; *The Appomattox Campaign*, pp. 105–107.
85. Benedict, p. 607; *The Civil War Battlefield Guide*, pp. 278–280; *The Appomattox Campaign*, pp. 107–111.
86. Benedict, pp. 607–608.
87. Thomas F. Broughton's military pension record; Peck, p. 47.
88. Benedict, p. 607.
89. Ibid., p. 608.
90. Ibid., pp. 608–609.
91. Ibid., p. 609.
92. Ibid.
93. Benedict, p. 610; *The Appomattox Campaign*, pp. 198–199.
94. James A. Cilley's military pension record.
95. Benedict, pp. 610–611; *The Appomattox Campaign*, p. 199.
96. Benedict, p. 611; *The Appomattox Campaign*, pp. 199–200; James A. Cilley's military pension record.
97. Benedict, p. 611; James A. Cilley's military pension record.
98. Samuel Crown's military pension, military service and court-martial records; Peck, p. 57.
99. Benedict, pp. 611–612; *Green Mountain Freeman*, XX July, 1865.
100. Benedict, pp. 612–614.
101. Ibid., pp. 122, 614–615.
102. Augustus A. Decelle, Civil War letters, Special Collections, Krietzberg Library, Norwich University, Northfield, Vermont, hereinafter cited as Augustus A. Decelle letters.
103. Augustus A. Decelle letters
104. Benedict, p. 123; *Green Mountain Freeman*; *Burlington Free Press*, 19 July 1865.
105. Euclid Farnham, *Tunbridge Past: A Pictorial History of Tunbridge, Vermont* (Tunbridge, Vt.: Tunbridge Historical Society and the Tunbridge Public Library, 1980), pp. 149–150; Benedict, p. v.
106. Jay S. Hoar, *New England's Last Civil War Veterans* (Arlington, Texas: Seacliff Press, 1976), pp. 144–146.

Bibliography

Published Primary Sources

Bates, Samuel P. *History of Pennsylvania Volunteers 1861–5.* vol. 2. Harrisburg: B. Singerly, State Printer, 1869.

Balzer, John E., ed. *Buck's Book; A View of the 3rd Vermont Infantry Regiment.* Burlington, Ill.: Balzer & Associates, 1993.

Bicknell, George W. *History of the Fifth Regiment Maine Volunteers.* Portland, Me.: Hall L. Davis, 1871.

Blight, David W., ed. *When This Cruel War Is Over: The Civil War Letters of Charles Harvey Brewster.* Amherst: University of Massachusetts Press, 1992.

Chase, Peter S. *Reunion Greeting, together with an Historical Sketch, and a Complete Descriptive List of the members of Co. I, 2d Regt., Vt. Vols.* Brattleboro, Vt.: Phoenix Job Printing Office, 1891.

Chittick, Geraldine F., ed. *In the Field: Doctor Melvin John Hyde, Surgeon, 2nd Vermont Volunteers.* Newport, Vt.: Vermont Civil War Enterprises, 1999.

Conline, John. "Recollections of the Battle of Antietam and the Maryland Campaign." in *War Papers Read Before The Michigan Commandery of the Military Order of the Loyal Legion of the United States,* vol.2. Detroit: James H. Stone & Co., 1898.

Early, Jubal Anderson. *War Memoirs.* 1912. Bloomington: Indiana University Press, 1960.

English Combatant. 1864. *Battle-Fields of the South, from Bull Run to Fredericksburg; with Sketches of Confederate Commanders, and Gossip of the Camps.* Reprint, Time-Life Books, 1984.

Grant, Lewis A. "The Old Vermont Brigade at Petersburg." in *Glimpses Of the Nation's Struggle, A Series of Papers Read Before the Minnesota Commandery of the Loyal Legion of the United States.* St. Paul, Minn.: St Paul Book & Stationery Co, 1887.

_____. "The Second Division of the Sixth Corps at Cedar Creek." in *Glimpses Of the Nation's Struggle, Sixth Series, Papers Read Before the Minnesota Commandery of the Loyal Legion of the United States, January, 1903–1908.* Minneapolis: Aug. Davis, Publisher, 1909.

Hardee, William J. *Hardee's Rifle and Light Infantry Tactics.* Memphis: E. C. Kirk & Co., 1861.

Hewett, Janet B., Bryce A. Suderow, and Noah Andre Trudeau, eds. *Supplement to the Official Records of the Union and Confederate Armies.* 80 vols. Wilmington, N.C.: Broadfoot, 1998.

Howard, Oliver O. 1907. *Autobiography of Oliver Otis Howard,* Major General, United States Army. vol. 1. Freeport, N.Y.: Books For Libraries, 1971.

Humphreys, Andrew A. *The Virginia Campaign of '64 and '65: The Army of the Potomac and the Army of the James.* New York: Charles Scribner's Sons, 1907.

Hyde, Thomas W. *Following the Greek Cross, or, Memories of the Sixth Army Corps.* Boston: Houghton, Mifflin, 1894.

Klynstra, Herbert, and John Stutsman, eds., *Letters of Jerome Cutler, Waterville, Vermont during his enlistment in the Union Army 2nd Vermont Volunteers 1861–1864.* (n.p., n.d.).

Lancaster, Dallas M., and Mary H. Lancaster, eds. *The Civil War Diary of Anne S. Frobel.* McLean, Va.: EPM Publications, 1992.

Newell, Joseph K. *"Ours," Annals of the Tenth Regiment: Massachusetts Volunteers in the Rebellion.* Springfield, Mass.: C.A. Nichols & Co., 1875.

Peck, Theodore, S. *Revised Roster of Vermont Volunteers and Lists of Vermonters who Served in the Army and Navy of the United States During the War of the Rebellion.* Montpelier, Vt.: Watchman Co., 1892.

Pond, George E. *The Shenandoah Valley in 1864.* 1883. Wilmington, N.C.: Broadfoot Publishing Company, 1989.

Rhodes, Robert H. *All for the Union: A History of the 2nd Rhode Island Volunteer Infantry in the War of the Great Rebellion as told by the Diary of Elisha Hunt Rodes.* New York: Orion, 1991.

Rosenblatt, Emil, and Ruth Rosenblatt, eds. *Hard Marching Every Day: The Civil War Letters of Private Wilbur Fisk, 1861–1865.* Lawrence: University Press of Kansas, 1992.

Smith, William F. *Autobiography of Major General William F. Smith 1861–1864.* Herbert M. Schiller, ed. Dayton, Ohio: Morningside House, 1990.

Stevens, George T. *Three Years in the Sixth Corps.* 1866. Reprint, Time-Life, 1984.

Stevens, Hazard. "The Storming of the Lines of Petersburg by the Sixth Corps," in *Personal Narratives of the Events in the War of the Rebellion Being Papers Read Before the Rhode Island Soldiers and Sailors Historical Society*, vol. 9. Providence, R.I.: The Society, 1903–1905.

Sturtevant, Ralph Orson. *Pictorial History, Thirteenth Regiment, Vermont Volunteers War of 1861–1865.* n. p., 1910.

United States War Department. *War of the Rebellion: A Compilation of the Official Records of the Union and Confederate Armies.* 70 vols. Washington: Government Printing Office, 1881–1902.

_____. *Revised Regulations for the Army of the United States,1861.* 1861. Reprint, Harrisburg: National Historical Society, 1980.

Walker, Aldace F. *The Vermont Brigade in the Shenandoah Valley, 1864.* Burlington, Vt.: The Free Press Association, 1869.

Webb, Alexander S. *The Peninsula: McClellan's Campaign of 1862.* New York: Scribner's, 1881.

Manuscripts

Barnes, Sanford R. Civil War letters. Special Collections, Bailey/Howe Library, University of Vermont, Burlington, Vermont.

Barton, Rollin W. Civil War letters. Special Collections, Bailey/Howe Library, University of Vermont, Burlington, Vermont.

Bixby, Orville. Civil War letter. In the possession of Ed Italo.

Blake, Horatio C. Civil War letter. Tunbridge Historical Society, Tunbridge, Vermont.

Bond, William. Civil War letters. In the possession of Thomas R. Baine.

Bromley, James W. Civil War letters. In the possession of Thomas R. Baine.

_____. Civil War letters. Vermont Historical Society, Montpelier, Vermont.

Brooks, William T. H. Civil War letters. U.S. Army Military History Institute, Carlisle Barracks, Pennsylvania.

Brown, Elijah S. Civil War letters. Vermont Historical Society, Montpelier, Vermont.

Butterfield, Joseph E. Civil War diary. In the possession of Kenneth E. Proehl.

Coburn, Curtis A. Civil War letter. Special Collections, Bailey/Howe Library, University of Vermont, Burlington, Vermont.

Cole, Nelson S. Civil War Recollections. In the possession of Douglas W. Ronaldson.

Decelle, Augustus A. Civil War letters. Special collections, Krieger Library, Norwich University, Northfield, Vermont.

Drury, Eben N. Civil War letter. U.S. Army Military History Institute, Carlisle Barracks, Pennsylvania.

Ellenwood, Eli. Civil War letter. W. Lang Collection. U.S. Army Military History Institute, Carlisle Barracks, Pennsylvania.

Emery, Edson. Civil War diary, 1861. Special Collections, Bailey/Howe Library, University of Vermont, Burlington, Vermont.

Felton, Joseph C. Civil War letters. Felton Collection, The Lincoln Memorial Shrine, Redlands, California.

Fifield, Edson H. Civil War letters. Special Collections, Bailey/Howe Library, University of Vermont, Burlington, Vermont.

Fisk, Wilbur. Civil War diaries. Library of Congress, Washington, D.C.

Franklin, Henry L. Civil War letters: Rare Book, Manuscript, and Special Collections Library, Duke University, Durham, North Carolina.

Fullam, Volney S. Civil War letters. Vermont Historical Society, Montpelier, Vermont.

Glines, Moses C. Civil War letters. In the possession of Kenneth E. Proehl.

Halpin, Philip. Civil War diary. Pittsford Historical Society, Pittsford, Vermont.

Hapgood, Charles M. Civil War diaries. Special Collections, Bailey/Howe Library, University of Vermont, Burlington, Vermont.

Harrington, Ephraim. Civil War Letter. S. Goldman Collection, U.S. Army Military History Institute, Carlisle Barracks, Pennsylvania.

Hayward, Henry R. "History of Co. E, 2nd Regt. Vt. Vols." Tunbridge Historical Society, Tunbridge, Vermont.

Holmes, James T. Civil War diary, 1863. In the possession of Kenneth E. Proehl.

Howe, Oramel G. *Three Years in the Civil War, 1861–1864.* n.p.: Vermont Historical Society, Montpelier, Vermont, 1912.

Hoyt, Timothy S. Civil War letter. In the possession of Douglas Williams.

Jackson, William C. Civil War letters. Vermont Historical Society, Montpelier, Vermont.

Janes, Dr. Henry L. Medical journal. Special Collections, Bailey/Howe Library, University of Vermont, Burlington, Vermont.

Johnson, Enoch E. Civil War letter. Vermont Historical Society, Montpelier, Vermont.

Johnson, Norman W. Civil War diary. Vermont Historical Society, Montpelier, Vermont.

Leach, Chester K. Civil War letters. Special Collections, Bailey/Howe Library, University of Vermont, Burlington, Vermont.

Leach, Orin T. "*Personal Reminiscences of the Civil War.*" Special Collections, Bailey/Howe Library, University of Vermont, Burlington, Vermont.

Leslie, Warren S. Civil War letters. Special Collections, Bailey/Howe Library, University of Vermont, Burlington, Vermont.

Merrill, George A. to Lucius E. Chittenden, 28 May 1861. In the possession of Ed Italo.

Montague, Hollis. Civil War letters. Special Collections, Bailey/Howe Library, University of Vermont, Burlington, Vermont.

Morey, Charles C. Civil War diaries. S. Goldman Collection, U.S. Army Military History Institute, Carlisle Barracks, Pennsylvania.

_____. Civil War letters. Leigh Collection, U.S. Army Military History Institute, Carlisle Barracks, Pennsylvania.

Nash, Horace. C. Civil War letters. Special Collections, Bailey/Howe Library, University of Vermont, Burlington, Vermont.

Noyes, William W. Civil War letter. In the possession of Ed Italo.

Nye, Cornelius. Civil War letters. Vermont Historical Society, Montpelier, Vermont.

Pingree, S. E., and S. M. Pingree. Civil War letters. Transcribed by Kelly A. Nolin. Vermont Historical Society, Montpelier, Vermont.

Rand, Kirk. Civil War letters. Sallie Joy White Collection,. Schlesinger Library, Radcliffe College, Cambridge, Massachusetts.

Reed, Carolus A. Civil War letters. In the possession of Bradley C. Limoge.

Reid, Albert J. Civil War diary. In the possession of Barbara F. Earle.

Richardson, Charles H. Civil War Diary. Library of Congress, Washington, D.C.

Rugg, Orin. Civil War letters. Internet. *www.gunsites.com/77th/letters.html*

Start, Storrs W. Civil War letters. Fredericksburg and Spotsylvania National Military Park, Fredericksburg, VA.

Stone, Lauriston L. Civil War letters. Special Collections, Bailey/Howe Library, University of Vermont, Burlington, Vermont.

_____. Civil War letters. Vermont Historical Society, Montpelier, Vermont.

Tillison, Charles. Civil war letters. Vermont Historical Society, Montpelier, Vermont.

Tilly, Hiram H. Civil War letter book. *The Pearce Civil War Documents Collection*, Navarro College, Corsicana, Texas.

Tracy, Amasa S. "*My recollections of the Battle of Cedar Creek.*" Harrisburg Civil War Round Table Collection. U.S. Army Military History Institute, Carlisle Barracks, Pennsylvania.

Worthen, Erastus. Civil War letters. Special Collections, Bailey/Howe Library, University of Vermont, Burlington, Vermont.

General Works

Barber, James G. *Alexandria in the Civil War*. Lynchburg, Va.: H. E. Howard, 1988.

Bearss, Ed. *First Manassas Battlefield Map Study*. Lynchburg, Va.: H. E. Howard, n.d.

Benedict, George G. The Service of the Vermont Troops: An Oration Before the Reunion Society of Vermont Officers, in Representatives' Hall, Montpelier, Vt., November 2, 1882 (Montpelier: Watchman and Journal Press), 1882.

_____. *Vermont in the Civil War*. 2 vols. Burlington, Vt.: Free Press Association, 1886 and 1888.

Bengtson, Bradley P., M.D., and Julian E. Kuz, M.D., eds. *Photographic Atlas of Civil War Injuries: Surgical Cases and Specimens, Otis Historical Archives*. Grand Rapids, Mich.: Medical Staff Press in association with Kennesaw Mountain Press, 1996.

Beyer, W. F., and O. F. Keydel. 1903. *Deeds of Valor: How America's Civil War Heroes Won the Congressional Medal of Honor*. Stamford, Conn.: Reprint, Longmeadow Press, 1993.

Boatner, Mark M. *The Civil War Dictionary*. rev. ed. New York: Vintage Books, 1991.

_____. *Military Customs and Traditions*. New York: D. McKay, 1956; repr., Westport, Conn.: Greenwood, 1976.

Cabot, Mary R. *Annals of Brattleboro Vermont*. Vol. 2. Brattleboro, Vt.: Press of E. L. Hildreth & Co., 1922.

Calkins, Chris M. *The Appomattox Campaign: March 29–April 9, 1865*. Conshohocken, Pa.: Combined Books, 1997.

Carleton, Hiram. *Genealogical and Family History of the State of Vermont*. 2 vols. New York: Lewis Publishing Company, 1903.

Catton, Bruce. *The Army of the Potomac: A Stillness at Appomattox*. Garden City, N.Y.: Doubleday, 1953.

_____. *The Army of the Potomac: Glory Road*. Garden City, N.Y.: Doubleday, 1952.

_____. *The Army of the Potomac: Mr. Lincoln's Army*. Garden City, N.Y.: Doubleday, 1951.

_____. *Reflections on the Civil War*. New York: Promontory Press, 1998.

Chapman, Craig S. *More Terrible Than Victory: North Carolina's Bloody Bethel Regiment, 1861–1865*. Washington and London: Brassey's, 1998.

Child, Hamilton. *Gazetteer of Orange County, 1762–1888*. Syracuse: Syracuse Journal Company, 1888.

Coffin, Howard. *Full Duty: Vermonters in the Civil War*. Woodstock, Vt.: The Countryman Press, Inc., 1993.

_____. *Nine Months to Gettysburg*. Woodstock, Vt.: Countryman Press, 1997.

Crockett, Walter Hill. *Vermont, the Green Mountain State*. New York: Century History Co., 1921.

Davis, Emma-Jo L. *Mulberry Island and the Civil War, April 1861–May 1862*. Fort Eustis, Va.: Fort Eustis Historical and Archaeological Association, 1968.

Davis, William C. *Battle at Bull Run*. Garden City, N.Y.: Doubleday, 1977.

Dodd, Ira S. *Song of the Rappahannock*. New York: Dodd, Mead, 1898.

Doubleday, Abner. *Chancellorsville and Gettysburg*. Charles Scribner's Sons, 1886.

Edwards, William B. *Civil War Guns*. Harrisburg: Stackpole, 1962.

Ellis, William Arba, ed. *Norwich University, 1819–1911: Her History, Her Graduates; Her Honor Roll*. Montpelier, Vt.: Capital City Press, 1911.

Farnham, Euclid. *Tunbridge Past: A Pictorial History of Tunbridge, Vermont*. Tunbridge, Vt.: Tunbridge Historical Society and the Tunbridge Public Library, 1980.

Furgurson, Ernest B. *Chancellorsville 1863; The Souls of the Brave*. New York: Knopf, 1992.

Gallagher, Gary W. ed. *The Wilderness Campaign*. Chapel Hill and London: University of North Carolina Press, 1997.

Gedney, William, compiler. *Descendants of Henry Wallbridge who Married Anna Amos, Dec. 25, 1688 at Preston, Connecticut*. Litchfield, Conn.: Press of Franklin Company, Phila., 1898.

A Genealogical Study of Some Families Who Came to Fletcher, Vt. Before 1850. Burlington, Vt.: Vantage Press, 1981.

Gould, Edward K. *Major-General Hiram G. Berry*. Rockland, Me.: Press of the Courier-Gazette, 1899.

Graham, Martin F, and George F. Skoch. *Mine Run: A Campaign of Lost Opportunities, October 21, 1863–May 1, 1864*. Lynchburg, Va.: H. E. Howard, 1987.

Greene, A. Wilson. *Breaking the Backbone of the Rebellion: The Final Battles of the Petersburg Campaign*. Mason City, Iowa: Savas, 2000.

Gregory, John. *1776–1876 Centennial Proceedings and Historical Incidents of the Early Settlers of Northfield, Vermont, With Biographical Sketches of Prominent Business Men Who have been and are now Residents of the Town.* Montpelier, Vt.: Argus and Patriot Book and Job Printing House, 1878.

Guernsey, Alfred H., and Henry M. Alden. *Harper's Pictorial History of the Civil War.* 2 vols. New York: Fairfax Press, 1866.

Hagemann, James. *The Heritage of Virginia.* West Chester, Pa.: Whitford Press, 1988.

Hardee, William J. *Hardee's Rifle and Light Infantry Tactics.* Memphis: E.C. Kiek & Co., 1861.

Harris, Joseph N. *History of Ludlow Vermont.* Charlestown, N.H.: Mrs. Ina Harris Harding and Mr. Archie Frank Harding Publishers, 1949.

Harrison, Noel G. *Fredericksburg Civil War Sites, December 1862–April 1865.* Lynchburg, Va.: H. E. Howard, 1995.

Hastings, Earl C., Jr., and David Hastings. *A Pitiless Rain: The Battle of Williamsburg, 1862.* Shippensburg, Pa.: White Mane, 1997.

Heitman, F. B. *Historical Register of the United States Army from Its Organization: September, 29, 1789, to September, 29, 1889.* Washington, D.C.: National Tribune, 1890.

Heller, Charles E., and William A. Stoft. *America's First Battles, 1776–1965.* Lawrence, Kans.: University Press of Kansas, 1986.

Hemenway, Abby Maria. *The History of the Town of Montpelier, Including that of the Town of East Montpelier, for the First One Hundred and Two Years.* Montpelier, Vt.: Miss A. M. Hemenway, 1882.

_____. *The Vermont Historical Gazetteer: a magazine, embracing a history of each town, civil, ecclesiastical, biographical and military.* 5 vols. Burlington, Vt.: Tuttle Co., 1923.

Henderson, William D. *12th Virginia Infantry.* Lynchburg, Va.: H. E. Howard, 1984.

Horn, John. *The Petersburg Campaign: June 1864–April 1865.* Conshohocken, Pa.: Combined Books, 1997.

Hotchkiss, Jedediah, and William Allan. *The Battlefields of Virginia: Chancellorsville.* New York: D. Van Nostrand, 192 Broadway, 1867.

Jeffery, William H. *Successful Vermonters (Lamoille, Franklin and Grand Isle Cities).* East Burke, Vt.: Historical Publishing Co., 1907.

Johnson, Robert U., and Clarence C. Buel, eds. *Battles and Leaders of the Civil War.* 4 vols. New York: Century, 1887–1888.

Keller, Roger S. *Events of the Civil War in Washington County, Maryland.* Shippenburg, Pa.: Burd Street Press, 1995.

Kennedy, Francis H. *The Civil War Battlefield Guide.* Boston: Houghton Mifflin, 1990.

Lane, E. H. *The Soldier's Record of Jericho, Vermont.* Burlington, Vt.: R. S. Styles, 1868.

Leech, Margaret. *Reveille in Washington, 1860–1865.* New York: Harper & Brothers, 1941.

Lewis, Lloyd. *Sherman, Fighting Prophet.* New York: Harcourt, Brace, 1932.

Lewis, Thomas A. *The Guns of Cedar Creek.* Strasburg, Va.: Heritage Associates, 1988.

Lord, Francis A. *Civil War Collector's Encyclopedia.* New York: Castle Books, 1965.

Marshall, Jeffrey D., ed. *A War of the People: Vermont Civil War Letters.* Hanover, N.H.: University Press of New England, 1999.

McWhitney, Grady, and Perry D. Jamieson. *Attack and Die.* University, Ala.: University of Alabama Press, 1982.

Melville, Dorothy Sutherland. *Tyler-Browns of Brattleboro.* New York: Exposition Press, 1973.

Mitchell, Reid, *Civil War Soldiers.* New York: Viking Penguin, 1988.

Morwood, James. *A Dictionary of Latin Words and Phrases.* Oxford: Oxford University Press, 1998.

Nebenzahl, Kenneth, ed. *Atlas of the American Revolution.* Chicago: Rand McNally Company, 1977.

O'Connor, Richard. *Sheridan the Inevitable.* Indianapolis: Bobbs-Merrill, 1953.

Olson, Sherry H. *Baltimore.* Baltimore: Johns Hopkins University Press, 1980.

Owens, William Miller. *In Camp and Battle with the Washington Artillery of New Orleans.* Boston: Ticknor and Co., 1885.

Peterson, Harold L. *Encyclopedia of Firearms.* New York: E. P. Dutton, 1964.

Pfanz, Donald C. *Richard S. Ewell: A Soldier's Life.* Chapel Hill and London: University of North Carolina Press, 1998.

Poirier, Robert G. *By the Blood of Our Alumni.* Mason City, Iowa: Savas, 1999.

Reese, Timothy J. *Sealed with Their Lives: The Battle for Crampton's Gap, Burkittsville, Maryland, September 14, 1862.* Baltimore: Butternut and Blue, 1998.

Report of the Adjutant & Inspector General of the State of Vermont, from November 1, 1862 to October 1, 1863. Montpelier, Vt.: Walton's Steam Printing Establishment, 1863.

Report of the Adjutant & Inspector General of the State of Vermont, from October 1, 1863 to October 1, 1864. Montpelier, Vt.: Walton's Steam Press, 1864.

Report of the Adjutant & Inspector General of the State of Vermont, from Oct. 1, 1864 to Oct. 1, 1865. Montpelier, Vt.: Walton's Steam Printing Establishment, 1865.

Rhea, Gordon C. *The Battle of the Wilderness, May 5–6, 1864.* Baton Rouge: Louisiana State University Press, 1994.

_____. *The Battles for Spotsylvania Court House and the Road to Yellow Tavern.* Baton Rouge: Louisiana State University Press, 1997.

Scott, Robert Garth. *Into the Wilderness with the Army of the Potomac.* Bloomington: Indiana University Press, 1957.

Sears, Stephen, W. *Chancellorsville.* Boston: Houghton Mifflin, 1996.

_____. *Landscape Turned Red: The Battle of Antietam.* Boston: Houghton Mifflin, 1983.

_____. *To the Gates of Richmond: The Peninsula Campaign.* New York: Ticknor & Fields, 1992.

Siegel, Alan A. *For the Glory of the Union: Myth, Reality, and the Media in Civil War New Jersey.* Rutherford, N.J.: Fairleigh Dickinson University Press, 1984.

Sifakis, Stewart. *Who Was Who in the Civil War.* New York: Facts on File Publications, 1988.

Stackpole, Edward J. *Drama on the Rappahannock: The Fredericksburg Campaign.* Harrisburg: Military Service Publishing Co., 1957.

Tarbell, Carroll R. *The History of Mount Holly.* Publisher unknown, 1987.

Tyler, D. Gardiner. *A History Pictorial Review of Charles County, Virginia.* Expert Graphics, 1990.

Waite, Otis F. R. *Vermont in the Great Rebellion.* Claremont, N.H.: Tracy, Chase and Co., 1869.

Wallace, William M. *Soul of the Lion.* Gettysburg: Stan Clark Military Books, 1960; reprint 1995.

Welcher, Frank J. *The Union Army, 1861–1865, Organization and Operations.* vol. 1. Bloomington and Indianapolis: Indiana University Press, 1989.

Wert, Jeffery D. *From Winchester to Cedar Creek: The Shenandoah Campaign of 1864.* Mechanicsburg, Pa.: Stackpole, 1997.

______. *General James Longstreet: The Confederacy's Most Controversial Soldier: A Biography.* New York: Simon & Shuster, 1994.

Wheeler, Richard. *Sword Over Richmond.* New York: Harper & Row, 1986.

Wiley, Bell Irvin. *The Life of Billy Yank.* Baton Rouge: Louisiana State University Press, 1986.

______. *They Who Fought Here.* New York: Bonanza Books, 1959.

Williams, J. C. *The History and Map of Danby, Vermont.* Rutland, Vt.: Printed by McLean & Robbins, 1869.

Williams, T. Harry. *Lincoln and His Generals.* New York: Alfred A. Knopf, 1952.

Wilson, Wright C. *Our Harford Heritage; A History of Harford County, Maryland,* 3d ed. Glen Burnie, Md.: French-Bray Printing Co., 1980.

Wilstach, Paul. *Tidewater Virginia.* New York: Tudor, 1945.

Wright, C. Wilson. *Our Harford Heritage: A History of Harford County Maryland,* 3d ed. Glen Burnie, Md.: French-Bray Printing Company, 1980.

Newspapers and Periodicals

Alexander, Ted. "Ten Days in July: The Pursuit to the Potomac." *North & South 2,* no. 6 (August 1999). pp. 27–28.

Bennington (Vt.) Banner.

The Black Water (Vt.) Tribune.

Brown, Kent M. "A Golden Bridge: Lee's Williamsport Defense Lines and His Escape Across the Potomac." *North & South 2,* no. 6 (August 1999). p. 60.

Burlington (Vt.) Daily Free Press.

Burlington (Vt.) Weekly Sentinel.

Eisenberg, Albert C., ed. "'The 3rd Vermont has won a name.' Corporal Albert C. French's Account of the Battle of Lee's Mill." *Vermont History 49,* no. 4 (Fall 1981). p. 227.

Harrison, Noel G. "Atop an Anvil." *The Virginia Magazine of History and Biography 106,* no. 2 (Spring 1998). p. 136.

Lamoille (Vt.) Newsdealer.

Montpelier (Vt.) Green Mountain Freeman.

The (Washington, D.C.) National Tribune.

Poughkeepsie Daily Eagle.

Ridout, D. Archie. "War at my Front Door." *Civil War Times Illustrated 37,* no. 3 (June, 1998). pp. 18–22.

Robbins, Peggy. "Bomb Brothers." *Civil War Times Illustrated 36,* no. 4 (August, 1997): pp. 40–66.

Rutland Daily Herald.

Rutland Herald.

Smart, Jeffery K. "Burning Bridges: The Events Leading Up to the Military Occupation of Harford County in 1861." *Harford Historical Bulletin 72* (Spring 1997). pp. 8–52.

Swift, Gloria Baker, and Gail Stephens. "Honor Redeemed: Lew Wallace's Military Career and the Battle of Monocacy." *North & South 4,* no. 2 (January 2001).

Tunnell, Ted. "With Banner, Gun, and Sword: Marshall Harvey Twitchell and the 4th Vermont Regiment Go to War." *Vermont History 59,* no.2 (Spring 1999). p. 80.

Vermont Watchman and State Journal.

Wickman, Donald, ed. "The 1864 Diary of Private John T. Kelly Second Vermont Regiment." *Rutland Historical Society Quarterly 24,* no. 2, (1994). pp. 18–43.

Index

*Numbers in **boldface** refer to pages with photographs or illustrations*